Jacob L. Wright
Rebuilding Identity

Beihefte zur Zeitschrift für die alttestamentliche Wissenschaft

Herausgegeben von
John Barton · Reinhard G. Kratz
Choon-Leong Seow · Markus Witte

Band 348

Walter de Gruyter · Berlin · New York

Jacob L. Wright

Rebuilding Identity

The Nehemiah-Memoir and its Earliest Readers

Walter de Gruyter · Berlin · New York

∞ Printed on acid-free paper which falls within
the guidelines of the ANSI to ensure permanence and durability.

ISBN 3-11-018319-6

Library of Congress Cataloging-in-Publication Data

Wright, Jacob L.
   Rebuilding identity : the Nehemiah-memoir and its earliest
readers / Jacob L. Wright.
       p.   cm. – (Beihefte zur Zeitschrift für die alttestamentliche
   Wissenschaft ; Bd. 348)
Includes bibliographical references and index.
   ISBN 3-11-018319-6 (cloth : alk. paper)
   1. Bible. O. T. Nehemiah – Criticism, interpretation, etc.   I. Title
II. Series.
   BS1365.52W75   2005
   222'.806–dc22
                                                          2004023892

Bibliographic information published by Die Deutsche Bibliothek

Die Deutsche Bibliothek lists this publication in the Deutsche Nationalbibliografie; detailed
bibliographic data is available in the Internet at < http://dnb.ddb.de >.

Printed in Germany
Cover Design: Christopher Schneider, Berlin

In Memoriam

Gerald L. Wright

יאדר זכרו

(Cf. Sirach 49:13)

Foreword

According to the thesis of this book, the Nehemiah-Memoir has gradually developed from a short building report into an account of Judah's Restoration, which in turn provided the theological impulses for the literary maturation of Ezra-Neh. Setting the precedent for Jewish histories written during in the Hellenistic age, the authors of Ezra-Neh employ the genre of letters, edicts, lists, etc., and present thereby Nehemiah's account as one "source" among others in the book. Although the authors of 1 Esdras removed this source from their history of the Restoration, a substantial segment of critical scholarship – equally influenced by Greek historiography – has pointed to 1 Esdras as support for the view that the Nehemiah-Memoir was interpolated at a late point in the composition history of the book. In taking this approach, it has failed to observe to what extent Ezra-Neh consists of responses from the first readers of the Nehemiah-Memoir. In each literary stage and in each building phase, the identity of the Judeans is defined anew. This concentration on identity takes its point of departure from the solidarity and fraternity established during the repair of Jerusalem's ramparts. The demarcation of space by the wall corresponds to the delimitation of an ethno-social group for which this edifice serves as a protective barrier. As the book matures, this space is differentiated into various spheres.

In contrast to the exponential amplification of Ezra-Neh, the present book represents an extensively abridged version of my dissertation completed for a Dr. theol. degree, which was granted by the Georg-August Universität, Göttingen in the summer semester of 2003. The 250 pages that were removed from the manuscript include a review of past research, a treatment of historical issues (e.g., the archaeology of Jerusalem and Judah, the problem of Nehemiah's governorship, the social and political situation of Judah in the late Persian and early Hellenistic periods), lengthier analyses of Ezra 1-10, and a discussion of the relevancy of H. Lefebvre's ideas and the theories of Urban Studies for the depiction of space in Ezra-Neh. These pages are presently being transformed into articles for publication.

As I prepare for my move to the University of Heidelberg and a new research-project, I cannot help but thinking back on the past eventful years in Göttingen and the people who made the work on Ezra-Neh a joyous task. I was fortunate enough to experience a past generation of "the Göttinger Gibborim," such as Rudolph Smend, Lothar Perlitt, and Robert Hanhart; their presence in the *Doktorandenkolloquium* is highlight in the history of the Old Testament faculty. Above all, I am indebted to their worthy successors, Reinhard G. Kratz and Hermann Spieckerman. Prof. Kratz recognized the need for a fresh analysis of the Nehemiah-Memoir and has guided the study along the way. Not only was he always there to lend an ear to my ideas and to share his insights on Ezra-Neh, but he also took a sincere interest in my personal welfare. I could not have hoped for a better *Doktorvater*. Prof. Spieckermann graciously served as my second advisor and contributed to the project in many ways. To Martin Hallaschka, André Heinrich, Peter Porzig, Hannes Bezzel, and all my other friends and colleagues in dear old Göttingen, many thanks for your forbearance throughout the years in which I must have seemed to be obsessed with Nehemiah. These non-native speakers offered their assistance in proofreading the manuscript; for the errors that remain I take full responsibility. Muchas gracias to Maribel Larrañaga for the expertly prepared indices. For the generous stipend from the German Research Society (Emmy Noether Program: "Christliches Gebet und seine jüdischen Ursprünge" under the direction of Niclas Förster) I am deeply grateful. Finally, I extend my gratitude to the editors of BZAW for publishing my work in their respected series.

This book is dedicated to the memory of my beloved grandfather, who passed away as it was nearing completion. He funded my education, encouraged the study of Nehemiah, and respected the direction I took. His life continues to provide inspiration for all who knew him.

Jacob L. Wright
Göttingen, August 2004

Contents

1. Spinoza and the Attempt to Isolate Nehemiah's First-Person Account

Hujus libri [Neh 1-13] maximam partem desumtam esse ex libro, quem ipse Nehemias scripsit, testatur ipse historicus v. 1. cap. 1. Sed quae ex cap. 8 usque ad v. 26. cap. 12. narrantur, et praetera duos ultimos versus cap. 12., qui Nehemiae verbis per parenthesin inseruntur, ab ipso historico, qui post Nehemiam vixit, additos esse dubio caret.

According to this Adnotatio XXIII from Spinoza's *Tractatus theologico-politicus*,[1] parts of "the book" of Nehemiah should not be ascribed to the pen of its eponymous author (cf. "The words of Nehemiah ben Hachaliah," Neh 1:1). Instead of attributing the interpolation of Neh 8:1-12:26 and 12:46f. to the hand of Ezra, Spinoza maintained that the book's final author was as an anonymous "historian" living in the second cent. BCE.[2] The doubt Spinoza raised with regard to the tradition was not welcomed by conservative commentators.[3] Thus, Starke maintained that the use of the first-person in the first and last chapters indicates that the entire book represents the *verba Neemiae*.[4] With regard to the third-person sections that Spinoza ascribed to a later hand, Hezel contended: "Nur einmal (Kap. 8,9) redet er in der dritten Person von sich, und zwar so und in solcher Stellung, daß man ihm auch dann weder jene Geschichte, noch viel weniger das ganze Buch würde absprechen dürfen, wenn man auch nicht wüßte, daß es unter Geschichtsschreibern gewöhnlich wäre, in der dritten Person von sich zu reden."[5] The pre-critical interpretation defended by Starke and Hezel faced greater obstacles, however. As Spinoza observed from the information offered by Josephus and Philo, Neh 12:11 and 22 refer to priests

---

1   1979 [1670]: 131f.
2   Ibid.: 132f. This historian was given a name (the "Chronisten") by Zunz (1832: 21ff.) and Movers (1834: 14). The popularity of their thesis is due not least to the early approval it received in de Wette's *Lehrbuch* (1845: 290).
3   According to the tradition transmitted in *b. Bat.* 15a, Nehemiah finished the book Ezra began. In *b. Sanh.* 93b, R. Yirmeyah ben Abba claims that the book is called "Ezra" because of the arrogance Nehemiah expresses in his זכרה-לי-prayers. – The doubt Spinoza raised has been more positively received, however, by early critical scholars, such as Michaelis (1783: 40ff.), as well as contemporary scholars who deny that the unity of 1-2 Chronicles and Ezra-Neh, such as Japhet (1968), Williamson (1977, 1985), Eskenazi (1988 [1 and 2]), and Throntveit (1992).
4   1744: 542. "[V]erba Neemiae" is the Vulgate's translation of Neh 1:1a.
5   1782: 324.

who must have lived long after the mid-fifth cent. BCE.[6] Responding to this difficulty, Starke claimed that the author enjoyed the lifespan of a Patriarch. For those whom this solution seemed farfetched, he made a significant exception, allowing for the possibility that the list of the priests in Neh 12 is "von einem anderen göttlich erleuchteten manne hinzu gethan worden seyn."[7]

Most scholarship of the last two centuries has not only conceded that the final author of the book must have lived after both Ezra and Nehemiah, but has also followed Spinoza in employing the use of the first-person as a criterion for isolating the original contours of Nehemiah's account. This criterion, however, soon proved to be inadequate. In 12:31 Nehemiah's words appear out of nowhere, only to disappear soon thereafter. In 13:4ff. they then reemerge and seem to refer to the activities portrayed in the preceding third-person passages ("but before this"). Similarly, the builder of Jerusalem discovers a genealogical record in 7:4-5 from which he quotes a lengthy passage (vv. 6-72). Without any noticeable seams between chaps. 7 and 8, the reader initially assumes that Nehemiah is narrating the middle section of the book. Hence, if one eliminates all the third-person material in Neh 1-13, the remaining account is extremely fragmented.

In the most influential modern commentary on Ezra-Neh, Bertheau proposed that the historian who edited the sources in the book, and who lived ca. 300 BCE, deleted a significant portion of the first-person account. Because the use of first-person does not resume after the list in Neh 7:6ff. and Nehemiah could not have quoted Ezra 1-6,[8] Bertheau identified chap. 11 as the original continuation of 7:4-5. Likewise, he maintained that the account of the dedication has been radically altered from its original form and that the introduction to Nehemiah's words in 13:4 indicates that immediately preceding chapters have not been transmitted.[9]

The solutions Bertheau advanced in defense of Spinoza's method prohibit one from appreciating the work of the later author(s), and thus Eskenazi argues for the advantages of a "literary approach."[10] While acknowledging that Ezra-Neh includes sources, she does not attempt to isolate them and instead devotes her attention to the contours of the book's final form. This holistic approach is to be commended for confining itself to the extant evidence and not speculating as to what the editor may have deleted from the original texts. Indeed, in reading Ezra-Neh as a unified whole, one notices that the tensions between the

---

6   1979 [1670]: 132.
7   1744: 542. See also Hezel (1782: 324).
8   Spinoza concluded that Nehemiah found the genealogical record, which he quotes (7:5ff.), in "the book of Ezra." (1979 [1670]: 133f.).
9   1862: 9f. et ad loc.
10   1988.

various parts of the book do not correspond to the sources which the last two-centuries of scholarship have postulated. Thus, while one searches in vain for significant disparities between the alleged sources and the narrative framework in Ezra 1-10 with respect to the presentation of the Golah as the protagonists of the Restoration, the introduction to Nehemiah's account (1:1-4) stands out against the backdrop of its transmitted surroundings (both Ezra 1-10 and Neh 1:5-13:31) by identifying the future builders of the wall with those who remained in the land after 587/6 BCE.

However, the advocates of the "literary approach" must still offer a compelling explanation for the friction and disparities within in the narrative. And they are by no means negligible: Whereas Zerubbabel and Jeshua form a harmonious diarchy, the relationship between Nehemiah and Eliashib is one of enmity. Furthermore, in simply acceding to his cupbearer's petition to build Jerusalem (Neh 2), Artaxerxes behaves much differently than he did a few years before as he followed in the tradition of his predecessors (Ezra 1-6) by giving priority to the institution of the temple and commanding "the people of Israel" from the realm of his reign (7:11ff.) to make Aliyah. So too, Neh 8 portrays festivities in the seventh month directed by a *sōfēr* and revolving around the Torah. In disregarding the temple, altar and sacrifices, it competes with the presentation of the activities during seventh month in Ezra 3.[11]

Moreover, if the "literary approach" intends to avoid an anachronistic interpretation, then it is necessary to know approximately when the author(s) wrote. Was it much later, at the same time, or perhaps earlier than the tenure of the final high priest in Neh 12? In order to answer this question, one must begin to differentiate between older and younger material. If it were to restrict itself to an exclusively synchronic reading, Ezra-Neh scholarship would fail to take advantage of an opportunity to recover valuable information regarding the history of the early Second Temple period.[12]

The present work develops a new approach by integrating the best of Spinoza's differentiation between the book and its sources, on the one hand, and Eskenazi's focus upon the final form, on the other. A primary objective of our study is the isolation of literary precursors to Ezra-Neh. This, however, does not mean that we neglect its canonical shape. To the contrary, our concerns relate equally to the process of the book's formation. Insofar as Ezra-Neh constitutes a *creatio continua*, one does injustice to the work by treating it as a static entity frozen in time. By retracing the maturation process, one digs deeper

---

11 See VanderKam (1992) and Kraemer (1993).
12 In failing to also perform a diachronic analysis of Nehemiah's account, J. Becker (1998) has fallen into the pitfall posed by exclusively synchronic exegesis and has interpreted the significant findings of his comparative work as indications that the whole work represents a late fiction written by "the Chronicler."

into the text and discovers older literary works surrounded by their first commentaries.[13] Such investigative work is not only indispensable for a reliable
assessment of the historical value of the supposed sources; it also recovers a
wide array of textual witnesses illustrating how generations of readers – not just
a late editor or "historian" – interpreted the works of their predecessors and
developed their views of the Restoration.[14]

Inasmuch as these readers respected the work they amplified and transmitted, they would have been very reluctant to delete portions of it. Thus, if several
of the passages in Nehemiah's account appear to be fragmentary, then they
probably have been composed as supplements to their narrative contexts. The
introduction to 13:4-31 ("but before this"), for example, need not be ascribed to
the "editor" of Ezra-Neh. Indeed, it provides an indispensable clue that the final
chapter originally stood closer to chaps. 1-6, from which it seems to have been
severed and gradually moved to its present position. The clue is disregarded
when one either simply assumes that the book consists of sources compiled by
an editor or doubts that we can reconstruct its composition-history.

That Nehemiah's account has matured over time does not represent a new
conclusion. It is already implicit in Spinoza's proposal that Neh 8:1-12:26 and
12:46-47 have been inserted into the first-person account. Following Spinoza,
many scholars maintain that a redactor has also interpolated the third-person
register of builders in 3:1-32. However, it is unlikely that someone who had
actually read Nehemiah's account, which portrays the priesthood and the aristocracy as the opponents to Judah's reconsolidation (5:1-13, 6:17-19, 13:4-9, 15-
22, 28-29), would have inserted a text in which the high priest initiates the construction and the nobles follow his precedent. According to the thesis defended
in the following chapters, this antagonism between Nehemiah and the priesthood prompted the composition of Ezra-Neh.

Nehemiah's account gradually developed from a brief building report (or
inscription) into an account of Judah's Restoration.[15] Its final form presents not
only the repair of Jerusalem's ramparts but also the Judeans recognizing their

---

13 The delight occasioned by the discovery of substrata in a text or of the connection between
    passages that are now separated (such as Neh 6:17-19 in 13:4ff.) is familiar to the
    Assyriologist who finds a "join" between broken cuneiform tablets, or the archaeologist
    reassembling an important piece of pottery, or the Qumran-scholar reconstructing a scroll.
14 This form of "redaction-"or "composition-historical criticism" has been developed above
    all by Zimmerli (1980, 1983), Steck (1989, 1991) and Kratz (1991). According to the
    principle, "Die Methode ergibt sich aus dem Gegenstand," the present study introduces the
    reader to this approach inductively, instead of devoting a considerable amount of space to
    an abstract discussion of texts and redactional phenomena.
15 Our reconstruction of Nehemiah's account shares much in common with the conclusions
    of Hurowitz (1992) and Kratz (2000). On the basis of ancient Near Eastern building
    inscriptions, Hurowitz proposes that the work can be isolated to a brief report in chaps. 1-6
    and 12 without the notices regarding the various antics of Sanballat, Tobiah and Geshem.
    Kratz comes to very similar conclusions by way of the internal literary evidence.

fraternity and the solidarity it necessitated (5:1-13), members of the aristocracy breaking off their relations with a foreigner (6:17-19) who was forced to forfeit his foothold in Jerusalem (13:4-9), the Levites returning to their rightful place (13:10-14), the nobles sanctifying the Sabbath (13:15-22), and the inhabitants of Judah relinquishing marital practices which jeopardized their ethnic identity they discovered in the process of rebuilding Jerusalem (13:23-31).

By identifying the future builders as "the remnant that were left after the captivity there in the province" (1:3) and describing the corruption in the temple, the authors of this first account of the Restoration provoked certain – presumably pro-priestly – circles to compose Ezra 1-6. This narrative affirms that the imperial court commanded the Golah to return and begin the Restoration with the construction of the temple. While Artaxerxes prohibits the building of wall (Ezra 4:7-22), Darius confirms Cyrus's decree (6:1ff.) and makes the completion of the temple possible. Before Artaxerxes takes advantage of his earlier proviso (4:21) and rescinds his decision (Neh 2), he commands Ezra to transport generous royal donations for the temple and make Aliyah with "the people of Israel." This story is told in Ezra 7-8, which bridge the temple-building narrative in Ezra 1-6 to Nehemiah's account by combining the contents of the former with the first-person form of the latter.

Although Nehemiah's account constitutes the point of departure for the composition of Ezra-Neh, the composition of Ezra 1-6 and 7-8, with its various "sources," presents it as an independent work integrated into the history of the Restoration. In distinguishing between the narrator and his sources, the book resembles other witness to Jewish historiography from the Hellenistic age.

In the third and final compositional stage, Ezra 9-10 and Neh 8-10 were inserted into the book. These texts, in contrast to Ezra 1-8, view Nehemiah's work more positively. Once Ezra arrives in Jerusalem, he realizes that Restoration was not complete with the construction and "glorification" (7:27) of the temple: "The children of Israel, the priests and Levites had not separated themselves from the peoples of the lands" (9:1). After Ezra reflects upon this situation in his prayer and before the composition of the third-person narrative in Ezra 10, the story continues with Nehemiah telling how he came from Susa, repaired Jerusalem's ramparts and built an ethnic "wall" around Judah. Because Ezra has acknowledged the importance of Nehemiah's work, he can join the builders in preparation for the dedication ceremonies (Neh 8). In stark contrast to Ezra 3, however, this celebration of the sacred seventh month neglects the role of the high priest, the temple, and the altar. Instead, the festivities revolve around the Torah, are led by a *sôfēr* and are celebrated throughout the entire city of Jerusalem. The confession in Neh 9 portrays the history of Israel in detail and as closely intertwined to obedience to the Mitzvoth, yet it fully disregards the temple. Thereafter (10:1-30), the community ratifies a new covenant to abide by the Torah. Taking their lead from Nehemiah's critique of the priesthood, the authors of this literary complex present Torah-reading and confession as an alternative to the temple-cult promoted in Ezra 1-6 (7-8). The final supplements to the book (10:31ff. and 13:30b-31a) counterbalance the concentration on Torah-study and penitence in Neh 8:1-10:30 by redirecting the reader's attention back to the temple.

For some circles, however, these short supplements were not enough. The authors of 1 Esdras, noticing the analogies between Ezra-Neh and Jewish-Hellenistic historiography, treated Nehemiah's account as one source among others in the book; they cut it completely out of the history of the Restoration and made changes to Ezra 1-10 that render the wall-building project superfluous.[16] The only text in Neh 1-13 for which they found a place is 8:1ff., but even it has been heavily reworked. Ezra is now only "the chief priest," no longer primarily "the *sōfēr*," and the celebration of Sukkoth without altar and sacrifices is omitted. Similarly, the legend recorded in 2 Macc 1:10-2:18 employs Nehemiah's name, yet assigns him a much different task than the one recounted in Neh 1-13: In coming from Persia and concerning himself solely with the reestablishment of the cult, he resembles the Zerubbabel of Ezra 1-6 and 1 Esdras.[17]

For the sake of space, the history of research and all other introductory matters will be discussed as the study progresses. The work is structured according to four parts, each with an introduction outlining the contents and rehearsing the main points of the preceding part. In the concluding chapter, the findings of the study are reviewed (§14.3) in preparation for a brief discussion of Neh 8-10.

---

16 For the differences between Ezra 1-10 and 1 Esdras pertaining to the building and repopulation of the city, gates and gatekeepers, the temple courts and city-streets, see Böhler (1997: 78ff.).

17 See also *1 Enoch* 89:72f., *Josippon* I 3.11d-12a, *Yal.* 2 §234, *Sanh.* 38a ("Zerubbabel...his real name is Nehemiah ben Hachaliah"), and *S. ʿOlam Zut.* (see Gelbhaus [1902: 46]). – Inasmuch as we argue that Nehemiah's account sparked the composition of Ezra-Neh and that 1 Esdras represents a later work from which Nehemiah's account has been excised, our thesis differs starkly from those scholars who have argued that latter has been secondarily inserted into the book; see, *inter alia*, Michaelis (1783: 40ff.), de Wette (1845: 291) Marquart (1896: 29), Torrey (1896: 57), Howorth (1901: 150f.), Mowinckel (1916: 23ff.), Hölscher (1923: 409ff.), Granild (1949: 37ff.), Galling (1954: 9ff.), Cross (1975 :11), Pohlmann (1970: 72ff.), Böhler (1997: 179ff.), Karrer (2001: 369) and Grätz (2004: 286f.). Our composition-model is most similar to, and indeed has been directly influenced by, that of Kratz (2000: 53ff.).

I. In Susa – 1:1-11

Introduction

The first lines of Nehemiah's autobiographical account, although drafted with economy, evince all the essential features of a masterfully designed prelude. Setting the scene, the narrator identifies the time, place and characters: It is the month Kislev of the twentieth year. Nehemiah ben Hachaliah is in the citadel in Susa (v. 1) where he encounters his brother, Hanani, and a group of men from Judah (v. 2a). While the episode revolves around a conversation, it nevertheless does not lack action or emotion: Nehemiah poses a question to his visitors, and upon hearing their response, he collapses in deep despondency (vv. 2b-4a). In keeping with the introductory function of this passage, the narrator allows the generated suspense to remain unresolved so that reader waits for the hero to arise from his mourning and to find a way to remedy the situation that has occasioned his despair. Stimulated by the uncertainty of whether the story will progress as anticipated, we continue reading and discover in the final words of his prayer (1:11) that he has devised a plan for his impending encounter with the king.

In contrast to the element of suspense that the author has consciously produced, Neh 1 creates an unintentional tension running at cross-purposes to the desired conflict. From the prayer's conclusion, "Grant your servant success today and give him favor in the sight of this man" (v. 11a), we expect Nehemiah later that same day to be mentally poised and ready to seize the opportunity furnished by his audience with the king. Yet the contrary is the case. In the next scene (2:1ff.), Nehemiah is busy performing his duties as a royal cupbearer and is taken aback as Artaxerxes notices his sorrowful countenance (v. 2b). He also seems to have suddenly found his time of fasting and intercession for the impending encounter to be insufficient, for as the king lends an ear to his request, he prays again to the God of heaven (v. 4b). Not only this perplexes the reader; one also wonders why Nehemiah is in Susa. For the answer, however, we must wait until v. 11b. So too, the dating of the episodes is confusing. While the scenes with the group from Judah and with the king are both set in the twentieth year, the date in 1:1 is incomprehensible without the reference to

Artaxerxes' reign that 2:1 (or Ezra 7) provides. And as Kislev is the ninth month, Nehemiah's appearance before the king in the month Nisan (the first month) would have occurred *before* the pivotal conversation in the citadel. The incoherency increases insofar as the account presents him making confession in 1:5ff. both immediately after he hears the despairing news (cf. the transition from v. 4b to 5) as well as on the same day as he appeared before the king (cf. היום in vv. 6a and 11a). Moreover, in reporting that the wall of Jerusalem is broken down and its gates burned with fire (1:3), Hanani and his entourage fail to inform Nehemiah how this happened. The reader of Ezra-Neh knows that Artaxerxes had previously prohibited the Judeans from rebuilding the city and its walls (cf. Ezra 4:6ff.), yet s/he has been told nothing about a recent destruction. If the condition of Jerusalem had not changed since the Babylonians razed its walls, it is bewildering that Nehemiah reacts as if the history of Judah during the last 140 years were unfamiliar to him.

Thus, the opening scene generates two forms of tension. On the one hand, the text fulfils the indispensable narrative function of introducing the conflict and providing a foreword to the story's action. It arouses the reader's interest so that s/he follows the story through until some sort of denouement is achieved. On the other hand, the critical scholar discerns under the surface an additional and subtler tension inasmuch as the chapter does not comport with the details of surrounding narrative. Just as the outer conflict engenders a desire in the reader for resolution, the inner discrepancies create the desideratum for an examination of the literary evidence and discovery of a solution.

With regard to the second form of tension produced by our text, scholarship has examined the literary evidence and discovered a wide range of solutions: At one end of the spectrum, many maintain that the incoherency results from the reader's false expectations. At the other end, a few suggest that an earlier version of the first-person account commenced in chap. 2. And in the middle is the majority to whom the unintended tension indicates that Nehemiah's original wording in chap. 1 has passed through editorial hands in the course of the text's transmission. Since the final group of scholars has isolated most of the friction to the prayer in 1:5-11a, we begin our analysis ("Chapter Two") of the opening scenes by inquiring whether this passage is integral to its context, and if not, what the perceptible redactional activity contributes to the first form of tension in the narrative. In "Chapter Three," we address the problem of the origins of Jerusalem's destruction and compare the information provided in Ezra 4:7-23 with that in Neh 1-2. Then, in "Chapter Four," we examine the introductions to Nehemiah's account and discover that the first chapter contains three strata that correspond to three compositional stages in Ezra-Neh.

2. Nehemiah's First Prayer – 1:5-11a

2.1 Introduction

Compared with Nehemiah's tersely formulated orisons, the confession in 1:5-11a is not only much lengthier, but it also employs the stereotyped phraseology of penitential prayers and betrays an unparalleled command of the biblical tradition. Because it deviates from the otherwise unconventional thought and style of the first-person account, scholarship has devoted much attention to the question of the "authenticity" of the passage.[1] Assuming that a royal cupbearer would have received only a Persian education, many doubt that Nehemiah could have composed a text that evinces such conversance with Deuteronomistic thought and diction.[2] Abandoning this source-critical approach, other scholars

---

1 With regard to the question whether the prayer constitutes a redactional insertion, the opinions are quite evenly divided. Those who believe the prayer to be an integral part of the chapter are: Bertheau (1862: 133ff.), Torrey (1896: 36), Siegfried (1901: 72), Bertholet (1902: 47), Johannesen (1946: 180f.), Rudolph (1949: 105f.), Granild (1949: 267f.), Gelin (1952: 15, 55), Plöger (1957: 46f.), De Fraine (1961: 74ff.), Myers (1965: 92ff.), Kellermann (1967: 75), Michaeli (1967: 308ff.), Clines (1984: 137ff.), Williamson (1985: 166ff.), Gunneweg (1987: 40ff.), Throntveit (1992: 62ff.) and Karrer (2001: 204-5). The scholars who treat the prayer as secondary are Winckler (1901: 473), Mitchell (1902: 87), Jahn (1909: 92), Batten (1913: 188), Mowinckel (1916: 30f.; 1964: 18), Hölscher (1923: 526), Noth (1944: 127, 148), Galling (1954: 218), Schneider (1959: 162f.), Blenkinsopp (1985: 208, 212), Steins (1995: 204-n. 134, 207), Schunck (1998: 26ff.), Kratz (2000: 69) and Reinmuth (2002: 44ff.). According to Bowman (1954: 666-70) and Steck (1967: 111f.), the prayer has been strongly reworked.

2 So, above all, Jahn (1909: 92), Mowinckel (1916: 30f.; 1964: 18), Hölscher (1923: 526), and Noth (1944: 127, 148). Williamson is one of the few who has responded to the critical objections: "Much of the prayer is a mosaic of earlier biblical phrases which had no doubt been absorbed into liturgical patterns and so were thoroughly familiar to Nehemiah. He need not, therefore, have been particularly conscious of their specific origin" (1985: 172). Similarly, Karrer supposes that the Deuteronomistic thought of the prayer would have been quite common to members of the Diaspora (2001: 137). These responses, however, warrant caution, for we cannot be sure about the ubiquity of Deuteronomistic language in the Persian period, the insistence to the contrary notwithstanding. The transmitted literature probably presents a very selective sample of the real religious thought and practices in Judah, and this assertion applies equally, if not also more, for the Diaspora. From the literature that has not been transmitted (e.g., the Elephantine papyri), one observes that Jerusalem in the late fifth cent. BCE is carrying on official correspondence with a Jewish community that worships in a manner clearly proscribed by Deuteronomy (and Nehemiah's prayer). Nevertheless, Karrer and Williamson are correct in pointing out that the use of this stereotypical Deuteronomistic language does not provide sufficient grounds for attributing the prayer to a later hand.

confine their studies to form- and tradition-critical analyses, without treating the
problems posed by the surrounding narrative.[3]

The problem with both of these approaches is that they bypass the exegetical
point of departure: the literary shape and setting in which the text has been
handed down to us. Regardless of the objective in studying a composition, the
task of inquiring after the function of the text in its present context deserves
priority. A sound methodology restricts the investigation of a work's compositional integrity to the literary level and confines the working assumptions as to
the historical circumstances of the putative author. This rigid *epoche* is necessary
in order to avoid the methodological hazards of drawing conclusions on the
unity of the passage based upon a presupposition regarding Nehemiah's
acquaintance with the scriptures. Since we know this figure only from his autobiographical work, we have no alternative than to focus our investigation on the
literary evidence, which means that our conclusions must be established on the
immanent criteria of the work's conceptual and stylistic consistency. At a subsequent stage, we will then test our findings by drawing upon historical analogies.

The present analysis begins by examining the relationship of the prayer to its
immediate context (§2.2). After presenting new arguments for its redactional
character, the investigation then moves on to consider the transition it provides
from Neh 1-13 to Ezra 1-10 (§2.3).

2.2 Diachronic Analysis

2.2.1 The Prayer in the Context of Neh 1-2

The possibility that the prayer represents a late redactional expansion is strongly
suggested by the several points of friction between the text and its context,
which were mentioned in the introduction to Part One. But instead of immediately concluding that the whole confession has been appended to the chapter,
one could attempt with Bowman and Steck to reconstruct a text that would
form a better continuation to the scene in v. 4.[4] Since after Nehemiah's
statement that he fasted and prayed (v. 4b) and the introductory ואמר (v. 5), the
reader is prepared for a sample of the initial supplications, one might consider
whether the dependant clause ולילה אשר אנכי מתפלל לפניך היום יומם in v. 6 has
been reworked. If the words יומם ולילה are a later gloss, the conjectured form
("that I pray today") would not presuppose a lengthy interval and consequently

---

3   Cf., e.g., Baltzer (1991), Mathys (1994), Newman (1996) and Boda (1999).
4   While Bowman (1954: 666ff.) was primarily interested in showing how the prayer at an
    earlier stage was better suited to the context, Steck's aim (1967: 111f.) was to recover the
    wording of an early exilic prayer that a editor fitted into its present context.

would be better suited the context.[5] The statement in 1:11aβ ("prosper your servant today and grant him mercy in the sight of this man"), which presages what comes unexpectedly on that same day (היום), could have been secondarily attached to the conclusion as a redactor sought to bridge the gap to chap. 2.[6]

The prayer may have undergone changes in the course of its transmission, yet even if one were to remove the putative editorial additions, it would still cause friction with the narrative. As Nehemiah hears about the calamity in Judah, he sits down, weeps and mourns for days (v. 4a). In an earlier edition of the account, the final clause, "and I was fasting and praying to the God of Heaven" (v. 4b),[7] was probably not meant to introduce the words of a prayer, but rather to inform the reader that Nehemiah made supplication over an extended period of time (ימים). After the participial construction ואהי צם ומתפלל, the transition to "and I said…" is extremely rough. If the author had intended to continue the passage with the prayer-text, he would have composed this clause with (way)yiqtol- and qatal-forms corresponding to v. 4a and 5a.[8]

The prayer probably intends to report Nehemiah's words which he spoke in preparation for his audience with Artaxerxes, rather than immediately after hearing the news from the province.[9] Yet the question arises, Why has this text not been included after the requisite information in 2:1a? In its present position, the prayer not only refers to "this man" before he is introduced, but it also mentions "today" before ever telling the reader that the date has changed. The wording would have been more felicitous had the narrator recounted how he finished his fasting in the month of Nisan and uttered this one final prayer before his decisive conversation with the king ("And it was in the month of Nisan, the twentieth year of King Artaxerxes that I prayed…").

Taking another glance at the formulation of v. 4, we notice that the introductory scene almost concludes in 1:4a ("for days"). However, the clause in v. 4b resumes the action: "And I continued in fasting and in prayer before the God of Heaven." The participial construction, ואהי צם ומתפלל, is unexpected

---

5   Proposed by Bowman (1954: 666ff.), while Steck (1967: 111f.) suggested that the whole phrase has been interpolated; לשמע אל-תפלת עבדך is said to have originally continued with ומחודה על-חטאות(ו).

6   Steck argued that also ואני ובית-אבי חטאנו in v. 6b is a secondary expansion that fits the prayer into the context of chap. 1. – In the newest work on Nehemiah's account, Reinmuth (2002: 54) contends that v. 11aβ constitutes an original part of the narrative, while the rest of vv. 5-11 is secondary. However, he does not explain why Nehemiah would have composed a prayer without an introduction and which presents more contradictions with his account than the "theologisch geprägte Sprache" in vv. 5ff.

7   The translation is from Blenkinsopp (1985: 203).

8   Against the backdrop of Dan 9:4 (ואתפללה ליהוה אלהי ואתודה ואמרה אנא וגו), not only the rough transition from the participial forms but also the repetition of אלהי השמים in vv. 4 and 5 is quite conspicuous. See also the introductions in Deut 9:26, 1 Sam 2:1, 2 Kgs 6:17, 19:15, Jon 2:1f. and 4:2.

9   Cf., e.g., Kellermann (1967: 11), Williamson (1985: 137f.) and Throntveit (1992: 63).

not only in the sequence of the *wayyiqtol* forms in 1:4a (ואבכה ואתאבלה), but also
after the duration of these activities has been specified (ימים). The verse would
have been much smoother, if the author had placed the expression "for days" at
the conclusion.[10] The best explanation for the unusual formulation is that an
editorial hand has appended the entire second sentence.

What would have motivated this addition in v. 4b? In his response to the
news from the province, Nehemiah merely weeps and mourns in v. 4a. By
supplementing his sadness with the actions of fasting and supplication, the
redactor confers a vertical axis to the original horizontal dimensions of the
passage.[11] The group from Judah came to Susa to notify an influential Persian
official of the desperate situation in Judah (vv. 1-3). This official in turn goes
before the monarch with a dejected countenance (v. 4a and 2:1ff.), yet before
taking this step, he has already occupied himself many days with fasting and
prayer before the sovereign God of Heaven (v. 1:4b).[12] The revision of the
opening scenes continues with the insertion of the prayer in 1:5-11a, which
requires the addition of v. 4b.[13] Now Nehemiah not only manifests his personal
piety by remarking that he spent many days in fasting and prayer; he also explicitly identifies the true cause of the ire at hand (vv. 6b and 7) and realigns all the
events reported later in the account as the fulfillment of the ancient promises
(vv. 8-10). By virtue of this introspective glimpse, the reader knows that what
Nehemiah seems never to have anticipated (2:1-5) had both been planned all
along and was brought to fruition by divine providence (v. 11a).

2.2.2 Prayers in other Biblical Narratives

The next section devotes more attention to the contribution the confession
makes to the reading of Ezra-Neh. First, however, we may briefly note that the
composition-historical phenomenon of amplifying texts with lengthy prayers is
by no means unique to Nehemiah's account.[14] Hence, a redactor is probably

---

10 The form צם is attested elsewhere only in 2 Sam 12:23, while the *qatal-* and *wayyiqtol-*forms
    appear numerously. Thus, if the clause ואהי צם ומתפלל ונו were original, it could have easily
    been formulated as ואצם ואתפללה ונו and positioned before ימים.
11 Cf. the examples of mourning and penitence in 2 Sam 1:12, Ezra 8:23, Esth 4:3, Dan 9:3,
    and Joel 2:12. In this regard, see Rudolph (1949: 105) and Myers (1965: 95).
12 In its present shape, the supplementary nature of the fasting and praying is unmistakable.
    The sense of the Hebrew in v. 4b is: "And (during this time) I was (*also*) fasting and pray-
    ing."
13 Throntveit (1992: 63) discerns a deeper meaning to the movement from vv. 4 to 5-11a:
    "Theologically speaking, it is important to realize that the bulk of the passage records
    Nehemiah's second response to the devastating news from Jerusalem. Following a period of
    grief (1:4, cf. Ezra 9:3-5), his initial response, Nehemiah demonstrates his faith by turning to
    the fount of his resources in prayer."
14 See Watts (1992).

responsible for Hannah's praise in 1 Sam 2:1-10, which severs the narrative join in 1:28 and 2:11.[15] David's psalm in 2 Sam 22:1ff. almost certainly represents a late addition to the book.[16] It is also widely accepted that Jonah's prayer of thanksgiving in 2:2-10 has been interpolated.[17] A later hand, furthermore, appears to have composed Tobiah's hymn in chap. 13. And empirical evidence for a movement to expand narratives with prayer-texts is not lacking. For example, the LXX to Dan 3 includes a prayer from a certain Azariah after v. 24 and is followed by a narrative interlude and the "Song of Three Young Men."

More pertinent to our study are the textual witnesses to the Esther-scroll. In both the MT and the LXX, Mordecai, upon learning of the plot to annihilate the Jews, clothes himself in sackcloth and ashes (4:1). Later, he follows Esther's command to fast for three days (4:16). In the MT, the narrative continues with the account of Esther's audience with the king on the third day (5:1ff.), which resembles Neh 2 in many ways. Yet the Add Esth, transmitted in the Greek versions, present her and Mordecai first petitioning for divine assistance (C 1-30). In this way, later authors have profoundly transformed the character of the protagonists. Whereas before the latter were motivated exclusively by a concern for the fate of their people, now they divulge in their private prayers that they had behaved in absolute accordance with the Mitzvoth. Thus, Mordecai avows that he did not intend to act with hubris as he refused to do obeisance to Haman (C 5). And in his supplication, which strongly echoes Nehemiah's prayer, evinces a facility with the tradition for Israel's deliverance. Likewise, Esther professes to abhorring the bed that she shares with an uncircumcised man and hating her crown just as much as her menstrual garments (C 27). She also claims to have never honored a royal feast with her presence or to have consumed wine offered to idols. Most significantly, the Esther of the Greek versions, as the Nehemiah in the transmitted form of his account, utters a prayer for success prior to her audience with the Persian ruler.[18]

In light of this "hard" textual evidence, I propose that the same redactional process that produced the amplified versions of Esther was also at work in the composition of Neh 1. Just as Mordecai exploits Esther's influence with Xerxes as he becomes aware of Haman's plot, so Hanani and the group from Judah inform Artaxerxes' loyal cupbearer of the adversity in the province. And in the later versions of both accounts, the actions of these highly-esteemed Persian courtiers manifest that it was not just their favor with the king and his benevo-

---

15　See Kittel (1923: 409ff.).

16　See McCarter (1984: 475).

17　Arguments against this consensus are provided by Stuart (1987: 470ff.).

18　See C 12-30. As for the genre of the "prayer for success" (Neh 1:11), see also Judith's prayer as she prepared to decapitate Holophernes in Jdt 3:4-5, 7.

lence, but also their intercession with God which brought about the ameliora-
tion of their people's sociopolitical plight.

2.3 The Function of the Prayer

In examining now what a later reader assumed Nehemiah to have said in his
final intercession, we will witness how the prayer in 1:5ff. consciously reinterprets both its immediate context and the book as a whole in new theological
categories. That the prayer is to be understood against the backdrop of its present context differs starkly from the opinions of many others who attribute the
passage to a later hand. For example, Bowman wrote disparagingly: "This prayer
[in Josephus] is appropriate to the occasion and has something of the
businesslike directness and simplicity of Nehemiah's language as it is known
elsewhere. In sharp contrast the biblical prayer is a rambling, indirect effusion of
stilted Deuteronomic phrases having little or no bearing on the situation that
evoked the prayer."[19] While Bowman may be correct in observing the multitude
of "Deuteronomic phrases" in the passage, we will observe that (i.) the prayer's
"rambling" character obtains from its false classification as a "penitential
prayer" or the like, (ii.) that it has been elicited by its immediate context, and
(iii.) that it serves as an introduction to Neh 1-13 in the final form of these
chapters.

2.3.1 The Influence of Solomon's Prayer in 1 Kgs 8

That the prayer was composed for its present literary setting is evident from the
chief request that its structure emphasizes. After the heading in v. 5, the corpus
of the confession opens in v. 6aα with ‑אל תהי נא אזנך‑קשבת ועיניך פתוחות לשמע
תפלת עבדך, what strikingly resembles v. 11aα: ‑אל אנא אדני תהי נא אזנך‑קשבת
תפלת עבדך. According to Throntveit, the text manifests the following chiasmic
structure:

> A Invocation (5-6a)
> > B Confession: Israel's sin (6b-7)
> > > X Appeal to covenantal promise of return (8-9)
> > B' Confession: God's Redemption (10)
> A' Invocation with supplication (11a)[20]

---

19 1954: 666. Cf also the opinions of Batten (1913: 188), Hölscher (1923: 526), Mowinckel
    (1964: 18), Steck (1967: 111-n. 11), Blenkinsopp (1985: 208ff.), and most recently,
    Reinmuth (2000: 58).
20 1992: 64.

In keeping with this view, the chiasmus serves to emphasize the middle sections of the confession and the promise of return in vv. 6b-10.

This approach encounters a problem, however. In comparison with similar prayer texts, the double petition to be heard in vv. 6a and 11a is unusual. Ezra 9, Neh 9 and Tob 3 lack this appeal, and Dan 9 and Bar 1:15-3:8 include it only once (vv. 17-19 and 2:14, respectively).[21] With regard to Nehemiah's prayer, it appears that vv. 6a and 11 do not simply function as a parenthesis around the contents in vv. 6b-10. Rather, we should probably understand the middle section as subordinate to the framing petitions. First, Nehemiah beseeches God: "Let your ear be attentive and your eyes open to hear your servant's prayer which I pray to you today night and day on behalf of your servants the children of Israel and with which I confess the sins of the children of Israel which we have committed against you" (v. 6a-bα).[22] In v. 6bβ-7, he then identifies and elaborates on these sins, and in vv. 8-10 reminds God of his promise to Moses. Thereafter, v. 11 resumes the petition that the prayers of God's servants be answered. Hence, vv. 6bβ-10 appear to constitute an interjection that explains the contents of the עבדך/עבדיך תפלת in vv. 6a and 11a). The text of 1:5-11a itself should not be confused with the prayers he made "day and night." Since it is to be distinguished from past confessions, Nehemiah's words cannot be properly ascribed to the genre of *Bußgebeten* or penitential prayer. Rather, they constitute simply a plea for supplications to be heard. This unusual character has been occasioned by the context: After spending many days in intercession (v. 4), Nehemiah makes a final request in vv. 5-11a that God would respond to his past supplications and prosper his impending audience with the king (v. 11aβ).

In relinquishing the attempt to fit this text into the form of penitential prayer, one notices that is shares many features with Solomon's dedicatory prayer in 1 Kgs 8/2 Chr 6. The address is quite reminiscent of 1:5b,[23] and the appeal to be heard appears – in contradistinction to the other confessions – both at the beginning and the conclusion.[24] Especially noteworthy is the correspondence of the final petitions. Nehemiah first calls attention to the people whom "you have redeemed by your great power and strong hand" (v. 10) before repeating his request that his and their prayer be heard (v. 11aα). Similarly, Solomon identifies the people as "your inheritance which you brought

---

21 Cf. also the use of the petition in the non-penitential prayer contexts of 2 Kgs 19:16/Isa 37:17, Ps 130:2 and Jdt 9:12b.

22 Throntveit (1992: 64), with many commentators (Williamson (1985: 165), Blenkinsopp [1998: 208]), reads v. 6bα together with the subsequent lines. This rendering, however, both assumes that the chief aim of the prayer is the confession and obfuscates the conjunction before "I confess." Cf. Rudolph's (1949: 104) and Gunneweg's (1987: 47) translations.

23 1 Kgs 8:23b/2 Chr 6:14b and Neh 1:5b. The introduction in 1:5, as well as Neh 9:32 and Dan 9:4, has most likely been formulated as a combination of this address and Deut 7:21 and 10:17. See Newman (1999: 101f.).

forth out of Egypt" before pleading that "your eyes be open unto the supplication of your servant and the supplication of your people Israel to hearken unto them in all that they call for unto you" (1 Kgs 8:51f.). In both texts, the ones praying identify themselves and the people of Israel with Moses by means of the title "your servant(s)." And while Nehemiah finishes with "prosper your servant today and give him favor before this man" (ותנהו לרחמים לפני האיש הזה), Solomon prefaces his conclusion with "and give them favor before those who have carried them captive that they may have compassion on them" (ונתתם לרחמים לפני שביהם ורחמום, v. 50b).[25] Yet Solomon does not only predict what would later occur in Neh 2;[26] also a central aspect of his prayer has made itself felt in the composition of 1:5-11a. Whereas Nehemiah pleads that God open his eyes and ears to heed his prior confessions that he is making day and night (v. 6), Solomon's prayer is nothing less than a demand that God open his eyes night and day to hearken unto all future intercession (v. 29). Finally, just as Solomon's supplication, by enumerating the many other occasions for prayer and intercession (vv. 31-53), gives expression to the importance that Israel makes confession,[27] so does Nehemiah highlight in his supplication the fact that he is praying.

Although Solomon's prayer has certainly influenced Nehemiah's, there are differences between the two. According to the former text, supplications must be made toward "this house" as the place of divine forgiveness. In the latter, the temple recedes into the background and is replaced by an emphasis on the commandments. By quoting Solomon's petitions to be heard, the author of Nehemiah's prayer is very selective and does not employ the phrase אל־הבית הזה contained in 1 Kgs 8:29.[28] In Neh 1:9b, Nehemiah mentions the "place where I have chosen to make my name dwell." While Solomon connects this Deuteronomic centralization-formula inseparably to the temple, Nehemiah redefines its meaning to include much more.[29] "Implicit in the promise is restoration; a

---

24　The opening petition manifests stark stylistic conformity to 1 Kgs 8:28f./2 Chr 6:19f.:

25　That this verse is missing in 2 Chr 6 indicates that (despite the correspondence between Neh 1:6 and 2 Chr 6:20, rather than 1 Kgs 8:29) the version in 1 Kgs 8 served as the *Vorlage* for Nehemiah's prayer. Relevant is this regard is also *TAD* A4.7 where Yedoniah greets Bagohi (=Bigvai) with "may the God of Heaven give you favor before Darius the king (ולרחמן ישימניך קדם דריוהוש מלכא) and the princes of the palace....".

26　Neh 1:11a and Ps 106:46 are the only biblical texts that correspond both semantically and conceptually to 1 Kgs 8:50b.

27　This enumeration of situations in which one should pray continues in such narratives as Tob and Jdt, which portray their protagonists making intercession even before sexual intercourse (Tob 8:4-9), as well as in 1QS IX, 26bβ-X, 8, which instructs the משכיל as to the times and occasions when he should utter his praises.

28　This contrasts with Jonah's declaration that his prayer "came unto your holy temple" (2:7). See also 2 Kgs 19:14ff./Isa 37:14ff., 2 Chr 20:5ff., Ps 18:7 (2 Sam 22:7), and 138:2.

29　The promise envisioned in vv. 8-9 is a mosaic of quotations from Deut 30:1-5. There the promise consists of bringing them to the *land* of their fathers. Inasmuch as the numerous

return to 'the place [...]' implies the Divine Presence dwelling with the restored community."[30] So too, Solomon pleads that God forgive his people when they turn unto him with their whole heart, simply admit that they have sinned (v. 47) and pray (vv. 33, 35, 38, 47). Nehemiah, on the other hand, reminds God of his promise to gather his people when they turn unto him, confess to not having kept the commandments, statutes and laws and then *keep them* (v. 9).[31] Thus, the reconciliation and forgiveness envisioned in 1 Kgs 8 for those who pray towards the temple has been replaced in Nehemiah's prayer with a legal *des et do* principle, mirroring the incipient tension between the temple and Torah.

2.3.2 The Prayer Between Ezra 1-10 and Neh 2-13

This emphasis on adherence to the Mitzvoth and the complete absence of the temple in the latter is all the more astonishing given the fact that other late "penitential prayer" accounts – even those which portray exilic situations – combine both of these religious aspects.[32] In, e.g., Ps 138:2, Dan 6:11, 9:21, Ezra 9:4-5, 10:1, Jud 9:1, and Bar 1:10, prayers are made either in the direction or vicinity of the House of God.[33] In light of these narratives and the attention given to Jerusalem in Neh 1:2-3, one would expect v. 4b, which appears to have been added, to affirm in some way that Nehemiah directed his prayer toward the temple.[34] How then should one explain that the redactors of chap. 1 appear to have consciously drawn upon the prayer for the dedication of the temple yet have avoided a reference to it both in Nehemiah's prayer and in the supplement in v. 4b?

Perhaps the easiest way to answer this question is to compare the vocabulary of the confession with that of the remaining sections of the book. The terms צום ,החסד ,הברית ,ידה *hit.,* מצות ,המשפטים ,החקים ,העבד משה, etc., while quite

---

lexical and conceptual echoes in v. 9 refer the reader to the quoted passage, s/he should link Jerusalem with the intended place of the promised return.

30 Williamson (1985: 173).

31 While 1 Kgs 8:58 and 2 Kgs 23:3 combine this formula with adherence to the commandments, Solomon's prayer does not. In providing an *apologia* for the temple, the prayer demotes the importance of the commandments by never even mentioning them, placing the emphasis much more on "this house" as the place of divine forgiveness. The only prerequisite is that one acknowledge his or her sin and that one pray towards it. "For there in no one who does not sin...." (v. 46). Although possibly a gloss, this thought mirrors the fundamentals of the prayer's theology of prayer (even if it is a gloss) and guides the suppliant of Ps 130 (v. 3) and 143 (v. 2). It is, however, quite irreconcilable with the prevailing Deuteronomistic expectation that one never break the Mitzvoth.

32 Therefore, it is not possible to attribute the prayer's peculiarities to merely a difference in the time of composition or provenance.

33 Some of these texts present the prayers being made at the time of the evening sacrifices.

34 Dan 6:11 presents Daniel not only praying before God, but also toward Jerusalem; the authors of Neh 1:4b or 5a could have easily inserted such a statement.

foreign to Nehemiah's style, appear *en masse* in the portions of the book positioned between the first-person account (chaps. 8-10).[35] As all the people gather
on the plaza before the Water Gate, they implore Ezra to bring the "Book of
the Torah that YHWH had commanded for Israel"(8:1). They then celebrate
Sukkoth in conformity to the ordinance (כמשפט, v. 18). Later in the month, they
reassemble to mourn, fast and confess their sins and the iniquities of their
"fathers" (9:2b; cf. 1:6b),[36] who received the "commandments, statutes and
Torah by the hand of Moses your servant" (v. 14, cf. 1:7b), but did not follow
them. The conclusion to the confession in vv. 31-37, which begins exactly as
1:5-11a (האל הגדול והנורא שמר הברית וחסד), descries the loss of Judah's autonomy. In chap. 10, the community signs a pact that they would "walk in the law
of God given by the hand of Moses, servant of God, and guard and do all the
commandments of YHWH, our Lord, and his judgments and statutes" (v. 30, cf.
עשׂה/שׁמר + מצות/חקים/משׁפטים in 1:5, 7, 9).

When taken at face value, the transition to chap. 8 from the list in 7:6ff. portrays a rehearsal of what Ezra 2-3 reports as having occurred almost a century
earlier, namely an assembly in the seventh month.[37] But whereas on the prior
occasion, the leaders, Joshua and Zerubbabel, are eager to rebuild the altar and
offer sacrifices, now "all the people" are intent on hearing the words of the
Torah and keeping the Mitzvoth. The section of Neh 8-10 both concentrates on
the Torah and passes over the temple in silence. While 1 Esdr presents the
people gathering in "the place of the gate east of the temple," Neh 8:1 and 3
makes no effort whatsoever to confirm that the meeting was held in the vicinity
of the temple.[38] Indeed, 8:13 portrays the priests gathering with the heads of the
families not in the temple precincts, but rather around "Ezra, the *sōfēr*." Instead
of the priests giving directions for the activities of the sacred seventh month,
Ezra and the council discover that Sukkoth – a feast associated in Deut 31:9-13
with Joshua (cf. 8:17) and the reading of the law – was to be celebrated in the
seventh month. Compared with the earlier time when Sukkoth was accompanied by sacrifices on the newly built altar (Ezra 3:4), the people now disregard
the precise prescriptions for offerings in Lev 23:25ff. and Num 29, and they
treat the temple in the same way as the domestic sphere: The booths are built

---

35 The following list by no means exhausts the semantic concentration of the prayer's themes
    within chaps. 8-10: צום: 9:1; חסד: 9:17, 22; הברית: 9:8, 32; ידה *hit.*: 9:2, 3; מצות: 9:13, 14, 16,
    27, 10:30, 33; משׁפטים: 8:18, 9:13, 9:29, 10:30; חקים: 9:13, 14, 10:30; משׁה: 8:1, 14, 9:14, 10:30,
36 ידה *hit.* + חטאת is relatively rare, occurring only in Lev 16:21, Num 5:7, Ps 32:5 and Dan
    9:20.
37 In addition to the long lists in Neh 7:6ff. and Ezra 2, which are more or less the same, cf.
    Ezra 3:1 ("And as the seventh month approached, the Israelites were in cities. And the
    people gathered as one man in Jerusalem") and Neh 7:72b-8:1a ("And as the seventh month
    approached, the Israelites were in their cities. And all the people gathered as one man in the
    place before the Water Gate").
38 See §14.3.

first on the roofs of their houses and in their courtyards, and then in the temple-courts and elsewhere. When they gather again to confess their transgressions against the commandments (9:1-3), they neglect the temple altogether.[39] More-over, the following thirty-seven verses of the Levites' confession in Neh 9 recount Israel's history since the beginning and in considerable detail, but not once do they mention the temple.[40] The focus is rather on the land (הארץ, referred to ten times) and the Torah. After acknowledging that it has lost its national sovereignty because "our fathers" had failed to hearken unto the Mitz-voth, the community enters into an oath to abide by the Torah (10:1, 30). And before vv. 31ff. expand upon the general oath by enumerating various stipula-tions, it seems that the temple had fallen into complete oblivion.

Without devoting more attention here to these texts, we may apply our ob-servations to the question concerning Nehemiah's prayer. This text, as we have seen, adopts several conceptual aspects and formulations from Solomon's dedi-catory prayer, yet omits the references to the temple in appropriating the peti-tions to be heard and does not identify "the place where my name will dwell" with the temple. After comparing the text with the rest of the book, one can explain these modifications and the superceding role of the commandments as part of the same tendencies in chaps. 7-10. Just as Nehemiah avoids a reference to the temple, so do these chapters appear to deliberately substitute central features in Ezra 2-3: "All the people" assume the role of Jeshua and Zerubbabel (cf. Nehemiah's concern with Judah's population in chap. 1). Instead of rebuilding the altar, they hear the Torah read. Instead of offering sacrifices, they celebrate Sukkoth in their homes and throughout the city. And instead of sacri-ficing, they make confession.

Expanding the purview to the final shape of the book of Ezra-Neh, one ob-serves similar tendencies distinguishing Ezra 1-10 from Neh 1-13: While the former part portrays the Persian court sending Sheshbazzar, Joshua, Zerubbabel and Ezra to rebuild and "beautify" (7:27) the house of God,[41] the latter part portrays the crown sending Nehemiah to Judah to rebuild only the city-walls and -gates. In these chapters, the temple is portrayed in an unprecedented nega-tive light. The institution poses a threat for Nehemiah, who, as a layperson, must intervene to amend the profound abuses in the priesthood. In 13:4-9, Eliashib prepares a temple-chamber for his antagonist Tobiah. Likewise, in

---

39 Contrasting with this, Ezra waited on a prior occasion to make his confession until the evening sacrifices (Ezra 9:4-5) and "cast himself down before the house of God" (10:1, 6).

40 The absence of the temple contrasts sharply with the prayers made in the vicinity of the temple in 2 Kgs 19:14ff./Isa 37:14ff. and 2 Chr 20:5ff.

41 Even the transmitted wording of the so-called firman (7:11-26) consists almost exclusively of directions for Ezra to carry the imperial gifts to Jerusalem for offerings in the House of God. Only vv. 23, 25-26 refer to the legal functions which presumed to be associated with his vocation as a sōfēr; everything else has to do with his role as a priest.

13:28, Nehemiah expels a descendant of the high priest who was the son-in-law of his archenemy Sanballat. Moreover, what belongs in Ezra 1-10 to the temple and its personnel alone is allocated in Neh 1-13 to the entire city and its inhabitants.[42] At the dedication ceremonies, for example, the priests and Levites not only purify themselves, as in Ezra 6:20, but also the people, the gates (cf. Neh 3:1f.) and the wall (12:30; see also the tithe of people who "freely offered themselves" to dwell in "the Holy City" in 11:1ff., the use of the gates to prohibit entrance to foreign merchants on the Sabbath in 13:19-22a, and the genealogical test of Jerusalem's future residents in 7:4-72).

In consideration of the shift from temple to city as a whole in Neh 1-13, it seems that a later reader expanded the opening scene to the second half of Ezra-Neh with a text that mirrors the chief tendencies in Neh 8-12, namely (1) the transfer of the sanctity of the temple and priests to the city and people in general,[43] and (2) the ever-greater importance of the Mitzvoth for the laypeople and their sovereignty in the land. Therefore, with the inclusion of the prayer, Neh 1 marks off Neh 1-13 from Ezra 1-10, preparing the reader for the critique of the temple/priesthood and the concomitant decentralization of Jerusalem.[44]

That the prayer reflects a tendency to place the commandments in the preeminent position of the temple thus indicates that it was not composed with merely the first-person account in view. In disputing the redactional character of the passage, Kellermann, followed by Karrer, pointed to the parallels with chap. 13, where Nehemiah pursues Torah-oriented reforms.[45] While the analogies between the prayer and this chapter (as well as chap. 5) are undeniable, we must also take note of several differences. On the one hand, the practical measures manifest not mere familiarity with the Pentateuchal legislation; their severity extends far beyond the "letter of the law." On the other hand, the speeches in 5:9, 13:17-18, 26-27 employ a different vocabulary than of the prayer. To describe the diction in both as "deuteronomistisch" obscures the fact that this category encompasses many nuances, if not contradictions, but is by no means monolithic. For instance, Nehemiah never uses in chaps. 5 and 13 the terms הברית, מצוה, המשפטים, החקים, משה, עבד אלהים, חטאת, ירה htp., etc., which we encounter in his prayer. In these passages, he predicates his arguments rather on the concepts central to the narrative in 1:1-4 (הרעה in 13:7, 18, 27 and חרפה in 5:8).[46]

---

42 The work of Eskenazi (1988) elaborates this point with deep exegetical insight.

43 This transfer begins already in Ezra 9.

44 Cf. the comments of Pichon (1997: 185) and Reinmuth (2002: 59, 381-84).

45 Both Kellermann (1967: 10) and Karrer (2000: 136) predicate the integrity of chap. 1 on the assertion that 13:18, 25-27 are *also* formulated in "deuteronomistischer Sprache."

46 Karrer (2000: 204-5) even admits the differences between the prayer and the first-person account: "Während der Gedanke des Bundes Gottes mit seinem Volk und des Bewahrens der Gebote für den Aufbau des ganzen Gebetes Neh 1,5-11 bestimmend ist, fällt in der ge-

Instead of introducing only the first-person narrative, 1:5ff. has been composed, I contend, in order to bring the narrative in 1:1b-4 into conformity
with final shape of Neh 1-13. This proposal is supported by the analogies with
passages that most likely constitute the youngest additions to the book, namely
Neh 9-10.[47] The people assemble in Jerusalem to confess their sins (9:1-3). Then
the Levites acknowledge in their prayer that the loss of the land is a consequence of disobedience (vv. 4-37). Finally, the community pledges itself to the
Torah (10:1ff.). This narrative sequence presents faithfulness (אמן, 9:8, 10:1) to
the commandments as the *conditio sine qua non* for a reversal of the current
political distress (ובצרה גדולה אנחנו: ובכל־זאת אנחנו כרתים אמנה, 9:37b-10:1a). In
a strikingly similar fashion, Nehemiah displays deep sorrow in 1:4a upon hearing
that the people in the province are in turmoil and reproach. In what follows, he
prays and implores God on the behalf of his people and land (v. 4b), and his
confession exposes the root of the problem at hand (vv. 5-11a). *Prima facie*, the
distress of Judeans who survived the deportation is merely connected to the loss
of their autonomy symbolized by the destroyed ramparts of Jerusalem. According to the confession, however, the Judeans themselves are responsible for their
fate by forgetting the key to Israel's political prosperity. Nehemiah, on the other
hand, proves in his use of the divine predicates that he is still cognizant of the
axiom: YHWH is one keeps the covenant with those who in turn love him and
keep his commandments (1:5b). The repetition of the expression שמר את־המצות
in vv. 7 and 9 signifies the intention behind the insertion of the prayer: The
calamity in the province cannot be removed exclusively with political means
(i.e., Nehemiah's influence upon Artaxerxes). Since this situation originated
exclusively from the failure to keep the commandments, obedience is the precondition for the process of reparation. From these observations, it appears that
the redaction of Neh 1 has been directly influenced by Neh 9-10.[48]

---

samten weiteren Nehemiaschrift kein Wort für 'Bund' oder Gesetz mehr." This observation
is then followed by the explaination: "Die Maßnahmen Nehemias in Neh 13,4-31 und 5,1-
13 sollen jedoch sicherlich in dem Sinn verstanden werden, daß er gegen den Bruch von
Geboten Gottes vorgeht bzw. vorbeugt." The diversity that Karrer observes may, however,
indicate the work of various authors. Accordingly, the author of the prayer reinterprets the
work of the authors of chaps. 5 and 13.

47 See the analysis in §14.2.2.

48 Finally, we may note how the prayer reinterprets the events and characters depicted in the
first-person account. For example, Jerusalem is referred to in the prayer as "the place that I
have chosen to set my name there" (v. 9). By way of this Deuteronomic sobriquet, the
author underscores the necessity that the city's present condition, with breaches in its wall
and its gates burned in fire (v. 3), be finally changed. So too, the prayer emphasizes that the
Judeans in 1:3 are none other than the בני ישראל (v. 6), "your people whom you have
redeemed by your great power and your strong hand" (v. 10). Implicit in this identification
is that the ancient promises to Israel (vv. 8-9) apply equally to the inhabitants of Judah who
had survived the captivity. More importantly, these inhabitants are not those who *remained* in
the land; rather, they have been gathered back (vv. 9-10) from Exile. Thus, following the
pattern of Lev 26:33ff., the prayer brings the narrative in 1:1-4 into conformity with the

2.4 Conclusions

The present chapter has demonstrated that Nehemiah's prayer in 1:5-11a has been added in the final stages of the composition of Ezra-Neh. That the prayer could not have belonged to the earliest edition of the first-person account is suggested first by the transition from the participial expressions in 1:4b ("and I wept and mourned for days, and *was fasting* and *praying* to the God of Heaven") to the *wayyiqtol* in v. 5a ("And I said…"). If v. 4b were designed as an introduction to the prayer, we would expect to read: "…and I *fasted* and *prayed*…and said…." Second, v. 4b seems already to have been added to v. 4a. Otherwise, the expression "for days" would most likely have followed "fasting and praying before the God of Heaven" (v. 4b). Without v. 4b, however, the prayer in vv. 5-11a lacks an introduction and must have been added even later. A closer inspection of the prayer confirms this conclusion: While we would anticipate to hear the words spoken during the days immediately after Nehemiah heard the sad tidings from Judah, v. 6 refers to act of praying "day and night" and v. 11a contains a petition for success "today." The author of the prayer has thus failed to inform the reader that several months had transpired. Moreover, in the court scene (1:11b, 2:1ff.), Nehemiah is taken aback as Artaxerxes demands an explanation for his downcast countenance, which conflicts with his prescience evinced in 1:11a as to what was to occur on that same day.

The addition of v. 4b already introduces a new dimension to the scene in vv. 1-4a: Upon hearing the news that the inhabitants of Judah were in distress and that Jerusalem was in ruins, Nehemiah does not just mourn and weep (v. 4a), but also prays and fasts before the sovereign "God of Heaven." In this way, he manifests his personal piety and affirms implicitly that only divine assistance could alter the desperate situation.

Golah-orientation of Ezra-Neh. Furthermore, Nehemiah refers to the Judeans also as "your servants" (עבדיך, vv. 6, 10 and 11). In his rejoinder to Sanballat and his cohorts in 2:20, he uses this designation in combination with אלהי השמים to distinguish himself and those who had already consented to the rebuild Jerusalem from those who would thwart the project. In the prayer, however, the epithet appears no less than eight times and in an explicit relationship to the commandments. Nehemiah is a servant like Moses not only in that he is fully conversant with these stipulations, but also in his intercession for the children of Israel, who constitute the final group of "your servants" (vv. 6, 10, and 11). The use of "servants" in 2:20 assumes new dimensions inasmuch as the Judeans' unity derives from their common subordination to the Mitzvoth commanded to Moses, the servant *par excellence*; see Baltzer (1991). And the opponents to the building project are dissociated from "your servants who desire to fear your Name" (v. 11). The implied reader, as a servant, should follow the thought of the prayer to its conclusions: Living in conformity to the Mitzvoth is tantamount to following Nehemiah's example of solicitous concern for the condition of Jerusalem and Judah's inhabitants; political quietism is not an alternative.

While 1:4b describes the actions of fasting and supplication, the space devoted to the content of his final prayer in 1:5ff. allows Nehemiah to demonstrate a thorough facility with the biblical tradition and explain *how* the situation portrayed in the narrative originated. The sociopolitical situation is not due to the impotence of Israel's God, but rather to its infidelity vis-à-vis the Mitzvoth. This contrasts with the rest of the first-person account, in which neither Moses nor the Torah is mentioned. On the other hand, the third-person passages found within Nehemiah's report (chaps. 8-10) correspond quite closely to the prayer. The closest analogies are found in chaps. 9-10, which probably constitute the final additions to Ezra-Neh. In the lengthy confession of chap. 9, Israel's history is reviewed and obedience to the Torah is presented as the precondition for political sovereignty. The temple, on the other hand, is never mentioned, and this corresponds to the silence with regard to the temple in Neh 9. Since Nehemiah does not pray toward his ancestral cultic center (contrary to what we would anticipate in a text that manifests such familiarity with the late biblical tradition), it seems that the prayer has been inserted in introductory scene to Neh 1-13 as an anticipation of the book's shift in focus – from temple to Torah. In what follows, we test the validity of this proposal.

3. The Origins of Jerusalem's Ruins

3.1 Introduction

Although the narrative in chaps. 1-2 is more coherent without the prayer, friction persists. In responding to Nehemiah's inquiry, Hanani and the men from Judah do not clarify how and when the calamity had occurred in Jerusalem (1:3). Most scholars consider it implausible that the Babylonians caused the devastation, as an event some 140 years earlier would not have prompted such an intense reaction from Nehemiah. According to the Artaxerxes-correspondence in Ezra 4:7-23, the reconstruction of the city was nearing completion (cf. v. 12). If these letters are authentic (or at least reliable), how can Hanani report a few years later that the wall and gates were in need of repair?

Continuing the composition-historical investigation of Ezra-Neh, the present chapter addresses the problems created by Neh 1 when read against the backdrop of Ezra 4. In §3.2, we examine several aspects of the narrative in 1:1-4 which suggest to many that the devastation had recently occurred. In §3.3, we then focus on Ezra 4 in an attempt to demonstrate that it contributes little to our historical knowledge of the period, yet much to the *Tendenz* of Ezra-Neh.

3.2 Examination of Neh 1:1-4

It is often assumed that 1:1-4 portrays the arrival of an official detachment commissioned by the Jerusalemite authorities to inform Artaxerxes' Jewish cupbearer of a turn of events in the province.[1] When one compares the passage with the depictions of Greek envoys, such an assumption appears tenable. V. 2 states that Hanani, one of Nehemiah's brothers,[2] and several Judeans came to the citadel in Susa, the same city in which the king received ambassadors according to Greek authors.[3] Hanani (and Nehemiah) may have belonged to an

---

1 This approach began with Wellhausen (1894: 161) and has been adopted by most modern commentaries, with the exception of Gunneweg's (1987: 42f.).

2 That Hanani was Nehemiah's blood brother and not merely his comrade (חבר), as Rashi and many subsequent commentators have maintained, is corroborated by 7:2. Moreover, Nehemiah does not refer to the other Judeans as his brethren in v. 2.

3 Cf., e.g., Herodotus, 7.133-137, Xenophon, *Hell.* 1.4.5, and Hofstetter (1972).

aristocratic family,[4] which would agree with the fact that the Hellenic legations consisted of men from the uppermost class.[5] Thucydides reports that an audience with the king was difficult to obtain.[6] In such a case, a mediator may have been sought. Thus, Plutarch tells how Themistocles turned to an important official to obtain a hearing.[7] For the court's decision, one was sometimes required to wait for a long time. Xenephon recounts how a Greek envoy was delayed for more than three years in Susa before they were informed of the decision.[8] Against the backdrop provided by the Greek material, it seems plausible that Hanani and his company had been sent as emissaries to the imperial court after a recent calamity in Jerusalem. Because they had either failed to obtain an audience with the king or were still awaiting a response, they turned to Artaxerxes' Jewish cupbearer, hoping that he would be able to represent their case.

Although this interpretation appears at first warranted, a closer examination of the text discovers insurmountable problems. First, Nehemiah is the one who inquires as to the situation in Judah: ואשאלם על-היהודים וגו. "[D]ie Initiative, so scheint es, geht bei der Begegnung von ihm aus, und nicht die Befragten sprechen zur Berichterstattung bei ihm vor. Dies scheint also gegen die Annahme zu sprechen, es habe sich um eine Gesandtschaft gehandelt."[9]

Second, had Hanani and his company been officially deployed, we would expect v. 2 not only to portray them *telling* Nehemiah before he asks, but also to make use of the verb שלח instead of בוא. This argument is substantiated by Neh 6, which describes several occasions of Sanballat and Nehemiah employing emissaries for communicative purposes. There it is always said that the messages/messengers were *sent* (שלח, six times in vv. 2-8).[10]

Third, if Hanani had failed in obtaining an audience with the king, Nehemiah, in keeping with the tendentious character of his account, would have surely reported this in order to contrast his own success with prior failures. In this way he would have been able to illustrate even more poignantly how his position and good rapport with the king were indispensable to securing the authorization to build: While the Judeans on their own were helpless, they gratefully had an influential servant of the imperial government on their side. However, the text merely presents the Judeans coming to Susa. The reader must, therefore, presume that the reason for their visit was not to seek permission to rebuild Jerusalem. Rather, Nehemiah emphasizes how he adventitiously learned

---

4   See Williamson (1985: 182, 242).
5   See Hofstetter (1972: 97).
6   1.137, where a petition for an appointment with the king is made in writing.
7   *Them.*, 27. See Junge (1940).
8   *Hell.* 1.3.13 and 4.1-7. See Hofstetter (1972: 101).
9   Gunneweg (1987: 42). Although interpreting the group as an official delegation, Blenkinsopp (1985: 207) notes the problem that Nehemiah is the first to speak.
10 6:5a provides the most detailed description of the manner of correspondence.

from his brother of the plight of the province. This awareness, with which the following narrative is set into motion, resulted from his own solicitude, as he took the initiative to inquire about the plight of people in the province and Jerusalem's welfare.[11]

Now if Hanani and his company, according to 1:1-4, neither formed an official legation commissioned by Judah nor were eager to inform Nehemiah that a misfortune had recently befallen Jerusalem, then caution is also recommended with regard to the conclusion that the condition of the city had recently taken a turn for the worse.[12]

According to the consensus of modern scholars, the report would not have elicited such a reaction from Nehemiah, as reported in 1:4, if the catastrophe had occurred many years before. Were the description of the city in v. 3 to relate to the condition after the Babylonian siege, this would not have been news to him, who presumably belonged to a family deported in 587/6 BCE. As he would have also kept himself up-to-date on all changes in his homeland, his reaction supposedly precludes the possibility that events in the distant past were the cause of the reported ruins.

There are, however, several arguments that gainsay this conclusion. First, one must take into account the tendentious qualities of the narrative. In depicting his conversation with his brother and the group from Judah, Nehemiah confines the account to the most indispensable details. The economy of the narrative functions to throw his own reaction into sharp relief: "And as I heard these words, I sat down and wept and mourned for days" (v. 4a). This statement causes the modern reader to presume that Nehemiah had heard something extremely unusual. Actually, however, he behaves in a stereotypical manner.[13] How else, moreover, would we expect Nehemiah to recount his response? Had he merely told his readers, "I was sad as I heard this," the story would lack the dramatic aspect and tension without which one loses interest. As it is, we know

---

11 Even an ancient reader so knowledgeable in diplomatic affairs such as Josephus did not understand the narrative as portraying a delegation from Jerusalem (*Ant.* 11.159ff.).

12 If Hanani is Nehemiah's actual brother, the problem with the theory that 1:2 describes an official delegation is even more problematic. The scene likely intends to illustrate how Hanani visited Nehemiah in Susa and how Nehemiah displayed his solicitude for his homeland and its capital by inquiring immediately about the situation in the province.

13 For example, as Ezra hears that "the holy seed had mingled themselves with the people of the lands," he tears his garments, plucks off his hair and beard, and sits down confounded (9:1-5). This exaggerated reaction constitutes a running motif in Ezra-Neh (Ezra 3:12, 10:1; Neh 8:9, 12:43). For a study of mourning rites, see Kutsch (1986). – One of the reasons that many pre-modern interpreters of Neh 1 linked the news in v. 3 with the condition of the city after 587/6 BCE may be that they did not find Nehemiah's reaction in v. 4 to be abnormal.

that Nehemiah was "a pious Jew who has not allowed preferment at a foreign court to dampen his ardour for Jerusalem and its honour."[14]

That 1:4 portrays a stereotypical response is indicated furthermore by the use of the ויהי כשמעי. In examining the literary structure of the first-person account, one cannot help but noticing the frequency of the similar expression, "and as he or they heard that…." While by no means rare in biblical narratives, the circumstantial clause with שמע occurs no less than nine times throughout the few chapters of the building report. In what follows, I refer to the structure it lends to the narrative as the "שמע-schema."

The "שמע-Schema" of the First-Person Account

1:4 When I heard (ויהי כשמעי) these words I sat down and wept, and mourned for days, fasting and praying before the God of Heaven.

2:10 But when Sanballat the Horonite and Tobiah the Ammonite official heard (וישמע), it displeased them greatly that someone had come to seek the welfare of the children of Israel.

2:19 But when Sanballat, the Horonite, and Tobiah, the Ammonite servant, and Geshem, the Arab, heard of it (וישמע), they mocked and ridiculed us, saying, "What is this that you are doing? Are you rebelling against the king?"

3:33 Now when Sanballat heard (ויהי כאשר שמע) that we were building the wall, he was angry and greatly enraged, and he mocked the Jews.

4:1 But when Sanballat and Tobiah and the Arabs and the Ammonites and the Ashdodites heard (ויהי כאשר שמע) that the repairing of the walls of Jerusalem was going forward and the gaps were beginning to be closed, they were very angry….

4:9 When our enemies heard (ויהי כאשר־שמעו) that their plot was known to us, and that God had frustrated it, we all returned to the wall, each to his work.

5:6 I was very angry when I heard (כאשר שמעתי) their outcry and these complaints.

6:1 Now when it was reported to (ויהי כאשר נשמע ל) Sanballat, Tobiah, Geshem, the Arab, and to the rest of our enemies that I had built the wall and that there was no gap left in it….

6:16 And when all our enemies heard of it (ויהי כאשר־שמעו), all the nations around us were afraid and fell greatly in their own esteem; for they perceived that this work had been accomplished with the help of our God.

Surveying the placement of the שמע-formula, one observes that it functions transitionally, either concluding or introducing a given conceptual unit. These units typically consist of (1) an advancement made in the restoration of the wall, (2) a disruptive maneuver by the antagonist, introduced with "and as P.N. heard," and then (3) Nehemiah's response or counteractive measures. For example, in 2:17-18 the people first resolve to commence the work, what in turn

---

14 Clines (1984:137), with references to Ezra 9:3, Dan 6:10, and Ps 137:5ff. See also Mowinckel (1964: 68f.). One should not forget that mourning for the destruction of Jerusalem has continued ever since the Babylonian destruction. Evidence ranging from the redactional history of Lamentations to the continuing significance of the Wailing Wall today renders it completely possible that Nehemiah is moved to grief by a tragedy long past.

provokes the contempt of their foes in v. 19: "But when Sanballat…*heard* this, they laughed us to scorn, and despised us." The contemptuous words of Sanballat and his cohorts are then finally met with Nehemiah's exclusivist rejoinder, which simultaneously motivates the builders to continue: "The God of Heaven, he will prosper us; therefore we, his servants, will arise and build. But you have no portion, nor right, nor memorial in Jerusalem" (v. 20). Depicting simultaneously reconstruction of the wall and reaffirmation of group-identity, the narrative progresses dialectically. In the third and final movement of each sequence, the builders gain starker profile as the adversary is rebuffed. Initially, Nehemiah achieves unity by way of a *common* enterprise – the building of the walls. This, in turn, engenders a *common* enemy, whose antipathy serves finally to boost the solidarity of the workers. Not only does the dialectic operate in the discrete literary units, but we also witness an escalation in the building report as a whole. From one section to the next, the enmity between protagonist and antagonist grows ever stronger until the wall is finally built, enabling Nehemiah to devote his attention to the equally critical, "extramural" issues (chap. 13).

The exceptions to, or variations of, this pattern are relegated to 1:4 and 5:6 – the two occasions when Nehemiah describes his own reaction.[15] The context of 5:6 pertains to the progress in the restoration only in an expanded sense. By means of the שמע-schema, the author establishes a continuity with the preceding passages. As Sanballat hears in 3:33 of the Judeans' initiative, he is *angry* (ויחר לו). As he and the other antagonists hear again in 4:1 that they were making steady advancements, they are *very angry* (ויחר להם מאד). Directly thereafter Nehemiah hears the complaint of the people against their Judean kinsfolk (5:1-5), and he too is *very angry* (ויחר לי מאד). In the present sequence of the narrative, his reaction contrasts sharply with that of his foes. While they are distraught by the headway made in the restoration, he is distraught by an *impediment* to the progress.

In 1:4 the שמע-formula also functions to juxtapose two ways of reacting. When Nehemiah hears Hanani's report, he is extremely displeased. As the prologue to the account, this scene provides the positive example with which the reader may compare the antagonists' behavior in the remaining narrative. We should not, therefore, be surprised when Nehemiah describes such an emotional response to the news from Judah.

Finally, it is worth considering whether the poignancy of Nehemiah's grief is related more to the situation of the Judean population (v. 3a) than to the con-

---

15 Clines (1984: 158, 165), Williamson (1985: 225), Blenkinsopp (1988: 225), Throntveit (1992: 59-60), and Reinmuth (2002: 93) all point out that the accounts of the enemies' reactions evinces this pattern, but have not noted that chaps. 1 and 5 also make use of the שמע-formula. Significantly, Blenkinsopp, Throntveit, and Reinmuth conclude that chap. 5 was not composed for its present context.

dition of Jerusalem (v. 3b). Hanani and the other visitors give priority to the
former and do not directly connect the physical ruins to the social calamity. It is,
therefore, surprising that most commentators interpret Nehemiah's sorrow as if
it were elicited primarily by the condition of the city. That he later concerns
himself primarily with the restoration of the wall should not prejudice the reading of the present passage.[16] The wording of vv. 3a and 4a points the reader to
the next appearance of the שמע-formula (2:10). In emphasizing his sorrow upon
hearing of the social distress (הנשארים ברעה גדלה), Nehemiah provides a point of
contrast to the distress (וירע להם רעה גדלה) of his enemies as they *hear* that
someone had come to seek the welfare of the children of Israel.[17] The building
enterprise is not yet in view in this description of Sanballat's and Tobiah's reaction. One may conclude from these striking parallels to 2:10 that Nehemiah's
chagrin was evoked above all by the plight of the people.[18]

Now, if the chapter places the plight of the population in the foreground,
Hanani and his company are not reporting what had recently transpired.
Nehemiah is merely told in v. 3a, in keeping with his inquiry as to the actual
situation in Judah, that the people are currently in great distress and reproach:
הנשארים אשר־נשארו מן־השבי שם במדינה ברעה גדלה ובחרפה. This nominal clause is
to be understood in the present continuous tense. If the condition of distress
had resulted from a recent incident, why do the Judeans not say this? From the
very ambiguous wording of the whole verse, which does not link the calamity
directly to the condition of the wall, both Nehemiah and the reader would have
to surmise that the sociopolitical situation in Judah had been precipitated by a
number of long-term factors. This would likewise comport with 2:17, which
presents the distress (הרעה) and reproach (חרפה) as an *ongoing* condition: ונבנה
את־חומת ירושלם ולא־נהיה עוד חרפה. Insofar as this applies to v. 3a, v. 3b also
does not portray a recent desolation. Corresponding to the statement that the
people are currently encountering adversity, this half of the verse simply describes the present state of the city: וחומת ירושלם מפרצת ושעריה נצתו באש. Significantly, the Judeans do not say that the wall *has been* broken down, but rather
that it *is* broken down.

---

16 We must treat 1:1-4 here on its own terms, since we have not yet established whether it has
been added to the building report.
17 Without having observed these literary connections to 2:10, Hölscher (1923: 525) arrived at
a similar conclusion: "Man mißversteht 1, 3 meistens dahin, als ob hier von einer neuerli-
chen Zerstörung Jerusalems die Rede wäre; aber das ist trotz Esr 4, 23 eine bloße Erfindung
der Ausleger. Was Nehemia erfährt und was ihn in Trauer versetzt, ist nicht die ihm natürlich bekannte Kunde von dem zerstörten Zustande Jerusalems, sondern die Nachricht von
der Not und Schmach, in der die Judäer leben."
18 Moreover, in expanding the opening scene with the prayer, which never mentions the
devastation of the city, later readers appear to have understood the plight of the people to
be the reason for Nehemiah's response in v. 4.

3.3 Neh 1-2 and the Artaxerxes-Correspondence

3.3.1 Comparison of the Texts

An examination of the Artaxerxes-correspondence in Ezra 4:9-22 bolsters our arguments. If one should interpret Hanani's report against the backdrop of this text, why does the latter never state that the Samarian officials, in implementing the directions of the court (Ezra 4:17-22), overstepped their commission and destroyed what had been built thus far?[19] According to most commentators, the great zest with which Rehum as the chancellor (בעל־טעם) and Shimshai as the secretary (ספרא) executed the king's edict provides the grounds for *supposing* that they also razed the city.[20] These grounds are admittedly quite shaky.

Why then do so many scholars believe that the devastation reported in Neh 1:3 was instigated by these two officials? The reason is the information contained in the correspondence. Rehum and Shimshai inform Artaxerxes that the Jews who had made Aliyah "are building the rebellious and wicked city. They are completing the walls and are joining the foundations" (Ezra 4:12). Responding to this complaint lodged against the Golah, the king prohibits the continuation of the work: "Therefore issue a decree that these men be made to cease and that this city not be rebuilt…" (v. 21). Thus, on the one hand, the building of Jerusalem had made considerable progress in the reign of Artaxerxes, and, on the other, Hanani reports that the city is still in state of extensive ruination. In order to avoid a contradiction between Ezra 4 and Neh 1, one must postulate that some catastrophe had occurred just before Nehemiah's encounter with the Judeans. According to the conventional approach, Rehum and Shimshai were directly responsible for this catastrophe, since our putative sources for this period in Ezra-Neh present these two figures as the chief opponents to the Golah. That 4:23 does not explicitly say that they caused the devastation is attributed to the narrator's lack of knowledge: "With no other source

---

19 V. 23: "Now when the copy of king Artaxerxes' letter was read before Rehum and Shishai the scribe and their companions, they went up in haste to Jerusalem and unto the Judeans and made them to cease by force and power (ובטלו המו באדרע וחיל)."

20 For example, Bertholet argued: "Die Judenfeinde scheinen von der ihnen dort erteilten königlichen Erlaubnis, den Wiederaufbau Jerusalems gewaltsam zu hindern, so energisch Gebrauch gemacht zu haben, dass als Resultat herauskam, was die historische Voraussetzung unseres Verses [Neh 1:3] ist" (1902:47). See also Galling (1954: 199) and Blenkinsopp (1988: 115). Williamson (1985: 64) has recognized the problem: "The king's order was only that the work be stopped, not that it be destroyed, and in his account the narrator does not indicate that Rehum and his colleagues overstepped this commission, though he paints as negative a picture as he can by introducing the strong element of force." Later, he writes: "This report cannot refer to the destruction of Jerusalem by Nebuchadnezzar some 140 years previously. A recent event, as yet unconfirmed in Susa, must be intended, and for this the destruction mentioned briefly in Ezra 4:23 presents itself as the ideal, and indeed only possible, candidate" (1985: 172).

of information than the copy of the letter itself, it is possible that he was un-aware of the fact that the walls were destroyed at this time...."[21]

While the documents in Ezra 4 clearly present Jerusalem in a much different condition than portrayed by Neh 1, an interpretation of the latter account on its own terms raises serious doubt as to whether the city had been destroyed in the reign of Artaxerxes.

First, it is problematic that Hanani does not identify the perpetrators. If Jerusalem's gates had recently been set on fire, Nehemiah would have certainly needed to know who committed this act prior to his audience with the king. Assuming that the imperial court had authorized the demolition, his response to Artaxerxes in 2:3 would imply, with the utmost impudence, that the king is re-sponsible for his depression. That Artaxerxes is not offended by Nehemiah's reply thus warrants against the conclusion that he had just issued a decree pro-hibiting the construction of the city-wall and permitting the destruction of what had already been built.[22] In responding tothe discrepancies between Ezra 4 and Neh 2, Blenkinsopp remarks, "It may seem surprising that Artaxerxes did not even bother to inquire further about the supposed hotbed of rebellion, the sub-ject of his response to Rehum's letter of complaint (Ezra 4:19-20)." Yet instead of following Wellhausen and Kosters in denying the historicity of the informa-tion in Ezra 4,[23] Blenkinsopp treats the inconsistency by speculating about the king's underlying motives: "The most likely explanation is that Artaxerxes was not 'taken in,' but decided that this was the opportune moment for reversing the decree (cf. Ezra 4:21), for shrewdly calculated political reasons."[24]

Second, one cannot doubt that an act of benevolence, boosting the relations with the community in Jerusalem, was in the political interests of the imperial government. Yet if Nehemiah had indeed succeeded in obtaining a reversal of

---

21　Williamson (1985: 64). This opinion assumes that the compiler of chaps. 1-6 carried over v. 23 in the process of appropriating the source for chap. 4. However, if the compiler was so selective as to include only an excerpt of this putative source, why did he not excise this verse and/or compose a new note that agrees with Nehemiah's account?

22　If the gates had, on the other hand, been burned during the administration of officially appointed magistrates who acted against the will of the imperial government, then it is sur-prising that both Artaxerxes and Nehemiah do not concern themselves with the culpable (cf. 1:4 and 2:4). In any event, the king would likely have first ascertained the identity of the miscreants before sending Nehemiah, so that the city would not suffer another catastrophe soon after it had been rebuilt.

23　In his historic dispute with Meyer, Wellhausen pointed to Nehemiah's depiction of the conversation with Artaxerxes as evidence that the city had not been recently destroyed. "[E]s ist nach Neh. 2 undenkbar, dass Artaxerxes selber die Zerstörung der Mauer befohlen habe." (1895: 170). Likewise, Kosters pointed out that Nehemiah does not allude ("mit keinem einzigen Worte") to the earlier command that prohibited the building and allowed for the devastation (1895:60). With a pat response to this argument, Meyer contended that Nehemiah's taciturnity is to be understood as a clever tactic: "Eine solche Dummheit sollte er [Kosters] doch dem gewandten Manne nicht zutrauen" (1896: 58-n. 2).

24　1988: 214.

Artaxerxes' decree, why has he bypassed the opportunity to tell his readers about this great accomplishment? In contrast to what we anticipate, his account only describes the king more or less casually granting permission to his beloved cupbearer.[25] Assuming that the contemporary readers were aware that this same ruler had previously banned the construction of "the seditious city" (4:15, 19), they would have realized that he was now rescinding the interdiction for the sake of Nehemiah.[26] Rather than concluding that the text aims to conceal the historical consequences entailed in Artaxerxes' acquiescence, it is consequently much more probable that the king had never even sent the prohibitive firman found in Ezra 4:17-22.

In his attempt to harmonize Neh 2 with Ezra 4, Meyer sought support in Artaxerxes' putative idiosyncrasies: "Er war ein gutmüthiger, aber in Folge dessen auch ein schwacher Herr."[27] That this ruler altered his decree is to be explained, therefore, by recourse to his putative capriciousness. Similar arguments have been occasioned by the mention of the queen consort in 2:6. "Nach allem was wir wissen, war Artaxerxes I. durch Frauen leicht zu beeinflussen; auch der Rebell Megabyzos verdankte dem Eintreten der königlichen Frauen für ihn sein Leben."[28] Surprisingly, this proposal – that feminine charms induced the king to assent to Nehemiah's request – has been widely accepted by commentators.[29] In turning to such psychological explanations, these scholars prove only that the plain sense of the text does not commend their conclusions.

Third, if the devastation was of late, Nehemiah would not tell Artaxerxes that "the city lies in ruins" (חרבה...העיר, 2:3). Why does he not say that city *has been* destroyed, instead of using a nominal clause, which expresses an ongoing situation? Once again, most commentators treat this problem psychologically, namely, as Nehemiah's canny attempt of concealment. Instead of explicitly mentioning Jerusalem, which Artaxerxes supposedly knew as "the rebellious and wicked city" (Ezra 4:12), he calls the city "the house of my ancestors' sepul-

---

25 Williamson describes this account superbly: "In realistic fashion, the king is portrayed as direct in his approach and yet totally relaxed, initially displeased at an apparent breach of etiquette (v 2), but then almost carelessly pleased to gratify a court favorite" (1985: 178).

26 This argument applies even more for those who presume that Nehemiah originally composed his account for the imperial court.

27 "Dass er da [bei den Finanzen] stutzig wird, ob die Massregeln, die er gebilligt hat, richtig waren, dass er die Inhibirung des Baus 'bis auf Weiteres' (v. 21) verfügt, ist doch eben so wenig auffallend oder gar 'undenkbar' [Wellhausen], wie dass er nachher einem Mundschenken zu Liebe, den er gern hat, die Ausführung des Mauerbaus gestattet"(1896: 57-58).

28 Rudolph (1949: 107). The arguments for the influence of women on Artaxerxes are presented in Olmstead (1948: 312, 344). That biblical scholars must question, with the consensus of Classicists (cf. Bigwood [1978]), the reliability of Ctesias account in general and the historicity of the Megabyzos' insurrection in particular has been emphasized by Hoglund (1992).

29 Cf., e.g., Hunter (1890: 294), Rawlinson (1891: 89), Clines (1984: 142-43) and Blenkinsopp (1988: 215).

chers" (בית־קברות אבתי).[30] Such an inference from this circumlocution is, however, quite arbitrary. If his intention was to convey the impression that
Jerusalem was a peaceful city, why does he not manifest any reservations about
informing Artaxerxes that "its gates have been consumed in fire"? The use of
אכל + באש instead of יצת *nif.* + באש (1:3 and 2:17) also does not suggest that
Nehemiah is describing the devastation in a less suspicious manner,[31] since אכל
+ באש appears in 2:13 where we would expect the ruins to be presented without
concern for the king's perception of the city.[32]

Moreover, Nehemiah begins his address in 2:17 by drawing attention to the
state of disrepair and despair: "Look at the sorry state in which we are – how
Jerusalem is in ruins (חרבה) and its gates destroyed by fire. Come let us build up
the wall of Jerusalem, that we be no more a reproach." According to Ezra 4,
however, the people were eagerly building until the chancellery forced them to
desist (4:23). In order to resume building, they would have only needed to hear
that Artaxerxes had changed his mind.[33] To be sure, Nehemiah would not have
been required to convince them by appealing to the current social calamity. As it
is, the building enterprise appears to constitute a new proposal, requiring motivation and organization (2:16ff.). Thus, in order not to contradict Ezra 4,
Nehemiah would have to tell his readers that his proposal was to *return to* the
building project that the people themselves had initiated (cf. Ezra 4:12). According to Ezra 4, Artaxerxes simply gave the word to Rehum and Shimshai,
and the construction work ceased.

If the king was later willing to allow the building to resume, why did he not
simply send another letter to these two officials? In that case, he would not have
had to forgo the services of his highly regarded cupbearer. The letters requested
by Nehemiah (2:7-8) consist of an order of safe conduct through the provinces
of the western satrapies and an order that the materials be furnished for the
construction projects. Yet, in addition to these edicts, a command to the
Samarian authorities to allow the city to be rebuilt is significantly not reported.[34]

It is also significant that Nehemiah, upon his arrival in Judah, does not tell us
of an encounter with the currently officiating magistrates. Given that so much
space of his account is devoted to the conflicts with his opponents, all of whom

---

30 See Myers (1965: 99) as well as Rudolph (1949: 107), Clines (1984: 141), Williamson (1985:
179) and Blenkinsopp (1988: 214).
31 See Batten (1913: 192).
32 Moreover, why does Nehemiah mention the gates, the most important component of a
fortification system? Similarly, the intended readers would not have believed that Artaxerxes
granted his permission and issued letters (2:7-8) without even knowing the name of the city.
They would have assumed that Artaxerxes knew the ethnicity of his cupbearer.
33 The report of the king's words form an addendum to his address (ואף־דברי המלך, 2:18aβ).
34 In §5.2.2, we conclude that the petition for these letters constitute a secondary expansion of
vv. 1-10. If this conclusion is warranted, it is surprising that redactors did not include a letter that reversed Artaxerxes' interdiction of building Jerusalem.

are mentioned by name, the silence with regard to Rehum and Shimshai is astonishing. If Artaxerxes, as generally supposed, intended to replace the latter two with Nehemiah as his new local official, then why does chap. 2 not portray him commissioning a new administrator? Instead, he sends his cupbearer with a single task: to build the walls of his ancestral city.[35]

3.3.2 The Authenticity of the Artaxerxes-Correspondence

How then should we explain the insurmountable inconsistencies between the documents in Ezra 4 and the account in Neh 1-3? On the one hand, Ezra 4 clearly states that Artaxerxes interrupted the ongoing construction of Jerusalem, and, on the other hand, Nehemiah presents the city in a condition of utter disrepair and appears fully oblivious to the existence of the edict in Ezra 4:17ff. Since one cannot presume that Ezra 4:12 refers to the wall built by Nehemiah,[36] another solution must be sought. According to the thesis defended here, the Artaxerxes-correspondence, rather than representing an authentic source, has been composed ad hoc for the book of Ezra-Neh.[37]

The first evidence supporting this thesis is the disparities between the letters in Ezra 4 and other official Aramaic documents from the same period. According to Williamson, the use of stereotyped formulae such as וכען ("and now") for transitions from one part of the letter to the next (vv. 11, 13, 14, 17, 21) and the introductory declaration ידיע להוא ל (PN) די ("let it be known to PN that," vv. 12, 13) "can be exactly paralleled in contemporary documents, a fact that becomes all the more striking when they are compared with the quite different practices of Greek letter-writing later on."[38] There is a significant problem with this argument: Both of these formulae continue to be used in letters incorporated in late works discovered at Qumran, and these letters provide a striking analogy to the epistolary forms in Ezra 4. In a fragment from the Aramaic "Book of Giants" (4QEnGiants³ ar [4Q203]), which was probably composed between the third century and 164 BCE,[39] a letter is reproduced that begins with

---

35 Hoglund (1992: 83-4), arguing against Alt's view of a non-autonomous Judah before Nehemiah, maintains that Rehum, Shimshai and others stationed in Samaria successfully assumed control over Jerusalem upon receiving the letter transmitted in Ezra 4:17ff. Shortly thereafter, Nehemiah was made governor. Although Hoglund's critique of Alt is justified, his proposal is problematic insofar as we are not told until the end of chap. 5, a passage that appears to have been added, that Nehemiah acted with gubernatorial authority.

36 According to Neh 6:15, the wall was completed within fifty-two days, while Ezra 4 presents the correspondence interrupting the construction apparently for a lengthy period.

37 This discussion of the historicity of the letters is confined to several new arguments.

38 1985: 60.

39 *Editio princeps* in Milik and Black (1976: 298-339). For the dating, see Stuckenbruck (1997: 28ff.).

the declaration ידיע להוא לכון די (line 7) and employs the transition marker וכען (line 12).[40] Likewise, Darius introduces the contents of his letter in 4QprEsther (4Q550ᵃ⁻ᶜ), which probably originated ca. 200 BCE, with ידיע להוא לכון די.[41] Insofar as the authors of these fabricated letters took great pains to mimic what they considered to be the form of official Aramaic documents from the Persian period, one cannot rule out the possibility that also the Artaxerxes-correspondence never existed independently of its transmitted context.[42]

The letter in 4Q550 is furthermore significant inasmuch as Darius employs the same salutation (שלם) as Artaxerxes in Ezra 4:17. In a helpful investigation of Northwest Semitic epistolography, Schwiderski has demonstrated that this form of greeting never appears in ancient and imperial Aramaic letters.[43] Contrasting with the varied and lengthier salutations in the official correspondence from the Persian period and in the Hebrew-Canaanite letters from the ninth to sixth cent. BCE, the Hebrew and Aramaic letters of the First Jewish War and the Bar Kochba Revolt confine the greeting to שלום or שלם, just as in Ezra 4:17 and 4Q550.[44] This monotony also characterizes the Greek epistolary tradition of the Hellenistic period, in which χαίρειν pervades as the salutatory expression. Inasmuch as χαίρειν represents the Greek equivalent to the Hebrew *Einwortformeln*,[45] Schwiderski has set forth a strong case for the influence of this Greek epistolary tradition on the composition of letters in earlier Jewish literature, including those in Ezra 4.

Additional aberrations from the imperial Aramaic letters are discernible. Schwiderski demonstrates that the salutation is not necessary when the sender holds a higher status. Thus, when Arsames reproaches the recipients of his letters or threatens them with punishment when they do not follow his directs, the greeting is conspicuously lacking.[46] In the case of Ezra 4:17ff. where Artaxerxes strongly admonishes Rehum and Shimshai (4:22a), we would expect the sender to forgo the greetings.[47] Astonishing is also that these petitioners fail to greet the king. Schwiderski notes that both the salutations differ widely in the official

---

40 This late text also still employs the Persian term (אגרתא...) פרשגן, as in Ezra 4:11. In Esth 3:14 and 4:8, this word is apparently misspelled: (הכתב) פתשגן. Meyer (1896: 22) regarded this as support for the antiquity of the letters in Ezra 4 since it spells the word correctly. Given the use in 4Q203, Meyer's argument is no longer tenable.

41 *Editio princeps* in Milik (1992).

42 In Add Esth B 1-7 (cf. also II Targum), 3 Macc 3:12-29 and Dan 3:31-32; 6:26-27, we notice the same attempt in Jewish literature from the Hellenistic period to draw upon official documental style. The first two examples are remarkably similar to both the form and *Tendenz* of Ezra 4.

43 This is easiest to observe from his comparative charts (2000: 220-23).

44 2000: 249-50.

45 Schwiderski (2000:318-n. 199). points to LXX Isa 48:22.

46 Cf., e.g., *TAD* A(5)6.8 and 10.

47 2000: 377.

Aramaic letters and the greeting is always very elaborate when the recipient is clearly a person of higher status. That Rehum and Shimshai forget the salutation in Ezra 4:11 is an insurmountable problem for the proponents of the letter's authenticity. "Ein Schreiben an den König als ranghöchsten Empfänger ohne Eingangsgruß hätte es mit Sicherheit nicht gegeben."[48]

Another problem is that the recipient would not be able to understand an important point of Artaxerxes' response without having first read the petition in vv. 12-16. In v. 19, the king says that he "gave a command and a search was made and it is found that..." (ומני שים טעם ובכרו והשכחו די). The difficulty consists in the fact that the reader does not know where they made the search, unless s/he glances back to v. 15. In presupposing the wording of the prior petition, Artaxerxes' response does not comport with the Aramaic epistolary tradition of the Persian period. As Janzen has demonstrated with regard to the Arsames-correspondence, we would expect a verbatim quotation of previous letters with the formula, PN *kn 'mr*.[49] Nothing of the sort, however, is found in Artaxerxes' response; to the contrary, his letter abbreviates Rehum's and Shimshai's request. While such a truncated style is not what one would expect in a letter composed by the imperial court, it appears frequently in Hebrew narrative. A prominent example is Neh 8:16a: "So the people went, brought and made themselves Sukkoth...." The antecedents – where the people went and what they brought – are provided in the foregoing verse (see also 8:12 with v. 10).[50] Insofar as the documents in Ezra 4 form a running narrative, one author appears to have composed both letters.

A comparison of the petition of Rehum and Shimshai with that of Tatnai and Shethar-bozenai in Ezra 5:6ff. is quite instructive. Both begin with the typical Aramaic epistolary formula ידיע להוא ל (PN) די and continue with a report of the ongoing building projects (4:12 and 5:8). Likewise, the writers of both letters petition that an inquiry be made in the records (4:15 and 5:17). In addition to these similarities, there are also differences: Tatnai and Shethar-bozenai not only make their request to Darius much more politely (וכען הן על־מלכא טב), but they also focus solely on the history of the Judeans' relations with the Persian empire: This appeal to the immediate past is fully in keeping with a conceivable imperial procedure and is what one observes in *TAD* A4.7. Rehum and Shimshai, on the other hand, are only concerned that a search be made in the record books in order to confirm their contentions that Jerusalem was a rebellious city "in

---

48 2000: 376.
49 Janzen (2000: 625ff.). This form is not restricted to one type of letter. Cf. *TAD* A3.3.4, A6.2.1-3, 22-23 and A6.8.1-2. Steiner (2001: 640ff.) has argued cogently against Janzen's findings for Ezra 7; his counterarguments do not apply, however, for Ezra 4.
50 "Go forth unto the mount and bring olive branches, and pine branches, and myrtle branches, and palm branches, and branches of leafy trees to make Sukkoth." Significantly, this line seems to have been informed the composition of Neh 8:15; see §14.4.

ancient times." The similarity between the course of action taken at the time of Darius and Artaxerxes indicates the possibility that the authors of the historically implausible letters in 4:8ff. utilized chaps. 5-6 as their *Vorlage*.[51] This possibility becomes a probability when we examine the analogies in the wording. Both petitioners request that a search should be made in the record books/geniza (יבקר in 4:15 and יתבקר in 5:17). Both kings give a command for the inquiry (ובקרו שים טעם in 4:19 and שם טעם ובקרו in 6:1). And on both occasions, the relevant information is found (והשכחו in 4:19 and והשתכח in 6:2).

Finally, the documents in Ezra 4 share features in common with Xerxes' edict in Add Esth, which few scholars would defend as authentic. Not only is it presented in the most credible manner; its contents are also very similar to that of the Artaxerxes-correspondence, in which both the officials in Samaria and the king himself consider Jerusalem to be a "rebellious" and "bad" city, with a history of "sedition." Haman, like Rehum and Shimshai, conspires against the Jews by winning favor with Xerxes, who then, just as Artaxerxes, writes a letter arguing that the Jews have always been – it belongs to their *ethnos* - bent on sedition. It is quite possible that the authors of this account have been influenced by Ezra 4. Yet it is equally likely that the Artaxerxes-correspondence, rather than an authentic source, originated in the same milieu as Xerxes' edict.

That the documents in Ezra 4 were drafted for their transmitted setting is indicated by the proviso in the king's response: "…the city should not be built until a command be given from me" (4:21b). In explaining the inclusion of this clause, Clines and Blenkinsopp contend that it may have been necessitated by a Persian legal custom according to which it was impossible to alter a law after it had been enacted. While this is possible, it is not probable. Artaxerxes appears fully convinced that Jerusalem is dangerous. Why should he then include a clause allowing the construction activities to continue at a later point? The most plausible answer to this question is that the same king in Ezra-Neh later grants permission to complete the restoration (Neh 2:4ff). Inasmuch as it is hardly coincidental that he makes an important proviso and then later draws implicitly on it, one may be confident that the author has created Ezra 4:21b to prepare the reader for the continuation of the *story* in Ezra-Neh.

Who is responsible for this proviso? Is he the author of the remaining portions of the letter, or is he only a glossator? In order to be able to maintain the authenticity of the letter, many scholars ascribe the proviso to a glossator.[52]

---

51 This proposal has nothing to do with the question whether the chaps. 5-6 are based on authentic documents. My point is only that this narrative presents a more plausible historical approach to the problem of building the temple and that the author of the Artaxerxes-correspondence drew upon these letters and/or account.

52 Galling (1954: 198), however, took a different approach and interpreted the addition of Ezra 4:21b in connection only with the completion of the *temple* in Ezra 5-6.

Warrant for this decision is, however, not provided by formal literary-critical criteria. Beginning with עַד, the clause constitutes a smooth continuation of the foregoing statement. The only evidence for the original omission of the clause is 1 Esdr 2:24. When making use of 1 Esdras as a witness to the oldest text, one must, however, be very selective, since this version has fully and consciously ignored the contribution of Nehemiah in its portrayal of the Restoration. Instead of the construction of the city as a whole and its fortifications specifically, the authors of 1 Esdras have focused solely on the building of the temple and the restitution of the cultic service; they are not concerned to tell us how and when the returnees built the rest of the city. Not only 2:24 but also other places in the Artaxerxes-correspondence – not to mention its setting – differ significantly from the MT.[53] Insofar as this book continues the effort initiated in Ezra-Neh to correct and counterbalance Nehemiah's account, one should not employ it in reconstructing the original wording of Ezra 4:21.[54] On the other hand, if the authors of 1 Esdras deleted Artaxerxes' proviso, then additional – albeit secondary – evidence surfaces that this command anticipates Neh 2 on a literary level.

3.3.3 The Function of the Artaxerxes-Correspondence in Ezra-Neh

In order to appreciate the function of the Artaxerxes-correspondence within the book of Ezra-Neh, we should begin by noting the space this work apportions to documents of all sorts.[55] This work not only contains two lengthy first-person accounts (Ezra 7-8, Neh 1ff.), but it also cites many lists (Ezra 2; Neh 3:1-32; 11:3ff.; 12:1-9, 11ff.), letters (Ezra 4:7, 8, 9-16; 5:6-17; Neh 2:7-9a and 6:1-9), genealogical records (Ezra 8:1ff.; Neh 7:5ff., 12:10ff.), edicts (Ezra 1:1-4; 4:17-22; 6:3ff., 6-12; 7:11-26), and a pact (Neh 10). Often these texts suit the purposes of the narratives so well that it would be surprising if many of them have not been composed freely, rather than representing historical sources.[56]

---

53 E.g., the authors have changed the foundations of the city in Ezra 4:12 to the foundations of the temple (2:17b). See also 2:15 and Böhler (1997: 119-140 and 216-304). Böhler's work on 1 Esdras is quite helpful inasmuch as it demonstrates how this work does not represent accidental variations that one can naively employ for text-critical decisions.

54 That 1 Esdras represents a later reworking of Ezra-Neh is strongly suggested by the fact that the temple is already built before the reign of Artaxerxes in both 1 Esdras and Ezra-Neh. The weightiest argument against Böhler's conclusions is that the development of Ezra-Neh takes its point of departure from Nehemiah's account, as the present work argues. Only when one neglects to examine the compositional growth of both 1 Esdras and Ezra-Neh, is it possible to posit the thesis of the priority of the former.

55 Eskenazi's work (1988) has given special attention to the role of documents in Ezra-Neh; her thesis has been developed by Schaack (1998).

56 Evidence for this premonition will be adduced as the investigation proceeds.

Among these various documents, Ezra 4 presents a special case. It not only quotes letters, but also the senders of the first letter request that a search be made for other documents (v. 15). The sender of second letter concedes to this petition (v. 19) and is successful in his search. The act of seeking and then (not) finding constitutes a popular motif in Ezra-Neh. For example, in Ezra 2:62/Neh 7:64, several priests search for their registration in the official list, yet do not discover it. After reviewing the people and priests before their departure, Ezra discovers that the Levites were missing (8:15). Later the community inquires and finds that many priests had married foreign women (10:16, 18). After convening the people to be enrolled, Nehemiah discovers a genealogical record with names written in it (7:5). When the heads of the ancestral houses gather around Ezra to study the words of the Torah, they find a written command (8:14-15). At the dedication ceremonies, the "Book of Moses" is read to the people and a written ordinance is discovered (13:1ff.). These passages portray the reading of texts with a reverence for the written word that corresponds to the respect displayed by Rehum and Shimshai for the authority of the Achaemenid records.

Turning to the immediate context of the Artaxerxes-correspondence in Ezra 5-6, we notice how Tatenai, Shethar-boznai and Darius search for the decree of Cyrus (cf. 5:17 and 6:1-2). While Ezra 5-6 probably antedate the Artaxerxes-correspondence and constitute the first narrative development in Ezra 1-6, it may be the work of a later author that combined two earlier texts (5:6-16, 17b and 6:[6-7]8-12).[57] The adaptation of the "seeking and finding" motif in chap. 4 serves to prepare the reader for the positive turn of events when Darius *later* discovers that the Jewish records coincide with the documents stored in the Babylonia geniza. Yet while Artaxerxes prohibits the building of the city-walls, Darius permits only the building of the temple.[58] The anticipation of Ezra 5-6 in Ezra 4 serves to underline the priority of the temple in Ezra 1-6 and 7-8. Not only do the Judeans begin their building activities with the construction of the temple, but also the imperial court itself postpones the repair of the wall to a later period ("when a command is given from me," v. 21). In Ezra 4, one observes a division between temple and city walls that resembles the reorientation from the temple and cult in Ezra 2-3 to the Torah, laypeople and land in Neh 7-10.[59] Consequently, we may relinquish both the transposition hypotheses for the

---

57 See Kratz (2000: 56ff.).

58 Whereas the use of the motif of "seeking and finding" in Ezra 4 may not have been directly influenced by the narrative in Ezra 5-6, it appears to presuppose a late stage in the development of Ezra-Neh, and thus the use of the motif elsewhere. That Ezra 4 is later than, for example, Ezra 7-8 seems likely from Artaxerxes' silence in these chapters with respect to his prohibition to build the wall. The date of Ezra 4 relative to the other texts in Ezra-Neh is, however, difficult to determine.

59 See §14.4.

Artaxerxes-correspondence,[60] as well as the view that "the editor" of the book intended merely to illustrate the hostility of Judah's neighbors.[61] With the imprint of authentic Aramaic documents,[62] these texts function primarily to increase the narrative tension, which is resolved in Ezra 6 and Neh 2, and to demonstrate that Artaxerxes, speaking for the imperial government(s),[63] agreed that the wall-building activities must await the completion (Ezra 6) and his own contribution to the "glorification" of the *temple* (chaps. 7-8; cf. לפאר in 7:27).

One notices additional points in which the letters are in particular agreement with their present context. For example, they mesh well with the emphasis that the redactors of Ezra-Neh place on illegitimate ancestry. The author of 4:2 presents the adversaries admitting to their foreign descent: They are those whom "Esarhaddon, king of Assyria, had brought up hither." Astonishingly, the writers of the letter do not hesitate to acknowledge with the narrator that they are not native to their resident lands. Rather, they are denizens whom "the great and illustrious Osnappar deported and resettled in the city of Samaria and in the rest of the province Abar Naharah" (v. 10). Conversely, these foreigners identify the builders in Jerusalem as none other than "Judeans," those who had previously lived in the land and had recently made Aliyah (v. 12).[64]

The documents are also well suited to the effort in Ezra-Neh to depict a general hostility of Judah's neighbors as characterizing the whole history of the Restoration. According to 4:5, "the people of the land" troubled the Judeans in their building and bribed counselors to work against them "all the days of Cyrus, king of Persia, and until the reign of Darius, king of Persia." Beginning with v. 6, we are told that they changed their strategy to writing accusations against the Judeans in Xerxes' reign and that this continued in the reign of Artaxerxes (vv. 7ff.). By means of this gradual compositional process, the whole time from Cyrus to Artaxerxes comes to be typified by opposition, which corresponds to the statement in 6:14 that the elders "built and finished their work according to the commandment of Cyrus, Darius and Artaxerxes king of Persia." With the theme of the builder's rebellion and sedition (מרד, 4:12, 15 and 19), the redactors have also bridged the gap to Nehemiah's account, which portrays Sanballat, Tobiah and Geshem accusing Nehemiah and the Judeans of insurrection: What is this thing that you are doing? Are you rebelling (מרדים) against the king

---

60 Cf., e.g., Meyer (1896: 15), Batten (1913: 160ff.), Rudolph (1949: 40f.) and Galling (1954: 197).
61 Cf., e.g., Williamson (1985: 59), Blenkinsopp (1988: 106), and Kratz (2000: 66).
62 Cf. Snell's suggestions to the question, Why is there Aramaic in the Bible? (1980).
63 If this text is late, whom does Artaxerxes represent? Do the authors of the correspondence aim to portray an historical figure with all his idiosyncrasies or an imperial ruler in abstract form? The second alternative would make much more sense for a reader living in a period after the downfall of the Achaemenid Empire.
64 See Torrey (1910: 150ff.).

(2:19)?" In 6:5-9, they bring these charges again: "It is reported that you and the Judeans are planning to rebel (למרוד), and this is the reason you are building the wall" (6:6). In Ezra 4, the redactors have included the letters containing the first allegations of insurgence. In this way, they explain not only why the reconstruction of the city was not completed before Nehemiah's arrival, but also cast shadows on any monarchical movements in Judah. At an earlier time, the accusations of sedition brought the work on the wall to a halt. Now, in strongly repudiating the same charges made by Sanballat, Nehemiah brings the wall successfully to completion.[65]

The inclusion of the letters thus provides a new framework for understanding Nehemiah's building enterprise. Herewith we know that the antagonism did not begin with his arrival in Jerusalem and a few isolated enemies. Rather, some time "during the days of Artaxerxes" (v.7) Rehum and Shimshai and "the rest of their colleagues" (4:17) were already occupied with foiling the restoration of the city. By tracing the accusations of sedition back to this group, the redactor identifies the ethnic origins of this antipathy. Nehemiah's foes persist in the same machinations as those who were deported from their homeland and resettled in the former territory of Israel (v. 10).[66] Likewise, we know now that Nehemiah did not initiate the rebuilding of the city: Earlier in Artaxerxes' reign, the Judeans had already commenced the renovation. Yet the builders did not await the appearance of an individual sent by the Persian court according to Ezra 4. Instead, all those who had made Aliyah were working collectively, both without a prominent personality and without the permission of the imperial government (v. 12a). On the one hand, the writers of the first letter report that the Judeans were making considerable progress (v. 12b). When Nehemiah later tells us that he motivated the people to build, we know, therefore, that he alone was not responsible for this accomplishment.[67] On the other hand, the second letter demonstrates also that the people could not witness success on their own.

---

65 The view of history provided in the correspondence of Ezra 4 corresponds to another passage in the Hebrew bible. When Artaxerxes points out that former kings in Jerusalem have ruled over the satrapy (v. 20), he seems to be quite familiar with the exaggeration in 1 Kgs 5:4, where Solomon is also said to have ruled over the whole of Abar Naharah, from Gaza to Tiphsah. In response to Galling's (1954: 198) and Williamson's (1985: 64) interpretation, it should be pointed out that the kings implied are not the Assyrians, Babylonians and Persians, but rather those who ruled *from* Jerusalem over the entire Abar Naharah. Moreover, Artaxerxes does not say that these kings destroyed the city, as in v. 15.

66 See Gunneweg (1985: 90). Mason (1989: 73) and Schaack (1998: 149f.) also interpret Ezra 4 in light of Nehemiah's account.

67 Making a distinction between sources and the narrative, Japhet has argued that a "close look at the narrative of the Restoration demonstrates how the author transfers the emphasis from the leader to the public or its representatives...." However, the putative sources for Ezra 4:7ff. evince this tendency even more clearly than vv. 1-5 (1982: 83). Karrer, picking up on Japhet's insightful comparison of Nehemiah's account with Ezra 4, argues that the latter manifests the emphasis on the people in contrast to Nehemiah's initiative (2001: 344).

Artaxerxes declares that the building be stopped. However, by means of the concluding proviso in v. 21 ("until a command be given from me"), he gives the reader hope. Apparently, the time and conditions were not right for the building of the wall. The temple must first be completed, and then Artaxerxes must send Ezra loaded down with royal donations to "beautify" it. Throughout the subsequent chapters, we anticipate the hope in 4:21 to be realized. And when this finally happens in Neh 2, we know that nothing can thwart the builders' success.

3.4 Conclusions

With regard to the question whether Hanani's report in Neh 1 alludes to recent destruction, we have seen that the common approach of interpreting this report in light of the "sources" in Ezra 4 must be abandoned. These texts do not report that a catastrophe befell Jerusalem in the reign of Artaxerxes. Instead of assuming what is not said, we have attempted to appreciate the tendentious qualities of the Artaxerxes-correspondence. Insofar as the report of Hanani predates these letters, the only history to which these documents relate is the *Rezeptionsgeschichte* of Nehemiah's account.

According to most pre-critical interpreters of this account, Nehemiah was the first to repair the city after the Babylonian destruction. Although dismissed by most modern scholarship, this view finds support in Neh 1:1-3. Since no one would dispute that הפליטה and נשארו מן־השבי refer to the Babylonian captivity, the prologue to the building account prompts us to understand Nehemiah's service for the people and Jerusalem in terms of the Restoration after the catastrophe of 587/6 BCE – the turning point in the history of Judah and Jerusalem. The pre-critical interpretation, therefore, has its origins in the first passage of Nehemiah's account.

Nevertheless, we need not assume that Jerusalem had remained in the same condition since the destruction in 587/6 BCE. It would be natural to suppose that during 150 years before the arrival of Nehemiah, the inhabitants of the city had undertaken a partial restoration of the city. Hag 1:4 refers to elaborate houses (בתים ספונים) that had been built throughout Judah and presumably also in Jerusalem. With the completion of temple, one may presume that the fortifications of the city had been partially rebuilt in order to protect the homes and sacred precincts. Some sort of demolition could have occurred during this long period leading up to the twentieth year of Artaxerxes' reign.

Caution is warranted, however. Although 2 Kgs 25 never states that the gates were burned (cf. Neh 1:3, 2:3, 13, 17), this account of the Babylonian siege has been confined to the essentials. V. 10 declares that the walls were broken down. The gates are not explicitly mentioned, yet their destruction is implied. As the weakest point in a fortification system, they were probably the first objects to be destroyed. That they were also burned is to be assumed, especially if the houses of Jerusalem were set aflame (v. 9). Moreover, Jer 17:19-27 aligns the burning of the gates with the divine punishment brought by the Babylonian armies.[68] Whether the gates had been rebuilt and subsequently destroyed may never be ascertained given the restrictions to archaeological work in Jerusalem. It is, however, noteworthy that although Nehemiah attempts to portray his enemies in the most negative light, he never ascribes to them the responsibility for the demolition of the wall and gates. That he never states who was responsible for the condition of the walls is all the more curious given that this condition is the focus of his account. The silence with regard to the culpable indicates that the destruction, while possibly not as old as 587/6 BCE, is not recent. Otherwise, one would expect Nehemiah to address the problem posed by the malefactors either before leaving Susa or as soon as he arrived in Judah.

While there are several possible explanations for the destruction of the walls and gates, the widely accepted solution based on the Artaxerxes-correspondence is not one of them. The present chapter has attempted to demonstrate that Ezra 4 has been expanded with letters that reinterpret the wall-building activities reported in Neh 1-6. Although the people begin to restore the walls on their own initiative, they fail without the permission that Nehemiah successfully obtains. In postponing the building of the fortifications to a later period when the temple had already been completed (Ezra 6) and beautified (Ezra 7-8), Artaxerxes acts in accordance with the priority given to the cult and the priests in Ezra 1-8. The *raison d'être* for a major passage in Ezra 1-8 is therefore Nehemiah's account.

Insofar as these letters are late, one must allow for the possibility that the authors intended to present Artaxerxes as a typical imperial ruler. Accordingly, we must accustom ourselves to reading Ezra-Neh from the perspective of an audience living after the Persian reign. Not only does the redactional evidence point to the final formation of the book in the Hellenistic age, but also its authors are largely *creating* history – not just *writing* it – in order to utilize it ideologically and pedagogically. In telling the history of Judah's successful relations with one empire (*viz.*, the Achaemenid), they illustrate the correct manner of interacting with its successors.

---

68 In §10.3.2, we examine the claim that Jer 17:19-27 has been composed with Neh 13:15-22 in view. According to our findings, the primary stratum of Neh 13:15 has nothing to do with the themes in Jer 17:19ff., but has been secondarily expanded on the basis of the latter.

4. A Prologue to the Amplified Account – 1:1b-4

4.1 Introduction

Taking a closer look at these introductory scenes in Neh 1-2, we observe several incongruities. First, the dates in 1:1 and 2:1 do not agree. If they are based on the Babylonian calendar, the encounter with the king in Nisan (the first month, 2:1a) occurred earlier than the conversation with Hanani in Kislev (the ninth month, 1:1a). Likewise, the truncated form of the date in 1:1 causes confusion insofar as the information "in the twentieth year" is meaningless without a point of reference. One must either flip back to Ezra 7 where Artaxerxes was last mentioned or read ahead to 2:1a. Finally, without the prayer in vv. 5-11a, the statement in 1:11b follows quite roughly upon v. 4: After telling us that he mourned for days, Nehemiah declares abruptly, "I was the king's cupbearer."

The present chapter follows these clues to further evidence indicating that, prior to the very late insertion of the prayer in 1:5-11a, an author composed a new introduction in vv. 1b-4. According to this thesis, the first-person account originally commenced with the scene of the audience with the king in 1:1a, 11b, and 2:1ff. Without the portrayal of Nehemiah's pious reaction to the news from the province, the narrative simply recounts how the king discerns the despondency of his faithful cupbearer and concedes to his request for a leave of absence. The passage in 1:1b-4, which transforms the building report into a sort of diary with entries for various dates (1:1, 2:1, etc.), has been composed for two reasons: 1) to explain why Nehemiah waits until the beginning of Artaxerxes' twentieth year to reveal his concerns to Artaxerxes, and 2) to introduce an amplified version of the first-person account in which the protagonist shifts his focus from the construction of the wall to the "extramural," socio-religious conflicts with Judah's inhabitants. The passage confers a new theological character to the narrative by presenting the repairs to the wall and the reforms in the province as Judah's Restoration after the catastrophe of 587/6 BCE.

4.2 Comparison of Neh 1 and 2

4.2.1 The Statement of Nehemiah's Position – 1:11b

In the opening scene of 1:1-4, the author identifies his name, the time, and the place, yet fails to divulge the position he occupied. Although we are told that his encounter with Hanani and the Judeans took place in the citadel in Susa, the reason for the location is not disclosed. The absence of this important detail at the beginning of the account becomes all the more conspicuous when precisely this information appears at the end of the chapter: "I was a royal cupbearer" (v. 11b).[1] Why does this statement not appear in 1:1, where we would expect it?[2]

In responding to this question, we may first note that the statement in v. 11b, rather than functioning as a continuation of the foregoing narrative or as a transition to the next episode, introduces the scene in 2:1ff.[3] Why the date in 2:1 appears after the information on Nehemiah's status is clear: V. 11b refers to a prolonged condition (Nehemiah's position as cupbearer) that existed before the month of Nisan.[4] Were 1:11b placed after 2:1a, the reader would be confused into thinking that Nehemiah acquired his post in Nisan.[5]

The formulation מַשְׁקֶה לַמֶּלֶךְ instead of מַשְׁקֶה לְאַרְתַּחְשַׁסְתְּא הַמֶּלֶךְ may be explained similarly. Literally, the designation means "*a* cupbearer to the king," and one should probably not render it as "the king's cupbearer,"[6] but rather as "*a* royal cupbearer."[7] This indetermination may indicate that Nehemiah served as a wine steward in the imperial court before Artaxerxes' ascension to the

---

1   Most commentaries and studies have not overlooked this problem. E.g., Blenkinsopp (1988: 205) writes, "[T]he opening of the first-person narrative is very abrupt. If this were the beginning of the Nehemiah Memoir we would expect the author to introduce himself, but for this we must wait until the end of the chapter (1:11b)."

2   The probability that the prayer in 1:5-11a has been inserted makes this question more poignant. Exactly this approach, however, has been taken in Reinmuth's study (2002: 54), according to which v. 11aβ-b originally followed v. 4b. The problems with this proposal are apparent when one reads the reconstruction: "and I was praying before the God of Heaven for days (v. 4b), and prosper your servant today and extend mercy to him in this man's presence. And I was a royal cupbearer (v. 11aβ-b). And it was in the month... (2:1ff.)."

3   This is suggested by the verse-division in the Peshitta, as well as by several commentators: Batten (1913: 190), Haller (1925: 163), Burrows (1954: 670), Blenkinsopp (1988: 212), and Throntveit (1992: 66).

4   Galling's solution (1954: 215) exchanges the parenthetic phrase יַיִן לְפָנָיו in 2:1a with v. 11b. This approach causes, however, the reader to wonder whether Nehemiah was a cupbearer before the first month of Artaxerxes' twentieth year.

5   Based on this and the following considerations, I cannot agree with Hölscher (1923: 525) and Kratz (2000: 69) that Neh 1:11b is a redactional gloss preparing the scene in 2:1ff.

6   See already Bertheau: "*und ich war einer von den Mundschenken des Königs* (nicht der Mundschenke des Königs, daher die Unterordnung durch ל)" (1862: 135 – italics original).

7   With Batten (1913: 190).

throne.[8] That a courtier's term of office was not thought to automatically termi-
nate with the death of a king is supported by Ahiqar's account. After
Sennacherib dies, the throne is assumed by Esarhaddon, who consents to the
Ahiqar's request to leave office and be replaced by his adopted son (Col. 1-2).[9]

Ahiqar's account is furthermore significant for the present inquiry insofar as
it consists of a narrative attributed to a functionary of an imperial court and
which begins by identifying the protagonist properly: After the heading, "These
are the words of Ahiqar" (אלה מ]לל אחיקר שמה]), follows a statement of his
vocation, "a wise and ready scribe" (ספר חכים ומהיר).[10] An introduction containing information on the function of its author is common to other first-person
commemorative inscriptions. Thus, the quotation of Wedjahor-Resenet's words
on his naophoros-statue is always prefaced with his title: "the chief physician
Wedjahor-Resenet, son of Atemirtis, says..."[11] In aberration from this pattern,
Nehemiah begins his account in chap. 1 by stating that he was "in Susa the
citadel" (v. 1bβ).

Confronted with the omission of information on Nehemiah's function in
Susa, one could follow many scholars in assuming that the introduction to the
narrative has not been reproduced *in toto* and/or has been reformulated.
Observing many analogies between Nehemiah's account and the ancient Near
Eastern commemorative inscriptions, Mowinckel pointed out that the latter
"fangen fast ausnahmslos mit der Selbstpräsentation des Betreffenden an.... Es
gehört auch zur ausnahmslosen Regel des Inschriftenstils, dass das betreffende
Ich auch sagt, was er ist."[12] Reconstructing an introduction to Nehemiah's
account that has more in common with its parallels, he proposed that the
original heading read: "Ich, Nechemja ben Chakalja, war (ein) Mundschenk des
Artaxerxes, Königs von Persien."[13] Since v. 11b is made redundant by this
proposal, Mowinckel insisted that the clause "ist nicht als eine generelle
Bemerkung über das Amt des Neh. gemeint, sondern ist ein Zustandsatz, der
auf eine konkrete Situation geht."[14] Hölscher was of the same opinion, although

---

8   As an alternative to this explanation, the necessity of including the name of the king in the
    date in 2:1a may have governed the formulation משקה למלך in v. 11b. Accordingly, the
    reference to Artaxerxes (לארתחשסתא המלך) (משקה twice in the same sentence would have
    been avoided due to the concern for economy and style.
9   According to Tob 1:22, Ahiqar also held the position of a cupbearer.
10 Reconstruction according to Cowley (1923: 226).
11 See Lichtheim (1980: 36ff). Moreover, the heading to the inscription consists of an
    exhaustive enumeration of all of Wedjahor-Resenet's functions and titles. Otto's collection
    of the Egyptian autobiographical accounts (1954: 130-199) contains numerous parallels
    supporting our proposed reconstruction (Neh 1:1a, 11b, 2:1ff.).
12 1964: 15.
13 Ibid.
14 Ibid. With "konkrete Situation," Mowinckel meant the period of mourning in v. 4.

he ascribed v. 11b to a redactor, who drew on the original wording in order to make the scene in 2:1ff. more comprehensible.[15]

With regard to the third-person introduction in v. 1a (דברי נחמיה בן־חכליה), Mowinckel and Hölscher established a consensus with the proposal that these opening words constitute an editorial note attached to the work at an early point.[16] Because the heading contains genealogical information that does not appear elsewhere in the account and is not formulated in the first-person,[17] an editor has supposedly reformulated the earlier title and has omitted the *Selbstpräsentation* in 1:1b. Although tenable, the supposition is unnecessary. Since such headings constitute a common caption to annals, collections, and first-person works (cf., e.g., "The Words of Agur," Prov 30:1),[18] it could either represent a literary convention used by Nehemiah himself or indicate that he employed a professional scribe to put his "words" into writing.[19]

While maintaining the transmitted heading in v. 1a, Kellermann conceded to Mowinckel and Hölscher that v. 11b is not in its anticipated position. He proposed that we reconstruct the opening lines accordingly:

V. 1a	דברי נחמיה בן־חכליה
V. 11b	(ו)אני הייתי משקה ל(ארתחשסתא ה)מלך
V. 1bα	ויהי בחדש־כסלו שנת (תשע עשרה למלך)
V. 1bβ	ואני הייתי בשושן הבירה

Although this transposition-hypothesis has the advantage that it requires less reformulation, one would like to know why a redactor moved v. 11b to its present position. If it originally stood after v. 1a, it still would have been near enough to 2:1. Instead of improving the narrative in chap. 2, the supposed rearrangement only creates an additional problem for the interpretation of 1:1b-4.[20]

---

15 1923: 525.
16 According to Schunck (1998: 19), the words could have been added by the archivist. Mowinckel (1967: 15) assumes that the original heading included information about the occasion and purpose of the work.
17 Neh 10:2, where his father's name appears, belongs to one of the latest additions to Ezra-Neh. See "Excursus I" at the end of Chapter Nine.
18 Cf. e.g., דברי־כוש בן in 2 Chr 29:30, דברי דויד ואסף החזה in 2 Chr 20:34, דברי יהוא בן־חנני in ימיני in Ps 7:1.
19 This type of heading serves both the purpose of providing a title to the work and of introducing the first-person account in the way the formula, "PN says," functions (cf., e.g., the Behistun inscription, Wedjahor-Resenet's account, and letters from Elephantine).
20 Aware of the problems posed by both v. 11b and past solutions, Gunneweg attempted to explain what could have motivated the transposition: The Chronicler, who is said to be responsible for the editing of the first-person account, moved this line from the heading to the scene of 2:1ff. in order to both demote Nehemiah's status from the royal cupbearer to almost a waiter (!) and to elevate Ezra's office (1987: 41-2). Gunneweg's explanation is

With earlier scholars, Williamson notes the absence of information about Nehemiah's status in v. 1, yet he recommends a healthy measure of skepticism. Acknowledging that v. 11b is firmly anchored in its context, he leaves the text as it has been transmitted, instead of proposing a different version of the transposition-hypothesis.[21] Williamson's approach is definitely preferable to the *ultima ratio* that a redactor extensively altered the wording of chap. 1 or only reproduced an epitome of it. As Galling contended against the latter assumption, the reason that Nehemiah begins his biography by recounting his conversation with Hanani and the Judeans is that it played "für das weitere Leben Nehemias eine entscheidende Rolle."[22] Therefore, one lacks a reason for presuming that his account reported any earlier episodes. Indeed, the tight connection between 1:1a and v. 11b suggests that later authors have added, not deleted, introductory material.

4.2.2 The Date in 1:1a

In support of the proposal that 1:1b-4 represents the work of a later author, the date in 1:1 provides an additional bit of evidence. Hitherto we have presumed that a time span of four months separates the scenes in chaps. 1 and 2. However, the text states something altogether different: According to 1:1b, the conversation with Hanani and the Judeans in the citadel took place in Kislev (the ninth month – November/December) of Artaxerxes' twentieth year. With this chronological information, 2:1a creates a contradiction by dating the audience with the king in Nisan (the first month – March/April) of the same year. Thus, the narrative depicts Nehemiah displaying his sorrow in the presence of the king some eight months *before* he learned of the situation in the province. How are we to make sense of the sequence of months?

According to a widely accepted solution to this question, the dates in chaps. 1-2, rather than presupposing an unchanging calendar, correspond to the exact day of Artaxerxes' accession to the throne.[23] If his reign commenced after Nisan yet before Kislev, then the date in 2:1a would follow the date in 1:1b. Although Bickerman and Depuydt cited evidence in support of this approach,[24] it poses several problems.

---

untenable, not least because an author could have more easily aggrandized Ezra by amplifying his account, rather than disrupting the narrative in Neh 1.

21 "While this view [with regard to Mowinckel] is certainly possible, it must not be concluded that v 11b itself can be removed" (1985: 166).

22 1954: 218.

23 See already Bertheau (1862: 135).

24 Bickerman (1981) and Depuydt (1995).

First, one must suppose that the author was writing for an audience that knew exactly how to interpret the dates in 1:1b and 2:1a.[25] Williamson, for example, maintains that in "so personal a composition, Nehemiah may be allowed to have used the calendar most familiar to himself, since he was not primarily addressing his Jewish compatriots in his memoir."[26] Similarly, Reinmuth argues that the first-person account may have been composed as a report for the Persian king or his representative in the province Judah.[27] On these views, however, one would have to assume that Nehemiah originally wrote in Aramaic, explain why his work was then translated into Hebrew,[28] and ascribe to a redactor all the explicit references to the tradition that would have confused a non-Jewish reader.[29]

Second, we do not know exactly when Artaxerxes ascended the throne. In maintaining that the enthronement took place in the month Ab, the fifth month of the Babylonian calendar (July/August), Bickerman committed a major mistake in his calculations. In 6:15, Nehemiah reports that the wall was finished on the twenty-fifth of Elul, the sixth month (August/September). Since he does not say in which year, we must infer that he means Artaxerxes' twentieth year. According to Bickerman's thesis, however, the day of completion must have been in Artaxerxes' twenty-*first* year.[30]

Finally, it was common in the ancient Near East to begin the regnal years of a king on the first day of Nisan in the year following the inauguration; the months prior to this date were then reckoned to the respective predecessor.[31] Hard evidence for this practice in the reign of Artaxerxes is provided by *AP* 6, which is dated to the twenty-first year of Xerxes *and* the first year of Artaxerxes: "On the eighteenth of Kislev, that is the seventh day of Thoth, in year 21, the beginning of the reign when (ראש מלוכתא) King Artaxerxes sat on his throne...."[32] Just as Neh 1, this document is dated to the month Kislev in Artaxerxes' reign, which renders it possible that the time of accession was

---

25 In view of this confusion caused by the dates, one may agree with Blenkinsopp (1988: 205) "that it would have been less misleading for Nehemiah to have referred to the months by number rather than by name."

26 1985: 170.

27 2002: 53.

28 Why would only this account, and not the material in Ezra 4-7, have been translated from Aramaic?

29 At one point in his commentary, Williamson's defends this position: "Even with these additions [5:14ff. and chap. 13] our present text cannot exactly represent the wording of this report. No doubt it would have been written in Aramaic, and the prayers (1:4-11, 3:36-37 [4:4-5] and 6:14) would probably not have been included" (1985: xxviii).

30 Williamson, Depuydt, and Reinmuth, who embrace Bickerman's proposal, fail to provide a solution to this problem. See Neuffer (1968) for the issues surrounding the unpublished Hellenistic tablet (LBART No. *1419).

31 See Begrich (1929: 91ff.).

32 See Cowley (1923: 16).

before Kislev but after Elul. Nevertheless, it is still dated to *Xerxes'* regnal years, and from it, we must presume that all documents *after* the interim period would be dated to Artaxerxes' reign beginning in the following Nisan (April 13, 464),[33] according to the long-established custom in Mesopotamia.[34]

Equally untenable, yet less creative, is the approach taken by those who, recognizing the insufficiency of the accession-dating thesis, simply change the text so that it reads what they would expect. Since we lack textual witnesses for other readings, Kugler's suggestion that 1:1b is corrupt and that it originally read "in Kislev of the *nineteenth year*," deserves to be treated with the utmost suspicion.[35] Why should one suppose that the words שנת תשע עשרה למלך were somehow lost and that a later hand mechanically inserted the year provided by 2:1a? If a copyist was so careful in reading the text to have noticed that the year was missing after the month in 1:1b, he would also have noticed that his attempt to correct the lacuna with the insertion of "in the twentieth year" creates more problems than it solves.

Schunck admitted that none of these approaches to the dates in Nehemiah's account is satisfying and proposed a new solution.[36] Turning the attention from 1:1b to 2:1a, he argued that we need only to insert a single word, אחת, between שנת and עשרים. Accordingly, the conversation with the king would have taken place in the twenty-first year. While such a proposal requires that we assume much less than on the prior views, it encounters a major obstacle in 5:14a, where Nehemiah dates his gubernatorial administration in Judah from the twentieth to the thirty-second year of Artaxerxes. Despite the redactional char-

---

33 See Parker and Dubberstein (1956).
34 In one of the most scholarly treatments of the problem, Neuffer states the matter clearly and apparently without knowledge of the problem posed by Neh 1-2: "The Persian reckoning means that his reign must have begun before Nisan 1, 464, because the Babylonian-Persian method was to postdate all reigns. That is, when a new king succeeded to the throne the scribes, who had been dating all kinds of documents by the day and month 'in the 21st [or whatever] year of King X,' would begin using the new date 'in the accession year [literally, "beginning of the reign"] of King Y,' and would wait until the next New Year's Day to begin dating 'in year 1 of King Y'" (1968: 60f.).
35 1922: 194. See also Haller (1925: 163), Rudolph (1949: 102), Galling (1954: 217), Kellermann (1967: 74-5), and Blenkinsopp (1988: 205).
36 "Es sind verschiedene Erklärungsversuche unternommen worden, die jedoch alle nicht befriedigen können" (1998: 15). Of these proposals, we may mention here that of Ararat (1976), according to which the original text in 1:1b, added by the editor of Ezra-Neh, was "the twenty-fifth year of Ezra." Nonetheless speculative is the suggestion made by Deliceto (1963) to understand the twentieth year as the time of Hanani's initial departure from Susa. Finally, Gunneweg (1987: 40) considers, and rejects as "wenig wahrscheinlich," the possibility that the twentieth year refers to Nehemiah's age or the twentieth year after beginning his service as cupbearer.

acter of this note,[37] it is improbable that the text was corrupt at such an early point in the development of the first-person account.

Likewise, one may discard the thesis according to which the date in 2:1a represents an interpolation.[38] Comparing 2:1a once more with 1:1b, we observe that Artaxerxes' name and title appear in the former (ויהי בחדש ניסן שנת עשרים לארתחשסתא המלך), while the latter ends abruptly with "in the twentieth year" (ויהי בחדש־כסלו שנת עשרים). If 1:1b is impossible to understand without knowing to whom or what the twentieth year refers, and 2:1a provides a complete and understandable form of the date, why should one believe that the latter has been inserted by a later hand?

With respect to the incomplete form of 1:1b, most scholars assume that the editor, in view of the prior reference to Artaxerxes in Ezra 7, omitted the words לארתחשסתא המלך. "[W]e must conclude that this points to the hand of the editor of Ezra-Nehemiah material. When he combined the accounts of their activities, he assumed that, following Ezra 7:1, 7, etc., there was no need to specify the reign again."[39] However, if the editor had been consistent, he would have not included Artaxerxes' name in Ezra 7:7 after it had already been mentioned in v. 1. More importantly, if we may be so sure that the editors did not consider it necessary to provide a complete and comprehensible date in 1:1b, why did they change their minds one chapter later? That they would have felt no inhibitions about excising an important part of the account is even more surprising when one considers that this decision achieves nothing except confusion.

Now, if we should not hold the editor of Ezra-Neh responsible for the alteration of 1:1b, how are we to explain the differences between it and 2:1a? The first-person account would certainly have not commenced with an incomplete date. But instead of assuming that only 1:1b has been secondarily altered, I submit that a later hand composed the whole passage of 1:1b-4. The findings of the present analysis support such a conclusion. Just as we are not told Nehemiah's occupation until v. 11b, so do we have to read ahead in order to understand the date in 1:1b.[40] It appears, therefore, probable that the author of 1:1b-4 had also already read the passage 1:11b, 2:1ff. Accordingly, the first

---

37 In §8.3.2, I follow several scholars in concluding that this chronological information has been supplied by a later editor, who added the information supplied in 2:1a with the tradition that Nehemiah served twelve years. Although Schunck discussed this problem briefly in the text-critical notes to 2:1 (and proposed that the gloss must be later than the corruption of the text), he unfortunately passed away before finishing his commentary on chap. 3-13.

38 Holscher (1923: 525) and Mowinckel (1964: 16).

39 Williamson (1985: 166).

40 See the comments of Ehrlich (1916: 183), Mowinckel (1964: 16), and Blenkinsopp (1988: 205).

edition of the account commenced with a scene set appropriately in Nisan – the beginning of the year.

Still, one must explain why the new introduction in 1:1b-4 is dated to Kislev. If the text is not corrupt or the author did not employ a regnal calendar that began after Elul (cf. 6:15) yet before Kislev, the conversation with Hanani is dated nine months *after* the conversation with Artaxerxes. In advancing a solution to these problems, one should observe that there are no textual witnesses for alternative dates in 1:1b. This surprising fact may indicate that later copyists thought that Nehemiah was using an autumn calendar beginning in Tishri (the seventh month). Scholarship has rejected this solution, since the use of the autumn calendar seems to have been confined to a small circle, and the dates in 2:1a and 6:15 attest to the use of the Babylonian calendar. But if Nehemiah did not have a direct hand in the composition of the opening scene, the hand responsible for this passage may have superimposed the autumn calendar on the first-person account. Although the Maccabees favored this division of the year, one need not suppose that the author of 1:1b-4 was writing at such a late date.[41] Already the authors of Ezra-Neh placed special emphasis on the activities in the month of Tishri (cf. Ezra 3:1, Neh 7:73, 8:2, 13, 9:1).[42] In expanding the introduction, the hand responsible for the new introduction may have intended to correct the importance assigned to Nisan in 2:1a by employing a calendar beginning in the seventh month.

It remains to consider in the next section (1) how the narrative beginning in 1:11b, 2:1ff. does not require 1:1b-4, (2) that Nehemiah's concern in the latter text encompasses much more than merely the condition of the city as in the former text, and (3) that it is difficult to account for these differences on the assumption that one author was responsible for both texts.

4.2.3 The Introduction to the Account in 1:11b, 2:1ff.

According to the present shape of his account, Nehemiah knows about Jerusalem's condition in 2:1ff. from his encounter reported in 1:1ff. Initially, one presumes that these two passages are inextricably connected. Yet, as we will see, the scene in 1:11b, 2:1ff. not only can exist independently of 1:1b-4, but it also makes better sense without this prologue.

First, the passage builds its own tension independently of 1:1b-4. Insofar as a courtier was required to be comely and present himself in the most "courteous" manner, Nehemiah's downcast demeanor constituted an open breach of

---

41 Schneider (1959: 163), Kellermann (1967: 75), Clines (1974: 36), and Kratz (2000: 69) have contended that the author was following the Seleucid calendar that began in the autumn.

42 See the discussion of these dates in §§13.3.2 and 14.2.3.1-2.

etiquette. Thus, when the king perceives that his wine-steward is depressed and demands an explanation for his appearance, Nehemiah is naturally terrified (v. 2b). At this point in the narrative, the king is awaiting a response. After 1:4, the reader already knows the reason for Nehemiah's moroseness, yet without the account of the news from the province, the narrative of 1:11b, 2:1ff. generates a greater element of suspense. Together with the king, the reader anxiously waits to hear what could have possibly occasioned such an infraction of propriety. In v. 3, both now learn for the first time why Nehemiah has committed this infraction of courtly etiquette: "And I replied to the king, 'May the king live for ever! How can my countenance not be troubled when the city where my ancestors lie buried is in ruins?'" Therefore, in portraying the scene, Nehemiah contrasts his own grief for Jerusalem with that of the imbibing and presumably jovial king. The cupbearer's duty is to contribute to the ambience, not to dampen the mood. Yet on one occasion Nehemiah failed to share in the merriment. With a touch of irony, he recounts how his unremitting anxiety for the condition of his ancestral city resulted in the failure to play the assigned role of a courtier and how this failure, in turn, brought about an alleviation of exactly what had sustained his anguish. Hence, the passage creates its own element of uncertainty, a significant aspect of which diminishes, however, when read as sequel to the preceding episode.

Second, Nehemiah, as a person of high status in the imperial court, would have had direct access to information on the conditions in Jerusalem and would have assumed that his readers could deduce this from the information on his position in v. 11b. Below we observe that the author responsible for 1:1b-4 was motivated not primarily by the need to explain how Nehemiah learned what he knows in 2:3, but rather by an interest to expand the theological dimensions of the restoration project. Moreover, we have already seen in §3.3 that the documents in Ezra 4 have been composed with Nehemiah's account in view and that the group of Judeans in 1:2ff. did not comprise an official delegation sent to report to Nehemiah on new developments in the province. Accordingly, we would not need to assume that some catastrophe had recently befallen Jerusalem. The state of the city described in 2:3 would probably not have changed in the time directly before Artaxerxes' twentieth year.[43]

---

43 It is widely supposed that Nehemiah belonged to a family that had been carried away in one of the Babylonian deportation. In his response in 2:3, 5, Nehemiah refers to Jerusalem as "the city (the house) of my ancestors' graves," which may indicate that he was of high birth, if not a Davidide (cf. Kellermann [1967: 11-13, 156-159, 166-70] and Williamson's comments and literature references [1985: 179]). Inasmuch as the deportees consisted of a small number of royalty and nobility, this is historically plausible. On the other hand, we know from the biographies of Ctesias and Wedjahor-Resenet that the Persians followed in the steps of their predecessors in securing the services of influential foreigners and aristocratic children from their provinces. Thus, Nehemiah may have enjoyed the advantage

Third, one must explain Artaxerxes' question in 2:2: "Why is your countenance so sad?" (מדוע פניך רעים). According to the present shape of his account, Nehemiah's appearance is to be interpreted against the backdrop of his reaction described 1:4, i.e., as his physical condition after a lengthy period of mourning and fasting. It is possible, however, to understand this question independently of 1:4. In Gen 40:7, Joseph poses the exact same question to Pharaoh's cupbearer and baker (מדוע פניכם רעים היום). Since the distress of these two courtiers lasted only one night, we would have to conclude from a reading of 1:1a, 11b and 2:1ff. that Nehemiah's face was merely troubled (cf. והנם זעפים in Gen 40:6), not that it showed signs of long days of mourning and fasting.[44] In keeping with his intention to illustrate the favorable relationship between himself and the king (cf. v. 5aβ), Nehemiah reports how Artaxerxes perceived, and was concerned by, his cupbearer's distressed frame of mind. It was thus the king's sensitivity and solicitude for the welfare of his Jewish servant that guaranteed the welfare of Judah and its capital. That Nehemiah is favored and granted a "request" (בקש, v. 4) belongs to a motif employed, inter alia, in Esther, Daniel, Ezra, 1 Esdras as well as the Joseph story and Ahiqar.[45]

Not only can one interpret the passage 2:1-11 without preceding episode, but this text also fails to provide an adequate continuation of the account of the conversation with the Judeans. In 1:2ff., Nehemiah is concerned primarily with the welfare of Judah's inhabitants, and his first question relates to those who had escaped the Babylonian captivity. Conversely, he does not even mention the inhabitants of Judah in 2:3ff.[46] One could explain this silence as Nehemiah's conscious attempt to avoid a reference to those whom Artaxerxes presumably knew as seditious and rebellious.[47] This explanation falters, however, on the evidence that the authors of Ezra 4 have most likely composed the Artaxerxes-correspondence *after* and expressly *for* Nehemiah's account.[48] In Neh 2, Artaxerxes displays the utmost admiration for his Jewish cupbearer. Had he been concerned with insurrectionist tendencies in Judah, why did he allow the Judeans to rebuild the fortifications of Jerusalem, with which they would be in position to secede from the empire? Since Nehemiah showed no inhibitions

---

of personally receiving an appointment from the court; his contemporary readers could have presumed this to be the case. Moreover, if he did not consider himself to be in exile, one could explain that he simply *comes* to Jerusalem (ואבוא אל־ירושלם, 2:11a). In contrast, Ezra makes Aliyah (Ezra 7:13, 28: לעלות).

44 See also Eccl 7:3.

45 While the protagonists in these texts are granted a "request" because of their outstanding performance or qualities, Nehemiah is granted a "request" even after his neglect of courtly etiquette represented by his downcast countenance. Insofar as the story masterfully employs the motif to build up its own suspense, it would not have required a preceding episode.

46 Cf. Kratz (2000: 69), who has also argued for the independency of Neh 2:1ff.

47 Cf. Ezra 4:12, 15-16, 19.

48 See §§3.2-3.

about complaining to the king that the gates of the city – the most important part of a fortification system – had been destroyed in fire, he could have also expressed his dissatisfaction with the plight of Judah's inhabitants. This would have certainly lent more weight to his petition inasmuch as good relations with its subordinate peoples are critical to the prosperity of an imperial government. Thus, both the scene in the citadel and the scene before the king emphasize Nehemiah's emotional disposition in order to illustrate his allegiance to Judah. Yet while in the former he grieves and mourns upon hearing that the Judeans are in dire-straits, in the latter he is disturbed only by the city's ruins.

Comparing the two episodes, we notice another inconsistency: Why does the king not notice his servant's distress on a prior occasion. To be sure, Nehemiah would have found it more difficult to hide his grief in the period immediately following the meeting with Hanani. It was during these days that he wept, mourned, and fasted. How then are we to explain that after four months he can no longer suppress his sorrow?

The solutions proposed for this time lapse are just as ingenious as they are unconvincing. Bowman explained the delay by supposing that Artaxerxes was absent in Babylon during the winter months.[49] However, we know that the Persian kings spent the winter months in *Susa* and the summer months in Ecbatana.[50] Moreover, Artaxerxes I appears to have preferred Susa to Ecbatana and spent the most of the year there.[51] Galling proposed that he was away on a military campaign.[52] According to another solution, there may have several royal butlers serving on a rota system.[53] Williamson is aware of the difficulty with all such assumptions and quotes Ryle's remark that "it does not seem likely that a cupbearer, who enjoyed the favor of the king, should have appeared so rarely in his presence…."[54]

Equally untenable is the most widely accepted suggestion that Nehemiah *waited* to make his petition until New Year celebrations in Nisan.[55] According to Herodotus (9:110f.), the Persian kings would usually organize a great feast (*tukta*) for their birthdays.[56] In order to display their generosity, they would grant anything requested of them. "[I]t is not impossible that…a similar practice was in effect on other occasions…,"[57] and Nehemiah, "who was not lacking in

---

49 Bowman (1954: 671).
50 See Xenephon (*Anab.* 3.5.15 and *Cyr.* 8.6.22).
51 Cf. Olmstead (1948: 352).
52 Galling (1954: 218).
53 Bertheau (1862: 135) and Siegfried (1901: 74).
54 1985: 178.
55 Kellermann (1967: 194).
56 Significantly, the Joseph story (Gen 40:20) also reports of Pharaoh's birthday when he pardoned his cupbearer and baker. See also Mark 6:22-23.
57 Williamson (1985: 178).

shrewdness, probably waited for such an occasion...."[58] While the reference to Nisan in 2:1 may indeed be an allusion to this type of festival, one must still explain why the king failed to notice his cupbearer's gloomy face for several months. The explanation offered for this problem is that, since hearing the bad news, Nehemiah "had kept up appearances and was now deliberately seeking an occasion to win the royal sympathy."[59] The only support for this supposition is found in the parenthetical note v. 1bβ: ולא־הייתי רע לפניו.[60] However, not only must one exchange לפניו with לפנים,[61] but also the statement, "Now up until now [or, previously] I had not been sad," does not make sense.[62] In fact, it flatly contradicts Nehemiah's statement in 1:4 that he was extremely distraught. Therefore, it is unwarranted to conclude from the putative original wording that he had intended all along to conceal his emotions until the New Year festivities. Most importantly, after the king comments on his appearance, Nehemiah says that he was struck by fear (v. 2b). If we take this statement at face value, we must dismiss the proposals that he waited until the right moment before "turning on" his emotions. The purpose of the text is to illustrate his heartfelt sorrow for Jerusalem and genuine fear that he would be punished. "[A] gloomy appearance, as well as a lack of courtesy, might well be interpreted as evidence of plotting against the king. The king's initial probing questions suggest such a suspicion on his part, making Nehemiah's fear understandable enough."[63]

In order to set forth the most compelling evidence for the thesis that Nehemiah began his work with the royal-audience scene, the following section considers how the composition of 1:1b-4 prepares the reader for the transformation of the building report into an account of Judah's Restoration.

4.3 The Reasons for the Composition of 1:1b-4

4.3.1 The Twofold Problem in the Province

While the belatedness of Nehemiah's solicitude and involvement for the cause of Jerusalem until the twentieth year of Artaxerxes' reign may have been one of the reasons for the addition of 1:1b-4, a closer examination of the passage reveals more significant reasons. Comparing his response in 2:3 with that of the

---

58 Blenkinsopp (1988: 213).
59 Ibid.
60 Either this means that Nehemiah was not out of favor with king or that he was not (or had never been) sad in his presence. See §5.2.1.
61 See Bertholet (1902: 49), Rudolph (1949: 106).
62 Williamson (1985: 177) recognizes the problem but, instead of rejecting this solution, assumes that *both* לפניו and לפנים were in the original text. Yet it is difficult to imagine that לפנים לפניו were written together.

Judeans' in 1:3, one notices that the two are quite different. Instead of mentioning Jerusalem's wall, Nehemiah says the city as a whole lies wasted (חרבה). And while the Judeans report that the gates are *burned* in fire (ושעריה נצתו באש), the king is told the gates are *destroyed* in fire (ושעריה אכלו באש). Rather than in conversation with Artaxerxes, the closest parallels to 1:3 are to be found in Nehemiah's plenary address after his arrival in Jerusalem (2:17). It both mentions the wall and describes the gates as *burned* in fire. The most significant parallel to 2:17 is the focus on the Judeans, who are passed over in silence in 2:3. Just as Hanani and his company report that the inhabitants of the province are in great trouble (ברעה גדלה) and reproach (ובחרפה), so does Nehemiah draw attention to his audience's trouble (הרעה) and implores them to remedy their reproach (חרפה). Given the number of common expressions, it is worth examining whether these texts also evince differences.

The Judeans' Report in 1:3	Nehemiah's Address in 2:17
And they said to me, "The remnant that are left of the captivity there in the province – they are in great <u>trouble</u> and <u>reproach</u>. Also the <u>wall of Jerusalem</u> is broken down, <u>and its gates are burned with fire</u>."	And I said to them, "You see the <u>trouble</u> that we are in, that Jerusalem lies wasted, <u>and its gates are burned with fire</u>. Come, we will build up <u>the wall of Jerusalem</u>, and we will no longer be a <u>reproach</u>."

The first thing to be observed is that Hanani and his company, corresponding to Nehemiah's twofold question, report two distinct problems: First, the inhabitants of Judah are suffering affliction, and, second, the wall is in ruins. By prefacing the description of the city with an elaborate statement on the sociopolitical distress, the latter is given priority. However, as he addresses the Judeans in 2:17, Nehemiah presents, in sharp contrast to the view in 1:3, the sociopolitical situation as tightly interwoven with the wall's state of disrepair. He begins by pointing out that the Judeans are in affliction: "Look at the *trouble* we are in..." (v. 17aα). He then defines this affliction: "...that Jerusalem lies in wasted..." (v. 17aβ).[64] For Nehemiah there is just one problem. Because the city is in ruins, the people are in disgrace. Continuing his appeal, he presents now the reason for his journey: "Come, let us build up the wall of Jerusalem..." (v. 17bα). In conclusion, he reiterates why this enterprise is necessary: "...so that we are no longer a *reproach*" (v. 17bβ). His address portrays, therefore, the repair

---

63 Williamson (1985: 179).

64 This use of אשר for כי is encountered often in the narrative. Cf., e.g., 2:3, 5, 10; 4:6; 7:65; 8:14, 15; 10:31; 13:1, 19, and 22.

of the wall as tantamount to the reversal of the sociopolitical situation. Predicating his argument on Judah's calamity, he promises that if Jerusalem is rebuilt,
the people will no longer have to endure the disgrace and humiliation
symbolized by the city's destroyed ramparts.

According to the primary strata of the narrative, to which 2:17 belongs, the
building of Jerusalem runs hand-in-hand with the construction of the ethnic
identity of the inhabitants of Judah. The demarcation of a physical sphere by the
eminently powerful symbol of the wall corresponds to the delimitation of the
ethno-political group for which this wall provides both the protective barrier
and the hallmark of its renewed strength. The interconnection of the building
enterprise with Judah's self-esteem and respect from its neighbors corresponds
to the dialectical manner of narration in the account, according to which every
stage of construction is met with the taunts and tactics of Sanballat and Tobiah
and the rest of Judah's neighbors (cf. 2:10, 19-20, 3:33-37, 4:1ff. and 6:1ff.).[65]
Specific details as to the actual work on the wall have been confined to a mini-
mum, while information on the interactions and conflicts with the antagonists
abounds. As the builders make headway, this enmity can only escalate. The
completion of the wall signifies the triumph: "And as all our enemies heard and
the nations round saw, they were much deflated and recognized that this work
was wrought by our God" (6:16a).[66] Here one can discern how, exactly as
promised in 2:17, the emergence of Jerusalem from its ruins brings about a
significant change in Judah's self-identity and the way it was viewed by its
neighbors.[67]

In comparison with Nehemiah's appeal in 2:17, Hanani and the Judeans
present a more differentiated view of things. The use of a simple coordinating
conjunction to begin 1:3b indicates that they do not consider the repair of
Jerusalem as the *conditio sine qua non* of redressing the social problem.[68] Their
report, in contrast to 2:17, not only draws a distinction between the problem
posed by Judah's disgrace and the problem of Jerusalem's ruins; it also down-
plays the significance of the latter by giving precedence to the former. And just
as the interweaving of these two in 2:17 prepares the reader for the building

---

65 See the table of the שמע-schema in §3.2 for a quick overview of these passages.
66 In this strand of the narrative, the central terms from 1:3 and 2:17 (רעה and חרפה) appear
    several times; cf. 2:10, 3:36, and 6:13.
67 Cf. also the implications of Sanballat's speech in 3:33f.
68 In an attempt to harmonize 1:3 with 2:17, one could interpret the *waw* in וחומת as an
    explicativum. Assuming, however, that both passages have been composed by the same hand,
    one must explain why the condition of the city in 1:3 has not been given the priority it has
    in 2:17. Furthermore, one must explain why the author has not employed the particle כי (or
    אשר, which replaces כי in many passages). Finally, the *waw-explicativum* is a highly subjective
    syntactical interpretation. One should hesitate to argue on this basis given the frequency of
    texts in which two statements are clearly distinguished rather than subordinated with the use
    of this conjunction.

narrative, so does the separation of the two in 1:3 coincide with sections of the first-person account. In these passages, corresponding more or less to chaps. 5 and 13, Nehemiah shifts his focus from the building of the wall to a treatment of various economic, social, and religious abuses throughout the province.

In chap. 5, the familiar rivals – Sanballat and his cohorts – are conspicuously absent in the scene of vv. 1-13. Playing the role of the antagonists are now the Judean nobles and officials, who learn that the success of the Restoration enterprise depends upon their willingness to concede to an economic policy in keeping with the fraternity of the community. Analogous to Hanani's distinction in 1:3, the remedy for this situation is an "extramural" reform. Indeed, the wall is not even mentioned once in this account. Incriminating the nobles and officials, Nehemiah asks, "Should you not walk in the fear of God because of the reproach (חרפה) of the nations, our enemies?" Exactly as in 1:3, the term חרפה is employed to describe a situation that exists independently of the city's ruins. This חרפה persists and will not desist unless the physical restoration of the ramparts is accompanied by an inner reformation of the entire province.[69]

A concern for the internal order of the community governs also chap. 13. Similar to the way chap. 5 depicts the establishment of a fraternal ethic as the precondition for redressing the חרפה of the people, the paragraphs in chap. 13 follow 1:3 in disconnecting the רעה נדלה from the mere restoration of the ramparts. While Nehemiah considers הרעה as the situation obtaining from Jerusalem's state of ruins, chap. 13 adds new dimensions to the meaning of the term. Eliashib commits הרעה by providing Tobiah a chamber in the temple-courts (v. 7). Likewise, the nobles commit הרע by not keeping the Sabbath. Because their fathers committed the same evil (v. 17), God brought הרעה הזאת־כל upon the people and upon the city (v. 18). Here the use of the term parallels most closely its meaning in 1:3, where the references to the captivity evoke the catastrophe in 587/6 BCE. Finally, in marrying alien women, the Judeans commit הרעה הזאת כל־הגדולה (cf. הרעה הגדולה in 1:3). The only time the wall is mentioned in these passages is vv. 19-22, yet instead of continuing to consider its reconstruction as the remedy to the הרעה, Nehemiah realizes that the wall is only an instrument with which one can prohibit הרעה that incurs from the presence of foreign merchants in the city on the Sabbath.

---

69 The connections between chap. 5 and 1:1b-4 are not relegated to their use of חרפה. In both passages, Nehemiah describes his reaction with the שמע-formula: "And *as I heard these words*, I sat down and grieved and..." (1:4). "And it angered me greatly *as I heard* their complaint *and these words*" (5:6). As already observed in §3.2, these are the only two places in the account where the שמע-formula describes Nehemiah's response rather than that of the antagonists. Now if 1:1b-4 constitutes a redactional expansion of the introduction, it may well have been originally drawn from 5:6 and used in 1:4 in order to prepare the reader for the later use of the formula.

Of utmost significance for our present concern is the opinion of many scholars that Nehemiah drafted chap. 5, together with the very similarly formulated paragraphs in chap. 13, for a second edition of his account. In chaps. 8-11 of the present study, we assess this opinion and conclude that, although Nehemiah most likely did not play the role of the redactor, these so-called "reform-accounts" could not have belonged to the first edition of the building report. If this conclusion is merited, then 1:1b-4 may well have been added as the introduction to an amplified account in which the wall-building narrative had been supplemented with reports of Nehemiah's additional measures to redress the reproach and disgrace throughout the province. The question whether the same author was responsible for these expansions does not require response at this point. Here it is important that we differentiate two basic layers. While the primary stratum presents the construction of the wall as a remedy to Judah's reproach, the final stratum, consisting above all of 1:1b-4 and the addition of chaps. 5 and 13,[70] reflects a more advanced phase in which the wall is already rebuilt, yet Judah's affliction continues.

To summarize, we have observed that Hanani and the Judeans, in reporting the dire-straights of the people (their הרעה and חרפה), disconnect the problem from the condition of the city. Conversely, in 2:17 Nehemiah presents the repair of the ramparts as the way in which the Judeans can change their plight. In rebuilding Jerusalem from ruins (the object of Judah's reproach), the province gains the respect of its neighbors. This conception corresponds to the conversation with Artaxerxes in which Nehemiah attributes his gloomy appearance to the disrepair of his ancestral city without mentioning the plight of his people. In amplifying this narrative, later authors have composed 1:1b-4 as a means of introducing the tension of the narrative in chaps. 5 and 13, which many scholars assign to a later edition of the building report. These texts place the work on the wall in relation to a more extensive Restoration. According to this later conception, Nehemiah's repair of the ramparts may have strengthened the province and brought about a sense of solidarity, but it did not solve the problems *in radice*. The trouble and reproach (הרעה and חרפה) persist until the people, and especially the aristocracy, treat each other as their own kindred (chap. 5), break off their "unholy alliances" (13:4-9), pay the Levites their portions (vv. 10-14), observe Sabbath rigorously (vv. 15-22) and abandon their practices of marrying foreign women (vv. 23-31). Insofar as 1:1b-4 gives priority to the situation of the people and relegates the ruins of the city to an ancillary problem, it corresponds to the focus on the social reforms and to the silence with regard to the wall in chaps. 5 and 13.

---

70 Other texts to be included in these strata are 6:10-14, 17-19 and 7:5-72.

4.3.2 The Concern for the Identity of the Judeans

In 1:1b-4, Nehemiah refers to the capital simply by name (v. 2b), while he designates the inhabitants of Judah, in contrast to the usual economy of the narrative, as "the Judeans that had escaped, which were left of the captivity" (v. 2b). As if this pleonasm did not suffice, Hanani and his company refer to the people with the same prolixity ("the remnant that are left of the captivity there in the province," v. 3a). Both in their verbosity and in their implications, these designations for Judah's inhabitants are unique in the first-person account. When referring to the people as a whole, Nehemiah employs various expressions: "the Judeans,"[71] "Judah,"[72] or simply "the people."[73] We search in vain, however, for a passage in which he identifies the people, as in 1:2-3, with "those who had escaped," who "were left of the captivity," or "the remnant."

The absence of this terminology is surprising inasmuch as the historical background implicit in this terminology would have certainly bolstered the argument of his address in 2:17. For example, he could have appealed to the fact that the inhabitants of Judah had survived the captivity and that the time was now due to begin the restoration: "Come, let us [who have escaped the deportation] rebuild the wall" (2:17b). Instead of taking this line of reasoning, Nehemiah presents the repair of the wall simply as a remedy to the sociopolitical disgrace and reproach. And rather than evincing a consciousness of the Judeans' deliverance, he recounts how various societal groups and classes in Jerusalem ("the Judeans, priests, nobles, rulers, and the remaining workers," v. 16b) form themselves into a construction crew and unanimously consent to his proposal.[74] The fact that Nehemiah fails to mention in this context that the future wall-builders had escaped the deportation has been corrected with the composition of 1:1b-4. In this text, the *dramatis personae* evince a strong consciousness of "the captivity" (השבי). Such redactional activity is anticipated inasmuch as the pivotal importance of the Babylonian catastrophe was developing in the historical consciousness of many Jewish groups throughout the late postexilic period and Hellenistic age.[75] In what follows, we briefly examine the new meaning that the terminology used in Neh 1:1b-4 assumes in the context of Ezra-Neh.

---

71   Cf. 2:16; 3:33; 4:6; 5:1, 8, 17; 6:6 and 13:23.

72   Cf. 4:4; 6:18; 13:12, 15, and 16. Given the possibility that many of these passages are late, it is all the more surprising that their authors did not make use of the terminology of 1:2-3.

73   Cf. 4:8; 4:19; 4:22; 5:1, 13, 15, 18, 19; 7:4, 5; 12:38.

74   Here again, a reference to the captivity could have been easily incorporated to subsume the various groups in this list.

75   Blenkinsopp writes: "In general, Nehemiah, unlike Ezra, is not at all concerned with return from exile, and the heavily charged language used here occurs nowhere else in the Nehemiah material" (1988: 207). – The assertion that the first drafts of the first-person account do not share this consciousness of the captivity appears to be invalidated by 7:4ff. Yet not only does this passage present the builders as those who returned from exile

One of the appellations for the Judeans in Neh 1:1-3 is הנשארים. This word
appears elsewhere in Ezra-Neh only in the first chapter of the book. There
"Cyrus king of Persia" proclaims to his empire that all the people of YHWH
should make Aliyah to Jerusalem and build the temple. "And whosoever still
remains (וכל־הנשאר), from any place where he dwells, let the men of his place
support him with silver and gold, with goods and livestock, together with any
freewill offerings for the house of God which is in Jerusalem" (v. 4). Many
scholars find it difficult to believe that a Persian ruler would employ a *terminus
technicus* that is used by biblical authors in heavily charged theological contexts.
While their concerns are warranted, their harmonizing solutions are not commended by an impartial reading of the syntax of this verse. One lacks a sufficient reason for dismissing the usual approach of taking אנשי מקמו as the subject
of the verb ינשאוהו. Accordingly, וכל־הנשאר וגו should be treated as a *casus
pendens* linked to the verbal suffix in ינשאוהו, and the specification "from any
place where he dwells" anticipates the subject "the men of his place." The
suggested alternatives to this reading indicate uneasiness with the fact that Cyrus
is familiar with the diction of biblical writers.[76] This anxiety is all the more
surprising when one considers the many other obstacles vv. 2-4 present for the
assumption that the passage is an excerpt from a historical decree, not to mention the inherent contradictions with the document Darius later discovers (chap.
6) and Haggai's and Zechariah's ignorance of this command to build the temple.[77] When we abandon the attempt to isolate an "authentic" Cyrus decree, its
literary connections with Nehemiah's account become obvious. By employing a

---

(instead of remain in the land), but it also appears to have been added at a late stage in the
composition of Ezra-Neh. See §13.3. – Not all scholars would agree that the terminology in
1:1b-4 signifies those who had *remained* in the land. Cf., e.g., Batten (1913: 183) and
Williamson (1985: 171). Isa 11:11ff. employs similar terminology for those who remaining
in the land, and one could argue with reference to this text that there is no disparity between
Neh 1:1b-4 and 7:4ff. The problem with this approach is that Isa 11:11ff. leaves no room
for doubt as to the origins of this remnant. This contrasts with the majority of texts in
which the term נשארים refers explicitly to those whom the Babylonians either killed or left in
the land as "the remnant of Judah" (2 Kgs 24:14; 25:12, 22; Jer 39:10; 40:6, 11, 14; 42:2, 15,
19; 44:12, 14, and 28). Therefore, I cannot embrace the position of Bertholet (1902: 47),
according to whom the term is to be interpreted, against Kosters (1895: 44f.), Marquart
(1896: 35) and, to an extent, Wellhausen (1895: 183ff.), in the sense provided by Neh 7:6.

76 Bickerman (1976: 84f.) followed recently by Schaper (2000: 72f.), argued that אנשי מקמו
renames וכל־הנשאר as the subject. This proposal must be rejected insofar as (1) the sing.
masc. suffix in ינשאוהו refers clearly to the sing. masc. subject וכל־הנשאר וגו and that (2) the
renaming of the subject and the switching from sing. to plur. is not what one would expect
after v. 3a, where a very similar syntax is used. While rejecting Bickerman's suggestion,
Williamson (1985: 5) does not offer a better alternative in arguing that אנשי מקמו is an
explanatory gloss.

77 See Galling (1964: 61ff.). A response to these arguments is presented in Bickerman (1946:
72-108), Williamson (1983), and Schaper (2000: 67-75). For the problem that Haggai and
Zechariah do not know about Cyrus' decree and the contradictions between Ezra 1:2-4 and
6:3-5, see most recently Bedford (2001: 114-180).

key designation from the introduction to the Nehemiah material (1:2-3), the author of the introduction to Ezra-Neh has redefined the character of the remnant survivors. Whereas the author of Neh 1:1b-4 employed the appellation הנשארים for all those remaining in the province and thus escaped deportation, Cyrus calls for כל־הנשאר in the Diaspora to return and build the temple.[78] Significantly, he (in contrast to characters of Neh 1) does not address, or even appear to be cognizant of those remaining in Judah.[79]

The second key term used by both Nehemiah and the rest of the book is השבי, "the captivity." Throughout Ezra-Neh, this word occurs frequently, yet in a different sense than in Neh 1:1b-4. For example, Neh 7:6 and its parallel in Ezra 2:1 identify "the children of the province" with those who had went up from השבי. This usage is encountered in other passages. Ezra 3:8 portrays "all they that were come out of the captivity unto Jerusalem" beginning the construction of the temple. In Ezra 8:35, "the children of the captivity, that were come out of exile" offer burnt offerings upon their arrival in Jerusalem. Neh 8:17 depicts "all the assembly of them that were returning from the captivity" celebrating Sukkoth. In his prayer, Ezra makes use of both the term השבי (9:7) and Nehemiah's and Hanani's third designation for the inhabitants of Judah: הפליטה (cf. vv. 8, 13, 14, 15). But while Nehemiah views the inhabitants of Judah from his place in the Diaspora as the ones who have escaped the captivity, Ezra brings "the escapees" from the Diaspora with him to Jerusalem and must attend to a situation in which "the children of the captivity" (cf. 9:4, 10:6, 7, 8, 16) had not separated themselves from the inhabitants of the land. The different meanings applied to the terms הפליטה and השבי in Ezra 9-10 and Neh 1 are even more significant if Ezra 9 has not only been patterned according to the Neh 1, but also serves as introduction to the entire first-person account.[80]

From these findings, we conclude that the authors of several important passages in Ezra-Neh have made conscious use of the designations for Judah's inhabitants in Neh 1:1b-4. One the one hand, this scene appears to constitute a redactional expansion of the introduction. It imparts to the first-person account an historical consciousness of the exile that is foreign to the primary stratum of the narrative, in which Nehemiah simply presents the building project as the means of consolidating the Judeans without drawing attention to the fact that they have survived the captivity. On the other hand, this new introduction must have been composed at an early point in the literary development of Ezra-Neh

---

78   Karrer writes: "Während die 'Übriggebliebenen von der Gefangenschaft' im Kontext der Nehemiaschrift zweifellos alle Bewohner Judas meint, die vom Exil verschont blieben, sollen im Rahmen der Gesamtkomposition die Judäer als 'Übriggebliebene' im Sinne von 'Rückkehrern aus dem Exil' verstanden werden "(2001: 314).

79   In this respect, the use of שאר by Cyrus corresponds to the use of this term in Ezra 9:8, 15.

80   See §11.2.2.

(and at a *late* point in the development of the first-person account). While Nehemiah is concerned with those had escaped the captivity and had not been deported from the land, the authors of the texts just discussed are concerned solely with those who had been carried captive and were later allowed to return. Inasmuch as they adopt the terminology of Neh 1:1b-4 and assign it a radically new meaning by combining it no less than thirteen times with the word הגולה,[1] it appears that their literary activity intends not least to qualify the identity of the protagonists in Nehemiah's account. With the composition of Ezra-Neh, "the survivors of the captivity remaining in the province" who later rebuild Jerusalem's wall and embrace Nehemiah's new policies (chaps. 5 and 13) are none other than the descendants of those who had formerly been deported and had returned with Sheshbazzar, Zerubbabel, Joshua, and Ezra in order to build and beautify the temple.[2]

4.4 Conclusions

The present chapter has reconstructed two introductions to Nehemiah's account. The first includes 1:1a, 11b; 2:1ff. – a scene set appropriately in the beginning of the year – and belongs to the earliest edition. Its form may be compared to the headings of several extra-biblical biographical works. The second introduction comprises 1:1b-4 and resembles the narrative style of the book of Esther (esp. chap. 2). Not only does the date in 1:1b disagree with 2:1, but also the statement of Nehemiah's title/function is expected at an earlier point. Instead of rearranging the text to the anticipated sequence, we have followed Kratz in noticing that the passage does not agree with 2:1ff. There Nehemiah does not mention the fate of his compatriots as a cause for his downcast countenance, even though this would have surely given Artaxerxes an incentive for approving his cupbearer's proposal.

In explaining why the paragraph has been inserted between 1:1a and 11b, we have observed that Hanani's answer in 1:3 responds to Nehemiah's speech in 2:17 by severing the social situation from the condition of the wall. Whereas Nehemiah presents the repair of Jerusalem's ramparts as the remedy to the "affliction" and "reproach," Hanani first reports that the people are suffering "affliction" and "reproach," and then adds that the wall and gates are destroyed. By both employing the terminology of 2:17 and placing the emphasis on the welfare of the Judeans rather than Jerusalem's ruins, this text shares the tenden-

---

81 This term is used for the exile in Ezra 1:11; 2:1; 4:1; 6:19, 20, 21; 8:35; 9:4; 10:6, 7, 8, 16; Neh 7:6.

82 The reader is encouraged to consult Karrer's work (2001), which discusses at length how many portions of Ezra-Neh expand the views espoused by Nehemiah's account.

cies of other passages (esp. chaps. 5 and 13) that both do not mention the wall and assign the responsibility for the "affliction" and "reproach" to the Judeans themselves. Since these passages are widely considered secondary insertions (composed by either Nehemiah himself or, as argued here, later authors), the conclusion suggests itself that 1:1b-4 has been prefaced to chap. 2 as an introduction to new and amplified edition of the building report. After the wall was already long finished and one noticed that the problems nevertheless persisted, the building report, instead of being regarded as solely an historical source, was transformed into an (didactic) account of Judah's Restoration.

That 1:1b-4 has been added after the composition of chaps. 5 and 13 explains why the latter do not refer to "the Judeans" as "the remnant that are left of the captivity." The author of 1:1b-4 confers a new historical consciousness to the first-person account inasmuch as the protagonist now weeps and mourns for days as he "hears" that the survivors of the Babylonian devastation were in distress (cf. the contrasting reactions of the antagonists in 2:10, 19, 3:33, 4:1, 9, 6:1, and 16 as they "hear" about Judah's progress). All of his actions – both the reparation of the wall and his communal reforms – are now to be understood as the turning point in the history of Judah after forfeiting its political autonomy in 587/6 BCE.

Although 1:1b-4 does not appear to have belonged to the earliest edition of Nehemiah's work, it seems to pre-date most parts of Ezra-Neh. Whereas the builders of the wall are now those *left* in the land after the Babylonian invasion, their ancestors are those who built the temple after *returning* from exile (Ezra 1-6; see also 7-8). In order to avoid any ambiguities, the authors of Ezra-Neh employ the terminology of Neh 1:1b-4. However, they impart a new meaning to it. Thus, "the survivors" (הפליטה) and those "who remain" (שאר *niph.*), rather than living "there in the province" (Neh 1:3), are the ones who return from "the captivity" (השבי). The analyses in "Part Two" will uncover further evidence for the priority of late editions of Nehemiah's account vis-à-vis the greater part of Ezra-Neh.

II. From Susa to Jerusalem

Introduction

The analyses in the preceding chapters have uncovered three strata in Neh 1, which correspond to three stages in the development of Ezra-Neh. In his prayer (vv. 5-11a), Nehemiah refers to "the children of Israel" whom YHWH promised to "gather," espousing thereby the Golah-orientation of Ezra 1-10. By emphasizing adherence to the Mitzvoth, the prayer prepares the reader for the portrayal of the dedication of the wall in Neh 7:1-13:3, during which the community takes a pledge to follow the Torah before celebrating the final stage in the Restoration of the Jerusalem and Judah. The older layer in 1:1b-4 precedes the composition of Ezra-Neh, inasmuch as the protagonists of the Restoration are those who remained in the land after the Babylonian captivity. This passage has been drafted as an introduction to the first-person account after it had grown from short building report to the history of Judah's reconsolidation. In dissociating the "affliction" and "reproach" in the province from the repair of the wall, it corrects 2:17 and confers a new historical consciousness to the Judeans. Accordingly, what primarily concerns Nehemiah is no longer the political humiliation symbolized by Jerusalem's destroyed ramparts, but rather the welfare of "the remnant." The oldest layer in 1:1a and 11b belongs to the earliest edition of Nehemiah's account. The heading it forms with 2:1 may be compared to the style of other autobiographical works, especially the vizier-inscriptions from Egypt.

In the following chapters, we turn our attention to Neh 2-6, which appear, with very few exceptions, to predate the composition of Ezra-Neh. Although older, these texts must have passed through the hands of several authors. A portion corresponds to the earliest edition of the building report in 1:1a, 11b, while the rest consists of a series of additions that necessitated the new introduction in 1:1b-4 as well as the creation of Ezra-Neh. "Chapter Five" begins with an analysis of 2:1-11a and then addresses three problems related to the account: the Achaemenid interest in Jerusalem's fortifications and the relationship of Neh 2 to Ezra 7-8. "Chapter Six" examines the lengthy section of 2:11b-4:17. With the working hypothesis that Neh 5 has been added at later stage, we investigate Neh 6 in "Chapter Seven" and show how the disparate paragraphs it contains have been adapted to the overarching theme of the enemy's attempt to intimidate Nehemiah. Finally, "Chapter Eight" returns to Neh 5 and finds that it has much in common with the units in Neh 13, thus setting the framework for the discussion of the additional reforms during the work on the wall in "Part Three."

5. Artaxerxes' Permission to Build – 2:1-11a

5.1 Introduction

The preceding chapter has already devoted considerable space to 2:1-11a in an effort to demonstrate that this passage, while failing to provide the expected continuation of 1:1b-4 (let alone 1:5-11a), forms – together with the heading in 1:1a + 11b – an inauguration account that renders the preceding episode in chap. 1 superfluous.[1] Taking our point of departure from this conclusion, the present chapter investigates the text with a different aim. After conducting a literary-critical analysis in the first half (§5.2), we consider in the second half (§5.3) the new light the proposed first edition of the passage and its redactional expansions shed on two historical problems.

5.2 The Composition of the Passage

The probability that later hands have amplified 2:1-11a at several places has been considered by Torrey, Wellhausen, Batten, Hölscher, Mowinckel and Galling. Without providing many counterarguments, Rudolph and Kellermann asserted that the account is unified. Unfortunately, their hasty conclusions have influenced most recent studies;[2] thus, the following subsections reassess the evidence for editorial activity. While Winckler, Kaiser, and Hoglund have voiced their skepticism with respect to the originality of even part of vv. 1-8,[3] we will see that a significant portion of this passage, with the heading in vv. 1a and 11b, belongs to the earliest edition of the building report. Indeed, the conversation with Artaxerxes in vv. 1-6, in contrast to the more substantial redactional activity in vv. 7-11, seems to have been amplified with only short glosses.

---

1 The court scene in Neh 2 belongs to a popular genre in ancient Near Eastern literature. Since it is a topic for itself and would take this investigation astray from its objectives, I have not included a comparative study here; it is planned to appear as an article. For a good introduction to the genre, see Meinhold (1975, 1976), Collins (1977) and Wills (1990).
2 The bibliographical information is provided below.
3 Winckler (1901: 473) and Kaiser (1984: 182-n. 15; 184). Hoglund contends that the court scene is the work of the author of Ezra-Neh "but is presumably based on some factual grounds" (1992: 208-n. 3). A discussion of Hoglund's claims is provided below.

5.2.1 The Integrity of VV. 1-6

We begin our investigation in 2:4b, where Nehemiah remarks that "I prayed to the God of Heaven." The author of this line appears to have employed the commentary style of vv. 1bβ and 2b to introduce a theological dimension to the scene. Assuming that the line is integral, one must explain the absence of similar references to praying elsewhere in passage. For example, a hymn of thanksgiving similar to that of Ezra's (cf. 7:27f.) would have been appropriate at the conclusion of the scene. Yet, as we observe below, even the reference to "the good hand of my God" in v. 8b seems to be secondary. Moreover, one must account for the differences between "the God of Heaven" (אלהי השמים) and "my God" (אלהי).[4] As proposed in §2.2.1, a redactor is most likely responsible for the remark in 1:4b, and it is formulated in similarly to 2:4b. Of course, the addition of 2:4b may have influenced 1:4b, but a direction of priority becomes quite tenuous when, as we shall see, all other references to praying and divine assistance probably represent late supplements, which attribute to Nehemiah a deep piety and propensity to pray at every occasion.[5] Before the addition of v. 4b, the account could be compared to the book of Esther MT, in which the Persian king grants his suppliant her requests solely because of a favorable rapport.[6] Wills points out that the absence of God is characteristic of "Court Legends."[7] Breaking away from this genre, the scribe responsible for v. 4b attributes Nehemiah's success not to his record of loyalty or to human causality, but rather to the sovereign supervision, if not direct intervention, of "the God of Heaven."[8]

---

4   For the similar use of the expression "God of Heaven," cf. Dan 2:18ff. (Kratz – 1991: 134ff.) and Jonah 1:9. It is also the exact same designation employed by Cyrus in 2 Chr 36:23 and Ezra 1:2. While its use in the late fifth cent. BCE is testified to by the Elephantine Papyri, one should not automatically assume that it always belongs to the first layers of Nehemiah's account. Karrer (2001: 202ff.) fails to point out that this expression appears quite often in Tob (7:12, 8:15) and Jud (6:19, 9:12; cf. also 5:8 and 11:17) as well as other late non-canonical literature. That also later authors are responsible for the expression in Nehemiah's account represents the conclusion of the many scholars who ascribe the prayer in 1:5-11a to a redactor.

5   The reshaping of the account that begins in Neh 2:4b continues in the prayer for success in 1:5-11a, with regard to which §2.2.2 has already noted the parallels to other narrative contexts that have been amplified with prayers.

6   "If your servant has found favor before you…" (v. 5). Cf. the variations of the expression ואם־על־המלך טוב (Neh 2:5) in Esth 1:19, 3:9, 5:4, 8, 7:3, 8:5, and 9:15. The term "request" (Neh 2:4) is used elsewhere in Est 5:3, 6, 7, 8; 7:2, 3, and 9:12. It can be traced back to a Persian custom (cf., e.g., Herodotus 9.110 as well as TAD A4.7.23). For Nehemiah's courteous responses, see the works of de Boer (1955: 225ff.) and Veijola (1975: 75).

7   1990: 22f.

8   This reworked form may be compared to the story of R. Johanan ben Zakkai's encounter with Vespasian (ARNA 4, ARNB 6; cf. also Lam. Rab. 1.5, b. Git. 56a-b.), Ep. Arist., Baruch, the Greek versions of the Esther story, both the Greek and Hebrew versions of the Daniel narratives, the transmitted version of "The Legend of the Three Bodyguards" in 1

The remaining glosses are likely older than v. 4b, but are also less significant for the theological reader. Indeed, the annotation in v. 6a, according to which the queen consort (Damaspia?[9]) was sitting beside the king, would have increased a later author's motivation for inserting v. 4b and ascribing the favorable outcome of the story to the suppliant's invocation of the God of Heaven, rather than to the presence of a woman and her influence on the king's mood. That the short clause itself has been interpolated is indicated not only by the way it disrupts the syntax (ויאמר לי המלך – והשגל יושבת אצלו – עד־מתי יהיה), but also by the fact that the author could have mentioned this figure earlier. The parenthetical notice should have been placed, if not in the introduction to the episode, at least before ויאמר לי המלך.[10] One must, therefore, concede the possibility that a later author has embellished the account with a detail that portrays the king in the company of his consort and consequently in a relaxed atmosphere. It may reflect the influence of the tradition known from Ctesias that Artaxerxes fancied many women and was thus a weak and capricious ruler.[11] Or perhaps the redactor even confused Artaxerxes with Xerxes and intended to suggest that השגל was no one other than Esther, whose legendary charm once again influenced the Persian king and the fate of her people.[12]

V. 6 seems to have accumulated a second gloss: "And I gave him a time." This clause creates first a conceptual incongruity, since the one to "assign a time" (זמן + נתן) would have been the king, not Nehemiah. The Peshitta portrays a more conceivable scenario: ויתן לי זמן ("and he set me a time"); nevertheless, the MT, as most scholars insist, has probably transmitted the original wording. That the clause has not been placed before v. bα ("and it pleased the king, and he sent me") augments the problem: After Nehemiah has already received permission, he would not have needed to inform the king when he would leave and return. Batten proposed that we simply move v. bβ to the position before v. bα.[13] Keil attempted to harmonize these statements by translating the *waw* in ואתנה temporally ("nachdem"), and Williamson takes this route, rendering v. b: "Thus it pleased the king to send me, *when* I had told him

Esdr, and, not least, Ezra 7. In the latter group of texts, the heroes are (1) either in the court or in the presence of a foreign king, where (2) they lead a most pious existence, predict the future or even pray before (3) they "find favor" and/or are granted their "requests." – For the expression "find favor," cf., e.g., Gen 39:4, 21, Tob 1:13, Bar 1:12 and 2:14. For a similar use of "request" (Neh 2:4), cf. most importantly the references to Esth above, Ezra 7:6, 21ff., and 1 Esdr 4:46, and then the *Ep. Arist.* 15ff. and 2 Macc 11:15.

9   Cf. *Pers.* 15.44.
10 So Batten (1913:193).
11 See Kellermann (1967: 194).
12 Before rejecting the latter suggestion as absurd, one should examine the Greek versions of Esth, for in naming the king Ἀρταξέρξης, they furnish evidence that later readers treated אחשורוש (probably Xerxes) as a variant of ארתחשסתא.
13 1913: 193f.

how long I should be."[14] While the translation may represent the most felicitous manner of presenting the text to modern readers, it does not resolve the tensions. V. bα provides the expected response to Nehemiah's request and hence appears to conclude the account. After the suppliant voices his wish in v. 5 ("if thy servant pleases thee, send me…"), the success is reported: "And it pleased the king, and he sent me."

Moreover, Artaxerxes' question in v. 6a, just as Nehemiah's question in 2:3 and most of the others in the first-person, may be meant somewhat rhetorically.[15] Although expressing it with finesse and humility, Nehemiah depicts how he was greatly respected and favored by the king. The account begins with a litotes: "And I was *not* in *disfavor* with the king" (v. 2bβ).[16] In order to illustrate his good standing, Nehemiah continues by reporting that the exalted ruler did not fail to notice his sad countenance (v. 3). Even after the infraction of courtly etiquette, which required that an attendant maintain a positive demeanor, he is granted a request (v. 4).[17] Finally, the king's question in v. 6 is clearly an expression of appreciation, if not also affection, for Nehemiah: "How long will you be away and when will you return?" Implicit in this response is not only the

---

14 See also Williamson (1985: 176f.)

15 In addition to 2:3, cf. 2:19; 3:33f.; 5:9; 6:3, 11; 13:11, 17f., 21, and 26f. (more than eighteen rhetorical questions in the first-person account!). Mowinckel (1964: 21) followed Hölscher (1923: 527) in treating v. bβ as the work of glossator who, misinterpreting the scene, presented Nehemiah responding to the king's questions.

16 The existence of this linguistic phenomenon in colloquial Hebrew has been demonstrated by Lande (1949: 60ff.). – In support of the suggestion, see Ibn Ezra's interpretation: כי חפץ שרותי. While admittedly disputable, this reading makes the best sense of the passage in which Artaxerxes insists that his cupbearer is רע after the latter has just claimed the contrary (ולא־הייתי רע לפניו). In attempt to harmonize the text, Bertholet (1902: 49) and Rudolph (1949: 106) proposed that we emend לפניו ("in his presence") to לפנים ("previously"). With respect to this approach, Batten wrote, "The Evs [=English versions] have tried to make black white by rendering the next clause, 'now I had not been beforetime sad in his presence.' But on what ground can we import 'beforetime,' and thus make the words imply the exact opposite of what they say?" (1913: 191f.). Although many have accepted Rudolph's proposal it creates another problem: If Nehemiah "had not been sad *previously*," what elicited his sadness at just this point? Recognizing the problem, Williamson (1985: 177) suggests that we add לפנים to the text. However, it is extremely unlikely that an author would have juxtaposed the words לפנים לפניו ("before this before him"). Instead of adding words to the text to gain a better sense, one should pay close attention to the differences in the expressions (רע לפניו and רע לב). Nehemiah claims that he was not in "disfavor" with the king, which implies that he was indeed very much *in favor* with him. This would explain why the king then takes an interest in his welfare, noticing that he was "depressed" (רע לב). As Batten pointed out (1913:192), such an approach makes the best sense of the various expressions for "sad" and "in favor" in the passage. See also Ehrlich (1914: 184f.).

17 See our discussion in §§3.3 and 4.2.3 as well as Herodotus 9.110, "The Story of the Three Bodyguards" in 1 Esdr, Esther's request in Esth 5:3, 7:2, etc., and Ezra 7:6.

approval of the request, but also sadness at the thought of his beloved servant's absence and a desire for his speedy return.[18]

5.2.2 The Supplements in VV. 7-10

More perplexing is the relationship of v. 6 to the rest of the passage. Hölscher and Mowinckel insisted upon the integrity of the immediately following verses, apparently recognizing that the repetition of "the king" in the statement v. 9b ("And the king sent officers of the army and cavalry with me") presupposes the preceding lines in which the subject alternates.[19] Torrey, Batten and Gunneweg contended that vv. 7-9a constitute an editorial insertion; consequently, they did not ascribe v. 6bβ to a glossator, so that the text flows smoothly ("And I set him a time [...] and the king sent officers...").[20] These proposals are confined by the gratuitous assumption that only one hand could have edited Nehemiah's account. When one allows for a succession of "active readers" (=redactors), it appears that v. 6bα ("And it pleased the king, and he sent me") originally continued directly in v. 11a ("And I came to Jerusalem"). Between these lines, a redactor inserted vv. 6bβ and 9b, creating a new framework for later authors to add vv. 7, 8b-9a and then v. 8a. With respect to v. 10, Winckler, Hölscher, Batten, Mowinckel, Galling and, most recently, Kratz agree that it does not belong to the earliest edition of the building report.[21] And they are most probably correct. The place of this verse in the composition of the passage is, however, difficult to determine and must be treated in relation to the rest of chaps. 2-6. The table below presents a reconstruction of the account's composition-history.

---

18 Cf. the author's own interpretation of the question: "Thus it pleased the king, and he sent me," (v. 6bα).
19 Mowinckel (1964: 21f.) and Hölscher (1923: 527).
20 Torrey (1896:37), Batten (1913: 194) and Gunneweg (1987: 55).
21 Kratz (2000: 72) proposes that all of vv. 7-10 without differentiating.

The Composition of 1:1-2:11a[22]

1:1 The words of Nehemiah ben Hacaliah [...]
> 1:1b-4a
>> 1:4b
>>> 1:5-11a
11 [...] I was a cupbearer to the king.
2:1 And in the month of Nisan, in the twentieth year of King Artaxerxes, wine was
before him.[23] **I carried the wine and gave it to the king. Now I was not in disfavor
with him.**
**2 And the king said to me, "Why is your face sad, since you are not sick? This
can only be sadness of the heart." Then I was very much afraid.**
**3 I said to the king, "May the king live forever! Why should my face not be sad,
when the city, the place of my ancestors' graves, lies wasted, and its gates
destroyed by fire?"**
4 Then the king said to me, "For what are you requesting?"
> And I prayed to the God of Heaven.

**5 And I said to the king, "If it pleases the king, and if your servant has found
favor with you, *I request* that you send me to Judah, to the city of my ancestors'
graves, so that I may rebuild it."**
6 Then the king said to me,
> and the queen consort was sitting beside him,

**"But how long will you be gone and when will you return?" Thus it pleased the
king, and he sent me.**
> And I set him a date.
>> 7 Then I said to the king, "If it pleases the king, let letters be given me to
>> the governors of 'Beyond the River,' that they may grant me passage until I
>> arrive in Judah;
>>> 8 and a letter to Asaph, the keeper of the king's forest, directing him to
>>> give me timber to make beams for the gates of the temple-fortress, [and
>>> for the wall of the city,] and for the house that I shall occupy."
>> And the king granted me what I asked according to the gracious hand of
>> my God that was upon me. 9 And I came to the governors of the province,
>> Abar Naharah, and gave them the king's letters.
> And the king sent officers of the army and cavalry with me.
>> 10 When Sanballat the Horonite and Tobiah the Ammonite official
>> heard this, it displeased them greatly that someone had come to seek the
>> welfare of the children of Israel.

11 And I came to Jerusalem....

---

22 For this stratification-table and those in the following chapters, the bold face indicates the
    oldest stratum, and the indentation signifies the successive layers. The square brackets mark
    small glosses.
23 Cf. Ehrlich's comment: "Der Ausdruck יין לפניו ist zu streichen. Das Sätzchen rührt von
    einem alten Schriftgelehrten her, dem der Artikel im folgenden היין im ersten Halbvers
    etwas über Wein vorauszusetzen schien. Aber der Artikel erklärt sich zur Genüge aus dem,
    was uns im Vorhergehenden über das Amt Nehemias gesagt ist" (1914: 184).

A good place to begin the defense of this reconstruction is v. 10, with respect to which there is the greatest level of scholarly consensus. Of all the notices describing the reactions of Nehemiah's nemeses (2:19f., 3:33-37, 4:1ff., 6:1ff.),[24] this may represent the youngest. The following chapter discusses the identity of Sanballat and Tobiah at greater length. Here it suffices to point out that the formulation of v. 10 appears to have been directly influenced by v. 19, where a *gentilicium* is provided for both Sanballat (החרני; cf. 13:28) and Tobiah (העמני; cf. 3:35). So too, these passages are unique in designating Tobiah as העבד. Moreover, 3:33, 4:1 and 6:1 present the full שמע-formula (ויהי כאשר שמע/נשמע ל; cf. also 1:4 and 5:6), whereas 2:10 and 19 contain the abbreviated form (וישמע). Yet the strongest point of similarity to 2:19f. is the presentation of the enmity as a sharp religious division. In 3:33ff., 4:1ff., and 6:1ff., Sanballat and Tobiah are angered as they learn about the progress made in the work on the wall. In 2:20, Nehemiah responds to the accusations of these two figures by drawing a clear line of distinction between them and those who consent to build, identified as "the servants of the God of Heaven." His response implies that Sanballat's and Tobiah's disapproval constitutes antagonism to the divine will. The composition of 2:10 continues in this direction, equating "the servants of the God of Heaven" with "the children of Israel." Likewise, Nehemiah's mission is no longer simply to repair the ruins of his ancestral city (cf. vv. 3-5); rather he is "someone who had come to seek the welfare"[25] of the Judeans. And it is precisely this newly defined mission that vexes Sanballat and Tobiah so greatly.[26]

It seems that a very late author intended that the reader understand the enmity of Sanballat, "the Horonite" and Tobiah, "the Ammonite" in terms of the same unrelenting hatred manifested by Israel's enemies in former days. This author, although making the *gentilicia* in v. 19 repetitive, has attempted to improve upon the earlier introduction of the enemy by portraying the conflict in more radical, and simultaneously more conventional, categories. While causing many commentators difficulties in dividing the paragraphs of chap. 2, the remark in v. 10 serves an important purpose. It employs one of characteristic features of the building account (*viz.*, the description of the enemy's reaction to

---

24 See the table in §3.2.

25 The feminine form טובה may have been influenced by v. 18b: "And they began this *good* (work; cf. מלאכה chaps. 4 and 6)." More probable is, however, that it is a wordplay on the name of Tobiah, as shown in the next footnote. See also Ps 122:9 for the use of this uncommon expression in relation to Jerusalem.

26 This formulation (וירע להם רעה גדלה) is found only in Jonah 4:1; cf. Golka (1986: 415ff.). The phraseology here may be explained by the *inclusio* formed by "good" and "evil": וישמע סנבלט החרני וטוביה העבד העמני וירע להם רעה גדלה אשר בא אדם לבקש טובה לבני ישראל. That the authors of Nehemiah's account would make a pun on Tobiah's name here is supported by the evidence in both 6:14 (play on 5:19 – "remember Tobiah"/"remember for good") and 6:19a ("his good works"/"Tobiah"); see §§7.5.1 and 8.2 for a discussion of these passages.

each stage of the building project with the שמע-formula) and presents the antagonism beginning *prior to* the construction activities. Instead of merely political concerns related to the wall, it was a deep-seated antipathy for "the children of Israel" and their "welfare" (טובה) that motivated Sanballat's and Tobiah's actions.

According to the present shape of the passage, what elicits Sanballat's and Tobiah's outrage is that Nehemiah was accompanied by royal troops. Without v. 10, however, the account makes much better sense: the army escort made safe arrival in Jerusalem possible (וישלח עמי המלך...ואבוא אל ירושלם, vv. 9b and 11a).[27] The incoherency created by v. 10 derives above all from the presentation of the antagonists learning "that a person *had come* (בא) to seek the welfare...," before Nehemiah had even arrived (ואבוא אל־ירושלם). Moreover, the following verses state explicitly that no one had been told of Nehemiah's plans (twice: vv. 12 and 16a). How then do Sanballat and Tobiah already know about them?[28]

The author of v. 10 may have not intended that we interpret v. 9b as the object of "hear," yet the lack of a better place in the passage made the infelicitous position of the verse inevitable. By supplementing the notice of the enemy's reaction, the first scene concludes in v. 10 (rather than v. 11a). It resembles the present shape of 2:11b-20 and 3:1-37, which likewise end with "and (as) Sanballat (and Tobiah) heard...."[29] Thus, the description of the enemy's reaction in v. 10 intrudes between vv. 9b and 11a and depicts the animosity beginning not with the commencement of the building activities, as in vv. 19-20, but already with builder's advent. Accordingly, Nehemiah's "mission" has a much greater objective, for it is no longer his grief for the ruins of the ancestral city, yet rather his solicitude (לבקש) for the טובה לבני ישראל that occasioned his journey from Susa to Jerusalem.

With regard to vv. 7-9a, Torrey, Batten and Gunneweg were most likely correct in contending that this passage been inserted between vv. 6bβ and 9b.[30] First, v. 9b would have been better positioned before v. 7, since Nehemiah first reports to having delivered the king's letters to the provincial governors, and then, as if he forgot to mention it, tells his readers that the king sent with him officers of the army and cavalry. In putting "the cart before the horse,"[31] the incoherency could not be greater. Williamson treats this as an example of

---

27 See Mowinckel (1964: 22).

28 Similarly, Batten (1913: 199).

29 Cf. also the use of the שמע-formula in 1:4. In contrast to 2:11ff. and 3:1ff., 4:1ff. and 6:1ff. confusingly *begin* with this formula. To what extent this situation is due to editorial hands remains to be seen in this study.

30 Torrey (1896:37), Batten (1913: 194), and Gunneweg (1987: 55).

31 Batten (1913: 194).

"dischronologized narrative."[32] However, v. 9b belongs also stylistically to v. 6, where Nehemiah already reports that the king "sent" him. Without vv. 7-9a, the repetition of שׁלח is much easier to explain (וישׁלח עמי...וישׁלחני ואתנה לו זמן המלך וגו).

There are additional arguments, which Wellhausen, Winckler, Torrey, Batten and Gunneweg furnished, yet have not been refuted by those who deny that these verses are secondary. First, the *wayyiqtol* in v. 9b does not suffice to fill in the missing information. "To avoid the difficulty by translating וישׁלח as *pluperfect*, is to ignore Hebrew syntax."[33] Second, "*to the king*" in v. 7 is unexpected after the pronoun "him" in v. 6bβ. Third, the question-and-answer style of the narrative ceases after v. 6. So too, in vv. 1-6 Nehemiah does not speak until the king poses a question, yet now he "presses on uninvited" and presents unabashedly a lengthy wish list.[34] Fourth, in contrast to the very general nature of the description of Jerusalem in vv. 1-6, which suits the king's unfamiliarity, Nehemiah mentions details in v. 8a that the king certainly would not have understood, let alone found interesting (e.g., the name of the forester). Fifth, we are never told elsewhere in the account that the fortress was ever built; it was probably constructed after Nehemiah was long gone.[35] Sixth, the timber is said also to be for the wall of the city (ולחומת העיר), yet "the wall," which is built of stone, not wood (cf. 3:34ff.; 4:4, 11ff.),[36] is remarkably absent from the conversation in vv. 1-6.[37] The *gates* of the city (cf. v. 3) are, conversely, not mentioned in v. 8a. Seventh, the lumber is also said to be for his own future house (ולבית אשׁר־אבוא אליו). "As Nehemiah's declared purpose was to rebuild *the city*, he is here by the Chronicler's [=the editor's] purpose removed rather far from his design."[38]

---

32 "Chronologically, of course, it belongs with v. 7, but Nehemiah holds back the reference to this point in order to give an almost cynical, but utterly characteristic, comment on the delivery of letters requesting safe conduct. To suggest that the intervening material must therefore be a later addition is to betray a woeful lack of literary sensitivity" (1985: 183). Schunck (1998: 45) and Reinmuth (2002: 62) embrace Williamson's argument. The expression, "dischronologized narrative," was introduced by Martin (1969).

33 Torrey (1896: 37-n. 1), Ehrlich (1914: 186), and Gunneweg (1987: 54f.).

34 Williamson (1985: 181).

35 See below.

36 Gunneweg wrote in this regard: "Die Risse in der Stadtmauer, von denen in der Nachricht aus Jerusalem gesprochen worden war, und überhaupt Bauschäden an der Stadtbefestigung werden doch nicht mit Holz, sondern mit Steinen ausgebessert und *verursachen auf jeden Fall keinen solchen Bedarf an Bauholz, dass zu seiner Deckung die Bestände des königlichen Forstes in Anspruch genommen werden müssten*. Das Holz soll zu Balken verarbeitet werden, was mit dem Verbum קרה Pi zum Ausdruck gebracht wird. Diese Vokabel begegnet außer in der Bauliste N 3 nur noch 2 Chr 34,11, hier im Zusammenhang einer Erzählung über Josias Tempelrestauration" (1987: 55 – my italics).

37 Building upon this observation, many of the same scholars who deny the redactional character of vv. 7-9a have argued that Nehemiah did not intend to mention the wall because of Judah's recent history (Ezra 4). Significantly, they do not explain the presence of v. 8a.

38 Batten (1913: 195 – my italics).

Likewise, if Nehemiah planned to be in Judah for only a short time, as Rudolph and Williamson argue,[39] why would he have desired to build a house for himself?[40] Eighth, Nehemiah claims in 5:16 that, "We did not buy a piece of land." Where then did he build his house? Ninth, he presents this long wish list not only without the king having first granted him an additional request, but also after he had *already* been sent and was no longer present in Susa: "And it pleased the king, *and he sent me*" (וייטב לפני־המלך וישלחני), not "that he would send me" (אשר שלחני; cf. אשר תשלחני, v. 5b).

Given the weight of these arguments, one may safely conclude that this case of "dischronologized narrative" originated with the insertion of vv. 7-9a between vv. 6 and 9b. After the editorial work, the statement וישלחני ואתנה לו זמן is severed from וישלח עמי המלך וגו, which confuses the reader into thinking that "the gracious hand of God" had caused only Artaxerxes' willingness to grant letters and not his provision of a military escort (v. 9b). The abiding problem is whether the insertion has been drafted by one hand. Resuming where Torrey, Batten and Gunneweg left off, I submit that v. 8a is later than vv. 7 and 8b-9a. In enumerating the additional requirements for the building project, which have nothing to do with the original purpose of the letters to convey Nehemiah safely to Judah, v. 8a is simply intrusive. Without it, the continuity and simplicity of an independent episode in the narrative in vv. 7, 8b-9a reemerges: The author of these lines, apparently inspired by the king's concern and generosity in v. 9b, portrays Nehemiah making a further petition for his own safety. The formulation of v. 7a seems also to have been borrowed from v. 5aα, which reads: ואומר למלך אם־על־המלך טוב.

In contrast to the information concerning the "letters" in vv. 7, 8b-9a, we are never told what happens to the "letter" in v. 8a. The reader searches the entire first-person account in vain for a reference to Asaph (an important Levitical name in Ezra-Neh and Chr), the timber, the temple-citadel (let alone their gates), or Nehemiah's house. What is the reason for this silence?[41] The answer to this question may be contained in the sequence of the purposes for the timber: It was to serve first for the gates of the temple-citadel, and then for the wall of the city (ולחומת העיר), and finally for Nehemiah's house. Thus, Nehemiah's concerns himself with the security and sanctity of the temple (cf. Simon's purification of the temple-citadel in 1 Macc 13:49-55) more than that of the Jerusalem as a whole. This order of importance corresponds precisely to that

---

39 Rudolph (1949: 108) and Williamson (1985: 181).
40 See below for the quotations of their work in the discussion of Nehemiah's house.
41 Galling (1954: 219) went to great lengths to explain the lack of denouement created by v. 8a: "Auf die Holzlieferungen kommt Nehemia nicht mehr zu sprechen. Das könnte damit zusammenhängen, daß Nehemia bei der Abfassung seiner Memoiren für den Mauerbaubericht in 3, 1-32 eine offizielle Liste heranzog, die ihrerseits keine Notiz über die Baumaterialen enthielt."

of Ezra 1-10. Following Cyrus' command and supported by liberal donations, the Golah returned, built the altar, laid the temple-foundation, and completed the work, before Nehemiah ever receives mere permission (without the generous imperial funds) to build the wall. In the midst of the construction of the temple, Artaxerxes prohibits the building of the city-wall "until a further decree be issued from [him]" (Ezra 4:19). There he seems to know that, after the completion (Ezra 6) and "beautification" (Ezra 7:27) of the temple, he would allow his Jewish cupbearer to build the rest of Jerusalem. And in Neh 2:8a, this same ruler donates timber – first, for the gates of the temple-fortress and, second, for the municipal wall.

Finally, v. 8a depicts Nehemiah as the builder not just of the fortress and the wall, but also of his own home. This phrase may constitute a late gloss, yet it leaves no room for doubt that a longer time was envisioned than just the fifty-two days of construction (cf. 6:15). While the request runs at odds to the nature of the mission in vv. 1-6, it agrees with the twelve-years of gubernatorial service reported in 5:14ff.[42] Instead of supposing with Rudolph and Williamson that Nehemiah was planning to just make a few repairs to an old family home where he was to stay for several months,[43] it is much more likely that "the house" refers to nothing other than the governor's mansion. A later author must have noticed the absence of a passage where the king appoints his wine-steward to the position of Judean governor. Accordingly, he supposed that Nehemiah received a full gubernatorial commission – not a mere leave of absence – on the occasion depicted in 2:1ff.

An additional problem created by v. 8a is that we are never told that the house was built (or repaired). Indeed, the only house that Nehemiah enters is that of Shemaiah (cf. ולבית אשר־אבוא אליו with ואני־באתי בית שמעיה; 6:10), which suggests not only that he was not a homeowner, but also that the temple (ההיכל) was the only place of asylum. Accordingly, the temple-citadel (הבירה אשר־לבית) may well have not existed as 6:10-14 was composed, since Shemaiah would surely have suggested it as a place of refuge.[44]

Since 2:8a presents the temple-fortress as already built, those scholars who do not dispute the integrity of vv. 7-9a must assume that it was completed between 536 and 445/4 BCE.[45] Yet in contrast to 1 Esdras (cf. 5:46, 7:9, 9:1), Ezra 1-6 does not mention the building of the temple-gates, let alone the gates of the citadel. Nor does the archaeological evidence support the assumption that

---

42   The problems surrounding Nehemiah's governorship in 5:14ff. are discussed in §8.3.
43   Rudolph (1949: 108) and Williamson (1985: 181).
44   In the analysis of Neh 6:10ff. (§7.5.1), I attempt to show that the reason sought to reproach Nehemiah was not an entrance into a sacred space but rather a manifestation of fear. Cf. Winckler's comments (1901: 474).
45   Cf., e.g., Bertholet (1902: 50) and Rudolph (1949: 107).

the citadel was already standing before 445/4 BCE.[46] Moreover, after Nehemiah just mentioned that the city-gates were destroyed in fire (2:3), Artaxerxes and the reader must suppose that the citadel was also part of the devastation. It must then have been built and destroyed within a very short time-span. Historically, this is most improbable. Therefore, if 2:8a is indeed younger than vv. 7, 8b-9a, one would not have to date the whole passage to the Hasmonean period.[47]

To conclude the literary-critical analysis, we turn briefly to the relationship of v. 9b to v. 6. In embracing the position of Torrey, Batten, Gunneweg, *et al.* that vv. 7-9a represents a late *relecture*, the reconstruction faces a problem: Without vv. 7-9a, the statement in v. 9b ("And *the king* sent officers of the army and cavalry with me") would follow upon the statement in v. 6bβ ("And I set him a time"). While this solution produces a smooth narrative, the analysis above has corroborated the conclusions of Hölscher and Mowinckel that v. 6bβ constitutes a gloss. Now it is necessary to explain the repetition of "the king" as the subject and "sent" as the verb in vv. 6bα and 9b. The best approach is to ascribe vv. 6bβ and 9b to later hand and to connect v. 6bα, which was probably the original conclusion of the court scene, directly to v. 11a. Even without the addition of vv. 7-9a, the remark in v. 6bα must be translated, as noted above: "And it pleased the king, *and he sent me*" (וישלחני), not "*that* he *would* send me," as v. 5b. Accordingly, Nehemiah reports succinctly that "he sent me, [...] and I came to Jerusalem" (v. 11a) before changing the scene in v. 11b ("After I had been there several days..."). The addition of v. 9b sustains the emphasis on Artaxerxes' appreciation for his cupbearer in vv. 1-6, inasmuch as the provision of royal troops demonstrates his concern for Nehemiah's prosperous journey and safe return (cf. "and when will you return" in v. 6).

---

46 For a bibliography of the excavation reports and discussions, see Bieberstein and Bloedhorn (1994: 91-94 and 104-108).

47 Already Wellhausen (1899: 174-n. 2; 251-n. 1.) proposed that the construction could not have preceded the reign of Antiochus IV, and he had good reasons to make this claim: Josephus (*Ant.* 15.403 §§91-92 and 18.91; see also 1 Macc 13:52) reports that Johannes Hyrkanos I built a citadel – the "Baris" – north of the temple. Had he known that the fortress existed prior to Hyrkanos's building project, he would have most likely formulated his account differently. The other possibility, which hitherto has not been considered, is to date the building of the citadel to the construction projects of Simon II (218-192 BCE), who "fortified" the temple according to Ben Sirach (50:1ff.). Whether this project consisted only of the walls mentioned in 50:2 is debatable. Therefore, in consideration of the additional evidence for Maccabean and Hasmonean expansions of the fortifications from the Persian period, I propose that a scribe from a much later time portrayed the citadel as an ancient construction already standing in monarchical times, destroyed (at least its gates) by the Babylonians, and restored by Nehemiah.

5.3 The Ramifications of the Analysis for an Historical Reconstruction

The remainder of the chapter treats the implications of the literary-critical analysis for two questions: (1) What type of building project is envisaged in the conversation with Artaxerxes? (2) How should one explain the significant differences between this account and Ezra 7-8? These problems involve many issues that cannot be addressed here. Our aim is only to establish a general direction for the present study, in the course of which we will marshal further evidence for our claims.

5.3.1 The Building Project and Achaemenid Strategic Concerns

According to the conventional conclusions based on an interpretation of 2:1ff., Nehemiah was sent to Judah solely to rebuild his ancestral city and that he was granted only a short leave-of-absence. In recent scholarship, these conclusions have been called into question. Thus, many would maintain that the author has intentionally concealed the "messy details" such as his appointment to the post of Judean governor (based on the information in 5:14ff.) or that it was the king who actually initiated the repair of Jerusalem's ramparts as part of the empire's military strategy. In the discussion of Neh 5 (§8.3), I investigate the problems surrounding Nehemiah's gubernatorial status. The present section endeavors to demonstrate that it is rather unlikely that the crown commissioned the building of the wall for military purposes. (Whether the wall later played a role in the defense of the empire is different issue.) Rather than planning to fortify the city and station troops there, it is more conceivable that Artaxerxes accepted the proposal of his Jewish minister with the aim of sustaining the loyalty of one of his subject peoples.

The best defense of the view that the rebuilding of Jerusalem's ramparts coincided with an imperial strategy is presented in Hoglund's study, *Achaemenid Imperial Administration in Syria-Palestine and the Missions of Ezra and Nehemiah* (1992). The author of this work has made a significant contribution to Ezra-Neh scholarship by assessing the historical problems of the mid-fifth century in the western Achaemenid empire. Many of Hoglund's conclusions merit acceptance.[48] Thus, it seems quite plausible that the imperial administration would have desired to tighten its control over the Levant after the intervention of the

---

48 Most importantly, Hoglund has emphasized to biblical research that Ctesias's account of the Megabyzos-rebellion is most probably completely unreliable.

Delian League and the continued Greek naval operations in the eastern Mediterranean in the decade of the 440's. Yet Hoglund also contends, "The actions reflected in the narratives regarding Nehemiah's mission are not a reward for past loyalty, nor the provision of special favors upon Jerusalem simply to ensure that the community continues in its obedience to the empire."[49] Accordingly, Hoglund speaks of "the mission of Nehemiah,"[50] according to which the imperial court enlists the Jewish cupbearer to refortify Jerusalem and build the citadel (2:8). "Presumably manned by imperial troops, this citadel not only would serve to protect a vulnerable portion of the city, but also place a concentration of imperial force just outside the city where it would be noticed by the inhabitants of Jerusalem." The mission encompassed more than just refortifying Jerusalem and building a citadel for Persian troops. The financial reforms reported in Neh 5, were necessitated, Hoglund claims, by the payment of taxes to support the imperial garrisons.[51] So too, the measures taken against mixed marriages described in chap. 13 are explained as the attempt by the "authorized reformer" to clarify the membership of the community, so that the empire could determine who belonged to Judah. These ethnic boundaries would have been important for the community that enjoyed imperial privileges and that was also required to pay imperial taxes. Hoglund summarizes "the primary facets of Nehemiah's mission" under three points:

> First, there was a strategic dimension, most dramatically represented by the refortification of Jerusalem by the restoration of the city wall system, but also including the establishment of an imperial garrison to the north of the city. Second, there were a series of economic reforms directed at lessening the impact of the increased imperial activity in the region. Finally, there was some form of reiterated opposition to intermarriage, circumscribing the community within a set of ethnic boundaries.[52]

In order to support these claims, Hoglund's points to various passages in Nehemiah's account. However, his treatment of the text is liable to the criticism of selective reading: What does not agree with his thesis, he attributes to "the author of Ezra-Neh." This selectivity is most pronounced with regard to audience-scene in Neh 2, which supposedly has been "reconstructed" by this author.[53] Yet it does not make sense that one hand was responsible for both the composition of the book and the rewriting of Neh 2:1ff. On Hoglund's thesis, we would have to conclude that the author failed miserably. One would expect this book to have portrayed the imperial government *commanding* Jerusalem to be

---

49 1992: 225.
50 Ibid.: 208.
51 Ibid.: 213.
52 Ibid.: 220.
53 No arguments are provided for this claim other than that it contradicts what is considered historical plausible.

fortified,[54] as this would have provided another example of the complimentary relationship between the imperial and divine will.[55] The same applies for the putative demand of the Achaemenids for an ethnically circumscribed community. Why has "the author" not reworked Ezra 9–10, Neh 5 and 13 in line with Ezra 1-6 (cf., e.g., Ezra 6:14) to show that the internal reforms were not only in keeping with the Torah, but also in the interest of the Persian empire?

Moreover, Neh 2 stands in great tension with Ezra 4:7-23, as we have seen in §3.3. Reading the former independently of the latter, one would never have imagined that Artaxerxes had just banned the construction of Jerusalem. Had the author of Neh 2 been cognizant of Ezra 4 and intended to present the king changing his mind, he could have at least indicated this in some way, instead of allowing the friction between these texts to persist. To be sure, the reader of Ezra-Neh is disappointed that Nehemiah does not say more about the success of finally receiving permission to build.

Neh 2:8 plays an important role in Hoglund's assertion that Nehemiah's "task" was to build the citadel, where imperial troops were to be established. In drawing upon the information in this verse, one should not disregard the caution urged by Torrey, Wellhausen, Winckler, Hölscher, Batten, Gunneweg *et al.* against employing precisely this verse for an historical reconstruction.[56] Even if v. 8a provided reliable information for the situation in Jerusalem in mid-fifth century, it is Nehemiah, not Artaxerxes, who desires to repair the gates of the citadel. Likewise, the only soldiers mentioned in the entire first-person account are those who simply convey Nehemiah to Judah (v. 9b).[57]

Since Neh 2 presents Artaxerxes merely allowing his faithful servant to build the city of his "ancestors' graves," what can one say about the *raisons d'état* – rather than just the *raisons de coeur* – of the imperial court? The best answer to this question is the very proposal Hoglund rejects, namely that if the court had any interest in seeing the restoration of Jerusalem, it was merely "as an inducement to greater loyalty by the show of imperial favor."[58] The security of the

---

54 For the commands and decrees of the kings, see, e.g., Ezra 1:1-4; 4:19, 21; 5:3, 9, 13, 17; 6:1, 3, 8, 11, 12, 14; 7:13ff.

55 To this subject, see most importantly Japhet (1982: 66-98) and (1983: 218-29).

56 See our analysis in §5.2.2.

57 In 4:5ff., Nehemiah mobilizes the people to face the attack from Sanballat & co. Where are the soldiers who were to provide for the peace? Is the silence with regard to them also due to "the author" of Ezra-Neh? And why is the only battle scene in the entire account depicted during the work on the wall and not after? Instead of portraying the wall as Jerusalem's defense system much needed in view of past aggression by the enemy, the author consistently presents it as the very thing that precipitates the aggression. Solely in 7:1-3 and 11:1ff. does the wall function as Jerusalem's fortification. Yet these passages, as pointed out in §13.3, not only do not correspond Nehemiah's primary emphasis on the consolidation of Judah brought by the restoration project, but they also appear to constitute additions from a much later time.

58 1992: 220.

Levant, which served both as a land-bridge to Egypt and bordered on the eastern Mediterranean, was certainly important. However, it remains to be seen whether Jerusalem itself was of concern to Artaxerxes for any other reason than the anticipated unity and loyalty the restoration of the city would secure in Judah.[59] On the assumption that the court *commissioned* Nehemiah to rebuild Jerusalem, one must explain why this city was allowed to rebuild its fortifications and not Samaria, which as a provincial capital played a considerably more important role. Moreover, the lack of municipal development in the central regions contrasts with what we observe along the coast: *Tell Abū Hawām, Gil'ām, Tēl Megādim,* Dor, *Tell Mubārak, Tell Abū Zētūn,* Jaffa, Lachish, *Tell-en Naṣbe* (=Mizpah?) and Hesbon all had fortification-systems. These walls, however, vary greatly in plan and are rather primitive.[60] Their modesty and the fact that most places remained unfortified may be due to the general tendency to employ small fortifications in the place of large city-walls as a defense system. In Hazor, Megiddo, Akko, *Tell el-Qasīle, Tell el-Ḥesī, Tell Ǧemme, Tell eš-Šeri'a,* and *Tell es-Sa'idīye,* large rectangular buildings with courtyards were erected that could be used for both administrative and military purposes.[61] Throughout the Persian period, the Via Maris was never part of Judah,[62] and all the other routes that passed through the vicinity of Jerusalem were subsidiary, serving only the immediate region. That the construction of fortresses and the renewal of city-walls concentrated itself along the coast and the important trade routes is directly related to their importance for the empire, which explains why no real municipal development is witnessed in the hinterland (Samaria and Judah).

How then should one view the construction of Jerusalem's wall by Nehemiah? Hoglund's response to this problem, if understood correctly, is that the court's interest in the building enterprise centered on the construction of "an imperial garrison to the north of the city." However, not only does Artaxerxes send troops merely to guard his cupbearer (2:9b), the text of 2:8a includes solely a request for wood to build the *gates* of the temple-citadel, the wall and Nehemiah's house. And it has been seen that this line stands in tension with the rest of the account: One searches futilely for a notice that the gates of the citadel were ever actually built. Moreover, inasmuch as the citadel was part of the temple-complex, it does not comport with the architectural pattern of fortresses elsewhere. Finally, it is questionable that this fortification even existed in the fifth or even fourth century BCE.[63]

---

59 For a general discussion of the Achaemenid attempts to solidify the loyalty of the provinces, see E. Meyer (1939: 26ff.), Dandamayev in Walser (1972: 15ff.), Hinz (1979: 55ff.), Frei/Koch (1996: 10ff.) and Briant (1996: 713ff.).

60 For a general discussion of the archeological finds, see Weippert (1988: 699f.)

61 See Stern (1982: 57ff.)

62 See Aharoni (1979: 45-54).

63 See §5.2.2.

According to a more tenable solution, the building of Jerusalem was undertaken as a communal effort, just as Nehemiah portrays it. After arriving, he
addresses the leaders and convinces them of the necessity of building, employing no other argument than that the ruins constituted a political scourge for the
inhabitants of Judah: "You see the affliction/dishonor we are in, how Jerusalem
is devastated.... Come let us build up the wall so that we are no longer a
reproach" (2:17). Later he tells them how "the hand of God was favorable"
upon him; only thereafter does he also recall "what the king had said" (2:18a).
The sequence of reasons presented here corresponds most likely to what
actually motivated the construction. Accordingly, Jerusalem occupied a central
place not in the strategic plan of the empire, but rather in the ethnic and political consciousness of the Judean leaders. With the restoration of its ancient
capital, Judah could begin a process of centralization and recovery of its former
political strength in the region. If the register of the builders in 3:1-32 provides
reliable information, the project began as a provincial effort to which the priests,
various guilds and above all the princes of the individual districts directly contributed. So too, they finished the work in fifty-two days according to 6:15; it is
inconceivable that the community could have accomplished anything more in
this short time than removing the ruins and making a few repairs. In any case,
the wall would certainly not furnished any real protection for Judah, let alone
the western Achaemenid empire.

Moreover, why does the king not finance the project? Even the transmitted
shape of the account portrays the king donating only timber, and Nehemiah
must even solicit this donation from him. Although the people are suffering
under the burden of heavy royal taxes (5:3) and although the crown does not
present them with any incentive for acceding to his putative plans to transform
Jerusalem into an imperial fortification, they build willingly. Thus, if one may
believe anything at all in Nehemiah's account, then it is that Jerusalem's wall was
not repaired with military-strategic concerns in view – especially those of the
Achaemenid empire. Rather, Nehemiah and the leaders of Judah undertook this
construction enterprise merely with the passive approval of the king (וייטב לפני־
המלך, 2:6). That they were eager to begin (cf. 2:18 and 3:38) and quickly complete the work despite the lack of financial support from the court indicates that
they must have had their own very compelling, political reasons. And as we will
observe in the course of the present study, these political reasons are qualified
anew with each expansion of the account.

5.3.2 The Relationship of Neh 2:1-11a to Ezra 7-8

The investigation of Neh 2:1-11a would not be complete without briefly discussing the relationship of the passage to Ezra 7-8. The following pages address the problems posed by the results of the literary-critical analysis above (§5.2), which initially appear to invalidate the claim of several scholars that Neh 2 has directly influenced the composition of Ezra 7-8.

To begin this discussion, we draw our attention to several expressions common to both Ezra's and Nehemiah's accounts. First, the king sends with Nehemiah "officers of the army and cavalry" (2:9b). Ezra, however, is "ashamed to require of the king an army and cavalry to 'aid us' against the enemy on the way" (Ezra 8:22). Second, Nehemiah receives what he "requests" (v. 4) according to "the favorable hand of God" (2:8; cf. also v. 18a). With regard to Ezra, the reader is told, "the king granted him all his request according to the hand of YHWH his God that was upon him" (Ezra 7:6). Similarly, Ezra explains the waiver of the king's soldiers and cavalry by affirming that that "the hand of our God is upon all them that seek him for good" (Ezra 8:22). References to "the good hand of God" are found also in Ezra 7:9, 28, 8:18 and 31. Third, Nehemiah reports in 2:11a that he "came to Jerusalem and was there three days." Likewise, Ezra announces, "And we came to Jerusalem and abode there three days" (Ezra 8:32). To these points of similarity may be added the facts that both accounts are formulated in the first-person, share a basic story-line (*viz.*, a Jew finds favor with Artaxerxes I, who grants him what he "requests" and then travels to Jerusalem), and have been transmitted in the same book.

These parallels have led Noth, Kellermann, In der Smitten, Gunneweg and Kratz to conclude that the author of Ezra 7-8 has drafted this material as a response to Nehemiah's account.[64] The letter in 7:12ff., or at least a part of it, is older and the narrative forms a midrash to it. These scholars stand over against the consensus according to which Ezra 7-8 predates Nehemiah's account.

In evaluating the conclusions of these scholars, one should consider that our literary-critical analysis above has shown that two of the expressions common to both texts represent redactional supplements (*viz.*, "the favorable hand of God" in Neh 2:8b and "army and cavalry" Neh 2:9a). Assuming the plausibility of these findings, the only explicit stylistic similarity between the two works is the statement of arrival in v. 11. As this is slim evidence for affirming a direction of dependency, it seems that our analysis supports the consensus view and that there is no reason to question the authenticity of Ezra 7-8. Furthermore, a

---

64 Noth (1943: 125f., 145ff.), Kellermann (1967: 56ff.), In der Smitten (1973: 54ff.), Gunneweg (1985: 121ff.), and Kratz (2000: 77ff.). Cf. also the older discussion in Fruin (1929).

closer examination of Ezra 8:22 reveals that it may constitute an interpolation.[65] If so, the reference to the band of soldiers and cavalry would parallel Neh 2:9a only because a redactor supplied it. Finally, it is possible that Nehemiah's use of the phrase "the favorable hand of my God" in 2:8b, which according to my reconstruction is younger than 2:9a, has been influenced by Ezra's account.[66] Hence, it would appear that the author of Ezra 7-8 was not familiar with Neh 2.

Problems persist, however. Even though the several stylistic points of contact between Ezra 7-8 and Neh 2 are probably due to the history of redaction, other more significant clues indicate that even the earliest edition of Ezra's account was composed for its transmitted context and thus is younger than Nehemiah's account. Accordingly, many of expressions discussed above originated in the redactional history of Nehemiah's account and have been incorporated by the authors of Ezra's account in order to highlight the differences between the two works.[67]

As pointed out in chap. 4, the introduction to Nehemiah's report seems to have originally included only 1:1a, 11b and 2:1ff., and may be compared to the form of many other first-person accounts and inscriptions in the ancient Near East. While only few scholars (Winckler, Kaiser, and Hoglund[68]) have suggested that an editor completely rewrote this introduction, no one would dispute the claim that the Ezra material does not begin with the anticipated form of introduction. In the place of the heading in Neh 1:1a (דברי נחמיה בן־חכליה), there is a narrative transition (ואחר הדברים האלה במלכות ארתחשסתא מלך־פרס, 7:1a) and a long genealogy (vv. 1b-5). Whereas Nehemiah first states the date and his function (1:1b, 11b; 2:1a) and then commences to recount his story, Ezra reports neither the date nor his function, and he does not begin narrating until after twenty-six verses.

How should one explain these discrepancies? According to Williamson, "the third-person introduction in 7:1-10 represents a rewriting of Ezra's original account by the editor who first combined the Ezra and Nehemiah material. He expanded some parts and abbreviated others to suit his purpose."[69] Although this approach is very popular, one must wonder why "the editor" would have decided to rewrite only the introduction to Ezra's account, changing it from the first- to third-person, while leaving Nehemiah's account in its original form. No

---

65 V. 23a (ונצומה ונבקשה מאלהינו) resumes the thought of v. 21, and the reader is confused into understanding "for this" (על־זאת) in v. 23 as referring to the conclusion of v. 22b.

66 As argued in the following chapter, an editor has probably added 2:18a.

67 Ezra 8:32 may have been influenced by Neh 2:11. The reference to the army and cavalry has almost certainly been drawn from Neh 2:9b. Yet the expression "the favorable hand of God" in Neh 2:8b, which postdates 2:9b, is probably native to Ezra's account.

68 Winckler (1901: 473), Kaiser (1984: 182-n. 15; 184), and Hoglund (1992: 208-n. 3). Perhaps one should include to this group the work of Eskenazi (1988), which consciously avoids any source-critical divisions.

69 Williamson (1985: 90).

one has even attempted to address this problem.[70] And this reticence is fully understandable considering the immensity of the problem. If any account should have been fully rewritten, it is Nehemiah's, not Ezra's. Assuming for the sake of argument that "the editor" indeed found the basic information contained in Ezra 7:1-10 in an older Ezran account, there would have been no reason to rewrite it. The most one would expect is the amplification of the text. Moreover, if the author of Ezra 1-6 desired to make the transition smoother to Ezra's account by reformulating it into the third-person,[71] one must also account for the transition from Ezra 10 to Neh 1ff.

Conversely, "the editor" would have had reasons aplenty to fully revise and revamp the Nehemiah's text with its unorthodox view of the Restoration. In 1:1b-4, Nehemiah is concerned only with those who had been left of the captivity in Judah. Disappointing the expectations of those who have just read Ezra 1-10, he does not inquire about the welfare of those who had returned – either recently or "in the beginning" (cf. Neh 7:5). In 2:1ff., he asks to be sent for reasons of personal piety (i.e., to rebuild "the city of his ancestors' graves"). Here he does not seem to be concerned with the temple, let alone transporting any additional donations for the sacrificial cult, which contrasts with the piety familiar to the reader of Ezra 1-10. As the king grants permission for the voyage, he does not follow Ezra in praising "YHWH, God of our ancestors…who has extended mercy unto me before the king…" (Ezra 7:27f.). Even Nehemiah's remark in 2:8 about "the favorable hand of my God" does not seem to be integral. And whereas Ezra makes Aliyah and gathers a group out of Israel to accompany him (7:28; cf. vv. 7, 9), Nehemiah simply "comes" (בוא rather than עלה) to Jerusalem, not bringing anyone with him except the king's soldiers and without appearing to consider his journey as a return from captivity.[72]

---

70 See, however, the analysis of Grol (1990). The works of Cazelles (1954), Cross (1975), Emerton (1966), Fernández (1921),Galling (1937), Green (1990), van Hoonacker (1924), Lefèvre (1960), Pavlovský (1957), Rowley (1952), Saley (1978), Talmon (1987), Tuland (1974), Widengren (1977), and Yamauchi (1980) focus on the issue of whether the historical Nehemiah preceded Ezra, rather than the priority of their *accounts*. None of them has seriously attempted to explain how "the original" Ezra-account began and why "the editor" altered of Neh 1-2.

71 For example, Japhet (1994: 208ff.), followed by Karrer (2001: 300ff.), divides the book into two halves: Ezra 1-6 and Ezra 7-10 + Neh 1-13. Accordingly, the third-person introduction in Ezra 7:1-10, which is lacking in Neh 1-2, is explained as the attempt by the author/editor to draw a decisive transition to the reign of Artaxerxes. The question arises, why did the author not introduce both Ezra and Nehemiah in Ezra 7:1-10 if his intention was to introduce both of these figures according to the diarchy of Jeshua and Zerubbabel? It would have been quite simple to do this: "And after these things in the reign of Artaxerxes, Ezra *and Nehemiah* went up from Babylon. These are the words of Ezra…"

72 Moreover, the very fact that 7:1-10 appears to have passed through many editorial hands suggests that the primary stratum of this section is still contained in the text and has not been rewritten from a first-person original.

There are other points to consider. For example, it is significant that the Artaxerxes of Ezra 7 does not resemble in any way the Artaxerxes of Neh 2. Is it possible that within the time-span of thirteen years this king had forgotten about his magnanimous decree for the Golah and temple? Rather than issuing another decree in Neh 2, he simply accedes to a request to repair the city and does not donate any silver or gold as he had earlier. Moreover, according to Ezra 7, he was much more pious than his Jewish cupbearer, who manifests knowledge of Torah only in the youngest additions to his account (e.g., Neh 1:5-11a). In contrast, the earliest portions of Ezra 7-8 present the non-Jewish king ordering Ezra to enforce the laws of "the God of Heaven" throughout Abar Naharah (7:25).[73]

In order to salvage the reliability of the Ezra material, one could argue that the so-called Artaxerxes-firman has been either heavily edited or interpolated. For example, Janzen has attempted to show that the letter does not correspond to the conventional manner of correspondence in which the king responds to a request by *quoting* the document in which the request is presented. Based on these and other new arguments, Janzen contends that the entire letter is not only inauthentic, but also historically unreliable. It "may have been composed as a kind of midrash on the rest of the Ezra narrative" and "[w]e do not need the letter to make sense of what Ezra does in the rest of the Ezra narrative."[74] Likewise, Karrer writes, "Die Unterschiede zwischen Brief und sonstigem Esra-Bericht lassen sich am besten erklären, wenn der Brief (in Teilen) als Dokument vorlag und sekundär, im Zuge einer redaktionell Überarbeitung, in den Esra-Bericht aufgenommen wurde."[75]

The problem with Janzen's and Karrer's proposals is that they assume that one can simply remove the letter without jeopardizing the rest of the narrative.[76] A closer examination of the text reveals that Ezra's only reason for making Aliyah was to deliver the royal donations to the temple referred to in vv. 12-23. It seems likely, as Karrer maintains, that the letter has passed through editorial

---

73 With regard to the identity of *dat* and *torah*, Rendtorff (1984) distinguishes between the two, while Kratz (1991: 227f. and 233ff.) considers them essentially equivalent. Willi (1995: 101ff.) interprets *torah* as teaching and *dat* as the ratification of "the commandments, statutes and judgments."

74 2000: 643. Cf., however, the important counterarguments made by Steiner (2001: 640ff.). Unfortunately, he does not address the results of Schwiderski's study (2000: 379f.). Most recently, Grätz (2004: 81ff.) has presented a compelling case for the inauthenticity of the letter.

75 2001: 230.

76 For the earliest layer of Ezra 7-8, Karrer seems to assert that it began in 7:6, 8 and continued directly in 7:28b, 8:15ff. The problem with beginning the narrative in 7:28b is that the expression "according to the good hand of YHWH my God that was upon me" presupposes the presence of the letter. In Neh 2:8b, Nehemiah uses the same expression (although without "YHWH"!) after Artaxerxes grants him *letters*.

hands.[77] However, the best approach to the tensions between this document and its present context is not to remove the former, but rather to allow for the possibility of redactional supplements throughout all of chaps. 7-8.[78] The narrative places the emphasis on the point that Artaxerxes and his court donated an incredible amount of gold and silver for the maintenance of the temple (cf. the central position of the praise in 7:27f.) and how Ezra organizes an Aliyah to deliver these donations (7:28b, 8:1ff.; cf. the order in 7:15). The story, while making perfect sense without a continuation in chaps. 9-10 and Neh 8, cannot survive without the letter in 7:11ff.*. On the other hand, Ezra 9-10 appear to presuppose an advanced stage in the composition of the preceding narrative.[79] If these conclusions are warranted and the narrative of Ezra 7-8 cannot exist without the letter, then the earliest strata of the material still includes the most problematic aspect: the presentation of Artaxerxes as a more pious devotee to "the God of Heaven" and his temple in Jerusalem than his Jewish wine-steward.

Those who maintain that the Ezra narrative was completed in the second half of the fifth century encounter insurmountable difficulties explaining why Nehemiah does not incorporate literary and conceptual features from his predecessor. If the latter thought that his audience would compare his account with that of Ezra, he would have certainly attributed his success to YHWH (cf. Ezra 7:28), rather than only to his positive relationship to Artaxerxes. So too, this ruler in Ezra's portrayal takes the lead without being prompted, ordering the treasurers of Abar Naharah to pay out everything required for the temple. Now assuming that Nehemiah had read the putative literary precursor to Ezra 7, why has he presented the king only consenting to his own request for Jerusalem? As witnessed above with respect to the court scene in 2:1ff, the author intends to relate to the reader that he was in favor with Artaxerxes and how his downcast countenance did not go unnoticed. If his intended audience had been familiar with Ezra's account, it would have had never been able to appreciate the fine nuances and the subtlety of his portrayal. Indeed, the reader would have likely concluded that Nehemiah did *not* enjoy good relations with the king.[80] Instead of

---

77 Cf., e.g., Kratz (2000: 82f.).

78 Accordingly, it seems that the earliest portion of the Ezra narrative (after 7:21ff.) is to be isolated in 7:1-6aα, b, 11a (without " the *sōfēr*"), 13 (without "the priests and Levites"), 15-21 (without "the scribe of the God of Heaven"), 22-23, 27f.; 8:1-15a, 21, 23-25, 28-29, 31-34. That the dates of Ezra's activities are not provided by the earliest layer, may be compared to the general dating in Ezra 4 (cf. esp. "in the days of Artaxerxes" of v. 7 with 7:1). The additions in which Ezra is also a *sōfēr* prepare the reader for the expansion of the material first in chap. 9-10 and then in Neh 8. Cf. Blenkinsopp's comments on the secondary character of the combination of priest and *sōfēr* (1988: 137).

79 As argued in §11.2.2, Ezra 9 presupposes the foregoing chapters and has been composed with Neh 1-13 in view.

80 These observations serve as a response to Emerton's comment in a review of Kellermann's work: "[I]f much of the narrative in Ezra vii-x and Neh. viii-xiii was invented by the

a recounting how he prompted the king, who then approved of his suggestion, Nehemiah should have attempted to depict the crown itself taking the initiative, commanding him to make Aliyah and build his ancestral city. The only tenable solution to this discrepancy is that Nehemiah (or the author of Neh 2) was writing for an audience that was not familiar with Ezra's account and that the latter was not composed until (long) after Nehemiah's.[81]

That the Ezra narrative was completed later and is largely fictitious would explain why Nehemiah does not seem to be aware of his more influential Jewish colleague. This obliviousness is quite strange considering that both of these figures supposedly were not only active at the imperial court at the same time, but also that Ezra received a large grant from Artaxerxes. If they had never encountered one another at the court, they surely would have come into contact in the small city of Jerusalem. The register of the builders in Neh 3:1-32 seems to refer to every important figure in Judah, yet Ezra's name does not appear. Scholars usually explain his absence in Nehemiah's account on the assumption that the former "failed" and was required to return to Babylon. While correctly questioning this negative view of Ezra's achievements, Williamson suggests the equally speculative solution that Ezra finished his work within one year and then voluntarily left Jerusalem.[82] Yet why would Ezra, after making Aliyah, have returned to the captivity whence he came? This would be even more incomprehensible if he had witnessed the profound social problems in Judah (chaps. 9-10). Moreover, Neh 8 presents him still in Jerusalem in 445 BCE, and the literary evidence allows for no other conclusion than that this chapter was composed for its present context.[83] Those who believe that Ezra actually came and went must also explain why Nehemiah a short time later observes an advanced situation in Judah in which the children were old enough to speak the language of their foreign mothers (13:24).

Chronicler with the aim of making Ezra overshadow Nehemiah, it is surprising that task was not fulfilled more efficiently" (1972: 183).

81 That the royal treasurers were to bestow everything the temple required (7:20, 23f.), assigning to Jerusalem the highest status in the satrapy, conflicts not only with Nehemiah's account but also with our knowledge that Judah did not belong to the most important of the provinces in the Achaemenid empire. Considering its insignificance, it is not surprising that the authors of Ezra 1-6 and 7-8 would have desired to present a much different view of their place in the world. The possibility that an author could have either fully transformed or even invented the Aramaic letter in Ezra 7 is supported not only by our study of Ezra 4:7ff. (cf. the references there to other clearly inauthentic letters in Jewish literature), but also by the Gadatas letter (cf. Meiggs and Lewis [1969: 20ff.]). Van den Hout has seriously called the authenticity of this text into question, arguing that it was composed by later priests with the aim of presenting the "ancient dignity of their sanctuary to Apollo" (1949: 147). The counterarguments of Wiesehöfer (1987) prove only that the letter could not have been written a long time after the Persian period, yet they do not refute van den Hout's suggestion that the letter is simply inauthentic and written after the reign of Darius.

82 1985: xlvii.

83 See §14.2.3.

Finally, that the royal treasurers were to bestow everything the temple required (7:20, 23f.), would assign to Jerusalem the highest status in the satrapy. This conflicts not only with Nehemiah's account, but also with our knowledge that Judah belonged to the less important provinces. Considering its insignificance, it is not surprising that the authors of Ezra 1-6 and 7-8 would have desired to present a much different view of their place in the world.[84]

How then should one explain the presence of Ezra 7-8? Since it most problematic to suppose that editors completely rewrote an earlier introduction to Ezra's account while retaining and expanding the more "heterodox" portrayal Neh 1-2, it appears safe to conclude that the Ezra narrative never existed independently of its present context.[85] That it was created for the position between Ezra 6 and Neh 1 explains why Ezra 6:16-22* provides the denouement to the story of the temple-construction, whereas only the latest addition in 6:21 shares features in common with the Ezra material (cf. the use of "separate" and "filthiness").[86] Similarly, the account of the dedication of the wall in 12:27ff. includes the name of Ezra only in the youngest portions.

Continuing the response to Nehemiah's account in Ezra 1-6, the author of Ezra 7-8 has bridged the reign of Darius to Artaxerxes by integrating the form of Nehemiah's account (i.e., a first-person report in which the protagonist finds favor with Artaxerxes and is sent to Jerusalem) with the basic theme of Ezra 1-6 (i.e., the solicitude of the Achaemenid empire for the temple and the repatriation of the Golah). In the earliest stage of Ezra-Neh, the imperial court commands the temple to be built before it acquiesces to the restoration of the wall.[87] Here the construction of the altar, temple and city-wall are simply paralleled. While presenting them as complimentary, it also emphasizes the proper (and probably historical) sequence of the building projects. After the composition of the correspondence in Ezra 4:7ff., the imperial court is presented as recognizing the seditious character of the Judeans and commanding the construction of the wall to be stopped until it issues another decree (v. 21). The temple is finished in Ezra 6, which is followed directly by Neh 1-2 (possibly only 1:1a, 11b, 2:1ff.) and thus the reversal of the decree in Ezra 4. But before changing his mind on

---

84 *That* the authors wrote what they wrote is the historical fact that deserves primary attention, and the question of the reliability of the contents is of secondary importance.

85 Kratz (2000: 78) rightly contends that the introduction to Ezra's account in 7:1a ("Now after these things…"), which presupposes the foregoing narrative (Ezra 1-6*), should not be ascribed to an editorial hand. On the assumption that the editor simply adapted the purported original introduction to its present literary setting, as required by most scholarly reconstructions, one must abandon all literary criteria for the analysis of Ezra-Neh's composition.

86 That Neh 1:1b-4 is *older* than Ezra 7-8 (*pace* Kratz [2000: 78f.]) would explain why the former does not know of a return and refers to the Judeans as "the remnant left of the captivity there in the province" (Neh 1:3).

87 For suggestions on the composition-history of Ezra 1-3, see §13.3.2.

the dangers inherent in the wall-building project, Artaxerxes sends Ezra weighted down with gold and silver to "beautify" the temple (7:27). The absence of the travel report in Neh 2:1-11 is compensated by the report of Ezra's Aliyah, which also places Nehemiah's permission to build in its proper framework.[88] The older portion of the Ezra-narrative continues in the direction established by Ezra 4:7ff., which counterbalances the building of the wall – and the political stance it symbolizes (cf. Ezra 4:12f., 19f.; Neh 2:19, 6:6f.) – with the joint-effort of the Achaemenids and the repatriated inhabitants of Judah to build the temple and altar.

5.4 Conclusions

The present chapter has demonstrated how the account of an encounter with Artaxerxes in 2:1-11a serves to legitimate the building project portrayed in the following passages. Following the litotes, "Now I was not in disfavor with the king" (v. 1aβ), Nehemiah reports how the king himself noticed his cupbearer's sorrowful countenance and demands an explanation (v. 2). Taking the lead of Nehemiah's loaded question (v. 3), he grants a request (v. 4). Nehemiah's wish is naturally to be sent to Judah so that he could build "the city of his ancestors' graves" (v. 5). After affirming that this suggestion "pleased the king and he sent me," the account has left no room for doubt that the building of Jerusalem's wall met with the approval of the imperial court. And just as Nehemiah emphasizes that the ruins of Jerusalem weighed heavy upon his own consciousness in 2:1ff., so does he affirm that the condition of the wall was a blight and scourge upon all Judah in 2:16ff.: "Look at the distress we are, how Jerusalem lies in ruins…. Come let us build up the wall that we be no more a reproach."

With regard to the thesis that Artaxerxes ordered the wall to be rebuilt for the strategic purposes of the empire, we have seen that this widely accepted suggestion is tenable only when one is willing to assume that Nehemiah's account is not reliable. Since "the author" of Ezra-Neh cannot be made responsible for 2:1-6, one must explain who rewrote the account or why Nehemiah would have not desired to show that Jerusalem was important to the security of the empire. The claim that Neh 2:1-6 and 17 reflect the true reasons for building the wall is supported by the probability that imperial soldiers were stationed in only small fortresses away from the urban centers. Likewise, the wall was built without the financial backing of the crown. If the leaders of the individual

---

88 Kratz writes: "Grundbestand und Zusätze rücken Esra und Nehemia immer näher aneinander und komplettieren die Analogie mit dem Paar Serubbabel und Jeschua und der Heimkehrergeneration aus Esr 1-6" (2000: 90).

districts in Judah contributed to the project and completed it in a very short time under the financial burden of imperial taxation, then they likely built with their own concerns in view.

The final section addressed the historical problems posed by Ezra's account. Instead of entering into the discussion of the parallels (or lack of them) between Artaxerxes' letter in Ezra 7:11ff. and official Aramaic epistolary form, it has approached the issue from a simple comparison of Neh 2 with Ezra 7-8. The latter text seems to be the oldest part of the Ezra narrative, and it cannot exist without the so-called firman. In contrast to Nehemiah's account, Ezra 7-8 appear to have never been transmitted apart from their present setting in Ezra-Neh. Those who insist to the contrary cannot explain why "the editor" would have fully rewritten an earlier beginning of Ezra's account, while only expanding Nehemiah's much more problematic introduction. Furthermore, if Ezra's account were written earlier, Nehemiah would have been most likely cognizant of it and worded his own work much differently. Accordingly, the long-debated issue of the priority of Ezra and Nehemiah must be replaced with the question whether Ezra's *account* is older than Nehemiah's.

The composition of Ezra 7-8 has been explained here on the supposition that it was written for the book of Ezra-Neh in order to bridge the temple-building narrative in Ezra 1-6 to Nehemiah's wall-building report. After the addition of Ezra 7-8, there are both a priest and layperson working in both halves of Ezra-Neh (Jeshua and Zerubbabel in Ezra 1-6 and Ezra and Nehemiah in Ezra 7-8, Neh 1-13*). The order of priority (Ezra then Nehemiah in the reign of Artaxerxes) corresponds to the governing interest in Ezra-Neh for the proper sequence of the Restoration: the building of the altar, the laying of the temple-foundation, the prohibition of the building of the wall until a later time, the completion of the temple, its beautification, and finally the construction of the municipal wall.

6. The Consolidation of the Builders – 2:11b-4:17

6.1 Introduction

The various paragraphs in the lengthy section encompassing 2:11b-4:17 pose two main problems. First, what motivates the building project according to 2:17 is the social and political disgrace symbolized by the destroyed ramparts of Jerusalem. However, the commencement of the construction only elicits greater scorn. Insofar as the "affliction" and "reproach" gradually become associated with the verbal and physical assaults of Sanballat, Tobiah and Geshem (3:33ff., 4:1ff., and esp. 6:16), one has reason to believe that later authors have added names and faces to what is only implicit in 2:2-3 and 17. Second, the "register of builders" in 3:1-32 presents both the beginning and *completion* of the work on the wall; the following passages report, however, that the work was only partly finished. Since the register most likely never existed independently of its present context, one must explain why its author did not portray the work only *commencing* and then add a list of the remaining names elsewhere (e.g., in chaps. 4 or 6). Moreover, the register conflicts with the rest of the account inasmuch as the authors portray the very same persons initiating the restoration work who are censured in 6:17-19 and 13:4ff. for their alliances with the enemy. It seems, therefore, that one or the other – the register or the better part of the first-person account – must have been drafted later.

In order to present a solution to these problems, we begin by retracing the growth of the account in 2:11b-15 from a succinct statement into an independent scene (§6.2). Against the backdrop of this detailed analysis, we can afford to be brief in examining whether the remaining units in this section have likewise matured from a primitive narrative strand (§6.3).

6.2 Nehemiah's "Night Ride" – 2:11b-15

6.2.1 Evidence of Editorial Activity

The account of the so-called "Night Ride" in vv. 11b-15 contains many clues that it has passed through editorial hands in the history of its transmission. Introducing the passage, Nehemiah reports that he was accompanied by a small group of men (v. 12aα). The continuation, however, does not employ the first-person plural, as we would expect. After recalling that *no one* had been told about *what God had placed in his heart to do* on the behalf of Jerusalem (v. 12aβ), he states a few lines later that several groups had not been told about *what he was planning* (ומה אני עשה, v. 16aβ). So too, the itinerary of the excursion is perplexing: While in vv. 12-14 the route is determined by the course of the wall, in v. 15 Nehemiah and his escort are suddenly in the valley. After encompassing half of the city, they inexplicably turn back, rather than proceeding around the other half of the city. Moreover, having already inspected "the walls of Jerusalem that were broken down and its gates gutted by fire" (v. 13b), he then "went up the valley at night, inspected the wall and then returned" (v. 15). The repetitiousness of this concluding line and its disparity with the preceding itinerary suggests most forcefully that the description of the nocturnal reconnaissance evolved from a brief statement.

With respect to the conclusion (ואהי עלה בנחל לילה ואהי שבר בחומה ואשוב, v. 15a-bα). Batten rightly noticed that the information "does not connect well with the preceding." The reader has already been told that the inspection tour took place "at night" (vv. 12, 13), which renders לילה in v. 15a fully superfluous. Likewise, the author reports already in v. 13 that he examined the ruins: ואהי שבר בחומת ירושלם, which may be translated "and I went, inspecting the wall(s) of Jerusalem."[1] In view of its incongruities, one may consider with Batten whether v. 15a constitutes a supplement. Were this the case, the tension created by the verse would be effectively resolved. However, one could not explain what would have motivated a later author to add v. 15a, especially as it reiterates in a more succinct fashion what Nehemiah reports in vv. 12-14. Consequently, an alternative solution must be sought, and I submit that v. 15, instead of representing a late addition, contains the oldest part of the account.

The description of the route creates the first point of friction with the conclusion. The company begins by following the course of the wall (vv. 13-14), and the narrator directs the reader's attention to a specific portion of the city, referring to the names of gates and other architectural landmarks. Comparing the route with the data provided in 3:1-32 and 12:31ff., one may be seemly certain that Nehemiah and his company, after exiting the Valley Gate, headed south. Most agree that we must locate the Dung Gate, the Fountain Gate and the King's Pool at the extreme southern end of the eastern hill (i.e., the City of David).[2] However, upon reaching this point, the description of topographical features suddenly ceases (v. 15). And whereas just before the company was in

---

1   Cf. Williamson (1985: 185) and Blenkinsopp (1988: 220).

2   According to 3:13, the Dung Gate was located 1000 cubits (450 meters) from the Valley Gate. For a very helpful treatment of the topographical issues surrounding the descriptions of the wall in Neh, cf. Williamson (1984).

the vicinity of the ramparts, now they are in the valley and must go up (עלה) in order to inspect the wall.

The statement "and there was no place for the beast to pass under me" (v. 14b) is difficult to interpret, but it probably indicates that Nehemiah was on the narrow ridge overlooking the Kidron Valley. The question arises, Why are we told that the company ascended (עלה) without having first descended (ירד)? The account of the itinerary lacks a transition to the statement that the group was in the valley. In order to harmonize v. 15 with the preceding, we "must suppose, therefore, that when he reached the Spring [or Fountain] Gate, Nehemiah was obliged by either the steepness of the hillside or by the rubble to leave the exact line of the wall and to move slightly downhill into the valley."[3] Although this may be what "we must suppose," it is not what is *said*. While in the preceding account Nehemiah is near the wall and carrying on his inspection, in v. 15 he has now suspended the investigation and is in the valley floor. He then "went up in the valley at night to inspect the wall and returned" (v. 15bα).

If vv. 12-14 constitute a secondary amplification, we can better account for the evidence that the statement of return in v. 15 has been expanded with information from the preceding account. "…And I inspected the wall and returned. And I entered the Valley Gate, and I returned." The repetition here demands an explanation. To correct the redundancy, one could assign the double ואשוב different meanings: "And I went up the valley by night and inspected the wall *before turning back* and re-entering the Valley Gate; *so I returned*."[4] Yet after being told that Nehemiah reentered by the same gate by which he departed (cf. v. 13), the reader already knows that the journey was complete. The second ואשוב, therefore, serves no purpose. As an alternative to this translation, one could connect the final word with the following verse: "*So kehrte ich zurück*, (v. 16) ohne daß die Ratsherren wußten, wohin ich gegangen bin und was ich getan hatte."[5] In stating that he returned through the Valley Gate, Nehemiah implies that the rulers, while knowing that he left the city, do not know *where* he went and *what* he was doing. On this interpretation, however, there is no transition from v. 16 to v. 17; he would then have disclosed his plan at night! Moreover, v. 16a functions as a transition to a new scene and the participial expression, ומה אני עשה, refers most likely to what he was planning, not what he did.[6] Given these obstacles, the easiest solution would be to follow many commentators in simply omitting either the first or second ואשוב: "Then I

---

3   Williamson (1985: 190). Blenkinsopp (1988: 222) shares this assumption, but locates the descent after the King's Pool. Schunck (1998: 64) explained the descent by combining Williamson's and Blenkinsopp's conclusions.

4   Williamson (1985: 185), who follows Siegfried (1901: 77) and Bertholet (1902: 52).

5   Rudolph (1949: 110) and Galling (1954: 220).

6   In v. 12, עשה refers to what God was placing in Nehemiah's heart *to do on the behalf of Jerusalem*. Cf. also the use of participles in v. 19 for the builders' future plans.

returned, entering the Valley Gate."[7] In taking this escape route, one cannot account for the presence of the doublet. I propose, therefore, that the verse originally comprised only ואהי עלה בנחל לילה ואהי שבר בחומה ואשוב (v. 15a-bα) and that the second ואשוב is a resumptive repetition with which ואבוא בשער הגיא (v. 15bβ) has been appended. Now Nehemiah returns to what v. 12 depicts as his point of departure.[8]

Surprisingly, the excursion is abruptly terminated in v. 15: "And I went up the valley at night, inspected the wall and then returned." The disruption of the journey is usually explained on the assumption that the demolition in the valley was so severe that just a brief glance sufficed. Although one may not be confident as to what v. 14b exactly means, many assume that it reports that the immense debris made the way impassable; consequently, they dismounted and decided to turn back. If, however, the path was not traversable, it is difficult to explain why he proceeded up the valley. So too, why did he previously investigate the ramparts in the vicinity of the Dragon Spring and the Dung Gate, which according to his own admission were "broken down and its gates gutted by fire"?[9] According to an alternative interpretation, he had already seen enough of the city's demolition or that he had caught a glimpse of the ruins in that area as he arrived.[10] All these solutions disregard the purpose of the account, treating it as a factual chronicle of the journey without a deliberate conception. Instead of mixing historical and literary lines of inquiry, we should recognize that vv. 12-14 intend to highlight a specific portion of the wall. The focus on the gates and other topographical features is interrupted by v. 15. Here Nehemiah inspects "the wall" and returns abruptly. If he had already made his way around half of the city, why does he not continue his reconnaissance along the ramparts and enter the Valley Gate from the north?[11] By taking a "round trip" (to the valley

---

7   Blenkinsopp (1988: 220). Cf. also Batten (1913: 206), Meyers (1963: 103), and Michaeli (1967: 311). Gunneweg (1987: 57) translates: "und ich ging wieder durch das Taltor hinein und kehrte zurück."

8   One may compare this editorial gloss with the composition of the register in 3:1-32, which in its final form portrays the builders finishing at the same gate where they began.

9   The description of the damage in v. 13 would not have been more favorable than what Nehemiah supposedly viewed in the valley, for in v. 17 he describes the massive destruction with very similar words to those in v. 13.

10   Blenkinsopp reckons with the possibility that "they saw as much as they needed to see, though from the lower route which they were obliged to take this could hardly have been more than a general impression...." To resolve the problems on this view, he assumes that "Nehemiah would have had an idea of the state of the northern peimeter [sic] on his first entrance into the city" (1988: 223). Cf. also Schunck (1998: 58), who suggested that "noch eine Besichtigung der Nordmauer anzuschließen verbot sich wahrscheinlich wegen der dann bereits zu weit fortgeschrittenen Nacht"(!).

11   He could have also entered by a gate on the east side (e.g., the Water Gate was much closer than the Valley Gate). By depicting Nehemiah re-entering through the Valley Gate, the editor of v. 15 may have not intended to explain why the rulers did not know where Nehemiah went or may have interpreted the reference to the valley as the Central Valley.

and back), he was required to retrace his way back through the difficult area (cf. v. 14b). Yet had he continued in the same direction, he could have saved time and inspected the entire circumference of the wall. As a solution to these incongruities, I suggest that the sudden disruption of the tour is a consequence of v. 15. If this verse contains the oldest part of the paragraph, the detailed route in vv. 12-14 may have been composed as an account of the journey prior to his inspection of the wall in the valley. The fact that he suddenly turns around and enters the city again through the Valley Gate, instead of continuing his inspection, has thus been determined by the wording of the original statement: "and I inspected the wall and returned" (v. 15aβ-bα).

Additional clues for the priority of v. 15 are provided by the participial constructions (ואהי שבר בחומה and ואהי עלה), which do not correspond to the immediately preceding *wayyiqtol* forms. Bertheau attributed ואהי עלה with the "längere Zeit in Anspruch nehmende(n) und mühsame(n) Hinaufsteigen und Besichtigen."[12] However pregnant the sense of the Hebrew participle may be, such an interpretation strains its meaning. The entire route would have certainly been rigorous, yet Nehemiah describes it consistently with the *wayyiqtol*. Seeking a more tenable explanation, we notice that the participial constructions recur twice more in the immediate context. The expression ואהי שבר ב- appears in v. 13b, yet there it is clearly premature and out of place. A quick glance at 3:1-32 and 12:31ff., which furnish the basis for our understanding of the city's current topography, reveals that there were *no* gates in the section of the wall between the Valley Gate and the Dung Gate. How then can Nehemiah declare that "its gates" were gutted by fire?[13] The declaration in v. 13b would have served well as the conclusion of the account, yet v. 15 already describes the inspection and return. Also the designation "the wall(s) of Jerusalem" obtrudes into its context: From vv. 11-12 we already know where Nehemiah is and that he is surveying the extent of damage to the city wall.

In explaining this repetition, it is significant that v. 13a joins smoothly to v. 14.[14] Batten was probably correct in asserting that "all or at least part of the clause is an addition by R [=the redactor]. The repetition interrupts the succinct story of the ride...and needlessly anticipates v. 15."[15] The wording of this clause resembles strikingly the report in 1:3b, Nehemiah's response in 2:3b and his appeal in v. 17. With v. 13b, he now confirms Hanani's report and prepares his readers for the following passage. Inasmuch as this statement seems to be

---

12 1862: 141f.
13 The commentaries are unusually silent on this point.
14 "And I went out by night by the Valley Gate, past the Dragon Spring and as far as the Dung Gate [...]. Then I passed over to the Spring Gate and to the King's Pool..." (vv. 13a, 14a).
15 1913: 200 and 205.

editorial, its formulation with the same participial construction found in v. 15 indicates that the latter contains an older portion of the narrative.

When the excursion took place is stated no less than three times in the passage (vv. 12, 13, 15). Many commentators are rightly disturbed by this redundancy, and some propose to emend the text.[16] Batten attributed the repetition to a later glossator, rather than to accidental corruption, yet this assumption cannot explain that the word appears three times. If a single editor "deemed it an essential part of the secret purpose of the trip," one occurrence at the beginning of the account (v. 12) would have fully sufficed.[17] I propose that the threefold repetition of "at night" corresponds to the three compositional layers of the account.

6.2.2 Three Compositional Layers

According to my proposal, v. 15a originally continued the participial construction in v. 11b (ואהי־שם ימים שלשה). The first expansion of the paragraph may be isolated in vv. 13-14 and 15b. Here Nehemiah reports to having exited and reentered the city via the Valley Gate. In amplifying the brief notice, "After I had been there three days, I went up in the valley at night, inspected the wall and returned...(vv. 11b, 15abα)," the authors of vv. 13-14 describe how Nehemiah arrived in the valley. There seems, however, to be a more significant reason for the addition of vv. 13-14 and 15b, namely to emphasize the route he takes. All of the topographical features in these verses occupy a special place elsewhere in the first-person account. After the two *Tôdôt*-companies had been organized at the dedication ceremonies in 12:31, they proceed along the Dung Gate, the Spring Gate, and around the City of David (v. 37). Not until v. 38 does the reader learn that one of the companies went in the opposite direction. The only gate not mentioned is the Valley Gate, but its absence signifies, as generally agreed, that it was the point of departure for the *Tôdôt*. Whatever way one chooses to understand the nature of these *Tôdôt* and the course they followed, it is clear that they begin where Nehemiah leaves the city and traverse the exact same section of the wall he inspected according to 2:13-14 and 15b.

Comparing now the account with the register of the builders in 3:1-32, we notice that the topographical features mentioned in 2:13-14 correspond to what Bertheau already recognized as a divergent segment of the register.[18] While vv. 1-12 connect the respective work forces with על־ידו or על־ידם ("at his/their hand"), vv. 16-32 alternate the formulation to אחריו ("after him"). Significantly,

---

16 Cf. Schunck's (1998: 54) proposal made in analogy to Galling's (1944: 220) emendation.
17 Ibid.: 201.
18 1862: 143ff.

the middle section (vv. 13-15) describes the repair of the same gates as those mentioned by Nehemiah in our passage: the Valley Gate, the Dung Gate, the Spring Gate. Thereafter, it recounts the restoration of "the wall of the Pool of Shelach appertaining to the King's Garden," which must be the name for the King's Pool before it was abbreviated.

Unfortunately, we cannot precisely define the relationship of 3:13-15 and 12:31ff. to one another. In mentioning the gates referred to in 2:13-14 and 15b consistently as a group, these passages indicate that there was something peculiar about the segment of the wall at the southern end of the city. One can only speculate what exactly that may have been. Perhaps the builders focused their activities in this area. Perhaps it was not built until a later period. Or perhaps certain circles wished to emphasize that this district of Jerusalem (and implicitly those groups which inhabited it) felt the brunt of the Babylonian destruction.[19] While the reason remains obscure, the evidence of 3:1-32 and 12:31ff. suggests that there was an interest in expanding the brief notice in v. 15 and drawing attention to the demolition to this particular side of the city. Whether the misplaced remark in v. 15b ("and I inspected the ramparts of Jerusalem which were breached and its gates gutted in fire") had already been inserted at this stage of the passage's composition is difficult to establish. At any rate, the redactor seems to have intended to emphasize that the destruction of specifically those ramparts and gates referred to in vv. 13a and 14a had occasioned Nehemiah's gloomy demeanor (2:2ff.).[20]

In the second and final layer found in v. 12, Nehemiah stresses the secrecy of his night ride. He takes only a few men with him (v. aα), tells no one of his plans (v. aβ), and restricts the means of transportation to a single animal (v. b). That this verse constitutes a second introduction to the account is once again indicated by the repetition of "by night" from vv. 13 and 15. Furthermore, the narrative in vv. 13-15, which is formulated consistently in the first-person singular, knows nothing of Nehemiah's escort referred to in v. 12. With the addition of v. 12, the singular predicates are to be understood as a variation of the *constructio ad sensum* inasmuch as Nehemiah is speaking on the behalf of a larger group. The first clause explains this identification: "And I arose in the night, i.e., I and a few men with me." The wording resembles that of 1:2bβ (ויבא חנני אחד מאחי הוא ואנשים מיהודה), but while the account of Nehemiah's conversation in the citadel properly employs the plural predicate (cf. v. 3:

---

19 For an analogy, cf. the eschatological expectations surrounding the expansion of Jerusalem "from the Corner Gate to the Tower of Hananel" in Jer 31:38; cf. also Zech 14:10 and Eskenazi (1988: 85ff.). Significantly, the mention of the Tower of Hananel in Neh 3:1 appears to be secondary.

20 In 1:3 and 2:17, the gates are "burned in fire" (ושעריה נצתו באש). The statement, ושעריה אכלו באש, occurs only here and in 2:3.

ויאמר לי), the formulation of 2:12ff. confuses the reader. Indeed, Nehemiah never employs the first-person singular elsewhere when speaking for his fellow builders (cf. esp. 2:17, 20; 3:33, 36, 38; 4:3, 9, 13, 14, 15). Here, the stress is on the small number of the group: "and a few (מעט) men with me." The author assumes (and perhaps rightly) that Nehemiah could not have made the tour alone. In emphasizing that the number of his company was limited, he explains how the rulers remained oblivious to the excursion (v. 16a).

This train of thought continues in v. 12b: "but there was no animal with me except for the animal upon which I was riding." The writer knew of the presence of an animal from v. 14b, the meaning of which is unclear.[21] It may simply explain why Nehemiah is suddenly in the valley in v. 15.[22] With the addition of v. 12b, however, the reader knows from the very beginning that Nehemiah was mounted on the animal. Here again, the emphasis is on the inconspicuousness. He took only a handful of men with him (עמי), and there was only one animal in the company (again עמי).

Insofar as v. 12aα forms a smooth join with the second half of the verse, the statement that Nehemiah had not told anyone of his plans (v. 12aβ) probably constitutes an insertion. That this remark belongs to the final redaction of the passage is difficult to deny when we recognize that its presence renders v. 16 superfluous. If it is integral to the account, why must Nehemiah affirm that he had not yet told the Jews, the priests, the nobles, the rulers, and the builders what he was doing (v. 16b)? After the all-inclusive negation ולא־הגדתי לאדם, the enumeration of these groups is not only excessive, but is also somewhat contradictory: While he claims to having told absolutely no one in v. 12aβ, he restricts the "no one" to specific groups in v. 16b. The insertion serves first to explain to the reader why Nehemiah took only a few men and one animal with him: he had not yet disclosed his purpose for coming to Jerusalem. If the passage originally consisted, as proposed, of a brief report that Nehemiah went up the valley at night to inspect the wall and that the rulers were oblivious to where he went and what he was planning, then the reader would not need to know that Nehemiah had kept his plans silent. Yet as the beginning of the account assumed greater proportions, such a statement became necessary.

Upon closer examination, however, there appears to be a much more significant reason for the insertion. In v. 16, Nehemiah remarks simply that he had not told the officials of his plans; here he affirms that no one had been made privy

---

21 Cf. Batten's comments (1913: 200).

22 "It would be natural to suppose that he had reached a point beyond which exploration was impossible. But as the mule could go almost any place a pedestrian could, it is far from clear why he describes the obstacle in this way" (ibid.).

of "what my God was prompting me to do on the behalf of Jerusalem."[23] Whereas the expansions in vv. 12aα, b, 13-14, 15bβ supply – what later readers considered to be – necessary details for understanding the nature of the nocturnal inspection, the interpolation of v. 12aβ serves a theological purpose. In the same sophisticated manner as his predecessors, the author of this clause corrects v. 16aβ by replacing Nehemiah as the subject of the participial construction ("…what I *was doing* [planning]") with Nehemiah's God: "…what my God was placing in my heart *to do* on the behalf of Jerusalem."[24] We may compare this reinterpretation of the account to the function of 1:4b,[25] 2:4b,[26] and v. 8b[27] in their respective contexts. All these passages attribute the king's authorization of the building to the direction of the divine sovereign, not merely to Nehemiah's personal influence on the mortal sovereign. In correlating the divine and imperial programs, the authors responsible for the final form of these texts intend to illustrate that God brought his plan for Jerusalem to fruition by way of the foreign overlord's permission.

While this presentation of the divine scheme dovetailing with that of the imperial government is due to a redactional process in Nehemiah's account, it represents the conceptual bedrock upon which already the *first edition* of Ezra's account rests. After receiving his writing of sanction, Ezra blesses YHWH "who has placed such in the heart of the king – to beautify the house of YHWH that is in Jerusalem" (Ezra 7:27). The formulation is strikingly reminiscent to Neh 2:12aβ. God is the subject, who places a plan in the individual's heart to do (infinitive) something for Jerusalem. That the author here has been directly influenced by Nehemiah's account seems quite probable in consideration of several factors: The expression לתת בלב appears in very few texts elsewhere. Often, we read that God *gives* someone a heart, be it wise, understanding, compassionate, etc., yet only rarely does God *put* something *in* an individual's heart.[28]

---

23 Past scholarship has failed to perceive the subtle shift from this statement and v. 16. Instead of comparing the two, Schunck (1998: 57), e.g., was concerned with the question whether Nehemiah's escort knew the reason for their unusual evening activities.

24 The connection between to the two passages is unmistakable not only as they are both participial constructions but also as מה and עשה appear in both texts. Moreover, the beginning of the v. 12aβ (ולא־הגדתי לאדם) uses the wording of v. 16b (ל־ לא הגדתי).

25 In this passage, which is integral to the immediately foregoing verses, Nehemiah not only mourns and weeps (v. 4a) but also fasts and prays before the God of Heaven.

26 Here Nehemiah prays again – although in an earlier version of his account (prior to the addition of 1:4b and 5-11a), probably for the first time – before the God of Heaven.

27 At this point, Nehemiah reports his success in receiving the letters from the imperial court with the remark "and the king gave (them) to me according to the good hand of my God was upon me."

28 Exod 31:6, Jer 31:33, and Ps 4:8. Although rightly bringing 2 Chr 30:12 into the discussion of other aspects of Neh 2, Reinmuth (2002: 70f.) fails to distinguish between the phrases לתת בלב ("to inspire") and לתת להם לב אחד, ("to give them *one* heart"). The latter expresses *unity* (in Judah to follow the king's commandment), not inspiration.

In Nehemiah's account, however, this idea appears twice (cf. 7:5). Moreover, Ezra continues with an expression that, as observed in the foregoing chapter, occurs twice in Neh 2: "according to the hand of YHWH my God that was upon me."[29]

However, there are differences between the final shape of Nehemiah's account and the earliest edition of the Ezra narrative. In the former, God inspires Nehemiah to rebuild Jerusalem's wall (2:12aβ). Artaxerxes, through the divine intervention instigated by prayer and "the providential hand of God" (1:4b, 5-11a; 2:4b, 8b), concedes to his servant's proposal. In Ezra's account, the same king does not wait for a proposal; to the contrary, he takes the initiative himself. Hence, Ezra is just an instrument of the king whom God inspires directly, and what he inspires is not the building of the city walls, but rather the beautification of temple (7:27f.). In respect to the direct actions for the temple by the Persian rulers, Ezra's account corresponds to the central accent of the temple building narrative in chaps. 1-6. In the first year of his reign, the founder of the empire proclaims that YHWH, God of Heaven, commissioned him to build the temple in Jerusalem. As the story proceeds, the court continues, by means of correspondence, to regulate the building – commanding it both to stop it and then to resume (4:6-6:15). In the end, the narrator can depict "the children of the Diaspora" celebrating Mazzoth "with joy, for YHWH *had turned the heart* (והסב לב) of the king of Assyria to them to strengthen their hands (חזק *hiph.* + יד; cf. רפה *piel* + יד in Ezra 4:4) in the work of the house of God, the God of Israel" (Ezra 6:22).

The Composition of 2:11-16a

11 **And I arrived in Jerusalem. And after I had been there several days,**
  12 I arose at night – that is, I and a few men with me.
    Now I had not told anyone what my God had put in my heart to do on the behalf of Jerusalem.
    But there was no animal with me, save the beast that I was riding upon.
  13 I went out by night through the Valley Gate and past (?) the Dragon Well and unto the Dung Gate,
    and I inspected the walls of Jerusalem that were broken down and its gates gutted by fire.
  14 Then I passed over to the Spring Gate and to the King's Pool, but there was no place for the beast to pass under me.
15 **I went up in the valley at night and inspected the wall and then returned.**
    And I entered by the Valley Gate and so returned.
16 **But the rulers did not know where I had went or what I was doing** (planning)....

---

29 Neh 2:8b and 18a. 2:8b is especially instructive, as it contains the adjective "good" in place of YHWH as in Ezra's formulation: כיד־אלהי הטובה עלי. Cf. also the use of חזק in Ezra 7:28 with Neh 2:18b.

6.3 The Commencement and Completion of the Wall – 2:16b-3:38

In the foregoing section, we observed how a transitional statement has gradually matured into an independent episode of the building report. While the extensive amplification has transformed the lines in v. 11b, 15*, 16a into "a passage of exceptionally enthralling narrative,"[30] it has also resulted in an imbalance with the concise continuation. In v. 16, Nehemiah reports that everyone was still "in the dark" with respect to his so-called Night Ride. Then, in v. 17, he abruptly recounts what he said to motivate the people to build the wall. Without being told how and when the people assembled, the reader initially presumes that he made his motivational speech at night. In v. 18b, the assembly is dissolved and the people begin the work just as unceremoniously as they gather.[31] The suddenness of the public announcement in vv. 16b-18 and its disparity with the disproportionately, lengthy account of the nocturnal inspection has led scholars to suppose that a portion of the narrative has been omitted.[32] Yet this supposition proves to be gratuitous once the possibility is conceded that vv. 12-15 have developed from a brief statement. In an earlier edition of the narrative, as reconstructed above, the report of the inspection of the wall in vv. 11-16 and the account of how he addressed the leaders were thus equally compact.[33] This, in turn, renders it likely that the scenes in 2:17-4:17 originally consisted of a concise narrative strand.

In what follows, we witness how the redactional activity of Nehemiah's readers, in expanding exponentially the first part of chap. 2 (not to mention chap. 1), corresponds to the development of several short lines into the present

---

30 Williamson (1985: 188).

31 In chap. 5, Nehemiah describes how he convoked a large assembly. In 7:5, he "gathers" the nobles, rulers and people to register their genealogies. Furthermore, chap. 4 recounts in detail how he organized the people to defend Jerusalem from an imminent attack (cf. also 12:31ff.). Why then does he not describe at this prominent place in his narrative how he assembled the people? It seems that the original edition of first-person account is characterized by an economy of words, as already observed in 1:1a, 11b; 2:1ff. In the later editions, this succinctness is replaced by an interest in illustrating the proper (Nehemiah's) response to socio-religious conflicts in the province.

32 Mowinckel (1964: 23) argued, on the basis of Josephus's more conceivable portrayal, for an omission of the text before v. 17 and after v. 18. Blenkinsopp, while recognizing the problem (1988: 224), rightly recommends caution in drawing upon Josephus here: (1988: 221). Nevertheless, Josephus does provide a good test case for how even early readers found Neh 2:11-18 to be disjointed.

33 Thus, the narrative suddenly shifts to a new scene in v. 16b. The third day after his arrival, Nehemiah and several others arise inconspicuously in the night to examine the condition of the city wall. This scene concludes in v. 16a with the remark that his night ride was successful inasmuch as he had kept the rulers in the dark. V. 16b depicts presumably the events of the following day – not during the night, as one presumes at first. At this point, when his fellow citizens had assembled, he finally discloses his reason for coming to Jerusalem.

form of 2:17-4:17. Everything else that is traditionally assigned to the primary author simply because it is formulated in the first-person proves upon closer inspection to be the work of later hands, which have also introduced a new form to the building report. The product is an account of successive building phases in which both the external animosity and the internal solidarity gradually increase. Although the entire compositional process in 2:17-4:17 is both interesting and important, it is unfortunately also very complex and largely impossible to reconstruct. We will, therefore, confine the discussion to the most important points, saving space for a more intensive analysis of chaps. 5-13.

6.3.1 The Address to the Leaders – 2:16b-18

According to most commentators, Nehemiah's reason for inspecting the wall at night was to conceal his plans from Sanballat, Tobiah and Geshem (v. 19) until the construction commenced.[34] This explanation, however, makes little sense. If he intended to present his enemies with the approval and inauguration of the building project as a *faite accomplie*, why does his response in v. 20 present the construction work as having not yet begun ("we will arise and build...")? Rudolph suggested that the encounter with the enemy reported in v. 10 was the reason why he "mit aller Heimlichkeit zu Werke ging,"[35] yet we have already seen (§5.2.2) that v. 10 was probably inserted at a very late stage in the composition of the first-person account. Since the reader is not told whether "it was at least a moonlit night" as Nehemiah made his tour,[36] we have no other alternative than to interpret the passage within the framework of the narrative and without speculation as to the historical situation. According to the text, the primary reason for the secrecy was to keep his plan concealed from the *leaders* until he made his official address (v. 17). This explains why he affirms in the immediately preceding lines that the *rulers* "knew not where I went and what I was planning" (v. 16a) and that "I had not yet told the Judeans, the priests..." (v. 16b). Sanballat, Tobiah and Geshem, however, are not present in vv. 11-18. The intention of the author is thus to allow the suspense to build, so that the reader waits expectantly to hear in vv. 17-18 what he said to inspire the people to build the wall. As this address has already been discussed (cf. esp. §4.3.1) and will be referred to often in the following chapters, we may focus our attention here on the addressees and their response.

---

34 Cf., e.g., Myers: "His plan of attack was kept secret so as not to arouse the people or tip his hand prematurely to the enemies within or without (vss. 12, 16)" (1965: 104).

35 1949: 108.

36 Williamson (1985: 188). This incongruity has been disregarded for the most part in prior scholarship. Batten (1913: 201), once again, represents an exception.

First, it seems likely that Nehemiah originally conferred solely with the rulers (הסגנים). From other texts one knows that this group constituted an independent administrative class with considerable power, and Nehemiah, without the authority of a governor, would have absolutely required their support if his project were to be a success.[37] Presuming that he was (already) a פחה, a later author misunderstood the official nature of the assembly and added the names of all the various groups in v. 16b, assimilating the scene to 5:1-13 where the entire community is represented. Accordingly, the statement in v. 16a ("But the rulers did not know where I went or what I was doing") continues smoothly in vv. 17-18a ("And I said to them, 'Ye see the distress that we are in…'"), and their reaction in v. 18b ("And they said, 'Let us arise and build!' And they strengthened their hands for the good (work),"). A closer examination of the verse supports this conclusion. In the first half, Nehemiah states that the rulers had not found out about his night ride. While the ואומר אלהם in v. 17 furnishes a felicitous transition, v. 16b continues to name the other groups which he had not yet informed. The formulation of this continuation, with a post-positioned predicate (עד־כן לא הגדתי) and a lengthy list beginning with the dative preposition ל,[38] suggests that it has been supplemented. The lack of a direct object requires that the reader link the verse-half with the foregoing statement. What he had not yet told the people, is thus "where I had gone or what I was doing." Similarly, the phrase, עד־כן ("until now"), which occurs only here,[39] refers to the night of the excursion. In view of v. 17, however, we must revise our initial interpretation: "Then I said to them, '…come let us build up the wall….'" What Nehemiah had not yet divulged is, therefore, his building proposal, not the fact that he had inspected the wall at night. This corresponds to his statement in v. 12aβ ("and I had not told anyone"), which does not refer just to his plans for that evening ("what my God was prompting me to do on the behalf of Jerusalem").

The repetition of "the rulers" (סגנים) constitutes a further clue supporting this conclusion. A single reference to this class of leaders would have sufficed. Had one author composed both verse halves, it would be difficult to explain the duplication. Williamson contends that סגנים is "a sufficiently flexible word to stand at the start of the verse as a general term for the leaders of the

---

37 Cf., e.g., *TAD* B2.3.13; B3.1.13, 18. Cross (1963:111) for the conclusion to one of the Samaria Papyri, Dan 3:2f., 27; Ezra 9:2; Neh 13:11; Isa 41:25. In Jer 51:23, 28; Ezek 23:12 and 23, they are also mentioned in tandem with governors (פחות). Cf. also Neh 5:17; 12:40 and 13:10-14.

38 וליחודים ולכהנים ולחרים ולסגנים וליתר עשה המלאכה. For המלאכה וליתר עשה ולסגנים ולחרים ולכהנים וליחודים, cf. Kaupel (1940).

39 Although עד־כן is a hapax, there is no doubt as to what the phrase denotes. In analogy to the expressions עד־פה, עד־כה, and עד־הנה, we can render it most suitably with "hitherto" or "up until then." Cf. the somewhat different meaning of the Aramaic עד־כען (Ezra 5:16).

community."[40] Yet this solution does not take into consideration the way the first-person account itself employs the appellation. In 4:8, 13, and 7:5, the סגנים clearly constitute an individual group to be distinguished from the nobles (חרים); in all of these places, the rulers are significantly mentioned *after* the nobles. This applies also for 5:7, where Nehemiah remonstrates with the nobles and officials for the fiscal abuses. In chap. 13, he then remonstrates with these groups separately.[41] Recognizing that סגנים is not an all-encompassing designation for officials, many commentators propose that we emend the text.[42] While others maintain the wording of the MT, they do not explain the duplication. As it is unlikely that the same verse employs the term in two different ways, the repetition suggests that a later hand has inserted v. 16b, which renamed the סגנים after the חרים in keeping with the pattern in 4:8, 13; 5:7 and 7:5.

As to why and when v. 16 has been expanded with the list, I suggest that its author was writing at a very early stage in the composition of the building account and has correctly understood that Nehemiah intended to bring about a sociopolitical change with the restoration of the wall. Whereas in 1:1-2:16 the subject is always "I," it changes to the first-person plural in 2:17-4:17.[43] This alternation is probably not coincidental, for with the use of "we," Nehemiah underscores the solidarity of the builders. Before reporting the beginning of the external antagonism, he has already portrayed how the construction activities brought about inner unity inasmuch as the community leaders unanimously sanctioned his proposal ("And they said, 'Let us arise and let us build,'" v. 18b). V. 16b expands upon this portrayal of unity by affirming that all Judah ("the Judeans, the priests, the nobles, the leaders, and the rest that were doing the work"), not just the rulers, approved of Nehemiah's plans.[44]

Before the סגנים voice their decision (v. 18b), Nehemiah had "told them that the hand of my God was good upon me and also the words that the king spoke to me." (v. 18a). There are several reasons for believing that these lines have been secondarily prefaced. First, the two other occurrences of "I told" (vv. 12αβ

---

40   1985: 191.
41   He assigns the rulers the guilt in 13:10-14 and the nobles in 13:15-22. Against the backdrop of 5:7, the intention of these passages seems to be a definition of their spheres of authority (and culpability). It is important to observe this nuance against the assumption based on chap. 13 that סגנים and חרים are interchangeable terms.
42   Galling (1954: 220) argued for השמרים in v. 16a, but could not account for the supposed corruption. More graphically similar to הסגנים is the word הסגרים ("gate keepers"), which several scholars have recommended. However, not only do we lack a textual witness for this proposal, but also the term for porters in Nehemiah's account and elsewhere is not הסגרים but rather השערים. Cf. Ezra 2:42 (Neh 7:45), Neh 7:1, 10:29 and 12:25.
43   The only exceptions are 4:7f., 13, 16.
44   Supplementing the account with the names of all the communal groups was necessary before v. 17, as this is the best (and probably only) point where one could expand the description of the audience.

and 16b: לֹא־הִגַּדְתִּי) seem to be redactional.[45] Second, Nehemiah always reports his actual words (and those spoken to him), not simply *that* something was said (cf. 1:1b-3; 2:1-6, 18b, 19-20; 3:33ff.; 4:8, 13, 16; 5:7ff.; 6:2-14; etc.).[46] Third, the use of the expression "the hand of my God" occurs elsewhere only in v. 8b, which belongs to the secondary passage vv. 7-9a that separates v. 9b from v. 6b.[47] The author of v. 18a seems to have been directly influenced by vv. 7-9a, for inasmuch as the rulers worshipped the same God as Nehemiah, we would expect "the hand of *our* God" (cf., e.g., Ezra 8:22). Fourth, the statement that "the hand of my God was favorable upon me," with which Nehemiah affirms that his enterprise was also divinely sanctioned, conflicts with the aim of the speech. The building project was to be a communal endeavor and would not require the involvement of a divinely inspired or charismatic leader. As we shall witness below, only later layers of the account shift the focus from the collective group to the person of Nehemiah. Finally, it is easy to conceive what would have prompted a redactor to include v. 18a. Without this line, the leaders consent to build merely because of the sociopolitical situation symbolized the ruins of Jerusalem's fortification. In order to emphasize their piety and their absolute loyalty to the empire, the redactor explains that before giving their consent, they had heard about the divine and imperial approval of the construction plans.

6.3.2 The Priority of the Register of Builders in 3:1-32

We may now turn to the most difficult problem relating to the earliest editions of the building account, namely the relationship between the register of builders in 3:1-32 and its context. That the register is integral to its context has often been denied. Already Wellhausen alluded to its secondary character ("ein allerdings wohl nicht zu den Memoiren gehöriges Verzeichnis"),[48] and this opinion has been espoused by a number of scholars since.[49] In 1934, Burrows could even claim that "[c]ritics are now fairly well agreed that it [the register] does not belong to the memoirs of Nehemiah."[50] Most recent studies, however, take issue with Wellhausen's position, contending that Nehemiah himself, while

---

45 Cf. §6.2.2.
46 So too, without the interruption of v. 18a, the account would resemble the dialogic style of 1:2-3; 2:1-6, 19-20; 5:7ff.; 6:2-4, 5-9 and 10-14.
47 Cf. §5.2.2.
48 1894: 168-n. 1.
49 Torrey (1895: 37f.), Batten (1913: 15, 206f.), Mowinckel (1916: 34, 1964: 109f.), Hölscher (1910: 529f.), Johannesen (1946:185f.), Gunneweg (1987: 75f.), and Blenkinsopp (1988: 231). Kratz (2000: 72) leaves the question open.
50 1934: 116.

not the author of the list, is responsible for its transmission in his account.[51] He either worded 2:19-20 with the introduction of register in view or adapted the latter to his own formulation.

Many who insist that the list has been inserted by an editor suggest that the notices in 2:19-20 and 3:34ff., which describe the reaction of Sanballat, belong together and are interrupted by 3:1-32.[52] This suggestion fails to recognize the structure of the account, which reports first progress and then the antagonism that its elicits (what I have called "the שמע-schema"). Nehemiah is sent to Judah; Sanballat and Tobiah *hear* about it and are irate (2:1-10). Nehemiah comes to Jerusalem and initiates the building; Sanballat, Tobiah and Geshem *hear* about it and proceed to scorn the Judeans and accuse them of sedition (2:11-20). The names of those who built are registered; Sanballat *hears* about it, and he and Tobiah resume their scoffing (3:1-37). The wall is half finished; all the enemies *hear* about it and plan to attack Jerusalem (3:38, 4:1-9). The builders return to the work; Sanballat and Tobiah *hear* that "I had built the wall," and then devise plans to intimidate Nehemiah 4:10-17 + 6:1-14. The wall is finished; the enemies *hear* the news and finally recognize their defeat (6:15-16). Hence, those who assume that the list in 3:1-32 can simply be removed have not paid close enough attention to the fabric of the narrative.[53]

However, this שמע-schema also causes problems for the assumption that the list is integral to its context. The present shape of the account portrays the work proceeding gradually, and every paragraph corresponds to a single phase of construction. The only paragraph that does not follow this pattern is 3:1ff., which recounts the completion of one section after another, concluding at the point of departure (the Sheep Gate).[54] After v. 32, the entire circumference of the wall has been erected, and the reader anticipates Nehemiah to report the success of the building project. However, v. 33 disappoints these expectations by describing Sanballat's response as he learned "that we were *building* the wall" (כי־אנחנו בונים את־החומה). Not until 6:15 do we hear that "the wall was finished on the twenty-fifth of Elul in fifty-two days," and the three chapters that separate this notice of completion from 3:32 recount at length what occurred during the fifty-two days: Instead of working in peace and harmony, the builders are both threatened with an attack from the surrounding nations (4:1ff.) and

---

51 Noth (1943: 127), Rudolph (1949: 113), Galling (1954: 221f.), Kellermann (1967: 14ff.), Clines (1984: 149) and Williamson (1985: 198ff.).

52 Cf., e.g., Mowinckel (1964: 110) and Rudolph (1987: 75f.).

53 Recognizing this problem, Gunneweg (1987: 75f.) suggested that a portion of the account was replaced by the list.

54 While the list also describes successive stages of building, these stages are merely sections of the wall – either gates or a מדה (cf. 3:11, 19, 20, 21, 24, 27, 30). And it – at least the second half (vv. 16-32) – does not present the entire circumference of the wall being erected *simultaneously*; rather, the builders work successively.

voice their dissatisfaction with the work (4:4f.). The wall is first built and then Nehemiah himself hangs the doors in the gates (cf. 6:1 and 7:1). In contrast to this, the list depicts the work *beginning* with the construction of the gates and the hanging of the doors. And it does not even mention Nehemiah. Similarly, the remaining account identifies the builders with the rulers, nobles and the rest of the people.[55] The list never mentions these groups; instead it refers to the princes (שׂרים).[56] Finally, we encounter several of the names referred to in 3:1-32 elsewhere, but always in a context of Nehemiah's enemies. For example, Meshullam ben Berechiah, who is commemorated twice in the list (vv. 4 and 30), intermarried his daughter to the son of Tobiah and was corresponding with him "also in those days" (6:17-19), which must refer to the fifty-two days of building in 6:15f.[57] Similarly, the high priest, Eliashib, is the one who initiates the work in 3:1 (cf. also 3:20), yet he and his descendants are castigated in the paragraph 13:23ff. (cf. v. 28), which, just as 6:17ff., begins with the expression "in those days." (Cf. also "Eliashib, the priest" in 3:21 with 13:4, 7). Inasmuch as the list never even mentions Nehemiah yet highlights the independent initiative of his opponents, its presence in the account could not be more problematic.

Those who contend that the historical Nehemiah was responsible for the present placement of the list often suggest that he included it as an independent witness to his success or in order to illustrate his superb organizational skills.[58] These explanations are quite tenuous, especially as Nehemiah never claims to have organized the work crews. As an alternative to this approach, one should consider the possibility that the register of names takes its point of departure from Nehemiah's response to Sanballat, Tobiah and Geshem in the immediately preceding passage (2:19f.). "And I answered them by saying to them, 'The God of Heaven, he will prosper us. We, his servants, will arise and build. But you have no share, right or memorial in Jerusalem!'" (2:20). Exactly what is denied those who scorn and deride the builders is granted to those who contribute to the work. Similar to the way a builder or donor to a building project commissions an inscription as memorial (זכרון) to his name,[59] the following passage 3:1-32 lists all the names of the donors to restoration of the wall. The register functions accordingly as a communal זכרון.[60] Likewise, the enemy must forgo

55 Cf. 2:16; 4:8, 13; 5:1-7, 17; 7:5; 13:11, 17.
56 3:9, 12, 14, 15, 16, 17, 18 and 19. They are mentioned elsewhere only in 12:31f. and in Ezra 7-10 and Neh 9-10.
57 Cf. §7.5.3.
58 Cf. Rudolph (1949: 113), Galling (1954: 222), Kellermann (1967: 15), Clines (1984: 149), Williamson (1985: 202) and Reinmuth (2002: 82).
59 For the use of סכר/זכר in both Aramaic and Canaanite inscription (many of which are specifically related to building projects, cf. *KAI* 18:6; 43:15; 53:1; 123:4; 161:5; 192:4; 214:16; 17, 21, 28, 30, 31; 215:22; 273:1.
60 Zech 6:14 refers a certain Tobiah, who is given a crown as a זכרון in the temple of YHWH.

any share (חלק) or claim (צדקה) in Jerusalem,[61] which implies that the names mentioned in the following passage have a portion and right in the city. Thus, instead of explaining the presence of the list simply as Nehemiah's attempt "die breite Beteiligung der Bevölkerung am Wiederaufbau der Stadtmauer zu dokumentieren,"[62] one must consider more closely the purpose it serves in the narrative.[63]

6.3.2.1 The Parallels between 2:19f. + 3:1-32 and 7:4-72

An examination of the literary function of the register is all the more worthwhile in view of the importance assigned to a list of names elsewhere in the building account. After the wall was finished (7:1), Nehemiah notices that "the city was large and great, but the people were few therein and there were no houses built" (v. 4). He gathers the nobles, rulers and the rest of the people in order to reckon them according to their genealogies. In this process, he discovers "a book of the genealogy of them that went up at the first" (7:5b), which consists of a long list of names (7:6-72). As we observe in the analysis of this text, the portrayal of Nehemiah "discovering" a "book" in which names "are found written," suggests that the authors, in keeping with the "realized eschatology" of Ezra-Neh, have composed a response to apocalyptic speculations about a new world order. Instead of placing their hopes in a new Jerusalem, they report that the present city was restored and repopulated "according to the book." Yet rather than a heavenly book, it is the historical record (e.g., Ezra 2) that is given attention. And instead of a time of judgment in the distant future, already in the past the one who rebuilt Jerusalem (cf. 6:1ff) "found" the book and employed it in deciding who was to reside in the city.

The only other place where Nehemiah cites a list is 3:1-32. This passage, which denies Sanballat, Tobiah and Geshem a place "in Jerusalem" and then names those who contributed to the work and thus possess a claim in the city, seems to have occasioned the composition of 7:4ff., which addresses the question whether even the *builders* themselves were eligible for residence in the same

---

61 Cf. *TAD* A4.7.27, where Bagohi is promised a צדקה before Yahu the God of Heaven if he consents to the building of the temple and *TAD* B2.11 for the usage of חלק.

62 Reinmuth (2002: 82).

63 That this task has not been undertaken hitherto may have much to do with the analogies between 2:1-10 and 11-20, both of which conclude by describing the reaction of the enemy. This has been seen by Galling (1954: 217ff.) and followed by Kellermann (1967: 11ff.), Williamson (1985: 177), Schunck (1998: 10f.), and Reinmuth (2002: 59). If 2:19-20 function also an introduction to 3:1-32, we must allow for the possibility that the structure created by 2:10 and vv. 19-20 is redactional. Galling has drawn attention to this structure; significantly, he also attributed *both* passages to an editor. As argued below, 2:19f. has been inserted as an *introduction* to the list, not as the conclusion to 1:1-2:18.

city they had restored ("the rulers, nobles and the rest of the people," 7:5; cf. 4:8 and 13). Significantly, this question and the inclusion of another list seem to have been prompted by the fact that several of the names included in the earlier register had intermarried (6:17-19, 13:4-9, 28f.) with the very ones who had ridiculed the restoration project. In the process of building the wall ("in those days," 6:17), Nehemiah observed that many of the aristocracy were intermarried with Sanballat and Tobiah. Conseqently, when he was finished building and God had inspired him to populate the city, he found it necessary to examine the genealogy of the people and to determine to what extent they belonged to the Golah (7:5).

Although 2:19f. appears to be older than 7:4ff., both of these texts present Jerusalem in line with a "realized eschatology." Each of the three terms used in 2:20 (חלק וצדקה וזכרון) is found in non-biblical contexts and is probably to be understood as "the civic, legal, and cultic rights in the Jerusalem community," as often maintained.[64] Nevertheless, their use here seems to reflect familiarity with their common biblical meanings. If Nehemiah draws on the language of late biblical poetry just a few verses later (3:36f.), we may compare his use of חלק to the Psalmist's expressions, such as "YHWH is my 'portion' in the land of the living" or "mortals who have their 'portion' in this life."[65] In emphasizing that labor is man's only "portion," Koheleth witnesses to the eschatological understanding of the term.[66] And the Rabbis continued this use of חלק, employing it often in their disputes about "who has a 'portion' in the world to come." A similar meaning is given to the terms צדקה and זכרון. With regard to the latter, the passages that refer to "a book of remembrances" are especially instructive (cf. Ex 17:14 and Mal 3:16).[67] Precisely this use of זכר is found in Nehemiah's work: both in his prayers for remembrance (cf. 5:19, 6:14, 13:14, 22, 29, 31) with which he addresses his entire literary work to the divine reader, and in his plea that God would not "wipe out" (אל־תמחה) the evil deeds of the enemy (3:37; cf. also 13:10b).[68]

To summarize, 2:20 serves as a preface to the register in 3:1-32 and anticipates the use of the list in 7:4-72. Whereas Nehemiah commemorates in 3:1-32 the names of those who built and thus were allotted a "portion" in the new(-ly built) Jerusalem, he realizes after the work is finished that some of the people he

---

64 Reinmuth (2002: 75) quoting Williamson (1985: 193). A similar approach is taken by Kellermann (1967: 156) and Blenkinsopp (1988: 226f.).

65 Ps 16:5, 17:14, 73:26, 119:57 and 142:5.

66 Eccl 2:10, 22; 3:22; 5:17, 18; 9:6, 9; 11:2.

67 Cf. also Ps 56:9, Eccl 1:11, 2:6 and Job 13:12.

68 Cf. Exod 17:14; 32:32f.; Deut 9:14; 29:19; 2 Kgs 14:27; Isa 43:25; 44:22; Jer 18:23; Ps 9:6; 51:3, 1; 69:29; 109:14; 1 Enoch 108:3 and Galling (1954: 220), who noticed the links between 2:20 and "Kult- und Stifterformeln, wie sie in 5,19 und 13,14 begegnen."

previously mentioned were ineligible for residency in "the holy city" (11:1) inasmuch as they were closely related to Judah's enemies.

6.3.2.2 The Composition of 2:19-20 and 3:33-37

While the parallels between 3:1-32 and 7:4-72 are certainly striking, they are most likely due to the hand of a redactor. Wellhausen argued that 3:1-32 does not represent an original and integral part of the "Memoiren" because we would expect it to follow 2:18b.[69] What he did not consider is that an earlier edition of Neh 2 might not have contained vv. 19-20 and thus that the register at one time did indeed follow v. 18. If so, the register 3:1-32 would have originally functioned much differently than the list in 7:4-72.

After hearing Nehemiah's speech, the rulers consent wholeheartedly, "We will arise and build," and then they initiate the work (ויחזקו ידיהם לטובה). As Blenkinsopp remarked, the natural implication of the latter expression is "that they actually made a start."[70] The antithetical idiom, "weaken the hands of another" (רפה piel + יד), means, "to disrupt the activities of another."[71] Williamson, however, translates the expression in 2:18b, "...and thus they encouraged themselves in the *preparation* for the good work."[72] This approach is understandable in view of Nehemiah's response in 2:20: "The God of Heaven, he will prosper us. We, his servants, shall arise and build (נקום ובנינו)." It is clear that the construction at this point has not yet commenced. However, if one does not allow vv. 19-20 to affect the understanding of v. 18b, then the latter seems to indicate that the work *began.*

A possible solution to this contradiction is that just 2:20 has been added. Since 2:10 simply describes the reaction of the enemy, a response from Nehemiah after 2:19 was not necessary. The questions ("What is this thing that you are doing? Are you rebelling against the king?") seem to be rhetorical, just as Sanballat's six questions in 3:34.[73] So too, the imprecation in 3:36-37 appears to have been added at a later point in the composition of chaps. 2-4, as several scholars have suggested and argued below. Accordingly, both 2:10 and 3:33ff. are not followed by a response from Nehemiah.

It is also surprising that the answer given in 2:20 does not correspond to the reason why the antagonists are distraught. Instead of declaring that the king had approved of the construction project, Nehemiah refers only to the God of

---

69   1894: 168-n. 1.
70   1988: 220.
71   Cf., e.g., 6:9 and Ezra 4:4.
72   1985: 185-my italics.

Heaven and leaves one wondering if they indeed were planning to rebel. With respect to the incongruity between the question and answer, Batten wrote, "The mention of the king's authority would be far more impressive to Sanballat than the grace of God...."[74] Yet instead of assuming "that a clause has dropped out" in 2:20 and that "the antecedent of 'his' [servants] should be Artaxerxes rather than 'God,'"[75] one should consider the possibility that a redactor has added v. 19b. Just as Sanballat's first question in 3:35 may have influenced the wording of the first question in 2:19, the second question seems to have been drawn from the rumors that Geshem (Gashmu) reported to him in 6:5f.[76] What may have motivated the redactor is the fact that Geshem plays a role *only* in 6:1-9 and 2:19. Without the questions in 2:19, the response in v. 20 makes much more sense. To the scoffs and jeers, Nehemiah replies by affirming that the God of Heaven would prosper their endeavors.

Therefore, we lack a reason to treat v. 20 as an addition to v. 19. The integrity of this passage is indicated furthermore by the introduction "as Sanballat...heard." The omission of the building activities as the object of "hear" in 2:19 (cf. 2:10), which contrast with 3:33, 4:1 and 6:1, combined with the declaration in 2:20 that "we shall arise and build," suggests that the author intended to date the episode to the time before the construction began and accordingly has reinterpreted the meaning of 2:18b.

Now if v. 20 cannot be separated from v. 19, then one must seek an alternative solution to the contradiction with 2:18b, which reports, in contrast to the following verses, that the work had already commenced. I submit that the register of the builders originally followed 2:18b.[77] This solution would account for the repetitious use of קום and בנה in 2:20. Moreover, after the leaders affirm, נקום ובנינו, and then "strengthen their hands," the most fitting continuation is the introduction to the list: "And Eliashib, the high priest, and his colleagues, the priests, arose (ויקם) and built (ויבנו) the Sheep Gate. They sanctified it...." Between 2:18b and 3:1, a redactor has squeezed in an *entr'acte*, postponing the initiation of the construction in order to introduce a new "elitist" dimension to the following list of names: Nehemiah first conveys the leaders' response in 2:18 (נקום ובנינו) to the antagonists in 2:20 with an exclusivist twist and then proclaims to his readers the fulfillment of his promise by recalling the names of the "the servants of the God of Heaven" who "arose and built" (ויקם...ויבנו, 3:1ff.).

---

73   One of these is almost exactly the same: Cf. מה־הדבר הזה אשר אתם עשים in 2:19 with מה היהודים האמללים עשים in 3:34.

74   1913: 204.

75   Ibid.

76   Cf. 6:6: אתה והיהודים חשבים למרוד על־כן אתה בונה החומה ואתה הוה להם למלך.

77   That 2:19-20 is younger than its context has been proposed by Batten (1913: 224f.), Galling (1954: 220) and Kratz (2000: 72). Against the proposal, cf. Kellermann (1967: 13-n. 28).

In order to adduce further evidence for this proposal, one may compare 2:19f. to 3:33f. In the latter passage, the final clause reads "and he derided the Judeans." In view of the presence of "we" in v. a (כי־אנחנו בונים את־החומה), one anticipates "and he derided *us*," not "the Judeans." While the clause seems to be editorial in 3:33, it is integral to 2:19a (וילעגו לנו).[78] Second, the following line in 2:19a (ויבזו עלינו) appears also to have been drawn from the imprecation in 3:36 (שמע אלהינו כי־היינו בוזה והשב חרפתם אל־ראשם ותנם לבזה בארץ שביה). Third, the author of 2:19f. must have known that 3:33ff. records the actual words of the enemy's provocation; otherwise, we would expect to have been told already in 2:19 what they said to insult the builders. Fourth, Geshem is not mentioned in 3:33ff. or 4:1ff., where "the Arabs" conspire with Sanballat and Tobiah without their leader. "Geshem the Arab" seems to make his appearance for the first time in the late additions 6:1-9. This explains the use of the *gentilicium* in 6:1 (הערבי). When introducing him earlier in the account, the author found it necessary to refer to him once again as וגשם הערבי, rendering thereby 6:1 superfluous and repetitive.[79] Similarly, Tobiah is called העמני already in 3:35, to which 2:19 adds העבד (cf. also 2:10).[80] All these points confirm the suspicion that a redactor is responsible for 2:19f.

That the list in Neh 3:1ff. originally followed 2:18 accounts for the fact that 2:19 includes all three of Nehemiah's nemeses in a single group, while 3:33 reports the reaction of just one figure. Given the usage of the שמע-formula in 2:10, 19; 4:1, 9; 6:1 and 16, it is peculiar that Sanballat alone is the subject of "heard" in 3:33. Only later are we told that "Tobiah the Ammonite was by him" (v. 35). If he had been there all along, v. 33 should read, "And as Sanballat and Tobiah heard...." That v. 35 is not integral to passage explains why Sanballat continues at length, while Tobiah confines his comments to one remark.[81] And this remark, in contrast to Sanballat's ironic questions, refers to the wall as *partially* built.[82] Moreover, aside from 2:10 and 19, the only other place where

---

78 Notice also that the prepositions vary between על and ל.

79 Originally, he seems to have played only an indirect role (6:5-9). Later, he became Sanballat's sidekick (6:2-4). And the latest layers refer to him as "Geshem the Arab" (6:1 and 2:19).

80 We have already witnessed this phenomenon with regard to composition of 2:10, after which the *gentilicia* in 2:19 are repetitive. According to my proposal, the names Sanballat and Geshem were not originally written with the *gentilicia*. However, once this practice of "name calling" began (probably in 3:35 with reference to Tobiah), the authors of 2:10 and 19 found it necessary to repeat the *gentilicia* as a way of introducing these figures. While the *gentilicia* were attached to the names of Geshem and Tobiah at early stage (6:1 and 3:35), it was not until 2:19 that Sanballat was referred to as "the Horonite."

81 The LXX has corrected this problem by assigning half of Sanballat's speech to Tobiah.

82 Both refer to stones, but Tobiah is sure that even fox would "break down the wall of their stones" (גם אשר־הם בונים אם־יעלה שועל ופרץ חומת אבניהם), while Sanballat speaks of the stones that must still be revived (היחיו את־האבנים מערמות העפר והמה שרופות), which may be

Sanballat and Tobiah cooperate is 4:1ff., where they, together with Arabs, Ammonites and Ashdodites, mount an attack on Jerusalem. Similarly, 6:1 appears to have been been reworked to include the name of Tobiah.[83] If this can be demonstrated as probable in our investigation of chap. 6, then the most historically trustworthy traditions (6:2-4, 5-9; 17-19 and 13:4ff.) do not present Sanballat and Tobiah working in tandem. Their alliances are accordingly due to a redactional process that brought them together (first in 3:33ff. and then in 4:1ff.).

Insofar as Tobiah has been introduced to the passage by a later hand, the imprecation in vv. 36f. must have been composed either at the same time or later. Noth has suggested the second alternative against Torrey's claim that all of 3:33-37 has been added.[84] According to v. 34aα, Sanballat "spoke before his brethren and the host of Samaria,"[85] yet v. 37b states that "they provoked you (?) to anger in the presence of the builders." This flat contradiction, which has never been satisfactorily explained, would seem to confirm Noth's suspicion. Closer inspection of the text reveals, however, that v. 34aα probably constitutes a late gloss. Otherwise, it would be difficult to explain the repetition of ויאמר after the clause.[86] So too, Nehemiah petitions God to recompense "them" in vv. 36f., which presupposes that a hand has already added v. 35 and introduced Tobiah to the scene.

What motivated the reparation of the wall according to 2:17 is the general situation of reproach (חרפה), and the completion of the work reversed this situation (cf. 6:16). It is important to note that originally the "reproach" was not in anyway related to the taunts of Sanballat, Tobiah and Geshem. Indeed, the reader of the final shape of the account must conclude that Nehemiah and the Judean leaders had defeated their purpose in building insofar as Sanballat and Tobiah ridicule and mock the Jews (2:19 and 3:33f.) only after they begin to erect the wall. As later authors introduced the שמע-schema to the building account, the reproach in 2:17 came to be identified with nothing other than the taunts and tactics of Sanballat and Tobiah (and the nations which they incite, cf. 4:1 and 6:1). The prayer in 3:36f. stands at the end of this literary development inasmuch as it employs this key term (והשב חרפתם אל־ראשם) in order to connect the motivation for building in 2:17 with the actions of Sanballat and Tobiah.

---

compared to the use of חיה *piel* in 1 Chr 11:8; cf. also the inscriptions of Yehimilk of Byblos and Karatepe.

83   In 6:2-4 and 5-9, Sanballat is associated solely with Geshem. The account in vv. 10-14 mentions him after Tobiah (cf. vv. 12 and 14), and the singular suffixes indicate to most scholars that his name has been supplemented. Cf. §7.5.1.

84   Noth (1943: 127-n. 2) and Torrey (1910: 225f.).

85   The חיל שמרון resembles the designation חילא יהודיא in the Elephantine papyri.

86   *Contra* Batten (1913: 226). That exactly v. 37aβ-b is not transmitted in the LXX[BA*] may be explained as an editor's attempt to reconcile the prayer to v. 34.

According to our findings, the passages relating to Sanballat, Geshem and Tobiah in chaps. 2-4 have both developed in the process of composing the building account and are not integral to their contexts. For the author of 2:10, the antagonism was not elicited by the commencement of the building as in 2:19f. and 3:33f., but rather by a deep-seated enmity for "the children of Israel" and "someone who came to seek their welfare." 2:19f. has been inserted between 2:18b and 3:1ff. in order to confer a new character to the register of builders. 3:33ff. originally consisted of only Sanballat's speech (without Tobiah's in v. 35 and the imprecation in v. 36f.) and must be older than the other שמע-notices,[87] yet its setting between the conclusion of the list and the statement that the work was half-finished suggests strongly that a later hand has inserted it too.

6.3.2.3 The Testimony of 3:1-32 to the Original Brevity of the Building Account

The presence of the list is the most important testimony to the original shape of the building account. In assuming that Nehemiah – or one author – was responsible for both the insertion of the register as well as the composition of the rest of the first-person account, one faces insurmountable problems. The paragraphs in 6:17-19, 13:4-9 and 28f. report that Eliashib, many priests and the aristocracy had entered into connubial and commercial alliances with Tobiah and Sanballat. Why would an author have placed a text reporting how Eliashib began the construction both directly after 2:19f., where Eliashib's own relatives scoff at the prospect of building and are denied "a portion, right and memorial in Jerusalem," and directly before 4:1ff., where Tobiah and Sanballat plan to attack not only all their political and commercial partners, but also their own sons and daughters![88] This author would have also presented Eliashib and his colleagues as the ones who initiated the construction (3:1ff.) at the same time as he recounted that the high priesthood had been "defiled" by virtue of its relationship to Sanballat (13:28f.) and that a priest "had committed evil" for his relative Tobiah (13:4ff.). Moreover, he would have commemorated Meshullam, Schechaniah and the rest of the nobles of Judah in 3:1-32, on the one hand, and rebuked them as traitors (6:17-19) and held them responsible for the present calamity (13:15ff.), on the other? Therefore, one or other – the register or

---

87　If 3:33f. is the oldest passage in the שמע-schema, it is significant that it employs שמע with חרה, which may be the original form of the literary devise. Cf. Gen 34:7; 39:19; Num 11:1, 10; Judg 9:3; 1 Sam 11:6, 17:28; 2 Sam 13:21; Neh 4:1, 5:6 and the Greek equivalent in, *inter alia*, 1 Macc 3:27, 5:11, 6:28, and 11:22.

88　E.g., the daughter of Meshullam ben Berechiah, who is commemorated twice in the list (vv. 4 and 30), was married to the son of Tobiah, and Sanballat's daughter was married to a descendent of Eliashib and would have been in Jerusalem as he scorned the Judeans and conspired to storm the city.

several other important passages of the first-person account – must be earlier, but it is difficult to conceive how one author was responsible for both and did not notice the contradictions he created.

The solution proposed here and defended in the remaining chapters of this study is that the list has both been inserted by a later hand and is older than the rest of 3:33-6:14 and 6:16-13:31.

Based on our analysis on 2:19-20 and discussion of the register in the preceding sections, we may agree with Wellhausen, and Batten that in the earliest edition of the building report 3:38 followed directly upon 2:18.[89] In response to his address, Nehemiah's audience proclaims, "We will arise and build." The following line reads: ויחזקו ידיהם לטובה. As already noted, this expression suggests that the work on the wall actually commenced. After the builders are already active in 2:18, the repetition of "arise" and "build" (בנה + קום) in 3:1 is thus unanticipated and provides the most cogent evidence for our proposal that the register has been inserted between 2:18 and 3:38.

Moreover, the use of "arise" and "build" in 3:1 suggests that the register has been drafted specifically for the context of 2:18b and 3:38. In order to explain the use of the terms in a document that was supposedly deposited in the temple archives, scholars must argue that Nehemiah altered the original heading to the register as he integrated it into his building account. Instead of resorting to such speculation, we suggest that the author of the text endeavored to recount how the entire province came together to rebuild the wall. By naming the donors for each section in an order that corresponds to the circumference of the wall, the list brings to symbolic expression the unity the building project promoted in Judah and its "districts" (פלכים). However, instead of Nehemiah, it is Eliashib and "his colleagues, the priests" who initiate the building (3:1). This fact speaks forcefully in favor of the suggestion that a later hand *composed* the passage for its present context in order to balance Nehemiah's contribution with that of the high priesthood.[90]

If the list is older than 3:33-37 and 4:1-6:14, one could explain why the latter passages refer to the construction only in passing. Karrer notes that the building report is "im Grunde eine Erzählung über die Abwehr der feindlichen Nachbarvölker."[91] It seems that this concentration on the antagonism elicited by the building (and the attention devoted to the reforms) is due to the authors responsible for drastically amplifying Nehemiah's originally brief report. And

---

89   Wellhausen (1894: 168-n. 1.) and Batten (1913: 224).
90   Most agree that the list emphasizes the priestly contribution (cf. Rudolph [1949: 113], Galling [1954: 222], Kellermann [1967: 14], Williamson [1985: 201], Gunneweg [1987: 74ff.], Blenkinsopp [1988: 231]), yet they also assume that it represents an archival document that was inserted by Nehemiah or a later hand.
91   2001: 181f. See also Gunneweg (1987: 80).

instead of merely describing how the wall was built, they employ the building report and Nehemiah's influential name to both criticize their enemies and to present their ideas of what the Restoration of Judah entailed.

In order to create space for their interpretations, these authors have edited 3:38. According to our thesis, the register, rather than being an archival document that was carelessly interpolated, has been drafted for the context of 2:18b.[92] Now, since it presents the wall as complete, one would anticipate its author to have linked the statement that the work commenced (2:18b) with the statement of its conclusion.[93] 3:33-37 recounts what occurred *during* the work, yet this passage appears to have been inserted between vv. 32 and 38. Accordingly, before the register in vv. 1-32 was written, v. 38 would have followed 2:18b, and as Batten recognized,[94] these two verses connect well. However, 3:38 affirms only that the work was *halfway* finished, which is not what we would anticipate both after the enthusiasm expressed in 2:18b and after the completion of the building in 3:32. So too, the statement itself is incoherent. Why does he praise the people for "having a heart to work" (v. 38b), when they had only succeeded in erecting half of the wall (ותקשר כל־החומה עד־חציה, v. aβ)? The best answer to this question is that v. 38 originally reported that the work was completely finished and comprised solely ונבנה את־החומה ויהי לב לעם לעשות, to which v. aβ has been added. The clauses in v. aα ("and we built the wall") and v. b ("and the people had a heart to do the work") join well both syntactically and conceptually: The ramparts were not only erected, but the people also undertook this task enthusiastically. The positive note connects well to 6:15, but everything in 4:1-6:14 provokes the reader to wonder why only the second half of the wall would have created so many problems (cf. 4:6ff.). Before the rulers consent to the construction project, Nehemiah pleads, "Let us build the wall of Jerusalem" (ונבנה את־חומת ירושלם, 2:17bα). When the same expression recurs in v. 38aα, we expect that the work had not merely begun, but rather was actually finished. Therefore, the notice of completion in 6:15 was very likely originally joined to 3:38, as Hurowitz proposes in consideration of many ancient Near Eastern building inscriptions.[95]

---

92 This explains the *Wiederaufnahme* of "arise and build" (בנה + קום) in 3:1.

93 Significantly, Karrer argues that 3:1-32 must represent "ein historisches Dokument," because if it were composed for its present setting, one would expect it to depict only the *beginning* of the work on the wall (2001: 134-n. 21). If, however, the earliest editions of the building report did not portray work on the wall after 3:32 and the next statement affirmed the conclusion of the construction, then one could explain why 3:1 employs the same expression as 2:18b: The author of 3:1-32 would have filled the space between the 2:18b and the notice that the work was finished.

94 1913: 224. Kratz suggests this as a possibility but leaves the issue unsettled (2002: 72).

95 I discuss Hurowitz's findings at greater length in §7.5, but here it suffices to quote one remark: "When all these passages [the accounts introduced by 'and as he/they heard…'] are excised from the memoirs, what remains (1.1-2.9; 2.11-18; 3.1-32 (38); 6.15 (16); 7.1-72a;

Two other observations attest to the possibility that 3:38 has been retouched in order to make room for the addition of material between it and 6:15. First, the statement that "the whole wall was joined until the half of it" (‫ותקשר כל־‬ ‫)החומה עד־חציה‬ does not make any sense.[96] While it is possible that the height of the entire wall was erected to its halfway point, the clause uses the word ‫קשר‬ *niph.*, which can only mean "to be tied" or "bound." How then can the full circumference of the wall be bound together, yet only to the halfway mark? The wording of the following passage contains the solution to this incoherency. As Judah's neighbors hear that progress had been made (4:1), they conspire (‫ויקשרו‬ ‫)כלם יחדו‬ to come and fight against Jerusalem. The author of this passage has employed the frequent expression ‫קשר‬ *qal* to portray "all of them" making a *conspiracy*, and the hand that reworked 3:38 used the less frequent ‫קשר‬ *niph* to create a metaphor and present "all the wall" being *tied together* as the reason for this conspiracy.

Second, 4:1ff. has clearly been altered so that later authors could portray the builders preparing for an attack *while* they were working. The passage may have originally comprised solely vv. 1-3, which describe how Sanballat, Tobiah, the Arabs, Ammonites and Ashdodites[97] heard about a change to the condition of Jerusalem, plan to storm the city. In preparation for the attack, the Judeans pray and post a guard day and night.[98] Yet what aroused the enemy? The first reason given is quite clear: ‫כי־עלתה ארוכה לחמות ירושלם‬. The expression ‫ארוכה‬ + ‫עלה‬ ("to be healed restored") occurs only four times elsewhere, three of which are in Jeremiah referring to healing of the people of Israel[99] and once in Chronicles referring to restoration of the temple.[100] All these texts leave no room for doubt that the first ‫כי‬-clause in Neh 4:1 portrays the enemy becoming "very angry" (‫)ויחר להם מאד‬[101] as they heard "that the walls of Jerusalem *had been restored*."[102]

11.1-2; 12.27-43) is nothing more than a building account written in traditional format" (1992: 120f.).

96 Commentators have a difficult time translating this verse and usually render it ambiguously: "So we built the wall, and the whole wall was joined up to half its height..." One must, however, account for the difference between this line and 4:1 ("the breaches were beginning to be stopped up"), which most scholars seem to have confused with the meaning of 3:38.

97 "The Ashdodites," which are not included in the LXX, may represent a supplement.

98 The rest of the passage (with the exception of v. 4) presents the "adversaries" making new plans not just to attack Jerusalem, but also to interrupt the construction. In emphasizing that the construction was not yet finished, it too arouses suspicion.

99 Jer 8:22 (‫)כי מדוע לא עלתה ארכת בת־עמי‬, 30:17 and 33:6.

100 ‫וריעשו עשׂי המלאכה ותעל ארוכה למלאכה בידם ויעמידו את־בית האלהים על־מתכנתו ויאמצהו‬: 2 Chr 24:13.

101 In 3:33, Sanballat is "angered" (‫)ויחר לו‬ and scorns the Judeans as he hears that they are "restoring themselves." The author of 4:1 portrays him as being "very angered" (‫ויחר להם‬ ‫)מאד‬ as he hears that the work was now finished.

102 Surprisingly, most commentators translate this line: "that the restoration of the walls of Jerusalem *was going ahead/progressing*." Cf. however the rendering of Rudolph (1949: 122) and Galling (1954: 223).

They then confederate to test the newly built fortifications of the capital of Judah (4:2). While this agrees with the proposal that 3:1-32 and 38 recount the completion of the work, 4:1 contains a second כי-clause: "i.e., that the breaches (cf. 6:1) *were beginning* to be stopped up" (כי־החלו הפרצים להסתם).[103] In using חלל *hiph.* to emphasize that the breaches were *not yet* repaired, the secondary character of this line is evident.[104]

Considering the confusion created by the composition of 4:1-6:14, it is not surprising that the LXX does not transmit 3:38. The only problem is explaining how 4:1-6:14 developed. While there are many possible solutions, it suffices to make several observations.

As already noted, 4:1-3 seems to have portrayed the enemy planning a raid when they heard that "the wall of Jerusalem had been healed/restored." A later hand has changed both 4:1 and 3:38 in order to present the attack during the construction activities (after "the whole wall had been joined unto the half of it" [3:38aβ] and as "the breaches were beginning to be stopped up" [4:1aβ]), and the rest of the chapter agrees with these changes. Without entering into a detailed discussion of the editing of vv. 4-17, I suggest that the earliest additions include vv. 5-6, 7b, 9 and 15abβ. Although v. 4 lacks a continuation in the present shape of the chapter,[105] the narrative originally related only to the *external* threat to the builders.[106] V. 4 has probably been inserted to illustrate how the external threat provided "Judah" with a new motivation for building. According to the transition from vv. 1-3 to vv. 5-9*, "the adversaries" develop a new plan: Now they

---

103 This is the only place where חלל *hiphil* ("begin") appears in Neh 1-13. The use is, however, very similar to that in such late texts as Ezra 3:6, 8; 1 Chr 27:24; 2 Chr 3:1, 3; 13:17; 20:22; 29:17, 27; 31:7, 10, 21; 34:3.

104 The same editorial phenomenon in 4:1ff. is witnessed in the introduction to chap. 6, the greater portion of which must be older than the account of the financial reforms in chap. 5. I will argue that 6:1 originally included only: "And as Sanballat…heard that I *had built* the wall and there was *no breach* remaining in it," to which the גם-clause has been added ("although at that time I had not yet hung the doors in the gates;" cf. the discussion in §7.3). Oddly, the גם-clause in 6:1b brings v. 1a into conformity with vv. 2-9 by creating a task for Nehemiah "at that time." The work he accomplishes between vv. 1 and 15 is the hanging of the doors in their gates, and here the redactor has plainly drawn upon the wording of 3:1-32, which employs the exact same expression (עמד *hiph.* + דלתות, cf. vv. 1, 3, 6, 13, 14, 15) to depict all the doors being hung before 3:38. Similarly, the introduction to 7:1 appears to have included only, "And as the wall *had been built* […], they appointed the gatekeepers," which a redactor, following 6:1b (and 3:1-32), has expanded with "and I had hung the doors" (cf. §12.3). Thus, the final redactors of the building account have created space for their accounts by drawing on the formulation of 3:1-32 to create successive building phases. Accordingly, 3:1-32 is now to be treated as a proleptic summary of what is recounted in detail and from a different perspective in the following chapters.

105 "And Judah said, 'The strength of the burden bearers is failing, and there is too much rubbish so that we are unable to work on the wall.'"

106 Kratz reconstructs the passage accordingly: "Die Arbeit ging zügig voran (3,38), dann ließen die Kräfte ein wenig nach (4,4), doch als Verstärkung kam (4,6a), kehrten sie wieder an die Arbeit zurück (4,9b)" (2000: 68). Cf. similarly Winkler (1901: 476ff.).

desire not merely to "come and fight against Jerusalem and cause confusion," but rather to "come in their midst and kill them *and cause the work to cease*." V. 6 describes how the builders were informed of the new plot. While Nehemiah recounts in v. 3 that "*we* appointed a watch," he acts alone in v. 7 (ואעמיד),[107] and thanks to his measures, the people can return to the work with new vigor (v. 9).[108]

The scene was first amplified with vv. 8, 10-12a, 17*.[109] After the people resume their activities in v. 9b, the reader presumes that the enemy no longer posed a threat. Yet the continuation in vv. 10-17 describes the builders "from that day on" working with only one hand and wielding a weapon in the other. So too, the builders are no longer simply "the people" (v. 7), but rather Nehemiah's "retainers" (v. 10),[110] "the officers," "the builders" (vv. 11-12), "the bearer of burdens" (v. 11), all of whom have not been mentioned until now.[111] The most important clue is v. 15, which according to the consensus did not originally include v. bα (it is also missing in the LXX) and is to be emended accordingly: "And we were laboring at the work [...] from the crack of dawn until the stars appeared." While this statement furnishes a fitting continuation to v. 9b, the addition of v. 15bα assimilates the statement to v. 10, which in turn has been formulated according to the pattern of v. 15abβ.[112] That v. 16 is not integral to its context would explain why it disrupts the participles in vv. 15 and 17 and employs the expression בעת ההיא instead of מן־היום ההוא as in v. 9.[113] Both v. 8 and vv. 12b-14 incorporate features of the "holy war" accounts,[114] yet the first passage, where Nehemiah pleads to "remember the Lord and fight,"[115] may be older than second, according to which the people must merely rally to

---

107 That v. 7a has been added is indicated by the repetition of ואעמיד.
108 V. 9: "As our enemies heard that we had been informed (כי־נודע לנו; cf. לא ידעו in v. 5) and that God had frustrated their plans, we returned to the wall, each to his own work." That "the enemies" in v. 9 are the same "adversaries" in v. 5 is confirmed by the parallel occurrence of איב and צר eighteen times in the Hebrew Bible. Most of the texts are poetic, which corresponds to the rhythmic character of v. 5. One lacks, therefore, a reason to attribute v. 5 to a different hand (*pace* Mowinckel [1964: 25]).
109 V. 17 appears to have been supplemented with אני ואחי ונערי ואנשי המשמר אשר אחרי.
110 That these "retainers" have to do with Nehemiah's gubernatorial office is made plain by v. 16, where all "the people" have "servants."
111 V. 10 refers also to "shields" and "armor," which are not mentioned in v. 7.
112 Cf. 15bα (וחצים מחזיקים ברמחים) with (וחצים מחזיקים וחצים מחזיקים והרמחים) חצי נערי עשים במלאכה in v. 10, which presupposes v. 15a and bβ (ואנחנו עשים במלאכה...מעלות השחר עד צאת הכוכבים).
113 The references to "night" and "day" may be explained as reinterpretation of the directly preceding verse.
114 For a list of the common features, cf. Kellermann (1967: 18), and for the portrayals of "holy war" or "YHWH-Krieg," cf. von Rad (1969), Stolz (1972) and Ruffing (1992). *Contra* Kellermann (and Karrer [2001: 185]), the use of קשר ("to conspire") does not belong to the conventional language of accounts of holy war; cf. Gunneweg's interpretation (1987: 81).
115 V. 8b: את־אדני הגדול והנורא זכרו והלחמו.

the sound of the shofar "and our God will fight for us."[116] If v. 8 was inserted at the same time as the first expansions in vv. 10-17, the otherwise inexplicable handicapping of the builders with weapons may be understood as the transformation of the actual work on the ramparts into a holy war.[117] With the supplements in vv. 8, 10-17, the composition of Nehemiah's building account has progressed considerably from 2:17 and 3:33f., which present the restoration of Jerusalem as the remedy to the general condition of Judah's affliction and reproach. Inasmuch as the building of the wall now creates more troubles than those that previously existed and is portrayed with features of the so-called "Conquest accounts," this redaction continues the theme of the second Exodus begun in Ezra 1.[118] Thus, although the Golah has returned in Ezra 1-6, the land has not been fully conquered until the fortifications are finally built and the enemy within (cf. 6:15) and without (6:17-19, 7:5ff. and 13:4ff.) is vanquished.

6.4 Conclusions

Our analysis has revealed the probability that the oldest editions of the building report, 3:38aαb followed 2:18b and continued in 6:15. Together with 1:1a, 11b; 2:1-6, 11, 15*, 16a, and 17, these verses were probably drafted by Nehemiah himself – perhaps originally for an inscription of some sort – to recount how he received a leave of absence from Artaxerxes, came to Jerusalem and motivated his compatriots to restore the disgraceful ruins of the wall that symbolized Judah's political humiliation. The rulers consent unanimously to his proposal (2:18b), so that he can announce: "Then we built the wall, and the people were eager to do the work. And the wall finished on the twenty-fifth of Elul – in fifty two days" (3:38aαb and 6:15). The first addition to this work is 3:1-32, which connects 2:18b with notice of conclusion (3:38* and 6:15) and commemorates the names of those who contributed to project. Because the register presents Eliashib "and his colleagues" commencing the work, the high priesthood was probably responsible for the first redaction of the account.[119]

The next expansions in 3:33ff. present the mirror-image of Nehemiah's speech in 2:17 and portray Sanballat spelling out – now negatively and

---

116 V. 14: ‏במקום אשר תשמעו את־קול השופר שמה תקבצו אלינו אלהינו ילחם לנו‎.

117 Cf. Karrer (2001: 187 – "Der Bau selbst wird zu einer Art 'JHWH-Krieg'").

118 In this regard, cf. Williamson's comments on Ezra 1 (1985: 8ff.) as well as Abadie's study (1998) on the Golah-ideology in Ezra according to which the land must be reclaimed from the non-exiled "Judeo-Samaritan populations."

119 With this first insertion, the struggle begins that will accompany the entire formation of Ezra-Neh, namely between the priesthood and Nehemiah in Neh 6:17-19 and 13:4-14, 28ff.; between the temple and the city as a whole in Ezra 1-6; between Ezra the priest and Nehemiah the cupbearer in Ezra 7-8; and between temple and Torah in Neh 8-10.

metaphorically – the aims of "these *withering* Jews" (היהודים האמללים) to *"revive* the stones out of the heaps of rubbish" (היחיו את־האבנים מערמות העפר) and *"restore* themselves" (היעזבו להם; "עזב II" in *BDB*).[120] Since 3:1 depicts the beginning of the construction, 3:33f. could not have been positioned before 3:1-32. Instead of disrupting the passage, the author presents Sanballat making his speech during the time recounted in 3:1-32 (כי־אנחנו בונים את־החומה, 3:33a). Because the clause, "and the whole wall was joined unto the half of it," has probably been added to v. 38, and because 4:1ff. describe the enemy's reaction to the completion of the "restoration" (ארוכה לחמות ירושלם), the only space for Sanballat's speech was between vv. 32 and 38. If the passage originally included solely Sanballat's speech, to which v. 35 has been added, then not only 4:1ff., which combines Sanballat and Tobiah as the subject of "heard," but also the imprecation in 3:36-37, which refers to "them," must have been composed after v. 35. The imprecation may be earlier than 4:1ff., however. Insofar as "[d]er Fluch klingt abschließend,"[121] it may have been composed for the notice of completion in 3:38 + 6:15.

Since 4:1-3 portrays Judah's neighbors plotting to storm the newly built wall of Jerusalem, we would expect it to follow 6:15. There are two possibilities why it has been placed between 3:38* and 6:15: Either the author who edited 3:38 found these three short verses on the margin and integrated them into the narrative as he added 4:5-9* and 15*, or the author of 4:1-3 was responsible for their present setting and intended to allow the date in 6:15 to remain the conclusion of the account. Whatever the case may be, 4:1-3 must be older than all of 4:4-6:14. If the reconstruction of 4:4-17 presented here is tenable, then the earliest amplification of the text concluded in either v. 9 ("and we returned to the wall, each to his own work") or v. 15abβ ("and we were laboring at the work from the crack of dawn until the stars appeared"). Both lines form a fitting transition to the notice of completion in 6:15 ("And the wall was finished…").

---

120 Karrer's writes on this passage: "Er spricht von היהודים האמללים. אמל bedeutet eigentlich ‚verwelken' und wird im allgemeinen von Pflanzen ausgesagt oder auch einem vertrocknenden Land [cf. however, 1 Sam 2:5; Jer 14:2, 15:9]. Was sind ‚verwelkende Judäer'? Nimmt man den metaphorischen Gehalt von חיה, ist es ein Volk, das keine eigene Lebenskraft mehr besitzt, das langsam und unauffällig dahinstirbt. Dem steht die Frage gegenüber, ob die Judäer etwa die Steine aus dem Schutthaufen beleben wollen. – ‚beleben' paßt semantisch nicht zu ‚Steinen'. Dagegen bildet es ein sinnvolles Gegenüber zu dem ‚Verwelken' des Volkes. Auch wenn die anderen Teile des Sanballat-Zitates nicht mehr richtig verständlich sind, so ist doch deutlich, dass Sanballat – als Hauptvertreter der gegnerischen Nachbarvölker – gezeichnet wird als einer, der voller Verachtung für das judäische Volk ist, es für kraftlos und langsam dahinsterbend hält. Der Mauerbau wird abgelehnt, weil er eine nicht erwünschte Belebung und Veränderung für dieses Volk mit sich bringt" (2001:184f.). From these observations, it is difficult to deny the connections between this passage and Nehemiah's speech in 2:17. Most importantly, both agree that the restoration of the wall served primarily sociopolitical, not strategic, purposes.

121 Kratz (2000: 72), who, however, discovers a Nehemian *Grundschicht* in chap. 4.

The Composition of Neh 4:1-17

1 **But when Sanballat and Tobiah and the Arabs and the Ammonites** and the Ashdodites **heard that the walls of Jerusalem had been restored**
   and the breaches were beginning to be stopped up,
they were very angry, 2 and all plotted together to come and fight against Jerusalem and to cause confusion in it. 3 But we prayed to our God, and set a guard as a protection against them day and night.
            4 But Judah said, "The strength of the burden bearers is failing, and
            there is too much rubbish so that we are unable to work on the wall."
   5 And our adversaries said, "They will not know nor will they see before we come upon them and kill them and stop the work." 6 And then the Jews who lived near them came and said to us, "???" [*txt. crrp.*]
            7 So I stationed in the lowest parts of the space behind the wall, in
            open places,
   So I stationed the people according to their families, with their swords, their spears, and their bows.
            8 And I saw, arose, and said to the nobles, the officials and the rest of the
            people, "Do not be afraid of them. Remember the Lord, who is great and
            awesome, and fight for your kin, your sons, your daughters, your wives, and
            your houses."
   9 When our enemies heard that it had been made known unto us, and that God had frustrated their plans, we all returned to the wall, each to his work.
            10 From that day on, half of my servants were working on the construction,
            and half were holding the spears, shields, bows, and body-armor; and the
            officers posted themselves behind the whole house of Judah, 11 who were
            building the wall. The burden bearers were carrying their loads in such a
            way that each labored on the work with one hand and with the other held a
            weapon. 12 And each of the builders had his sword strapped at his side
            while he built. [The man who sounded the trumpet was beside me.]
            13 And I said to the nobles, the officials, and the rest of the people,
            "The work is great and widely spread out, and we are separated far
            from one another on the wall. 14 Rally to us wherever you hear the
            sound of the trumpet. Our God will fight for us."
   15 And we labored at the work,
            and half of them held the spears
   from break of dawn until the stars came out.
            16 I also said to the people at that time, "Let every man and his
            servant pass the night inside Jerusalem, so that they may be a guard for
            us by night and may labor by day." 17 So neither I nor my brothers
            nor my servants nor the men of the guard who followed me
   And none of us took off our clothes; each ??? [*txt. crrp.*].

The Composition of Neh 2:11-4:17

2:11 And I came to Jerusalem, and after I had been there several days…
            vv. 12-14*
15 I went up in the valley at night and inspected the wall and returned…
16 But the rulers knew not whither I went, or what I did;
            And the Jews, the priests, the nobles, the rulers, and the rest that did the work
            and I had not told until then.
**17 And said I unto them, "You see the distress that we *are* in, how Jerusalem *lies*
waste, and the gates thereof are burned with fire: come, and let us build up the
wall of Jerusalem, that we be no more a reproach."**
                        18 Then I told them of the hand of my God which was good
                        upon me; as also the king's words that he had spoken unto me.
**And they said, "Let us rise up and build." And they strengthened their hands for
the good (work).**
                                    19 But when Sanballat the Horonite, and Tobiah the
                                    servant, the Ammonite, and Geshem the Arabian, heard,
                                    they laughed us to scorn, and despised us,
                                                and said, "What is this thing that you are doing?
                                                Are you rebelling against the king?"
                                    20 Then I returned a word to them, and said unto them,
                                    "The God of Heaven, he will prosper us; we his servants
                                    will arise and build: but ye have no portion, nor right, nor
                                    memorial, in Jerusalem.
            3:1-32

                                    33 But it happened that when Sanballat heard that we built the wall, he was
                                    wroth, and took great indignation,
                        and mocked the Jews.
                        34 And he said
                                    before his brethren and the army of Samaria, and said,
                        "What are these withering Jews doing? Will they restore themselves? Will
                        they sacrifice? Will they make an end in a day? Will they revive the stones
                        out of the heaps of the rubbish which are burnt?"
                                    35 Now Tobiah the Ammonite was by him, and he said, "Even if
                                    they are building, if a fox go up, he shall even break down their
                                    wall of stones."
                                    36 Hear, O our God; for we are despised: and turn their
                                    reproach upon their own head, and give them for a prey in
                                    the land of captivity:
                                    37 And cover not their iniquity, and let not their sin be
                                    blotted out from before you: for they have provoked you to
                                    anger before the builders.
38 So built we the wall;
            and all the wall was joined together unto the half thereof:
And the people had a heart to do the work.
                        4:1-3* (For vv. 4:1-17, see the above.)
                                    v. 4
                                    vv. 5-9* and 15*
                                        vv. 10-17*
(6:15-16*)

7. The Intimidation of the Builder – 6:1-19

7.1 Introduction

The preceding chapter concluded that the oldest portion of 6:1-19 is to be found in the notice reporting that the work was complete (v. 15), which appears to have originally followed directly on 3:38*. The present chapter embraces this conclusion only as working hypothesis in order to take a fresh look at the literary evidence in chap. 6. Its aim is to test the integrity of the chapter and its place in the building report. According to the interpretation defended here, the chapter intends (1) to warn Judah's leaders about the danger of diplomatic relations with their neighbors (vv. 1-4), (2) to distinguish a strong and refortified province from an independent and rebellious province (vv. 5-9), and (3) to manifest the corrupt tendencies among the prophets (vv. 7 and 9-14) and the upper-classes (vv. 17-19). We begin by appreciating the unity of the chapter.

7.2 The Unity of the Chapter

Neh 6 portrays several episodes revolving around a single theme: the intimidation of the builder. V. 1 introduces the antagonists who play a central role throughout the chapter, but abandon the scene in 7:1ff. The thematic unity of five sections (vv. 2-4, 5-9, 10-14, 15-16 and 17-19) distinguishes them both from chap. 4, which treats the failed attempts to discourage the builders by means of military incursions, and from chap. 5, whose topic is only indirectly related to the building of the wall. In the present chapter, the concentration is on the leader of the builders, whom the enemy before "the closing of the gates" (cf. 6:1 with 7:1) endeavors to eliminate from the scene.

In order to achieve this aim, the enemy resorts to an array of ruses and intrigues. First, Sanballat and Geshem attempt to lure Nehemiah away from Jerusalem to a place where they could physically harm him (vv. 2-4). Since they were unsuccessful, Sanballat sends a letter reporting alleged rumors (vv. 5-9) with the intention of bringing the work on the wall to a halt. After failing once again, he joins forces with Tobiah. Together, they attempt to frighten Nehemiah so that he would commit a fatal *faux pas* (vv. 10-14). And finally, Tobiah exploits his alliances with the Judean nobility to obstruct Nehemiah (vv. 17-19). The common denominator of these accounts is the term ירא ("fear" in *qal* or "intimidate" in *piel*), which appears five times – in reference to Nehemiah (vv. 13, 14, 19), the Judeans (v. 9), as well as the enemies (v. 16). The antagonists are thus united in their resolve to assassinate Nehemiah – or at least his character.

Other shared features connect the various paragraphs. For example, Nehemiah is petitioned three times to meet somewhere or with someone (v. 2a, v. 7b, and v. 10bα). A central motif of the chapter is also the sending of messages: the reader encounters the verb שלח no less than seven times. The senders are Sanballat, Geshem, and Tobiah, as well as God (v. 12a). Most importantly, the focus in all these accounts is on the person of Nehemiah. He is the one who builds the wall (v. 1a), hangs the doors in the gates (v. 1b), is doing "a great work" (v. 3), allegedly aspires to rule as king (v. 6), the object of a murder plot (v. 10) and intimidation (vv. 13, 15, 19), etc. Chaps. 2-4 present the building project as a communal endeavor. The narration is generally in first-person plural: "we will arise and build" (2:20), "we built the wall" (3:38), "we returned to the wall" (4:9), "we were building from the break of dawn till the stars came out" (4:15), etc. In these passages, the building account presents the repair of ruins of Jerusalem as an effort to consolidate the inhabitants of Judah. In order to achieve this, the account portrays the Judeans as a unified ethnic group over against their neighbors who reproach them (2:17, 6:16). Contrasting with this emphasis upon unity, chap. 6 depicts the repair of the walls as Nehemiah's personal achievement (cf. vv. 3, 6, 9b). The enemy, accordingly, shifts its attention from the builders (cf. 3:33ff.; 4:1ff.) to their leader.

To what extent does this observed unity obtain from the first author of the chapter, and how much must we attribute to redactional activity? Are the similarities of the recounted episodes simply due to historical coincidence? If not, what does the literary composition contribute to the building report? In order to respond to these questions, I submit the chapter to a diachronic analysis in order to establish whether the various paragraphs were formulated simultaneously or have developed piecemeal. If the chapter is composite, it is important to determine for which context the authors drafted the individual units. We begin the analysis with an examination of the heading in v. 1.

7.3 The Heading – V. 1

As elsewhere (2:10, 19; 3:33; 4:1), the depiction of the (final) conflict with the enemies in chap. 6 is introduced with the שמע-formula, which presents both the protagonist ("that I built the wall") and other the *dramatis personae* as well as the phase of building in which the episodes took place. In order to add precision to the general statement of progress in v. 1aα,[1] the narrator provides two additional details in v. 1aβ-b, according to which everything happened as "there was no breach left in it (the wall), although at that time I had not set up the doors upon the gates."

In comparison with the customary use of the שמע-formula, one observes several peculiarities in v. 1. First, the כי-clause ("that I had built the wall") contrasts sharply with the כי-clause in 3:33 ("that we were building the wall"). This variation may be explained in light of the new focus. As noted above, the chapter revolves around the person of Nehemiah, whereas the remaining builders, in contrast to chaps. 2-4, are not in view. A similar explanation must be sought for the appearance of the *niphal* form of שמע, which contrasts with the *qal* where the שמע-formula appears elsewhere.[2] Except for v. 1, this form occurs rarely in the book (12:43 and 13:27), yet twice in chap. 6 (vv. 6, 7). It seems, therefore, that the שמע-formula has been adapted to the contents and style of the following paragraphs.

Despite these observations, v. 1 has probably been prefaced secondarily to the chapter. This suggestion accounts for the pronounced discrepancy between v. 1a, according to which the wall is already complete, and Nehemiah's reply in v. 3 ("I am doing a great work…").[3] One initially assumes that the work refers here to the hanging of the doors, which v. 1b presents as a still unfulfilled task. However, v. 6aβ ("…for which cause you are building the wall…") and 9aβ ("saying, 'Their hands will be weakened from the work so that it will not be done'") equate the work with the building of the wall. The contradiction is most blatant in vv. 15-16, which identify "this work wrought of our God" with the completion of the wall. Significantly, nothing is said about the gates. How then can Nehemiah state in the introduction that he had already built the wall and then in the following paragraphs describe what occurred as he was building it, waiting until v. 15 to finally report that the construction was complete?

Comparing the syntax of the שמע-formula elsewhere, we notice that the subject is consistently named only once, so that the following clause beginning with a *wayyiqtol* form is inseparable from the preceding relative clause.[4] In 3:33, for example, the subject is introduced with ויהי כאשר שמע and is not repeated in the main clause (ויחר לו ויכעס הרבה וילעג על־היהודים). In contrast, the syntax of 6:2 is fully independent from the foregoing introduction. Indeed, one could describe the latter as a fragment in contrast to the complete sentence in v. 2.

---

1   "Now it came to pass, when Sanballat, and Tobiah, and Geshem the Arab, and the rest of our enemies, heard that I had built the wall…."
2   See §3.2 for the comparative table of the שמע-schema.
3   The participle (אני עשה מלאכה גדולה) contrasts with the *qatal* form of בניתי in v. 1.
4   If the name "Tobiah" has been inserted by an editorial hand, as most scholars agree (see §7.5.1), then the repetition of the subject in v. 2 is even more problematic.

In combination with the stylistic features drawn from the chapter itself (נשמע
and כי בניתי את־החומה), these contradictions and anomalies warrant our conclusion that a redactor has prefixed v. 1 to vv. 2ff. The attribution of the wall-
building to Nehemiah alone sets the tone for the following passages, in which
strategies are described to distract and eliminate him as the instigator and super-
visor of the building project. Before the addition of this introduction, the passage must have been composed for another context. We search for that context
in the following section.

This contradiction with the remaining account augments with the final גם־
clause ("...although at that time I had not yet hung the doors in the gates").
Several commentators have suggested that this line constitutes a late gloss,
assuming that the removal of it would resolve the tension in v. 1a.[5] While this is
not the case (v. 1a already poses a serious incongruity), we must agree that the
conjunction גם lends itself well to the insertion of supplementary material. It
seems that a later author has added the clause in an attempt to resolve the tension between v. 1a, according to which the wall is finished, and vv. 2-9, which
report what occurred during the building.[6]

With the addition of 6:1a, the episodes reported in vv. 2-19 occurred
between two stages in the construction: as no breach remained in the wall and
before the doors had been set up in the gates. While the latter is reported in 7:1,
the breaches are mentioned in 4:1aβ. The analysis of 4:1ff. concluded that this
clause has been inserted to transform the account of the first attempted attack
after "the wall of Jerusalem had been healed" into an attack on the city as "the
breaches were beginning to be stopped up."[7] With regard to these headings (4:1,
6:1, 7:1), one observes how the narrative gradually assumes finer temporal
contours. The redactional activity has pressed pre-existent material into a
chronological schema of successive building phases. Whereas before the addition of v. 1, the conflict occurs during a loosely defined period (as Nehemiah
was building the wall; cf. vv. 3, 6), the incidents assume greater significance as
they are dated to an independent (and final) stage of the construction project. In
the eyes of later readers, the attempted calumny and assassination of Nehemiah
constitute a new chapter (both literally and metaphorically) in the history of the
wall's restoration. Accordingly, what began as a collection of disparate episodes
becomes an individual epoch. The heading of 6:1, therefore, parallels the

---

5   See Mowinckel (1963: 28), Ehrlich (1914: 196) and Hölscher (1923: 536).

6   If v. 1b is secondary, it follows that 7:1aβ (ואעמיד הדלתות) has been added at a later point.

7   It appears that the redactor of 4:1 has drawn on the wording of 6:1, and this is supported by
     the reference to "the rest of our enemies." The author of 4:1 names these enemies: "the
     Arabs, the Ammonites and the Ashdodites." As many scholars have proposed and as argued
     below, the absence of a preposition before "Tobiah" in 6:1 seems to indicate that the name
     has been inserted. In 4:1, however, Tobiah and Sanballat cooperate, which agrees with the
     addition of 3:35 and the late supplements in 2:10 and 19f.

redactional activity in chaps. 2-7 that creates construction phases: in 2:19-20 (and 3:1-32), the building begins; 3:33-38 relates the progress until "the whole wall is joined until the half of its height" (3:38aβ); 4:1-17 (and 5:1-19) recount the attack on the workers (and socio-economic reforms) as "the breaches were beginning to be stopped up" (4:1aβ); 6:1-19 portray the various attempts to eliminate Nehemiah "as no breach remained in the wall although at that time I had not hung doors in the gates" (6:1aβ-b); and 7:1ff. conclude the building account by describing the measures taken to ensure Jerusalem's security as "the wall had been built and I had hung the doors" (7:1a). Each of these sections begins with the ויהי כאשר שמע(ו), except for 7:1, which is introduced simply by ויהי כאשר נבנתה.[8]

7.4 Nehemiah's Correspondence with Sanballat and Geshem

Chap. 4 recounts how the enemies of Judah plot an attack on Jerusalem. Once their plans are exposed, the builders can return to the work (v. 9b). Now, in chap. 6, Sanballat (vv. 2-9) and Geshem (vv. 2-4) invite Nehemiah to meet together in Hakkephirim. Because their offer is declined four times (v. 4), Sanballat decides to operate alone and sends him a letter reporting how the nations perceived the Judeans' building project. The letter concludes by repeating the offer to meet and "take counsel with one another" (v. 7b).

From an historical vantage point, this account makes little sense. Had Sanballat really wished that Nehemiah finally take him up on his offer to come to the conference, he would most likely not have sent a letter filled with accusations. Far from persuasive, this approach would have only made Nehemiah

---

8   Importantly, the account of the building of the temple evinces a similar periodization to that of the wall-building account. Ezra 1-2 recount how the Golah returns to Jerusalem (cf. Neh 1-2). The first phase of building is described in Ezra 3:1-7; Joshua and Zerubbabel "arose and built" the altar (cf. the use of "arise and build" in Neh 2:18, 20 and 3:1). The passage of Ezra 3:8-4:24 depicts the second building phase in which the builders lay the temple-foundations. Adopting the שמע-schema (Ezra 4:1) from the wall-building account, the author describes how the adversaries (cf. Neh 4:5) hear that "the children of the Golah" were building, offer to help, are repudiated and then begin "to weaken the hands" (cf. Neh 2:18b and 6:9) of the builders. This is the beginning of the antagonism encountered during the construction of the wall. In the final building phases (chaps. 5-6), the construction of the temple concludes with a dedication ceremony that strongly resembles the *ḥanukkah* of the wall in Neh 12:27ff. – One may compare this periodization of postexilic history in Ezra-Neh to the "Enneateuch," the authors of which have aligned individual episodes in Israel's and Judah's history, with ever-increasing precision, into a sequence of epochs prior to Judah's exile. Redactors have then gradually marked off these epochs into separate books by expanding their opening and/or closing chapters. Accordingly, the demarcation of books in Gen-Kgs parallels the formation of chapters in Nehemiah's account. The inclusion of the prayer in 1:5-11a witnesses to a developing demarcation of "the book of Nehemiah" from "the book of Ezra."

more resolute in his decision to continue doing the "great work" (v. 3). It is also fully incomprehensible that Sanballat desired to meet with one whom he had just accused of seditious activities (v. 7). After warning Nehemiah that the king would find out about his plans to assume the throne, the best course of action would have been to distance himself from the rebel, not to meet with him and "take counsel together." Moreover, after Nehemiah had recently armed the builders to counter their military strike, how could Sanballat and Geshem expect him to be willing to come to a conference? We would anticipate Sanballat and Geshem to first send a delegation to bring about a rapprochement and to pave the way for possible future negotiations. To be sure, a casual offer to meet after a display of violence and without further explanation is quite inconceivable. With good reasons, therefore, the recipient of the message presumes that "they were only devising to do me harm" (v. 2b).[9]

7.4.1 Nehemiah as an Indefatigable Builder - VV. 2-4

Instead of dismissing the possibility of ever understanding Sanballat's and Geshem's intentions or assuming that the author of the account has concealed facts from the reader, one should first attempt to interpret the passages in vv. 2-4 and 5-9 independently of their present, incongruous, literary settings (i.e., after chap. 4). In doing so, we notice that the combination of יחדו and יעד or יעץ (as in 6:2) always appears in portrayals of subterfuge and conspiracies. For instance, the "kings met together...to fight with Israel" in Josh 11:5. The Psalter frequently portrays Israel's or the psalmist's enemies plotting together.[10] Also Num 14:35 (16:11 and 27:3) describes the Israelites gathering together against YHWH. It appears then quite plausible that the authors of vv. 2-9 have drawn upon יחדו + יעץ/יעד to present, with negative undertones, Sanballat and Geshem recognizing Nehemiah as Judah's representative and inviting him to join their league.

The suggested place of meeting in vv. 2-4 is in "Hakkephirim in the valley of Ono." Since it is not known whether this site belonged to Judean territory or constituted a neutral zone at the time of composition,[11] one cannot be sure why this location was chosen. The intention seems to be the remoteness of the site. Claiming that an excursion to this place would involve a considerable pause from his building project, Nehemiah turns down their offer: "I am doing a great work, so that I cannot come down. Why should the work cease while I leave it

---

9   As Clines remarks, "it is hard to see what Sanballat hoped to achieve just at this time, and his unimaginative importunity (v. 4) is not the work of a constructive statesman" (1984: 173).

10 Cf., e.g, Ps 71:10; 83:4 and 6.

11 Williamson has provided a good discussion of these alternatives (1985: 254).

and come down to you?" That he also meant what he said is indicated by his repetition of this response (four times, v. 4).

According to most modern interpreters, however, Nehemiah's answer illustrates only his sense of humor. He "shows a nice wit in making his excuse for not coming when he knows quite well that the intention of the invitation is to stop his work."[12] That we should not take seriously the answer he sent to Sanballat would explain why he gives his readers a conflicting reason for rejecting the offer: "But they were only planning to inflict injury upon me." The actual reason for not accepting the proposal was, accordingly, not his resolve to finish the task he had begun, but rather a fear for his life.

Upon closer examination, this interpretation – that Nehemiah's response is meant ironically – is unconvincing. First, the authors of the composition of v. 2b have availed themselves again of the language of the Psalter. Ps 21:12; 35:4; 41:8; 140:3 all employ the verb חשב together with the noun רעה to describe the plotting of the psalmist's enemies to do him harm. We may, therefore, embrace Reinmuth's suggestion that "die entsprechenden Wendungen aus den Psalmen mitklingen, die auf je ihre Weise um die Rettung vor den Feinden bitten oder im Falle von Ps 21,12 dem König sogar solche Rettung zusagen."[13] The function of the remark is to point out that Sanballat and Geshem wished only ostensibly to join forces with the Judean leader; actually, they were conspiring to injure him. By declaring their underlying motives, Nehemiah warns his readers that Sanballat and Geshem – two prominent representatives of Judah's neighbors – may have seemed to be interested in cooperating, yet their true aim was to cause him (and the Judeans as a whole) harm. Instead of falling into a trap and consenting to their diplomatic proposals, Nehemiah continues to do the "great work" of building Jerusalem's wall. In this assessment of what motivated the diplomacy of these two foreign leaders, the isolationist tone of Nehemiah's account is quite audible.

The final passage of the chapter (vv. 17-19) also depicts written correspondence, yet with a considerable difference. Whereas Nehemiah sends letters only to reject the offers of Sanballat and Geshem, the nobles initiate the correspondence (v. 17).[14] The authors of these passages have drawn a contrast between Nehemiah, on the one hand, who considered the building of the wall as a means of centralizing the province and separating it from foreign influence, and the aristocracy, on the other hand, who supported the building project, yet out of

---

12   Clines (1984: 173). See also Rudolph (1949: 135), Gunneweg (1987: 94) and Blenkinsopp (1988: 268).
13   2002: 197.
14   In 2:16, 4:8 and 12, the nobles are portrayed as contributors to the building project. 6:18 even mentions a name that appears twice in the 3:1-32 (cf. also Eliashib in 3:1 and 13:4-9, 27-29).

concern for their own commerce were opposed to a separatist policy and the centralization of Judah.

Since the response in v. 3 is probably not to be understood as simply Nehemiah's attempt to be humorous, one must explain the differences between it and v. 2b. Without v. 2b, Nehemiah's response, rather than constituting wit or irony, would have to be taken seriously. One may thus conjecture that the original purpose of the passage is to display Nehemiah as a fervent and unrelenting builder. Vv. 2a and 3-4 depict an opportunity for Nehemiah to take advantage of his position and accumulate more influence by "meeting" with Sanballat and Geshem. Rather than succumbing to this temptation, he recognizes that his present task deserves undivided attention. Even a short absence would involve the cessation of the "great work" (v. 3b). Hence, these verses both portray his presence as requisite to the progress on the wall and depict him as one who is firmly determined to build.

The last place where Nehemiah emphasizes his personal involvement in the building is 5:14ff. In this review of his lengthy period of selfless gubernatorial service (vv. 14-18), he maintains that "I also continued in the work of this wall, we acquired no land, and all my men were gathered there to the work" (v. 16). The recurrence of the term המלאכה, the emphasis that both he and his servants participated, and the claim that they were not distracted by the acquisition of personal wealth may be compared to the message of 6:2a, 3-4. Indeed, the entire chap. 5, but especially the passage of vv. 14-19, contains similar accents and follows the same intention of portraying Nehemiah as an ideal leader. The difference between the two texts is that 5:14ff. present Nehemiah as an ideal governor, while 6:2b, 3-4 presents him only as a dedicated and single-minded builder. Moreover, 5:14 present Nehemiah working on the wall for twelve years! If a later author has expanded the building account with 5:14-19, the account in 6:2ff. must have been composed for another literary setting. 5:1-13 does not present a possible alternative: This passage has nothing directly to do with the building and, in depicting a reform in the province, contradicts Nehemiah's insistence in 6:2ff. that he would not abandon his construction enterprise.[15] The next, and most likely, candidate for the context of 6:2ff. is chap. 4, which concludes with a description of the indefatigable workers: "And we did the work from the crack of dawn until the stars came out..." (v. 15). Here, in contrast to 5:14ff., the passage has been formulated with participles, and the wording and theme resembles 6:3.[16] In light of these similarities, the portrayal of the people's industriousness in chap. 4 appears to have been formerly connected to 6:2-4* in

---

15 That 5:1ff. has been added at a late stage is argued in §8.2.

16 Cf. מלאכה גדולה אני עשה (v. 3a). ואנחנו עשים במלאכה מעלות השחר עד צאת הכוכבים with מלאכה גדולה אני עשה. That 4:15 has been reworked with the phrase "and the half of them were holding the spears" is generally acknowledged.

which Nehemiah, as an assiduous builder, is resolved not to "relax" (v. 3) and attend to other business.[17]

The depiction in 6:2-4 resembles the motif of the "Relentless Builder" in many building inscriptions from the ancient Near East. With respect to Ps 132:3-5, Weinfeld has pointed to the depiction of Gudea building Eninnu: "For the sake of building the house for his master, he slept not nights, nor rested the head at noon" (cf. the use of רפה in Neh 6:3).[18] In studying the motif of "The Untiring Temple Builder," [19] Hurowitz observes that in "The Curse of Agade," Inanna goes without sleep in order to do good things for Agade (i.e., as she is building the temple and city).[20] This portrayal may compared to inscriptions from Šulgi, Nebuchadnezzar I and Nabonidus. With regard to Assyrian texts, one hears of the kings exerting themselves, becoming exhausted, yet not being negligent. Especially noteworthy is the inscription of Tiglath-pileser I reporting the building of the Anu and Adad temple: "the pure temple…[I] planned and did not desist and was not negligent in building but speedily completed [it]."[21] Insofar as this motif appears in a wide range of Northwest Semitic texts, it may have informed the composition of 6:2a, 3-4, which idealizes Nehemiah, in line with the great kings, as both one who was an indefatigable builder and without whom progress on the wall was impossible.[22]

While vv. 2a, 3-4 make sense against the backdrop provided by this motif, v. 2b complicates the meaning of the passage. Now we do not know whether Nehemiah really was intent on finishing the "great work." Indeed, the reader is confused into thinking that the response in v. 3 was meant ironically or was simply afraid to meet with Sanballat and Geshem. Since without v. 2b the repetition of the same answer becomes easier to interpret (i.e. as an indication of Nehemiah's resolve), the reason given to the reader may very well be the product of a *relecture*.[23] In any case, both it and its context serve the same ideological purposes: (1) They emphasize that the success of the building enterprise depends upon the presence of a great leader (v. 3b). (2) They present an image of this prototypical leader – one who is a fervent builder of Jerusalem and whom power does not distract from the "great work" for the province (v. 3a). And (3) they expose the dangers of diplomatic relations with Judah's neighbors insofar as Sanballat and Geshem were only devising to injure its representative (v. 2b).

---

17 רפה *hiph.* means both "to abandon" and "to relax."
18 Cylinder A XVII 7-9. Weinfeld (1992: 48).
19 Cf. 1992: 324f. Hurowitz, however, has not mentioned Nehemiah's account in this context.
20 Line 24. Cf. Kramer's translation in *ANET*, 647 b 1.24.
21 *AKA* (Budge and King) 101, 102 VIII 17-21.
22 Significantly, vv. 5-9 treat the rumors that Nehemiah aspired to become Judah's *king*.
23 This is the conclusion of Winckler (1901: 480-481).

7.4.2 The Builder's Royal Prerogatives – VV. 5-9

Turning now to vv. 5-9, I suggest that this passage functions didactically. Its authors, by reporting Sanballat's unsavory proposal to "take counsel together" (v. 7b) and to discuss the Judeans' insurrectionist plans, make a sharp distinction between the building of the wall and reestablished autonomy it symbolizes, on the one hand, and the use of the fortification to rebel against the empire, on the other. Although Nehemiah is a relentless builder, he has no intentions of reigning and has not taken advantage of venal prophets to proclaim his kingship. Sanballat has simply invented (כי מלבך אתה בודאם, v. 8b) what he claims to be rumors among the nations. Implicit in this response is that all those who anticipate an (eschatological) reestablishment of the monarchy after the restoration of Jerusalem join with Judah's enemies in misconstruing Nehemiah's intentions.[24]

According to the formulation of v. 5, Sanballat makes these allegations in a letter which he sends "a fifth time in like manner" (כדבר הזה פעם חמישית). Upon closer inspection, one notices that the author has employed the expression כדבר הזה improperly. In v. 4, the expression, occurring twice, means "according to this word"[25] and refers clearly to the *contents* of messages in v. 2a and v. 3. However, the letter sent by Sanballat the fifth time contains a wholly different message. Williamson translates כדבר הזה with the ambiguous phrase "in the same way." Accordingly, it refers to the message itself in v. 4, yet to the medium of communication in v. 5.[26] Blenkinsopp avoids this equivocation by rendering the expression in two different ways: "the same message/answer" and "in the same way."[27] Insofar as the manner of correspondence in vv. 2-4 differs from that in vv. 5-9,[28] כדבר הזה has been employed correctly in v. 4, yet falsely in v. 5.

Before dismissing the misuse of the expression in v. 5 as a minor error or deleting it as an "erroneous repetition,"[29] we should observe that it belongs inseparably to the continuation פעם חמישית. The author has clearly the formulation in v. 4 in view: כדבר הזה ארבע פעמים. Most noteworthy is the reading of v. 5 transmitted in the LXX[BAℵ]: "Then Sanaballat sent his servant to me with an open letter in his hand." Since even most modern scholars have overlooked the discrepancy in the MT, one should probably not assume that the LXX repre-

---

24 Cf. Gunneweg (1988: 96) and, most recently, Karrer (2001: 188).
25 One may compare the use of the expression, e.g., in Gen 32,19 and כדברים האלה in vv. 7-8.
26 1985: 247.
27 1988: 265.
28 Cf. Batten (1913: 252). In vv. 5-9, Sanballat sends his servant with a letter (vv. 5b-6aα"). Conversely, the author of vv. 2-4 is not specific as to the type of communication chosen by Sanballat *and Geshem*. Cf. the ambiguous לאמר.
29 1913: 261.

sents a correction of its *Vorlage*. If the latter contains an earlier reading,[30] it provides the first evidence that redactors have integrated vv. 5-9 with its present literary setting.

The second clue supporting this possibility is found in v. 7b, which resembles v. 2aβ (cf. לכה ונועצה יחדו with ועתה לכה ונועצה יחדו). Since vv. 6-7 follow the Hebrew epistolary tradition (with ואגרת פתוחה describing the type of the letter, כתוב בה introducing the contents of the letter, and ועתה marking the transition to the objective), the repetition of clauses beginning with ועתה in v. 7, which is unparalleled in both Hebrew-Canaanite as well as ancient Aramaic epistolary forms,[31] deserves an explanation. Most commentators reckon with two meanings of this particle or simply avoid translating the first (following the LXX and Vulgate). A possibility they have overlooked is that the second clause constitutes a new conclusion to the letter.[32] While Nehemiah explicitly declines the offer in the first paragraph (v. 3aβ), he does not even refer to an offer in the second paragraph. Inasmuch as the reasons for the meeting are dismissed, Sanballat receives an implicit answer to his petition.

Nevertheless, questions remain for the reader: What is the purpose of the letter? Does its sender aim to threaten the recipient, so that he takes fright and abandons his building project?[33] Or does he really expect the recipient to accept the repeated invitation? If the latter were the case, then it would remain inexplicable that Sanballat first assures Nehemiah that the king will be told of his alleged monarchic aspirations. Instead of a stimulus, the warning would have made Nehemiah even less eager to finally come to the meeting. While the letter in vv. 5-9, just as the first messages in vv. 2-4, aims to bring about the cessation of the building, its contents differ substantially: Nehemiah should refute the rumors about his ulterior motives by stopping the construction.[34] Once he desists from building the wall, no one would be able to accuse him of aspiring to be king. Hence, the proposal to meet is appropriate in vv. 2-4, yet is incongruous in vv. 5-9. In consideration of both the discrepancy between the purpose of

---

30 Cf. esp. καὶ ἀπέστειλαν πρός με ὡς τὸ ῥῆμα τοῦτο καὶ ἀπέστειλα αὐτοῖς κατὰ ταῦτα. It is indeed peculiar that Sanballat and Geshem sent a message "four times" and then Sanballat a message alone "a fifth time." If it were original, the LXX would have no reason to alter it. However, v. 4 may have been added to emphasize that Nehemiah remained determined to finish his task. Or "four times" may simply represent a reworking of פְּעָמִים, "a couple (several) times."

31 Cf. most recently Schwiederski (2000: 55ff., 155ff., and 250ff.).

32 Pardee remarks that "the marker of transition ועתה occurs twice in v 7." An explanation is sought by arguing that "as in Jer 29:27, its function here is not specifically epistolary" (1982: 179). Yet v. 6 introduces the contents with the quotation formula, כתוב בה, and what follows is reported with direct speech. The repetition is thus unanticipated. For a general discussion of the use of transition ועתה, cf. Brongers (1965).

33 This intention is explicitly declared in v. 9a.

34 That the letter is described as open, ואגרת פתוחה, is difficult to understand; cf. Jer 32:11, 14. For a helpful discussion of the problem, see Williamson (1985: 256).

the letter and the repetition of ועתה, we may conclude that the petition in v. 7b has been supplemented according to the contents of the first message.

If this conclusion is permitted, the offer to "take counsel together" may be understood as portraying Sanballat with seditious ambitions. We have already seen that יעץ + יחדו carries pronounced conspiratorial overtones. After he already accused Nehemiah of aspiring to become king and warning that the court would surely hear about these aspirations, Sanballat would have committed a grave error by meeting with a potential insurgent.[35] While the proposed consultation in v. 7b does not make sense from the original rationale of the letter, it may represent an attempt by a later hand to impute an insurrectionist motive to Sanballat.

Another indication that vv. 5-9 have been integrated into their context is found in v. 7aα. Here Sanballat expands his allegations (וגם), claiming that Nehemiah had appointed prophets to proclaim in Jerusalem that there is a king in Judah. That a redactor is responsible for this remark appears likely insofar as it positioned after the accusation: "and you will become their king – according to these things" (v. 6b). Assuming that these verses were composed simultaneously, one must explain the presence of v. 6b. V. 7aα suffices to express Nehemiah's monarchical aspirations and renders v. 6b superfluous. So too, the clause is formulated with the *qatal*, which contrasts with the participles in v. 6. In introducing a new thought into the passage (the corruptibility the prophets), it creates tensions with the continuation of the narrative in vv. 10-14. Once Sanballat had accused him of appointing prophets to proclaim his kingship, Nehemiah would have committed a major *faux pas* by entering the house of a prophet (v. 10a) immediately thereafter. It is much more plausible to assume that the author of v. 7aα has integrated an aspect of the following paragraph into the account.[36] The reason for this editorial activity is apparent. With the inclusion of v. 7aα, Sanballat presents the prophets in Judah as prone to venality and later Nehemiah confirms this claim (cf. v. 12).

Finally, v. 9a deserves consideration. In this כי-clause, Nehemiah addresses his readers directly, describing what motivated his enemies' actions: "For they all were making us afraid, saying, 'Their hands shall be weakened from the work so that it be not done.'" A later hand has probably supplemented this remark, since the plural subject and object (כי כלם מיראים אותנו) do not suit the context.[37] While Sanballat cooperates with Geshem in vv. 2-4, he acts alone in vv. 5-9. So too, their intention in vv. 2-4 was to frighten (ירא, *piel*) neither Nehemiah nor

---

35 Cf. Batten (1913: 254).
36 The "prophets" in v. 7aα may refer to those identified by name in v. 14b.
37 That the clause is redactional was also the opinion of Batten (1913: 254f.).

the Judeans. Rather, they wished to *distract* him from the building.[38] Moreover, Nehemiah alone is the object of their machinations in these verses, and thus neither the plural object in v. 9aα (אותנו) nor the verb (מיראים) agrees with the formulation of the passage. In the second paragraph, conversely, Sanballat's aim was indeed to intimidate, but again it seems that he was interested in only "weakening" Nehemiah's hands (cf. 9b).

One can adduce additional evidence for the redactional character of v. 9a. First, it employs expressions from its context. For instance, כלם מיראים אותנו has been formulated almost exactly like the last clause of the imprecation in v. 14. But while the subject is clearly defined in v. 14, the reader of v. 9aα requires the redactional v. 1 to understand the reference to "all of them." Likewise, the continuation of v. 9aα employs the vocabulary as Nehemiah's response in v. 3b.

Second, v. 9b (ועתה חזק את־ידי) sticks out from its literary surroundings. Many of the English versions read it as prayer, adding the words "O my God." Yet, as Williamson correctly points out, Nehemiah's ejaculatory prayers are always clearly marked by the inclusion of the vocative אלהי. Williamson construes חזק as "an inf abs doing service for a finite verb" and translates "but in fact I continued with even greater determination."[39] The problem with this rendering is that the ועתה "cannot refer to the past."[40] Significantly, Sanballat's letter concludes with ועתה, and thus the best approach to this clause would be to include it as the final clause of Nehemiah's response. The meaning may very well be that Nehemiah would now increase his industriousness (cf. the LXX). If the form represents a corruption of אחזק, then the author responsible for v. 9a could have misunderstood its original intent, inserting the remark that "their hands will be weakened from the work" (cf. חזק את־ידי with ירפו ידיהם).

That vv. 2-4 have been composed as a prelude to the following paragraph is indicated furthermore by the way they develop features from the latter. Both texts describe diplomatic correspondence. Yet whereas Sanballat is alone the sender in vv. 5-9 and refers to Geshem only in passing, he and Geshem act together in vv. 2-4. And while v. 5 depicts Sanballat sending his servant with a letter in his hand, v. 2 simply states that Sanballat and Geshem "sent" to Nehemiah.[41] Thus, we "learn for the first time that Sanballat had been using his נער [...] to act as an intermediary."[42]

---

38 While Nehemiah maintains in v. 2b that they wished to cause him harm, this was not their professed purpose.

39 1985: 246, 249.

40 Clines (1984: 174).

41 The use of לאמר in comparison with כתוב (v. 6) does not indicate that Sanballat and Geshem sent oral messages while Sanballat alone sent a written message (*pace* Batten 1913:252). לאמר is often used to introduce the contents of letters; cf., e.g., 1 Kgs 21:8-9; 2 Kgs 5:6; 10:1-2.

42 Williamson (1985: 255).

7.4.3 The Priority and Purpose of VV. 5-9

Insofar as foregoing analysis has demonstrated that redactors expanded vv. 5-9 with features of both the preceding (vv. 5aβ, 7b, 9aβ) and following (vv. 7aα, 9aα) paragraphs, it warrants the conclusion that the passage is older than its context. While vv. 2-4 correspond, as we have seen, to the emphasis on the assiduousness of the builders in 4:9ff.,[43] Sanballat's enmity is well suited to the censure of Sanballat in 3:33ff. and 4:1ff. Compared to the foregoing paragraph, vv. 5-9 would also provide a better continuation to these texts. Here Sanballat's intention remains to intimidate. If v. 7b indeed constitutes a supplement, he would not have petitioned Nehemiah to come to a conference.[44] His only aim would have been to discourage him by reporting the surrounding nations' perception of the builders', and especially their leader's, motives.

Because vv. 10-14 never refer to the building, we may consider the possibility that vv. 5-9* were composed directly for the notice of the completion of the building in vv. 15-16.[45] Between 3:38* and 6:15f., this paragraph implies that Sanballat, who has already been portrayed acting alone (cf. 3:33ff.), recognized that his tactics of jeering (2:19, 3:33ff.) and violence (4:1ff.) were to no avail. He then resorted to defamation, the purpose of which was to "dishearten" the leader of the builders (cf. 3:38b). By intimidating the one who is indispensable to the progress of the restoration (cf. 6:3b), he could efficiently obstruct the building enterprise. Despite this sly strategy, Nehemiah returns to the work (6:9b) and "the wall was completed on the twenty-fifth of Elul after fifty-two days" (6:15).

Whereas Nehemiah describes in chaps. 2-4* how he inspired his fellow Judeans and cooperated with them, in 6:2-9 he is no longer concerned to validate his position and to receive recognition for his accomplishment. Rather, his name already possesses symbolic authority, and his words carry considerable influence. The authors both presume that the reader is interested in his political viewpoint (i.e., Judah must occupy a subordinate position in relation to the empire) and enhance his self-portrait by depicting him as a leader fully committed to Jerusalem's restoration (vv. 2-4).

The composition of vv. 5-9 witnesses a developing tradition that identified the repair of the wall as an accomplishment of Nehemiah. The maturation of this tradition seem to be already presupposed in vv. 2-4, where Nehemiah

---

43 The author of 6:2-4 could have been inspired by the portrayal of the Judeans' industry in 4:9ff. to present Nehemiah as a "tireless builder" who does not pause from his "great work" to meet with the representatives of neighboring lands.

44 We have noted in the preceding chapter that Sanballat's and Geshem's nonchalant petition to come together in vv. 2-4 poses an incoherency for the reader who knows that Sanballat and the rest of Judah's enemies had just mounted an attack on Jerusalem (4:1ff.).

45 The following section provides a further defense of this thesis.

claims all responsibility for the "great work" and assumes that his absence would prevent its progress (v. 3). Independent evidence for the existence of this tradition is furnished by Sirach's *Laus patrus* (early second century), from which we know that later generations did not extol him as one who merely inspired the building project, but rather as one who was exclusively responsible for it: "Nehemiah, glorious is his memory! – Who raised up our ruins, – And healed our breaches, – And set up doors and bars" (49:13).[46]

Sirach's praise is furthermore instructive as it illustrates that Nehemiah was also considered as an early proponent of the movement in Judah toward autonomy. Nehemiah belongs to the final figures to receive acclaim before the all-surpassing panegyric for the high priest, Simon ben Jochanan (chap. 50). Significantly, the government of the latter is eulogized for organizing construction projects in Jerusalem that increased the security of the city: the fortification of the temple (v. 1), the construction of the wall (v. 2) and the pool (v. 3; cf. Neh 2:14), and the security of the people and city (v. 4) – all aspects of Nehemiah's restoration project according to the present shape of the first-person account. In this regard, one should compare 1 Macc 14:10, 2 Macc 1:10-2:18, and *1 Enoch* 89:72f., which also demonstrate that the building of the wall and the name of Nehemiah were identified with the political developments of the Hasmonean period.

Although vv. 2-4 present Nehemiah, in analogy to royal building inscriptions from the ancient Near East, as an "indefatigable builder," vv. 5-9 clarify that he did not arrogate to himself the kingship associated with the construction of a city wall. If the latter passage was written by Nehemiah, it lacks significance. His contemporary readers would have known that he did not assume royal prerogatives. Conversely, for generations from the mid-fourth cent. BCE onwards, the text would have contained a highly polemical message. The readers who consider the heroic builder of Jerusalem as an advocate of Judean autonomy or the reestablishment of the monarchy must identify themselves with non-Judeans and especially with the archenemy, Sanballat. Nehemiah's response speaks directly to this political movement: "There are no such things done as you say, but you are fabricating them out of your heart. Now I will strengthen my hands" (vv. 8, 9b). In repudiating the claims and ascribing them to an assumption made by the enemy, he effectively emphasizes the point that a monarchy is not a suitable form of government for the new Judah.

---

46 Of course, Sirach presents Israel's history as a sequence of the acts of great men, so that one might expect him to disregard the cooperation of others. Nevertheless, he could have portrayed Nehemiah as one "who guided us as we rebuilt our ruins" instead of simply "who rebuilt our ruins." Cf. the attention he gives to the people at the time of Hezekiah (48:19-20) and Simon (chap. 50).

In the following section, we turn our attention to the rest of the chapter and, independently of our present conclusions, test the hypothesis that vv. 10-14 have been inserted between vv. 5-9 and vv. 15-16.

The Composition of Neh 6:1-9

1 Now it came to pass as Sanballat *and Tobiah*, and Geshem the Arab, and the rest of our enemies heard that I had built the wall and that no breach remained,
    although at that time I had not set up the doors upon the gates
2 Then Sanballat and Geshem sent unto me, saying, "Come, let us meet together in Hakkephirim in the plain of Ono."
    But they thought to do me mischief.
3 And I sent messengers unto them, saying, "I am doing a great work, so that I cannot come down. Why should the work cease, while I leave it and come down to you?"
4 Yet they sent unto me [four] several times (פְּעָמִים) in this way, and I answered them in the same way.
5 Then sent Sanballat his servant unto me
    in this way a fifth time
with an open letter in his hand, 6 wherein was written: "It is reported among the nations, and Gashmu says it, that you and the Jews think to rebel. For this reason you are building the wall. And you will become their king,
    according to these words.
        7 Also you have appointed prophets to proclaim of you in Jerusalem, saying, 'There is a king in Judah.'
and now shall it be reported to the king according to these words.
    Come now therefore and let us take counsel together."
8 Then I sent unto him, saying, "There are no such things done as you say, but you are fabricating them out of your heart."
        9 For they all were making us afraid, saying, "Their hands shall be weakened from the work, that it be not done."
Now, [I will] strengthen my hands.

7.5 The Notice of Completion (VV. 15-16)
in the Context of VV. 10-19

The remaining portion of chap. 6 can be divided into three units: vv. 10-14, which recount Nehemiah's encounter with Shemaiah; vv. 15-16, which report the date of completion and the reaction of the Judeans' enemies and the surrounding nations; and vv. 17-19, which describe the exchange of letters between Tobiah and the Judean nobility. Our primary aim in this section is to determine the relationship of the middle unit (vv. 15-16) to its context.

7.5.1 Nehemiah's Encounter with Shemaiah – VV. 10-14

The first paragraph has provoked, and continues to provoke, a considerable amount of discussion from scholarship relative to the attention given to the rest of the chapter. Because so many facets of the account are completely obscure to the modern reader, the most advisable approach is to admit our ignorance and to advance our conclusions with the utmost caution. Many have boldly claimed that later editors have heavily reworked the text, while asserting that the rest of the chapter faithfully reflects Nehemiah's formulation. The first claim is occasioned by several incoherencies in the text.[47] However, the assumption that the author of the passage was also responsible for the rest of the chapter cannot account for the fundamental incongruity with the foregoing passage (vv. 5-9). It is difficult to conceive, as observed above, why Nehemiah would enter the house of Shemaiah, who was presumably a prophet,[48] after Sanballat had just accused him of appointing prophets in Jerusalem to proclaim his kingship (v. 7aα). Indeed, one would expect him to the steer clear from all mantic figures, so that Sanballat would lack any evidence for the rumors he supposedly heard. Although it has gone largely unnoticed in the discussion of the passage, Kellermann recognized the problem and proposed that vv. 10-14 recount an

---

47 First, by removing the second line of Shemaiah's oracle in v. 10 (אל־תוך ההיכל, "into the midst of the temple"), the remaining parts evince a *parallelismus membrorum*:

> "Let us meet in the House of God,
>   And let close the doors of the temple.
> For they are coming to kill you,
>   Yea in the night, they are coming to kill you!"

Second, the reason for the addition to the oracle may be linked to Nehemiah's later – more pious – reason for not accepting Shemaiah's offer ("Should one as I enter the temple and live?" v. 11aβ). If this line were integral to the passage, we would expect it to precede Nehemiah's first response ("And I said, 'Should such a man like me flee?'" v. 11aα). Although Nehemiah could have had two reasons for not acceding to Shemaiah's petition (cf. Williamson [1985: 259]), one must acknowledge that according to the present wording, Nehemiah first argues on the basis of his position and honor and only secondarily out of concern for the sanctity of the temple. Instead of assuming that Nehemiah regarded his own honor more than that of the temple, we may conclude that the second reason has been appended to the first. Third, in v. 13a Nehemiah refers to the action of entering the temple as sin (וחטאתי). If this *qatal* form denotes finality to the *wayyiqtol* forms (למען־אירא ואעשה־כן), then we cannot explain why the following clause is also formulated in the perfect (היה להם לשם רע). Thus, one can not rule out the possibility that וחטאתי has been inserted. Fourth, the parts of the passage resemble strikingly 2 Chr 26:16-20; 27:2, where Uzziah enters the sanctuary and later dies. In light of these observations, we follow Hölscher (1923: 536), Rudolph (1949: 137), Mowinckel (1964: 45), Kellermann (1967: 22f.), Gunneweg (1987: 97f.), and Karrer (2001: 137f.) in concluding that the text has been reworked to underscore Nehemiah's piety for not entering the temple. Cf. a further discussion of the passage, cf. Ivry (1972) and Carroll (1992).

48 Although his occupation is not certain from v. 10a (והוא עצור, the meaning of which is fully uncertain), this is surely to be inferred from v. 12b, which describes the word he utters in v. 10b as a prophecy: כי הנבואה דבר עלי.

episode prior to the ones reported in vv. 2-9. The passage is said to show that "Nehemia einen Anhaltspunkt für diesen Verdacht zugestehen muß, den er nun seinerseits in der NQ [=Nehemia-Quelle] ins rechte Licht rücken will."[49] However, the suggestion cannot claim textual support. Adopting Galling's description of the narration,[50] Kellermann argued that the switch to the *qatal* and the emphasis of the subject in v. 10 signifies a flashback to the time before the events recounted in vv. 2-9. Yet not only does this interpretation strain the grammatical and syntactical differences, but we would also expect the narrator to explicitly indicate the flashback, as he does in 13:4.[51]

Seeking a more tenable solution to the incoherency, the preceding analysis has demonstrated that v. 7aα, which repeats v. 6b and which also alternates to the *qatal*, has been inserted in order to introduce the central theme of vv. 10-14 (the venality of the prophets) into vv. 5-9.[52] These findings do not require the assumption that vv. 10-14 have been composed simultaneously with earliest layer of vv. 5-9. To the contrary, it seems likely in view of the transition from the conclusion of the account to v. 15 that only a late hand could have drafted the account of Nehemiah's encounter with Shemaiah. The paragraphs of the building report have been arranged according to an alternation of progress and interruption.[53] Thus, before Nehemiah can report that the wall is finished (v. 15), he must affirm that Sanballat's tactic was again unsuccessful and that the work continued. Yet the conclusion of vv. 10-14 does not report any progress. Indeed the whole passage does not refer – even indirectly – to the work on the wall; instead, it focuses solely on the opposition presented by Tobiah, Sanballat, Shemaiah and the rest of the prophets. Where then does Nehemiah state that he continued the work? While v. 4b ("and I answered them according to this word") does not provide a conceivable transition, v. 9b is just what we would expect. The idiom with חזק *piel* and יד appears also in 2:18b (ויחזקו ידיהם לטובה), which describes the commencement of the construction. Insofar as the reciprocity of progress and opposition characterizes the narration of the building report, Nehemiah's response in v. 9 ("And now I will strengthen my hands") appears to have been composed directly for the notice of completion in v. 15. And since the passage in vv. 10-14 severs this join, we must attribute it to an editorial hand.

Additional support for this assertion is provided by the list of the antagonists in v. 1. While the names of Sanballat and Geshem as well as "the rest of our

---

49   1967: 180.
50   1954: 229.
51   ולפני מזה, cf. בימים ההם in 6:17, 13:15, 23.
52   The problem posed by the sequence of v. 7aα and vv. 10-14 only becomes more acute when one recognizes the probability that the account of Nehemiah's encounter with Shemaiah has been composed later than vv. 5-9.
53   Cf. the discussion of the שמע-schema in §3.2.

enemies" all begin with a ל, Tobiah's name lacks the dative preposition. Recognizing this anomaly, most scholars have concluded that the name is a gloss that supplements the names of Sanballat and Geshem – the *dramatis personae* in the following verses – with the name of the third antagonist.[54] Significantly, the main culprit in vv. 10-14 is Tobiah; it is quite unusual for the building report that Sanballat here is not mentioned before Tobiah.[55] Now if the missing ל before טוביה in v. 1 indeed indicates that the list has been altered from its original wording, the main culprit in vv. 10-14 would not have been originally included in this heading to the chapter. Tobiah's name may well have been inserted in v. 1 together with the composition of vv. 10-14 in order to introduce the remaining antagonist in the final building phase.

The use of the word יעד ("meet") in v. 10bα also merits attention. Since the two figures are already together, we would anticipate Shemaiah's petition to be "let us go" (נלכה) or נבואה) to the temple.[56] Assuming, moreover, that Nehemiah is reporting here the actual wording – couched in poetic form – of the prophecy (הנבואה), one finds it difficult to explain that Shemaiah employs the very same term that appears in Sanballat's and Geshem's first messages (v. 2a; cf. also v. 7b). Were, however, the author of vv. 10-14 writing after vv. 2-9 had been composed, it would be easy to account for Shemaiah's petition "to meet" the temple. And to this argument, one may add the appearance of שלח in v. 12a ("And I perceived that God had not sent him"), a verb encountered frequently in the surrounding text (vv. 2, 3, 4, 5, 8, 19). The author of vv. 10-14 seems to have been intended to put a new twist on this word.

This conclusion – that vv. 10-14 are younger, not older, than vv. 5-9 – has considerable consequences for our investigation of the development of the building report. The previous section attempted to demonstrate that vv. 2-4 and 5-9 do not represent indispensable portions of the first-person account. Insofar as the analysis of chap. 4 has exposed a primary literary stratum that describes Judah's neighbors planning an attack as they hear that the construction was already finished, it confirms our working hypothesis that 3:38aα (ונבנה את־) החומה) has employed the expression from 2:18bα (ונבנה את־חומת ירושלם) to recount the completion of the building. The only text before 6:15-16 yet to be investigated is chap. 5. For the present, we may assume with several scholars that this chapter was inserted at a later stage in the composition of the building report. We have thus found no compelling literary evidence in 4:1-19 or 6:1-14 that would invalidate the conclusion that 3:38* was originally connected to 6:15.

---

54 Batten (1913: 249), Hölscher (1923: 536), Rudolph (1949: 134), Galling (1954: 227), Mowinckel (1964: 28), Kellermann (1967: 22-n. 71), Gunneweg (1987: 93), Williamson (1985: 248 – undecided).

55 Cf. 2:10, 19; 3:33, and 4:1.

56 יעד always means meeting or coming together when two or more entities are separated.

In keeping with the concern of this study for the entire maturation process, the following discussion attempts to answer what the passage of vv. 10-14 contributes to its context.

First, the transition to the episode is very abrupt. The reader does not know what occasioned a visit to the house of Shemaiah and the nature of his condition.[57] Hitherto, the opponents had attempted to eliminate Nehemiah by diverting his attention (vv. 2-4) and by intimidation (vv. 5-9). Now they are now coming to murder him in the night. "As stated here, the proposal does not make good sense. According to 4:1ff. and 5:13ff.,[58] Nehemiah had an armed retinue at his disposal and had no need to take refuge in the temple in order to save his skin. Up to this point, we have been given no indication that the situation was desperate enough for him to seek sanctuary...."[59]

After the exciting introduction, the conclusion to the account is disappointing. Just as the reader waits in vain for a thrilling battle story in chap. 4, so does s/he learn now that there was no assassination plot. Indeed, the enemy had planned to assassinate only his character (v. 13). While the lack of action dissatisfies, the depiction agrees with the tenor of chap. 6 in which Nehemiah alone is responsible for the progress on the wall and the opposition is aimed solely at him. Although vv. 10-14 do not portray him building, it does expand the theme of opposition. And it is noteworthy that this opposition aims to cause to the *person* of Nehemiah exactly what inspired the community to undertake the restoration project. According to v. 13, Shemaiah was hired so that Nehemiah would take fright, act according to his suggestion and sin, "so that they might have a bad name with which they could reproach me."

Here the sequence of שם רע ("bad name") and חרף (*piel*, "reproach") brings unavoidably to mind Hanani's report that the inhabitants in Judah are in רעה גדולה and חרפה (1:3a). In §4.3.1, we saw that this report draws directly upon the wording of 2:17, where Nehemiah draws attention to the condition of רעה and presents the building of the wall as the means of redressing Judah's חרפה. In contrast to 2:17, the report in 1:3 separates רעה and חרפה from the condition of the wall and relegates the latter to an afterthought. The separation and diminution of the importance of the building project prepares the way for the developments in chaps. 5 and 13, where Nehemiah notices that the recalcitrant רעה (cf. 13:7, 18, 27) and חרפה (cf. 5:8) cannot be remedied simply by the construc-

---

57 The parallels between v. 10a and Ezek 8:1ff. are evident. The prophet is sitting in his house and the elders of Judah are sitting before him when the hand of YHWH falls upon him. Therefore, the phrase והוא עצור, which has occasioned an interminable discussion, should probably be interpreted as "in ecstasy." Cf. Kutsch (1952). V. 10b accordingly contains the words of his oracle.

58 While 4:1ff. may postdate this passage, 5:1ff. must be earlier since 6:14 presupposes 5:19. See below.

59 Blenkinsopp (1988: 270).

tion of the wall. Since they necessitate a radical approach, he undertakes "extra-mural" reforms. Finally, the accounts of these reforms and 6:10-14 not only lack a notice that the construction advanced,[60] but they also conclude with זכרה-prayers.[61]

These findings commend two important conclusions. First, it seems that the authors of vv. 10-14, just as those responsible for 1:1-4, 5:1-13 and 13:4ff., have intended to highlight and reinterpret the two central terms in the building account: רעה and חרפה. "Whereas the object of reproach had been the sorry state of Jerusalem and the survivors in chapters 1 and 2, narrowed down to the builders in chapters 3 and 4, the object of reproach in 6:1-7:3 is Nehemiah himself."[62] This explains the appearance of the imprecation in v. 14. Without the introduction "and I prayed to the God of Heaven" (cf. 1:5), the text forces the reader to re-pray Nehemiah's words. Similar to the way one relives the antago-nism experienced by the psalmist in praying the words of the Psalter,[63] the reader re-utters Nehemiah's imprecation and identifies him- or herself with this hero, who in turn underwent in his life what the Judeans experienced in their social existence.

Second, the noted lexical parallels between vv. 10-14 and chaps. 5 and 13 encourage us to read v. 14 as concluding a literary unit (consisting of vv. 1-14). A characteristic feature of chaps. 5 and 13 is that each respective paragraph concludes with זכרה-prayer (cf. 5:19; 13:14, 22, 29 and 31). The only other place where this so-called "Gedächtnismotiv" occurs is 6:14: "Remember, O my God, Tobiah and Sanballat according to his works...." Here it is evident that the author is playing on the formulation of the prayers in 5:19 (cf. "Remember me, O my God, for *good* for all that I did" with "Remember, O my God, *Tobiah* for all his deeds").[64] Insofar as a new unit commences after each זכרה-prayer in chaps. 5 and 13, we may be quite confident that the presence of the same in v. 14 indicates that the author of vv. 10-14 considered v. 15 as the beginning of a new paragraph. Accordingly, 6:1-14 concludes in the same way as the preceding section (5:1-19). In §§8.2 and 9.2.2, we will observe that 13:4ff. was probably composed as the continuation of 6:19. If so, a pattern emerges: One after the other and without interruption, the five passages surrounding the notice of completion (6:15-16) – 5:1-19; 6:1-14; 6:17-19 + 13:4-14; 13:15-22; 13:23-29(30-31) – all conclude with זכרה-prayers.[65] In §8.2, we discuss the significance of

---

60 Cf. 5:16 and 13:19-22, which presupposes the completion of the building.

61 Cf. 5:19; 6:14; 13:14, 23 and 31.

62 Throntveit (1992: 84f.).

63 Cf. Watts (1992) and Erbele-Küster (2001).

64 זכרה אלהי לטוביה [ולסנבלט] כמעשיו אלה וגו׳/זכרה־לי אלהי לטובה כל אשר־עשיתי על־העם הזה.

65 And, anticipating our analysis of chap. 13, the three passages after the notice of completion in 6:15-16 begin with the expression "and in those days" and are formulated with participles: 6:17-19 + 13:4-14; 13:15-22; 13:23ff.

these findings in refuting the influential thesis that the first-person account consists of two separate works, a building report and a later text documenting the provincial reforms, which either Nehemiah or a later editor combined.

7.5.2 The Completion of the Building – VV. 15-16

It seems quite certain that v. 15 constitutes an original part of the building account. While the verse sticks out in its present context, there is no reason it should have been interpolated. That it probably predates all of 4:1-6:14 is supported by the parallels to other building accounts. Hurowitz has assembled a large number of ancient Near Eastern building inscriptions that conclude both with the dates of the respective construction projects and with the expression *šlm* (cf. החומה ותשלם).[66] While noticing that these inscriptions share much in common with Nehemiah's wall-building report, Hurowitz found nothing that is similar to the account of the attack, the financial reforms and the intimidation of the builder in 4:1-6:14. Significantly, he asserts that without these passages, what remains "is nothing more than a building account written according to the traditional format."[67]

The preceding section concluded that v. 15-16* represents the earliest portion of vv. 1-14. Insofar as this conclusion is warranted, v. 15 must have been composed as the continuation of the first-person remark that "we built the wall...for the people had a heart to work" in 3:38*. Hurowitz's remarks with regard to the connection between 3:38 and 6:15 deserve to be quoted at length:

> Chapter 3 depicts the work on the walls and describs [sic] the walls and gates themselves (3.1-32, 38).... Completion of the work is mentioned in 6.15.... At this point, the building account is linked to the account of disturbances which concludes with a prayer (for curses) in 6.14. [...] The building account and the account of the disturbances are joined by literary links at two points: 3.38 and 6.16. The account of the disturbances presupposes the building account, but the building account is not dependent to the same degree on the story of the disturbances. Removing the accounts of the disturbances as well as some additional secondary material not directly related to the building of the walls does not affect the continuity of the building story. In addition, all the "extraneous" material is well defined literarily by use of stereotyped introductory and/or closing formulae. From all this, it becomes clear that the building story is the backbone and torso of Nehemiah's memoirs, to which everything else is secondarily attached.[68]

Thus, Hurowitz argues on the basis of other building accounts that the use of ותשלם in 6:15 originally continued the statement that "we built the wall" in 3:38.

---

66 1992: 224-242.
67 Ibid.: 121.
68 Ibid.: 122f.

And he provides a long list of witnesses for the inseparability of "built" and "finished" (*banû, epēšu, rasāpu* // *šuklulu, quttû* and the like).[69] The numerous analogies presented by Hurowitz support the results of our analysis of chaps. 3-6. The placement of the building register in its present position, while contradicting the accounts in chaps. 4:1-7:1 in which the wall and the gates had not yet built, makes perfect sense if 3:38* reports the conclusion of the building.[70]

According to thesis of the present work, the original formulation of Nehemiah's building account comprises more or less 1:1a, 11b, 2:1-6*, 11, 15-18*; 3:38* and 6:15. This reconstruction resembles much more closely the parallels Hurowitz adduced. The disparities between this reconstruction and other building inscriptions are to be explained by the fact that the builder of Jerusalem's ramparts is not a king. Nehemiah must affirm that Artaxerxes granted him permission to rebuild the city's ruins, and he has done this in 1:1a, 11b, 2:1-6 following the pattern of the royal audience accounts in Egyptian and Aramaic sources. Because he was not a recognized authority in Judah, he has emphasized that the building was a communal enterprise (2:16-18 and 3:33-38).

6:15 reports that the wall was completed on the twenty-fifth of Elul after fifty-two days. Since a new year has not been mentioned, we are to assume that this is the sixth month of Artaxerxes' twentieth year (cf. 2:1). Josephus (*Ant.* 11.5.8) claims that the work continued for two years and four months. One need not give priority to this information, as Mowinckel did, unless it is assumed that Nehemiah's account originally contained the building register in 3:1-32. This register recounts a much more extensive construction enterprise than that which could be accomplished in fifty-two days. Its topographical description of Jerusalem probably applies to a later time, and is to be treated as "fictional" insofar as it depicts the builders building all the gates and the entire of the wall. We must assume, contrary to the information in the list, that most of the wall had not been destroyed. It serves not only as a "map" of Jerusalem, but also as a memorial to the generation of Judeans who followed the initiative of the high priest and who worked in unity with one another.

If the builders did not establish a new line of the wall and were content to undertake only extensive repairs of the existing ramparts, Nehemiah's account would make sense. In 2:1-6, Artaxerxes grants his cupbearer permission to rebuild the city of his fathers' graves. Likewise, instead of predicating his address in 2:17 on strategic and military strength, Nehemiah encourages the Judeans in 2:17 to repair the wall as remedy to their sociopolitical reproach. Kidner, quoted by Williamson, points out that "it is the disgrace, not the insecurity of their

---

69 Ibid.: 238ff.

70 This confirmation is even more rewarding as I discovered Hurowitz's investigation only after searching for analogies to 6:15.

position which strikes him."[71] It seems that Nehemiah and the Judeans wished
to demonstrate to their neighbors that they had restored Jerusalem from its state
of humiliation and devastation. And in order to accomplish this, they would not
have needed to rebuild the entire wall and all the gates.

This demonstration of Judah's regained sociopolitical strength to their
neighbors is exactly what Nehemiah reports after the notice of completion in v.
16. Instead of continuing to reproach them, the nations are demoralized as they
learn of the Judeans' achievement, and their self-esteem decidedly diminishes.
Since the disgraceful situation is only illustrated by Sanballat's and Tobiah's
jeering in 3:33ff. yet not limited to it, one need not identify the enemies in 6:16
with these figures. Were only these three figures intended, we would expect their
names to be listed here as in 2:19, 3:33ff., 4:1, 6:1. Only with the amplification
of the account in 4:1-6:14 (cf. esp. 6:1) are Sanballat and his cohorts to be
understood as the leader of Judah's enemies. "All our enemies" must refer, as in
4:1 and underlined by the parallelism in 6:16a, to "all the nations round about."

That 6:16 constitutes, however, an early amplification of v. 15 is quite likely.[72]
Not only do many building accounts conclude with date formulae analogous to
Neh 6:15 (cf. not least 1 Kgs 6:38 and Ezra 6:15), but also this verse Ps 118:23
may be quoted. If the Psalm does not antedate the late fourth century BCE, the
only way Neh 6:16 could be integral to the building account is if its author drew
on the words of Nehemiah's work, as some have argued.[73] Such a view cannot
be categorically dismissed since v. 23 has a quite different sense than 6:16 and
the Psalm consists of a compilation of disparate material.[74] Yet it also cannot be
ruled out that Ps 118:23 integrated Neh 6:16 after it had undergone expansion.

The last clause (v. 16bβ) seems to interpret the fact that the wall was finished
in fifty-two days as a miracle. In 6:3, Nehemiah claims, "I am doing a great
work." Similarly, the aim of the enemy according to v. 9a is to weaken the hands
of the builders so that "the work" would not be done. Describing the מלאכה as
a divine accomplishment (כי מאת אלהינו נעשתה המלאכה הזאת), this clause may
have been added to balance the non-theological depiction in vv. 2-4, 5-9. Insofar as these primary strata of these paragraphs probably constitute expansions of
the building report, as argued above, it is difficult to conceive that their authors

---

71 1985: 191.

72 The strongest argument for supplementary nature of this verse is provided in the next
    section, in which we observe that the introduction to v. 17, "in those days," refers to the
    "fifty-two days" of v. 15. With the insertion of v. 16, however, the antecedent of "those
    days" is no longer apparent to the reader.

73 Several features of this conclusion to the building account ("and all the *nations* round about
    saw and it was *incredible* in their *eyes*") are very reminiscent of passages from the prophets.
    Cf., e.g., Mic 7:15-16, Zech 8:6, Isa 52:10, 52:15, 62:2, 66:18, and Ezek 39:21.

74 For example, the remark about the cornerstone in v. 22 seems to have been influenced by
    Jer 51:26 and Isa 18:26.

composed the statements in vv. 3 and 9 without a reference to God and with the same phraseology of the explicitly theological statement in v. 16bβ. Much more conceivable is that the latter reinterprets vv. 2-9.[75]

7.5.3 Tobiah's Correspondence with the Judean Nobility (VV. 17-19) and the Increasing Significance of the Notice of Completion (V. 15)

In turning our attention now to vv. 17-19, we observe how the date in 6:15 has been interpreted as the conclusion of "the Restoration" in the fullest sense of the term – i.e., not just of the walls, but also of Judah. Up until the twenty-fifth of Elul, when the building concluded, many of the Judean nobles remained in contact with the Tobiah, to whom they had sworn allegiance (v. 18). The reader is to infer that after the completion of the walls they discontinued their collaboration with this inimical figure. Thus, simultaneous with the completion of the building project, the corruption among the aristocracy ceased.

This interpretation – that the date in vv. 15-16 represents the climax of the narrative and that vv. 17-19 describe activities before the completion of the building – appears at first to be an untenable reading of the passage. Representing the conventional approach, Blenkinsopp contends that the activities reported in this passage "need not be contemporary with the rebuilding of the wall."[76] Similarly, Karrer dates the exchange of letters after the completion of the wall: "Die Erzählung über den Mauerbau kommt also zu ihrem Ende, ohne das Thema der 'Gefahr durch äußere und innere Feinde' wirklich abzuschließen."[77]

Yet why would Nehemiah remark that the nobles began corresponding with the enemy immediately after he reports the success of the building? To explain this, many assume that the passage has been transmitted in the wrong place or that its original wording has been lost.[78] Such speculation and proposals to move the text before vv. 15-16 are, however, unwarranted. The formula (גם בימים ההם) introducing v. 17 backdates the activities of correspondence before the "Heilsdatum" in vv. 15.[79] Accordingly, this paragraph, just as the passages in 2:19-6:14, treats the opposition to the building. Yet while the latter passages report individual episodes that disrupted the progress on the wall or character-

---

75 We have already witnessed a similar theological correction of 2:16a ("what I was doing") in 2:15aβ ("what my God was placing in my heart to do"). See the analysis of Nehemiah's night ride (2:12-16) in §6.2.

76 1988: 273.

77 2001: 189.

78 Cf., e.g., Mowinckel (1916: 44; 1964:29), Hölscher (1923: 537) and Myers (1965: 139).

ized the respective stages of the building, the paragraph in vv. 17-19 describes the deleterious activities that accompanied the *whole* period of the building. In order to make plain that the corruption of the Judean nobility was not isolated to a single occasion or a single building phase, the text has been placed after the notice of completion in v. 15 and is dated to "those days" (= the "fifty-two days" in v. 15). On this view, one can account for not only the introduction with גם ("also"), which resumes the narrative in 6:1-14, but also the formulation with participles (durative) instead of the *wayyiqtol* that characterizes the narration of isolated events in the remaining account.[80]

Although the passage does not explain why the aristocracy was sending letters to Tobiah, the meaning is nonetheless clear. Written correspondence is the manner of communication with the enemy outside Jerusalem and Judah, just as in vv. 2-9.[81] Here, however, the authors have given it a new twist. Nehemiah's letters contain only negative answers to Sanballat's and Geshem's letters, yet instead of replying to the enemy, the aristocracy *initiates* the correspondence.[82] Moreover, that the letters "were going" and "coming" symbolizes the ongoing contact between the upper class and an influential neighbor. Tobiah was apparently not in Jerusalem (cf. 13:4-9). Nevertheless, he was continuing to make political encroachments into the province by way of the correspondence with the Judean nobility and *mariages de convenance* with them.

---

79 With the insertion of v. 16, the antecedent of "those days" in v. 15 is admittedly more difficult to ascertain.

80 According to a literal rendering of the v. 17a MT, the nobles of Judah "were making many their letters (which were) going to Tobiah" (מַרְבִּים חֹרֵי יְהוּדָה אִגְּרֹתֵיהֶם הוֹלְכוֹת עַל־טוֹבִיָּה). The Judeans thus did not begin their correspondence during the work on the wall, they were only increasing (מַרְבִּים) it. This reading, however, cannot be correct, for the participle should follow the subject. Moreover, the two participles (מרבים and הולכות) are fully incongruous and superfluous. Yet instead of resolving the problem by either replacing the מ before חרי יהודה (רבים מחרי יהודה) or adding another ה before הולכות, as has been done hitherto, I contend that the consonantal text is correct. When the מ is understood as the preposition "from" as the counterpart of אל (ואשר לטוביה באות אליהם), the verse makes good sense: "*from many of* the nobles of Judah [their] letters were going (מרבים חרי יהודה אגרתיהם הולכות) to Tobiah and Tobiahs's (letters) were coming to them." Therefore, instead of increasing their correspondence with Tobiah, the text states that the nobles were merely exchanging letters with this pen pal during the period of building.

81 This also corresponds to the evidence of the Elephantine papyri. See below.

82 The only exception to this is v. 19b where Tobiah sends letters directly to Nehemiah to intimidate him (אגרות שלח טוביה ליראני). This conclusion fits the passage neither conceptually (the emphasis is on the nobles' alliances with Tobiah, not on what Tobiah was doing; the latter is never the subject), nor syntactically (we would expect a participle as in vv. 17-19a not a *qatal* form). Since the description of the sending and receiving in v. 17 employs different vocabulary than שלח, and since שלח appears six times in vv. 2-14, this statement has probably been appended to the paragraph to integrate it with the paragraphs in vv. 2-14. Support for this proposal is provided by the intention of Tobiah's letter ("to intimidate me"), which is exactly what we encounter also in vv. 2-14 (cf. vv. 9, 13, and 14).

That the nobles are sending letters to the enemy as the building progresses is surprising. Chap. 4 depicts this group cooperating in the work and arming themselves as Sanballat and his cohorts prepare to attack Jerusalem. It is difficult to explain that the nobles were communicating with Tobiah and reporting his good deeds to Nehemiah at the same time ("in those days") as Tobiah was planning to act violently against their city.[83] The building register (3:1-32), which must have been inserted at an early stage, presents the high priest and Meshullam ben Berechiah (3:1, 4, 30) as prominent contributors to the building project. These two figures, however, were also allied with Tobiah according to the notices in 6:18; 13:4-9, 27-28. And these notices probably contain historically accurate information. We have independent evidence that Yedoniah and his colleagues sent a letter to Bagohi (Bigvai), the governor of Judah, petitioning for support to rebuild the temple in Yeb (*TAD* A4.7, which is dated to 407 BCE). They also claim to have sent a letter "to Delaiah and Shelemiah the sons of Sanballat governor of Samaria" (l. 29).[84]

While it has certainly been adapted to the narrative of the building report, valuable historical information is to be found vv. 17-19. The next time we hear about "the nobles of Judah" is in 13:15ff. (cf. v. 17) where Nehemiah notices that they were continuing production of goods on the Sabbath. Their industry and commerce was apparently jeopardized by the centralized province that could impose regulations and taxation. Similar to landed gentry in other places and times, it was in the interests of the Judean nobility in the late Persian and early Hellenistic periods that the province remained decentralized. To counterbalance the focus of power in Jerusalem made possible by the restoration of the city, the nobles allied themselves with Tobiah – probably already in the late fourth century.[85] Hence, the alliance between the aristocracy and Tobiah constituted a centripetal force that threatened this consolidation.

In order to understand why later authors would have expanded the building account with criticisms of both figures, it is important to note that the Tobiads and Sanballatids allowed their presence to be felt in Judah for many years after Nehemiah. Thus, we know from the papyri from Wâdi ed-Dâliyeh that a second

---

83 Cf. Grabbe (1998: 49).

84 The approval of Bagohi and Delaiah is found in *TAD* A4.9. – As Cowley commented, "The fact that the Jews of Elephantine applied also to Delaiah and Shelemiah at Samaria and mention this to the authorities at Jerusalem, shows that (at any rate as far as they knew) no religious schism has as yet taken place" (1923: 110). In a later article (1928: 382ff.), he went so far as to claim Nehemiah must have come to Jerusalem in the reign of Artaxerxes II 384 BCE and thus after the peaceful relations between Jerusalem and Samaria in 407 BCE.

85 Williamson writes: "[T]he fact itself makes clear that there was an influential Tobiad party in Jerusalem with whom Nehemiah must have had difficulty in dealing, even though rarely surfaces in our texts. Perhaps they wished to continue with an open policy toward Judah's neighbors in the interests of commerce and trade" (1985: 261).

Sanballat lived in the mid-fourth cent. BCE,[86] and as will be argued in the discussion of 13:28f., it is this Sanballat whose daughter was married to one of the descendants of Eliashib. If the authors of these accounts reflect the sentiments of their times, then we may suggest that the increasing polemical nature of the texts (3:33f.–» 4:1ff. –» 6:2-9*–» 6:1–» 2:19f., –» 2:10) corresponds to the ever-widening gap between Judah and Samaria. What would have been a more effective means of voicing one's criticism against Samaria than presenting the antagonism beginning with the restoration of Jerusalem and instigated by the eponymous head of the Samarian governors?[87]

With regard to the Sanballat of Nehemiah's account, *TAD* A4.7 confirms that he was on the scene in the late fifth century, although he would have been extremely young. Whether he was already governor in the year 445 as he was in 407 is rather unlikely.[88] In 6:5-9, he refers to the rumors relayed to him by Geshem (v. 6), who may have occupied a higher position and would have been able to report the putative seditious movement in Judah to the king (v. 7).[89] If one may identify the Geshem who yielded extensive power over the Syrian desert and North Arabia with the "Gashmu" and "Geshem, the Arab" in Nehemiah's account,[90] it is understandable why Sanballat substantiates his claims by referring to him.[91]

As far as Tobiah is concerned, the more reliable passages (6:10-14, 17-19 and 13:4ff.) do not associate him with Sanballat or Geshem. Hübner writes: "Tobija war nichts anderes als ein um die Mitte des 5.Jh. v.Chr. [...] in der Provinz-Hauptstadt Samaria eingesetzter Beamter, der die Aufgabe hatte, von dort aus die Subprovinz Ammon zu verwalten." In support of this conclusion, Hübner

---

86 Cf. Cross (1963: 11ff.; 1969: 43ff.; 1974: 18ff.; and 1988: 18ff.).

87 Further evidence for this proposal is found in Ezra 4:1-3, which incorporates central features from Neh 2:19-20 and presents those whom Esarhaddon "had brought up" sacrificing to YHWH (outside of Jerusalem), desiring to participate in the building of the temple, rebuffed, and then causing trouble. The authors of this late passage date the beginnings of the Samaritan schism to the building of the temple, rather than the wall (as in Neh 2:19f.).

88 Cf. Williamson's comments (1985: 182).

89 For the silver vessel found at Tell el-Maskhuta (=Sukkoth) in Lower Egypt and the Lihyanite inscription (JS lih 349) found at Arabian Dedan, cf. Rabbinowitz (1956: 2), Gibson (1975 – n. 25) and Lemaire (1989: 102f.). Herodotus refers also to Gusam and "the king of the Arabs" (4.3). Finally, the LXX to Gen 45:10 (καὶ κατοικήσεις ἐν γῇ Γεσεμ ᾿Αραβίας) and 46:24 (ἐν γῇ Γεσεμ ᾿Αραβίᾳ) indicates that the name Geshem stood for Arabia in general and at still a much later time (cf. Williams 1992: 995]). It should be emphasized that the attempts to quickly identify names from inscriptions with figures in biblical accounts is extremely hazardous. The extra-biblical evidence only confirms that there were rulers in Arabia named Geshem from the early fifth until the third centuries BCE (and probably later).

90 Cf. Cross (1955: 46-47), Rabbinowitz (1956: 1-9), Dumbrell (1971: 33ff.), Williams (1992), Knauf (1989: 104f. and 156f.; 1990: 202ff.).

91 Not only the fact that Sanballat's sons were consulted by the Jews of Elephantine in a cultic matter, but also their theophoric names and the fact that his daughter was married to a descendent of Eliashib indicate that most Judeans even after the time of Nehemiah would have placed themselves and Sanballat in the same religious categories.

claims that the appellation העבד in 2:10, 19 signifies "das untergeordnete Verhältnis des Tobija gegenüber seinem Vorgesetzen Sanballat."[92] While Hübner's
conclusions, which are quite reminiscent of Williamson's,[93] are possibly merited
by a reading of the end-text, a closer inspection reveals that Tobiah carries the
title העבד only in the youngest additions (2:10 and 19). The insertion 3:35 refers
to him simply as "the Ammonite." The passages 6:17-19 and 13:4-9 (as well as
6:10-14) omit any title whatsoever and present him acting alone. His cooperation with Sanballat is a product of an extended compositional process and has
less – if anything – to do with the historical situation.[94]

If the nobles were interested primarily in their own industry (cf. 13:15ff.) and
in maintaining their trade with Judah's neighbors, Tobiah may have been an
important financial partner. This would explain not only his connubium with
the nobles, priesthood and the "many" in Judah who had entered into contracts
with him (6:18), but also why he was given a chamber in the temple precincts –
the fiscal center of the region. The presence of the register (3:1-32) indicates
that the authors of the earliest editions of the building account were not in the
least critical of the nobility. The "hardliners," who have made their presence felt
in the composition of the late editions, corrected this image. As Nehemiah came
to town (13:7ff.), he threw Tobiah out of his chamber and pointed his finger at
the priesthood.[95] Given that the Oniads as the opponents of the Tobiads
regarded Nehemiah as a hero who fortified Jerusalem (cf., e.g., Sir 49:13 with
50:1ff.), the placement of Tobiah's name after Sanballat's (2:10, 19f.; 3:35; 4:1ff.
and 6:1), rather than indicating that he was actually Sanballat's subordinate,
represents an attempt to associate him with the despised northern neighbors.
Although he probably never militantly opposed the building of the wall, these
authors, by defaming his name, identify his descendants and their aristocratic
friends as the enemies of a strong and independent Judah.[96]

---

92 1992: 214.
93 1985: 183f.
94 Even the late notices 2:10 and 19 do not call him "his (i.e., Sanballat's) servant."
95 That the polemics against the Judean aristocracy in vv. 17-19 would have had relevance for
later generations is supported also by TAD A4.7, which demonstrates that "nobles of Judah"
(חרי יהודה, v. 17a and 13:17) is not an expression unique to Nehemiah's account. The
recipients of this letter from Yedoniah and the priests in Yeb are, inter alia, "the nobles of
the Jews" (חרי יהודיא). In contrast to 6:17-19, they were not eager to correspond to
Yedoniah (אגרה חדה לא שלחו עלין). In light of this evidence one may be confident that (1)
the יהודיא/יהודה חרי represented an established group that continued to exist for many
years after the mid-fifth century BCE, (2) that they exercised considerable influence in Judean
affairs, (3) that they maintained diplomatic relations by way of written correspondence, and
(4) that they remained in contact with later generations of Nehemiah's enemies.
96 It is difficult, therefore, to accept Hübner's proposal that the Tobiah of Nehemiah's
account should not be identified as the predecessors of the Tobiads in the Hellenistic
period. Can it be only coincidental that "Tobiah the Ammonite" – who possessed a pied-à-
terre in Jerusalem, who was allied both connubially and commercially to the priesthood and
aristocracy – has nothing to do with the Tobiad family a century later which was also closely

We return now to our first observation in this section, namely that the passage of vv. 17-19 presents the written correspondence as taking place only "in those days" and not after the twenty-fifth of Elul. This contradicts what we know about the continuing influence of Tobiads in Judah during the early Hellenistic period. Rather than abandoning its alliances with Tobiah, the aristocracy probably only strengthened them after the building of the wall. Were the authors of vv. 17-19 reporting the facts, they would certainly not have introduced the passage with the formula בימים ההם. Why then does the text restrict the exchange of letters to the time of building?

This limitation may be explained by the growing significance of the completion of the building that one observes in the composition of Ezra-Neh. The disparate material in Neh 1-13 has been fitted in between two fixed points: the date in 6:15 and the dedication in Neh 12:27ff. Chap. 5, for instance, tells of Nehemiah's remonstration with the leaders and nobles in the midst of the work on the wall. The lack of a reference to the building, while interrupting the narrative in chaps. 4 and 6, probably indicates the authors' intention to portray a problem that runs deeper than the originally envisioned promise of the construction enterprise in 2:17. Yet regardless of how one explains the composition of this chapter, the transmitted shape of the first-person account demands that one interpret this reform in the historical setting before the twenty-fifth of Elul. The account of a fiscal reform illustrates paradigmatically that the building cannot be completed until the Judean aristocracy recognizes the fraternity of the Judeans (אחיהם היהודים, v. 1) in distinction to "the nations our enemies" (v. 9). The episode concludes with the nobles and leaders promising to do as Nehemiah says. Thereafter, the building progresses (chap. 6). With the composition of chap. 5, the completion of the wall on the twenty-fifth of Elul increases in significance. What appears incredible in the eyes of the surrounding nations (6:16) is now to be understood as both the completion of the wall as well as the unity brought by the reforms that accompanied the work on the wall.

The composition of the accounts of the population measures and the pledge to the Torah in 7:4-12:26 is to be explained similarly. In keeping with our endeavor to take seriously the transmitted shape of the text, the analysis of these accounts will attempt to show that the wall cannot be dedicated and the completion celebrated until the community gathers to read the Torah (8:1-12), put into effect what they learn (vv. 13-18), confess its sins (chap. 9), commit itself to keep the commandments (chap. 10), and repopulate "the holy city" (chap. 11).

---

related to the priesthood and established itself as a quasi-autonomous power in the Ammonite region? Cf. the inscriptions from 'Iraq el-Emir (RÉS Nr. 1889; CIJ Nr. 868) that refer to a *Twbyh* (Naveh [1970: 62f.]); the so-called Tobiah-legend transmitted by Josephus (*Ant.* 12.160-236 and the discussion in Hengel [1969: 486ff.] and Goldstein [1975: 87ff.]); 1 Macc 5:10-13; 2 Macc 12:17; and the Zenon papyri (Tscherikower [1937: 11ff.]).

Only once all this is accomplished can the people express their unrestrained joy (12:43). Just as the aristocracy must pledge themselves to a new fiscal policy before the building concludes,[97] so must the people pledge themselves to the Torah before the wall can be dedicated.

These general observations on the formation of Neh 1-13 assist us in understanding why the nobles are portrayed in vv. 17-19 as corresponding with the enemy only during the period of the construction. In contrast to the nobles in chap. 5, they are not presented in vv. 17-19 as changing their behavior prior to the completion of the work. Nevertheless, it appears that the authors of this passage did not wish to detract from the significance of the date in 6:15. Although these verses follow the notice of completion, they report what was occurring before the twenty-fifth of Elul and thus actually contribute to the climatic character of this *Heilsdatum*.[98] With a review of "those days," the authors can, on the one hand, correct the positive portrayal of the nobility in chaps. 2-5: Throughout the whole period of building, many were collaborating with the enemy. On the other hand, by way of this device the authors can maintain the climatic character of the date. "Mit 6,15 ist der Zielpunkt erreicht, auf den die ganze Darstellung Nehemias zueilt: trotz aller Angriffe und Schikanen von außen und trotz aller Schwierigkeiten im Inneren wird die Mauer am 25. Elul fertig."[99] The contact with the enemy continues throughout the period of building, yet it ceases simultaneously with the completion of the building. Inasmuch as the wall around Jerusalem is to be interpreted as a blockade against foreign influence in the politics of the province,[100] the Judean reader in the late Persian or early Hellenistic period is encouraged to draw an imperative from the indicative character of these three verses: The aristocracy must discontinue their intercourse with their neighbors before the Restoration can be considered complete.

---

97 Cf. 5:12-13 for clear allusions to a covenant ceremony.

98 This can be compared to the account in 6:10-14, which has nothing directly to do with the building theme. However, the authors of this account have not placed it somewhere after vv. 15-16 in order not to detract from the climax.

99 Rudolph (1949: 139).

100 This symbolic significance of the wall, while only implicit in vv. 17-19, is made explicit in chap. 13. In vv. 4-9, Nehemiah casts Tobiah's belongings out of the chamber in the temple precincts. Similarly, the v. 16 describes Tyrians selling their wares to the Judeans "and in Jerusalem." Here, the wall serves to prohibit the entrance of foreign traders to Jerusalem on the Sabbath. Finally, in vv. 27-29 Nehemiah extradites a descendant of Eliashib who had married into Sanballat's family. In all these passages, Nehemiah focuses on "intramural" reforms in Jerusalem necessary to redressing the situation of distress and reproach in the province as a whole.

7.6 Conclusions

According to our findings, the oldest layer of chap. 6 is to be found in vv. 15-16*, which probably belong to the original formulation of the building report. Vv. 5-9 have been composed for this notice of completion, and vv. 2-4 expand upon vv. 5-9. V. 1 was then added as the heading to vv. 2-9 and vv. 15-16. When vv. 17-19 were drafted, is difficult to say. While the paragraph seems to be older than vv. 10-14, which severs the connection between v. 9 and v. 15, its adaptation of the correspondence-motif suggests that it was added to vv. 2-9 + 15-16*.

Whether or not one embraces this reconstruction, it seems quite certain that the authors of chap. 6 have not endeavored to simply report what occurred as the wall was being built, but rather to interpret the significance and implications of the building for later generations in Judah. In explaining the motivation for adding vv. 2-14 and 17-19, we observed that in chaps. 2-4 Nehemiah presents the building project as a communal endeavor. The earliest editions of the building account depict the repair of ruins as an effort to centralize the province and to consolidate the inhabitants of Judah. The account emphasizes the Judeans' ethnic unity over against their neighbors who reproach them (2:17, 6:16). Contrasting with this portrayal of unity, chap. 6 presents the building of the walls as Nehemiah's personal achievement (cf. esp. vv. 3, 6, 9b). The enemy, accordingly, shifts its attention from the builders (cf. 3:33ff. and 4:1ff.) to the intimidation of the builder.

With regard to vv. 2-4, this paragraph not only must have existed before the introduction in v. 1, but it also poses an incongruity for the reader who knows that Sanballat and friends had just mounted an attack on Jerusalem (chap. 4). The nonchalant invitation to meet is fully unanticipated and, indeed, inconceivable from an historical point of view. Instead of assuming that the author has hidden the facts from the reader, we have attempted to read the account independently of its problematic context. In so doing, it could be demonstrated that the passage functions to illustrate Nehemiah's fervor as a builder. Rather than taking a pause from the "great work" and meeting with two prominent political figures, he responds by pointing out that if he abandoned the building (or "rested"), it would not be done. The passage incorporates the widespread motif of the indefatigable builder found frequently in royal inscriptions. That it does not constitute an integral part of the first-person account seems probable since it does not comport with the basic aim of the building report, in which Nehemiah tells how he motivated and assisted the Judeans in repairing the ruins of Jerusalem. It is more plausible to assume that the account was written as his name had already attained authoritative status. Employing the *verba Neemiae*, the author of vv. 2-4 warns later generations of rulers against rapprochement between Judah and her neighbors.

What is made explicit in v. 3 is only implicit in vv. 5-9, namely the recognition that the builders would no longer be able to finish the wall without Nehemiah. The most important contribution this text makes to the building report is Nehemiah's response to those readers in Judah who saw him as one who paved the way for Judah's complete autonomy (v. 8). That the erection of walls was a royal prerogative in the ancient Near East can be seen both from monarchical inscriptions as well as biblical accounts (especially the building notices in 2 Chr), which portray the righteous kings restoring exactly those portions of the wall mentioned in Nehemiah's account.[101] By depicting the enemy as the one making the connection between wall-building and kingship, the authors of vv. 5-9 both identify the readers supporting Judah's autonomy with a non-Judean attitude and effectively proscribe the reestablishment of a king as a legitimate alternative for the future government of the province. While vv. 5-9 appear to have been composed after the first edition of the building account as Nehemiah had already won the respect of the reader, the passage is probably earlier than the text in which it is embedded. That it predates vv. 2-4 is supported by the evidence of redactors who have expanded the former with features from not only the latter, but also vv. 1 and 10-14. Thus, v. 7b probably constitutes an expansion, especially since one cannot explain why Sanballat would make the proposal to "take counsel together" in the same letter in which he warns that the king would hear of Nehemiah seditious plans. It seems also that v. 7b has been drawn from v. 2a. Similarly, v. 7aα has likely been added to assimilate the passage to vv. 10-14. Finally, v. 9a appears to be a late supplement that presupposes vv. 1, 2-4 and 10-14.

The final passage of the chapter (vv. 17-19) presents "many of the Judean nobles" entering into contact with Tobiah through an exchange of letters. While Nehemiah sends letters only to reject the offers in Sanballat's and Geshem's letters, the nobles are initiating correspondence with Tobiah (v. 17a). Likewise, vv. 10-14 point out that the prophets, instead of aiding the building project, had also been corrupted by the enemy to inflict upon Nehemiah the very same reproach which the building project was to remedy (2:17). While 6:10-14 presupposes the new introduction to the first-person account in 1:1b-4 and the reform-accounts in chaps. 5 and 13, the paragraph is 6:17-19 appears to be older. The authors of these texts intend to warn Judah of the dangers to the Restoration posed by those groups that "may have been happy to see the city

---

101 Cf. the classic work on the building "topoi" in 2 Chronicles by Welten (1973).

repaired without committing themselves in the least to the more separatist policy of which Nehemiah regarded the wall as a major symbol."[102]

The Composition of Neh 6
V. 1*
V. 2-4*
VV. 5 –9* [See the table in §7.4.3.]
10 I came unto the house of Shemaiah ben Delaiah ben Mehetabeel, who was shut up. And he said, "Let us meet together in the House of God,
in the midst of the temple,
and let us shut the doors of the temple: for they are coming to kill you – yea, in the night they are coming to kill you." 11 And I said, "Should such a man as I flee?
And who am I to go into the temple and live?
I will not go." 12 And I perceived that God had not sent him, but he pronounced this prophecy against me: for Tobiah [and Sanballat] had hired him.
13 Therefore was he hired,
that I should be afraid,
and do so, and sin,
and that they might have matter for an evil report, that they might reproach me. 14 My God, think thou upon Tobiah [and Sanballat] according to his works,
and on the prophetess Noadiah, and the rest of the prophets,
that would have put me in fear.
15 So the wall was finished on the twenty-fifth day of Elul – in fifty and two days!
16 And it came to pass, that when all our enemies heard it, and all the nation round about us saw it, and they were much cast down in their own eyes; for they perceived that this work was accomplished by our God.
17 Moreover in those days the nobles of Judah sent many letters unto Tobiah, and the letters of Tobiah came unto them. 18 For there were many in Judah sworn unto him,
because he was the son in law of Shechaniah the son of Arah; and his son Johanan had taken the daughter of Meshullam the son of Berechiah.
19 Also they reported his good deeds to me and uttered my words to him.
Tobiah sent letters to put me in fear.

---

102 Williamson (1985: 261). This statement aptly expresses our findings insofar as one understands "Nehemiah" here as the figure of tradition, not history.

8. The Socioeconomic Reforms – 5:1-19

8.1 Introduction

The preceding chapter presented evidence for our working hypothesis that the building narrative did not originally comprise 5:1-19, the section in which Nehemiah recounts his socioeconomic reforms. The analysis has shown that Nehemiah's unwillingness to take a break from the work on the wall in 6:2-4* dovetails with the assiduousness and celerity reported in 4:15-17*. Given both the thematic and the tight stylistic and semantic correspondence, these passages appear to have been previously conjoined. In the present chapter, we address the problem of how and when these passages became disjoined. According to our proposal, the account in 5:1-13 has been composed in order to amplify the building report into a history of Judah's Restoration.

Upon depicting the internal difficulties and the external opposition during the course of the work on the walls simultaneously in 3:33-4:17, the narrator focuses his attention in chap. 5 on the former, namely on the domestic conditions in Judah. Beginning in vv. 1-13, he tells about his actions to bring about a *restitutio in integrum* upon hearing the desperate outcry of the Judeans. Thereafter, in vv. 14-18, he considers in retrospect his twelve years of gubernatorial office during which he selflessly waived his income of "the governor's bread." Finally, in v. 19, he turns to God in a prayer for remembrance of his service on behalf of the people. To the uncritical reader, the three sections present themselves as parts of a unified whole centering on the recurrent theme, "all that I have done for the sake of this people" (v. 19b). However, three scholars – Winckler, Batten and Williamson – have asserted that these paragraphs could not have been composed at the same time, and it is their denials of the perceived integrity of Neh 5 which have most affected the existing solutions to the problem to be addressed in the present chapter.

In an essay published in 1901, Winckler remarked quite succinctly to vv. 1-13: "jüngerer zusatz auch dem inhalte nach? wenigstens sind keine alten bestandteile festzustellen."[1] While subsequent German scholarship ignored the

---

1   1901: 479.

proposal,[2] Batten put it to use. Now, instead of solely vv. 1-13, the entire chapter is said to have been added to the building report, since it "breaks the story of
the rebuilding of the wall," and "Neh. would scarcely have stopped work to
hold an assembly, esp. in view of the pressing danger, which never ceased until
the last stone was laid and the last gate in place."[3] With regard to the second
section of the chapter, Batten remarked that "the date in v. 14 shows that we are
at the end of the twelve years of Neh.'s rule."[4] Although Nehemiah is the one
who authored the chapter,[5] a "compiler" reassigned it to its present context.[6]

In recent years, the *status quaestionis* relating to Neh 5 has been shaped to the
greatest extent by the proposal made by Williamson, which we have already
begun to assess in the preceding chapters. He suggests that Nehemiah himself,
in the process of updating his building report, added not vv. 1-13, but rather the
final paragraph with the prayer (vv. 14-19) as well as chap. 13.[7] Noting that a
prayer for remembrance occurs in the conclusion of four separate accounts
(5:14-19; 13:4-13; 15-21; 23-30), all of which "can be linked in some way with
chap. 10," Williamson posited that "after the pledge of chap. 10 had been
sealed, Nehemiah may have felt that justice was not being done to him within
his own community… [H]e was thus moved to rework his old report, adding to
it a number of short paragraphs dealing specifically with those points for which
he felt he was not being given due credit."[8] While Williamson provides a solution to "the evident chronological discontinuity" between vv. 1-13 and vv. 14-
19,[9] the question remains how the opening account of the debt remission relates
to the building narrative. That the socioeconomic troubles "probably arose
during the course of the wall-building" explains the historical setting for the
account, but what about the problems which Batten and many others after him
observed with regard to its literary setting?

Responding to this question, Throntveit has argued on the basis of the
remarkable formal parallels between chap. 5 and the reform accounts in chap.
13 that the former text in its entirety could not have originally belonged to the
building narrative. Combining these results with Williamson's thesis, he returned
to Batten's proposal and suggested that the *whole* of chap. 5 formed a continua-

---

2   Cf. Mowinckel's comments on the proposal (1964: 27). Gunneweg (1987: 84) expresses
    doubt as to the originality of the context but comes to no final decision.
3   1913: 237.
4   Ibid.
5   Ibid.
6   "The placing of this c. so that it breaks the story of the rebuilding of the wall indicates that
    the compiler regarded these hard conditions as due to the work on the walls" (ibid.). Cf.
    Michaeli (1967: 327), Bowman (1954: 705), Blenkinsopp (1994: 202), and Kratz (2000: 69f.).
7   Cf., e.g., Throntveit (1992: 122) and the recent works by Karrer (2001: 145f.) and Reinmuth
    (2002: 328ff.), all of which follow the direction established by Williamson.
8   1985: xxviii. A more thorough discussion of this position is provided below.
9   Ibid.: 235.

tion to chap. 13. Nehemiah drafted all the accounts for second memoir, and an editor has transposed chap. 5 to its present setting.[10] Despite its advantages, Throntveit's view fails to account for the discontinuity between vv. 1-13 and 14-19, which Winckler and Williamson discerned.

In resisting the contemporary skepticism with regard to the possibility of recovering the literary precursors to biblical literature, Williamson and Throntveit have made a deep impact on the way we approach the problems posed by chap. 5 as well as of the entire first-person account. Their proposals serve therefore as the point of departure for the following analysis. After a closer inspection of the parallels between the text and the reform accounts in chap. 13, we turn to a detailed analysis of the composition of the account with the aim of understanding what it contributes to the building report.

8.2 Comparison of the Reform Accounts in Neh 5 and 13

As already observed, chap. 5 occupies an unusual place in the wall-building report. The other units in the narrative commence with a שמע-formula, which introduces the reaction of the adversaries upon learning of the progress on the walls: "As p.n. heard that the wall…" (cf. esp. 2:10, 19; 3:33; 4:1, 9; 6:1 and 6:16).[11] Contrasting sharply with this pattern, chap. 5 begins with ותהי. In keeping with this variation, the account broaches a topic that the narrator has hitherto left untreated: the credit policies practiced within the province. Significantly, in reporting the reforms he instituted, Nehemiah never even mentions the wall. Consistent with this thematic digression, the familiar opponents – Sanballat and his cohorts – are conspicuously absent in the scene of vv. 1-13. Now the Judean nobles and officials play the role of the antagonists. Given the latter's exemplary willingness and cooperation thus far with regard to building project (2:16-18; 4:8, 13), it is all the more surprising that they are now portrayed in a negative light. Also peculiar is the concluding passage (vv. 14-19), in which Nehemiah touches upon the subject of the wall only in passing (v. 16) and belatedly informs the reader that he served as governor.

Given the weight of this evidence, we may accept that opinion of several scholars that the building report did not originally contain chap. 5. Although the narrator achieves a certain degree of unity with the surrounding passages in concentrating on his own person and achievements, the text is bereft of too many features of the surrounding account to qualify as an indispensable episode of the story. Of course, one cannot exclude the possibility that one author, in com-

---

10 1992: 122-25.
11 Cf. the discussion of שמע-schema in §3.2.

posing the entire account, intentionally made an excursus from the main story line and then (in 6:1ff.) returned to it. We must admit, however, that this is extremely unlikely in the present case. The text intrudes without warning into the narrative and detaches the material in chaps. 1-4 from its necessary conclusion in chap. 6. If this chapter and its context were conceived simultaneously, one would expect some sort of transition. Hence, the question posed for our remaining investigation is not *whether* the text has been added to the building report but rather *why*.

We begin with a form-critical consideration of three other passages in Nehemiah's account: 13:10-14; 15-22; 23-31. The resemblance these accounts bear to one another is striking. Not only do all three employ a similar vocabulary, but they also follow a common pattern. Specifically, each begins with (*i.*) Nehemiah's detection of a particular deficiency. He "finds out" (ואדעה) that something has not been performed or "observes" (ראיתי) an abuse. He then (*ii.*) remonstrates (ואריב/ואריבה) with the offenders. Those he takes to task in the first two cases are the leaders of the community (הסגנים or חרי יהודה). To the malefactors he then (*iii.*) poses an incriminating question. Thereafter, he (*iv.*) takes physical measures to repair the problem and then (*v.*) reports that the problem was resolved. Concluding each unit is a (*vi.*) short זכרה־לי-prayer that God would take account of the respective good deed. These six features and the pattern they form are illustrated in the following synopsis of the passages.

	13:10-14	13:15-22	13:23-31
i. Detection of a Deficiency	v. 10	vv. 15-16	vv. 23-24
ii. Remonstration	v. 11a	v. 17a	v. 25
iii. Question	v. 11a	v. 17b-18	vv. 26-27
iv. Immediate Measures	v. 11b	vv. 19-21a	vv. 28-29; cf. v. 25
v. Success	vv. 12-13	vv. 21b-22a	vv. 30-31
vi. Prayer	v. 14	v. 22b	v. 31

Comparing these three accounts from chap. 13 with chap. 5, we observe that each of the characteristics isolated above appears in the narrative. First, Nehemiah hears (שמעתי) the grievances of the people against their Judean brethren (v. 6). Second, he remonstrates with (v. 7) both the nobles and the officials; only here and in chap. 13 does the term ריב occur in Ezra-Neh. Third, he poses an incriminating question (vv. 7 and 9).[12] Fourth, he takes action by petitioning

---

12 The unusual word-order of v. 7aβ (ואמרה להם משא איש־באחיו אתם נשאים), which
    Williamson also recognizes (1985: 233), probably indicates that it is to be understood as an

the creditors to return the properties they seized (vv. 10ff.). Fifth, he reports that they promised to do as he proposed and that they kept their word (vv. 12-13). And lastly, he calls upon God that he would credit him with all that he did for the people (v. 19). To reiterate, only here and in chap. 13 does Nehemiah appeal that his achievements be remembered.

There are several other features common to both chaps. 5 and 13. First, we notice an "extramural" orientation insofar as Nehemiah, rather than focusing solely on Jerusalem and the restoration of her walls, recounts his activities in the greater province. Thus, in 13:10-14, he reports his success that "all Judah brought the tithe of the grain, wine and oil into the storehouses." The initial problem in vv. 15-22 concerns the fieldwork on the Sabbath "in Judah," and the walls are presented as already built. In vv. 23-31, furthermore, those who have espoused international women are "the Judeans." Likewise, the complainants in 5:1-13 utter their grievances against "their Judean kindred," while Jerusalem is not mentioned. And in vv. 14-18, Nehemiah states that he was appointed governor "in the land of Judah."

Moreover, each of the remonstrations is formulated with expressions or clauses contained in the communal pact of chap. 10. In 13:11 Nehemiah inquires, "Why is the house of God abandoned?" repeating *expressis verbis* the communal pledge in 10:40b, "We will not abandon the house of our God." So too, in 10:31 the people promise not to "give our daughters to 'the peoples of the land,' nor take their daughter for our sons." In 13:25, they swear again to this end. And although they are opposed to trading wares with the "people of the land" on the Sabbath or holy days in 10:32a, Nehemiah reports in 13:16 that they were buying fish and other wares from the Tyrians on the Sabbath. Finally, in 10:32b they affirm their commitment to the acquittal of debts every seventh year; the word מַשָּׁא appears elsewhere only in 5:7 and 10.

Furthermore, chaps. 5 and 13 contain similar dates. According to 5:14, Nehemiah held the office of governor for twelve years – from the twentieth to the thirty-second year of Artaxerxes' reign. And in 13:6, he informs his readers that in the thirty-second year of Artaxerxes he returned for a time to Babylon.

From these findings, we may draw a tentative conclusion that corresponds to the approach many scholars have taken to explain the development of Nehemiah's account. The similarities in style, subject matter, and form bear witness to the possibility that chaps. 5 and 13 were not originally conceived for the wall-building report. The texts either represent excerpts of a second "memoir" or were composed as an addendum to the report. The present shape of the first-person account is consequently the product of an editor who interpolated chap.

---

interrogative, rather than declarative, sentence: "Are you exacting interest from one another?" Cf. 13:11 and 17, where a question, introduced with וָאֹמְרָה, follows directly upon the remonstration. The LXX has also read this line as a question.

5 and left chap. 13 at the end of the work. While the earlier report could have been written at the earliest occasion after the completion of the restoration project, we must infer from 5:14 and 13:6 that Nehemiah began writing again after his twelve-year gubernatorial tenure. In keeping with this thesis, the aim in compiling the latter work would have been to counterbalance the one-sided image emerging from the first account, namely that Nehemiah's only commendable achievement during his time in Judah was the reparation of the walls. We are now told how he made his presence felt throughout the province, bringing to its inhabitants an appreciation and observance of the social and religious ethic of the Torah and showing them that they were delinquent in their adherence to the pact in chap. 10. In this regard, the priests and communal leaders, who once enjoyed a good rapport with him, are found to be especially culpable and are consequently more severely censured.

While at first glance, this proposal appears to be the most plausible explanation for our findings, it proves upon closer inspection of the literary evidence to be in need of qualification at several critical points.

First, assuming that Nehemiah originally composed chaps. 5 and 13 for a second memoir, it is difficult to cite a reason for the transposition of the former text from its original and presumably more felicitous setting.[13] What does the editor achieve with an interpolation that severs the transition from chap. 4 to chap. 6? By attributing the insertion of chap. 5 to a later hand rather than the primary author, the assumption fails to solve the first problem and creates an additional one. We must now explain both the text in its original setting and the editorial intention in transposing it to its present context. Moreover, the chapter begins quite abruptly ("And there was…"). For this introduction, which lacks any parallels in chap. 13, there are two possible approaches: Either one can speculate that a reviser has excised the original introduction with which the text was purportedly connected to chap. 13, or one can focus on the transmitted text. In opting for the second alternative, we have the advantage of being forced to explain what motivated the expansion of the building report with these paragraphs and what they in turn contribute to their context.

Caution is also recommended with respect to the identification of the author of chaps. 5 and 13. If Nehemiah – or the author of the building report – also wrote chaps. 5 and 13, how then should one account for the conspicuous stylistic differences between these chapters and the remaining work? An example of the disparity between chaps. 5 and 13 is the orthography of "I said." Throughout the building report, Nehemiah employs the anticipated *yiqtol* form (ואמר) seven times and the *qatal* (אמרתי) just once. In chaps. 5 and 13, however, he uses *exclusively*, and no less than nine times, a *yiqtol* form with the ה-para-

---

13   Throntveit admits this disadvantage to the proposal (1992: 124).

gogicum (ואמרה).[14] This observation is all the more significant as (ואמרה) appears elsewhere only in Jud 6:10; Ezra 8:28, 9:6; Dan 9:4, 10:16, 19, and 12:8. With regard to all these texts, numerous scholars have suggested dates – independently of this orthographical consideration – that are later than what is commonly proposed for the building report.[15] Since the ה-*paragogicum* is used with other verb stems in chaps. 2-4, we cannot not attribute this stylistic anomaly to the work of copyists. Inasmuch as the appearance of ואמרה coincides with a thematic shift in chaps. 5 and 13, one also cannot be certain that Nehemiah, or the author of building report, was also responsible for these redactional texts. Instead we must reckon with the work of anonymous authors, as with respect to a great extent of ancient Jewish literature.[16]

With regard to the connections between the pact in chap. 10 and the reform accounts in chaps. 5 and 13, it is quite unlikely that the latter texts quote the former. Indeed, as many have contended, the wording of the reform accounts has directly influenced the formulation of the stipulations in 10:31-32, 40b.[17] In keeping with this view, Nehemiah quotes the pact, because it is *younger* than the first-person account. While the composition-history is probably more complex than usually assumed,[18] the widely shared opinion – that the stipulations which share expressions with chaps. 5 and 13 have been formulated with the latter texts in view – requires that we exercise caution with an historical reconstruction according to which Nehemiah composed the reform accounts in an attempt to claim more credit for the community's pledge to the Torah.[19]

---

14 The only other occurrence of this form in first-person account is 6:11, which, as we have already seen, is part of a late portion that also concludes with a זכרה-prayer! The non-paragogical verb forms occur only chaps. 1-4, which we propose are older than 5:1-6:14 and 6:16-13:31. – Two other stylistic features common to chaps. 5 and 13 deserve mention here: First, the use of the preposition מן with a substantive for an indefinite subject or object occurs in Chronicles more than 25 times and is found in the Memoir in 5:5 and 13:19, 25b and 28. Second, the preposition ל before a time designation – also a favorite in Chronicles – occurs in the Memoir only in 5:18 (cf. 2 Chr. 21:19 an 29:17) and 13:6 (cf. 2 Chr. 18:2).

15 With regard to Judg 6:10, one notices that the Gideon story, beginning in v. 11, has been framed with Deuteronomistic passage in vv. 1-6 and that the account of the anonymous prophet, in vv. 7-10, forms a tertiary introduction, severing v. 6 from v. 11. That this section is most likely very late is illustrated by the Qumran manuscripts in which exactly vv. 7-10 are absent. Cf. the remarks of Auld (1989: 260).

16 While many scholars have proposed a gradual development of Nehemiah's account, they have for the most part attributed the redactions to Nehemiah himself. That the Persian cupbearer was a skilled author is plausible, but that he was also an adept editor is an assumption that proves to be untenable in the light of the number of redactional stages one can isolate in the narrative.

17 To mention only the most important contributions: Hölscher, (1923: 545f.), Noth (1943: 129f.), Kellermann (1967: 37ff.) and Blenkinsopp (1988: 312).

18 Cf. Excursus I at the end of Chapter Nine.

19 Therefore, I cannot share Williamson's optimism in retracing the exact historical developments behind the editorial process (*viz.*, chap. 5 – or at least vv. 14-19 – and chap.

In considering the dates in chaps. 5 and 13, they appear at first sight to have much in common. A closer examination, however, reveals that they are in irreconcilable tension. Presuming that Nehemiah composed 5:14ff. *simultaneously* with 13:4ff., it is baffling that after describing his magnanimous policy for twelve years (5:14a) he would then begin to discuss his reforms *after* the twelfth year (13:6b). The reader is compelled to wonder how Nehemiah conducted himself vis-à-vis the socioeconomic trouble in the province (reported in 5:18b) during this later period.[20] Are we to presume that he relented from his selflessness?[21] The analysis of 13:4-9 supports the conclusion of several scholars that the notice in v. 6 has been inserted.[22] Now if the date is not original, we lack a basis for supposing that Nehemiah composed chaps. 5 and 13 twelve years after his first account.

The introduction to 13:4 ("but before this") is also instructive. As suggested in the preceding chapter and defended in the analysis of 13:4ff., this expression probably refers not to the few short days preceding the dedication ceremonies, but rather to a time prior to the activities described in 6:17-19. The nobles were exchanging letters with Tobiah "also in those days" – that is, during the period of the building. If 13:4-9 describes that earlier Tobiah had possessed a chamber in the temple and that he was dismissed as Nehemiah arrived for the first time in Jerusalem, then the reader would understand why he was forced to further his encroachments into Judah by way of correspondence. The significance of this observation is that we could no longer neatly distinguish between a building report and an account of reforms (chaps. 5 and 13), for every passage after chap. 4 would conclude with a זכרה-prayer (5:1-19; 6:1-14; 6:15-19 + 13:4-14; vv. 15-22; vv. 23-29; and vv. 30-31) and each passage after 6:15-16 would begin with the expression "in those days." In the preceding chapter, we saw that 6:14 makes a pun on 5:19.[23] Assuming that chap. 5 has been transposed or composed at a later point than 6:10-14, one cannot appreciate this wordplay. Insofar as these four verses presuppose the insertion of chap. 5, we must relinquish the attempt to distinguish between a building report and a later account of provincial reforms.[24]

All these points render our tentative conclusion implausible. While chap. 5 evinces a number of significant parallels with chap. 13, one lacks grounds for asserting that the author drafted it for an independent literary setting. In

---

13 were composed by Nehemiah himself as a response to the ratification of the communal pact).

20 We discuss this problem at length below.

21 Reinmuth's contention (1992: 126f.) that one can better understand the dates in chap. 5 if the text has been composed for an independent literary setting thus warrants doubt.

22 See §9.2.1.

23 זכרה־לי אלהי לטובה כל אשר־עשיתי על־העם הזה / זכרה אלהי לטוביה כמעשיו אלה.

24 This is all the more necessary if 6:10-14 itself has been inserted between vv. 9b and 15.

assuming that it was secondarily moved to its present position, one creates the additional problem of explaining why an editor disrupted the transition from chaps. 4 and 6 rather than leaving it in the context for which it was intended. Moreover, one cannot account for the composition of the text in light of ratification of the pact recorded in chap. 10 since, as many scholars argue, several stipulations quote chaps. 5 and 13. So too, a closer comparison of the dates in 5:14 and 13:6, far from confirming the simultaneous composition of chaps. 5 and 13, prove to be in serious tension. The assertion that Nehemiah is the author of both chapters warrants doubt, since the style and orthography of the two chapters differs from that of the building account. Most importantly, the prayer in 6:14 clearly plays on the wording of 5:19.

Before offering a different explanation for the presence of vv. 1-13 in its transmitted setting, we examine the paragraph in vv. 14-19, which appears to have been composed first.

8.3 Nehemiah as an Ideal Leader – 5:14-19

8.3.1 Introduction

In 5:14ff., Nehemiah continues to depict himself as an exemplary leader, yet here we encounter something which we did not anticipate in his self-portrait. In the foregoing narratives, he has sketched an image of one who, distraught by the inimical conditions prevailing in his homeland, comes to Jerusalem in order to organize the repair of her ramparts. Now, instead of organizing a construction project, rallying the builders to carry on in the face of provocation, and settling internal disputes, he describes how he faithfully served the people in the role of *governor* and generously entertained them at his court.

In this passage, the narrator has retouched his self-portrait with masterly finesse. Instead of first establishing exactly how and when he entered office and then describing the manner in which he performed his duties, he affirms with just a single stroke of the pen that he has been a selfless governor. And there is a good reason for this economy of words, for in placing the emphasis on his altruism instead of on his appointment, he restricts the discontinuity created by the presentation of the ancillary and belated information. Inasmuch as he focuses on the same positive leadership traits exemplified elsewhere, he imparts to the narrative an accent to which the reader is accustomed.

So skillfully composed, this text also compels the reader to revise his or her interpretation of the story, just as 6:17-19 corrects the image of the nobles' actions "in those days." Following the cross-reference to the twentieth year of Artaxerxes in v. 14a, we leaf back to the account in 2:1-9 where the king grants

Nehemiah his request and sends him to build Jerusalem. Although we are not told *expressis verbis* that Nehemiah was appointed governor at this time, we presume that this must be said somewhere between the lines. Furthermore, we now know that Nehemiah's success hitherto in consolidating the people is not merely due to his charismatic personality or powers of persuasion, but also to his puissance as a *peḥah*. It is thus instructive that he rarely puts this authority to use. Instead of coming to Jerusalem and authoritatively foisting his plan upon the people, he exercises great caution, inspecting the construction site at night and then proposing the project as a communal enterprise (2:11-18).

In giving the story this *relecture*, we are most likely complying with the intentions of late redactors. Not only does chap. 5 seem to be secondary, but also vv. 14-18 probably antedate vv. 1-13 and v. 19. If so, we could explain why Nehemiah predicates his arguments in the latter on the fraternity of the Judeans (cf. the use of אח in vv. 1, 5, 7, 8, 10) yet never refers to the people as his kindred in the former. Given the form-critical parallels to the reform accounts in chap. 13, it seems quite likely v. 19 was composed by the same hand which drafted vv. 1-13. Moreover, vv. 14ff. appears to have developed in two stages. That vv. 14-15 have been secondarily prefaced to vv. 16-18 is indicated by the repetition of the introductory גם in v. 14 (cf. v. 16) and the differing reasons for the waiver of the governor's daily allowance ("the fear of God" in v. 15b versus the "heavy load on this people" in v. 18b). In v. 18b, Nehemiah simply remarks that he "did not request the bread of the governor" despite the number of people he entertained daily. In vv. 14-15, however, he says explicitly that he served as governor and compares his selfishness with the egoism of the previous officeholders. Finally, the formulation of vv. 16-18 resembles the insertion in 4:16. Both begin with גם. Both refer to המלאכה, "the work," (cf. 4:9, 10, 11, 13, 15, 17 as well as 6:3, 9 and 16). And, most importantly, both are formulated with the *qatal* instead of the usual *yiqtol*. In the preceding chapter, we saw how the celerity of the workers in 4:15 and 17 coincides with Nehemiah's refusal to take a break from his construction activities in 6:2-4. It seems that these two texts were once conjoined and that 5:16ff. was the first paragraph to sever them.

This reconstruction creates a problem. We know that Nehemiah was governor only from 5:14-15. If the composition of these verses takes its point of departure from the statement in v. 18b, what can one say about the historicity of his governorship? With regard to Neh 2, one observes that (1) Artaxerxes only allows his cupbearer to travel to Judah to rebuild the city of his fathers' graves; (2) in asking when his servant will return (v. 6), the king clearly does not appoint the latter to the position of governor; (3) the building plans are presented to a gremium of leaders in 2:16ff., and a governor in Judah is not mentioned. One could assume that Nehemiah's tenure began soon after he arrived in Jerusalem. As Blenkinsopp writes, "it does not seem that he was appointed governor before his departure from Susa, though he must have been shortly after his arrival in Jerusalem."[25] This assumption is extremely tenuous, however. Why would Nehemiah leave Susa without an appointment only to receive it presumably in a letter "shortly after he arrived" in the province? Although they are widespread in the interpretation of Nehemiah's account, such explanations merit only caution and a search for a better solution. Moreover, if the passage of 13:4ff. continues 6:17-19 and recounts the reforms *during* the building of the wall, as we will argue in the next chapter, then the first-person account contains only six verses (5:14-19) that recount the activities of the twelve-year procuratorship. And in these verses, we are told little more than that Nehemiah governed selflessly and did not tax the people. The historian must take this evidence seriously in reconstructing the establishment of a governorship in Judah. And this is all the more urgent if the only text that reports Nehemiah's gubernatorial status (5:14ff.) has been secondarily attached to a redactional passage.

Since the full weight of these arguments cannot be felt until the next chapter, we discuss vv. 14-18 in what follows without presupposing the conclusions made above. Our aim is to investigate the composition of the passage and to make several observations for those who read this text as the work of the historical Nehemiah.

8.3.2 The Date in V. 14

"And from the day I was appointed to be governor in the land of Judah – from the twentieth to the thirty-second year of King Artaxerxes, i.e. twelve years – neither I nor my brothers ate the bread of the governor" (v. 14). Here Nehemiah has presented his readers with no fewer than three temporal details: 1) מִשְּׁנַת עֶשְׂרִים וְעַד שְׁנַת שְׁלֹשִׁים שְׁתַּיִם לְאַרְתַּחְשַׁסְתְּא הַמֶּלֶךְ (2 מִיּוֹם אֲשֶׁר־צִוָּה וגו 3) שָׁנִים שְׁתֵּים עֶשְׂרֵה. Much scholarly attention has focused on the doublet formed by the second two details. Insisting that Nehemiah was only interested in the duration, Hölscher restricted the original formulation of v. 14a to the first and third detail. While it is conceivable that a glossator supplied the corresponding regnal years, adding the sum of twelve to the other dates of the memoir, the awkward phrasing of this verse-half without the second detail poses a serious problem. The expression, גַּם מִיּוֹם, does not fit well to an absolute quantity such as שָׁנִים שְׁתֵּים עֶשְׂרֵה. After a prepositional phrase with the temporal מִן, one would expect a construction with the temporal עַד. Exactly that is provided in the

---

second detail. Due to this syntactical inconsistency, Williamson rejects Hölscher's proposal and insists on the integrity of v. 14a.

However, one should not disregard a persisting conceptual problem. The primary aim of this verse is to declare that Nehemiah from the very start of his tenure never availed himself of the share allotted to the governor. This could have been expressed with only the first temporal detail: "And since the day I was appointed to be governor in the land of Judah neither I nor my brothers have eaten the bread of the governor." That *both* the regnal years and the absolute quantity constitute an afterthought is suggested by the placement of dashes or parentheses around these phrases in modern translations. These two phrases introduce information that is not directly relevant to the interpretation of their context[26] and hence indeed appear to stem from a foreign hand.[27] This conclusion explains why the reference to *years* in these second two details does not concur with the initial mention of a *day*. The latter has been conditioned by the diurnal nature of the "bread of the governor." Later editors appear to have found the first remark to be a suitable point at which they could both provide the reader with missing information on the length of Nehemiah's administration as well as emphasize the duration of his altruistic policy. In removing this information, the Hebrew syntax becomes much smoother.

Although both of the latter two details appear to be secondary, it is nevertheless, as Hölscher argued, difficult to imagine that they were inserted simultaneously. Williamson's contention that the third temporal detail, שָׁנִים עֶשְׂרֵה שָׁתֵים, requires the second "as its antecedent to be intelligible" explains only the final arrangement of these phrases. Most plausible is that the reference to the twelve years originated as an interlinear or marginal gloss based on information regarding Nehemiah's governorship in Judah. Whether this information has been reliably transmitted or constitutes a scribal assumption is difficult to say.[28] Later, an editor may have correlated this quantity with the date in 2:1, inserting the exact number of Artaxerxes' regnal years during which Nehemiah held office.

That the date in 13:6b did not serve as the source for 5:14a is most probable. It seems that the hand responsible for 13:6b drew upon the mention of thirty-second year in 5:14a for the date when Nehemiah left and returned to Jerusalem. While originally the remark in 13:6b was intended only for the immediate context, the consequence of this insertion is that the three following

---

26 That they can be read independently of their context is illustrated by the amount of individual attention devoted to them in Nehemiah-scholarship.

27 Galling (1954: 226f.) has similarly proposed that both dates are secondary.

28 The time span is actually misleading insofar as it provokes the question whether Nehemiah intended to continue his policy in the years ahead. Thus, the date is more conceivable as an explanatory gloss for a later generation.

accounts in 13:10-14, 15-22, 23-31 must be interpreted as having occurred after the thirty-second year. Now if the editor responsible for the dates in 5:14a had been aware of these activities after the thirty-second year reported in chap. 13, why would he have restricted Nehemiah's commendable policy to only the first twelve years of his term of office?[29]

The suggestion that a later hand has added the dates has implications for the way we interpret the immediate context. With the insertion of a definite time span ("twelve years"), the perspective necessarily changes. While לא אכלתי was originally meant to be understood as a durative or present perfect ("have not eaten"), in the final form of the verse this negated verb must be rendered with the simple perfect ("did not eat") to express an action within a closed time frame. This switch in tense resulting from the insertion of the dates applies also for the remaining first-person *qatal* forms. Thus, the transmitted text portrays Nehemiah reflecting in retrospect on an already terminated administration: After twelve years, he is still alive and working on his memoirs, yet he is no longer officiating as governor. Contrasting with this, the earlier version of the account presents him simply reviewing his actions *adhuc*, not writing after his tenure.

From the original formulation of 5:14-19, the reader would have to conclude that Nehemiah never left office. I have argued above that the chronological information originated with the gloss of the third temporal detail שנים שתים עשרה. While twelve years sounds like a rounded-off sum, it could very well be based on a reliable tradition. Equally likely is that this quantity refers not to when Nehemiah is thought to have composed the passage, but rather to the length of Nehemiah's activity in Judah. Accordingly, Nehemiah's death may have occurred in his twelfth year of administration. That his tenure was life-long would agree with what we know about official posts in the Persian period.

These findings have significant consequences for our approach to Nehemiah's career and motivation in composing his memoirs. Inasmuch as in the original formulation of the passage Nehemiah portrays himself as still holding office and the information in 13:6b has been derived from the edited version of 5:14, one lacks support for the thesis that he compiled his memoir as an *apologia pro domo sua* upon leaving office.[30] According to this view, charges were brought against Nehemiah at the imperial court that eventually lead to his dismissal from office after twelve years of service. The polemical tone in the first-person account (specifically, in chaps. 5, 6 and 13) is said to be a direct consequence of the purported indictment. If, however, even the redactional section

---

29   Batten avoids the contradiction between 13:6b and 5:14a by reading between the lines: "He merely says here that he served for twelve years without pay, but the implication is that his whole period of service is included."

30   This thesis informs many commentaries, but is voiced most clearly in the work of Kellermann (1967).

of 5:14ff. did not originally include the length of Nehemiah's procuratorship and presents him as composing his memoirs during his administration, then this thesis, as well as the intrigues against Nehemiah which it presupposes, warrant skepticism. Instead of linking the polemical tone to the Nehemiah's concern to defend his actions, I contend that the authors of chaps. 5, 6, and 13 intended to correct the image presented in the earlier editions of the building account. Rather than the surrounding nations (chaps. 2-4), the Judeans themselves are at fault for the situation of affliction and reproach that necessitated the building of the wall.

8.3.3 The Portrayal of Nehemiah's Governorship

The question deserves to be posed, who commanded Nehemiah to be governor according v. 14a? Assuming that the Persian court must have made such an appointment, the missing subject to צוה merits attention.[31] According to most widely accepted solution proposed by Rudolph, צוה אתי is to be emended to צואתי as an equivalent to the צויתי. Although the grammatical problem may be solved, the reader would still like to know who made the appointment. If it was the king, why does Nehemiah not say this? One might presume that the mention of the king in the date implies this, yet even Rudolph is of the opinion that this information has been supplemented.

Taking an alternate route and giving the present shape of the text priority, we discover in the immediately preceding sentence (v. 13bβ) a masc. sing. subject: העם.[32] If vv. 14-18 are to be understood according to transmitted setting as the continuation of vv. 1-13, this textual arrangement may imply that the Judean "people" appointed Nehemiah to his post. If, however, the paragraph originally followed chap. 4, as suggested above, then the subject would be "the nobles, the rulers and the rest of the people" – the protagonists of chap. 4 (cf. esp. vv. 8 and 13). That this might well be the case is indicated by the designation for governor: פֶּחָם, a form of פֶּחָה which is grammatically impossible. Many commentators simply emend the text to read פחה, without explaining how the present reading originated or why the same verse also contains the proposed reading. The best alternative is the suggestion that the intended form is פֶּחָתָם,

---

31 Cf. Ezra 5:14 where Cyrus names Sheshbazzar governor. The verb צוה occurs elsewhere always with a defined subject. That it was lost in the process of inserting the dates is however difficult to prove.
32 Here the verb of this subject is in the singular and not, according to *constructio ad sensum*, in the plural.

"their governor," which served as the *Vorlage* for the LXX.[33] Hence, another possible reading of v. 14 is: "And since the day *they* appointed me to be *their* governor in the land of Judah, I and my brothers have not eaten the bread of the governor." Admittedly, it is difficult to conceive that the Judeans considered themselves authorized to appoint someone to be governor, yet we must concede that on the basis of the transmitted Hebrew text, which allows for several inter-pretations, one cannot be certain that the Persian court appointed him.[34] As Eskenazi points out, "This equivocation, or rather the missing subject of Neh 5:14, may be an accurate reflection of the reported reality; no one has been specifically mentioned as one who commanded Nehemiah to be governor."[35] His account could have been much clearer with respect to these important details, and widely accepted emendation – "I was appointed to be the governor" – does not change our predicament.[36]

What the designation פחה exactly implies in this paragraph is not clear. Significantly, the only other reference to Nehemiah as governor, 12:26, does not specify his jurisdiction, what contrasts with the normal usage of this term (e.g., פחת שמרין or פחת יהודה).[37] It is also revealing that פחה has been linked not with the official term מדינה (cf. 1:3), but rather with the vague expression ארץ יהודה.[38] This use resembles "the *governors* of the land" in 1 Kgs 10:15 (2 Chr 9:14); as we observe below, there are other parallels between Neh 5:14ff. and 1 Kgs 1-10.

The presentation of Nehemiah's governorship in this paragraph presents us with an additional problem. According to v. 18, the gubernatorial kitchen pre-pared daily one ox, six sheep, and a selection of fowl. Thus, more than 2,500 head of cattle – not to mention the fowl – were consumed every year only by Nehemiah and his entourage. From an historical vantage point, this is quite improbable. According to Carter's demographical estimates, the population of Judah during this period (450-332 BCE) probably amounted to no more than 17,000 inhabitants.[39] If so, Nehemiah's yearly rations would have sufficed for the meat consumption of the whole province! One could dismiss the informa-tion provided in v. 18 as an exaggeration in order to maintain the accuracy of Nehemiah's claims in the rest of the passage, yet such a selective reading is precarious.

---

33 *Pace* Hölscher (1923: 535). Rejecting Guthe's proposal, Batten comments, "But as the sf. has no antecedent, I should prefer פחה" (1913: 248). That, however, a plural suffix can follow הָעָם is illustrated in 5:1.

34 13:6b, which reports of a trip to the king in Babylon, should not be cited as evidence in this discussion, since its information is based on the equally unreliable information in 5:14a.

35 1988: 150.

36 Cf. also Gunneweg's important observations (1987: 90f.).

37 Cf. e.g., Hag 1:1, 14, etc. and *TAD* A4.7.29.

38 The book of Esther (3:12 and 8:9) connects the פחוות with the מדינות.

39 1999: 195-213.

Although our knowledge of the conditions surrounding Nehemiah's appointment and the nature of his authority leaves much to be desired, we can be more confident as to what the text imparts to the image of Nehemiah. One cannot help but noticing several allusions to biblical texts. First, the closest parallel to Nehemiah's daily allowances in vv. 14-18 are to be found not in documents found from other satrapal courts in Persian times, but rather in 1 Kgs 5:2-3, the list of Solomon's royal mensal requirements. The formulation ויהי לחם־שלמה ליום אחד is so close to לחם הפחה in vv. 14 and 18 and to היה נעשׂה ליום אחד ואשׁר in v. 18 that one may presume that there a genetic link between these two texts. Given the mention of עבר הנהר in 1 Kgs 5:4, which otherwise is only found in Ezra 8:36, Neh 2:9 and 3:7, we may reliably date this editorial work to the postexilic period. The fanciful information itself was most likely created at this same time.[40] Whereas the historicity of both Solomon's royal and Nehemiah's gubernatorial mensal requirements is quite suspect,[41] the *Tendenz* of the texts is plain to see. Similar to the way Solomon manifests the greatness of his empire in preparing a generous table, Nehemiah endows Judah as the territory of his governorship with prestige in entertaining a large number of guests with meat each day. The differences between the two is that the reader of 1 Kgs 1-10 wonders how Solomon financed his pretentious court, while Nehemiah, who does not endeavor to be king (6:5-9), emphasizes that he waived his right to "the bread of the governor" and fed his dinner-guests from his own purse.

That the bread of the king was utilized as a sort of royal *beneficium* is illustrated in a several texts. Thus, David proves himself a gracious leader with regard to Jonathan's lame son, Mephibosheth, in 2 Sam 9:7.[42] Likewise, 2 Kgs 25:27ff. (Jer 52:31ff.) reports that Jehoiachin was pardoned and allowed to eat bread before the king continually. Although Nehemiah in 5:14-18 does not draw on the institution of table invitations as a means of pardon, he does evince his magnanimity as a ruler by entertaining not only the 150 officials, but also those without financial means (v. 17).

Finally, Nehemiah describes his predecessors as ones who oppressed the people: הכבידו על־העם (v. 15). Since כבד *hiphil* is used here absolutely, Joüon proposed on the basis of the Lucianic reading that a second על, with the

---

40 The repetitive resumption of 4:7 in 5:7 indicates that the list in 4:8-19 was the initial insertion. 4:20-5:6 may also have been added; they sever the earlier connection between 4:19 and 5:7. The editing of these verses is quite complex so that it no longer possible to arrive at a reliable reconstruction. Nevertheless, 5:4 depends upon the subject in v. 1, thus making the insertion of the royal mensal requirements in 1 Kgs 5:2-3 very late.

41 Arguments for the historicity the information in Neh 5:14ff. are provided by an important article from Williamson (1988 and 1991). Because space is scarce in the present book, my discussion of this work must be published elsewhere.

42 Cf. also 2 Sam 19:29 and David's direction to Solomon in 2 Kgs 2:7.

meaning of "a yoke," has been lost due to haplography. Therefore, the original text may have read: "And the former governors placed a heavy yoke upon the people."[43] However one explains the syntax, this expression refers the reader back once again to the depiction of Solomon's kingship. While 1 Kgs 1-10 present Solomon in all his glory and without criticism, chaps. 11-12 introduce the down side of his policies. In his accession to the throne, Rehoboam rejects the advice of the elders to serve the people (12:7) instead of treating them as his father who "made our yoke heavy" (הכביד את־עלנו, 12:10, cf. v. 14). Thus, Rehoboam follows in his predecessor's footsteps and continues to lay a heavy burden upon the people, whereas Nehemiah reforms the policies of the former governors and lightens the burden on the people (cf. Neh 5:18bβ with 1 Kgs 12:4). Moreover, the reason for his break with the tradition established by the first governors ("But I did not do this out of fear for God" v. 15b) follows David's last words in 2 Sam 23:3: "One who rules must be just, ruling in the fear of God." The expression יראת אלהים corresponds exactly to Nehemiah's words, and only here do we encounter the fear of God as an explicit requirement for rulers.

To summarize, the paragraph vv. 14-18 provides the reader with the belated information that Nehemiah also served as governor. The placement of the passage resembles the addendum in 6:17-19, which corrects the positive of image of the nobles presented in chaps. 2-4. Although we may agree with Williamson that the paragraph has been appended, it remains highly questionable that Nehemiah himself was involved in this editing, since the context for which it was composed also appears to be redactional. As we observe in Part Three, the earliest form of 13:4ff. portrays reforms, as in 5:1-13, that were undertaken *during* the building of the wall. Accordingly, the first-person devotes only six verses to the activities of Nehemiah's lengthy governorship. So too, he receives only a leave of absence in 2:1ff. and addresses various groups of rulers yet no governor in 2:16f. One may, therefore, advance a very tentative solution to the conflicting information in 2:1ff. and 5:14ff.: The institution of governor – if it ever existed before Nehemiah – was not *firmly* established in Judah until after Nehemiah, and he himself did not serve in this capacity. Given the evidence of the Elephantine papyri and the Yehud coins, which of all the extra-biblical material can be most reliably dated, one cannot preclude the possibility that authors in the fourth cent. (or later) have designated Nehemiah *peḥah* in 5:14ff. and made the changes to 2:1ff. ("the house I shall enter" in v. 8) with the intention of contrasting him with the contemporary governors (cf. esp. "But the governors who were before me oppressed the people," 5:15).

---

43 1931: 87.

8.4 Nehemiah's Call for a Cancellation of Debts: VV. 1-13

In vv. 1-13, Nehemiah recounts how he reacted to the people's desperate out-cry. Instead of complaining that the work was too difficult (cf. 4:4) or that they could not continue in the face of the threat posed by their enemies (cf. 4:1ff), the Judeans now voice their grievances against their own *kindred.* In the final shape of our account, the word אח ("brother") is used no less than six times. The people and their wives complain to their Judean brethren (v. 1). They also point out that they are of the same flesh and blood and their children are equal (v. 5). Nehemiah accuses the nobles and officials of mistreating their brethren (v. 7). He claims to have bought back those who sold themselves into slavery to non-Judeans (v. 8). and that he and his brothers had advanced them loans (v. 10).[44]

In seeking to explain why later authors have inserted this account into the building report, the highlighting of the Judeans' fraternity furnishes an impor-tant clue. It seems that the composition of this account has taken its point of departure from the prevailing concentration on Judah's consolidation in the early versions of the building report. Initially, Nehemiah achieves unity among the people and groups in Judah (2:16b) by way of a common enterprise. This, in turn, engenders a common enemy, whose antipathy serves finally to boost the solidarity of the workers and the urgency of repairing of the wall. Although the common enemy does not make an appearance in this chapter, the problem it poses remains the point at issue. In his interrogation of the nobles and rulers after hearing the people's charges, Nehemiah argues on the same basis on which he predicated his first plenary address in 2:17: "It is not good what you are doing. Should you not walk in the fear of God because of the reproach (חרפה) of the nations, our enemies?" The difference between chap. 5 and its context is the identity of the culpable. Whereas in the surrounding building account, Sanballat and his cohorts play the role of the antagonists over against the workers as the protagonists, here the crisis arises within. "And there was a great cry of the people and their wives against their *brethren,* the Jews" (v. 1). The con-centric lines of demarcation and identity represented by the wall and its builders have already been drawn. Advancing beyond the simple scenario of *nos versus eos,* this passage treats the more developed problem of the internal relations of an already defined community.

In drawing upon the terminology of Nehemiah's address in 2:17, this text is not alone. Also the very first passage of the account (1:1b-4) mentions the "affliction" (הרעה) and "reproach" (חרפה) that inspired the Judeans to build.

---

44 Moreover, the use of the first-person pl. in v. 8 and 10b may represent an attempt to emphasize Nehemiah's solidarity with his "kindred."

There, however, the problems are separated from the condition of the wall, as seen in §4.3.1. For independent reasons, I have suggested that this passage has been inserted between 1:1a and 1:11b and that it serves as a new introduction to the building report after it had been amplified with account such as 5:1-13.[45] It has already been seen that the passage in 6:10-14, which interrupts the connection between vv. 9b and 15, not only makes use of the terms רע and חרף, but also concludes with a זכרה-prayer. Likewise, each of the paragraphs in 13:4ff., which we investigate in the next chapter, employ the keyword הרעה, follow the structure of 5:1-13 and conclude with זכרה-prayers. While all these texts were likely not composed by the same hand,[46] they do follow the same line of thought. Insofar as their authors either separate הרעה and חרפה from the condition of the wall (1:1b-4) or do not even mention the it (5:1-13, 6:10-14, 13:4ff.), they reflect the realization that the building enterprise has not really solved the problems in the province. While Judah may have regained respect from its neighbors as promised in 2:17, the situation of הרעה and חרפה has continued. These two, rather ambiguous, terms have been imputed with new meaning throughout the first-person account. The authors apparently intend to "rück- und vorweisend vielfach Formulierungen aus dem Schriftganzen aufgreifen, auf andere Redaktionsformulierungen der Schrift verweisen, Kontexte mit älterem Formulierungsgut neu strukturieren und akzentuieren und so sachlich Leseanleitung für das Schriftganze in einem redaktionellen Sinn geben."[47]

Prima facie, the problem in vv. 1-13 centers only on the economic rifts between various classes in Judah. The people complain that they must pledge their children and property to buy grain and survive (vv. 2-3).[48] In his response to the problem, Nehemiah treats the problem *in radice*: The Judeans have lost consciousness of the fact that they are all kindred (אחים). By emphasizing their commonality and fraternity directly in the middle of their work on the wall, the account illustrates how the objective of the building enterprise was much more than the mere restoration of Jerusalem's fortifications. Nehemiah aims to achieve nothing less than the restoration of a sense of ethnicity and fraternity.

In taking a closer look at the structure of the passage, we notice that the first-person narration does not begin until v. 6. What is the reason for this delay? In v. 1 the people and their wives voice their complaint not *against*, but rather *to*

---

45 This thesis explains why 1:1b-4 and 5:1-13 are the only two passages which employ the שמע-schema to describe Nehemiah's rather than the enemy's reaction. Cf. the variations of the שמע-schema in 2:10, 19; 3:33; 4:1, 9; 6:1, 16 and the table in §3.3.

46 Cf. §6.3.2.3, where it is shown that 5:1-13 presupposes an amplified version of chap. 4. A more precise conclusion on the relationship of these passages to each other must await the analyses in the following chapters. Cf. the table in §14.3 for the relative dating of the texts.

47 Steck (1989: 77-78).

48 To the issue of debt slavery, cf. Chirichigno (1993).

their Judean brethren.[49] Moreover, the participles in vv. 2, 3 and 5 indicate that
their grievances were ongoing and hence falling on deaf ears. Now finally someone reacts: "And it vexed me sorely as I heard their outcry and these words" (v.
6).[50] In paying heed to the complainants and expressing extreme dissatisfaction
with the situation, Nehemiah distinguishes himself as one who, in contrast to
the original addressees, sympathizes with the plight of the people. In the
absence of a juridical institution, he proves his solidarity with the people by
taking it upon himself to resolve a matter that "their Judean brethren"
neglected. Therefore, the alternation from the third- to the first-person in v. 6ff.
serves to contrast and emphasize the response of the narrator.[51]

Just as in 13:4-9,[52] the portrayal of Nehemiah's reaction is paradigmatic and
serves a didactic function. Although the people do not appeal to him, he
responds to their grievances and, in so doing, assumes a typical leadership role.
A זעקה/צעקה is normally directed to the king Ex 5:15; 2 Sam 19:29; 1 Kgs
20:38ff.; 2 Kgs 6:26, 8:3, 5.[53] But Nehemiah does not just fill the traditional
judicial, function of the king. The combination of שמע + צעקה/זעקה occurs
elsewhere – not only often, but also exclusively – with regard to the *divine*
response to a complaint.[54] To cite an instructive example, Ex 22:21-23, 26
promises that if one afflicted or oppressed cries (צעק) unto God, he will hear
(שמע) their complaint (צעקה). Significant is not only that this passage appears
directly before the laws on interest in vv. 25-27, which Neh 5 probably has in
view, but also that the divine reaction to the oppression is very reminiscent of
Nehemiah's (cf. the anthropomorphism in v. 24, וחרה אפי, with the phraseology
in 5:6, ויחר לי מאד). So too, the Priestly version of the Exodus story begins in
2:23f. with the Israelites crying (זעק) to God because of their slavery and oppres-

---

49 While commentators have hitherto translated אל־אחיהם, "against their brethren," it is clear
    from the use of צעקה / זעקה התו אל elsewhere (cf. Exod 5:15, 2 Sam 19:29, 1 Kgs 20:39; 2
    Kgs 4:1; 6:26; 8:3, 5) that the preposition carries its usual directional sense.
50 ואת הדברים האלה (v. b) refers likely to the specific grievances in contrast to את־זעקתם, which
    signifies the complaint in general. The use of זעקה instead of צעקה (v. 1) does not indicate a
    change of hand, as these two terms are used interchangeably in unified texts.
51 This conclusion departs from the usual approach that interprets the people as appealing
    directly to Nehemiah.
52 One observes this same compositional technique in 13:4-9. Both there and in 5:1-13, the
    reaction to the problem (5:6 and 13:7) is prefaced with a lengthy description (5:1-5 and 13:4-
    6), whereas the remaining reform accounts commence with the perception of the offense
    (13:10, 15, 23). Moreover, both accounts do not conclude with a זכרה־לי-invocation. Only
    when read together with the following paragraphs (5:14ff. and 13:10ff.) do they incorporate
    this chief characteristic of the other ריב-passages.
53 Cf., however, situation in 2 Kgs 4:1, which evinces many parallels with our text: A woman
    (5:1), whose husband feared YHWH (cf. v. 9) cries (צעק, cf. vv. 1 and 6) to Elisha that a
    creditor (נשה, cf. v. 7) has come to seize her sons (cf. vv. 2 and 5) to be his slaves (לעבדים,
    cf. v. 5).
54 Cf. e.g., Gen 27:34; Num 20:16; Deut 26:7; Isa 30:9; Ezek 22:30; Jer 11:11; Mic 3:4; Hab 1:2;
    Ps 34:18; Neh 9:27, 28 and 2 Chr 20:9.

sion (עברה, cf. 1:13-14 and Neh 5:2-5, 16, 18) who hears (שמע) them. Given the number of parallels, it worth considering whether Nehemiah is portraying his reaction as an *imitatio dei*.[55]

After considering the matter (וימלך לבי עלי),[56] Nehemiah decides to take action by indicting the offenders (v. 7). In defending the rights of the oppressed by contending (ריב) with the oppressors, he continues to emulate the divine protector. According to Isa 19:20, when the Egyptian Diaspora cries (צעק) to YHWH, he will answer them by sending a מושיע who will deliver them also by way of a ריב. Likewise, in Isa 3:13ff. "YHWH rises to argue his case (ריב)…and enters into judgment with the elders and princes of his people: It is you who have devoured the vineyard; the spoil of the poor is in your houses. What do you mean by crushing my people, by grinding the face of the poor?" Just as Nehemiah identifies the culpable with the nobles and officials, who have seized land from their debtors (cf. vv. 3, 5, 11), so does YHWH align the wicked with the elders and princes, who have robbed the property of the poor.

Also the incriminating question which YHWH poses in Isa 3:13ff. finds a parallel in Nehemiah's interrogation of the culprits, משא איש־באחיו אתם נשאים. As there is no consensus as to how to render this statement,[57] we must briefly reconstruct its meaning. First, the unusual word order, with the prefixed accusative object, may indicate that the clause is not a statement, but rather an incriminating question. If so, it would correspond to the interrogation that directly follows the remonstrations in 13:11, 17, 26.[58] Second, we should probably link the word משא, which appears elsewhere only in v. 10 and 10:32, as variation of משאה. The latter occurs in Prov 22:26 in combination with the term with ערבים ("placing as surety"), the same participle which we find on the lips of the complainants in vv. 2-3. The only other text in which we encounter משאה is Deut 24:10, where it appears in combination both with נשה/נשא + ב as in Neh. 5 and with the collection of collateral.[59] In light of the evidence provided by all three texts, one can conclude that the expression משא with נשא + ב probably

---

55 This would not be surprising, as a righteous ruler is concerned with justice. In the absence of such a ruler, the complainant cries to God to reestablish justice.

56 This unique expression is probably an Aramaism (cf. also the Akkadian, *milku* and *malaku*). That it means "to take counsel" or "to consider the matter" seems likely from the meaning "my counsel" for מלכי in Dan 4:24.

57 A number of manuscripts and the LXX read נשאים/משא instead of נשאים/משא. Noting the conflict with v. 10b, in which Nehemiah asserts to doing exactly what he censures in v. 7, Rudolph (1949: 130) follows this textual tradition and translates: "ein Last legt ihr einer wie der andere auf seinen Brüder." Although disputing Rudolph's decision, Blenkinsopp (1988: 253) renders the Hebrew similarly: "You are distraining the persons and property of your kinsfolk." Recognizing the difficulties, Williamson (1985: 231) translates loosely: "Each of you is acting the creditor against his own brother." Others (e.g., Gunneweg [1987: 84]) connect the charges with the practice of usury.

58 The LXX also reads a question.

59 Deut 24:10 refers to the advanced stage when the creditor collects the collateral.

does not refer to excessive interest (usury), but rather to lending against surety or collateral. Yet whatever type of lending practice the expression implies, Deut 24:10 clearly does not forbid it. Indeed, while these laws describe the proper procedures for seizing the collateral, Nehemiah looks negatively upon משא and the whole lending practice associated with this term.

How then is one to understand Nehemiah's censure?[60] I suggest that Nehemiah is arguing along the lines of Lev 25:35-37. While there is a slight difference between "interest" (נשך) and the lending against collateral (משא + נשא/נשה) in Neh 5,[61] in both texts the kinsperson (אח) and the creditor, who lends food (אכל, cf. 5:2-3), play a role. So too, the return in vv. 10, 13, 27, and 28 corresponds to Nehemiah's petition in v. 11. Assuming that the author of Neh 5 was cognizant of Lev 25, we could more easily explain the fact that Nehemiah's next incriminating question in v. 9b ("Will you not walk in the fear of our God...?") is predicated on the same precept on which the prohibition is based ("But fear your God," Lev 25:36).[62] The continuation of this question connects this command to fear God from Lev 25 with point of departure for the building enterprise: the reproach (חרפה) of the nations (cf. 1:3 and 2:17).

One cannot, however, overlook a significant difference between Neh 5, on the one hand, and Lev 25:35ff. and the remaining three so-called מוך-passages (v. 25ff., v. 39ff., v. 47ff.), on the other. In the former, Nehemiah never argues on the basis of impoverished conditions. Although the people complain that they must put up their progeny and property as surety in order to survive (vv. 2-3), the charges brought against the nobles and officials are much more rigorous, namely that they are even entering into a creditor-lender relationship with their own *brethren* (איש־שאחיו). The emphasis on the fraternal aspect of the conflict could not be stronger. Thus, in v. 5, the people point out: "Now we are of the same flesh and blood as our kindred (אח), and their children are just like our children. Behold, we are bringing *our* sons and daughters into bondage" (cf. אחים also vv. 1 and 8). Contrasting with the importance of fraternity *per se* in Neh 5, Lev 25 prescribes how one should treat his or her kin in the case of privation of financial support. The same applies to Ex 22:24: "If you lend money to my people, the poor among you, you should not be to him as a creditor, you (pl.)

---

60 Prior research has presented a wide range of answers to this question. Since a satisfying discussion of this research both would require too much space here, I refer to the Reinmuth's helpful reviews (2002: 129ff.).

61 On the basis of Isa 24:2, we can differentiate two general types of lending: לוה and נשא בו. Ex 20:22 sheds more light on the matter: "If you lend money to my people [the first category in Isa 24:2], the poor among you, you should not be to him as a נשא, you should not place upon him נשך. From both these texts, we may be seemly certain that לוה means lending (*hiphil*) or borrowing (*qal*) in the most general sense; cf. meaning II in *BDB*. Thus, נשה would signify the more particular type of lending on interest.

62 Cf. also vv. 17and 47.

should not place upon him interest." So also, Deut 15:7ff. applies only for the poor comrade (אביון מאחד אחיך). Now if the point at issue in Neh 5 is also the abuse of the poor, why does Nehemiah not mention them? The author could have easily formulated v. 1, "And there arose a great outcry of the poor...." Instead, the account treats the people and their kindred as a whole. In view of the number of accounts in which the destitute cry to God,[63] the unparalleled prominence of the term אח and the absence of an explicit reference to the poor in our text deserve an explanation.

The closest parallel is to be found in Deut 23:19f.: "You shall not charge interest to your kinsperson (אח); interest on money, interest on provisions, interest on any thing that is lent. On loans to a foreigner you may charge interest, *but on loans to your kinsperson you may not charge interest....*" This ruling constitutes nothing less than a universal prohibition on lending upon interest to *any* kinsperson. In contrast to Ex 22:24, Lev 25:35ff., and Deut 15:7ff. which proscribe only lending upon interest to a brother without financial means, Deut 23:19ff. allows one to make a loan only when he or she is willing to forgo interest to a fellow citizen.[64]

What then remains as the incentive for the provision of credit? The first stimulus is Deuteronomic love (ואהבת את יהוה אלהיך, 6:5), which evinces itself in solicitude for the communal solidarity – the essence of the Deuteronomic code.[65] Lending is then no longer business, but rather comradely compassion. On the other hand, Deuteronomy makes an essential proviso, namely the promise of great international transactions ("And you shall lend unto many nations, but you shall not borrow," 15:6; "On loans to a foreigner you may charge interest," 23:21). Because, however, the Judeans are a reproach among the nations and build the wall as a defense against them (cf. v. 9), Nehemiah does not concern himself with alternative international markets for lending or the problems that incur when the most basic forms of credit are banned. In its place, he emphasizes the fraternity-ethic of Deuteronomy and the command to fear God in Lev 25. Inasmuch as an economy with neither domestic nor international credit opportunities is incomprehensible, Neh 5:1-13 depicts a situation that, despite the wishes of the authors of this text, probably never existed in Judah. Inasmuch as this text portrays Nehemiah drawing the consequences of the Judeans' fraternity and calling for the termination of all lending to kindred, our attempt to read the text as a literary composition continuing the "us vs. them" polarity created in the building report appears all the more justified.

---

63 Examples for outcries from the poor are numerous. Cf., e.g., Exod 22:23; Deut 15:9; 24:15; Job 34:28; Ps 86:1-3; Prov 21:13.

64 For the development of the fraternal ethics in Deuteronomy, cf. Perlitt (1980: 29ff.).

65 Cf. the insightful study of Spieckermann (2001: 160ff.).

We have now observed what motivated the amplification of the building account with the report of Nehemiah's reform of the lending practices in Judah. In its present shape, the building account in chaps. 1-4 and 6-7 focuses less on *how* Jerusalem's walls were restored and much more on the reason *why* the Judeans accept Nehemiah's proposal to build: They are a *reproach* among the nations (cf. 1:3 and 2:17). In his incrimination of the nobles and officials, Nehemiah asks, "Should you not walk in the fear of God because of the *reproach* of the nations, our enemies?" (5:7). Hence, the two go hand in hand: In order to remove the reproach, the Judeans must not only rebuild Jerusalem's wall, symbolizing their restored unity to the surrounding nations; they must also, in the midst of their work and faced with an imminent attack from the enemy, acknowledge the fraternity of all Judeans by agreeing to discontinue their lending practices with their kindred.

8.5 Conclusions

The present chapter has investigated the new accents Neh 5 contributes to the context into which it intrudes. We began by evaluating the influential thesis that Nehemiah composed the text with chap. 13 for an account of his later gubernatorial reforms and that an editor moved it to its present context. While one notices several significant features common to all the reform-accounts contained in these chapters, this thesis creates more problems than it solves: We must not only explain why an editor interrupted the flow of the building narrative, but also account for the significant disparities between chaps. 5 and 13. The best approach is to treat the text as an expansion of its present context. In failing to do this, prior scholarship has noticed neither the parallel between 5:19 and 6:14, both of which conclude the foregoing paragraphs with זכרה-prayers, nor that 6:14 makes a pun on 5:19. Assuming that chap. 5 has been transposed or composed at a later point than 6:10-14, one cannot appreciate the wordplay.

Neh 5 appears not only to have been composed for its present context, but also to have developed in three stages: The earliest stratum is to be found in vv. 16-18 and bears striking resemblances to 4:15ff., which it may have originally followed. In attaching vv. 14-15 to vv. 16-18, a redactor has extrapolated the statement in v. 18b. Originally Nehemiah affirms that even though he feed many mouths each day, he "did not request the bread of the governor." With the addition of vv. 14-15, he now claims to have actually served as governor and compares his policy with those of his predecessors. If these verses have been secondarily prefaced to vv. 16-18, one could account for the repetition of "also" (v. 14 and v. 16) and the more pious reason for the waiver of the governor's allowance ("because the burden on this people was heavy," v. 18b; "because of the fear of God," v. 15b).

The final stratum includes vv. 1-13 and 19. Whereas Nehemiah never refers to the Judeans as his "kindred" in the review of his gubernatorial policies, the Judeans' fraternity is the focus of vv. 1-13. That the prayer in v. 19 belongs to this stratum is indicated by both the wording ("all that I have done for this people") and the form-critical parallels between vv. 1-13 and the other reform accounts in chap. 13. Given the wordplay between this prayer and the invocation in 6:14, the composition of 5:1-13, 19 presupposes the insertion of 6:10-14 between 6:9 and 6:15.

We observed how vv. 1-13 and 19 develop the depiction of solidarity in the earliest redactions of the building report. These redactions focus on the antagonism elicited by the building activities. The repair of Jerusalem's ramparts first consolidated the various groups in Judah. This in turn provoked a common enemy, which finally boosted the solidarity of the builders and illustrated the necessity of erecting the wall. In chap. 5, the external enemy recedes to the background in order to demonstrate that the Judean aristocracy itself is responsible for the affliction of the province. Because of the reproach of the nations (v. 9), which originally necessitated the building enterprise (2:17), the nobles and rulers must terminate their credit practices that deny the basic fraternity of the Judeans. In repeatedly underlining the kinship of the people with the designation אח, the passage introduces a new aspect to the fundamental division between "we" and "them" expressed in chaps. 2-4. It must have been composed as its authors realized that the affliction in the community persisted in spite of the repair of the ramparts. The province needed to experience internal reform before the completion of the restoration could be reported.

In comparing the account with the Pentateuchal ordinances for lending, we saw that it has much in common with Deut 23:19ff. Both texts completely proscribe lending to kin. While the ruling in Deut 23:19ff. permits credit transactions with the nations, the only incentive it leaves for domestic loans is neighborly love. Since Nehemiah considers the nations to be enemies (cf. 5:9) and forbids all contacts with Judah's neighbors (cf. esp. 6:17-19 and 13:4ff.), he does not address the possibility of international lending as in Deut 24. Instead, he emphasizes the Deuteronomistic conception of fraternity and the fear-of-God motif from Lev 25.

The Composition of Neh 5

4:15ff.*

1 Now there was a great outcry of the people and of their wives against their Jewish kin. 2 For there were those who said, "With our sons and our daughters, we are many; we must get grain, so that we may eat and stay alive." 3 There were also those who said, "We are having to pledge our fields, our vineyards, and our houses in order to get grain during the famine." 4 And there were those who said, "We are having to borrow money on our fields and vineyards to pay the king's tax. 5 Now our flesh is the same as that of our kindred; our children are the same as their children; and yet we are forcing our sons and daughters to be slaves, and some of our daughters have been ravished; we are powerless, and our fields and vineyards now belong to others." 6 I was very angry when I heard their outcry and these complaints. 7 After thinking it over, I brought charges against the nobles and the officials; I said to them, "You are all taking interest from your own people." And I called a great assembly to deal with them, 8 and said to them, "As far as we were able, we have bought back our Jewish kindred who had been sold to other nations; but now you are selling your own kin, who must then be bought back by us!" They were silent, and could not find a word to say. 9 So I said, "The thing that you are doing is not good. Should you not walk in the fear of our God, to prevent the taunts of the nations our enemies? 10 Moreover I and my brothers and my servants are lending them money and grain. Let us stop this taking of interest. 11 Restore to them, this very day, their fields, their vineyards, their olive orchards, and their houses, and the interest on money, grain, wine, and oil that you have been exacting from them." 12 Then they said, "We will restore everything and demand nothing more from them. We will do as you say." And I called the priests, and made them take an oath to do as they had promised. 13 I also shook out the fold of my garment and said, "So may God shake out everyone from house and from property who does not perform this promise. Thus may they be shaken out and emptied." And all the assembly said, "Amen," and praised YHWH. And the people did as they had promised.

14 Moreover from the time that I was appointed to be their governor in the land of Judah, [from the twentieth year to the thirty-second year of King Artaxerxes, twelve years,] neither I nor my brothers ate the food allowance of the governor. 15 The former governors who were before me laid [a heavy yoke?] upon the people, and took food and wine from them, besides forty shekels of silver. Even their servants lorded it over the people. But I did not do so, because of the fear of God.

16 Moreover I devoted myself to the work on this wall, and acquired no land; and all my servants were gathered there for the work. 17 And there were at my table one hundred fifty people, Jews and officials, besides those who came to us from the nations around us. 18 And that which was prepared for one day was one ox and six choice sheep; also fowls were prepared for me, and every ten days skins of wine in abundance; yet with all this I did not request the food allowance of the governor, because of the heavy burden of labor on the people.

19 Remember for my good, O my God, all that I have done for this people.

III. Additional Reforms during the
Work on the Wall – 13:4-31

Introduction

We have already noticed the numerous stylistic and conceptual features shared by the reform-accounts in Neh 5 and 13. Given these strong commonalities, some scholars maintain that Nehemiah composed these passages simultaneously, as an account of his activities many years after the completion of the wall. Against this conclusion, we adduced a wide range of evidence indicating that chap. 5 is the product of anonymous authors who intended to add a new dimension to the building project: The objective of the enterprise is no longer merely the reparation of Jerusalem's ramparts and the concomitant respect from the surrounding nations (see esp. 2:17 and 6:16). Rather, the "Restoration" means also that the Judahite aristocracy must terminate a credit policy that denies the fundamental fraternity of Judah's inhabitants.

If Neh 5 was composed for its present literary setting and has always depicted the community embracing the socioeconomic reforms *during* the building activities, it is surprising that the reforms in Neh 13 are dated to twelve years *after* the completion of the construction (cf. 13:6). The initiation of these reforms in the midst of the work on the wall would have certainly contributed to the social significance of the restoration project, which we have observed in our study of Neh 5 and 6. Beginning with this observation, the following investigations defend the suggestion alluded to in the preceding chapters, namely that a later hand inserted the date in 13:6.

Whereas some scholars have argued that v. 6 constitutes the work of a later author, no one has yet considered the possibility that the account in 13:4ff. continues the notice in 6:17-19. Significantly, this notice begins just as 13:15ff. and 13:23ff. with the expression "also in those days." Inasmuch as the expression in 6:17-19 clearly refers to the time before the twenty-fifth of Elul, *all* the reforms reported in chap. 13 are to be dated to the building period, as we would expect after our investigation of chap. 5.

Three paragraphs in chap. 13 (vv. 4-9, 10-14, and 23-31) make perfect sense if they report what took place during the building activities. A problem, however, is caused by vv. 15-22, in which Nehemiah orders the gates to be closed in order to prohibit foreign traders from entering Jerusalem. Assuming that he gave these instructions during the work on the wall, we must explain the reference to the gates. If one could shut them, they were already built; consequently, the construction work must have been finished as he notices the abuses on the Sabbath. We respond to this difficulty by showing that the account in 13:15-22 has probably undergone heavy editing. If it can be demonstrated that vv. 19-22a do not belong to the earliest edition, then it is quite likely that originally the reform-accounts in chap. 13, which parallel 5:1-13 both in structure and terminology, did indeed depict Nehemiah instituting the reforms simultaneous to the building activities.

Thus, our aim in this part of the book is to show that the reforms in chap. 13, just as the reform reported in chap. 5, were instituted before the conclusion of the building. Accordingly, the notice of success in 6:15 includes more than the completion of Jerusalem's physical wall. Indeed, an ethnic wall around Judah had been erected insofar as the Judahites had acknowledged their fraternity by embracing a new fiscal policy (5:1-13), the aristocracy and the priesthood had relinquished their contacts with Tobiah (6:17-19; 13:4-9), "all Judah" had begun delivering the Levitical portions (vv. 10-14), a strict view of Sabbath observance had been embraced (vv. 15-23), the Judean men had renounced their marriages to women from neighboring lands (vv. 23-27), Nehemiah had expelled a descendant of the high priest who had intermarried with the Sanballatides (vv. 28-29), and, finally, the Temple-cult had been reorganized (v. 30).

9. The Cultic Reforms – 13:4-14

9.1. Introduction

The present chapter consists of two main parts corresponding to the two paragraphs in 13:4-14. The first section (§9.1) treats the account of the Eliashib-Tobiah affair in vv. 4-9 and attempts to show that, before the insertion of v. 6, this text was connected to 6:17-19. The second section (§9.2) considers the ramifications of this conclusion for understanding the account of the Levitical reforms reported in vv. 10-14. In addition, it presents a critique of the assumption that the information on the Levitical guild provided in this and other passages in Nehemiah's account is historically trustworthy.

9.2 The Eliashib-Tobiah Affair – 13:4-9

9.2.1. The Interpolation of V. 6b

Against the backdrop of the third-person account in 12:44-13:3, the narrative in 13:4-31 stands out in sharp relief. While the paragraphs concerning the appointment over the chambers and treasuries in 12:44-46, the delivery of the portions in 12:47, and the expulsion of multiethnic Judeans in 13:1-3 are all formulated either in the third-person or passive voice, the remainder of chap. 13 allows Nehemiah to relate first-hand how he *alone* perceived and brought about an awareness of the abuses which the community *later* decided to correct (ולפני מזה, v. 4).[1] Inasmuch as the communal resolutions in 12:44-13:3 reflect his prior influence, he can pride himself in the concluding chapter of the book as the initiator of the reform.[2] Thus, the reader must "regard the whole of 13:4-31 as pluperfect, 12:26-13:3 forming the abiding climax" of the story in Neh 1-13.[3]

---

1 Whether ולפני מזה should be interpreted as referring originally to the directly preceding material in 12:44-13:3, is discussed below, yet the contrast of Nehemiah's own report to the preceding third-person account of similar activities indicates to the "naïve" reader that ולפני מזה functions to predate Nehemiah's acts in 13:4-31 *before* the changes undertaken during the ideal time ("on that day") depicted in 12:44ff. Cf. Ibn Ezra's interpretation of this phrase: וקודם זה ההבדל.

2 Our treatment of the arrangement of these paragraphs differs drastically from previous scholarly attempts to see 12:33-13:3 as downplaying Nehemiah's achievement. For example,

Insofar as 13:4ff. was not composed for its present literary setting, such a reading of this text is not the intention of the original authors. While most scholars agree on this point, they are odds with regard to the presence of ולפני מזה directly after the redactional compositions of 12:44-13:3. How could Nehemiah have referred to that which, on all accounts, was written subsequently to his own work? Attempting to resolve this historical conundrum, some commentators contend that before the addition of the material in 12:44-13:3, the summary pronoun זה referred to everything that had been recorded in the building report.[4] Others argue that the introduction has always served to predating the incident depicted in 13:4ff. to a time before the events recounted in the immediately preceding paragraphs (12:44-13:3). Yet they also ascribe these two words to an editorial hand.[5]

Determining which of these approaches to ולפני מזה is more plausible requires that we consider another question: If the introduction originally referred to the prior events recounted in the building report, how should one explain v. 6? Here Nehemiah affirms that "in all this (ובכל־זה) I was not in Jerusalem, for in the thirty-second year of Artaxerxes king of Babylon I went to the king." According to this statement, the incident must have occurred during or sometime after the thirty-second year of Artaxerxes' reign, but the consecration of the wall in 12:27-43 as well as all of the events reported in chaps. 1-7 must have taken place in the twentieth year of his reign. Thus, Nehemiah reports in v. 4 that "before" the building of the wall (the twentieth year) Eliashib prepared a chamber in the temple for Tobiah, while v. 6 implies that the incident took place during or subsequent to the thirty-second year. Since the dates do not agree, something must be amiss in the formulation of the passage. Scholarship has rightly recognized that either the introductory phrase in v. 4 or the date in v. 6 has been added.

The decision to make a later reader responsible for v. 6 instead of the phrase ולפני מזה in v. 4 has serious consequences. Since the next paragraph (vv. 10-14), which concerns Nehemiah's measures to ensure the payment of the Levitical portions, lacks a time reference, the reader would have to date these actions to the period after his return from Babylon. Likewise, the two remaining accounts

---

Eskenazi writes: "Neh 12:44-13:3 describes what the *people* themselves have done: they gladly provided for the cultic personnel and separated from foreigners. In Neh 13:10-13 Nehemiah himself energetically imposes these measures, acknowledging no overt support from the community" (1988: 124 – author's italics). It is difficult, however, to conceive why later authors would desire to detract from the accomplishment of the very one whose account they were responsible for transmitting. Much more plausible is a development in the other direction: At the instigation of the pious governor, the community enacts reforms.

3   Williamson (1985: 383f.).
4   Cf. Mowinckel (1964: 35), as well as Winckler (1901: 484), Hölscher (1923: 559), Kittel (1929: 648ff.), Noth (1943: 150), Kellermann (1967: 49f.), and Gunneweg (1987: 166).
5   Clines (1984: 238f.) and Williamson (1985: 380ff.).

of Nehemiah's Sabbath and marriage reforms in v. 15ff. must be understood as having taken place during this second period. Yet without 13:6, there would be no second period, and the general date "in those days" introducing the reform-accounts (13:15 and 23) would refer to the time during which the wall was built.

Given this complication, why do many scholars insist that the date in v. 6 is the work of an editor? Surely, the strongest motivation for this approach is the insoluble tension created by the notice when read together with 5:14ff., a passage in which Nehemiah reflects retrospectively on his twelve years of selfless gubernatorial service. His magnanimity expressed itself in his willingness to forgo his gubernatorial compensation. With regard to this text, Gunneweg remarks pointedly that if Nehemiah can pride himself of his altruism for all twelve years, then this must mean the *entire* time during which he held office.[6] His intention was, of course, not to say that after these twelve years he relented in his benevolence. Such is, however, what 13:6 unintentionally implies, insofar as it introduces a return to Jerusalem subsequent to his initial period of service.[7] On the other hand, without 13:6 there would be no room for doubt that he behaved equally unselfishly and imbued with the official powers of a governor as he indicted the offenders in chap. 13. Moreover, if one assumes that he is responsible for the composition of the entire passage of 5:14ff., he must have been writing after Artaxerxes' thirty-second year. Yet 13:6 presents him at this time visiting the imperial court and returning to continue his aggressive administrative policies. Hence, the reader must infer that Nehemiah is drafting the passage 5:14ff. some time after the thirty-second year, reporting that his administration lasted only twelve years, and at the same time instituting the reforms reported in chap. 13.[8]

The designation for Artaxerxes in 13:6 ("the king of Babylon") poses another problem. The first-person account mentions the king more than fifteen times yet always simply as "the king" and never "the king of Persia," let alone "the king of Babylon." Rudolph replied to this argument by pointing out the likelihood that the account did not originally contain chap. 13 and was only later added to it.[9] While we agree with Rudolph and those who follow him on the point that 13:4ff. belongs to a later edition of the building report, it does not make sense that Artaxerxes requires an introduction. Inasmuch as the passage

---

6   1987: 166.

7   Of course, Nehemiah could not have undertaken the reforms in the same year as he left. Travel back and forth between Babylon and Jerusalem required more than half-year and Nehemiah stays in Jerusalem for a period of time (ולקץ ימים).

8   That such corresponds to the historical facts would be difficult to maintain since nowhere in his Memoir does Nehemiah depict himself wielding such authority and influence as in the accounts of the law suits in the final chapter.

9   1949: 203.

has been composed as a continuation of Nehemiah's account, which has already identified this ruler, a general reference to "the king" would have sufficed.[10]

Now if the incident with Eliashib and Tobiah is not to be dated to the time after Artaxerxes' thirty-second year, when did it take place? The best response to this question is that the passage originally reported Tobiah's dismissal as Nehemiah arrived in Jerusalem. One notices the analogies between the formulation of 13:6a + 7a and the notice of his first arrival in 2:11: ואבוא אל־ירושלם ואהי־שם ימים שלשה//ובכל־זה לא הייתי בירושלם...ואבוא לירושלם. When separated from the immediately preceding clauses (13:6b), Nehemiah's statement in 13:7 that he came to Jerusalem and noticed the evil that Eliashib had committed for Tobiah is fully comprehensible. Yet the inclusion of v. 6b, which explains that he left and went to the king, creates confusion: Instead of "and I came (ואבוא) to Jerusalem," one would have expected: "and I returned (ואשוב)."[11] Thus, we may embrace the view of the above named scholars that the passage originally presented Tobiah's expulsion upon Nehemiah's first arrival in Jerusalem.[12]

Since it is probably not merely coincidental that both 5:14 and the present passage provide chronological information for Nehemiah's administration and mention the thirty-second year of Artaxerxes' reign, it seems that 5:14 has directly influenced the date in 13:6 merits serious consideration.[13] In drawing on the *terminus ad quem* in 5:14, the author of 13:6 has probably intended to portray Nehemiah returning to the king once he had finished his tenure as governor.[14] After some time (ולקץ ימים), Nehemiah pleads for a leave of absence (נשאלתי מן־המלך). The evidence of שאל *niph.* ("ask leave of absence," *BDB*) as it used elsewhere (cf., e.g., 1 Sam 20:6, 28) does not permit the conclusion that the king appointed his cupbearer to a second term of governorship. It indicates rather merely a short furlough to visit Jerusalem. The author of 13:6 apparently desired to portray Eliashib acting as if he did not expect Nehemiah to return after he had finished his term of office in Judah (cf. 5:14 with 13:6).[15] The redactional

---

10 Rudolph also argued that 13:4ff. was composed as an appendix to the building report, and not for a separate account. Cf. Ezra 8:1, which refers to Artaxerxes as the "king of Babylon." Since Ezra's account was probably composed after Nehemiah's (cf. §5.3.2), it supports the present conclusion.

11 Cf. 2:15b in relation to 2:13a.

12 Williamson's counter-arguments (1985: 382) apply only to Kellermann's attempt (1967: 153, 196) to link this episode, which he presumed to be historical fact, to the time before the commencement of the building. This seems to be a case of making literary-critical decisions primarily on the basis of historical consistency.

13 An explanation for this tension is even more urgent given the probability that the former is due to redactional activity, as many scholars maintain. If 5:14 has been retouched with chronological information, the date in 13:6 is almost certainly redactional.

14 *Pace* Hölscher (1923: 559).

15 One may compare the depiction in 13:4-9 to *TAD* A4.7 which reports that in the fourteenth year of Darius II the priests of Khnub, who were in league with the governor

activity has, however, placed the historicity of the account in doubt. With regard to the information provided in v. 6, Hölscher observed that it " schon deshalb nicht angenommen werden kann, weil die persischen Statthalter auf Lebenszeit ernannt wurden."[16]

If the interpretation of vv. 4-9 is eased by the removal of v. 6, how should one account for the editorial activity? Karrer is most likely correct in dismissing the assumption that the author wished to excuse Nehemiah by emphasizing that he was absent during the incident.[17] According to her solution, the twelve years are to be understood as an attempt to present a lengthy interval between the signing of pact in chap. 10, which makes explicit reference to the reforms, and the point when Nehemiah notices the community's failure (13:4ff.). The problem with this solution is that according to 5:14 Nehemiah is present in Judah during these twelve years. The reader thus wonders why he does not notice the abuses earlier? Nevertheless, we may follow Karrer in bringing the pact in chap. 10 to bear on the problem. It seems that the interpolation of 13:6 intends to reinterpret both the pact and the reform accounts in chap. 13. Rather than attempting to undercut "Nehemiah's own egotistical assertions by subsuming [his] implementations. . .to the prior communal decision,"[18] it is more likely that the editor desired to illustrate how the community requires a central authority (represented by the person of Nehemiah) that ensures its adherence to the Torah. While it had fulfilled its obligations for the twelve years during which Nehemiah was in office, it was delinquent after the thirty-second year, when he left the government of the province in the hands of the rulers (v. 11) and nobles (v. 17). Instead of recounting a gradual decline after the pledge made on the

---

Wiadrang, destroyed the temple of Yahu as Arsames "departed and went to the king" (line 4f.). The similarities are indeed undeniable, but there are also considerable differences. While Arsames is still governor as he made his journey, the author of 13:6, by presenting Nehemiah traveling to Babylon in Artaxerxes' thirty-second year, does not depict a mere trip of the governor. Rather, Nehemiah returns after leaving office. Otherwise, he would not have needed to request a leave of absence (שאל niph.). Whereas TAD A4.7 describes the Jews' enemies taking advantage of Arsames absence to destroy the Yahu temple, Eliashib's and Tobiah's behavior suggests that Nehemiah was not planning to return (or, according to the proposed original meaning, that he had never been in Jerusalem). By providing Tobiah a chamber in the temple precincts, Eliashib and those he represents make a symbolic gesture: "Provision of space in the temple was no doubt connected with commercial concessions. The word translated "room" (liskah) connotes both residence and storeroom, but the latter is more common in Second Temple texts (1 Chron. 9:26; 2 Chron. 31:11; Ezra 8:29; Neh 10:38-40 [37-39]). Commercial interest, either as supplier or as middleman, was therefore the reason for wanting a pied-à-terre in the temple" (Blenkinsopp (1988: 354)). Inasmuch as the temple was the center of political and commercial activity, Tobiah has a place in Jerusalem's governmental affairs. Thus, it is quite unlikely that the original authors of 13:4ff. intended to portray Eliashib making this significant political move for only the short time of Nehemiah's absence. Here is the main difference with TAD A4.7.

16   1923: 559.
17   2001: 141.
18   Eskenazi (1988: 101).

seventh month of the twentieth year, the author of v. 6 shows how the community leaders failed to enforce the pledge *as soon as* Nehemiah left office. When the latter is again granted a leave of absence and visits the province, he immediately observes that the pledge had been broken. He then identifies and prosecutes the offenders (vv. 11, 17, 25), quoting the individual stipulations of the pact – themselves quotations of Neh 13. The inclusion of v. 6 demonstrates that without the strong hand of a pious ruler, who is the first to commit himself to the Torah (10:2), the province reverts inevitably and without delay to the same situation it had promised to change.

In addition, the authors of the pact intended that we read the prosecutions in chap. 13 in light of the principle, sine lege nihil crimen. Before the insertion of v. 6, Nehemiah's remonstrations are to be understood as simply his own progressive policies which he introduced "before this" and which the community embraced in their pledge. After the author of v. 6 contradicts the introductory phrase in v. 4 and dates the reforms to a later period,[19] Nehemiah no longer institutes new reforms. To the contrary, he demonstrates the community's failure to keep what it previously acknowledged as the requirements of the Torah.[20] Whereas the interpretation of Nehemiah's remonstrations originally did not presuppose chap. 10, they assume greater significance once the community has already taken an oath. Now when he returns from Babylon (13:6), he comes in prophetic fashion and indicts (ריב) the offenders for the sins against the Torah itself.[21]

If the date had not yet been inserted in v. 6, the authors of 12:44-13:3 would have found the introductory phrase ולפני מזה in v. 4 to be a suitable place before which they could "show that the outcome of the dedication [of the wall;

---

19 That the author of 13:6 has been directly influenced by the wording of the pact is supported by the presence of several literary connections discussed in the following chapters. Here, it should be pointed that the opening phrase ובכל זה, which occurs only in 13:6 is strikingly similar to the first words of the pact: ובכל זאת (10:1).

20 The pact may even have originally consisted only of a general pledge to the Torah (vv. 1-30*), which was then amplified successively with individual stipulations. Cf. the excursus at the end of this chapter.

21 One may compare this composition history in chaps. 10 and 13 to literary developments elsewhere, such as the relationship created between the Decalogue and Hos 4. In the latter, Hosea pronounces YHWH's indictment (ריב) with "the inhabitants of the land." "Swearing, lying, and murder, and stealing and adultery break out; bloodshed follows bloodshed" (v. 2). Against the backdrop of the Decalogue, this passage refers to the second, eighth, fifth, seventh and sixth commandments, respectively. Insofar as the claim is merited that the Decalogue has developed from this and other passages in the Prophets (cf. Jeremias [1983: 61ff.] and Kratz [1994: 214ff.]), the authors of the former have transformed Hosea's indictment against social abuses to a reminder and enforcement of the covenant ratified on Sinai. Similarly, Nehemiah's actions assume new weight with the amplification of chap. 10 and the insertion of 13:6. He now indicts the community for breaking the previously ratified pledge to follow the Torah, and this Torah is likewise the covenant behind Hosea's prosecutions.

12:27ff.] was support for the cult and maintenance of its purity"[22] and that "before this" Nehemiah had already brought these issues to the community's attention.[23] By portraying the community both celebrating the completion of the wall and continuing in the direction established by Nehemiah, the composition of 12:27-13:3 takes the narrative in 13:4ff. one step further.

9.2.2 The Original Literary Setting of 13:4-9

Since the immediately preceding paragraphs have been drafted to present the community continuing what Nehemiah instigated in his reforms and ולפני מזה in v. 4 should not be ascribed to a later redaction, the question poses itself, What was the original antecedent of זה in this introductory phrase? That it should be identified with the occasion when the community celebrated the completion of the wall, as suggested by Kellermann,[24] seems most unlikely given the lack of the time between it and the twenty-fifth of Elul. The antecedent could be the date in 6:15, yet this is equally improbable since Eliashib would have assigned Tobiah the chamber in Nehemiah's presence.[25]

A possibility not yet considered is that ולפני מזה refers to what is reported in 6:17-19. If the antecedent were the introductory phrase in v. 17, "also in those days," with which the author means the fifty-two days of construction (6:15-16), then the introduction in 13:4 ("but before this/previously") would date the actions in vv. 5-9 to the time prior to Nehemiah's first arrival in Jerusalem. If so, the passage reports that before the nobles were exchanging letters with Tobiah, the priest Eliashib had placed a temple-chamber at his disposal. As Nehemiah came to town, he dismissed this figure from his toehold in the seat of the province. We know now that because Tobiah had "previously" lost his pied-à-terre, the nobles were forced to communicate by way of written correspondence (6:17) in order to maintain their relations with the one to whom they had sworn allegiance (v. 18).

In order to test the proposal that 13:4-9 was originally connected to 6:17-19, we may first examine the purpose of passage in order to see that the primary author was neither concerned to simply document another episode of the antagonism between Nehemiah and his foes depicted in chaps. 2-4 and 6:1-9,

---

22 Williamson (1985: 383).

23 Assuming the integrity of v. 6, which dates Nehemiah's reforms to more than twelve years after "that day" of the dedication, one cannot explain the composition of 12:44-13:3, since then the reader could no longer understand the phrase "but before this" as referring to an occasion prior to the community's actions.

24 1967: 50.

25 V. 7 states clearly that as Nehemiah arrived in Jerusalem, Tobiah already possessed the chamber.

nor intended merely to illustrate his service for the temple-chambers. Were this the case, one could argue that passage fails to form an appropriate continuation of 6:17-19, which calls into question the loyalty of the Judean nobles and their commitment to the Restoration.[26] Yet if the analysis can show that this paragraph censures Eliashib and that the other topics – the sanctity of the temple-chambers and Tobiah's antagonism – are subsumed to this goal or constitute secondary additions, then the author would follow the same polemical *Tendenz* introduced in 6:17-19.[27]

It is undeniable that the transmitted form of the account pays particular attention to the temple-chambers. נשכה/לשׁכה occurs no less than five times in these six verses. While Nehemiah commences by describing the conditions which made possible the desecration of these rooms (v. 4), he concludes by reporting that they were finally cleansed (v. 9a). The account achieves denouement with the note in v. 9b that the temple-vessels, meat offering and frankincense were restored; previously, it had mentioned these cultic items as the former contents of the misappropriated chamber (v. 5). The placement of the passage between 12:44ff. and 13:10-14 adds to the impression that the passage is primarily concerned with the temple-chambers and the measures Nehemiah takes to ensure their maintenance and purity. First, in the following paragraph, all Judah brings tithes of corn, new wine and oil into the treasuries (v. 12). V. 5b mentions these items in the exact same order. It continues with the statement "as prescribed for the Levites, and the singers and the porters, and the offerings for the priests," which is quite reminiscent of 12:44. Second, Eliashib was "placed over" the temple-chambers (v. 4). In v. 13, Nehemiah appoints new officials over the treasuries (v. 13), and 12:44 refers to the appointment of men over the chamber. Third, 12:45 mentions the ward of purification, and in 13:9a Nehemiah orders that the chambers be purified. Finally, Nehemiah prays in v. 14b that God remember his good deeds for the *temple* and its services.

Although it seems that 13:4-9 shares the focus of its context, a diachronic analysis reveals that the similarities between this passage and its context are due to editorial hands. For example, both the vocabulary and syntax of v. 7bβ render it likely that an editorial hand has appended this clause to the foregoing statement. The statement ואבינה ברעה אשר עשה אלישׁיב לטוביה would have sufficed after vv. 4-5aα, and the continuation לעשׂות לו נשכה lags behind. So

---

26 Reinmuth considers this to be the case (2002: 283). Cf. also Gunneweg (1987: 164ff.) and Blenkinsopp (1988: 353).

27 The fact that these verses do not conclude with a prayer for remembrance, while vv. 10-14 do not begin with dating formula as in vv. 4, 15, 23, does not warrant the conclusion that vv. 4-9 represents a section of vv. 4-14 (*pace* Karrer [2001: 166] and Reinmuth [2002: 267f.]). This approach is heavily influenced by the division of paragraphs in chap. 13 according to the use of the prayers for remembrance. Cf. the table in §8.2 which omits vv. 4-9 from the comparison of 5:1-13; 13:1-14, 15-22, and 23-27.

also, the rest of the passage consistently spells the word for chamber with a ל
(לשכה; vv. 4, 5, 8, 9), not with a נ (נשכה). Finally, this chamber is said to be in the
courts of the temple, what should have already been stated in vv. 4-5aα. The
reason for this proposed addition is probably not to clarify the ambiguous
formulation of v. 7aα, but rather to emphasize that the "evil" perpetrated by
Eliashib consisted in that he gave Tobiah a place within the sacred precincts
(בחצרים).[28] If v. 7 originally consisted of only ואבוא לירושלם ואבינה ברעה אשר
עשה אלישיב לטוביה, it would constitute the first evidence indicating that the
primary author of the passage was less concerned with the sanctity of the temple
than with the priesthood's connections to Tobiah.

V. 9a provides further evidence in this direction. The foregoing verses report
that only one chamber had been misappropriated. Why then does Nehemiah
order that all the chambers be purified? While it is likely that the author
considered Tobiah's presence to have polluted all the chambers, it also likely
that this author is not responsible for the first edition of the passage. What so
deeply perturbs Nehemiah (v. 8a) is not *that* but rather *how* Eliashib had
desecrated the temple precincts. The tight connection between v. 8b to v. 9b
suggests that v. 9a has been inserted: "All the things of the house of Tobiah" are
replaced with "the things of the house of God." Just as Nehemiah "throws out"
(ואשליכה...החוץ מן־הלשכה), he also "restores" (ואשיבה שם). V. 8b, however,
severs this join. Furthermore, the antecedent of the preposition שם is "the
chamber" in v. 8a, yet the transmitted shape of the passage causes the reader to
link it with "the chambers" in v. 8b.[29]

Finally, we noticed above that v. 5 both highlights the significance of the
chambers and shares many features in common with the context of vv. 4-9.
Were one to take the information in this verse at face value, the chamber would
have previously (לפנים) served as the storeroom not only for the grain offering,
incense and vessels, but also for the tithes belonging to the Levites, singers and
gatekeepers and the priestly offerings. That all these items were kept in a single
large room taxes the credibility of the account. One cannot rule out the possibility that the author of 13:4ff. has intentionally exaggerated the facts. However,
Nehemiah restores only the vessels, the grain offering and incense. in v. 9b [30] If

---

28 While v. 5a is interested in the size and nature of the property (לשכה גדולה, "a large
    chamber"), v. 7bβ is concerned with its location.

29 This conclusion would explain that טהר (*piel/hit.*) appears elsewhere in Nehemiah's account
    only in places (13:22a and 30a) where editorial activity has been posited (cf. the analysis of
    vv. 15-22 and 23-31 in the following chapters). With the addition of v. 9a, the term recurs in
    each section of chap. 13, thus increasing the stylistic and structural unity of these texts.
    While the term probably does not belong to earliest formulation of chap. 13, it is integral to
    late texts in Ezra-Neh (Ezra 6:20 and Neh 12:30).

30 While v. 9bβ may have been appended by an editor, it can hardly be coincidental that v. 5aβ
    includes the same tithes v. 12 mentions – and in the same order.

v. 5 originally enumerated solely these items, the expansion may have been directly influenced by the following paragraph, which identifies the portions for the Levites and singers with the exact same triad ("the tithes of grain, new wine and oil," v. 12). "Man muß ferner beachten, daß es sich 13,5aα um Opfermaterialen (Opfermehl, Weihrauch) und die entsprechenden Aufbewahrungs- und Meßgefäße handelt, während 13,5aβb von Abgaben zur Erhaltung des Kultpersonals spricht, die erst 13,12 behandelt werden."[31] Kellermann rightly concludes from this that a later hand added v. 5aβb.[32]

According to the analysis, the earliest edition of the passage comprised the following:

> Before this, however, Eliashib the priest, who was appointed to be in charge of the chambers in the House of our God, was a relative of Tobiah and provided for his use a large chamber where there had been previously kept the grain offering, the incense and the vessels. [...]. As I came to Jerusalem and realized the evil that Eliashib had done for Tobiah [...], I was very angry and threw all the things belonging to the house of Tobiah out of the chamber [...] and restored the things belonging to the House of God.

If all the other lines of the paragraph indeed belong to a later layer, Eliashib does not place at Tobiah's disposal a chamber where all the offerings for the cultic officers were previously stored (v. 5aβb),[33] nor was Nehemiah enraged that Tobiah was allowed to pollute the sacred precincts (vv. 7bβ and 9a). It appears, therefore, justified to conclude that the authors of the passage were primarily interested in censuring Eliashib rather than emphasizing Nehemiah's acts of piety for the temple or his conflict with Tobiah. This would explain why Eliashib is consistently the subject of the action (cf. esp. v. 5aα and v. 7abα).

The connections between this passage and 6:17-19 are striking. Both passages present Tobiah as a foil for the criticism of "many of the nobles in Judah" (6:17) or "the priest, Eliashib" (13:4). He is neither mentioned first (cf. 6:17 and 13:4), nor does he play an active role. Moreover, only in these passages does Tobiah act alone, which contrasts with seven other passages where he appears in tandem with Sanballat.[34] Furthermore, the culpable in both passages are said to have entered into political alliances with this figure. 6:17-19 states that the Judean nobles were exchanging letters with him (v. 17) and that "many in Judah" had sworn allegiance to him (v. 18a). 13:4-9 likewise reports that Eliashib had placed a chamber at his disposal. So too, both passages report that the guilty parties were directly related to him. Not only was he the son-in-law of

---

31 Kellermann (1967: 49).
32 Followed by Gunneweg (1987: 165), Steins (1995: 205) and considered by Williamson (1985: 386).
33 This is rather unlikely since Eliashib would have been concerned not to aggravate his own priestly guild.
34 Cf. 2:10, 19; 3:33ff.; 4:1; 6:1, 10-14.

Shecheniah ben Arah, but his son had also married the daughter of Meshullam ben Berechiah (6:18b).[35] In 13:4, we are told that Eliashib was a relative (קרוב) of Tobiah.[36]

It was noted above that the formulation of 6:17 corresponds to that of 13:4 (a general time reference + the identification of the culpable + a participle) and that the introductory expression ולפני מזה, which cannot be ascribed to an editorial hand, refers to the exchange of letters between the nobles and Tobiah. Thus, the account in 13:4-9 fits hand in glove to the subject of 6:17-19: The nobles sustain their relations with Tobiah by way of written correspondence after he had lost his pied-à-terre in Jerusalem and then sought to perpetuate his encroachment in the province with a different approach. These findings render it quite probable that 6:17-19 and 13:4-9 were originally conjoined.[37]

The claim that these two passages were directly connected in a former edition of the building-report is substantiated by the results of the analysis of chap. 6. Although vv. 17-19 clearly continues the theme of diplomatic corre-spondence begun in vv. 2-4 and 5-9, the terminology is different. In the preceding paragraphs, messages are "sent" (שלח, vv. 2, 3, 4, 5, 8, 12). However, in vv. 17ff., letters are "going" (הולכות) and "coming" (באות). Likewise, we observed that 6:19b has probably been appended to the paragraph. The foregoing account is consistently formulated with participles, yet this clause, which lacks a conjunction, switches to the *qatal*. Furthermore, the nobility, not Tobiah, is the subject in the foregoing verses. That he sought to intimidate Nehemiah (אגרות שלח טוביה ליראני) corresponds to vv. 1-14 (cf. the use of ירא in vv. 9a, 13a and 14b). Hence, it seems quite likely that as the connection to 13:4-9 was lost, this statement has been added to v. 19a in order to integrate the passage with the theme in foregoing verses and thus to integrate vv. 1-19 into an individual "chapter." Originally, a new unit must have begun already in v. 17, rather than in 7:1. Before the notice of completion in vv. 15-16, the reader encounters a זכרה-prayer (v. 14). The preceding unit, chap. 5, also concludes with a זכרה-prayer (v. 19), and between it and 6:14 there is an unmistakable word-play.[38] Now if the זכרה-prayer in 6:14 functions to delimit a literary unit as in chaps. 5 and 13, the notice in vv. 17-19 is left dangling between vv. 15-16 and the introduction of a completely different theme in 7:1ff. Recognizing its

---

35　Significantly, the building register depicts the latter person repairing the wall opposite his chamber (נגד נשכתו, 3:30).

36　Whatever type of relationship this may have been, the implication is that the personal tie to Eliashib is the necessary background for understanding how Tobiah obtained a chamber in the temple.

37　Since the first-person material in chaps. 7-12 neither mentions Tobiah or the rest of enemies, nor continues the portrayal of the contacts between the aristocracy and the enemy, 13:4ff. represents, in the transmitted shape of Ezra-Neh, the *Wiederaufnahme* of 6:17-19.

38　Cf. §§7.5.1 and 8.2.

"suspended" character, Torrey and Rudolph suggested that the passage was added later, while Mowinckel, Hölscher, Myers, *et al* contended that it was originally located before the notice of completion in vv. 15-16.[39] What these scholars failed to consider, however, is that vv. 17-19 originally continued in 13:4ff. If this is indeed the case, the זכרה-prayer in 6:14 may have been employed so that 6:1ff. concludes in the same way not only as 5:1-19 but also as the succeeding paragraphs (6:17-19 + 13:4-14, vv. 15-22 and 23ff.).[40] Likewise, each of the passages after 6:15-16 begins in the same way: with the expression ("in those days") followed by participles (cf. 6:17ff.; 13:15ff. and 23ff.).[41]

9.2.3 The Historicity of Episode

In chap. 2, Nehemiah arrives in Jerusalem and inspects the wall at night (2:11ff.). He emphasizes that he waited to tell the rulers of his plans (2:16a). When he does inform them, he uses caution and deference, appealing to the common situation of affliction and reproach (2:17; cf. the emphasis on the אנחנו). As anticipated, the building enterprise consolidates the inhabitants of Judah in chaps. 2-4. On the other hand, Nehemiah reports in 13:4-9 that he was not at all concerned to make friends with the ruling classes as he arrived in Jerusalem.[42] This account does not record an isolated incident of tension between Nehemiah and a single priest, for the intended reader would have known that Eliashib could not have made "this gesture of defiance to Nehemiah's political-religious policies if he did not have the support of a number of priests, and perhaps also of the high priest himself…(cf. 13:28)."[43] Just as 13:28-29, this passage censures the entire Jerusalem priesthood and creates thereby an incongruity with 2:16ff., where Nehemiah attempts to secure the approval of the priests. Testimony that he actually succeeded is furnished by the

---

39 The latter assumption is based heavily on v. 19b. If this clause indeed constitutes an addendum, as argued above, the assumption is even more gratuitous.

40 In §7.4.3, we saw that 6:5-9 was composed for the notice of completion in vv. 15-16. The addition of vv. 10-14 serves to distinguish a *new* unit (vv. 1-14), which creates a pattern with 5:1-19 and 6:17-19 + 13:4-14, 15-22, 23ff.

41 Hölscher's wrote with respect to the insertion of v. 6: "Der Interpolator meinte, daß die Denkschrift die Taten Nehemias in *chronologisch-biographischer Form* erzähle…" (1923: 559-my italics). "Die Denkschrift Nehemias berichtete über die Taten des Statthalters nicht in biographisch-chronologischer Folge, sondern im aufreihenden Stile der Inschriften und ähnlicher Literatur. Das Hauptwerk Nehemias, der Mauerbau, steht an der Spitze und wird am ausführlichsten behandelt. Nun folgen in einfacher Aneinanderreihung allerlei andere verdienstliche Taten Nehemias" (1923: 558).

42 Here the "we" is almost completely absent; cf. solely "the House of *our* God" in v. 4.

43 Clines (1984: 239). Hölscher (1923: 559) was likely correct in assuming that the author was referring to the high priest, Eliashib. Both he and Meshullam ben Berechiah feature prominently in the building register and are censured in 6:18b and 13:28.

building register, in which the high priest, Eliashib, sets the precedent for the other builders (v. 1). Hence, from an historical vantage point, Nehemiah's behavior in 13:4-9 contradicts the portrayal of the same in chaps. 2-4. One finds it, therefore, difficult to believe that he both needed the approbation of the priesthood and at the same time overruled their decision with respect to the use of the chambers. Even if we disregard the plain sense of chap. 2 and assume that he held the office of governor as he came to Jerusalem, the violation of the priesthood's sphere of sovereignty would have certainly precluded their cooperation.

These observations should not cause doubt with respect to the conclusion that v. 6, which dates the incident to many years after the building of the wall, has been inserted by a later hand. That Nehemiah expelled Tobiah as he was just visiting Jerusalem causes even more tension with the rest of the account. Instead of speculating when this incident may have occurred, one need only to compare this text to the redactional motivation behind 5:1-13; 6:10-14, 17-19 and 13:10ff., which correct the positive image of the ruling classes in chaps. 2-4. In reporting that the prophets (6:10-14), nobles (vv. 17-19) and priesthood (13:28f.) had been corrupted by Nehemiah's enemies or were allied with them, the authors could not have portrayed these groups in a more critical light. Historically, it is possible that Tobiah was forced to forfeit his temple-chamber as Nehemiah came to the province in an official capacity.[44] It is also probable that there existed the same connubial and political ties between Sanballat, Tobiah and the upper classes in Judah recorded in Nehemiah's account. Yet, it is quite unlikely that Nehemiah took it upon himself to treat this problem, especially at the time and in the way reported in 13:4-9. Much more conceivable is that he contented himself with the support of these groups in order to gain the unity necessary to the success of his plans. Focused single-mindedly on finishing the work (cf. esp. 6:2-4) and not wishing to jeopardize the unity he established, he would surely not have attempted to solve all social and religious abuses in the province.

That the priesthood established close links through marriage to promote their political and economic interests (*connubium et commercium*), not only in the Persian period but also in later ages, cannot be doubted.[45] In the secondary layers of his building account, Nehemiah gradually addresses himself to the threat posed by these connubial ties.[46] Accordingly, chap. 13 adds a considerable nuance to his opinion expressed in 2:17a that the ruins of the wall represent the

---

44 "Die scheinbare Einzelmaßnahme, die im Hinauswerfen von Tobija bestand, ist im großen Zusammenhang der verwaltungsmäßigen und kultrechtlichen Verselbständigung Judas zu sehen" – Gunneweg (1987: 167).
45 Cf., e.g., Josephus, *Ant.* 11.302f..
46 Cf. the drastic measures he takes in 13:28f.

source of הרעה. Now we are told that as he comes from Susa, he noticed that Eliashib had perpetrated הרעה (13:7). In each passage that begins with the expression, "in those days," and concludes with a זכרה-prayer in chap. 13, he repeatedly corrects his initial view expressed in 2:17 and shows that הרעה is a condition that obtained neither from Jerusalem's state of disrepair nor from the reproach of the surrounding nations, but rather from the Judeans themselves (cf. vv. 17 and 27).[47]

9.3 The Reinstallation of the Levites and Singers – 13:10-14

With the groundwork already laid in §9.1, the following discussion of the account in vv. 10-14 can afford to be succinct. Here we will observe how the authors of these verses intended to portray Nehemiah gathering the Levites to Jerusalem as one of his first achievements after his arrival (§9.3.1) and that one should neither accept the historicity of this account nor assume that Nehemiah favored the Levites over the priests (§9.3.2).

9.3.1 The Historical Settings

We noted above that the tensions created by v. 6 indicate that v. 4ff. did not originally include this verse. If this proposal is tenable and the expression ואבוא לירושלם in v. 7a originally meant, "when I *arrived* to Jerusalem" (not "when I *returned* to Jerusalem," as required by v. 6), then vv. 10-14 dates Nehemiah's actions for the Levites to the twentieth year of Artaxerxes' reign. Without a new introduction in v. 10 (as in vv. 4, 15, 23) Nehemiah "notices" that the Levites had not received their portions at the same time as he "discovers" (v. 7) that Eliashib had provided Tobiah with a temple-chamber. After he recalls the Levites and singers from their fields and appoints them to their places (v. 11b), he can report that, "all Judah brought the tithes of grain, new wine and oil in the storerooms" (v. 12). One may, therefore, agree with Winckler that Nehemiah recounts in 13:10-14 his actions as he came to the province for the first time.[48]

Although disputed by a number of scholars,[49] this reading makes much more sense than the transmitted shape of the text. The situation that forced the Levites to abandon their posts in order to support themselves could not have

47 For a further defense of this thesis, cf. §4.3.1.
48 1896: 484f. This view is also espoused by Mowinckel (1916: 69f.), Hölscher (1923: 538f.), Kellermann (1967: 153, 196), and seems to be assumed by Gunneweg (1987: 166f.) and Karrer (2001: 140-n. 44).
49 Cf. ad loc. the commentaries of Bertheau, Siegfried, Bertholet, Rudolph, Myers, Clines, Williamson, Blenkinsopp.

arisen over night. How then should one conceive that the inhabitants of Judah had consistently delivered the Levitical portions for the twelve years of Nehemiah's procuratorship only to withhold these portions after he returned to the imperial court? If they had ceased tithing their grain, new wine and oil (v. 12) *as soon as* he left the province, they would have certainly not have been particularly eager to tithe the same *before* he arrived. Since the Judeans probably did not undergo a change of opinion vis-à-vis the Levites during his administration, this paragraph must refer to a situation that already existed before the wall was repaired and present the reappointment of the Levites and singers as one of Nehemiah's earliest achievements.

The paragraph continues the theme of Judah's consolidation and centralization introduced in chaps. 2-6. Initially, Nehemiah required the acquiescence of the סגנים before the construction could commence (2:16a, 17, 18b), yet now he informs his readers that he possessed independent authority and even indicted (ריב) the local authorities for their negligence (13:11a). That the סגנים consented to his proposal and supported the project despite his confrontational manner portrayed in 13:10-14 is certainly surprising and poses an insurmountable problem for the assumption that the passage is integral to Nehemiah's account. Nevertheless, we must appreciate the intention of its authors. Although a Persian cupbearer came to Judah simply in order to restore the ruins of his ancestral city (2:3, 5), soon after his arrival he realized the need for a more extensive restoration. The Levites and singers had been forced to seek their subsistence elsewhere, and before Jerusalem could be restored to its central place in the province, Nehemiah must make it possible for them to resume residence in the capital.[50]

The first redactional response to the account is found in 12:44ff. At the time when they dedicated the wall (12:27ff.), the whole community corrects the abuse to which Nehemiah "previously" (v. 4) had drawn its attention:

> On that day they appointed men to take charge of the chambers for the stores, sacred contributions, the prime offerings, and the tithes, to gather in them from the rural fields the portions prescribed by the Torah for the priests and Levites; for Judah delighted in the appointed priests and Levites.

One should observe the new accents this addition introduces to the account. While Nehemiah is the one who appoints new officials in v. 13, the people ("they") now take it upon themselves to make the appointments. So too, the

---

50 In *Ant.* 11.159-183, Josephus presents Nehemiah recalling the Levites after he had noticed that the city was poorly populated, thus connecting 13:10-14 to 7:4-5a. Most likely, Josephus understood the appointment of the Levites not just as an example of Nehemiah's solicitude for this guild, but also as a part of the centralization of the province. What may have motivated his conjoining of these passages is the phrase "and I gathered" that appears in 7:5 and 13:10.

Levites are now mentioned after the priests. The assertion that "Judah delighted" in both of these groups may have been influenced by v. 12: "And *all Judah* brought the tithes…into the storerooms." According to 12:44, however, the people do not bring the tithes in to the storerooms; rather, the newly appointed officials themselves go to the fields and collect the contributions. All these observations strongly suggest that the paragraph has not only been composed after 13:4ff., but also reflects the innovations – or at least the view – of a later time.[51]

The passage underwent the next *relecture* with the addition of v. 6. We saw above (§9.2.1) that the presence of this verse is to be explained in light of the ratification of the pact (Neh 10). In 13:11a, Nehemiah remonstrates with the leaders and accuses them of abandoning the temple (ואמרה מדוע נעזב בית־ האלהים).[52] The formulation of this indictment parallels the final stipulation of the pact: ולא נעזב את־בית אלהינו (10:40). Before the reforms recounted in chap. 13 were re-dated to the period after the thirty-second year, the סגנים are rebuked "merely" for their negligence. The inclusion of v. 6 presents this rebuke in a wholly different light. Now the reader must understand Nehemiah's remonstration not as his *own* solicitude for the Levites, but rather as an accusation of the community leaders for failing to impose the stipulations of the pact they had previously signed (10:38).[53] His accusation is all the more serious inasmuch as the community has already affirmed that the individual stipulations represent the requirements of keeping "the Torah of God given by the Moses the servant of God (10:30). Hence, the leaders are doubly culpable: Their negligence with regard to the Levites constitutes not only a breach of the pledge made more

---

51   Cf. §14.2.1 and Reinmuth (2002: 253ff.) for a further comparison of the details in 12:44.

52   V. 11a may constitute an insertion: In v. 11b, Nehemiah assembles "them" and appoints "them" to their posts. The present shape of this verse causes the reader to initially understand that the group mentioned in the preceding clause (הסגנים) were assembled. It becomes much clearer when we remove v. 11a: "And I perceived that the Levitical portions had not been delivered so that the Levites and singers who did the work had all fled to their fields. And I gathered them and appointed them to their posts. Then all Judah brought the tithes…." That the leaders were responsible for the Levites' absence is required by the inclusion of v. 11a, yet it is more likely that the priests, whom vv. 4-9 censure, were primarily responsible (with Schaper [2000: 234ff.] and *pace* Kippenberg [1978: 75]). The proposed redactional activity may have been influenced by the formulation of the following paragraphs in which Nehemiah remonstrates with the nobles (v. 17) and the Judean men (v. 25); cf. also 5:7. With v. 11a, the reader is to understand that Nehemiah considered the absence of the Levites to represent the neglect of the *whole* temple (נעזב בית־האלהים).

53   Here the authors have made a compromise between the depiction in 13:12 and 12:44. In v. 38a, the people promise to bring the tithes themselves in the temple-chambers (as in 13:12), and in v. 38b they affirm (as in 12:44) that the Levites are the ones who go to all the cities and take the tithes (עשׂר, *piel*).

than twelve years before, but also a violation of the Torah that Moses received centuries before.[54]

9.3.2 Nehemiah's Levitical Partisanship

More problematic is the issue of the historical Nehemiah's relationship to the Levites. A formative study undertaken by Vogelstein[55] and most recently the work of Schaper[56] have not questioned the transmitted text and conclude that Nehemiah was a important benefactor of the Levitical guild in the mid-fifth century BCE. Although widely accepted, this conclusion warrants criticism. It is certainly conceivable that Nehemiah viewed the Levites more positively than the priests, since many of the latter had intermarried with the Tobiads and Sanballatids (cf. 13:4 and 28f.). Nonetheless, the claim that the historical Nehemiah "trusted" the Levites is based, according to our findings, upon an end-text reading of an account that originally emphasized Nehemiah's effort to *consolidate* the Judeans and to which editorial hands have added passages resounding with a factious tenor.[57] Without the latter, one lacks a reason to doubt that Nehemiah played the role of a conciliator.

So too, caution is merited with regard to other texts in which Nehemiah assigns the Levites important tasks. For example, 7:1b reports that the porters, singers and Levites "were appointed" once the wall had been built. Significantly, many scholars treat this reference to Levites as a gloss.[58] In the only other first-person passage in which the Levites figure prominently (13:22a), Nehemiah commands them to "purify themselves and come to guard the gates to sanctify the Sabbath." Inasmuch as he had already appointed his servants to guards the gate (v. 19b) and not required their purification, it is likely that this line also represents a late supplement that emphasizes the superiority of the Levites.[59] Therefore, while we cannot deny that in several passages Nehemiah displays sympathies for the Levitical guild, these texts appear to be the work of anonymous authors writing in Nehemiah's name.

If 7:1-3 and 13:22a have been added by late redactors, what can one say about the age of 13:10-14? It has already been seen that this passage seems to presuppose the foregoing paragraph of vv. 4-9, which belongs together with

---

54 Duggan notes that "the last word in the community's covenant renewal becomes the first word in Nehemiah's reforms" (2001: 285). Steins (1995: 174) points out that not only does Nehemiah begin with the final stipulation, but also that the following two reform accounts in chap. 13 correspond in reverse order to the first stipulations.

55 1889: 21f.

56 2000: 230ff.

57 "Die Leviten genossen also das Vertrauen Nehemias. . . " (Schaper [2000: 237]).

58 Cf. the literature cited in §12.3.

59 This passage is studied in the next chapter.

6:17-19 and thus represents an addition to the building account. The question is whether the same hand is responsible for the primary strata of these three texts.[60] I suggest that a later author was inspired by the censure of the priesthood in vv. 4-9. Accordingly, he may have inserted vv. 10-13 between vv. 9b and 14a in order to demonstrate that Nehemiah, after finding the Jerusalem priesthood culpable of a close rapport with the enemy, recalled the Levites from their fields back to Jerusalem and appointed a new council over the storerooms.

This proposal can explain why the passage shares much in common with the *redaction* of vv. 4-9. What originally disturbed Nehemiah is that Eliashib was related to the enemy and placed a chamber in the temple precincts at his disposal. With the addition of v. 5aβ, the priest perpetrates a crime also against the Levites, since Tobiah's chamber previously contained "the tithes of grain, new wine and oil prescribed for the Levites, singers and gate-keepers."[61] As Tobiah forfeited his chamber and as Nehemiah recalled the Levites and singers, "all Judah brought *the tithes of grain, new wine and oil* in the storerooms" (v. 12).

Vv. 10-14 introduce a new accent to the foregoing paragraphs (6:17-19 + 13:4-9), and thus it surprising that they conclude with Nehemiah's plea that God would "not wipe out my good deeds that I have done for the temple and its services" (v. 14b). If one ascribes this half of the prayer to a later hand, v. 14a ("Remember me, O God, for this") would form a fitting continuation to v. 9. That v. 14b has been added would also explain the disparity between it and the זכרה-prayer in v. 22b. In the latter, Nehemiah prays that God would spare him according to the greatness of his חסד.[62] In v. 14b, however, Nehemiah is more confident of his standing with God insofar as he prays for remembrance of his own חסדים.[63]

That a different hand has drafted vv. 10-13, 14b explains Nehemiah's familiarity with cultic vocabulary. Many have attempted to make the Nehemian authorship of the passage more tenable by excising v. 10bβ ("the Levites and singers that did the work"), which appears to be a supplement. Representing the consensus, Kellermann remarked, "Der Satz erläutert הלוים von 13,10a durch

---

60 The possibility of "prolevitische Redaktion" of Nehemiah's account has also been briefly considered by Kaiser (1992: 139, 141f.), who ascribes this activity, however, to the editorial hands responsible for the insertion of the account between Ezra 1-10 and Neh 8.

61 The placement of the reference to the "the offerings for the priests" in v. 5b after the gatekeepers may signify that this reference has been inserted after v. 5aβ. This would solve the incongruity that Eliashib would have caused himself and his priestly colleagues injury by assigning Tobiah the chamber where their offerings were stored. If this reference constitutes a gloss, it may have been influenced by both 13:10ff. and 12:44a.

62 Here מחה, "erase," is the antonym of זכר, "reckon to my account," and seems to refer to an act of heavenly bookkeeping by the divine judge. Accordingly, it may correspond to the late additions to the building account in 3:37 and 7:4ff., both of which incorporate this conception.

die schon bekannte Unterscheidung von Leviten und Sängern. Er muß nach Stil und Konstruktion dem nachchron. Interpolator als Glosse zugeschrieben werden. Der übrige Text geht auf die NQ [Nehemia-Quelle] zurück."[64]

When one compares vv. 10-13 and 14b with other texts, Kellermann's claim that the rest of the account should be ascribed to the hand of Nehemiah becomes difficult to accept. The point at issue is the "the portions of the Levites" (13:10). While one encounters the general, non-cultic semantic use of the term מנת in the Psalms (11:6, 16:5, and 63,11) and in Jeremiah (13:25), its specific cultic usage is very rare. Except for Neh 12:44 and 47, direct parallels are to be found only in our passage and in 2 Chr 31:4, where Hezekiah commands that inhabitants of Jerusalem "to give" (cf. נתנה, Neh 13:10) the מנת הכהנים והלוים.[65] In his accusation of the rulers, Nehemiah inquires, "Why is the house of God forsaken?" (13:11a). The verb here for "forsaken" (עזב) is not rare in the Deuteronomistic History, yet it appears more frequently (twenty-six times) in 1-2 Chr. With it, the authors refer most often to the neglect of the *temple* and the retribution it incurs.[66] In 13:11b, Nehemiah gathers the Levites (ואקבצם). Similarly, 2 Chr 23:2 describes the Levites being gathered from out of all the cities of Judah and being brought to Jerusalem (cf. also 2 Chr 24:5). After gathering the Levites, Nehemiah appoints them to their places. In order to see that he uses עמד in its technical sense in 13:11b, one need only to examine the frequency with which it occurs throughout 1-2 Chr in contexts describing how cultic officers were appointed to their places (for עמדם על-, cf. 2 Chr 30:16 and 35:10).[67] Finally, Nehemiah pleads to be remembered for what he did for the temple and its "services" (ובמשמריו), a very rare, cultic term (cf. Neh 12:24). This comparison has been limited to the most salient examples of the *termini technii* in the passage. Not all the texts mentioned above are earlier than 13:10-13 and 14b. Nonetheless, it appears that the authors of vv. 10-13, 14b presuppose the

---

63 Cf. 2 Chr 6:6 (זכרה לחסדי דויד עבדך), 32:32 and 35:26, all of which pertain to figures who perform "great deeds" for the cult in Jerusalem.

64 1967: 51.

65 Cf. also 2 Chr 34:3.

66 Corresponding to the verdict of the Deuteronomistic History – "and so and so did that which was evil in the eyes of YHWH," - this *terminus technicus* together with its antonym דרש serve as compositional devices for the Chronicler's depiction of the history of Israel. In 1 Chr 28:9f., David admonishes Solomon, "If you seek (דרש) him, he will be found of you; but if you forsake him (עזב), he will cast you off forever." Beginning with a portrayal of how Rehoboam forsook YHWH, the Chronicler exemplifies in the account the Judean kings how the "נוח from the enemies round about" is directly occasioned by seeking (דרש) YHWH. This, in turn, evidences itself in faithfulness to *the temple and its priesthood*.

67 In 1 Chr 6:16ff., we encounter the *hiph.*, and namely with reference exclusively to the Levites whom David sets (העמיד) in their posts. Cf. further 2 Chr 23:18 and 35:2ff. In Ezra-Neh, על-עמדם occurs only here and in 8:17, 9:15. Insofar as the people stand "in their places," the authors may have intended to depict the people assuming the role of cultic officers in Ezra 3.

sense that *many* of these rare terms possess in Ezra-Neh and Chr, which renders it equally unlikely that they were responsible for vv. 4-9.

Finally, we may consider the evidence of the passage's context. The paragraph of vv. 4-9 manifests marks of editing precisely where we encounter similarly technical terminology (vv. 5aβb, 7bβ, 9a). In vv. 30b-31, Nehemiah "appoints" the wards for the priests and Levites. These lines almost certainly constitute a supplement based upon the wording of the pact in chap. 10 (vv. 35ff.). In view of the editorial activity in vv. 4-9 and 30b-31, it is even more difficult to maintain that the authors of vv. 10-13 and 14b, in which the cultic terminology is integral, also composed the substrata of vv. 4-9 and 23ff., which editors have amplified with cultic terminology. These findings correspond to the evidence indicating that the passages which emphasize the role of the Levites (7:1-3 and 13:22a) represent very late additions to the building report.

In sum, the earliest layers of chap. 13, which itself appears to be an addition to the building report, lends support to the contention that the historical Nehemiah, in contrast to the claims of later tradition, was not concerned to promote the Levites.

9.4. Conclusions

The present investigation began by discussing the tension created by the compact notice in v. 6 that Nehemiah returned to Babylon in Artaxerxes' thirty-second year and then asked for a leave of absence some time later. One finds it difficult to understand why he served as governor for twelve years without accomplishing anything of significance other than waiving his right to the governor's *per diem* allowance (5:14ff.), and then *after* his tenure undertook several major reforms. Moreover, the introductory phrase, "but before this," in v. 4 dates the Eliashib-Tobiah affair to a *prior* period. Instead of following many scholars and ascribing this phrase to an editorial hand, we have concluded that v. 6b represents a supplement. That this line is not integral to its context explains the composition of 12:44-13:3 inasmuch as these paragraphs present the community following the precedent set by Nehemiah's actions ("before this") against the influence of an Ammonite in "the congregation of God" (13:1-3) and for the temple-chambers and maintenance of the cult (12:44ff.). The presence of v. 6 is to be explained in light of the pact in chap. 10, several stipulations of which are formulated with the same words of Nehemiah's indictments in chap. 13. Before the insertion of 13:6, the reforms represent Nehemiah's progressive policies that he introduced "before this" and that the community included in their pledge to the Torah. Yet once the redactor employed the information in 5:14 to present Nehemiah leaving office in the thirty-second year and returning some time thereafter, chap. 13 no longer reports *progressive* reforms. To the contrary, Nehemiah's remonstrations are now to be understood as the enforcement of what the community previously acknowledged as the requirements of the Torah (10:30ff.).

In searching for the original literary setting of 13:4-9, we have proposed that 6:17-19 formerly continued directly in 13:4-9. This suggestion is supported by the findings of a literary-critical analysis: The first formulation of the account does not emphasize the antagonism between Nehemiah and an Ammonite nor his deeds for the temple, as the authors of the surrounding passages and many modern exegetes have read the account. Rather, it censures Eliashib who had entered into alliances with Tobiah. Both here and in 6:17-19, the Judeans of the upper class are the antagonists, not Tobiah (who appears without Sanballat in only these two passages). Moreover, 13:4-9 continues the thought begun in 6:17-19: "In those days," the nobility were communicating with Tobiah by way of an exchange of letters (6:17-19), "but before this" the priest Eliashib had placed a temple-chamber at his disposal (13:4-5). As Nehemiah came to Jerusalem, he expelled Tobiah from his chamber (vv. 7-9), which forced those who had "sworn allegiance" (6:18) to Tobiah to maintain their diplomatic relations with him by way of written correspondence. In an earlier version of the first-person account, each paragraph after chap. 4 (5:1-19; 6:1-14; 6:17-19 + 13:4-14; vv. 15-22 and 23ff.) concluded with the זכרה-prayer. So too, each of the units after the notice of completion in 6:15-16 began with the same expression ("in those days") and was formulated with participles (cf. 6:17ff.; 13:15ff. and 23ff.).

Without the date in v. 6, the passage in 13:10-14 makes much better sense: As Nehemiah arrived in the province, he noticed that the Levites were not where they were supposed to be. One of his first accomplishments in Judah was thus to recall them and reinstall them in their places. From v. 6, the reader must understand that they left their places after Nehemiah's gubernatorial tenure. Yet if the Judeans were opposed to supporting the Levites after Artaxerxes' thirty-second year, they would have been even more opposed to supporting them before his twentieth year. This passage appears to have been inserted between vv. 9 and 14b. It employs a technical vocabulary and stereotypical expressions that occur only in the later layers of the surrounding passages. The authors may have found the censure of the priesthood in vv. 4-9 to be suitable place to present Nehemiah's positive stance vis-à-vis the Levites. Inasmuch as it belongs to later tradition, one must be very cautious in employing this text in an historical reconstruction.

The Composition of 13:4-14

6:17-19*

4 Now before this, the priest Eliashib, who was appointed over the chambers of the house of our God was related to Tobiah, 5 and prepared for him a large room where they had previously put the grain offering, the frankincense, the vessels,

> and the tithes of grain, wine, and oil, which were given by commandment to
> the Levites, singers, and gatekeepers,
>> and the contributions for the priests.

6 While this was taking place I was not in Jerusalem,

>> for in the thirty-second year of King Artaxerxes of Babylon, I went
>> to the king. And after some time I asked leave of the king.

7 And as I came to Jerusalem, I discovered the evil that Eliashib had done on behalf of Tobiah,

> preparing a room for him in the courts of the house of God.

8 And I was very angry, and I threw all the things of the house of Tobiah out of the room.

> 9 Then I gave orders and they cleansed the chambers,

and I brought back the things of the House of God, with the grain offering and the frankincense.

> 10 I also found out that the portions of the Levites had not been delivered, so
> that they all had fled to their fields
>> the Levites and the singers, who conducted the service.
> 11 And I remonstrated with the officials and said, "Why is the house of
> God forsaken?"

And I gathered them together and set them in their stations. 12 Then all Judah brought the tithe of the grain, wine, and oil into the storehouses. 13 And I appointed as treasurers over the storehouses the priest Shelemiah, the scribe Zadok, and Pedaiah of the Levites, and as their assistant Hanan son of Zaccur son of Mattaniah, for they were considered faithful; and their duty was to distribute to their associates.

14 Remember me, O my God, for this!

> and wipe not out my good deeds that I have done for the house of my God
> and for the service thereof.

Excursus I: The Composition of Neh 10:1-40

Neh 10 purports to be a copy of the compact ratified by the Restoration community on the twenty-fourth of Tishri in conclusion to the many days of reading in the Torah and confessing "the sins of their fathers." Examining this document more closely, we notice several inconsistencies with regard to the relationship of the passage to the foregoing chapter. While 9:1-5 introduces the people as the בני-ישראל without distinction or class, 10:1-29 presents the nobles and the governor in the foreground. Furthermore, the confession in chap. 9 does not prepare the reader for the community's commitment to perform the specific statutes enumerated in 10:31-40. According to the prayer, the distress "this day," as in former periods of foreign subjugation, is directly occasioned by the sins of "the fathers" against the Torah that God revealed "by the hand of Moses, thy servant" (9:14). This correlates very well to the general pledge in 10:30 to "walk in the Torah of God, which was given by the hand of Moses." However, the continuation of the pledge in 10:31-40, with detailed provisions for the maintenance of the temple and its cultic ministers as well as the specific prohibitions of *connubium* and *commercium* with "the peoples of the land" has nothing in common with the prayer. In fact, chap. 9 mentions neither the temple nor sins with the "peoples of the lands." While these observations initially suggest that the chapter represents an archival document, they actually only indicate that the original edition of the chapter has been thoroughly reworked and edited after the original edition was attached to the prayer in chap. 9. Accordingly, the individual stipulations have various origins, and several presuppose the youngest redactions of the Nehemiah's accounts. Their interpolation into the pact gives Nehemiah's reforms in chap. 13 new meaning: The builder has now become a prophet who prosecutes his *rîb*-lawsuits according to the terms of the renewed covenant in the same manner as the redactors of the prophetical books depict the prophets as defendants of the covenant made on Sinai. We begin with an analysis of the introduction to the pact.

THE HEADING: V. 1

Chap. 10 portrays the response to the prayer as the ratification of the אמנה. That this rare term signifies some sort of pact or unilateral agreement is clear from the formulation of v. 1. Like a covenant (ברית), it is "cut" (אנחנו כרתים אמנה)[68] and then fixed in written form v. 1 (וכתבים). The parties seal it with their names and bind themselves to its terms with a curse and oath (v. 30). In past treatments of chap. 10, the introductory words ובכל־זאת have both posed translation problems and been ascribed to a late redaction. Most English commentaries have rendered this expression either "And because of all of this" or "And in spite of all this." The limitation to these two alternatives is all the more surprising when one compares this phrase to similar formulations elsewhere. For example, in Neh 13:5 we notice that the introduction with the masc. demonstrative pronoun (ובכל־זה) simply means, "And during (or in) all this." The best approach is thus to begin with the literal translation, "And in all this," and to confine ourselves to the present context for the determination of its original setting. The demonstrative pronoun זאת requires an antecedent. If we are to understand it as a feminine sing., we could link it to concluding fem. noun in

---

68 Cf. the covenant initiated by Shechaniah in Ezra 10:3, as well as the reference to the covenant cut with Abraham in Neh 9:8. See also Muilenburg (1959), Kalluveettil (1982).

9:37: ובצרה גדולה. Understood as a common pl., it would refer to the generally portrayed situation in the final lines of the prayer. Regardless of which alternative one favors, we must take the present shape of the text seriously in order to avoid unverifiable speculation as to the pact's original historical or literary setting.

The error of many older analyses has been the examination of the pact independently and in exclusion of the prayer.[69] These approaches require that we either regard ובכל־זאת as secondary or the assumption that the entire wording has been altered. Yet the striking of the transmitted introduction is problematic, for it strips the pact of a conceivable syntactical opening.[70] That the original text no longer exists represents the *ultima ratio*. Furthermore, when we separate the pledge from the prayer, the problem arises how one should explain that both texts are formulated in the first-person. If the narrator was simply drawing on source material, he could have simply recounted the ratification of the pact, as in Ezra 10, for example. Most importantly, if the text were a copy of a legal document that was ratified by the community, deposited in the archives, and thus *familiar* to all, the editor responsible for its inclusion in Ezra-Neh would certainly not have tampered with the wording, especially with that of the introduction.

On the other hand, when one does not delete ובכל־זאת, the account fits well into the pattern of covenant-renewal ceremonies. The end of the prayer, in which the present dire straits of people are directly attributed to a neglect of the Torah, provides the backdrop to the pledge. Here, in the conclusion to the foregoing confession, the Levites plead for an end to the prevailing situation of Judah's subjugation to foreign rule. V. 36f.: "And so now today we are slaves . . . here in the land which you gave to our ancestors . . . And we are in great distress." 10:1 follows up on this complaint with the response of the community: "In spite of all this [distress] we make a pact [namely, to keep the law of God (cf. v.30)]." The אנחנו here is the same אנחנו in the directly preceding confession. The unique designation for the pact (אמנה) lends support to this reading. It is best explained as a play on the use of the same root in 9:8, where God likewise ratifies (כרת) a covenant with Abraham as a reward for the latter's faithfulness.[71]

---

69 Clines writes: "There can be little doubt therefore, as most scholars agree, that this chapter belongs chronologically after Neh 13...." (1984: 199). That "most scholars agree" with the transposition of Neh 10 after Neh 13 is due not least to the work of Bertholet (1902), who noted the implausibility of the coincidence that the community in chap. 13 infringed exactly all those regulations which it had singled out in its pledge to keep the Torah in chap. 10. He proposed that chap. 10 should be read after 13:31 In contrast, cf. Ibáñez Arana (1951).

70 "We write" is inconceivable as an introduction.

71 Cf. Holmgren (1992). In light of these considerations, we must take exception to the interpretations of Fishbane, Blenkinsopp, Williamson, and others, which negate the primacy of the chapter's present literary setting. Williamson, e.g., maintains on the basis of a proposed independent origin for the prayer that it "follows automatically that the join with

Conversely, for those who insist on the unity of chaps. 9 and 10, a different set of problems emerges. If the same person was responsible for the insertion of both prayer and pact, why do the two vary so thoroughly with regard to their themes? As noted in the introduction to this excursus, the confession (as well as the whole narrative in chaps. 8-9) fails to anticipate the commitment to perform the specific provisions enumerated in vv. 31-40. According to the former, the distress "this day," as in former periods of subjection to foreign reign, is the direct consequence of the sins of "the fathers" against the Torah that God revealed "by the hand of Moses, thy servant" (v. 14). While this corresponds perfectly to the general pledge in 10:30 to "walk in the Torah of God, which was given by the hand of Moses," the continuation of the pledge in vv. 31-40, with detailed provisions for the maintenance of the temple and the priests as well as the specific prohibitions of *connubium* and *commercium* with the עמי הארץ, has nothing in common with the prayer. In fact, chap. 9 refers neither to the עמי הארץ nor the temple.[72] It mentions the prior inhabitants of Canaan only as a foil to the main objective of recounting the bestowal and forfeiture of sovereignty in the land. Moreover, why does 9:1-5 introduce the people as the בני-ישראל without distinction or class, while 10:1-29 gives priority to the aristocracy and leaders such as Nehemiah?

The dissonance could be the author's intentional narrative strategy. For example, Eskenazi contends with regard to the prominence of the temple in 10:33-40 and its absence in the prayer that it "indicates that the older temple does not hold great significance in this book. I suggest that one reason for such silence is that the older temple does not fully correspond to Ezra-Nehemiah's notion of the house of God and therefore does not merit great emphasis."[73]

Neh 10 must also fall into the same category" (1985: 337). Similarly, Fishbane sees the chapter as "a subsequent ratification and codification of the *ad hoc* measures discharged by Nehemiah during the course of his procuratorship" (1985: 134). The origin of the pact is thus identified with an independent legal document deposited in the temple-archives and subsequently appropriated for the narrative context. The assumption at the base of these approaches – that the original opening to the pact is no longer extant – creates more problems than it solves, for how are we to explain that the one responsible for the sequential arrangement of these chapters tampered with the wording of a public legal document?

72 Eskenazi (1985: 105) is one of the few scholars who draws attention to this shift: "Whereas the first three scenes of Nehemiah 8-10 (Neh 8:1-12; 13-18 and 9:1-37) ignore the house of God, Nehemiah 10 reverses this tendency. It is, in many ways, a counterpart to Neh 8:1-12, with this difference: as 'people' was the *Leitwort* of Neh 8:1-12, the 'house of God' is the *Leitwort* of Neh 10:33-40. Neh 10:30 declares primary commitment to the Torah; the rest of the chapter spells out this commitment largely in terms of commitment to the house of God. The expression 'house of *our God*' recurs eight times in the seven verses of Neh 10:33-40, with every single verse reiterating the concern of the house of God. It is, indeed the final word of this section, which closes as follows: ולא נעזב את־בית אלהינו, 'We will not neglect the house of our God' (Neh 10:40)."

73 Ibid.

This suggestion merits serious consideration, yet one should also not overlook the possibility that later readers have expanded the pact with the individual stipulations in vv. 31-40.[74] In order to test this suggestion, we briefly examine the formulation of vv. 1-30 and 31-40.

THE LIST OF SIGNATORIES: VV. 2-29

The declarative voice, after having been established in v. 1 with the use of first-person pl. participles, is immediately interrupted by four groups of names in vv. 2-9, 10-14, 15-28, 29 and then resumes in v. 30. While it is not inconceivable that the register of signatories has been positioned in conformity with the documentary style that was customary of the time,[75] the traces left behind in vv. 2-28 suggest that another reader had assumed the tedious task of composing the long list.[76] Not only does the repetition of the החתום ועל of v. 1 in v. 2 come unexpectedly,[77] the rubrics in the list do not agree with the wording "our princes, our Levites, and our priests." According to the list, vv. 2-9 record the priests who signed their name, vv. 9-14 contain the names of the Levites, and vv. 15-28 the lay leaders. However, the last group of signatories is not referred to as השרים as in v. 1 but rather as ראשי העם. Furthermore, all of these titles lack the first-person pl. suffixes of v. 1. The placement and formulation of these headings is also not uniform. While we are told who the first person is, the following names are not identified until the subscription in v. 9 (אלה הכהנים). The Levites and laity are on the other hand introduced with superscriptions. Yet while והלוים in v. 10 is followed by a conjunction before the first name, a *waw* has neither been prefixed to ראשי העם in v. 15 nor to the succeeding name.[78]

THE FIRST POINT OF THE PACT: VV. 29-30

If we are justified in treating the list of signatories as an interpolation, the question arises, Do other parts of the pact also manifest traces of an editorial

---

74 That the stipulations have been expanded is rarely denied by scholars. Some have even proposed a very small substratum in vv. 31-40. See Rudolph (1949: 178ff.), Galling (1954: 241f.), Gunneweg (1987: 138f.), Steins (1995: 171ff.) and Reinmuth (2002: 211ff.). The commonalities between vv. 33-40 and 11:1 indicate that the latter has influenced the composition of the former, not vice versa (*pace* Böhler [1997: 334ff.]).

75 Cf. Tucker (1965).

76 With regard to the secondary nature of the catalogue of signatories in vv. 2-28, most commentators do not share the reservations expressed in Gunneweg's question, "Worüber soll sich eigentlich der sogenannte listenfreudiger Ergänzer gefreut haben?" (1987: 138). Cf. Tucker (1965).

77 Albeit in the plural: החתומים ועל.

relecture? In responding to this question, we need only to follow the path created
by v. 1. On the way, one must bypass several detours, the first of which is the
clause (ועל החתום שרינו לוינו כהנינו, v. 1b). Not only does it detract from the
flow of participles in vv. 1 and 30a, but it also switches to the third-person pl.
and thus appears to represent an expansion by a later hand. Whether it is older
than the list, is difficult to say. Although the first-person pl. nominal suffixes
agree with the previous sentence better than the rubrics of the list, the
composite nature of the signatures and headings permits nothing more than a
tentative answer.

That vv. 29-30aαα (including אדיריהם) have also been added appears probable
inasmuch as the formulations switch from the first-person declarative in v. 1a to
the third-person narrative, and the wording, ושאר העם הכהנים וגו, presupposes
the presence of a preceding list of signatories. Although at first sight, this verse
refers to two groups already mentioned in vv. 2-14 (the priests and Levites), all
of the present groups distinguish themselves from those of the list in that they
belong to lower classes; their entrance into the curse and oath of the pact
illustrates their support of their *noble* brethren (v. 30). After this expansion, one
is tempted to understand that only the lower classes of v. 29 are the ones who
are uttering the pledge in v. 30, yet this runs contrary to v. 1a, in which the
impetus to ratify the pact originates with the broadly defined אנחנו. The author's
intention in adding this note was possibly to correct the list in which only the
upper classes are involved by including the whole Restoration community.

Without vv. 1b and 29-30aαα in the way, we are in a better position to
determine where the trail from the first sentence, ובכל־זאת אנחנו כרתים אמנה
וכתבים, leads. However, the combined usage of ambiguous masc. pl. participles
in vv. 1 and 30a complicates matters. They can be read together with both the
first-person pl. subject (v. 1) and the third-person pl. subjects (v. 29). The
answer hinges ultimately on how much of v. 30 one ascribes to the sentence of
v. 29, which requires nothing more than מחזיקים על־אחיהם אדיריהם. The
remainder of v. 30a fits well to v. 1. A second alternative is to strike וכתבים from
v. 1a and seek the resumption in ללכת וגו of v. 30a. "And we write" may have
resulted from the same thought behind the redactions of v. 1b and the list,
namely that the pact is a written contract. The second proposal has a greater
aesthetic quality, yet the first requires less editing and is hence preferable. With
vv. 1a and 30aβ-b, a well-rounded statement remains:

---

78 Cf. Jepsen's study of the names (1954), which, however, draws rather speculative
    conclusions with regard to the age of the pact.

> And because of this, we hereby make an agreement (and write it) […] and enter into a
> curse and into an oath to walk in the Torah of God, which was given by the hand of
> Moses the servant of God and to keep and do all the commandments of YHWH our
> Lord and his ordinances and his statutes.

What follows in vv. 31ff. both applies the Torah casuistically to specific situations and supplements it with additional provisions and detailed instructions.
After even a cursory glance at these paragraphs, one cannot help being
impressed by the composite nature of the material.[79] The disparate stipulations
are so loosely structured that the reader who attempts to find a method to the
madness of their arrangement faces a daunting task. Surprisingly, those exegetes
who have been most reluctant to embrace a diachronic approach to other texts
exhibit relatively few inhibitions of engaging in literary-critical operations on
these verses. The most critical analyses have nonetheless insisted that at least a
part of this material is "authentic."

The individual terms of the contract are introduced in various ways. With the
subordinate conjunction ואשר (v. 31), a series of self-imposed prohibitions
begins, and they are all formulated in the first-person pl. *qatal*. The first three are
expressed negatively: לא־נתן (v. 31a) and לא נקח (twice in vv. 31b and 32a).
These points are held together by their exclusivist character. The fourth point,
in which the exaction of all debts is promised, lacks the לא, but is semantically
negated. The futurist tempus of all these first four terms serves to underline that
the community is renewing their commitment to apply older laws to specific
situations. One should thus describe them as casuistic reflexive prohibitions. Yet
the people have not restricted themselves merely to re-enforcing what had been
previously instated; the next point (v. 33) treats a new fiscal ordinance. The
syntax of the verse sets it apart from the preceding lines with a verb in the
perfect followed by an infinitive construction, and it is positively formulated. V.
34 explains then to which purposes this tax is to be employed. The subject
matter has herewith alternated to the cultic, which is maintained throughout the
remaining points. V. 35, with a construction similar to v. 33, describes an action
that has already been accomplished. Contextually, the infinitives of vv. 36 and
37 depend upon the action of v. 35. V. 38 then reverts to the first-person
wayyiqtol forms of vv. 31-32, while v. 39 switches to third-person and confines
the subject to the Levites and priests. The כי-clause of v. 40a continues in this
modus, while broadening the subject again to בני־ישראל and בני הלוי. V. 40aβ
explains in the present tempus, with the implied verb היה, the function of the
indirect object in v. 40. Finally, v. 40b reverts again to the first-person *qatal* form
of v. 38, although it resembles more the negatively formulated לא-constructions
in vv. 31-32.

---

79 *Pace* Gilatt-Gilad (2000).

The interconnection of the various contractual terms is indeed confusing, and therefore it is not surprising that so many exegetes reckon with expansions within these verses.[80] What however has not yet been considered is the possibility that this *entire* section forms an addendum to the pact. We search in vain for a good literary join between v. 30a and one or more of the provisions enumerated in the following verses. If one is reticent to accept this proposal, it must nevertheless be conceded that v. 31a provides a well-rounded closure to the foregoing and that nothing else thereafter is necessary for the structure of the passage. Moreover, one cannot deny that these statutes are already syntactically subordinated to the general pledge to abide by the Torah. The following paragraphs of the pact do not clarify what this pledge entails, but are additional stipulations and sub-points.

While this is clear from the Hebrew wording, the modern translations have tended to smooth out the transition to the specific provisions in vv. 31ff., interpreting them as elaborations of the commitment in v. 30. Despite the widespread insistence to the contrary, there is no reason to consider the usage of ואשר (the introduction to the stipulations in v. 31ff) as exceptional and render it "to wit..." or "nämlich, daß..." Taking this subordinate conjunction at its semantic face value, one would have translate it simply: "and that." At least this rendering corresponds to its usage in a wide range of biblical texts and more specifically legislative contexts, in which it is employed to annotate and adapt previous rulings (cf., e.g., Ex 21:13; 30:33, Deut 11:4ff.; 19:5; 28:4).Whether the same applies for the present case must be decided on the basis of the conceptual and stylistic consistency. In keeping with standard syntax, we would expect the use of an infinitive construct after an antecedent participle, such as we already have in v. 30. Whereas one cannot rule out the possibility of the present usage, the rough break from a formulation with present participles and infinitive constructs to first-person *qatal* forms is nevertheless difficult to explain as coming from one and the same hand. A simple infinitive form like לא־לתת would have been both clearer for the reader and easier for the author. Yet without the use of an infinitive construction, vv. 31 and 32 are only loosely connected to the oath and pledge in v. 30, and it is likely that the author intended to make these stipulations as the natural expression of v. 30 rather than merely supplementary.

With regard to surrounding context, one has also trouble conceiving why after the general wording of the prayer and pact the community has decided to include these very detailed individual provisions. The most fitting response to the broad confession of forsaking the Torah in the prayer is a renewed commitment to the whole Torah. As noted above, nowhere in the prayer are sins of

---

80 For a good overview of works of these scholars and valuable alternative suggestions to the origins of the material, see Steins (1995: 171ff.) and Reinmuth (2002: 211ff.).

the fathers defined as abuses against the temple or with the עמי הארץ. The pact makes much more sense as a continuation to the prayer without these additional stipulations. In the latter passage, the ancestors, after having received the Torah on Sinai by the hand of Moses, the servant of God (9:14), prove repeatedly to be negligent of the commandments. Consequently, they lose control over the land, which is returned to foreign dominion. Concluding the confession is a plea for regained sovereignty.[81] For the author of the pact, however, the political activism of the time must be balanced with Torah-obedience. The present social distress has been brought about by the failure of the ancestors, and before experiencing miraculous intervention again as in times past, the community enters into a sure agreement "to keep the law of God given by the hand of Moses, the servant of God" (10:30). In appending chap. 10, the writer thus reutilizes the depiction of Israel's beginnings in the prayer as an historical prologue to the pact.[82]

CONCLUSIONS

To conclude, we may reiterate here that the amplification of the pact with the stipulations emphasizing the community's concern for the maintenance of the temple should be seen in terms of the reciprocal compositional process at work in Ezra-Neh. After supplements to Nehemiah's account criticize the temple and its personal, Ezra 1-6 and 7-8 respond by giving priority to this institution and portraying the most positive relationship possible between it and the Persian rulers. To this, the authors of (Ezra 9 and) Neh 8:1-10:30 respond by intentionally neglecting the temple in favor of a society centered on the Torah. And finally, the secondary stipulations to the pact in Neh 10 are added to counterbalance this presentation by showing that obedience to the Torah involves a willingness to promote the importance of the temple.

---

81 The unique statement in vs. 37, "and they rule over us according to their will" calls into mind the use of the same phraseology in Esth 9, Dan 8 and 11. Because of these parallels, it is difficult to deny the late (Maccabean?) provenance of the prayer (or of at least vv. 32-37).

82 The parallels to this familiar covenantal structure are numerous and well documented. The text most instructive for the interpretation of our passage is 1QS I,18-II,18, the liturgical formula of the covenantal renewal ceremony from the so-called "Manual of Discipline." There we read, "And at their entrance into the covenant, the priests and Levites should praise all the salvific acts of God and his works of truth. And all who come into the covenant should confess after them: We have done wrongly, we have sinned, we and our fathers before us, by transgressing his statutes. Right and just is his judgment upon us and our fathers. But his longsuffering mercy retributes us from age to age" (see Baltzer [1960: 51ff.]). The similarities between this text and Neh 9, in which the Levites praise God and confess their sins in almost the exact same language, as well as Neh 10, in which the community enters into a covenant, are indeed remarkable.

10. The Sabbath-Reforms – 13:15-22

10.1 Introduction

According to present shape of chap. 13, Nehemiah noticed the abuse of the Sabbath during a second leave of absence (v. 6b).[1] The preceding chapter has concluded that an editorial hand is responsible for this dating. Not only does v. 6 create many incongruities; the statement in v. 7 is also formulated according to the analogy of 2:11, and when read independently of the preceding notice, cannot refer to a *return* to Jerusalem. The paragraph vv. 4-9, which is undoubtedly older than 12:44-13:3, must have originally continued the narrative in 6:17-19. The latter passage recounts the written correspondence between the Judean aristocracy and Tobiah that occurred not twelve years after, but rather during the work on the wall ("in those days"). If 13:4-14 were formerly joined to this passage, each remaining literary unit of the first-person account, beginning with 5:1-19 and 6:1-14, would conclude with a זכרה-prayer. So too, Nehemiah would not have carried out the actions portrayed in 13:4-31 during a second visit to the province. While the paragraphs of vv. 4-9 and 10-14 must recount his first accomplishments after his arrival in Jerusalem, the question remains, When did he enact the Sabbath- and marriage-reforms?

The building account in 1:1-6:16 follows the שמע-schema to present discrete building phases. This schema discontinues, however, after the notice of completion in 6:15-16. The introductory phrase "in those days" and the use of participles in 6:17-19 is to be explained by the fact that the activities of the nobles were not restricted to a single building phase, but rather characterized the whole period of building. Significantly, the only other two paragraphs that begin with the expression "in those days" (13:15-22, 23ff.) also employ participles to depict the problems that Nehemiah addresses (cf. vv. 15-18 and 24). One would thus expect that he also addressed these problems before the completion of the wall.

Such expectations are disappointed by the account of the Sabbath-reforms in 13:15-22. In vv. 19ff., Nehemiah orders that the gates be closed in order to

---

1   For a general discussion of the issues relating to Sabbath in the Bible, cf. Robinson (1988) and Veijola (1989).

prohibit traders from entering Jerusalem. If he gave these instructions during the work on the wall, as is initially assumed from the introductory expression "in those days," one must explain how the wall and gates could prohibit entrance to the city. It seems then that the construction work must have already been finished. Hence, 13:15-22 poses a serious problem for our proposal that all the reforms were introduced before the twenty-fifth of Elul.

In addressing this problem, one should not exclude the possibility that the paragraphs in 13:10-14, 15-22, 23-31 represent successive expansions of vv. 4-9. Insofar as it is quite probable that 6:17-19 has been secondarily attached to the original conclusion of the building report (v. 15), the account in 13:4-9 and the rest of the paragraphs in chap. 13 did not belong to the first editions of Nehemiah's account. So too, the introductory formulae in vv. 15-22 and 23-31 resemble the expression "on that day" used in 12:43, 44 and 13:1. Most commentators agree that the report of the dedication ceremonies concluded with the description of Jerusalem's joy in 12:43 and that the material in 12:44-13:3 constitutes the work of later authors. Thus, Blenkinsopp represents the consensus in suggesting that the paragraphs of 12:44ff. and 13:1ff. "could be read as supplements, both introduced by the same phrase, 'on that day' (*bayyôm hahû*), which often marks additions to prophetic collections in the postexilic period (e.g., Zech 12-14)."[2] Now if the phrase "often marks additions" in other contexts, why could it not also indicate that Nehemiah's account has been supplemented with 13:15ff.?[3] Therefore, it is possible that the account of the Sabbath-reforms has been added after the interpolation of v. 6 and that its authors have used the expression, "and in those days," in a different way than in 6:17 and 13:23.

While this possibility is worth consideration, the following analysis shows that the introductory formulae originally functioned as anticipated. We will isolate an older stratum of the account which presents Nehemiah instituting the Sabbath-reforms before the twenty-fifth of Elul. This narrative strand treats the desecration of the Sabbath throughout the province of Judah as a whole (vv. 15a, 16*). Those whom Nehemiah finds guilty are "the nobles of Judah" (v. 17a). Inasmuch as the narrative originally concluded with the interrogation and "sermon" (vv. 17b-18*, 22b), it has an analogy in 13:23ff. And without vv. 19-22, the passage would no longer pose a problem for dating the reforms in chap. 13 with those in chap. 5 to the period of building.

---

2   1988: 353.

3   That this possibility has never been considered is to be explained by the formulation of the passage in the first-person, which represents the chief criterion for ascribing contradictory texts in Neh 1-13 to the same author. Yet were one to consequently adhere to this criterion for the composition-history of other corpora, the redactors of, e.g., Deutero- and Trito-Isaiah, who copy the style of the earliest layers of Proto-Isaiah, must be identified with the eighth century, Judean prophet.

10.2 Synchronic Analysis

Whereas the profanation of the Sabbath represents the overarching theme of
13:15-22, Nehemiah depicts the abuse in several ways. In the introduction to the
account, he describes the work on the Sabbath in the province as a whole (v.
15aα): "In those days I saw in Judah (some) treading wine presses on the
Sabbath." After declaring the guilt of all Judah, he then turns to the particular
case of the capital, (v. 15aγ): "...they were bringing to Jerusalem on the Sabbath
day."[4] In v. 16, he introduces yet another aspect to his report: Tyrian merchants
were selling fish and other wares to "the children of Judah."[5] Thus, what initially
disturbs Nehemiah is that the work in the winepresses was compromising the
sanctity of the Sabbath. Contrasting with this, the second problem he observes
concerns the import of goods into Jerusalem. Despite the insistence of many
commentators that this statement depicts the Judeans entering into trade in
Jerusalem, it seems that the desecration of the Sabbath was caused solely by the
transport of burdens to the city.[6] If they intended to market their goods on the
Sabbath, why does he warn the perpetrators "on *the day* when they sold their
wares" (v. 15b).[7] While v. 15aβ reports that some were simply "bringing" their
commodities to Jerusalem, v. 16 – corresponding to the third problem noted by
Nehemiah – declares that the Tyrians who dwelt in Judah were "bringing" fish
and all manner of merchandise and *selling* them on the holy day to the Judeans.
Because the Judeans, in contrast to the foreign merchants, were not allowed to
purvey their wares on the Sabbath, "many must have felt that the law set them
at an unfair commercial disadvantage."[8]

Upon closer examination, Nehemiah not only recounts three measures he
took to enforce Sabbath observance (vv. 17-22a), but he also presents them in
the same sequence as he described the abuses (vv. 15-16). First, he remonstrates
with the Judean nobles (vv. 17-18). It is quite likely that this group would have
been responsible for allowing operations in the wine presses to continue on the

---

4 The description of the work done on the Sabbath in the first half of the verse cannot be
   understood as subordinate to the transport of wares into Jerusalem as if they were
   producing wine on the Sabbath and transporting it to Jerusalem all on the same day. The
   first and primary problem is that the Judeans were working in the winepresses on the
   Sabbath.
5 The use of participles in vv. 15-16 describes persisting conditions in Judah and Jerusalem.
   The alternation to non-participial verb-forms in v.17ff. signifies accordingly Nehemiah's
   discrete reactions.
6 This interpretation is supported also by Jer 17:19ff., which is discussed §10.3.2.
7 Ehrlich (1914: 211) suggested that we emend the text to: "And I warned *them* not to sell
   their food." Against this emendation, see Williamson (1985: 392). – The situation of the
   markets being closed on the Sabbath is reflected in Amos 8:4ff., where the accused
   complain that they were not allowed to sell their grain on the Sabbath.
8 Williamson (1985: 395).

Sabbath, and thus vv. 17-18 correspond to the first abuse reported in v. 15: "And in those days I saw in Judah the treading of winepresses on the Sabbath" (בימים ההמה ראיתי ביהודה דרכים־גתות בשבת), v. 15aα).[9] This interpretation explains the lack of subject before the participle.[10] V. 19 describes the second measure taken to enforce the observance of the Sabbath: Nehemiah issues orders that the gates remained closed until after the Sabbath (v. 19a), and then he stations some of his retainers at the gates to ensure that no load enters Jerusalem (v. 19b). These actions represent a response to the second abuse reported in v. 15: "And they were bringing their heaps of grain…to Jerusalem on the Sabbath day." Finally, the activities reported in vv. 20-21 correspond to the situation described in v. 16.[11] After instructions had been given to keep the gates closed during the Sabbath, the traders were spending the night outside Jerusalem. Once they are threatened with physical removal, they do not return.

10.3. Diachronic Analysis

The composition and organization of the disparate material in this passage generates a significant amount of dissonance. Not only is the narrative much more complicated than other parts of the account; it is also unbalanced. The first line produces the tension by reporting the operations in the winepresses on the Sabbath in *Judah*. But instead of resolving this tension, the lengthy conclusion treats the measures to ensure the sanctity of *Jerusalem*, introducing thereby new conflicts (vv. 20-21). Since the initial and main problem of the passage concerns fieldwork throughout the entire province, vv. 19-22a fail to produce denouement.

There are two alternative explanations for the imbalance of the account: one can attribute it either to the historical conditions or to later revisions. Hölscher has offered an interpretation in keeping with the first approach: "Die Adligen, die Nehemia schilt, wohnen natürlich auf dem Lande, erzwingen kann er dort

---

9   That this line constitutes a complete thought is indicated by the end position of בשבת.

10 Instead of taking Joüon's approach (1931: 89) and treating ביהודה in v. 15a as an abbreviation of בני יהודה, the formulation probably intends to prepare the reader for Nehemiah's identification of the real perpetrators in v. 17.

11 Galling's claims notwithstanding (1954: 253), the Tyrians of v. 16 are clearly the merchants referred to in v. 20f. The term הרכלים refers most often to foreign merchants and seven times specifically to Tyrians merchants. Cf. 1 Kgs 10:15 and Ezekiel's lamentation over Tyre in Ezek 27. This claim is also supported by the inversion of וכל־מכר ומכרים (v. 16) in v. 20 (ומכרי כל־ממכר). The building register in chap. 3 also depicts the merchants (הרכלים, cf. vv. 31, 32) building along side the goldsmiths. However, they are probably not the Tyrians in 13:16, for the phrase ישבו בה refers to Judah (ביהודה), as demonstrated below. Moreover, Nehemiah warns the רכלים from residing outside Jerusalem (13:20f.). This contradicts 3:31, which states that they shared a house in Jerusalem (with none other than the Nethinim).

die Sabbatruhe nicht. In Jerusalem dagegen tut er, was er kann."[12] This solution is, however, not compelling. The use of ריב here as elsewhere does not signify mere chiding ("schelten"), as Hölscher renders the verb, but rather much more serious legal procedures. In 5:1-13 and 13:10-14, Nehemiah not only indicts (ריב) the leaders and nobles, but also initiates reforms that affect the entire province. Therefore, his jurisdiction, at least for the author of these passages, included more than Jerusalem.

Hölscher, however, did not hesitate to critically reconstruct the original formulation of the passage. With several other scholars, he suggested that the references to Jerusalem in vv. 15-16 are the work of redactors.[13] V. 15 begins by describing simply the work in the winepresses on the Sabbath; it then takes a turn, employing ומביאים no longer for the collection of the heaps of grain, but rather for the transport of goods to Jerusalem (ומביאים ירושלם ביום השבת). The reader can only infer from the following statement (v. 15b) that these goods were also sold in the capital. Consequently, Hölscher concluded that the verse has been revised according to v. 16, which describes the Tyrians *bringing* fish and other wares and *selling* them to the Judeans.

While these conclusions merit serious consideration, they also pose a problem: Without a reference to Jerusalem in vv. 15-16, the account has not introduced the abuse that Nehemiah's addresses in vv. 19-22a (the transport to and sale of goods in Jerusalem on the Sabbath). Now if v. 15 originally reported only fieldwork on the Sabbath, we would have to conclude that later editors have added vv. 19-22a.[14] In mentioning the gates, they are also inconsistent with the dating of the events to "those days" (v. 15), which according to the analogy of 6:17 one would expect to refer the period before the completion of the building activities. Since the question whether these concluding verses belonged to the earliest edition of account depends upon the integrity of the references to Jerusalem in the introduction, we begin by devoting attention to v. 15.

10.3.1. The Final Redaction

The introductory statement in v. 15 ends with בשבת: "And in those days I saw in Judah the treading of winepresses on the Sabbath" (v. 15aα*). Thereafter, the text becomes quite confusing so that it is difficult to determine the relationship of the various clauses to each other. While ועמסים על־החמרים ("and they were

---

12 1923: 560.

13 1923: 560. Winckler (1901: 486), Mowinckel (1963: 39f.), and Gunneweg (1987: 170).

14 This paragraph begins suspiciously with ויהי כאשר, which is not only a formula used to introduce new topics, but is also, as one witnesses elsewhere, a device with which redactors append supplementary material (cf. the analysis of Neh 4:1, 6:1, 14, and esp. 7:1-3).

loading asses") does not require a direct object,[15] the clause ומביאים ירושלם ביום השבת ("they were bringing to Jerusalem on the Sabbath day") is deficient without one. Furthermore, the אף-phrase continues a previous thought other than the one directly preceding it. The most likely candidate is ומביאים הערמות ("and they were bringing heaps of grain").

With regard to the latter clause, we notice several peculiarities: If the reader should understand that the Judeans were collecting or harvesting grain, then the use of קבץ or אסף is expected.[16] However, the term ערמה does not refer elsewhere to sheaves, but rather to piles of threshed grain.[17] Therefore, one should probably translate ומביאים in the same way as מביאים in v. 16 ("and they were *bringing*"). This conclusion raises the question, What was the destination of the transport of the heaps? It is probably not merely happenstance that v.15aγ provides a fitting answer: "...they were bringing (ומביאים) to Jerusalem on the Sabbath day."[18] In the case of v. 15, in which the word ומביאים occurs twice, I propose that the original continuation of ומביאים הערמות is to be found in ירושלם ביום השבת (cf. vv. 16b and v. 21b: לא־באו בשבת). A later hand expanded this description first with a list of additional wares (the אף-phrase), which was then disconnected from its requisite verb with the insertion of ועמסים על־החמרים. This clause refers simply to loading asses for a journey, as in Gen 44:13, and explains how they transported the wares to Jerusalem.[19]

Thus, in an earlier edition of the account, the first line of v. 15 ("And in those days I saw in Judah the treading of wine presses on the Sabbath") was followed by the shorter statement, "And they were bringing heaps of grain to Jerusalem on the Sabbath day." While the first part of v. 15 both forms a complete thought that ends with בשבת and is structurally indispensable to the account, the continuation is unanticipated. That a later hand appended the second line to the first is suggested by the repetition of "on the Sabbath." The reader already knows *when* the wares were being brought to Jerusalem. One can explain neither why the author found it necessary to reiterate that the work was being done on the Sabbath nor why he varies the designation for the Sabbath (ביום השבת instead of בשבת).[20] Furthermore, the statement in v. 15b ("and I

---

15 Cf. Gen 44:13.
16 Cf., e.g., Mic 4:12 and Ruth 2:7.
17 Cf. Hag 2:16 and Ruth 3:7.
18 Significantly, one of the few passages where the term ערמה appears (2 Chr 31:6ff. – four times) describes the Judeans bringing their cattle and produce to *Jerusalem*, where they were stored in the chambers (לשכות; cf. Neh 13:4ff.). – The truly bewildering formulation of Neh 13:15 is an example of "resumptive repetition." When a text has been amplified to such an extent that the initial thought has been sidetracked and interrupted by subsidiary information, a word is repeated in order to signify where it resumes.
19 This addition may have been influenced by the prohibition in Deut 5:14 of employing asses on the Sabbath.
20 The proposed first stratum of the account employs only בשבת.

warned [them] on their market day [?]") is in tension with the remaining passage.[21] In v. 21, Nehemiah also warns the foreign merchants, and here the form
ואעידה (with the ה-paragogicum) is consistent with the style of all other first-
person sing. verbs in the chapter. V. 15b employs, however, the form ואעיד
without an object.[22] While Nehemiah neither states whom he admonished nor
what they were told in v. 15b, he both names the perpetrators and reports what
he said in vv. 17-18 and 21. Finally, one must infer from v. 15b that he warned
the people who were involved in the labor and transportation of the goods to
Jerusalem. In v. 17a, however, we learn that those whom Nehemiah found guilty
were the nobles, who probably would not have engaged in physical labor.[23]

If v. 15 originally concluded with בשבת, one could better explain the formulation of v. 16. First, the preposition בה in the ישבו בה refers to province in
general rather than specifically the capital.[24] Were it to refer to the city, as most
scholars assume,[25] the verse would not make any sense: "And the Tyrians who
dwelt in (Jerusalem) were bringing fish and all manner of wares and selling them
on the Sabbath to the Judeans *and in Jerusalem*." In v. 20 Nehemiah reports that
the foreign merchants were staying over night (וילינו; cf. 4:16) outside Jerusalem.
After he threatens them with physical removal, they do not return. As noted
above, the use of הרכלים elsewhere for foreign merchants – and most often
Tyrian merchants – indicates that this term in v. 20 refers to the subject of v. 16.
This is supported by the inversion of כל־מכר ומכרים (v. 16) to ומכרי כל־ממכר
(v. 20). Now if בה in v. 15 refers to Jerusalem, one cannot explain that v. 20f.
portrays the foreign merchants *coming* to the city (באו, v. 21b) and lodging
outside the wall.[26] Finally, the assumption that v. 16 refers to Tyrian settlements
in the city rather than in Judah neglects that the phrase ישבו בה appears many
times elsewhere in which the antecedent of בה is הארץ (cf., e.g., Deut 2:10, 20;

---

21 Hölscher (1923: 560) also observed the terminological differences between vv. 15b and 18.
22 We would expect the indirect object בהם as in v. 21a. The use of העיד absolutely is very rare.
23 Inasmuch as the participle in v. 15aα lacks a subject, the statement joins well to v. 17a,
   where Nehemiah identifies the perpetrators. This agrees with the other reform accounts in
   5:1-13 and 13:10-14, which delay the naming of offenders until Nehemiah begins his
   accusation (cf. 5:7 and 13:11). How then are we to explain the warning in v. 15b? I propose
   that the author has rightly recognized that the indictment of the nobles for their wine
   production in v. 17f. does not concern the ones who were actually involved transporting the
   goods to Jerusalem. He thus found it necessary to report that also the laborers were
   admonished to suspend their Sabbath activities.
24 One must, however, concede the analogies to Tyrian settlements in foreign cities. See, for
   example, Herodotus's description of Memphis (2.112), as well as 1 Kgs 20:34.
25 Although Kellermann (1967: 52) did not accept the conclusions of Hölscher and
   Mowinckel, he also noted that this phrase can only refer to Judah.
26 That vv. 20f. have been appended to v. 19, as we propose below, does not obviate this
   argument. To the contrary, it only demonstrates that early readers also understood that the
   Tyrians in v. 16 did not reside in Jerusalem. Cf. also the interpretations of these early readers
   in 10:32, which provides for the situation when the peoples of the land "bring" their wares
   and sell them to Judeans on the Sabbath.

Ezek 37:25; and Ps 68:11). Hence, the antecedent of בה is probably "Judah" (cf. "in the *land* of Judah," 5:14). This conclusion is confirmed by the parallel use of ב in both formulations: ביהודה and ישבו בה.

Our findings bear significant consequences for the interpretation of v. 15. After Nehemiah reports that the Judeans were bringing their wares to Jerusalem on the Sabbath and that he warned them on their market day (v. 15aβb), the phrase ישבו בה in v. 16 is not only far removed from its antecedent ביהודה in v. 15aα, but the reader is also tempted to follow many modern translations and commentators in identifying the antecedent with the next feminine object – the city, Jerusalem, in v. 15aβ. Without the second half of v. 15, however, this confusion would not obtain.

If v. 15 has been extensively expanded as Hölscher maintained, then Nehemiah would have prohibited the opening of the gates on the Sabbath in order to deny only the Tyrians access to Jerusalem on the Sabbath. While this reading is perfectly conceivable, in v. 19b Nehemiah places his retainers in charge of the gates so that no burden could be brought into the city. As witnessed in the synchronic reading above, this measure corresponds to v. 15aβ, which contains a long list of the items which the Judeans brought to Jerusalem. Moreover, v. 15aγ is formulated quite similarly to v. 19b (cf. וכל־משא ומביאים ירושלם ביום השבת with לא־יבוא משא ביום השבת). Since v. 15 has probably been amplified, we must consider whether an editorial hand has added v. 19b to the foregoing statement.

The evidence for redactional activity in v. 19 is not lacking. In the first part of the verse, Nehemiah expressly commands that the gates were not to be opened until after the Sabbath. Why then must he station his men at the gates?[27] Moreover, why does he first give the instructions before he had appointed the gatekeepers? Without v. 19b, the narrative also flows more smoothly: The gates are closed to prohibit foreign merchants from entering on the Sabbath. Thereafter, the merchants lodge outside Jerusalem (v. 20) and before the wall (v. 21a). Yet if v. 19b is integral to its context, why does the continuation in vv. 20-21 concern only the foreign merchants and not the Judeans who were bringing burdens into Jerusalem? Finally, v. 19b employs ביום השבת just as in the second part of v. 15, yet the surrounding context employs consistently בשבת.

In sum, vv. 19a, 20-21 form a stylistically and conceptually unified narrative: Nehemiah closes the gates to prevent the foreign merchants who come to capitalize on the prohibition of mercantile activities for Judeans on the Sabbath.

---

27 Winckler pointed out that, "da die tore geschlossen sind, kann keiner herein. das aufstellen militärischer wachen ist also völlig überflüssig. der jüngere bearbeiter ist ausserdem deutlich an der erweiterung: keine last" (1901: 487). Likewise, Mowinckel remarked with a touch of irony, "die Jägersleute – bezw. die tryrischen Fischverkäufer – dachten doch noch nicht, die verschlossenen Tore zu erstürmen" (1964: 41).

V. 19b interrupts this thought. Now the gates are closed to prohibit the Jerusalemites themselves from bringing burdens into the city on the Sabbath day. Since it cannot be merely coincidental that this line both creates friction and continues the thought and vocabulary (בוא, משא, ירושלם, ביום השבת) of the second part of v. 15, it is quite probable that a redactor has amplified the account in both vv. 15 and 19 in order to apply Nehemiah's measures to the inhabitants of Jerusalem who were bringing "all manner of burdens" through the city-gates. With the addition of v. 19b, Nehemiah recounts three solutions in vv. 17-21 in the same order as he presents the three abuses in vv. 15-16 as observed above in the synchronic reading.

10.3.2. The Affinities of the Final Redaction to Jer 17:19ff.

The expansion of the account in vv. 15 and 19 poses a problem: Of all the ways one could have desecrated the Sabbath, why is Nehemiah disturbed by the activities of bringing provisions to Jerusalem on the Sabbath? And why does he take precautionary measures to prevent them from transporting any burden through the *city-gates*? If carrying burdens were prohibited on the Sabbath, the closing of the gates would only ensure Sabbath observance within Jerusalem. How then should one explain Nehemiah's actions?

A response to these questions requires that we turn our attention to Jer 17:19-27, where YHWH calls the prophet to stand in the gates of Jerusalem and to warn the Judeans against bringing a burden through the gates on the Sabbath. If they fail to hear, he will kindle a fire in the gates and palaces of Jerusalem.

> 19 Thus said YHWH to me: "Go and stand in the People's Gate, by which the kings of Judah enter and by which they go out, and in all the gates of Jerusalem, 20 and say to them: 'Hear the word of YHWH, you kings of Judah, and all Judah, and all the inhabitants of Jerusalem, who enter by these gates. 21 Thus says YHWH: For the sake of your lives, take care that you do not bear a burden on the Sabbath day or bring it in by the gates of Jerusalem (והבאתם בשערי ירושלם).... 24 'If you listen to me,' says YHWH, 'and bring in no burden by the gates of this city on the Sabbath day (לבלתי הביא משא בשערי העיר הזאת ביום השבת), but keep the Sabbath day holy (ולקדש את־יום השבת) and do no work on it, 25 then there shall enter by the gates of this city kings who sit on the throne of David, riding in chariots and on horses, they and their officials, the people of Judah and the inhabitants of Jerusalem; and this city shall be inhabited forever.... 27 'But if you do not listen to me, to keep the Sabbath day holy, and to carry in no burden or bring it in through the gates of Jerusalem on the Sabbath day (ולבלתי שאת משא ובא בשערי ירושלם ביום השבת), then I will kindle a fire in its gates; it shall devour the palaces of Jerusalem and shall not be quenched.'"

The parallels in both content and formulations are so numerous and patent that few would deny that a genetic relationship exists between the two texts. Most of the recent studies maintain that 17:19ff. represents a late redactional text that presupposes Neh 13:15ff.[28] Although Jer 17:19ff. may have been composed at a late stage in the growth of the book, it seems most improbable that it presupposes Nehemiah's account. Otherwise, one cannot explain why the authors have only elaborated on a single aspect of Neh 13:15ff. (*viz.*, the transport of burdens through the gates of Jerusalem), while disregarding the first and third problem Nehemiah notices (*viz.*, the treading of wine presses and the presence of foreign merchants). Moreover, these recent studies of Jer 17 are governed by the age-old assumption that the first-person portions of Neh 1-13 must have been drafted by the historical Nehemiah, who would not have known late redactional texts from the prophets. However, our investigation thus far has produced evidence that the building account has passed through editorial hands, and this necessitates a fresh examination of the parallels between 13:15ff. and Jer 17:19ff.

First, we may observe how Jer 17:19ff. appears to have developed from literary precursors in the book. Several times elsewhere YHWH calls Jeremiah to stand in a gate and declare his words (cf. 7:1ff., 19:1ff., and 22:1ff.). One of these passages (22:1ff.) probably served as the model and provided the framework for the composition of 17:19ff.[29] If so, the authors of 17:19ff. have not only expanded the form of the precursor, but have also introduced a new subject. Mere social justice is no longer required; one must also observe the Sabbath in a more rigorous manner than required by the Torah. To drive home this point, the gates of Jerusalem, where Jeremiah had often delivered his prophecies to Judeans, function symbolically. If "kings of Judah, and all Judah, and all the inhabitants of Jerusalem, who enter by these gates" (v. 19; cf. 22:2) intend to avoid divine judgment, they must take care "to not bear a burden on the Sabbath day or bring it in by the gates of Jerusalem" (v. 21). And if they heed YHWH, "then there shall enter by the gates of this city kings who sit on the throne of David" (v. 25; cf. 22:4; also 1:15).[30] The author of this text, therefore, combines the language and motifs of other Jeremian passages (e.g., the gates of Jerusalem) with a rigorous interpretation of one of the Torah's prohibitions (i.e., work on the Sabbath) in order to increase the ramifications of YHWH's warnings

---

28 Cf., e.g., Briend (1985: 23ff.), Holladay (1986: 509), Carroll, (1986: 368), McKane (1986: 417f.), Veijola (1989: 255ff.), and already Volz (1928: 190f.).

29 22:1ff.: "**Thus says YHWH: Go** down to the house of the king of Judah, and speak there this word, 2 and say: **Hear the word of YHWH, O King of Judah** sitting on the throne of David-- you, and your servants, and your people **who enter these gates**. 3 **Thus says YHWH:** Act with justice and righteousness, and deliver from the hand of the oppressor anyone who has been robbed. And do no wrong or violence to the alien, the orphan, and the widow.... 4 For if you will indeed obey this word, **then through the gates of this house shall enter kings who sit on the throne of David, riding in chariots and on horses, they, and their servants, and their people. 5 But if you will not heed these words,** I swear by myself, says YHWH, that this house shall become a desolation."

30 Briend (1985) provides a good discussion of the parallels in this passage to other texts in Jeremiah.

elsewhere (esp., 22:1ff.). The evidence of the literary influence of 22:1ff. on 17:19ff. means that we need not suppose – and it is indeed difficult to maintain – that the account in Neh 13 served as the source for Jer 17.[31]

In a study that demonstrates the late character of Jer 17:19ff., Veijola concludes that the author intended to reinterpret Nehemiah's measures in terms of YHWH's warning.[32] This conclusion, however, fails to take into account that the interpretation of Neh 13:15ff. requires familiarity with Jer 17:19ff. One searches in vain for biblical texts that prohibit the carrying of burdens on the Sabbath, let alone bringing burdens to Jerusalem. The reader of Neh 13:15ff. is consequently bewildered: Why does Nehemiah command that the gates of Jerusalem remain closed until after the Sabbath (v. 19a)? Conversely, the account makes perfect sense when read against the backdrop of YHWH's warning recorded in Jer 17:21: "For the sake of your lives, take care that you do not bear a burden on the Sabbath day or bring it in by the gates of Jerusalem." Neh 13:15ff. has interpreted this prohibition of bringing a burden through the gates of Jerusalem, which makes use of the symbols and forms of the book of Jeremiah, quite literarily. Thus, while Jer 17:19ff. is a product of a literary development within the book and can be understood independently of Neh 13:15ff., the interpretation of latter requires familiarity with the former.

Moreover, if the authors of Jer 17:19ff. intended to reinterpret Nehemiah's actions in terms of Jeremiah's woe oracle, why does YHWH not command the kings of Judah to keep the gates closed on the Sabbath? This would have been a perfect opportunity for the authors of Jer 17:19ff. to refer the reader of Nehemiah's account back to their text. In the present form of these passages, Nehemiah goes above and beyond what is required: In order to ensure that no burden be brought through the gates of Jerusalem, he interprets Jeremiah's oracle with the rigor of a pious reader of the prophets, commanding the gates to be closed as soon as it began to grow dark on Erev Shabbat and remain closed until the day after the Sabbath (v. 19a).[33] Although YHWH does not demand this of the Judean kings, Nehemiah illustrates his piety by taking all precautionary measures. Yet without having first read Jer 17:19ff., one can neither understand why Nehemiah is opposed to the transport of burdens through the gates nor

---

31 That the Sabbath is not mentioned elsewhere in Jeremiah does not mean that the author must have drawn upon Neh 13:15ff. since Nehemiah's account also does not mention the Sabbath elsewhere. In both passages, the profanation of the Sabbath is presented pars pro toto as the failure to keep the covenant and thus grounds for divine judgment.

32 1989: 258. See Reinmuth's lengthy defense of this approach (2002: 295f.).

33 Tigay (1987: 362ff.) suggests that the expressions לפני השבת and אחר השבת mean, as they do in other texts, "Friday" and "Sunday," respectively. Accordingly, we may compare Nehemiah's orders for the closing of the gates to the attention given to the length of the Sabbath in such late texts as M. Shabbat XXII 2 (לפני השבת) and LXX Ps 92:1; 2 Macc 8:26; Jdt 8:6; Mark 14:42. With regard to אחר השבת, cf. T. Ket. 1.1, KAI 200:5f., and 2 Macc 8:28.

appreciate the rigorous and practical implications that he – as depicted by the redactor – exegetically draws from Jeremiah's prophecy.[34]

Upon closer inspection of Neh 13:15ff., one notices that only several lines of the account presupposes Jer 17:19ff., and exactly these lines correspond to the redaction isolated above. Not only do vv. 15aα* (ending with בשבת), 16-19, 20-21, 22a have nothing in common with Jer 17, Nehemiah's indictment of the nobles (vv. 17-18) refers to the profanation of the Sabbath (ומחללים, v. 17; לחלל, v. 18). This language is Priestly and Ezekielian,[35] yet is foreign to Jer 17:19ff. If the author of the latter drew on the formulation of Neh 13:15ff. as Veijola and others contend, one must explain why he has not employed the expression לחלל את־השבת in the many places where we would anticipate it.[36] Conversely, the material in vv. 15aβb, 17bβ, 19b, and 22a, which corresponds to the final redaction(s) in our reconstruction,[37] is formulated with the same expressions found in Jer 17:19ff. (ולקדש את־יום השבת ,בוא + משא ,ירושלם שערי ,ביום השבת) and provides a new reason for the closing of the gates. In order to understand this reason, we must have already read Jer 17:19ff. Without these lines, however, Neh 13 does not require familiarity with Jer 17 and may even be older.

---

34 Hence, the older view according to which Jer 17:19ff. predates Neh 13:15ff. is preferable insofar as it can explain that Nehemiah seems to presuppose the prophecy in Jer 17:19ff. and expands it implications. Cf., e.g., Rudolph (1968: 119-121), Thiel (1973: 205f.), Williamson (1985: 395), and Blenkinsopp (1988: 359). Nevertheless, this view also faces serious obstacles: If "Nehemiah bases his formulation and condemnation on Jer 17:19-27," as Fishbane maintains (1985: 131), one must explain why the expression "to sanctify the Sabbath" (ולקדש את־יום השבת), which appears three times in Jer 17 (vv. 22, 24, 27), is relegated only to Neh 13:22a. This half-verse also likely belongs to a secondary layer of the account. It flatly contradicts v. 19b, where Nehemiah already reported that he placed his retainers over the gates. If both lines are from the same hands, why is purification not required for the first group of gatekeepers? (V. 21a thus agrees with other late texts that Jerusalem, her wall and her gates were holy. Cf., e.g., 12:30 and the Temple Scroll, which even prohibits toilette facilities within the city.)

35 Cf. Ezek 20:13, 16, 21, 24; 22:8, 26; 23:38. The expression appears also in Exod 31:14 and Isa 56:2, 6.

36 Both Neh 13:18 and Jer 17:22f. mention the "fathers." With respect to the first passage, I propose that it belongs to the original formulation of the account. Jer 17:22f., however, appears to have been inserted: Not only does the form of prohibition switch from אל (v. 21) to לא, but also the prohibition of carrying burdens out the houses is not repeated in vv. 24ff., as the other prohibitions. Now if the author of Jer 17:19ff. follows the formulation Neh 13:15ff., one must explain why the reference to the "fathers" is not integral to its context. As Reinmuth rightly points out, the insertion of the "Geschichtsrückblick" in Jer 17:19ff. has probably developed from 1 Kgs 17:14, Jer 7:26 and 19:15, not Neh 13:18.

37 That v. 17bβ has been added seems likely insofar as the questions in vv. 17bα and 18a are interrupted by "you are profaning the Sabbath day." Comparing v. 17bα to 5:9a ("the thing you are doing is not good"), we would expect only אשר אתם עשים הזה הרע מה־הדבר. Cf. also 13:11aβ. Without v. 17bβ, the עשו of v. 18a follows directly on the present participle אתם עשים. Moreover, v. 18b would no longer unnecessarily repeat "profaning the Sabbath" (cf. ומחללים את־יום השבת in v. 17bβ with לחלל את־השבת in v. 18bβ). However, it is certainly possible that v. 17bβ has been appended earlier than the expansions in vv. 15, 19-22a.

This analysis of the relationship between Neh 13:15ff. and Jer 17:19ff. provides the most compelling evidence for our proposal that an earlier edition of the former did not include vv. vv. 15aβb, 17bβ, 19b, and 22a. Since the tension and friction felt in Nehemiah's account is created precisely by those aspects that presuppose Jeremiah's prophecy, we may safely suppose that a redactor amplified Neh 13:15ff. in order to establish a direct connection to Jer 17:19ff., the authors of which may have been acquainted with the earliest editions of the building account.[38] By means of this amplification, Nehemiah draws practical implications from Jeremiah's woe oracle, employing Jerusalem's ramparts and gates that he had built to protect the city from the judgment caused by the desecration of the Sabbath. The didactic intention in portraying Nehemiah's practical measures for Jerusalem contrasts with the polemical nature of the proposed first edition of the account, which sharply censures the Judean aristocracy.

10.3.3 The Earliest Editions

The analysis thus far has demonstrated that an earlier edition of Nehemiah's account comprised only vv. 15aα [until "the Sabbath"], 16-17abα, 18-19a*, 20-21, 22b. In this reconstructed edition, one can isolate two distinct narratives corresponding to the normal and boldface texts:

15 **In those days, I saw in Judah the treading of wine presses on the Sabbath** [...]
16 And the Tyrians who lived there were bringing fish and all kinds of merchandise and selling them on the Sabbath to the people of Judah, and in Jerusalem.
17 **And I contended with the nobles of Judah and said to them, "What is this evil deed that you are committing?** [...]
18 **Did not your ancestors act in this way so that our God brought upon us all this evil and on this city? Yet you bring more wrath on Israel by profaning the Sabbath."**
19 When "it began to be dark" [meaning uncertain] at the gates of Jerusalem before the Sabbath, [...] I gave orders that they should not be opened until after the Sabbath. [...]
20 Yet the merchants and sellers of all kinds of merchandise spent the night outside Jerusalem once or twice.

---

38 In v. 27, YHWH promises to kindle a fire in Jerusalem's gates if the Judeans did not heed his warning. Only here and in Neh 1:3 and 2:17aβ do we find שערים together with יצת and אש in reference to Jerusalem's destruction. Since it appears that Jer 17:19ff. belongs to a late revision of the book, I propose that the author must have known the earlier editions of Nehemiah's building account and thus the formulation of 2:17, which represents, as argued in the present study, the point of departure for the editorial expansions in 1:1b-4; 5:1-13, 6:10-14; 13:4ff. If 2:17 played such an important role for the later authors of Nehemiah's account, it may have been important also for the authors of Jer. Alternatively, 2:17aβ may represent a late supplement influenced by Jer 17. In v. b, Nehemiah petitions the people to build the wall; nothing is said about the gates. Moreover, it is difficult to explain why Nehemiah repeats "Jerusalem" in v. b.

21 And I warned them and said to them, "Why do you spend the night in front of the wall? If you do so again, I will lay hands on you." From that time on, they did not come on the Sabbath. 22 [...] **Remember this too in my favor, O my God, and spare me according to the greatness of your steadfast love.**

While the material in vv. 15, 17-18, and 22 contains the introduction to the account so that it is indispensable to the structure, the narrative in vv. 16, 19-21 cannot exist on its own. In reporting that the Tyrian merchants were bringing their wares and selling them to the Judeans on the Sabbath, v. 16 introduces a "foreign" aspect into the account.[39] Whereas in vv. 15, 17-19 only the Judeans and especially the upper class are to blame, now Nehemiah points his finger at the Tyrians who had settled in the province. From the formulation of the verse, we know that the author considers the Tyrians to be the problem, not the Judeans who were purchasing their goods. Elsewhere the offenders are always mentioned first (cf., e.g., 6:17a; 13:4, 5, 7, 23); the same applies for v. 16. Moreover, not only the offenders but also the offenses are fully distinct. Inasmuch as v. 16 severs the remonstration of "the nobles of Judah" from the description of the treading of the winepresses "in Judah," one may be confident in assigning the two narratives isolated above to a first edition (vv. 15aα, 17abα, 18, 22b) and a revision (vv. 16, 19-21).

If subsequent authors were responsible for vv. 16 and 19-21, the original edition of the account would have been much shorter and have concluded with the words of Nehemiah's sermon (and his prayer). While at first this may be surprising, we should compare the proposed length with the terseness of most other passages in Nehemiah's account. So too, the next chapter attempts to demonstrate that the redactors of the final paragraph of chap. 13 (v. 23ff.) conclude the account also with Nehemiah's sermon (v. 26f.). If so, it is quite probable that also v. 15ff. originally concluded with the sermon in v. 18 and that the redactors responsible v. 23ff. have attempted to assimilate the account to the form of v. 15ff.[40]

How should one explain the composition of the first edition? I suggest that this brief passage continues the censure of the aristocracy already witnessed in other passages of the first-person account. In 13:4-9, Nehemiah recounts that the Jerusalem priesthood had entered into alliances with the enemy Tobiah. Similarly, he recalls in 6:17-19 that many of "the Judean nobles" were sending letters to Tobiah during the work on the wall. In the present passage, he indicts

---

39 Only Galling has recognized this (1954: 253); his reconstruction is, however, problematic.

40 That vv. 23-25 originally concluded with the oath in v. 25b, just as 5:1ff. (cf. v. 12b) and has been expanded with vv. 26-27 indicates the likelihood that even the earliest edition of v. 15ff. has been added after v. 23ff. and 5:1ff. The latter texts present the *rîb*-accusations as a preparation for an oath, while the authors of vv. 10-14 and 15-22 report the accusations in isolation. Insofar as Bovati's conclusions (1986: 19-148) are merited, we would expect something like an oath after the accusation.

again "the Judean nobles."[41] While 6:17-19 exposes the aristocracy by reporting that they were entering into diplomatic or financial relations with a prominent figure who militantly opposed the restoration of Jerusalem, 13:15-22* does the same by reporting that this same group greedily allowed operations in the winepresses to continue on the Sabbath.

Indeed, Nehemiah's condemnation of the nobles in 13:17-18 is harsher than in 6:17-19, for he attributes the present affliction in the province (כל־הרעה הזאת) to the ancestors of the nobles: "Did not *your* ancestors act in this way so that *our* God brought upon *us* and this city all this evil? Yet you bring more wrath on Israel by profaning the Sabbath." As in the prayer (9:26f.), prophetic texts (Isa 56:1ff.; Ezek 20:1ff.; 44:24, Jer 17:19ff.), and the final shape of the legislation concerning the Sabbath (Ex 20:8-35:3; Lev 19:3, 30; 23-26), the profanation of the Sabbath in Neh 13:17-18 represents *concretum pro abstractum* Israel's breach of the covenant. Because the forefathers of the Judean aristocrats acted wickedly (מה־הדבר הרע הזה אשר אתם עשים//הלוא כה עשו אבתיכם), Judah is in a state of affliction. The present generation has not learned the lesson from Israel's history, and thus instead of facilitating the Restoration, they are prolonging the divine ire.

The proposed first edition agrees with the composition of 5:1-13 and 6:17-19 + 13:4-14, which transform the building report into an account of Judah's Restoration. The dating of the indictment of the חרי יהודה to "those days" (13:15) is parallel to 6:17ff., which recounts that the חרי יהודה were corresponding with the enemy during "those days" of the building activities. Both passages are formulated with participles to express the ongoing nature of activities. Yet the most substantial support for this proposal is provided by the expression "all this evil" (כל־הרעה הזאת) in v. 18. In 2:17, Nehemiah ascribes הרעה to the situation of Jerusalem's ruins and the attendant sociopolitical disgrace (cf. also 1:3). Once the wall is built, he declares that the nations no longer disdained the Judeans (6:16). Now if the nobles were profaning the Sabbath after the wall had already been built, as required by v. 19-22a, how can Nehemiah still speak of the affliction in the province? Assuming that the Sabbath reforms were introduced at some point after the work on the wall, Karrer has recently followed Blenkinsopp in suggesting that "all this evil" refers to the situation of Judah's subjugation to the Persians.[42] If correct, Neh 13:18 would be the only passage in the first-person account that presents a negative image of the Achaemenid reign.[43] However, the passages 1:1b-4; 5:1-15; 6:10-14; 13:4-9 and v. 23ff. employ the terminology of 2:17, ascribing "the affliction" and

---

41 This designation appears only here and in 6:17.
42 2001: 195. Cf. also Blenkinsopp (1988: 360).
43 A similar formulation appears in Ezra's prayer (ואחרי כל־הבא עלינו במעשינו הרעים in 9:13), and there "all that is come upon us" clearly refers to the judgment of 587/6 BCE.

"reproach" to the situation in Judah and the condition of Jerusalem *before* the completion of the wall. Insofar as the earliest layer of Neh 13:15ff. presented "the affliction" continuing after the twenty-fifth of Elul, it would detract from the significance of this *Heilsdatum*.

So too, the deixis הזאת identifies the present condition with הרעה. How then are we to account for the reference to Jerusalem: ועל העיר הזאת (v. 18aβ)? If the city had already been built, then Nehemiah could not have drawn attention to "all this evil that our God has brought upon us *and on this city*." V. 18 makes sense only when Nehemiah could demonstrate the noble's culpability by pointing, in a gesture reminiscent of the prophet's symbolic acts,[44] to the physical ruins of Jerusalem. Since after the twenty-fifth of Elul these ruins and the concomitant sociopolitical distress no longer existed,[45] the formulation of v. 18 substantiates the proposed isolation of the primary stratum in v. 15-22.[46] Accordingly, the author employs the expression "and in those days" in the same way as it is used in 6:17 and portrays Nehemiah illustrating how the nobles' profanation of the Sabbath has led to the very ruins they were repairing.

If the first edition of Neh 13:15ff. did not include vv. 16 and 19-21, the entire account would not have been composed at a very late date. In v. 15b, Nehemiah does not utter his warning on the Sabbath, but rather "on the day they sold their food" (ואעיד ביום מכרם ציד).[47] Not only this late addition but also v. 16 reflects a time when the Judeans were not allowed to market their wares on the Sabbath. Such a prohibition is attested, as already noted, in Amos 8:4ff. This passage – an exposition of the fourth vision – is probably postexilic, as

---

44 Significantly, the first reform account also depicts a symbolic act; cf. 5:13.

45 This applies, at least, for the presentation of the building report.

46 It cannot be ruled out this phrase in v. 18 has been supplemented by a later hand. In its present location the phrase lags behind as if were an afterthought. We would expect it to have been placed directly after the first indirect object ("upon us"). That God "brought all this evil upon us" is a formulation that is not by any means unique to this verse. In 1 Kgs 9:9 (2 Chr 7:22) we encounter almost the exact same wording. Equally similar are Jer 2:3; 23:17; 32:23, 42; 36:31; 42:17; Job 2:11; 42:11; Dan 9:12, 13, 14, etc. This evidence supports the conclusion drawn from the awkwardness of the syntax in Neh 13:18. It appears that the hand that inserted the phrase "and upon this city" assimilated the original formulation to a number of passages which warn of the evil that God would bring upon Jerusalem: 2 Kgs 21:12, 16, 20; Jer 19:3, 15; 35:17; 44:2; Ezek 14:22; 2 Chr 34:24, 28 etc. Significant is that none of these texts places the direct object (כל-הרעה הזאת) between two indirect objects, as in Neh 13:18. This conclusion agrees with the view espoused by Jahn (1909: 172), Mowinckel (1916: 88-n. 1; 1964:71), Hölscher (1923: 561), Rudolph (1949: 207), and Bowman (1954: 813). It also explains why Nehemiah begins his account in Judah and then, without saying how, is suddenly in Jerusalem. Cf. Williamson's solution: "he may have preferred not to follow the offenders to Jerusalem until after the Sabbath" (1985: 395). – If the phrase constitutes a gloss, it must have been inserted at a very early stage, since the identification of the evil with the condition of the city to which Nehemiah refers contradicts vv. 19ff., which presuppose that the city has already been built.

47 This interpretation is in keeping with the consensus; cf., e.g., Williamson (1985: 395).

Wolff argued compellingly.[48] Veijola has demonstrated that v. 5a – the line which corresponds to Neh 13:15b – has been inserted between vv. 4b and 5b.[49] Since the only texts which refer to the closing of the markets on the Sabbath are Amos 8:5a and Neh 13:15ff.,[50] Veijola concludes that the passage presupposes Nehemiah's account.[51] This conclusion faces difficulties, however, when one recognizes that Neh 13:15ff. presents the Judeans merely *carrying* their burdens to Jerusalem and solely the foreign merchants selling their wares on the Sabbath. The hand responsible for the insertion of Amos 8:5b does not seem to be aware of Sabbath markets in Judah organized by foreign merchants. Now if Amos 8:5b presents the accused complaining that they cannot sell their grain on the Sabbath and Neh 13:15aβb-16 reflects a situation in which only foreign merchants do business on the Sabbath, then Neh 13:15aβb-16 is later, not earlier, than Amos 8:5b. Since the latter must have been added to its context at a very advanced stage in the editing of Amos, as Levin has made probable on the basis of independent evidence,[52] one must date Neh 13:15ff. to an even later period. However, when one concedes that only supplements to the reform account presuppose that the Judeans are prohibited to market their goods on the Sabbath, the original formulation of Neh 13:15ff. could be older than Amos 8:5a.

In view of this evidence, it seems that Neh 13:16 mirrors a more advanced situation when Tyrians had settled in Judah and recognized the financial possibilities contained by the prohibition of Sabbath mercantile activities for Judeans. Given the lack of archeological evidence for settlements of Phoenician traders in Judah during the fourth cent. BCE, our proposal merits serious consideration.[53]

---

48 Cf. Wolff (1969: 372ff.).
49 Veijola (1989: 254) identifies vv. 5a and 6b (the bold face) as a *relecture* of Amos 8:4ff., since these lines interrupt the use of infinitives (the italics) in vv. 5b and 6a. Moreover, only vv. 5a and 6b can be understood as the words of the accused, what does not apply for vv. 5b and 6a. It exactly the proposed addition of the passage which corresponds to Neh 13:15b, where Nehemiah warns them on the day they sold their wares not on the Sabbath: "4 Hear this, you that trample on the needy *to bring to ruin* the poor of the land, **5 saying, 'When will the new moon be over so that we may sell grain; and the Sabbath, so that we may offer wheat for sale,** *to make small* the ephah and *to make great* the shekel, *to practice deceit* with false balances, 6 *to buy* the poor for silver and the needy for a pair of sandals, **and selling the sweepings of the wheat.'"** As Reinmuth (2002: 296) helpfully points out, the pair "new moon and Sabbath" appears frequently in very late texts (cf., e.g., Isa 66:23; Ezek 45:17; 46:1, 3; Eccl 2:16; Neh 10:34; 1 Chr 23:31; 2 Chr 2:3; 8:13; 31:3).
50 Cf., however, 10:32a, which is undoubtedly younger that Neh 13:15ff.
51 1989: 254.
52 1997: 407ff. and 2001: 257ff.
53 According to Galling, "Im 3. Jh. v. Chr. gab es an verschiedenen Orten, wie Sichem und Maresa, Sidonierkolonien; so wird es auch – kaum vor 200 v. Chr. – in Jerusalem eine Tyrerkolonie gegeben haben" (1954: 253). Galling's conclusions, based on Bliss's and Macalister's excavations of Marissa (Tell Sandakhanna), still represent the present state of

The situation in Judah may be compared to present-day disputes both in Europe regarding Sunday shopping-hours and in the modern state of Israel, where Jewish citizens frequent Arab markets on the Sabbath in, for example, the Old City of Jerusalem. Despite the latter analogy, it appears that v. 16 originally referred to Tyrians selling their wares in the province generally, not in Jerusalem specifically. The initial problem posed by the merchants is that they are selling their wares on the Sabbath "*to* the Judeans." With the final phrase, the problem posed by these foreign traders is not that they are selling to the Judeans on the Sabbath, but that they were practicing their trade on the Sabbath "*in* Jerusalem."[54] If the verse had not passed through editorial hands, we would expect to read "*in the cities of* Judah and in Jerusalem." or "to the inhabitants (ישבי) of Judah and Jerusalem." Yet instead of moving the phrase with Rudolph to the beginning of the verse,[55] it is much more tenable to assign it to a later revision.[56] Accordingly, the verse depicts the Tyrians bringing their wares and selling them at the Judean markets on the Sabbath. Without the phrase "and in Jerusalem," one can now appreciate the contrast between "the Tyrians" and "the children of Judah."[57]

That ובירושלם must have been appended to v. 16 has substantial consequences for the treatment of vv. 20-21, where Nehemiah notices several times that the foreign merchants were spending the night outside Jerusalem. If v. 16 originally depicted the Tyrians selling their wares to the inhabitants of the province as a whole and an editorial hand has supplemented ובירושלם to assimilate the verse to the emphasis of Jerusalem in the rest of the passage, then the primary author of v. 16 has not prepared the reader for vv. 20-21.

---

knowledge concerning Tyrian colonies in Judah. Blenkinsopp (1988: 359) can only presume that the Sidonian settlement dates back into the Persian period. We also know of "the Sidonians of Shechem" from both Josephus (*Ant.* XI. 344) and the exchange of letters between this community and Antiochus. Finally, it is possible that there was a Tyrian colony in Rammoth-Ammon (cf. Polybius 5.71: 1-10). In all three cases, the evidence for Phoenician colonies is restricted to the Ptolemaic and Seleucid times. Even if scattered groups of Tyrians moved eastward prior to this time, the *colonies* began after the campaign of Alexander the Great. The Tyrians of Neh 13:16, 19-21 were thus most probably in Judah and Jerusalem at much later time than the end of the fifth century BCE. With regard to the remaining evidence of Phoenician trading colonies, cf. Moscati (1968: 82-7), Luria (1970: 363ff.), Ap-Thomas (1973: 259ff.), and Janzen (2002: 143).

54   The formulation לבני יהודה ובירושלם resembles vv. 15 and 18a inasmuch as the abuse of the Sabbath in Jerusalem is secondary to the Sabbath profanation in the province as a whole.

55   1949: 206f.

56   Cf. Hölscher (1923: 560), Mowinckel (1923: 560), and Gunneweg (1987: 169).

57   Whether the ו before "Jerusalem" is to be interpreted as a *waw explicativum* with Kellermann (1967: 51-n. 236) and Williamson (1985: 391 – who translates "to the people of Judah – in Jerusalem itself!"), is difficult to determine. This question has, however, little bearing on the problem of the integrity of the phrase, for the *waw explicativum* is also an editorial device. In any case, Kellermann's and Williamson's approach is preferable to Blenkinsopp's (1988: 357), according to which we should simply delete the ו.

The findings of this analysis seem to pose a problem. If both וּבִירוּשָׁלַםִ in v. 16 and vv. 20-21 belong to a later expansion, Nehemiah would have failed to report how he handled the situation of the Judeans buying from the Tyrians on the Sabbath. Upon second glance, however, the account does provide a response to the activities of Tyrian merchants in Judah on the Sabbath. According to v. 16, these merchants were selling to the בְּנֵי יְהוּדָה. Since the statement, as noted above, intends simply to contrast the foreign Tyrians with the Judeans, the reader should not understand that *all* the inhabitants of the province were patronizing the Sabbath markets. Indeed, the average Judean in both the Persian and Hellenistic periods led a simple agricultural life and was largely self-sufficient; s/he would not have been able to afford the luxury-items imported from the coast. On the other hand, "the nobles of Judah" (v. 17a) would have constituted a lucrative clientele. In patronizing the Tyrians, they would have departed from the agricultural ideal and aversion to city-life shared by many conservative circles in Judah (cf., e.g., Prov 24:30-34; 27:23-27; Eccl 2:4f.; 5:8; Sir 7:15; 20:28).[58] Thus, the Tyrian merchants in Neh 13:16, by importing "fish *and all manner of wares*," represent foreign influence: "Der Handel ist ein Kontrahieren, das fremde Kultur und sicherlich auch fremde Religion im Gefolge hat."[59] In this respect, one may compare the identification of the merchant with the Canaanite (כְּנַעֲנִי) in the Hebrew Bible. Similarly, the absence of the Canaanites/traders in Jerusalem characterizes the Day of YHWH (cf. Zech 14:21).[60] It appears, therefore, the Chassidic circles in Judah after the Persian period, which must have viewed Nehemiah as an early representative of their views (cf. Sir 49:13; 2 Macc 1:10-2:18; *1 Enoch* 89:72f.), found in the account of the remonstration with nobles for profaning the Sabbath – an institution that was elevated to the *status confessionis* of Judaism in the third century[61] – an appropriate context for adding a new aspect to the criticism of the cosmopolitan tendencies among the aristocracy (cf. 6:17-19; 13:4-9, 28f.). As Hengel remarks: "[I]n den Kreisen der strenggläubigen Frommen stand man den phönizisch-kanaanäischen Händlern, die fremden Luxus, die Versuchung fremder Kulte und rituelle Unreinheit ins Land brachten, mit äußerstem Mißtrauen gegen-über."[62] Thus, Nehemiah's remonstration of "the nobles in Judah" in vv. 17-18 represents a response to the problem posed by "the children of Judah" (=the wealthy) purchasing the wares of the Tyrians "living there" (= in Judah). And inasmuch as the censure of the aristocracy in Neh 13:17-18 is general enough to

---

58 Cf. Boström (1935: 64ff. and 72ff.).
59 Boström (1935: 92).
60 Cf., e.g., Hos 12:8; Ezek 16:29; 17:4; Job 40:30; Pr 31:24. With regard to the Phoenicians specifically, cf. Zeph 1:11 and Isa 23:11.
61 Cf. Jdt 8:6, 10:2; 1 Macc 1:34, 43, 45; 2:32, 34, 41; 6:44; 9:34, 43; 10:54; 2 Macc 5:25; 8:26, 27, 28, 12:58; 15:3.
62 1969: 66.

treat the issue of trade between affluent Judeans and foreign merchants in v. 16, a continuation of the account – especially the one in vv. 19-22a – comes unexpectedly.

The evidence of the communal pledge (chap. 10) substantiates our findings. "And if the peoples of the land bring in merchandise or any grain on the Sabbath day to sell, we will not buy it from them on the Sabbath or any holy day" (v. 32a). Since this stipulation of the pact employs the same wording as 13:16 (cf., e.g., the parallels of המביאים and למכור), one may expect it to provide a window into the reception and development of Nehemiah's account. With regard to the remaining stipulations, we notice that they surpass the implications of the reforms in 5:1-13; 13:4-14 and 23ff. Conversely, Nehemiah's Sabbath-reforms in 13:15ff. surpass the requirements of the community's pledge in 10:32a. While prohibiting the patronization of "the peoples of the land" when they "bring their merchandise or any grain to sell on the Sabbath day," the latter fails to provide for the specific case of Jerusalem. Duggan's remarks with regard to 10:32a bear repeating:

> [I]n terms of content, the community's Sabbath stipulation provides a catalyst – but not a predetermined agenda – for Nehemiah's activities. Nehemiah's Sabbath reform (13:15–22) *exceeds the bounds of the community's Sabbath stipulation* (10:32a). Specifically, the stipulation does not address the activities that Nehemiah observes the Judahites performing on the Sabbath.... The stipulation focuses on the Judahites who might buy (10:32a), whereas Nehemiah directs his concern to those who sell (whether Judahites or foreigners [cf. 13:15–16]). Moreover, Nehemiah not only prohibits the foreigners from selling at the gates, but even prevents their entering the city during the Sabbath.[63]

What Duggan notes from a synchronic perspective may be directly applied to the present diachronic analysis. Since the people do not follow Nehemiah's example by pledging themselves to prevent foreign merchants from entering the city (cf. the concentration on Jerusalem in vv. 33-40), it appears all the more likely that v. 16 did not contain the final ובירושלם. In the thirty-second year of Artaxerxes, Nehemiah returns to the province and notices that the Judean leaders (10:1-28, 30ff.), despite their promise to the contrary, were patronizing foreign merchants on the Sabbath. 10:32a indicates that the earliest readers of the account interpreted v. 16 as imputing guilt to the aristocracy that purchased these imported wares. This interpretation is much more possible without the specification "in Jerusalem" in v. 16 and the depiction of the practical measures for the city in vv. 19-22. Accordingly, a later author re-dated the Sabbath-reforms to a time after the ratification of the pact and the building of the wall (v. 6) and thereby paved the way for the amplification of 13:15ff. with ובירושלם in vv. 16 and vv. 19-22a. Now Nehemiah, in order to guard the city from foreign

---

63   2001: 275 – my italics.

influence on the Sabbath, closes the gates of the wall that had been restored more than twelve years earlier. That the gates could be closed stands in tension not only with the introductory expression "in those days," but also with v. 18, where he draws attention to the ruins of the city (v. 18a; cf. above). Hence, the evidence of 10:32a indicates that early readers interpreted 13:15-18 just as one would anticipate if vv. 19-22a, as proposed, were appended later.

10.4 Conclusions

With regard to the tenability of our approach to Nehemiah's reforms in chaps. 5 and 13, the present analysis has produced positive results. The only account that poses a problem for dating the reforms to the fifty-two days of building is 13:15ff., and we have seen that it underwent several expansions. In the earliest editions, Nehemiah employs the introductory expression "and during those days" in the same way as in the foregoing unit 6:17-19 + 13:4-14, namely to recount additional activities before the twenty-fifth of Elul. As the wall was being built, "the nobles of Judah" (6:17, 13:17) were both exchanging letters with the enemy and profaning the Sabbath. The assumption that chap. 5 reports the activities of a later time and was composed for the context of chap. 13 is, therefore, gratuitous. Although these reform accounts portray what is historically improbable, one must respect the attempt of their authors to continue the transformation of the building report into a depiction of Judah's social and religious Restoration.

According to our reconstruction, the account of the Sabbath reforms origi-nally comprised only vv. 15aα (including בשׁבת), 17-18* and 22b. This form resembles an earlier version of the following paragraph that concludes with the interrogation and sermon in vv. 26-27. Moreover, Nehemiah refers to "all this evil" (הזאת [הגדולה] כל־הרעה, v. 18). In 2:17a, he identifies הרעה with the condition of the wall. If he remonstrates with the Judeans during the construc-tion, this expression would have the same meaning as it does in 2:17a and the inclusion of "and upon this city" in v. 18 (a reference to the *present* ruins) would make sense. The differences between 2:17 and 13:7, 17, 27 is that Nehemiah now places the blame for הרעה on the Judeans themselves. Accordingly, the remedy to הרעה is not simply the repair of the wall, but a change of behavior.

The Composition of Neh 13:15-22

15 **In those days I saw in Judah the treading of wine presses on the Sabbath,**

> and the transportation of heaps of grain
> > and loading them on donkeys;
> > > and also wine, grapes, figs, and all kinds of burdens,
> > *and the transportation* to Jerusalem on the Sabbath day; and I warned
> > them on they day when they sold food.

16 And the Tyrians who lived there [i.e., in the land of Judah] brought in fish
and all kinds of merchandise and sold them on the Sabbath to the inhabitants
of Judah,
> and in Jerusalem.

17 **Then I remonstrated with the nobles of Judah and said to them, "What is this
evil deed that you are committing?**
> > You are profaning the Sabbath day.

18 **Did not your ancestors act in this way so that our God brought all this
disaster on us** and on this city? **Yet you increase the wrath on Israel by profaning
the Sabbath."**

> 19 And when the gates of Jerusalem grew dark (were to be closed?) before
> the Sabbath,
> > I commanded that the doors should be shut
> I gave orders that they should not be opened until after the Sabbath.
> > And I set some of my servants over the gates, to prevent any burden
> > from being brought in on the Sabbath day.
> 20 Then the merchants and sellers of all kinds of merchandise spent the
> night outside Jerusalem once or twice.
> 21 But I warned them and said to them, "Why do you spend the night in
> front of the wall? If you do so again, I will lay hands on you." From that
> time on they did not come on the Sabbath.
> > 22 And I commanded the Levites that they should purify
> > themselves and come and guard the gates, to keep the Sabbath day
> > holy.

**Remember also this in my favor, O my God, and spare me according to your
great faithfulness.**

11. The Marriage-Reforms – 13:23-31

11.1. Introduction

The preceding chapter has attempted to show that the introduction to 13:15-22 ("in those days") originally served the same function it still does in 6:17ff., namely to date the Sabbath reforms to the fifty-two days during which the wall was restored. Since the account of the marriage-reforms in v. 23ff. also begins with this expression, and since its contents do not indicate that the restoration was already finished, "those days" must likewise refer to the period of building.

This conclusion improves the interpretation of the text. Rather than waiting a year or more, Nehemiah takes notice of the situation – that the Judeans had married women from neighboring lands whose children were speaking their respective languages – already in the first months of his stay in Judah. Inasmuch as he "heard" the people's complaint (5:6), "perceived" Eliashib's misdeed (13:7), "noticed" the absence of the Levites (v. 10) and "saw" the treading of the winepresses on the Sabbath (v. 15) either soon after his first arrival in Jerusalem or as the construction was in progress, we may presume that he also "saw" the abuse described in vv. 23-24 before the twenty fifth of Elul.

While this reading enables us to appreciate how later authors have transformed the building report into an account of Judah's Restoration, it raises serious questions with regard to the historicity of the reforms. If Nehemiah had taken the Judeans to task after the completion of the wall, one would not necessarily have to question the reliability of the account. However, few would disagree that the offenders, after they had been cursed, beaten and plucked hairless (v. 25a), would have been willing (or able) to continue supporting the construction enterprise. Moreover, it is difficult to conceive how Nehemiah would have had enough time during the fifty-two days of construction to address such a complicated issue as the Judeans' marital practices.

Even more problematic for an historical reconstruction based on 13:23ff. is the contradiction between this account and the third-person narrative in Ezra 10. If Ezra had organized a mass divorce from all "outlandish women" (הנשים הנכריות), why does Nehemiah only thirteen years later observe "that the Judean men had married Ashdodite, Ammonite and Moabite women" (13:23)? Since "laws against intermarriage are notoriously difficult to enforce in any age," Cross argues that Nehemiah found the people backsliding.[1] This solution does not, however, stand up to closer inspection: Since the children of these families were old enough to speak יהודית, Nehemiah cannot be reporting a turn of events long after Ezra's time.[2] Insofar as these two figures do not appear to be acquainted with one another, one could alternatively follow van Hoonacker in dating Ezra to the reign of Artaxerxes II.[3] Yet this approach is equally untenable; it poses the problem of explaining why Ezra never refers to Nehemiah, although he would have continued the precedent established by the latter and have even borrowed his modification of Deut 7:3 (cf. Ezra 9:2, 12 and Neh 13:25b).

With the aim of discovering a more tenable solution for these historical difficulties,[4] the following analysis begins by focusing on the literary evidence (§11.2). Thereafter (§11.3), we briefly consider the attendant historical problems.

11.2 The Literary Development of 13:23-26 and Ezra 9-10

11.2.1 Analysis of 13:23-26

To date, the best proposal for the literary development of vv. 23-31 has been advanced by Pichon, who isolates vv. 23aα, 24a, 25a (28) and 31b as "le récit primitif." The deficient situation depicted and treated in this extract from "les Mémoires de Néhémie" is that, "des fils de Judéens ne parlent plus la langue paternelle mais 'l'ashdodien.'"[5] Later, the primary edition underwent expansions in vv. 23aβ, 24b, 25b-27, with which the redactors have revised Nehemiah's account "dans la ligne de la réforme d'Esdras, décrite en Esd. ix-x."[6] In distinguishing between these two layers, Pichon points out rightly that we would not expect an account composed by Nehemiah to manifest such familiarity with the biblical tradition. Otherwise, it is difficult to reconcile the text with the redactional character of the passages in chaps. 1-6, in which Nehemiah is well versed in the scriptures (e.g., in 1:5-11a). On the other hand, our analyses have already shown that all of 6:17-19 + 13:4ff. may have been added to the building report. Consequently, one should be cautious in attempting to harmonize the tenor of chap. 13 with the earliest layers of chaps. 1-6. As already observed, the reader

---

1   1975: 18-n. 69.
2   That these children are not very young is indicated by the use of בנים instead of ילדים as in Ezra 10:1, 3; Neh 12:43.
3   Van Hoonacker (1924).
4   Janzen unfortunately never addresses the relationship of Ezra 9-10 to Neh 13:23ff. in his recent study of Ezra's account (2002). As Smith-Christopher urges Ezra-Neh scholarship (1994: 265), an *historical* inquiry with respect to the mixed-marriage crisis in Yehud should begin with Nehemiah's account.
5   1997: 192.

must be quite conversant with the biblical tradition in order to appreciate or even understand the foregoing paragraphs in this chapter, which concern the reappointment of the Levites to "their places" and the observance of the Sabbath in Judah. It would thus be surprising if one could isolate with Pichon a substratum of the account in 13:23ff. that "ne connaissait pas la Loi."[7]

With regard to the introduction, Pichon follows the *opinio communis* in assigning עמוניות אשדודיות, which are not joined by a copula, to an editor who was influenced directly by the quotation of Deut 23:4 in the unquestionably late text 13:1-3 (לא־יבוא עמני ומאבי בקהל האלהים עד־עולם). While this conclusion will be accepted here, it is not supported, as often assumed, by v. 24. Ever since Batten argued for the priority of the LXX reading for v. 24,[8] scholars have commonly attributed the second half (וכלשון עם ועם), which refers to the language of Ammon and Moab, to a glossator in order to eliminate the incoherency in the verse: "And half of their children spoke Ashdodite – and none of them knew how to speak the language of Judah – and the languages of the respective peoples." Reading the verse without the dashes, one is confused into thinking that merely the fact that the children were monolingual disturbed Nehemiah. Without v. 24b, this confusion does not obtain.[9] Moreover, if half (=many) of the children spoke Ashdodite, yet none of the children spoke the language of Judah, what did the other half speak? The verse has probably been supplemented not with v. b but rather with v. 24aβ (ואינם מכירים לדבר יהודית). This solution both explains the alteration from מדבר to מכירים לדבר and provides a better reading: "And half/many of their children were speaking the language of Ashdod or the language of the respective people."[10]

The problem with this solution is that it presupposes v. 23 in its transmitted form. Since וכלשון עם ועם refers clearly to אשדודיות עמוניות, one must either contend, against the consensus, that the second half of v. 23 does not constitute a gloss or conclude that even the earliest part of v. 24 (aα,b) has been inserted between vv. 23 and 25. Insofar as the latter conclusion is more reasonable, the most important part of Pichon's reconstruction is redactional. Since the Nehemiah of this passage is not primarily concerned with the survival of the Judean language, he must consider the connubium wrong in and of itself. On the other hand, if his objective is the survival of יהודית, as Pichon, suggests, one cannot explain other points of the narrative. Elsewhere, the offenders are always named first (cf., e.g., 6:17; 13:4, 5, 7, 28), which means that the malefactors in v.

---

6 1997: 199.
7 Ibid.
8 1913: 300.
9 In simply following the LXX, Batten's solution is, however, weak, for ואינם in v. 24aβ means "none of them" (cf. 4:17). The *versio Syriaca* attempt to correct the misunderstanding.
10 That v. 24b is missing in the LXX only indicates that later readers have noticed the same problem.

23ff. are the Judean men who married Ashdodite women. This agrees with v. 25a, where these men are cursed, beaten and plucked hairless. In resorting to these violent extremes, Nehemiah does not intend to persuade these men that they should prohibit their wives from speaking Ashdodite at home or that they should organize *ulpanim* throughout Judah. What evokes his vehemence is rather that the Judeans had even contracted marriages with non-Judeans.

It seems that a later hand has added v. 24aα,b in order to demonstrate the consequences of this connubium for the solidarity of the Judean people, which required a common language. After this insertion, the emphasis in the building account on the consolidation of the province strikingly resembles the transmitted shape of Gen 11:1-9, which however *censures* the building of a city (cf. עיר ויאמרו הבה נבנה־לנו [v. 4a] with ויאמרו נקום ובנינו [Neh 2:1]) and the concomitant ethnic and linguistic unity.[11] So too, the emphasis in v. 24aβ on the language of Judah – whatever that may have been – suggests that this *relecture* is very late. It presents Nehemiah, who may have originally composed the building report in Aramaic,[12] as a champion of "Yehudit."

The conclusion that v. 24 does not belong to the first edition of the account determines the treatment of v. 25. After inflicting pain upon the offenders, Nehemiah makes them swear that they would discontinue their activities: "You shall not give your daughter to their sons nor take (נשא) any of their daughter for your sons or for yourselves." The wording of the oath clearly has been adapted from Deut 7:3b: "you shall not give your daughter to his son, nor his daughter shall you take (לקח) for your son." Significantly, Ezra also adds "for yourselves" and uses נשא instead of לקח when he quotes Deut 7:3b (cf. Ezra 9:2 and 12).[13] It is quite unlikely that both Nehemiah and Ezra modify this text in the same way yet independently of each other. Since other first-person passages in Neh 1-13 that draw heavily on the biblical tradition have probably been formulated by later authors, Pichon proposes that a redactor has appended the second half of v. 25 to bring Nehemiah's reforms for the Judean language into conformity with Ezra's marriage reforms.[14] This proposal, however, proves to be untenable if an editorial hand is responsible for v. 24.

More recently, Reinmuth has proposed a more radical solution: Nehemiah does not quote Ezra's reading of Deut 7:3b. Rather Deut 7:3 quotes Nehemiah

---

11 The best study of the unity of language and building themes in this text is that of Uehlinger (1990, esp. pp. 4-6-512) It investigates the parallels with extra-biblical building inscriptions, which could represent the general thematic background for the insertion to Neh 13:24.

12 Cf. Williamson (1985: xxviii).

13 Cf. Pichon (1997: 183).

14 As already noted, Pichon's analyzes Neh 13:23ff. under the assumption that the historical Nehemiah drafted the earliest version. Yet insofar as all of 6:17-19 + 13:4ff. amplifies the presentation of the building activities, it is not surprising that the primary author of 13:23ff. draws on the biblical tradition in the formulation of the account.

and the mixed-marriage polemics elsewhere (Exod 34:11-26, Judg 3:5f., Jer 29:6f., Ezra 9) are younger than Nehemiah's account.[15] While all these passages indeed appear to be late expansions of their contexts,[16] it is unlikely that they are a "Reflex auf die Darstellung in Neh 13,23-31." With regard to Deut 7:3b, it is admittedly "nicht fest im Kontext verankert." Nevertheless, one may easily account for it, with Hölscher, as a development of 7:2 + 6 against the background of Exod 34:11-26.[17] In discussing Neh 13:25b, Reinmuth unfortunately fails to respond to Pichon's observations that the wording of the oath does not suit the context. The offenders at issue in vv. 23-24 have long married and fathered children; it would then have been too late for Nehemiah to make them swear that they would not intermarry. Moreover, the beginning of the oath ("You shall not give your daughters to their sons...") does not apply to the situation at hand. Now if the author of Deut 7:3b has reformulated the oath, as Reinmuth insists, why does the latter, in contrast to Deut 7:3b, not correspond to the depicted situation? In assuming that Nehemiah must have composed the text because he would not have known a late passage in Deuteronomy, Reinmuth advances solutions which are incompatible with the literary evidence.

Why does Nehemiah, in formulating the oath, quote a text that does not correspond to the problem portrayed in v. 23? Instead of following Pichon in ascribing v. 25b to a later hand, one should first concede that the account does not report an historical situation and response. In doing so, a direct connection between v. 23 and 25 can be established: The problem of Judeans who have already married Ashdodites serves merely as foil for the quotation of Deut 7:3b. Nehemiah probably never cursed, beat and plucked out the hair of the offenders, yet in reporting these actions, the author depicts his exemplary fervency for the prohibition of intermarriage and underscores the point, already expressed in 5:1-13, that the consolidation of the province requires compliance with the Deuteronomic code.

Insofar as he can assault the offenders and expect them to know why he assaults them, even the earliest edition of the passage presupposes the reader's awareness of the prohibition of connubium with foreigners.[18]

---

15 2002: 213-215, 305ff.
16 To Exod 23:11-26, cf. Blum (1996: 363ff.); to Jer 29:5-7, cf. Schmid (1996: 211-n. 53); to Judg 3:5f., cf. Reinmuth's own observations (2002: 309f.).
17 Hölscher (1922: 170f.).
18 The formulation היהודים instead of מין־היהודים (cf. 1:1; 5:5b; 13:19, 28) indicates that v. 23 has been formulated with the general oath (v. 25b) in view. With respect to the formulation of v. 23, Karrer remarks that "Die Beschuldigten werden nicht als Angehörige einer Gruppe sondern als Angehörige des Volkes der Judäer angesprochen" (2001 :154 – italics original).

Whether or not one should speak of a "Prophetic Lawsuit" in other biblical texts,[19] the narrative certainly follows a familiar pattern in Neh 1-13. In chap. 10, the community takes an oath to follow "the Torah of God" (v. 30). The first stipulation of this pledge resembles Ezra's and Nehemiah's modification of Deut 7:3b: "and we will not give our daughters to the people of the land, nor take their daughters for our sons" (v. 31). After the community has already sworn not to contract mixed marriages, the oath in 13:25b is repetitive. The authors of the final shape of the book, however, present Nehemiah returning years after the ratification of the pact, opening a lawsuit in prophetic style, and then, in making the Judeans swear, renewing the pact of chap. 10.

Because chap. 10 and especially v. 31ff. (beginning with ואשר) are most likely much later than the earliest edition of 13:23ff.,[20] one must seek an earlier analogy. The best candidate is the account of the reforms in chap. 5: After hearing the complaint (שמעתי, v. 6; cf. ראיתי in 13:23), arraigning (ואריבה, v. 7; cf. 13:25a), and interrogating (vv. 7aβ, 8-9) the malefactors, he makes them swear (ואשביעם in both v. 12b and 13:25b) to a new lending-policy. There is, however, a difference: Whereas in 5:1-13 the administration of the oath (v. 12b) follows the interrogation (vv. 7aβ, 8-9), Nehemiah continues in 13:26-27 with a sermon and interrogation. After v. 25b, the offenders have already been beaten and, most importantly, have taken the oath. Why then does Nehemiah continue, now in a much more rational manner, with the sermon and interrogation?[21] Since it is difficult to conceive how one hand could be responsible for this incongruity, we cannot rule out the possibility that a redactor has added vv. 26-27.[22]

11.2.2. Comparison with Ezra 9-10

In order to test our reconstruction of Neh 13:22-27, a brief glance at Ezra 9-10 is necessary. As already observed, the wording of Nehemiah's oath employs the modification of Deut 7:3b found in Ezra 9:12. It cannot be merely coincidental that both passages quote Deut 7 in the same way, as Pichon contends. I suggest, however, that Ezra 9:12 has been influenced by the formulation of the oath. If, as Pichon claims, the redactor of Neh 13:23ff. intended to realign Nehemiah's reforms for the language of Judah according to Ezra's marriage reforms and

---

19 Cf. De Roche (1983).
20 Cf. Excursus I at the end of chapter nine.
21 Without the introduction ואמרה (cf., e.g., 5:7; 13:11, 17), the presence of vv. 26-27 is even more problematic.
22 Cf. Noth (1943: 150). That the sermon in vv. 26-27 has been added to v. 25b explains also the terminological differences (cf., e.g., נשים נכריות in vv. 26b and 27b). – With respect to this addition, they show, as Rudolph wrote, "wie sehr Nehemia in der Geschichte der Vorzeit zu Hause war " (1949: 209).

draw a direct parallel between the two, one would expect the oath to include more of Ezra 9:12. For example, the clause, "nor seek their peace or their wealth for ever...," is perfectly suited to the situation depicted in Neh 13. Significantly, this line quotes Deut 23:7. Since the plus of Ezra 9:12 vis-à-vis Neh 13:25 corresponds exactly to the quotation of Deut 23, the common modification of Deut 7:3b in Ezra 9 and Neh 13 suggests that Ezra 9 has been composed with Neh 13:23ff. in view. While the latter quotes only Deut 7:3b, the passage Ezra 9:10ff., as Blenkinsopp points out, consists of a collage of key expressions from Deut 1:38f.; 6:11; 7:1, 3; 18:9; 23:7; 2 Kgs 10:21; 16:3; and 21:2.[23] Thus, Ezra 9 appears to draw on the quotation of Deut 7:3b in Neh 13:25b with the aim of expanding its theological (i.e., Deuteronomistic) horizon.[24]

Karrer has helpfully noted also the differences between Ezra's and Nehemiah's use of Deut 7:3b and their presentation of mixed marriages:

> In der Nehemiaschrift wird dieses Verbot im Sinn einer ethnischen Abgrenzung interpretiert. In der Esraschrift hingegen ist die Abgrenzung wesentlich religiös bestimmt. Die 'Fremden' sind durch ihre 'Greuel' und ihre 'Unreinheit' gekennzeichnet, die mit der als 'heilig' verstandenen Gemeinschaft nicht in Berührung kommen dürfen. Diese religiös bestimmte Abgrenzung wird also an den Personen selbst festgemacht. Die Verwendung des Ausdrucks 'heiliger Same' verweist darauf, daß die Heiligkeit mit genealogischem Denken in Verbindung gebracht wird. Das sakralrechtlich orientierte Denken der Esraschrift radikalisiert das Verständnis der Mischehen gegenüber der Nehemiaschrift. Es handelt sich nicht mehr um den Bruch eines Gebotes unter anderen wie in Neh 13, sondern um eine Infragestellung der Existenz Israels, da in diesem Denken die Verletzung der 'Heiligkeit' das Gottesverhältnis selbst zerstört.[25]

When one confines what Karrer refers to as the "Nehemiaschrift" and the "Esraschrift" to Neh 13:23-25 and Ezra 9 respectively, these comments describe superbly the differences between the two texts and rightly affirm that Ezra radicalizes the problem of mixed marriages of his successor. If the earliest edition of Nehemiah's account comprised only vv. 23-25, the presentation in Ezra 9 of the mixed-marriage problem in the most profound existential categories must indicate that it represents the younger text. One arrives at different conclusions, however, when s/he includes the expansions in vv. 26ff. and the third-person narrative in Ezra 10. Neh 13:26ff. employ not only the verb מעל, which is found in Ezra 9 (vv. 2, 4, 6), but also the expression נכריות נשים, which occurs seven times in Ezra 10 (vv. 2, 10, 11, 14, 17, 18, 44) yet not once in

---

23   1988: 184f.
24   In referring to the abominations (תועבה), which are mentioned 16 times in Deut and which Rehoboam, Ahaz, and Manasseh commit, the author of Ezra 9 aligns the problem presented in Neh 13:23-25 with what directly occasioned the demise of Israel and Judah in the Deuteronomistic History.
25   2001: 278f.

Ezra 9. Since Nehemiah describes his actions as purification (מכל־נכר וטהרתים,
v. 30a) and portrays the problem in terms of God's relationship to Israel (v.
26), we cannot follow Karrer in claiming that Neh 13 does not manifest "sakral-
rechlich orientierte[s] Denken" or depict mixed marriages in the category of
"Heiligkeit." Hence, if one includes v. 26ff., Nehemiah's account appears to be
even younger than Ezra 9. On the other hand, when one reads Ezra 9 together
with chap. 10, the narrative depicts Ezra treating the problem of mixed
marriages with more deliberation than Nehemiah. Accordingly, the Ezra
account would be younger than the final edition of Nehemiah account.

Given the confusing state of evidence for the relationship between Ezra 9-10
and Neh 13:23ff., the attempt to determine the order of priority and
dependency appears futile. Neh 13:23-25* seems to be older than Ezra 9, yet
Neh 13:26ff. could be younger. While this corresponds exactly to our proposal
that v. 26ff. have been appended to v. 25b, confusion arises when Ezra 10 is
included. If this text were drafted at the same time as Ezra 9, one could not
explain the fact that Neh 13:26ff. appears to be younger than Ezra 9. In view of
this discrepancy, we must consider the possibility that the third-person narrative
in Ezra 10 has been added to first-person account.

Since the commentary of Bertheau, it has been commonly assumed that the
compiler of Ezra-Neh simply recast several sections of Ezra's "memoirs" into
the third-person.[26] Why he did this, no one can explain. Even more surprising is
that he apparently left Nehemiah's account in its original form. In taking Ezra
10 at face value and abandoning the speculative premise that editors reformulated this text from the first- to the third-person, we can begin to appreciate its
intention.

First, the switch from the first- to third person suggests that "the author" of
Ezra-Neh intends to draw a sharp distinction between excerpts from the source
material in 7:12-26 and 7:27-9:15, what he does not present as his own words,
and his own account in 7:1-11 and 10:1ff.[27] That chap. 10 was composed by
Ezra rather than the author of Ezra-Neh — even if this were to correspond to
the historical facts — runs completely at odds with the intention of the book and
thus represents a critical construct. Theological commentaries do a great
disservice to their readers when they fail to make this point clear and neglect the
narrative contours of Ezra-Neh.[28]

---

26 1862: 8. Cf. Bertholet (1902: XIV), Rudolph (1949: XXIV and 93), Williamson (1985:
    145ff.), and Throntveit (1992: 48ff.).
27 This does not apply to Neh 8, where the transition from the list in 7:6ff. to the narrative is
    seamless. The authors may have intended to present Nehemiah telling this story.
28 In not following this trend, Throntveit's commentary (1992), which manifests influence
    from Eskenazi's work (1988), is to be commended.

For the purposes of critical scholarship, however, one should note the differences between Ezra 9 and 10 which indicate that the latter is just what it purports to be: the work of a later hand. For example, the reader would not have known from chap. 9 that Ezra prayed in the vicinity of the temple; only chap. 10 specifies – indeed emphasizes – this location (cf. "before the house of God," vv. 1 and 6). Not just the place but also the time is defined very precisely by chap. 10. From Ezra's own words in chaps. 8-9, however, one would have presumed that the incident occurred in the middle of the fifth (or perhaps the sixth) month (8:31; cf. also 7:9), but not the ninth and tenth months (cf. 10:9, 16). Moreover, 9:4 disrupts the join between vv. 3 and 5 and appears to be an interpolation.[29] Not only the *Wiederaufnahme* in v. 4b but also the use of אסף instead of קבץ as in 10:1, 7, 9 makes it quite probable that the author of this verse intended to both provide an etiology for the חרדים and to prepare the reader for 10:1ff.[30] Yet without the information that "those who trembled" had gathered around Ezra, we do not know that he prayed in public. This too emerges solely from the narrative in chap. 10, which, however, describes the assembly in much different manner.[31]

These narrative differences correspond to the terminological variations. As already noted, only chap. 10 refers to the נכריות נשים. So too, only it mentions the קהל (cf. vv. 1, 8, 12, 14), although this term would have suited the context of 9:1-2. On the other hand, chap. 9 refers to זרע הקדש (v. 2) and תועבה (vv. 1, 11, 14) – words which never occur in chap. 10. Finally, it consistently employs "the people of the lands" (עמי הארצת, vv. 1, 2, 7, 11), while chap. 10 uses only the singular "the people of the land" (עמי ארץ, vv. 2, 11).[32]

---

29 Cf. Kratz (2000: 86).

30 9:4 and 10:3 may have been directly influenced by the late passages in Isa 66, the only other place where the חרדים make an appearance (cf. 9:4 with Isa 66:2b and 5a).

31 With these differences in view, Eissfeldt (1966: 544) and Blenkinsopp (1988: 187) posit two independent sources for Ezra 9 and 10. This thesis is untenable first on literary grounds: The author, in contrast to the other places in the book, has not given us any indications that he is citing a source. Blenkinsopp points to the parallels between 9:4 and 10:1ff. It appears, however, that v. 4 constitutes an interpolation. Without v. 4, we do not know that Ezra was praying in public. Even with v. 4, we do not know that he was praying "before the house of God" (10:1). Thus, if chap. 10 is based on a source, it disagrees with Ezra's depiction even on this point. Eissfeldt's and Blenkinsopp's thesis does, however, confirm the findings that chaps. 9 and 10 contain disparate depictions and information.

32 Thus, one must question the approach of denying any significance to the use of first- and third-person for the literary development of the Ezra narrative, which is followed by Torrey (1896: 21), Batten (1913: 16f.), Hölscher (1923: 493), Noth (1943: 126), Kapelrud (1944: 79), Mowinckel (1964: 75ff.), Gunneweg (1985: 173) and most recently by Janzen (2002: 37ff.). Cf. Williamson counterarguments to Mowinckel's proposal that the author intentionally switched from the first- to third-person (1985: 145ff.).

That chap. 10 is not integral to the account poses a problem. In chap. 9, Ezra is told of the problem of mixed marriages, mourns and then prays. Without a continuation, the narrative would leave the reader hanging.

In response to this problem, it must first be conceded that the break between chaps. 9 and 10 is a problem facing also those who contend that the author of chaps. 9 and 10 intentionally switched from the first- to third-person or that an editor altered the formulation. Why did he decide to employ two different voices? After chap. 9, the reader is disappointed to hear only the comments of the narrator. Moreover, if the author of Ezra-Neh had "source material" available to him, he would have certainly employed it. Otherwise, one cannot explain the abundance of all sorts of ostensible documents in Ezra-Neh.[33]

Chap. 9 places the emphasis on the prayer in vv. 6-15. Inasmuch as the narrative, which is less than half the size of the prayer, serves simply to present the problem and Ezra's reaction, this account does not require a continuation. Those who insist that the account must have also existed independently of its present context in Ezra-Neh, could accordingly maintain that Ezra 9 was composed to evoke a similar response from the community as that depicted in chap. 10.

The internal evidence, however, indicates that chap. 9 was drafted solely for it present position in the book. The investigation in §5.3.2 adduced evidence for the view that Ezra 7-8 both do not require a continuation and presuppose the temple-building narrative in chaps. 1-6. Since one cannot explain why the historical Artaxerxes would have generously financed Ezra to beautify the temple, yet merely have consented to Nehemiah's petition for permission to build the city, the authors of Ezra 7-8 most likely intended to sustain the priority given to the temple in chaps. 1-6 and prepare the reader for Nehemiah's "secular" activities in Neh 2-6*. After Artaxerxes, in the midst of the temple-construction, prohibits the building of the city-wall until a later time (Ezra 4:21), he sends Ezra loaded down with gold and silver for the maintenance of the temple. Once the latter had delivered these donations (8:33f.), he has fulfilled his original commission (7:11a, 12-13, 15-23) and can finish his report. With the addition of the notice in vv. 35-36, a redactor has concluded the narrative in the same way it begins (i.e. in the third-person). We would, therefore, not anticipate a continuation of the account.[34]

Even more surprising is that this continuation in chap. 9 no longer portrays success. In espousing Torrey's view, Williamson explains the change of mood by positing that Neh 8 was formerly in the first-person and was located between Ezra 8 and 9. "Thus within the original Ezra narrative it was the community's

---

33 Cf. the discussion of these documents in Eskenazi (1988).
34 Cf. Kratz (2000: 84).

understanding and acceptance of that law which pricked their leaders' con-
sciences into bringing their confession to Ezra."[35] Despite its popularity, this
proposal does not stand up to closer inspection. Not only is it difficult to conceive how Neh 8 could have been formulated in the first-person, but the chapter also manifests substantial differences to Ezra 9. In Neh 8, "all the people"
(כל־העם, occurring nine times, but not once in Ezra 9) call for Ezra to read the
Torah. In Ezra 9, on the other hand, the Torah is never mentioned (cf. solely
10:3) and the people are referred to as העם ישראל. The people also fail to recognize their sins, which is astonishing given their desire for the Torah and willingness to make confession in Neh 8-9. In Ezra 9 only the princes come and report
the sins of the people; in Neh 8:1-9:3 (cf. ראשי האבות in 8:13) the princes are
completely absent. Instead of drawing upon 1 Esdr in order to harmonize these
texts, one should consider the possibility that Neh 8 was composed for its
present literary setting.[36]

How then should one explain the sudden change of mood in Ezra 9? Kratz
appears to have correctly assessed the composition of Ezra-Neh in suggesting
that Ezra 9 has been composed with Neh 1 in view. The main argument
advanced for this proposal is the similarity of Ezra's and Nehemiah's prayers.[37]
The study of Neh 1:5-11a has demonstrated, however, the likelihood that this
prayer – with its emphasis on מצות, חקים and משפטים that is absent in Ezra 9 –
has been composed to prepare the reader for the shift from temple in Ezra 1-10
to Torah in Neh 8-10.[38] If this conclusion is tenable, the author of Ezra 9 could
not have known Neh 1:5-11a. Nevertheless, this author does appear to have
been familiar with Neh 1:1-4, where Nehemiah reacts to the news of the
province with continual prayer (v. 4b). Just as Hanani and other men from
Judah come and report to Nehemiah about the situation among the people in
the province, so do the princes come and report to Ezra about the situation
among the people of Israel. Both Ezra and Nehemiah "hear this word/these
words" (Ezra 9:3 and Neh 1:4aα). Both then proceed to "sit down" (cf. ואשבה
משומם in Ezra 9:3b with the simple ישבתי in Neh 1:4aβ).[39] Thereafter, both pray
(Ezra 9:6ff. and Neh 1:4b). In his confession, Ezra employs the terminology of
the narrative in Neh 1:1b-4. For example, he refers to the פליטה in vv. 8, 13, 14,
15. Aside from Neh 1:2, this term occurs only here in Ezra-Neh. In two places
(vv. 8 and 15), Ezra links this term to שאר as Nehemiah does (cf. הפליטה אשר־
נשארו in Neh 1:2 with להשאיר לנו פליטה in Ezra 9:8 and נשארנו פליטה in v. 15).

---

35 1985: 127.
36 Cf. Noth (1943: 128ff.). The analysis in §14.2.3 provides further support for this solution.
37 2000: 84f. Cf. also Plöger (1957: 46f.).
38 Cf. §2.3.
39 Ibn Ezra noticed these connections in his commentary and supplemented the words
    "astonished" from Ezra 9:3b, 4b to "and I sat down" in Neh 1:4.

Against the backdrop of the similarities between Ezra 8 and Neh 2, the narratalogical and terminological parallels between Ezra 9 and Neh 1 are sufficient to propose a genetic relationship between the two texts. Yet not only the first passage but also the final passage of Nehemiah's account shares much in common with Ezra 9. Before Ezra sits down, he pulls out his hair (ואמרטה, v. 3b) in despair for those "who had taken their daughters for themselves and for their sons" (v. 2). In Neh 13:25, Nehemiah reacts by pulling out the hair (ואמרטם) of the offenders and by making them swear by God that they would "not take their daughters for their sons and for themselves." Only these two passages of the Hebrew Bible depict someone pulling out his own hair (מרט) or that of another.

In addition to these similarities, we notice not only that the author of Ezra 9 has incorporated central features from Nehemiah's account and made subtle changes and reversals, but also that he draws primarily on the first (1:1b-4) and final passages (13:23ff.).[40] Most significantly, our study has shown that 1:1b-4 has been drafted to introduce the account after it had been expanded with texts such as 13:23ff.[41]

The conclusion is unavoidable: Just as Ezra's first-person account in chaps. 7-8 bridges the gap between Nehemiah's first-person wall-building report in Neh 2-6* to the third-person, temple-building narrative in Ezra 1-6, so does the addition of Ezra 9 prepare the reader for the expanded version of wall-building account by pointing him or her to the first and final passages. That Ezra presents the situation in greater theological dimensions yet does not attempt to treat the situation with any practical measures, indicates that the author is writing with Neh 13:25b in mind. Nehemiah is the one who solves the situation by taking an oath from all the Judeans (היהודים, v. 23). Insofar as the author draws on the wording of the first and final passages of the building account, he expects that we read the latter in the conceptual framework provided by Ezra's prayer.

As intended by the author of Neh 1:1b-4, the one responsible for Ezra 9 understood the protagonists in chaps. 1-13* as הפליטה and הנשארים (cf. Ezra 9:8-15). The composition of Neh 1:1b-4 already represents an adept reinterpretation of the building account: While the latter never portrays the protagonists as those who remained in the land after the captivity, 1:1b-4 makes these origins

---

40   Without Ezra 10, the next passage in the book would be Neh 1. The terminology, manner of depiction and conception of the first-person account in Ezra 9 would thus flow smoothly into the beginning of the Nehemiah's first-person account. Accordingly, the personal views of both figures agree with one another a multiple levels.

41   13:23ff. belongs to the same redactional level as 5:1ff.; 6:10-14, vv. 17-19 + 13:4ff., all of which de-emphasize the building of the wall and focus on the social problems. 1:1b-4 concerns itself first with the survivors of the captivity in the province and then the building of the wall, as a comparison of 1:3 and 2:17 clearly demonstrates. Cf. §4.3.1.

very clear, presenting thereby the reforms and building of the wall as the Restoration after the devastation of 587/6 BCE. Ezra 9 continues this reinterpretation of Neh 2-13* begun in 1:1b-4: The פליטה and the נשארים are not those who never went into captivity, as we must understand from Neh 1:1b-4. They are rather those who accompany Ezra as he returned from Babylon.

Furthermore, Neh 1:1b-4 presents the reforms and wall-building as the transformation of Judah after her judgment, and Ezra 9 integrates epexegetically this restorative aspect with the matrimonial reforms in Neh 13:23-25 into a single entity. The Judean-Ashdodite unions now constitute a problem of existential and exilic proportions requiring the repair of the wall and the separation that it symbolizes (cf. 13:16, 19-22a). For the author of Ezra 9, Nehemiah's final reform is the key to understanding all his activities in Judah. In assimilating the priestly focus in Ezra 1-8* to the theme of Judah's consolidation in Neh 1-13*, Ezra 9 presents the building of the wall not only as part and parcel of the Restoration of Judah, but also as the necessary conditions for maintaining a wall of separation (גדר, v. 9) between the people and "filthiness" of "the peoples of the lands" (cf. 1 and 14). As long as Judah does not confront its problem and separate itself, it is in danger of incurring complete judgment – without any survivors in the province for Nehemiah to inquire about thirteen years later. In the final passage of his work (v. 23ff.), which describes the time before the completion of the wall ("in those days), he makes the Judeans swear that they would not "take their daughters," thus not only restoring the חומה around Jerusalem, but also refortifying the גדר around Judah (cf. Ezra 9:9).

These observations with regard to Ezra 9-10 lend considerable weight to our reconstruction of the earliest edition of Neh 13:25ff. Ezra 9 has been composed with the oath of v. 25b in view. The third-person narrative in Ezra 10, which reports another oath (וישבע, v. 5) and consequently renders 13:25b (ואשביעם) superfluous, was composed probably by a much later generation of writers who actually believed that Ezra wrote chap. 9. It too has been influenced directly by Nehemiah's account, especially Neh 5.[42] That someone decided to compose Ezra 10, instead of leaving the original connection between Neh 1 and 13, must be explained by the different accents that it introduces to the account. A further analysis of the text cannot, however, be undertaken here.[43] Yet it seems certain both that Ezra 9-10 has developed in a complex literary process which took its

---

42 The unusual expression for "marrying" in Neh 13:23 (ישׁיב *hiph.* + אשׁה, cf. also v. 27) appears repeatedly in Ezra 10 (cf. vv. 2, 10, 14, 17f.). The parallels with Neh 5 are indeed undeniable. Aside from the manner of resolution in which Ezra and the congregation resemble Nehemiah and the assembly, there are stylistic correspondences. Cf. esp. Ezra 10:5 and 12 with Neh 5:12 and 13b.

43 The chapter appears to have influenced the composition of Neh 13:26ff. (both, e.g., use the expression נשׁים נכריות).

point of departure from Nehemiah's account and that the earliest edition (chap. 9) cannot be understood without Neh 1-13*.

In light of our findings, one must exercise extreme caution with regard to the attempt to employ Ezra 9-10 in a reconstruction of the social conditions in Judah during the fifth and fourth centuries. In recent studies of Ezra 9-10, it is often assumed that the mixed-marriage problem reflects the attempt by one segment of the community (those who had returned from captivity) to divest another segment (those who had remained) of its place and property.[44] The problem with this assumption is threefold.

First, it is based primarily upon Ezra 10,[45] which, as we have seen, presupposes the addition of Ezra 9 to Ezra 7-8 and thus the penultimate compositional stages of Nehemiah's account. It was probably composed after the fourth century.[46] That the text is so late would explain the fact that most of the parallels to the "temple-communities" date to the Hellenistic period.[47]

Second, the assumption that land is the real issue behind the intermarriage problem does not do justice to the silence of the text with regard to this kind of property. 10:8 refers the confiscation of only moveable possessions (כל־רכושו). Although this is often cited as evidence,[48] one should observe that only those *who did not come* to the assembly within three days were subject to the penalty. Nowhere is it said that the merely marriage to "foreign women" resulted in loss of moveable property, let alone land.

Third, and most importantly, the earliest texts relating to intermarriage in Ezra-Neh, namely those in Nehemiah's account, do not involve a distinction between the Golah and those who were left home. Indeed, Nehemiah in 1:1b-4 is interested in the welfare of none other than those who remained in the province. Since these earlier texts do not know of a repatriation of Judah after

---

44 Cf., e.g., Weinberg (1992), Blenkinsopp (1991), Carroll (1991), Smith (1991).

45 It is not surprising that Ezra 9 does not play a large role in these theses, since its stereotypical and theological character – without dates or specific details – makes it difficult to gather details for an historical reconstruction.

46 *Pace* Hoglund (1991: 67).

47 Blenkinsopp admits this: "While much of the evidence adduced here comes from a time later than the Persian period, it may be taken to illustrate a type of temple economy which flourished during those two centuries, at least in Asia Minor" (1991:29). – The weakest aspect of the thesis is the fact that the priests, who were supposedly in charge of "the temple-community" were the worst offenders in the issue of intermarriage (cf. Ezra 9-10, but esp. Neh 13:4, 28f.). Moreover, why does Ezra 9-10 state explicitly that the "congregation of the Golah," and not those who were found in the land, had sinned in taking foreign wives? – It should be noted here that a critical part of Weinberg's thesis is the parallels between the Netinim and temple slaves. The passages that mention the Netinim however, represent probably the latest texts in the Hebrew Bible. Their existence began most likely in the Mid-Hellenistic period and this would agree with the parallels discussed in McEwan's study (1981: 58f.). For a superb evaluation and convincing refutation of Weinberg's thesis, cf. Williamson (1998).

48 Cf. Blenkinsopp (1991:50) and Hoglund (1991:67).

the captivity, as the later passages of Ezra-Neh, the problem of intermarriage originally had nothing to do with a land-dispute initiated by those who returned from the Babylonian captivity. Rather, it was elicited by the emphasis on the consolidation of the province in the building account. In order to maintain the ethnic and religious unity in Judah, Nehemiah censures the inhabitants of the province for exogamy and defines it as a sin against the Deuteronomic code.

11.3. The Banishment of Eliashib's Descendant – 13:28f.

11.3.1 The Notice 13:28f. in its Context

As seen in the analysis hitherto, all the paragraphs in 13:4ff. expand the building account by presenting Nehemiah introducing reforms before the twenty-fifth of Elul. Now if 13:23ff. did not belong to the earliest editions of Nehemiah's account, does it contain historical information with regard to the banishment of Eliashib's descendant by Nehemiah?

In responding to this question, we must concede that the passage depicting the expulsion does not agree with even the late expansions of vv. 23-27. Pichon has noticed the narrative tensions.

> Le transition par un simple waw n'est pas suffisante pour dissoudre la tension: les vv. 28-30a concernent le sacerdoce et en particulier la grand-prêtrise, alors qu'il n'etait question auparavant que des 'Judéens' (v. 23). L'alliance avec Sanballat rend compte de mariages avec les Samaritains; l'opposition de Néhémie ne visait que les Ashdodiens dans le récit primitif des vv. 23-31, les 'Ammonites et Moabites' étant un ajout ultérieur. Aux vv. 23-7, Néhémie n'ordonne pas l'expulsion des fautifs, alors qu'il 'chasse loin de' lui de Yoyada (v. 28). Toute porte ainsi à penser qu'il s'agit d'un événement indépendant de ce qui précède.[49]

If Nehemiah is simply content to make that Judeans swear that they would "not take their daughters for their sons" in vv. 23-25, yet "chases away" the son of Joiada in v. 28b, the latter text may report an incident from a different time. But it is questionable that, as Pichon asserts, v. 28 represents an excerpt of Nehemiah's "Mémoires," which the author of chap. 13 integrated with the purportedly Nehemian material in vv. 23-25*. How could "le récit primitif" have included the note in v. 28 directly after v. 25b (or even v. 25a) and without an introduction? If the same author were responsible for the combination of v. 23ff. with v. 28, we would expect a tighter connection between the two passages. Moreover, Pichon cannot explain why or for what context Nehemiah originally composed v. 28.

---

49 1997: 196.

There are further arguments for the late character of vv. 28-29. In v. 30a, Nehemiah reports that he "cleansed them from everything foreign" (וטהרתים מכל־נכר). The antecedent of "them" is not found in vv. 28-29, as is often assumed. The first candidate would be "the Levites" in v. 29, yet since the latter are not at fault, an alternative is required. In order to solve this problem, Reinmuth emends the text in v. 29b from "the priesthood and Levites" to "the priests and Levites" and then identifies the antecedent of "them" with both of these groups.[50] Yet if the editor responsible for v. 30b also searched for the antecedent in the conclusion to Nehemiah's prayer, how are we to explain that he repeated the reference to the priests and Levites? Instead of taking this harmonizing approach, one should probably connect v. 30a directly to v. 28b. Accordingly, the phrase "to marry foreign (נכרי) women" agrees with "everything foreign (נכר)." Since vv. 26-27 must have been added to v. 25b, the notice in vv. 28-29, which intrudes between vv. 27b and 30a, must have been composed at a very advanced stage in the composition of the chapter.[51]

A closer look at the formulation of v. 28 supports this conclusion. Nehemiah refers to Sanballat as "the Horonite" (החרני). The only other places where the *gentilicium* occurs after Sanballat's name are in 2:10 and 19, which in the present shape of the account introduce the leading antagonist. Why then does it recur only here, at the end of the account, and not in 4:1, 7; 6:1, 2, 5, 12 and 14? The author seems to have intended that we connect Sanballat's daughter with the "Moabite women" of v. 23 (cf. "Tobiah, the Ammonite servant" in 2:10, 19). Inasmuch as עמוניות מואביות represents a gloss to v. 23, as most agree, the passage vv. 28-29 has been added to a reworked edition of the account. Whether החרני in 2:10 and 19 bears the same disparaging tone as it does in

---

50 2002: 304. In response to Reinmuth's comparisons, we should note that in 12:30 and 13:22a (the priests and) the Levites cleanse *themselves*.

51 I have suggested above that earliest edition of the passage encompassed vv. 23-25* and the זכרה־לי-prayer in v. 31b. The account has been expanded first with vv. 26-27, 30a and then vv. 28-29*. While v. 30a summarized, in later stage of the composition, the foregoing account in vv. 23-29, the remaining material in vv. 30b-31 refers to additional measures that are completely unrelated to the subjects in vv. 23-30a. That v. 30b has indeed been inserted much later is suggested above all by the similarity between v. 30b and 12:45. Nevertheless, v. 30b could have been composed to present Nehemiah replacing the banished priest with new priestly and Levitical assignments. The author presents Nehemiah idealistically and in line with the righteous kings in Chronicles, who perform pious deeds in support of the cult. With regard to the first half of v. 31, we must have first read Neh 10:35f. in order to know what Nehemiah did with these materials. Given the reference to the cultic appointments in v. 31b, the author of this supplement apparently noticed that Nehemiah recounts in chap. 13 how he enforced the pact. Since the passages in 13:4ff. refer to only several of its stipulations, he has added v. 31a in an attempt to fill the lacuna. Galling (1954: 252f.) and Blenkinsopp (1988: 366) have suggested that all of vv. 29-31a was added, while the most recent works (Steins [1995: 174] and Reinmuth [2002: 305]) propose only the first half of v. 31 represents a late supplement.

13:28f. is difficult to say, yet it seems certain that the author of the latter has drawn on the information in 2:10 and 19 for his censure of the high priest.

Therefore, Pichon must be correct: 13:28f. reports the developments of a later time. Yet insofar as the 13:28f. must be younger than the addition to the building account in 6:17-19 + 13:4-9 as well as vv. 23-25*, this time is probably much later than just a decade.

In order to determine when this incident could have occurred, we must consider several factors. Nehemiah reports that one of sons of Joiada ben Eliashib "was the son-in-law" of Sanballat. The use of חתן indicates that the marriage was not recent; otherwise one would expect to be told that Joiada's son "took the daughter of Sanballat." For example, 6:18 reports that Tobiah "was the son-in-law" of Shechaniah (v. 18aβ). Of course, Tobiah had not recently married Shechaniah's daughter, for his son Johanan "had taken the daughter" of Meshullam (v. 18b). Now if Joiada's son had also not recently married Sanballat's daughter, one may safely presume that Joiada was much older than fifty. It is most unlikely that his father, Eliashib, would still have been living.[52]

This observation renders it very improbable that Nehemiah could have banished Joiada's son. From the register of builders in 3:1-32, one may assume that Eliashib was a contemporary of Nehemiah. The register in chap. 3 presents him initiating the building (3:1f.) and even refers twice his house (vv. 20-21). Since Joiada is not mentioned in the register or elsewhere, he may have not been old enough to be of significance. Thus, Cross may be correct in dating Eliashib's birth to ca. 495.[53] Accordingly, as Nehemiah came to the province, the high priest would have been fifty years old; his son, Joiada, could not have been older than twenty-five. And his grandson who married Sanballat's daughter would probably not even have been born. This study has shown that the earliest editions of the first-person account treats only the activities in the time span of one year. Now even if Nehemiah had been active in the province for twelve years (cf. 5:14 and 13:6), Joiada's son would have been in his early teens as he was chased away, assuming that the incident occurred in the last year of Nehemiah's tenure. This age, however, does not comport with חתן, which indi-

---

52 As most commentators rightly note, the formulation of v. 28 may suggest that Joiada occupied the office of high priest at the time. While "the high priest" is placed after "Eliashib," the author could not have worded the verse differently. So too, the reader would have known that both Eliashib and Joiada were high priests. If Eliashib is no longer in office, he was almost certainly no longer alive.

53 1975: 16. Admittedly, Cross's reconstruction of the succession of the high priests is tenuous and founded on many assumptions of papponymy and haplography; cf. Windengren (1977: 506ff.). Yet on the dating of Eliashib, most scholars are in agreement. With regard to the list in Neh 12:10, it appears that the compiler had only the names beginning with Joiakim at his disposal. The name of Jeshua was found of course in Ezra 1-6, but the names between him and Joiakim were no longer known at the presumably very late date when the list of high priests was compiled.

cates that he had already been married for some time. Moreover, he would probably not have been banished if he did not already occupy an important function in Jerusalem.

In approaching the problem from the side of Sanballat we notice the same contradictions. According to *TAD* A4.7, Sanballat was still serving as governor of Samaria in the seventeenth year of Darius II (407 BCE). If he were even as old as sixty-five (which is a significant assumption), he would have been about thirty as Nehemiah came to the province. And even if Nehemiah waited until the last days of his putative twelve-year tenure, Sanballat would have been only in his early forties as his daughter and her husband were banished from Jerusalem. While this is possible, it is not likely insofar as the use of חתן suggests that her marriage to Joiada's son was not recent. Moreover, Yedoniah claims in *TAD* A4.7 to have sent a letter to his Sanballat's sons Delaiah and Shelemiah, and *TAD* A4.9 reports the response of Delaiah (and Bagohi).[54] Significantly, these sons are not mentioned in Nehemiah's account, which adds weight to the proposal that Sanballat was a young man in Artaxerxes' twentieth year. If so, it is quite likely that his sons and daughter were not yet on the scene. Hence, not only has the notice in 13:28-29 been inserted at a late stage in the composition of the passage, but it also falsely presents Nehemiah as active in Judah when Eliashib's grandson was a grown man.

If the information in this passage is inaccurate, one could better explain both the historical improbability that Nehemiah would have been in the position to expel a member of the high-priestly family[55] and the disparity between it and other passages. As observed above, 13:28 emphasizes, in contrast to chaps. 3-6, that Sanballat was a "Horonite." While we do not know exactly what החרני signifies, there is no doubt with regard to Tobiah's *gentilicium*: העמני (2:10, 19) clearly identifies his origins as Ammonite. This creates a problem: 6:18 reports that Tobiah was the son-in-law of Shechaniah and that the daughter of Meshullam had married his son. So too, Eliashib, "the priest," was "related" to Tobiah according to 13:4. Why then does Nehemiah "chase away" only one who was married to an חרני and not also the family members of an עמני?

---

54 That the sons are addressed and not their father indicates only that they had been assigned responsibilities for the administration and does not require that Sanballat was too advanced in age to handle official business.

55 That Nehemiah "chases him away" (ואבריחהו מעלי), while somewhat incongruous here, may constitute a play on the same root in 13:10, which reports that the Levites and singers "had fled to their fields" (ויברחו איש־לשדהו). While Nehemiah gathers the latter back to their rightful "places" in Jerusalem which they (because of the priests?) had been forced to abandon, he forces Eliashib's descendant to abandon the place which his marriage to Sanballat's daughter had made him ineligible to occupy. If v. 28f. plays on the formulation of v. 10ff., then v. 28f. must be either contemporary with or later than vv. 10-13, 14b, which we have posited as an insertion between vv. 9b and 14a.

That Eliashib's grandson received unjust treatment permits us to draw two conclusions: 1) the passage is probably younger than 6:17-19 + 13:4ff.; 2) there may have been another reason for the banishment, assuming that it does correspond in some way to an historical event. Accordingly, the author of vv. 28-29 has attributed the expulsion solely to the fact of the *connubium*, in keeping with the censure of every form of intermarriage in vv. 23-27.

11.3.2 Possible Historical Backgrounds to 13:28f.

Since the ages of Joiada, his son and Sanballat's daughter do not agree with the date of Nehemiah's activities in Judah, one may either assume that the addition to 13:23ff. is completely legendary or attempt to date it a later occasion. Opting for the second alternative, we find two intriguing parallels in *Ant.* 11.7.1 §§297-301 and 11.7.2-8.2 §§302-312.

In the first passage, Josephus reports that Eliashib died and his son Jodas (=Joiada) succeeded him. As his son, Joannes (=Johanan), became high priest, he caused Bagoses, the στρατγός of Artaxerxes, to both enter – and thus defile – the sanctuary and to impose tribute on the Jews. Earlier Bagoses had promised Jesus, the brother of Joannes, the high priesthood. As Jesus reported to Joannes what Bagoses had promised, they quarreled in the temple and Joannes murdered his brother.

There is no reason to question the fundamental reliability of this story.[56] As Grabbe has recently proposed with convincing arguments, Bagoses is likely the Bagohi of *TAD* 4.7-8, who is referred to as the פחת יהוד.[57] The Elephantine papyri also mention "Johanan, the high priest." If the Artaxerxes of the story is the successor of Darius II,[58] it would not be inconsistent with *TAD* 4.7-8, according to which Bagohi was governor in the seventeenth year of Darius'

---

56 *Pace* Williamson (1977), who argues that the Bagoses of the *Ant.* cannot have been a Jew, while the Bagohi of the Elephantine papyri (cf. below) must have been, since it is otherwise difficult to explain that a continuity of governors in the other provinces. This argumentation is unconvincing. We can be quite sure that Judah did not have a dynasty of governors (as in Samaria, for instance), and we cannot be sure that Nehemiah actually served as governor (Neh 5:14ff. is late); cf. also Grabbe's arguments (1991). Secondly, Williamson draws on the chronology of Josephus and his identification of Darius II and III and Artaxerxes II and III to date the incident to the end of the Persian period. Yet Josephus's telescoping of the end of the fifth and the entire fourth centuries allows us also to date the affair to the reign of Artaxerxes II rather than the III.

57 1991: 50ff.

58 It is not clear why, as Marcus remarks (ad loc.), the failure to specify which Artaxerxes requires that we identify him with Artaxerxes III. This comment is assigned significant weight by Williamson (1977:57).

reign.[59] Grabbe is, therefore, probably correct both in contending that the affair has an historical basis and in dating it to ca. 400 BCE.

The parallels between this account and Neh 13:28f. may shed some historical light on the latter. Both present Joiada inheriting the office of high priest, and both censure his son. Although we cannot be sure that the son of Joiada in Neh 13:28 is Johanan, we also cannot rule it out. Similar to the way the source employed by Josephus attributes fratricide to Johanan, the author of Neh 13:28f. criticizes his marriage to Sanballat's daughter. On the other hand, the son of Joiada in Neh 13:28 may be Jesus, who makes alliances with foreign powers (Bagoses in the *Ant.* and Sanballat in Neh). In any case, if one may confidently trace the struggle between Joiada's sons to the last years of the fifth century, it would be extremely unlikely that Nehemiah could have accomplished what 13:28b ascribes to him. At this time, he was likely no longer on the scene.

The tradition behind the account of Josephus provides evidence for the existence of circles that were still interested in criticizing the actions of much earlier generations of the high priests. According to the consensus, Josephus could not have invented all of what he writes in §§297-301, and thus we must assume that he has a source, either oral or written.[60] From a source-critical perspective, this assumption is well founded. One observes that for Josephus (or a later version of the story), the most unfortunate side of the episode is that Bagoses entered the temple and imposed tribute on the Jews (297b). It is however conceivable, as Williamson argues, that the original version of the story centered on the fratricide among the Jerusalemite priesthood and the necessity of a Persian-appointed ruler to resolve the situation. That Bagoses imposed tribute is, accordingly, the fault of Joaida's sons, who cause the Jews many problems. The same *Tendenz* of the supposed source behind *Ant.* §§297-301 is witnessed in many of the additions to Nehemiah's account that criticize the nobility and especially the priesthood (cf., e.g., 6:17-19 + 13:4ff.). Significantly, in the very late paragraph 6:10-14, Nehemiah refuses to enter the temple, which contrasts with the behavior of Bagoses. In 5:14ff., Nehemiah claims to have not taxed the people; this too contrasts with the policy of the latter. The parallels are

---

59 Darius reigned for only three (or four) more years.
60 Williamson provides a superb analysis of the evidence for the use of a source by Josephus (1977:50-56). Most important are his observations with regard to the editorial method employed by this historian: "In the narrative proper...the result of the affair is given first (297b), namely that when Joannes was high priest, Bagoses 'defiled the sanctuary, and imposed tribute on the Jews'. The incident which led to this result is then recounted (298-301a), whilst a conclusion explicitly links the cause and its effect ('This, then, being the pretext which he used, Bagoses made the Jews suffer seven years for the death of Jesus', (301b). Finally, and of special interest, we must point out the phrase by which the transition is made between the two main parts of the narrative: 'The reason for this was the following happening' (298a)" (ibid.: 50).

even closer when one concedes with Grabbe and others that Bagoses is the same Bagohi who was governor of Judah shortly after Nehemiah's activities.

Several other paragraphs of in the *Ant.* (11.7.2, 8.2 §§302-303, 306-312, 321-325) provide an alternative for reconstructing the historical background to the banishment of Joaida's son in Neh 13:28f. In these sections, Josephus reports that when Joannes "departed this life," his son Jaddus (=Jaddua) succeeded him as high priest. Like his father, Jaddus was at odds with his brother, whose name was Manasseh. To the latter, Sanballat "gladly gave his daughter Nikaso, in marriage, for he believed that this alliance by marriage would be a pledge of his securing the goodwill of the entire Jewish nation" (303). Later, "the elders of Jerusalem" required Manasseh to "either divorce his wife or not approach the altar" (306f.). Manasseh then went to his father-in-law and told him "that he loved his daughter Nikaso, nevertheless the priestly office was the highest in the nation and had always belonged to his family, and that therefore he did not wish to be deprived of it on her account." In response, Sanballat promised him "not only to preserve the priesthood for him but also to procure for him the power and office of high priest and to appoint him governor of all the places over which he ruled, if he were willing to live with his daughter; and he said that he would build him a temple similar to that in Jerusalem on Mount Garizein" (310).

The parallels to Neh 13:28f. are so patent that some scholars treat the account as a "tendentious retelling" of Nehemiah's account.[61] While one cannot preclude the possibility that Josephus was influenced directly by Neh 13:23ff. and other texts from Ezra-Neh,[62] there are several details that are inexplicable on the assumption that everything in "the Manasseh episode is merely a midrashic expansion on Neh 13:28 and has no independent historical value...."[63] For example, Josephus must have either invented the names of Manasseh and Nikaso or have possessed independent information.[64] More

---

61 Williamson (1985: 401) and Blenkinsopp (1988: 365).
62 Cf., e.g. 303 with Ezra 4:15-16 and 1 Esdr 2:22-24 (this is rightly observed by Hjelm [2000: 201]). Moreover, 307f. appears to have been informed by Neh 13:25b-27 and esp. Ezra 9: "...for they considered this marriage to be a stepping-stone for those who might wish to transgress the laws about taking wives and that this would be the beginning of intercourse with foreigner. They believed, moreover, that their former captivity and misfortunes had been caused by some who had erred in marrying and taking wives who were not of their own country. They therefore told Manasses either to divorce his wife or not approach the altar." However, the thought begun in 306 continues in 308b: "Now the elders of Jerusalem, resenting the fact that the brother of the high priest Jaddus was sharing the high priesthood while married to a foreigner rose up against him.... [...] And, as the high priest shared the indignation of the people and kept his brother from the altar, Manasses went to his father-in-law Sanaballates...." It is thus possible to isolate an earlier version of the tradition just as Williamson has done with regard to §§297-301.
63 Grabbe (1987: 237).
64 With regard to Manasseh, Grabbe points out the Samaritans considered themselves the descendants of Joseph, i.e, the Ephraimites and Manassites. He believes that Josephus expanded the tradition by giving a name to the characters (1987: 237) and had no other

importantly, Josephus could not have known from Nehemiah's account that Sanballat was a satrap in Samaria. Nehemiah refers to Sanballat solely as "the Horonite" and never states his official status. Only 3:34 mentions Sanballat in relation Samaria: "and he said before his allies, and the army of Samaria, and he said...."[65] While this applies for the Hebrew tradition, Josephus most probably employed a Greek translation either identical to 2 Esdr or very similar to it.[66] Inasmuch as the latter has identified "his allies" with ἡ δύναμις Σομορων,[67] Josephus could have inferred that Sanballat was somehow affiliated with Samaria. Nevertheless, even the Greek tradition would not have permitted him to suppose that Sanballat was the leader of "the Samarian host," not to mention the governor of the entire province. That he was an official in Samaria, as Josephus claims, was corroborated first by the discovery of the Elephantine papyri and then the Samaria papyri. Thus, it seems that Josephus employed a different source than Neh 13:28f.[68]

Third, Josephus foreshortens the whole fourth century and dates Jaddua, Eliashib's grandson, to the beginning of the Hellenistic age. The alternation of the names of Darius and Artaxerxes probably led him to assume that only three generations separated Nehemiah from Alexander. This confusion is understandable and may be considered as a precursor to *Seder Olam Rab.* 30, which telescopes the events in the Persian period to a time-span of some thirty years. However, the Jaddus in Josephus is clearly the great-grandson of Eliashib. This means that the episode must have occurred the middle of the fourth century, yet Josephus presents it contemporary with the appearance of Alexander. Instead of completely discrediting the information from Josephus or following him in dating the Manasseh-Sanballat affair to the end of the Persian period, one should allow for the possibility that Josephus has embellished the story by interweaving it with Alexander's campaign, which he dated a half-century earlier.

Although much recent scholarship has dismissed the possibility of doing source-criticism of Josephus, the evidence for an editorial technique of splicing together two different accounts is readily available in these sections. The first

---

source of information than Neh 13:28. Yet even if Manasseh's name has been invented, one should not negate the historicity of the whole story. Otherwise, we would also have dismiss Nehemiah's account, which does not seem to know the name of Joiada's son. Furthermore, one need not suppose that Josephus simply invented the name, Nikaso, and that the latter is Greek. As Marcus suggested (ad loc.), the name is probably "the hellenized form of a Semitic name, possibly Aram. *nik'sâ* 'sacrifice' (?)," and even Grabbe admits that "the omega ending seems strange for a Greek name" (1987: 238-n. 29).

65 Cf. §6.3.2.2.

66 This is probable insofar as Josephus presents Nehemiah praying before his audience with the king. The prayer in Neh 1:5-11a, as we have seen, presupposes the book of Ezra-Neh.

67 ...καὶ εἶπεν ἐνώπιον τῶν ἀδελφῶν αὐτοῦ αὕτη ἡ δύναμις Σομορων.

68 If Josephus, as many maintain, wished to employ the information in 13:28 in order to remedy his paucity of sources for the gap between Nehemiah and Alexander, one must explain why he did not also make use of Nehemiah's notices regarding Tobiah and Geshem.

story concerns only Darius, Alexander and the high priest, Jaddus. It begins in §§304-305, resumes in §§313-320 and then again in §§325b-339 (§§320b and 325b are joined by the siege of Gaza).

In view of the way that Josephus skips back and forth between this account and that of the Sanballat-Manasseh affair, it is quite probable that he drew information from independent sources and spliced the account of the Sanballat-Manasseh affair into the framework provided by the Alexander-Jaddua legend. This thesis explains the fact that the references to Darius in the Sanballat-Manasseh account are only loosely connected to their contexts. For example, the formulation of §§302-303 allows us to easily remove the center-section, in which Josephus voices his anti-Samaritan polemics and which interrupts the sentence.[69] So too, Sanballat promises in §310 that he would procure the office of the high priest for Manasseh and "appoint him governor of all the places over which he ruled if he were willing to live with his daughter." After the thought appears to conclude with the stipulation that the marriage could not be terminated, the continuation comes unexpectedly: "…and he said that he would build a temple similar to that in Jerusalem on Mount Garizein…" (§310b). The earlier thought resumes later: "Elated by these promises, Manasseh stayed with Sanaballates" (§311; "promised" and "promises" form the connection). Here the story attains denouement: Manasseh leaves Jerusalem with many whom Sanballat supplied "with money and with land for cultivation and assigned them places wherein to dwell, in every way seeking to win favor for his son-in-law." The reader does not anticipate a continuation of this account, which resembles the censure of an earlier generation of the Jerusalemite priesthood in the foregoing sections.[70] Finally, the passages in §§315 and 321-325 are easy to bracket from the narrative.

It is thus quite possible to distinguish an account of the Manasseh-Sanballat affair (§§302-303, 306-312) and a story about Alexander and Jerusalem (§§304-

---

69 "…he had a brother named Manasses, to whom Sanaballetes – he had been sent to Samaria as satrap of Darius the last king, and was of the Cuthean race from whom the Samaritans also are descended –, gladly gave his daughter, called Nikaso in marriage […] knowing that Jerusalem was a famous city and that its kings had given much trouble to the Assyrians and the inhabitants of Coele Syria."

70 The middle section in §311, however, prepares the reader for the later events: "…believing that he would obtain the high priesthood as the gift of Darius, for Sanballates, as it happened, was now an old man." Everything here agrees with the Alexander account in §§313-326 (e.g., that Sanballat is old agrees with §325). Yet after the foregoing line ("Elated by these promise, Manasses stayed with Sanaballates"), which refers to the initial promises before the stipulation, we do not anticipate a continuation. The proposed earlier version of the story resembles strikingly the affair between Joannes and Jesus, for whom Bagoses *"promised"* to obtain the priesthood" (§298). Since in this earlier episode, which undoubtedly derives from an independent source, Bagoses does not tell him how he would procure the high priesthood for Jesus, it is certainly conceivable that everything pertaining to Darius and Alexander has been added by Josephus, who attempted to integrate two narrative strands.

305, 313-320 and 325b-339). And it is equally possible that Darius and
Alexander were originally absent from the first account. Accordingly, Josephus
has not only juxtaposed the two, but has also reworked them. This proposal
agrees with the findings of Williamson's study of §§297-301, according to which
Josephus has reworked earlier material. Both of the posited sources censure the
priesthood and have been embellished with anti-Samaritan polemics. Now if
one can isolate an independent account before Josephus edited and integrated it
into his history, it need not be assumed that the original version of the
Manasseh-Sanballat legend was situated in the last reign of the Achaemenids.

This conclusion assists us in making the next connection. We know from the
Samaria papyri that there was Sanballat on the scene in the mid-fourth cent.
BCE. Cross dates his birth to ca. 435 and suggests that he served as governor of
Samaria.[71] Although one may readily accept this proposal, Cross then posits "by
virtue of the practice of papponymy" that there was a third Sanballat who was
born ca. 385 and who is to be identified with the Sanaballetes in Josephus.[72]
Josephus, however, presents the affair clearly three generations after Eliashib,
which would have been in the middle of the fourth century, and our source-
criticism of his account demonstrates that this may be the correct date.[73] Significantly, Cross's chart of the succession of the high priests and governors of
Samaria presents "Sanballat II" in the same generation of Jaddus/Jaddua.[74] As
Cross does not allow for the existence of an earlier source in Josephus that did
not include a reference to Alexander and Darius, he must posit a Sanballat III.
Instead of following Cross in this regard, we may simply agree that the evidence
for the existence of a second Sanballat in the mid-fourth century confirms the
sources in Josephus, which present Sanballat as a leading figure in Samaria and,
most importantly, as a contemporary of Eliashib's great-grandsons.

Finally, it should be pointed out that the Jaddus of Josephus is the son of
Joannes, the grandson of Jodas, and the great-grandson of Eliashib. Grabbe has
made this clear.[75] Curiously, however, many assume that the reprobate was the
brother of Jaddua in Josephus (Manasses) but the son of Jaddua in Neh 13:28.[76]
This is false. In both accounts, he is a direct descendant of Jodas/Joiada. The
only difference between Josephus and Neh 13:28 is that Josephus depicts the

---

71 Cf. Cross (1963: 120; 1969: 41-62; 1975: 5).
72 1975: 5.
73 Josephus reports: "Sanaballates, as it happened, was an old man" (§311). However, this
    comment may represent an attempt by Josephus to integrate the story of the Sanballat-
    Mannaseh affair with the Alexander-Jaddua story (and perhaps also Nehemiah's account).
74 1975: 17.
75 1987: 243f.
76 Even Grabbe is somewhat confusing here: "The strongest argument for saying that the
    Manasseh pericope is different from Nehemiah 13 is that the reprobate is the brother of
    Jaddua in Josephus, whereas he is the son of Jaddua in Nehemiah" (1987: 238).

grandson of Jodas/Joiada ben Eliashib married to Sanballat's daughter, while Nehemiah banishes simply "one of the sons" of Joiada ben Eliashib.

Hitherto, we have followed the consensus in assuming that the expression "one of the sons" refers to the son of Joiada and grandson of Eliashib. Yet in examining the use of ומבני elsewhere, one notices that it does not mean specifically, "one of the sons," but rather much more generally, "one of the descendants." Of the ninety-five places where the expression appears, one searches at length to find an instance where it refers to the first generation of descendants. If the author meant the son of Joiada, he would have expressed this with the simple ובן. Why then has he not explicitly named the figure that Nehemiah banished? He may have simply attempted to portray the situation more plausibly. It would be certainly difficult to conceive how Nehemiah could have both reported that Eliashib built the wall (3:1ff.) and banished one of his late descendants. More likely, however, is that the author has aimed to cast dark shadows on the entire high-priestly line from Eliashib to his son Joiada and his unnamed descendent. They have "polluted the priesthood and the priestly covenant."

All of these points render it very likely that Neh 13:28f., which has been inserted at late point in the composition of its context, reflects an historical event from the mid-fourth century BCE. If ומבני refers not to the grandson of Eliashib but rather to an even younger descendant, then it is impossible that Nehemiah would still have been alive to banish the malefactor. Furthermore, it is difficult to assume that Josephus has no other source for his information than Neh 13:23ff. yet knows details that he could not have gathered from the latter. Since even modern commentators normally assume that ומבני refers to the grandson of Eliashib, Josephus may well have had a source for the Manasseh-Sanballat affair, as is usually assumed with regard to the Joannes-Bagoses affair and the Jaddua-Alexander legend. I suggest, therefore, that Neh 13:28f. mirrors either an historical struggle for the office of high priest between the great-grandsons of Eliashib or at least a legend which developed about this generation of high priests similar to that of the former generation (*Ant.* §§297ff.). If historical, it seems that Jaddua's brother, in order to gain support for his case, sought the help of his father-in-law, Sanballat, who was presumably an important political figure of the time. This situation would have provided many opponents of the priesthood with an occasion for voicing their criticism. Accordingly, the traditions transmitted in Nehemiah and Josephus represent (originally) independent responses to the same political dispute.

That the criticism of the priesthood in the mid-fourth century and their relations to foreign aristocracy has made itself felt in the composition of Neh 13:23ff. lends considerable weight to the claims in this study. Since a Sanballat in the mid-fourth century was exercising influence in the affairs of Jerusalem, some

of the Sanballat-notices elsewhere (2:10, 19ff., 4:1; 6:2-9) may represent projec-
tions from later periods (and subsequent Sanballatids) back into the time of
Nehemiah. Likewise, we may rest assured that there was a milieu in Judah in the
mid-fourth century and later in which one criticized the Judean nobility and
Jerusalemite priesthood for their alliances with foreign powers. Here we must
locate the *Sitz im Leben* for texts such as Neh 6:17-19 + 13:4-9.

11.4 Conclusions

The present chapter has attempted to demonstrate the earliest edition of the
account comprised vv. 23-25* and 31*. After Nehemiah administers the oath (v.
25b), the sermon in vv. 26-27 is superfluous. If it were integral to the account,
the author would have placed it before v. 25b. In concluding with the oath
(ואשביעם, v. 25b), the earliest edition resembles the reform account in 5:1ff. (cf.
ואשביעם, v. 12b). These findings permit us to propose that 13:10-14 and vv. 15-
22, which do not report an oath, represent later adaptations of the *rîb*-form
preserved in 5:1-13 and 13:23ff. So too, our analysis of 13:15ff. has shown that
the measures for enforcement of the Sabbath in Jerusalem described in vv. 19ff.
have been appended to vv. 17-18. If the account originally concluded with the
sermon to the Judean nobles and prayer (v. 22b), then it may have been patterned according to the expanded edition of the marriage reforms, which likewise concluded with a sermon (vv. 26-27) and prayer (v. 31b). This means that
the first edition of the account of the Sabbath-reforms is younger than the
amplified edition of the account of marriage-reforms. Significantly, the latter
begins in exactly the same way as 6:17-19 + 13:4-9, 14a (גם בימים ההם), while the
introduction to the former is somewhat different (בימים ההמה).

With regard to Ezra's account of the so-called "mixed-marriage crisis," we
have adduced considerable evidence that the third-person narrative in Ezra 10 is
just what it purports to be: a text that was composed later than Ezra 9. The
expansions in 13:26-27 employ the language of the third-person narrative in
Ezra 10 and may postdate the composition of the latter. Given the astonishing
similarities between Neh 1:1b-4; 13:23ff. and Ezra 9, it appears likely that a
redactor, before the composition of Ezra 10, has drafted Ezra 9 in order to
reinterpret the entire work of Nehemiah. If the account of the Sabbath-reforms
in Neh 13:15-23 was not extant as the author drafted Ezra 9, we may posit that
the accounts relating to the issue of mixed marriages in 6:17-19 + 13:4-9, 14a
and 13:23ff. have influenced the author of Ezra 9 to understand intermarriage as
the primary problem facing the Restoration community. Accordingly, he
presents Nehemiah's repair of the wall as the necessary step to separate Judah
from the "filthiness" of "the peoples of the lands." Insofar as Ezra 9-10 are a

product of redactional activity within the book of Ezra-Neh and do not report an historical situation, the future study of intermarriage in the Second Temple period must begin with Nehemiah's account.

In our study of 13:28f., where Nehemiah "chases away" a descendant (not son) of Joiada ben Eliashib (vv. 28-29), we have observed that it and an account in the *Ant.* (11 §§306-312). may be based on a common source. If the sources used by Josephus in §§297ff. provide a basis for assuming that circles in the fourth century BCE and later were voicing disapproval of the priesthood, it is quite likely that they also were using Nehemiah's work as an influential context to publish their criticisms.

Finally, with respect to vv. 30b-31a, we have seen that they were added at the latest stage in the composition of the passage in order to complete the assimilation of chap. 10 and chap. 13.

The Composition of 13:23-31

23 **Also in those days I saw (that) the Judeans had married Ashdodite women,**
Ammonite, Moabite
> 24 and half (=many) of their children spoke the language of Ashdod,
> > yet none of them could speak the language of Judah,
> and the languages of the respective peoples.

25 **And I contended with them and cursed them and beat some of them and pulled out their hair; and I made them take an oath in the name of God, saying, "You shall not give your daughters to their sons, or take their daughters for your sons or for yourselves.**
> 26 Did not they cause King Solomon of Israel to sin? Among the many nations there was no king like him, and he was beloved by his God, and God made him king over all Israel; nevertheless, foreign women made *even him* to sin. 27 But should it be heard of *you* to do all this great evil and to transgress against our God by marrying foreign women?"
> > 28 And one of the sons of Joiada ben Eliashib, the high priest, was the son-in-law of Sanballat, the Horonite; and I chased him away from me. 29 Remember them, O my God, for they have defiled the priesthood and the priestly covenant,
> > > and of the Levites.
> 30 And thus I cleansed them from everything foreign,
> > > and I established the duties of the priests and Levites, each in his work; 31 and for the wood offering at appointed times and for the first fruits.

Remember me, O my God, for good.

IV. The Dedication of the Wall (12:27-13:3) and the Formation of a New Climax (7:1-12:26)

Introduction

"Part Three" has shown how the composition of 13:4-31 continues the trans-formation of a report of the construction of the wall into an account of Judah's social and religious reconstitution after the catastrophe of 587/6 BCE. Originally, all of the reforms were presented as Nehemiah's activities during the brief period in which he repaired the wall. With the addition of 13:4-31 and the accompanying texts, the redactors of the building report have conferred greater significance to the twenty-fifth of Elul, which is the day on which not only the wall of Jerusalem, but now also the Restoration of Judah was finished. A later author has given the reforms in chap. 13 a new historical setting with the inter-polation of 13:6. Instead of during the construction work, Nehemiah imposes the changes in Judah twelve years later. While 6:17-19 + 13:4-31 originally represented "footnotes" to the depiction of the time from Nisan to Elul in 2:1-6:16, the author of 13:6 has adapted these texts to the chronological narration of 1:1-6:16.

Turning our attention back to the material in 7:1-13:3, we observe that also it reports in a chronological manner what took place after the twenty-fifth of Elul. Once the wall is built, the gatekeepers are appointed (7:1), the city is repopulated (7:4ff.), the people gather for the reading of the Torah (8:1ff.), etc. This chronological narration, however, poses a major problem: it disrupts the con-nection between 6:17-19 and 13:4ff., passages which report what happened before the twenty-fifth of Elul. How then are we to explain the literary setting of this material?

The following chapters advance a simple solution: Instead of assuming that a single compiler rearranged his sources and disconnected 6:17-19 from its con-tinuation in 13:4ff., I maintain that *all* of the material in 7:1-13:3 is later than the framework in 6:17-19* and 13:4ff.* and has developed in a gradual maturation process. Accordingly, the first text that was inserted is the account of the dedi-cation ceremonies "on that day" in 12:27ff.; it was originally in the third-person and has been composed specifically with 13:4ff. in view (i.e., the introductory expression "but before this" as well as the theme of the cultic arrangements in

vv. 4-14 and 30b). That it has not been placed *before* 6:17-19 suggests strongly that the author read the latter as an integral part of the portrayal of diplomatic correspondence and the intimidation of Nehemiah in 6:1-14.

With the insertion of the dedication account in 12:27ff., later authors have introduced a new fixed-point into the building report. Originally, "that day" (12:43, 44) referred to the twenty-fifth of Elul when the wall was finished (6:15), yet after the successive expansions in 7:1-12:26, it must be identified with an occasion in the seventh month or later (cf. 7:72b; 8:2, 13; 9:1). Just as redactors have conferred a new dimension to the date of completion by expanding the building report with accounts of provincial reforms, so do these successive additions in 7:1-3, 4ff.; 8:1-13, 14ff.; 9:1-3, 4ff.; 10:1-30, 31ff.; 11:1ff.; 12:1-26, while repeatedly postponing the dedication of the wall to later dates, provide new reasons for the celebratory activities by portraying ever more elaborate preparations. The development of this new climax began with the insertion of the account of activities "on that day" (12:27ff.), and thus we begin our investigation with this passage.

12. The Account of the Dedication Ceremonies (12:27ff.) and the Analogy of 7:1-3

12.1 Introduction

In preparation for the following chapter in which we discuss the original context of the account of the dedication ceremonies in 12:27ff., the present chapter examines how the first-person strand in this account relates to its immediate narrative surroundings. According to the conventional approach, Nehemiah's description of a simple circumambulation can be isolated in vv. 31-32 and 37-40, which developed into a depiction of dedication ceremonies as later authors added vv. 27-30, 33-36 and 41-43. With regard to 12:44-13:3, these paragraphs are usually identified with even younger supplements. This solution is, however, quite inadequate since we must reckon with heavy editing not only of the conclusion but also of the introduction. On the other hand, the third-person framework in vv. 27-30 and 43ff. is fully self-sufficient (i.e., one can understand it without Nehemiah's words). Insofar as the first-person account lacks a beginning and an ending, it probably does not represent the indispensable substratum of vv. 27ff. That this view became the consensus is due not least to the premise that later authors would not have employed Nehemiah's voice in expanding a text. After testing this premise in §12.2, we turn our attention in §12.3 to 7:1-3. The short passage represents another example of a narrative that has been reworked with first-person material, and as we attempt to demonstrate in the next chapter, it appears to be one of the first texts to have been inserted between 12:27ff. and 6:17-19.

12.2 Analysis of the Composition of 12:27-43

12.2.1 The Abrupt Beginning in v. 31

For the attempt to isolate the putative first-person substratum in the account of the dedication, v. 31 presents itself as the best point of departure. Here Nehemiah begins by bringing up the princes upon the wall (v. 31a). In comparing this clause with the rest of the verse, we notice that it unnecessarily repeats the phrase מעל לחומה. Not only does the reader already know after v. 31a that the princes of Judah are "on the wall," but it is also quite peculiar that Nehemiah waits until they had ascended to organize them into two processions. Moreover, the information contradicts the present formulation of the passage. Initially, the reader presumes that the Tôdôt consists solely of the princes. However, v. 32 portrays this group *following* the processions. So too, only "half of the Judean princes" are with Hoshaiah in succession to the Tôdôt. In v. 38, Nehemiah reports that he and "half of the people" followed the second procession. What happened then to the other half of Judean princes?

Instead of assuming that Nehemiah forgot them or that they got lost on their way to the temple, one should consider the possibility that v. 31a has been attached by an editorial hand. If the account originally began with v. 31b ("And I organized two large Tôdôt…"), we would not have to ascribe the repetition of מעל לחומה to dittography.[1] So too, it makes more sense that Nehemiah organizes the Tôdôt before they ascend the wall.

In view of the abrupt beginning formed by v. 31 (both by the first and second halves), many scholars have proposed that part of the present introduction in v. 27 (ובחנכת חומת ירושלם) was originally a part of Nehemiah's words.[2] This is, however, quite doubtful.[3] Not only do we lack an indication that the introductory expression is not integral to its context, but also its syntax does not suit the *wayyiqtol* forms in v. 31 (ואעלה and ואעמידה).[4] According to another view, the original introduction to v. 31 has been lost.[5] Since such a proposal cannot be verified and does not assist us in arriving at a scholarly consensus, we should treat it as the *ultima ratio*. Nevertheless, the fact that many have proposed that the first-person account must have begun with either part of v. 27 or some other phrase indicates that v. 31 does not provide the anticipated introduction to the passage. And indeed in examining the rest of the building report, we notice that (ואעמיד(ה, although a favorite expression, does not introduce any other paragraph in the first-person account.[6] We may thus conclude that Nehemiah's words in 12:27ff. lack an appropriate beginning.

---

1   Burrows (1935: 31ff.) also noticed the doublet formed by the use of מעל לחומה in v. 31b, yet he treated it as a case of dittography. Because Burrow's proposal to simply omit this phrase cannot be defended either text-critically or from the rationale of a later editor, one must search for another solution. Burrows did not consider the possibility that v. 31a has been added. To the place of the processions, see Fullerton (1919: 171ff.).
2   Noth (1944: 131-n. 3), Rudolph (1949: 196), Mowinckel (1964: 31), and considered by Kellerman (1967: 46). According to Galling (1954: 247), all of v. 27a is original.
3   Steins (1995: 190) also rejects this suggestion.
4   Instead, we would expect a *qatal* as provided by the present, and most likely original, setting of the phrase: ובחנכת חומת ירושלם בקשו את־הלוים מכל־מקומתם להביאם ונו.
5   Cf., e.g., Batten (1913: 279).
6   Cf. 4:3, 7b; 6:1, 7; 7:1, 3; 13:11, 19, 30. Moreover, none of these passages belong to early editions of the building report. ואעלה only occurs in this passage.

12.2.2 The Continuation of v. 31b in v. 37

With the help of a process of elimination, we can trace the path leading from v. 31 throughout the rest of the text by initially subtracting all the material that clearly disrupts the first-person strand. This includes not only the portrayal of the preparations for the ceremonies in vv. 27-30, which is examined below, but also the lists of the participants leading up to the description of the route in v. 37. The reason for asserting that a later hand inserted vv. 32-36 is not that the list of names interrupts the narrative flow, but rather that the sequence of prepositional phrases in v. 37 is impossible to translate without a verb. Instead of assuming with many scholars that a portion of the text has been omitted as vv. 33-37 were interpolated, we need only to connect v. 31b directly to v. 37.[7]

> And I organized two great *Tôdôt* which then were proceeding (? – see below) toward the right on the wall to the Dung Gate (v. 31b), over the Spring Gate, to the steps of the City of David on the ascent of the wall, past the House of David and finally to Water Gate on the east" (v. 37).

Once the intervening material in vv. 32-36 is removed, the description of the route in v. 31b ("on the wall southward to the Dung Gate") continues very smoothly with the mention of the Spring Gate in v. 37,[8] and a new sentence begins thereafter (ונגדם עלו וגו). That v. 32 constitutes an editorial expansion is indicated also by the incongruity of a plur. masc. suffix in אחריהם; the antecedent is a plur. fem. noun (שתי תודת גדולת or ותהלכת).[9]

If this literary evidence requires us to seek the original beginning of the first-person account in vv. 31b and 37, then "the princes of Judah" are not mentioned in the first edition of the account. What would have motivated a redactor to include this group as participants in the ceremonies?[10] Their presence on this occasion certainly poses a problem, for instead of the שרים, we would expect the חרים and the סגנים to be chief participants in the festivities. These two groups

---

7   According to the most commonly accepted opinion, the interpolation begins in v. 33. This position has been defended recently by Steins (1995: 187). He posits that v. 32 was transposed from its original place after v. 31aβ with the insertion of vv. 33-36, for which it was reformulated as the introduction.

8   Williamson (1985: 370) argues rightly that v. 32 has been inserted with vv. 33-36.

9   V. 38 does not make this mistake.

10 Against v. 31a, I have argued that it contradicts v. 32, leaving the other half of the princes unaccounted for. Yet if v. 32 is redactional, my argument against v. 31a would seem to constitute a *petitio principii*. Against appearances, this is not the case: In v. 31a, Nehemiah peculiarly brings the princes up on the wall before organizing two processions, and v. 31b forms a doublet with מעל לחומה. With regard to v. 32, I have argued that v. 37 lacks a verb and that it and v. 31b form a join. If both vv. 31a and 32 are secondary but nevertheless contradict each other, it appears that they have been drafted by separate hands. As to the question, which of the two is older, any proposal would be too speculative to be of value.

represent the ruling classes elsewhere in the first-person narrative.[11] Although
the שׂרים appear several times in the building account, we never encounter a
group called שׂרי יהודה. The appellation שׂר refers rather to the military officers
who escort Nehemiah to Jerusalem (2:9) and who later protect the people as
they build (4:10). 7:2 refers also to "the ruler of the citadel" (שׂר הבירה). In the
wider context of Ezra-Neh, however, one notices a usage of שׂרים very similar to
that in the description of the wall-processions (cf. 9:32, 34; 10:1; 11:1 and Ezra
8:20, 24, 25, 29; 9:1, 2; 10:5, 8, 14).[12] The most significant parallel is, however,
the list in Neh 3, which probably did not belong to the first edition of the
building report. This passage not only registers the names of all the שׂרים who
rule the "half part" of a particular district in Judah (cf. vv. 9, 12, 14, 15, 16, 17,
18, 19), but it also refers, just as 12:43ff., to the gates and other architectural
landmarks in Jerusalem. Since the first-person account only rarely pays attention
to topographical details, it seems that those responsible for the revision of
12:31f. intended to present the princes of Judah as forming the processions that
traverse exactly those points in the wall which the princes rebuilt according to
3:1-32. Given the tight connections between the two texts, we may safely conclude that the amplification of the first-person substratum in 12:27ff. has been
heavily influenced by the interpolation of the register in 3:1ff.

12.2.3 The Lists of the Participants in vv. 32-36

Examining vv. 32-36 more closely, one notices that this insertion includes a
confusing array of names and groups. We are told about:

1. a presumably prominent figure named Hoshaiah – v. 32a;
2. half of the princes of Judah – v. 32b;
3. seven other characters of unknown function: (a) Azariah, (b) Ezra, (c) Meshullam,
   (d) Judah, (e) Benjamin, (f) Shemaiah, (g) Jeremiah – vv. 33-34;
4. Zechariah, "a son of the priests," whose genealogy is traced back six generations to
   Asaph (v. 35b),
5. and eight of his colleagues with "the instruments of David:" (a) Shemaiah, (b) Azarel,
   (c) Milalai, (d) Gilalai, (e) Maai, (f) Nethanel, (g) Hanani, (h) Judah – v. 36a;
6. Ezra, the *sôfēr*, directing the way – v. 36b.

What unites these disparate names and groups is their position in relation to the
processions: All of them are said to follow the *Tôdôt*-companies (וַיֵּלֶךְ אחריהם,
"and after them went..."), with the exception of Ezra, who takes the lead

---

11 Cf. 2:16; 4:8; 4:13; 5:7, 17; 6:17; 7:5; 13:11, 17. The סגנים appear also in the immediate
    context; cf. v. 40.
12 That שׂרים is employed in the same manner as 12:31ff. solely in secondary passages of
    Nehemiah's account as well as in the Ezra-narrative only makes the problem more acute
    (*contra* Steins [1995: 189]).

(לפניהם, "was before them"). This information, however, creates a serious incoherency: After v. 31a, the reader assumes that the *Tôdôt* consisted of the princes, yet v. 32 states that princes followed the *Tôdôt*. That v. 31a is also redactional compounds, rather than diminishes, the problem: Although describing tediously the arrangement of the groups trailing the *Tôdôt*, the interpolation in vv. 32-36 fails to tell us how what is most important, namely how the *Tôdôt* themselves were configured.[13]

Since the mention of the trumpets in v. 35a and other instruments in v. 36a corresponds to the musical associations of the word תודה,[14] vv. 35-36 most likely intends to present Ezra (v. 36b) leading the *Tôdôt* that consist of "the sons of the priests" (vv. 35-36a). Conversely, we should probably understand the seven names in vv. 33-34 as those who join Hoshaiah and the group of the princes in the rear. While this certainly seems to be the best reading of the passage, it has not been made explicit. To the contrary, the introductory phrase וילך אחריהם initially prompts the reader to place the figures referred to in vv. 35-36a in a position posterior to Hoshaiah, the princes, and the following seven figures in vv. 33-34. Why then has the author not marked in some way the differences between vv. 33-34, which describe the trailing groups, and vv. 35-36, which describe the *Tôdôt* themselves?[15] The reason for this, I submit, is that more than one author have composed vv. 32-36.

That vv. 32-36 may have undergone revision is not a new proposal. Thus, many insist that the reference to Ezra in v. 36b, which is the first time Nehemiah mentions his predecessor, constitutes an annotation to the information in vv. 32-36. Arguing that the editor of Ezra-Neh has drawn his information from a reliable source, Williamson claims that this statement was not found in the source material and attributes it to an addition by a glossator.[16] If, however, one relinquishes the attempt to ascribe any historicity to these verses, it appears likely that the reference to Ezra in v. 36b is actually older than vv. 35-36a.[17] We observed above that the latter passage, although it probably identifies the actual members of the *Tôdôt*, has not been introduced properly inasmuch as the reader is confused into thinking that these cultic musicians followed the *Tôdôt*. If a later author inserted the name of Zechariah, his

---

13 We may compare this to Ps 68:25, which reports exactly what was in the middle of the preceding and succeeding groups.

14 These associations are certainly present in v. 27b: "to celebrate the dedication with rejoicing, with thanksgivings (ובתודות) and with singing, with cymbals, harps, and lyres."

15 Whom does Ezra lead? According to the present shape of the text, a new list begins in v. 35 with ומבני הכהנים בחצצרות זכריה ונו. Thus, the antecedent of the plur. masc. suffix in לפניהם are the names in vv. 35-36a. But this group of musicians probably does not represent the original antecedent.

16 1985: 371f.

17 Support for this proposal is provided by the reference to "half of the princes" in v. 32. Cf. also Snaith (1967).

genealogy, and the following names of his colleagues between vv. 33 and 36b, then the statement "and Ezra, the *sōfēr*, went before them" would have originally been in closer proximity to the phrase "and behind them went...." Moreover, the prepositional phrase לפניהם without a verb in v. 36b presupposes the presence of וילך in v. 32, and prior to the insertion of vv. 35-36a, the reader would not have to search at length for the antecedent.

> And behind them went Hoshaiah and half of the princes of Judah (v. 32). And Azariah, Ezra, Meshullam (v. 33), Judah, Benjamin, Shemaiah, and Jeremiah (v. 34). And the *sōfēr*, Ezra, went in front of them (v. 36b).

According to this reading, Ezra leads not just the musicians listed in vv. 35-36a, but rather the whole procession. This makes much more sense since לפניהם forms a close analogy to אחריהם. The placement of this material is easy to explain: If a redactor had appended the list of the musicians to v. 36b, then the musicians would accompany Ezra as leaders in the procession. Such a scenario apparently did not correspond to the intended depiction, which bears a close resemblance to Josh 6:9.[18]

An examination of the first group of names in this passage suggests that also vv. 32-34 may have been retouched. The mention of Ezra in v. 33 (not v. 36b) duplicates the preceding name of Azariah, an alternative spelling of Ezra or Azrael. So too, a conjunction is missing before his name. Already Bertheau suggested that it constitutes a gloss,[19] and since then, many scholars have either accepted or seriously considered this correction.[20] The only problem with the solution is that the author of vv. 33-34 seems to have intended to list seven priests in analogy to the group at the temple (v. 41), so that the removal of a name would distort the desired quantity. All the names refer to priests who are attested either as signatories to the pact (10:3-9) or in the register of Jerusalem's residents (chap. 12). The only exception is Judah, who may have been a Levite.[21] Significantly, his name also lacks a conjunction. So too, Hoshaiah is referred to without a title (v. 32). From his position before the princes, we must assume that he was an important lay figure and thus commentators are at loss to explain why we do not hear about him elsewhere. These peculiarities attest to the probability that Hoshaiah is to be grouped with the rest of the figures whose position is not specified. The phrase "the half of princes of Judah" in v. 32 would have been inserted according to the analogy of the other half-groups in vv. 38 and

---

18 Both passages describe priests (cf. Josh 6:4ff., 13) making music as they encircle city-walls, albeit with altogether different motives. In view of these analogies, one wonders whether Josh 6 may have even influenced the redactional formation of Neh 12:35-36a.

19 1862: 257.

20 Bertholet (1902: 87), Williamson (1985: 368, 371), Blenkinsopp (1988: 343). Cf. Rudolph (1949: 196), who emended the text with LXX[B].

40b. Before this insertion, the princes would have made up the *Tôdôt* (cf. v. 31a) instead of following them. Likewise, Ezra would have lead the same group which on a prior occasion informed him of – and assisted him in resolving – the crisis in Judah.[22] As an earlier edition of these verses, I propose therefore: "And following them were Hoshaiah, and Azariah, and Meshullam, and Ben(Mi)jamin,[23] and Shemaiah, and Jeremiah and the *sôfēr*, Ezra, went in front of them."

If vv. 32-34* originally continued in v. 36b, we must date vv. 35-36b to a very late compositional stage. This conclusion is corroborated by a comparison of v. 35 with Neh 11:17. Both passages provide an account of one genealogical line starting at the same point. But while 11:17 traces it only four generations down to Mattaniah, 12:35 includes the names of Mattaniah's son, grandson, and great-grandson. The time gap is compounded by the probability that Mattaniah was not even a contemporary of Nehemiah. The catalogue in which 11:17 is embedded refers to a Shilonite named Maaseiah ben Baruch ben Kolhozeh (v. 5). As Mowinckel contended, the very rare name Kolhozeh is probably the same person as Shallum's father in 3:15. Maaseiah would then be the nephew of Shallum and a generation later than Mattaniah.[24] According to these findings, one must account for at least five generations. Assuming that the author of 12:35-36a thought of Zecheriah as a contemporary of Nehemiah and thus much older than his present generation, there would be many more than just five generations separating the composition of the first-person stratum of the dedication and the insertion of these verses. Most important, however, are the findings indicating that the expansion of the first-person stratum is younger than chap. 11. As we shall observe in the following chapter, this contrasts with the third-person narrative in 12:27ff., which does not present the Levites as residing in Jerusalem and which consequently must be older than chap. 11.

The second clue for the late dating of vv. 35-36b is the designation of David as "the man of God" (v. 36a). We encounter this appellation elsewhere only in 12:24 and 2 Chr 8:14b. The latter passage is instructive insofar as it presupposes and corrects, as Steins points out, the Davidic ordinances in 1 Chr 23:25-32.[25] Significantly, "the instruments of David" in v. 36a appears also in 1 Chr 23:5.[26] Since 1 Chr 23:25-32 appears to be redactional or at least belongs to a larger

---

21 Cf. 12:8 and Ezra 10:23.
22 Cf. Ezra 9:1, 2; 10:5, 8, 14.
23 LXX[L]. This could have been altered to Benjamin as the name Judah was introduced. Cf. Rudolph (1949: 197).
24 1964: 150.
25 1995: 289f.
26 Cf. also 2 Chr 7:6 and 29:26.

interpolation (chaps. 23-27),[27] the reminiscent wording and subject matter of
Neh 12:35-36a indicates that its author was also writing at a very late date.[28]

12.2.4 The Second *Tôdah*

V. 38 portrays a second *Tôdah*: והתודה השנית ההולכת למואל. This additional
information creates a substantial incongruity, for in v. 31bα Nehemiah reports
that he organized two *Tôdôt* and that these "processions" (וְתַהֲלֻכֹת) took the
common route described in vv. 31bβ and 37. In v. 41, we are told that the two
processions "stood" at the temple v. 40 (וַתַּעֲמֹדְנָה שְׁתֵי הַתּוֹדֹת [v. 40a]; cf. שׁתי
תודת גדולת ותהלכת [v. 31b]). Are we to understand that they separated and then
later convened at the temple? While this seems to be the implication of v. 38-39,
it has certainly not been made explicit in v. 31b. How then should one account
for the report of the second procession in vv. 38-39?

According to the consensus, the text in v. 31b must be emended. In an
attempt to harmonize v. 31b with the reference to the second procession in v.
38, Smend Sr. posited as the original text: וְהָאַחַת הֹלֶכֶת ("and the first [*Tôdah*]
was going...").[29] Most scholars have accepted this conjecture – often uncriti-
cally.[30] Before following in this tradition, one should take into account several
factors that indicate the form ותהלכת does not amount to a mere text-critical
problem.

First, all textual witnesses of the LXX either attempt to render ותהלכת or
omit v. 38.[31] Assuming that the register of the builders presents an accurate
description of Jerusalem, this omission only creates further problems: The
processions would follow the circuit of the wall until the Water Gate (v. 37) and
then cross back through the city, resuming their course in the opposite direction
(v. 39a). For this reason, one must be very cautious in drawing upon the testi-

---

27 Cf. Noth (1943: 112ff.), Rudolph (1955: 152), Galling (1954: 63-71), Williamson (1979), and
    Wright (1989, 1991, 1992).

28 These two clues suggest that not only the editing of the first-person narrative continued into
    the Hellenistic period, but also that, even at this time, an Asaphite (Zechariah) and his
    colleagues were not considered Levites. Thus, we must take issue with Schaper's thesis,
    according to which the inclusion of the Asaphite phratry among the Levites is to be dated
    already in the late Persian period (2000: 279ff.). Moreover, if Neh 12:35-36a and Ezra 3:10b
    do not simply present two different views on the status of the Asaphites, the latter text
    would reflect a later development; otherwise, "the sons of Asaph" would not be equated
    with the Levites. Inasmuch as Ezra 3:10a originally continued in v. 11b, v. 10b would
    however not determine the dating of its context.

29 1881: 11-n. 13. Cf. also Kosters (1895: 50).

30 Barthélemy (1982: 573) has presented compelling and wide-ranging evidence that the text is
    not corrupt here.

31 Rudolph (1949: 196) was wrong in affirming the contrary, since the phrase καὶ διῆλθον
    ("and they passed...") represents the best attempt to translate this *hapax legemenon*.

mony of the LXX. Nevertheless, these witnesses do illustrate that later readers found ותהלכת to pose an incoherency and endeavored to correct it.

Second, the widely accepted emendation proposal (והאחת הלכת) does not agree with v. 38 (והתודה השנית ההולכת למואל), which is formulated analogously to v. 31b.[32] Consequently, it is suggested that we delete the article before ההולכת in order to produce an analogy to the proposed emendation in v. 31b.[33] Such a procedure is, however, quite tenuous.

Third, we must explain the formulation of v. 32. If the author of this verse meant to recount those following one *Tôdah*, why has he said "after them" instead of "after it" as in v. 38 (אחריה) corresponding to (והתודה השנית?

Fourth, one must account for the presence of the insertion in vv. 32-26 and the absence of comparable redactional expansions within vv. 38-39. Many commentators contend that vv. 41-42 contain the names of those in the second procession and that the two evince remarkable balance and order. According to a commonly accepted approach, we should delineate the groups as follows:[34]

	I. First Group	II. Second Group
a. Processions	"The First *Tôdah*"(v. 31ff.)	"The Second *Tôdah*" (v. 38f.)
b. Prominent layperson	Hoshaiah (v. 32)	Nehemiah (vv. 38, 40)
c. Half of the lay-leaders	The Princes (v. 32)	The rulers (v. 40)
d. Seven priests with trumpets	(v. 33-35a)	(v. 41)
e. Precentor	Zechariah (v. 35b)	Izrahiah (v. 42b)
f. Eight Levitical musicians	(v. 36)	(v. 42)

Examining this table more closely, one notices that it imposes a symmetry on the processions that does not correspond to the information in the text. Vv. 41-42 registers the names of the musicians present at the temple, not those who followed the second *Tôdah*. In order to correlate the processions in the manner presented in the table, we must assume that these verses have been placed after v. 40 for lack of space. Yet such an assumption requires that we deny the editor any compositional proficiency. If he intended to identify the participants in the second *Tôdah*, why did he not insert these names between vv. 38 and 39 according to the analogy of vv. 31 and 37?[35] Moreover, the number and character of the names in vv. 32-36 do not agree with those in vv. 41-42. V. 41

---

32 The best rendering of the MT is, "And I appointed two large thanksgiving companies *proceeding* southwards" (v. 31b) and "The second thanksgiving company *proceeding* forwards" (v. 38a).

33 Cf., e.g., Williamson (1985: 369).

34 Cf. Rudolph (1949: 199), Meyers (1965: 204), Williamson (1985: 371), Blenkinsopp (1988: 345). This table presents how all these scholars have delineated the processions.

35 Williamson (1985: 370) has observed this problem and refers to "the odd placing in the narrative of what must be intended as the description of the second procession (vv 40-42); it would have been more natural in v 38."

identifies seven "priests with trumpets," while vv. 33-34 lists seven names of unknown origin. The phrase "and of the sons of the priests" (v. 35a) most likely introduces the Asaphite, Zechariah, and his colleagues in vv. 35-36a.[36] Likewise, v. 42a enumerates eight names that are not necessarily to be identified with the singers referred to in v. 42b. Finally, this interpretation cannot explain why only the first procession has a leader (Ezra; v. 36b).[37] Faced with this dissymmetry, one must wonder why redactors have focused their attention on the first procession, leaving only Nehemiah and "half of the people" (v. 38) following the second procession.

In consideration of the problems created by the emendation of the text in vv. 31-32 and 38, I suggest an alternative: Vv. 38-39, which depict a separate route for one of the *Tôdôt*, have been added to the account.

This conclusion seems at first fully implausible. According to the description of the wall in 3:1-32, the city-wall in 12:31ff. is separated into two hemispheres, and each of the *Tôdôt* traverse the course of one half of the wall. Just as they diverge (presumably at the Valley Gate; cf. 3:13), so they also converge later at the temple (12:40). However, when one edits 12:38-39, both *Tôdôt* advance together from one side of the city to the other. After the work on the entire circumference, why would only half of the wall play a role in the festivities?

Before offering a solution to this incoherency, it should be pointed out that, other than Nehemiah's account, we lack information on the topography of Jerusalem in the Persian period. Archaeological work in the city is not only severely limited, but it has also all too often searched for Nehemiah's wall rather than investigating the finds independently of the biblical text. This is all the more unfortunate in view of the fact that the repair and construction of the wall continued, with occasional interruptions, until the end of Persian Period and throughout the Hellenistic Age. Hence, it is difficult to establish whether a given portion of a gate or section of the wall was actually built during the fifty-two days before the twenty-fifth of Elul in the twentieth year of Artaxerxes' reign or some time later. This situation forces us to focus on the text, which contains two other descriptions of Jerusalem: 2:11-15 and 3:1-32.

The register in 3:1-32 – the most important of the two passages – can be divided into two halves.[38] In vv. 1-13, the named figures build or repair the segments of the wall between the gates "next to" (ידו/ועל-ידם) each other. After vv. 13-15, which refers only to the reparation of three gates, a new formulation

---

36 Cf. the analogies to this form of introduction in Ezra 8 and 10 and the arguments presented above.

37 As shown above, there are good reasons not to follow most scholars in treating the reference to Ezra (v. 36b) as gloss to the interpolation of vv. 32-36a.

38 Cf. esp. the article from Burrows (1933-34), who analysed the list in detail according to this distinction.

begins. Instead of "next to," now the builders repair the segments of the wall "after" (אחריו) each other. Significantly, these two halves correspond to the route of the two processions: The "two *Tôdôt*" in 12:31b, 37 traverse the section of the wall described in 3:14ff., while "the second *Tôdah*" in 12:38-39 proceeds along the half of the wall described in 3:1-12, beginning with "the broad wall" in v. 11 and continuing to the Fish Gate in v. 1.[39] The only gate not mentioned in 12:31ff. is the Valley Gate in 3:13, and we should probably follow most commentators in identifying it as the point of departure for the processions. Finally, while the names of the points along the wall in 12:31b, 37 do not always agree with 3:14ff., the itinerary of "the second *Tôdah*" corresponds exactly to the presentation in 3:1-12.

The account of the inspection tour in 2:11-15 parallels our findings in 3:1-32. After several days in Jerusalem, Nehemiah arises at night and exits the city through the Valley Gate. This gate occupies the center point of the register in chap. 3 and represents probably the place where the *Tôdôt* began their processions in 12:31ff. After Nehemiah is outside the city, he investigates "the walls of Jerusalem that were broken down and its gates that had been consumed in fire" (2:13b). Noteworthy are the places and gates mentioned in this passage: They correspond to the section of the wall repaired in the second half of the register (3:13ff.) and the description of the common route taken by the two *Tôdôt* (12:31b, 37). Instead of continuing and inspecting the first half of the wall (3:1-12), which "the second *Tôdah*" traverses (12:38-39), Nehemiah terminates his "night ride" and returns through the Valley Gate.

These considerations lend considerable weight to the assertion that a later author, who was influenced directly by the first half of the building register (3:1-12), expanded the account of the dedication ceremonies in 12:27 with the portrayal of a second procession in vv. 38-39. Without the latter, we need not emend the whole account (i.e., v. 31b to read "and the first went," v. 32 to "after it," and v. 38a to "and the second *Tôdah* went northwards"). That vv. 38-39 have been added would furthermore explain why later authors have so heavily expanded vv. 31b, 37 with the names of those who followed the processions: As these lists were inserted, there probably did not yet exist a second procession to which names of priests and musicians could have been added. V. 40 resumes the description of the two *Tôdôt* and may have followed directly on v. 37 in an earlier edition of the text. If so, one could account for the tension between it and vv. 38-39: After Nehemiah has already stated that he followed the second procession (v. 38a), why does he need to explain that he

---

39   The correspondence would be even closer if v. 39 did not originally include the clause, "and they stood at the Prison Gate." In comparison to the conclusion of the itinerary in v. 37 (ועד שער המים מזרח), we would expect v. 39 to have concluded with וְעַד שַׁעַר הַצֹּאן. It is generally agreed that ועד in both cases indicates the terminus of the respective processions.

was with the two *Tôdôt* at the temple? Moreover, why is he accompanied by "half of the officials" rather than "half of the people" (v. 38b)? The most reasonable answer to these questions is that vv. 38-39 have been added after the other first-person lines in the account.

If vv. 38-39 represent a tertiary supplement, Nehemiah would have originally depicted the two *Tôdôt* proceeding along the course of the wall that he inspected soon after his first arrival in Jerusalem (2:11ff.). Our analysis of that account has demonstrated the likelihood that the earliest stratum is to be isolated in vv. 11, 15* ("And I went up the valley at night and inspected the wall and returned") and 16a.[40] After the first redaction, the account mentions certain sections of the wall by name, and it is precisely these sections which correspond to both 3:13ff. and 12:31b and 37. What motivated the redactor of 2:11ff. to draw attention to only this half of the wall is difficult to determine. Possibly, it bore special significance, or it could have been built at later time. Whatever the case may be, the evidence of the editorial activity both here and in the corresponding verses of the building register (3:13ff.) renders it quite possible that a later hand expanded the account of the dedication in 12:27ff. with Nehemiah's words in vv. 31b, 37, 40 in order to draw attention again to a specific part of Jerusalem.

12.2.5 The Conclusion in v. 43 and the Priority of the Third-Person Narrative in vv. 27 and 43

That a redactor has inserted Nehemiah's words in vv. 31-40* is suggested most forcefully by the absence of a conclusion. While many argue that v. 31 provides an adequate introduction, the majority of scholarship agrees that the first-person account could not have ended with the notice in v. 40 that "the two *Tôdôt* stood in the temple – I and half of the rulers with me." This statement leaves the reader hanging. What happened after they arrived in the temple?[41] V. 43 supplies a fitting answer to this question: "They offered up great sacrifices that day and they rejoiced…." Several scholars have assigned this conclusion, however, to the same layer as vv. 31-32, 37-40.[42] Yet this notice clearly resumes the third-person account in vv. 27-30. Accordingly, the "they" refers to those who "sought the Levites from all their places" (v. 27a – or, less likely, to "the priests and Levites" of v. 30) and cannot be distinguished from those responsible for the appointment of the men over the chambers in v. 44. Since the subject is masc., it cannot refer to the *Tôdôt*; the only other option would have been the first-person plural. Moreover, the formulation is not what we would expect from Nehemiah.

---

40 Cf. §6.2.2.
41 Cf. most recently Karrer (2001: 142) and Reinmuth (2002: 232).
42 Williamson (1985: 370), Throntveit (1992: 120), Kratz (2000: 69).

Indeed, Ezra 3:13 and 6:22 appear to have provided the pattern for the author of Neh 12:43.[43] If the latter verse seems to presuppose the depiction of joy in Ezra 3:13 and 6:22 and attempts to surpass it with the repetition of שמח (no less than five times), then it is quite unlikely that Nehemiah's account would have originally concluded in this way. The only way this could be possible is if the earliest edition of the wall-building report were drafted after the final edition of the temple-building report in Ezra 1-6, and these scholars rightly do not consider the possibility of such a compositional sequence.[44]

If Nehemiah's words lack a conclusion, how may one maintain that they predate their immediate context? The response most commonly offered to this question is that the original conclusion has been replaced. As Rudolph wrote, "die Ausdrucksweise ist chronistisch (Esr 6, 22; 3,13), aber die Sache selbst muß auch bei Nehemia gestanden haben."[45] Similar remarks have been made by Meyer, Bertholet, Hölscher, Mowinckel, Kellermann, Gunneweg and Blenkinsopp.[46] Although popular, this approach encounters immense problems in explaining what motivated the editors to excise Nehemiah's words. Instead of deleting material, one would expect them rather to have corrected and amplified it, as we have observed in the analysis of vv. 31ff.

Apparently recognizing the weakness of these proposals, Steins (followed by Reinmuth) contends that the earliest layer in 12:27 consisted only of vv. 31f, 37-40, which portrays simply a "Mauerbegehung," and may have followed directly on 7:1-3.[47] That redactors have transformed an earlier account into a description of "the dedication of the wall" (12:27) is certainly quite conceivable, yet it is rather unlikely that the earliest layer originally concluded in v. 40a. Since Steins and Reinmuth agree with many scholars that 13:4-31 has been appended at a later point, the difficulties created by their reconstructions are severe: The first edition of the building report would have concluded with the statement, "And the two Tôdôt stood at the House of God." Were this the final line before the addition of 13:4ff., the work would have been extremely open-ended.

It is probably not merely coincidental that the processions advance toward the House of God without performing any action there. I suggest that the author of vv. 31b, 37, 40 formulated these lines in order to present Nehemiah himself organizing these "two large Tôdôt" that traverse the same section of the wall that he inspects in 2:11ff. If v. 43 did not already exist before the composition of this first-person account, one would expect Nehemiah to ascribe to the

---

43   Cf. §13.4.
44   Nevertheless, the dependency of Neh 12:43 on Ezra 1-6 is acknowledged to an extent by Throntveit (1992: 113ff.).
45   1949: 198.
46   Meyer (1896: 94), Bertholet (1902: 86), Hölscher (1923: 536), Mowinckel (1964: 31f.), Kellermann (1967: 46), Gunneweg (1987: 160) and Blenkinsopp (1988: 344).
47   Steins (1995: 193) and Reinmuth (2002: 226).

Tôdôt a specific function at the temple. That these groups are not mentioned after v. 40 indicates strongly that v. 43 continues an earlier line. The best candidate is v. 27.

> V. 27: "At the dedication of the wall of Jerusalem *they sought* out the Levites in all their places, to bring them to Jerusalem to celebrate the dedication with *rejoicing*, with thanksgivings and with singing [cymbals, harps and lyres]."[48]
>
> V. 43: And *they offered* great sacrifices that day and *rejoiced*, for God had made them *rejoice* with great *joy* [the women and children also *rejoiced*].[49] And *the joy* of Jerusalem was heard far away."

V. 27 suffices to describe the celebration. Inasmuch as the services of the Levites are required for the dedication of the wall, the composition of this notice can be compared to other short, pro-Levitical additions to the building report (cf., e.g., 7:1b; 13:10-13, v. 22b). Moreover, if the whole passage may be reduced to this verse, it could have been composed as a continuation to 7:1-3, which, as we shall see below, may also be isolated to a third-person narrative.

Yet it is quite likely that the first layer included not only v. 27 but also v. 43. The subject of both verses is the all-encompassing subject "they." So too, the Levites are brought to Jerusalem for one purpose, namely to organize a great celebration. Just as v. 27 emphasizes the joyousness of the occasion (לעשׂת + חנכה and שׂמחה as well as בתודות and בשׁיר), v. 43 employs the word joy (שׂמחה) five times (cf. also v. 27b).

Whether the earliest layer comprised more than vv. 27 and 43 is difficult to say, yet these short lines would have provided a sufficient basis for the expansions in vv. 31b, 37 and 40, where Nehemiah claims to have organized two large processions. Since תודות with the meaning "thanksgiving choirs" is encountered only here, it is quite plausible that the authors of these supplement were the first to use the term in this manner and, more importantly, that they were inspired by the presence of בתודות in v. 27b.

In §13.4, we witness how these two verses severed the original connection between 6:17-19 and 13:4ff. That a third-person account has been interpolated into Nehemiah's account should not be surprising. There is actually no other way around this conclusion, for the whole center-section of Neh 1-13 consists of third-person material. Moreover, one must not forget that the third-person building register (3:1-32), which may even refer to Nehemiah,[50] has been positioned directly in the middle of the first-person account. In order to provide an analogy to the insertion of Nehemiah's words in a narrative framework, we turn

---

48 That v. bβ has been added, cf. Steins (1994: 193).

49 The כ-clause may be a late insertion influenced by the crying of "the women and children" in Ezra 10:1.

50 Cf. 3:5 and the commentaries *ad loc.*

our attention to 7:1-3, the earliest layer of which appears to have been formulated in the third-person.

The Composition of 12:27-43

27 And at the dedication of the wall of Jerusalem, they sought out the Levites in all their places, to bring them to Jerusalem to celebrate the dedication with rejoicing, with thanksgivings and with singing, cymbals, harps, and with lyres.

> 28 The companies of the singers gathered together from the circuit around Jerusalem and from the villages of the Netophathites; 29 also from Beth-gilgal and from the region of Geba and Azmaveth; [for the singers had built for themselves villages around Jerusalem.]

> 30 And the priests and the Levites purified themselves; and they purified the people and the gates and the wall.

> 31 And I brought the princes of Judah up on the wall,

And I appointed two large *Tôdôt* and went in procession to the right on the wall to the Dung Gate;

> 32 and after them went Hoshaiah [and half the princes of Judah],
> 33 and Azariah, Ezra, Meshullam,
> 34 Judah, Benjamin, Shemaiah, and Jeremiah,

>> 35 and of the descendants of the priests with trumpets: Zechariah son of Jonathan son of Shemaiah son of Mattaniah son of Micaiah son of Zaccur son of Asaph;
>> 36 and his kindred, Shemaiah, Azarel, Milalai, Gilalai, Maai, Nethanel, Judah, and Hanani, with the musical instruments of David the man of God;

> and the *sôfēr*, Ezra, went in front of them.

37 At the Fountain Gate, in front of them, they went straight up by the stairs of the city of David, at the ascent of the wall, above the house of David, to the Water Gate on the east.

>> 38 The second *Tôdah* went toward the south (?) [– and I followed them with half of the people –] on the wall, above the Tower of the Ovens, to the Broad Wall, 39 and above the Gate of Ephraim, and by the Old Gate, and by the Fish Gate and the Tower of Hananel and the Tower of the Hundred, to the Sheep Gate;

>> and they came to a halt at the Gate of the Guard.

40 And the two *Tôdôt* stood in the House of God, and I and half of the rulers with me;

>> 41 and the priests Eliakim, Maaseiah, Miniamin, Micaiah, Elioenai, Zechariah, Hananiah with trumpets; 42 and Maaseiah, and Shemaiah, and Eleazar, and Uzzi, and Jehohanan, and Malchijah, and Elam, and Ezer

> - and the singers made themselves heard – and Jezrahiah the leader.

43 And they offered great sacrifices that day and rejoiced, for God had made them rejoice with great joy, and the women and children also rejoiced. **And the joy of Jerusalem was heard far away.**

12.3 The Third-Person Substratum in 7:1-3

That Nehemiah's words have been inserted in the third-person narrative in 12:27ff.*, while appearing at first untenable, parallels the evidence adduced by diachronic analysis of 7:1-3.

The account begins (7:1aα) in the passive mood ("And as the wall had been built"). This is surprising given that the similar introduction in 6:1 reads, "And as it was heard that *I had built* the wall" (cf. also 3:33). Reinmuth has attempted to assimilate these two expressions by reading נבנתה as a first-person pl. ("And as we built the wall").[51] However, the expected form would be ונבנה, and the absence of a direct object marker before החומה ̄ indicates that text has not been altered.[52] The use of בנה *niph.* also agrees with 7:1b, which is formulated in the passive mood ("...they appointed the porters, singers and Levites").

The formulation of v. 1b causes a problem insofar as the directly preceding clause contains Nehemiah's words: "...I hung the doors" (7:1aβ). Not only is the transition very rough, but one must also wonder, Why does Nehemiah claim to have performed the task of hanging the doors alone, while stating that others made the more important decisions of assigning the gatekeepers? Williamson offers an explanation: "Nehemiah, in all probability, left the detailed arrangement of the guards to the leaders mentioned in the next verse; it is unlikely, otherwise, that 'were appointed' would be cast in the passive mood."[53] Thus, we must assume that "they" in 7:1b are not identified until v. 2. This solution is, however, quite tenuous, especially since Nehemiah himself appoints gatekeepers in 13:19b and 22a (cf. also 4:7 and 13:30b for similar activities).

Seeking a more tenable approach, one notices that 6:1b ("And also at that time I had not hung the doors in the gates") is probably secondary, as Ehrlich, Hölscher, Mowinckel et al. suggested. In v. 1a, Nehemiah asserts that the wall is already complete, while vv. 2-9 depict further construction. Mowinckel remarked that "erst in 6:15 ist die Mauer fertig, und auch dort ist nur von der Mauer, nicht von den Toren die Rede. Die einzelnen Episoden während des Mauerbaus hat N offenbar in chronologischer Reihenfolge erzählen wollen. Noch in v. 9 ist die Arbeit nicht fertig, und das in vv. 1-6 Erzählte streckt sich über mehrere Tage oder Wochen."[54] In order to resolve this tension, an editorial hand has supplemented passages with the גם-clause v. 1b, assigning Nehemiah a still unfinished task. Since all of 6:1 has probably also been prefaced to vv. 2-9, as demonstrated in §7.3, the first-person clause in 7:1aβ seems to have been inserted in order to report that Nehemiah had completed the task of hanging

---

51   2002: 174.
52   Cf. 2:17 and 3:38.
53   1985: 269.
54   1963: 28. Cf. also Ehrlich (1914: 196) and Hölscher (1923: 536).

the doors in the gates. This conclusion not only explains that 7:1 appears to be an abbreviation of 6:1b,[55] but it also provides for much smoother syntax in 7:1. The relative clause is followed by a single independent clause in the passive mood: ...ויהי כאשר נבנתה החומה...ויפקדו השוערים.[56] A closer glance at the tempora in v. 1 lends weight to this proposal. As Rudolph concluded, "ואעמיד הד' ist also nicht Nachsatz, sondern steht parallel zu נבנתה."[57] The best approach to v. 1aβ is to connect it to the circumstantial clause in v. aα. While Williamson, Blenkinsopp and most other commentators translate the verse accordingly, they do not address the incongruity created by the sudden change from *qatal* (נבנתה) to *wayyiqtol* (ואעמיד).

With regard to v. 3, one notices that it, similar to the passive mood in v. 1*, is formulated in the third-person – at least according to the *Ketib* (וַיֹּאמֶר לָהֶם). Most often the text is emended to the first-person, yet this only creates a further tension with v. b: והעמיד משמרות. Although the Massoretes have vocalized והעמיד as an inf. abs., the form elsewhere is always a simple *hiph.* (וְהֶעֱמִיד). Furthermore, commentators agree that וְאָחֹזוּ in v. aβ must be emended to a *wayyiqtol* (cf. the preceding ינִיפוּ הדלתות). Since they are most likely correct, the transition to an inf. abs. for והעמיד after these third-person pl. forms is all the more unexpected. Therefore, we should probably follow the MT, whose אתנח-accent indicates the beginning of a new clause, and render the clause משמרות והעמיד: "and he appointed divisions of watches...."[58] That v. 3b is to be understood as a third-person sing. confirms the *Ketib* in v. a (ויאמר) and enables us to understand the sense of the verse. In the first part, "he" gives instructions for the opening and closing of the gates and, in the second part, "he" appoints the inhabitants of Jerusalem to additional watches "each in his own division and each over against his own house."

If the text in v. 3 should not be emended, the question arises, Who is the subject and to whom does "he" issue the orders for the opening of the gates (להם)? In v. 2, Nehemiah recalls that he placed his brother Hanani and Hananiah the governor of the fortress in charge of Jerusalem. ויאמר cannot refer in this case to both persons. Thus, Blenkinsopp, who does not emend v. 3a, suggests with Hölscher, Mowinckel, Bowman, Galling and Gunneweg that ואת־חנניה constitutes a gloss to את־חנני אחי.[59] One cannot preclude the possibility

---

55 Cf. ואעמיד הדלתות (7:1) with דלתות לא־העמדתי בשערים (6:1) גם עד־העת ההיא.

56 It is quite likely that the singers and Levites have been appended to this verse. One could compare this editorial activity to 13:22a, where Nehemiah replaces his own retainers (cf. v. 19b) with the Levites as gatekeepers.

57 1949: 138.

58 That this statement has been formulated in the third-person is supported by a Latin MS, which consistently alters "and he said" and "and he appointed" to the first-person.

59 1988: 275. Cf. Hölscher (1923: 538), Mowinckel (1964: 29), Bowmann (1954: 724), Galling (1954: 228), and Gunneweg (1987: 102).

that v. 2 has undergone expansion, especially since the כי-clause in v. 2b ("for he
was a more dependable and God-fearing man than most") refers to a single
person and has been included probably "in view of anticipated charges of nepo-
tism."[60] Moreover, it is unlikely not only that two men were ever in charge of
Jerusalem, but that they also bore such confusingly similar names. While we may
agree that one of these names have been added, Blenkinsopp's solution, nevertheless, makes for an extremely awkward and complex account: V. 1aα begins in
the passive mood, switches in aβ to the first-person, then to the third-person in
v. b, then back to the first-person in v. 2, and thereafter a new subject begins in
v. 3a, where Nehemiah reports what Hanani said to the gatekeepers mentioned
in v. 1b. Finally, he recounts in v. 3b that his brother commanded the
gatekeepers to appoint watches from the inhabitants of Jerusalem.

    Searching for a better reading, we observe elsewhere that, with the exception
of the building register in 3:1-32, the subject of עמד *hiph.* is always Nehemiah
(4:3 ["we set a משמר"], 7 [mobilization of the people]; 6:1, 7; 7:1; 12:31; 13:11, 19
[appointment of guards], 30; cf. also 4:16 where he commands the people to
remain in Jerusalem to serve as a משמר in the night). Nehemiah is thus most
likely also the subject of the verb in 7:3b (והעמיד משמרות) as well as of ויאמר
להם. This third-person formulation should not be attributed to textual corruption; it is more difficult to argue that a later scribe made a mistake here than to
suppose that the primary author was responsible for the wording. We may
compare ויאמר להם to the redactional insertion of ויאמר in 5:9.[61] So too, the
following first-person passage 7:4ff. must also constitute a very young insertion.[62] The analysis of the next section will support the widely held opinion that
in an earlier edition of the building report 7:1-3 was followed directly by
12:27ff., and we have seen above that the composition of the latter probably
began with a third-person narrative.

    One notices, finally, that the introduction in v. 1 emphasizes the appoint-
ment of the gatekeepers: "Now when the wall had been built [...], they
appointed the porters." While v. 2 no longer has the gatekeepers in view, v. 3
places them once again in the center of attention: "And he (=Nehemiah) said to
them (=the porters)...." Blenkinsopp appears to be correct in identifying
"them" in v. 3 with the newly appointed gatekeepers, rather than with Hanani
and Hananiah (v. 2). Indeed, if one should follow Hölscher, Mowinckel, Galling,
Bowman, Gunneweg and Blenkinsopp and treat the mention of Hananiah as
secondary, then there is no alternative than that Nehemiah is speaking to the
gatekeepers.

---

60 1988: 276. The insertion includes most likely the whole phrase ואת־חנניה שר הבירה since
    על־ירושלם depends upon the verb, not הבירה.
61 Cf. the analysis of this passage in §8.4.
62 I attempt to demonstrate this in §13.3.1.

I suggest that v. 2 does not even belong to the first edition of the account, since it interrupts the transition from v. 1 to v. 3. After the gatekeepers had been assigned, they should receive their instructions. In the present shape of the account, however, Nehemiah speaks only to his brother and Hananiah. It would have been easier and more sensible to address the gatekeepers directly. Inasmuch as יפתחו in v. 3aα has been vocalized in the *niph.* (in contrast to the indirect speech in 13:19b), the best approach is to identify the addressees with the porters, who are the focus of v. 1:

> Now when the wall had been built, [...] they appointed the porters (הֹשּׁוֹעֲרִים) [...]. And he said to them, "The gates (שְׁעָרִים) of Jerusalem are not to be opened until the sun has grown warm (...?)."[63] And he assigned guard divisions from the inhabitants of Jerusalem, each in his own division and each over against his own house.[64]

Inasmuch as the reader has trouble identifying the addressees, our conclusion appears tenable. The account in v. 1aαb and 3aαb recounts the measures taken for the defense of the city after the fortification had been repaired. It appears, therefore, that the author of v. 2 was inspired by the description of the appointments to include additional information regarding the Hanani's commission. This verse has, however, little to do with Jerusalem's security, and if ואת־חנניה שׂר הבירה is indeed secondary, it would be even less related to the topic.[65]

That v. 2 has been inserted directly before "and he said" (v. 3) lends additional weight to the suggestion that it originally included only the name Hanani and that a redactor composed it in the first person ("and I commanded my brother...") in order to adapt the third-person account to the foregoing chapter. Accordingly, the speaker of v. 3a and the actor of v. 3b are now to be

---

63 The continuation is incomprehensible. My translation of the first part departs from that of Williamson and Blenkinsopp, who render it: "The gates of Jerusalem are *not to be left open during the hottest part of the day.*" Against this approach, cf. 1 Sam 11:9, which indicates that the expression חם הַשֶּׁמֶשׁ is idiomatic and refers to the time after first-light; cf. also 1 Sam 11:11.

64 Williamson has argued against this interpretation: "[T]he orders given refer to a third party, themselves most easily understood as the gatekeepers. It is thus most probable that Nehemiah is here addressing the two leaders" (1985: 266). An interpretation must do justice to the meaning of עד, which is used in the preceding clause with it usual meaning "until (the sun has grown hot)." Williamson, however, translates the clause, "but while they are still on duty they must shut the doors." This does not make sense, for the gatekeepers would of course still be on duty as the gates were closed. It seems more likely that the switch from "the gates of Jerusalem" to "the doors" indicates that the verse has passed through editorial hands. Comparison with the analogous line in 13:19 ("and I commanded that they should not open them [=the gates of Jerusalem] until [עד] after the Sabbath") indicates that v. 3a could have originally concluded with "until (עד) the sun burns." Because the clause in v. 3aβ is, as generally acknowledged, corrupt, the safest approach is, however, to not allow it to influence the interpretation.

65 Further support for this proposal is provided by the unnecessary repetition of "Jerusalem" in vv. 2 and 3. Without v. 2, or at least v. 2aβ, the text would not contain this incongruity.

identified as Hanani rather than Nehemiah. Whether v. 2, which must be very young, transmits historically reliable information is irrelevant to the present investigation. Important is only that one recognize the probability that the earliest layer of 7:1-3 has been formulated in the third-person and that it has been expanded with two-first person statements (vv. 1aβ and 2).

That the earliest layer in 12:27ff. did not contain Nehemiah's words is substantiated by these findings, which are all the more significant if the dedication account formerly stood directly after 7:1-3.

The Composition of 7:1-3

1 **Now it came to pass, when the wall was built,**
    and I had set up the doors,
and the porters [and the singers and the Levites] **were appointed,**
        2 That I gave my brother Hanani,
            and Hananiah the ruler of the palace,
            charge over Jerusalem: for he *was* a faithful man and feared God above many.
3 **And he said unto them, Let not the gates of Jerusalem be opened until the sun be hot;**
            and while they stand by, let them shut the doors, and bar *them* [As generally acknowledged, this line is corrupt.]
and he appointed [re-vocalized] **watches of the inhabitants of Jerusalem, every one in his watch and every one over against his house.**

12.4 Conclusions

The present chapter has considered the implications of the fact that Nehemiah's words in the dedication account in 12:31ff. lack both an appropriate beginning and ending. The conclusion we have drawn is that the first-person account has been inserted into the earliest stratum of the surrounding narrative (possibly only vv. 27 and 43). So too, the description of "the second *Tôdah*" in vv. 38-39 may have been added to vv. 31, 37 and 40, which report that the two processions followed a common route. While the course of "the second *Tôdah*" appears to have been formulated according to the wording of the first half of the register in 3:1-12, the common route taken by "two large *Tôdôt*" corresponds only loosely to the description of the wall in the second half of the register in 3:13ff., yet significantly mentions the same section of the city which Nehemiah examines on his "night ride" (2:12ff.). The hand that inserted vv. 31, 37 and 40 (as well as 2:13-14) seems to have intended to portray Nehemiah focusing on this section of the city. Subsequently, the addition of vv. 38-39 may have been influenced by 3:1-32. Given the evidence of editorial activity in this passage (as well as in 2:12ff. and 3:1-32), caution is advised in drawing on its topographical information for an historical reconstruction of the extent of "Nehemiah's Jerusalem."

That Nehemiah's voice is suddenly, although quietly, heard amidst the third-person voices in 7:6-13:3 makes sense if it had been introduced at a later point and if the whole passage once stood in closer proximity to chaps. 1-7. Significantly, we notice this same redactional phenomenon in 7:1-3. An examination of this paragraph has shown that its earliest layer can also be isolated to the narrative framework (vv. 1aα, b and 3) and that the first-person strand appears to have been added secondarily. Accordingly, one need not assume that only a late copyist made a mistake in writing "and he said" in v. 3. It is much more likely that this represents the earliest wording and that a later hand added v. 2 in order to present Nehemiah reporting what his brother said to the gatekeepers of v. 1.

Taking its point of departure from these findings, the next chapters attempt to show that and how redactors have successively inserted the short third-person notices 12:27 + 43 and 7:1-3 + 11:1ff. (and then later 7:4ff., 8:1ff., etc.) between 6:17-19 and 13:4ff.

13. The Account of the Dedication Ceremonies and the Growth of Chaps. 7-13

13.1. Introduction

While the dedication of the temple in Ezra 6:16ff. follows directly upon the notice of completion in 6:15, the dedication of the wall is postponed for days (cf. Neh 6:15 with 12:27ff.). Most critical scholars make a compiler responsible for the delays. Accordingly, the account of the celebration in 12:27ff. – a portion of which is presumed to have been drafted by Nehemiah – originally appeared in closer proximity to the notice of completion in 6:15-16. For instance, Rudolph contended that the earliest stratum of 12:27ff. followed 6:16 (or 7:3) and that it was moved to its present position by the Chronicler "um dadurch ein Gegenstück zur Tempelweihe am Schluß des 1. Teils (Esr 6) und zu der feierlichen Verpflichtungsfeier am Schluß des 2. Teils (Neh 9/10) zu schaffen."[1] In suggesting that the transmitted context of the account is due to an editorial hand, Rudolph doubted that the activities reported in 8:1ff. would have necessitated that the community defer the dedication of the wall. He thus assumed that the text's original literary setting must correspond to its historical setting.

Although representing the consensus, Rudolph's opinion must be challenged. Instead of extricating the account of the dedication from its original context and transposing it to a new context, we would expect later authors to have followed the usual method of redaction and to have simply amplified the narrative surrounding 12:27ff. With regard to transposition hypotheses, one must be wary of scholarly attempts to rearrange the text so that it agrees with what one considers historically probable. As Torrey remarked with respect to the proposal that Neh 8 originally stood behind Ezra 8, "Any attempt to 'restore the original form' of an ancient document, by *rearranging* its chapters, paragraphs, or verses, ought to be met with suspicion and subjected to the severest criticism."[2] This suspicion

---

1 1949: 195.
2 1910: 252 – my italics. While Torrey could explain the present context of Neh 8 as an *accidental* misplacement, he was not prepared to assume that a later author *intentionally* rearranged the material after the notice of completion in 6:15. Thus he assigned, and rightly so, all of the material after 6:15 to the work of a later author.

appears all the more warranted in view of the quantity of proposals for the original context of Neh 12:27ff.[3]

In this chapter, we offer an alternative to these transposition hypotheses, taking our point of departure from the following question: If 7:1-3 began, as we concluded in §12.3, with a third-person notice reporting Nehemiah's actions and was later transformed into a first-person account, how should one explain that this paragraph's immediate context in chap. 6 and 7:4ff. has been formulated in the first-person? Our solution to this problem entails four arguments: (1) The first-person account in 7:4ff., which presupposes (and reinterprets) the presence of the list in Ezra 2, must be younger than 7:1-3*. The repetition of Ezra 2 occasioned the composition of Neh 8-10, which belongs to the final additions to Ezra-Neh. (2) Before the composition of 7:4ff., the third-person notice in 7:1-3* originally continued in 11:1ff. (3) Likewise, the notice in 7:1-3, prior to the insertion of 11:1ff., stood between 6:17-19 and 12:27ff. (4) The first text to interrupt 6:17-19 and 13:4 was the third-person account of the dedication in 12:27 and 43. We begin the analysis by examining the evidence indicating that 12:27, which belongs to the proposed primary stratum of the dedication ceremonies, must be older than the lists in 11:3ff. (and 12:1-26) as well as the first-person account in 13:10ff.

13.2 The Priority of 12:27 vis-à-vis 11:3ff. and 13:10ff.

That the author of 12:27ff.* was the first to sever 6:17-19* from its continuation in 13:4-31* is rendered likely by an examination of the surrounding material. According to a common view, 12:27 has not only been added to the first-person account in vv. 31ff., but also presupposes the lists in 11:3ff.[4] With regard to the first assertion, the previous chapter has shown that Nehemiah's words lack both an adequate beginning and ending, so that it is easier to suppose that they have been inserted into the third-person narrative. This narrative, which begins in v. 27, appears to have *preceded* the insertion of the list in 11:3ff. To organize the dedication of the wall, "they sought out the Levites from all their places to bring them to Jerusalem...." As Hölscher perceptively remarked, "12,27a ist natürlich älter als 11,15-18, wo bereits 284 Leviten in Jerusalem sind."[5] Similarly, Williamson observes that v. 27 implies "that the Levites and singers were living away from Jerusalem. As far as our information goes, this was the case at the time the walls were built *before* the events described in chap. 11 (whose dating is,

---

3   6:15, 6:16, 6:19; 7:3, 7:5bα,7:5bβ, 11:20 and 11:36 have all been suggested as the original contexts.

4   1994: 193.

5   1923: 556.

however, uncertain), and again later (cf. 13:10) until the pledge described in chap. 10 rectified the situation."[6]

These observations with respect to the relationship of chaps. 10 and 11 to 12:27 are invaluable for a tenable reconstruction of the composition-history in chaps. 7-13. Insofar as the Levites are presented as still dwelling outside Jerusalem, 12:27 must be older, as Williamson points out, than the list in 11:3ff. and the pact in chap. 10, as well as Nehemiah's account of his reforms for the Levites in 13:10ff. According to the latter passage, the failure to deliver the מניות־הלוים had forced the Levites and singers to seek their subsistence elsewhere. As Nehemiah comes to Jerusalem and notices this situation, he takes the rulers to task, gathers the Levites and singers, and assigns them to "their places." The investigation in §9.2.1 provided support for the widely accepted opinion that 13:6 constitutes a late addition which dates the reforms to a time after the ratification of the pact in chap. 10. Before this editorial work, the statement in v. 7 ("and I came to Jerusalem…") must refer to Nehemiah's arrival in the twentieth year of Artaxerxes' reign. Had the author of 12:27 known that the Levites and singers returned to Jerusalem already before the completion of the wall, he would certainly not have reported that they were still absent as the wall was about to be dedicated. In §9.3.2, we saw that 13:4-9 appears to have originally concluded with v. 14a and that 13:10-13, 14b was inserted at an advanced stage in the composition of the chapter. Thus, the author of 12:27ff.* could have severed 6:17-19 from its continuation in 13:4ff. without contradicting the account.[7] That the third-person notice in 12:27 (and 43) is older than a portion of the first-person account in chap. 13 also validates the assertion that Nehemiah's words in 12:31ff. and 7:1aβ, 2 are younger than their narrative contexts.

In order to cite another example of a redactor inserting Nehemiah's words into a narrative, we turn now to the literary link formed by 7:1-3 and 11:1-2.

13.3 The Literary Link between 7:1-3* and 11:1-2

Just as it possible to isolate Neh 13:10-13, 14b from its context so that not all of 13:4-31 must be later than 12:27 (*pace* Williamson), it is also not necessary to ascribe the entirety of chap. 11 to the same hand. Thus, the text may have origi-

---

6   1985: 370 – my italics.

7   Moreover, 13:14 refers to both the Levites and the singers. Despite insistence from many to the contrary, the reference to "the singers" is probably integral to the account. In 12:27ff., on the other hand, the community petitions only the Levites to come to Jerusalem, yet the singers "gather themselves" (vv. 28-29). Here, one may be quite sure that the reference to the singers in vv. 28-29 is editorial, which provides further evidence that 13:10-13, 14b represents a very late addition.

nally concluded with v. 20.[8] So too, the list has three headings (vv. 1-2, 3*, and 4), and comparison with 1 Chr 9 in both the MT and LXX suggests to some scholars that the section in vv. 3ff.* was transmitted independently and adapted to diverse purposes.[9] With regard to vv. 1-2, this introduction refers the reader back to the theme of Neh 7:5ff. Since both passages concern the repopulation of Jerusalem, many contend that 7:5a (or all of 7:5a-72) was connected to 11:1ff. before the interpolation of chaps. 8-10,[10] or that "the editor" of Ezra-Neh added 11:1-2 in order to direct the reader to the resumption of the subject in 7:4ff.[11] More probable, however, is that 11:1-2 existed before the addition of vv. 3ff. and was drafted as the continuation of a third-person note in 7:1-3*. Accordingly, it is quite possible that an earlier edition of the building report presented the dedication account directly after 7:1-3 + 11:1-2. If so, the narrative, without the notice in 11:15ff. of 284 Levites already living in Jerusalem before the dedication of the wall, would not have contradicted 12:27.

13.3.1 The Enrollment of the Residents of the "New" Jerusalem in 7:4-72

In the present shape of chap. 7, vv. 1-3 form a short remark on the security measures for Jerusalem. This paragraph, however, leaves the reader hanging, for in vv. 4-5 Nehemiah is more concerned with taking a census and proving the people's exilic genealogy than with the population and defense of the city. It is often assumed that 7:5b and vv. 6ff. have been added to the "authentic" portion of Nehemiah's account.[12] Before accepting this conclusion, we should note that already 7:4 is in tension with vv. 1-3. That "there were no houses built" (v. 4b) flatly contradicts v. 3b, where "he appointed guards from the inhabitants of Jerusalem...*each over against his own house*." Without an indication that "house" in v. 4 possesses a different meaning than "house" in v. 3, the reader is confused.[13]

---

8   Williamson (1985: 349) and Blenkinsopp (1988: 322).

9   See, e.g., Böhler (1997: 332ff.). Knoppers (2000) compares the Neh 11 and 1 Chr 9 in both the MT and the LXX, seeking to demonstrate that an order of dependency is impossible to reconstruct. For a defense of the older position, see the literature cited by Steins (1995: 396ff.).

10 See Meyer (1896: 94-102), Batten (1913: 266f.), Hölscher (1923: 551), Rudolph (1949: 181), Mowinckel (1964[I]: 145f.), Myers (1965: 186), Fensham (1982: 242), Clines (1984: 211), McConville (1985: 136), Gunneweg (1987: 140f.), Blenkinsopp (1988: 322f.), and Grabbe (1998: 59f., 168).

11 See Williamson (1985: 348ff.), Eskenazi (1988: 111ff.), Throntveit (1992: 111f.), and Lipschits (2002: 427).

12 Most recently Karrer (2001: 142) and Reinmuth (2002: 197) have taken this route.

13 It also contradicts the more reliable information in 3:20, 29; 4:8, and Hag 1:4. To witness how scholars struggle to solve this contradiction, see Blenkinsopp (1988: 277 – v. 4 "cannot be taken literarily"), Clines (1984: 179 – "no new buildings had yet been erected"), and Reinmuth (2002: 206 – "vielleicht [waren] *einige* Häuser noch nicht wieder aufgebaut und die Stadt [war] noch nicht in *vollem* Maße wieder bewohnt" [italics original]).

In contrast to the friction between the passages vv. 1-3 and vv. 4ff., the latter contains no inner tension, so that one lacks a reason to doubt that it originally continued with vv. 5b-72. That Nehemiah gathered the people "to examine their genealogy" (להתיחש, v. 5a) indicates that the author was responsible for not just v. b (cf. ואמצא ספר היחש), but also 7:6-72 (נמצא ולא המתיחשים כתבם בקשו אלה, v. 64a). The root יחש in v. 5a appears elsewhere only in the late passages Ezra 2:62/Neh 7:64, Neh 8:1, 3 and Chronicles (thirteen times).[14] Consequently, its use by Nehemiah is quite problematic.[15]

The mention of "the nobles and rulers" in 7:5a presupposes the additions of 5:1-13; 6:17-19; 13:10-14, 15-22. In these texts, Nehemiah demonstrates that exactly these two groups thwarted the progress on the wall by failing to acknowledge their fraternity with their fellow Judeans (5:1ff.), entering into commercial and connubial contracts with Tobiah (6:17-19), failing to pay the Levites an emolument (13:10-14), and continuing their business on the Sabbath (in the winepresses and with the Tyrians; 13:15-18).

Hence, instead of attempting to reconstruct a fragment of the text that Nehemiah could have drafted, it is much more tenable to treat the whole as a late insertion with which the author corrects 1:1b-4. In the latter passage, which introduces the late editions of the first-person account,[16] the protagonists refer to the inhabitants of the province as "the Judeans, the escapees, which are left of the captivity" (v. 2) and "the survivors that are left of the captivity there in the province" (v. 3). Although this text is most probably the work of a later author and has been inserted between v. 1a and 11b, both it and Ezra 5:1-6:15 do not agree with the historical ideology presented in the final editions of Ezra-Neh. The latter employ the same terminology found in Neh 1:1b-4 ("all those who remain" [כל־הנשאר, Ezra 1:4] and "escapees" [הפליטה, Ezra 9:8, 13, 14, 15]) for those who *returned* from Babylon, not those who simply *survived* the catastrophe. Similar to way the composition of Ezra 1-4 and 6:16ff. corrects the building account in 5:1ff. by identifying the "elders of the Jews" with the Golah, the addition of Neh 7:4-72 makes another change (after 1:1b-4) to the wall-building account by assigning new meanings to the terms הנשארים and הפליטה.

In the opening scene, Nehemiah inquires about those still living in the province after the Babylonian captivity and, just as Ezra 5:1-6:15*, does not seem to know about a return. After completing the repair of the wall, he notices that the city was "expansive and great" (7:4) but not yet populated. God places

---

14 Despite his commendable effort to examine the reception of Nehemiah's account in the Hebrew Bible, Reinmuth surprisingly does not mention that Nehemiah shares here the same concern for genealogies witnessed in Chronicles and Ezra 1-10.

15 That the term appears in Ezra 8:1, 3, which is integral to the earliest layers of Ezra's account, supports our findings that Ezra's account not only espouses a different view of the Restoration than the earliest layers in Nehemiah's account, but also that it was written later.

16 See §§4.2-3.

in his heart a new plan for Jerusalem (ויתן אלהי אל־לבי, 5aα – an adaptation of אלהי נתן אל־לבי לעשות לירושלם in 2:12), namely to take a census of those who had worked on the wall (ואקבצה את־החרים ואת־הסגנים ואת־העם, v. 5aβ; cf. the triad in 2:16, 4:8, 13 and 5:1-7). He then discovers a genealogical record of those who made Aliyah long before. After quoting this "book," the narrative continues seamlessly in the third-person. Inasmuch as we do not how he employed the book, we must presume that only those who could prove their exilic descent were allowed to inhabit the city (cf. v. 64f.). Herewith, Nehemiah espouses a view that differs radically from that in 1:1b-4, yet agrees with the final authors of Ezra-Neh.[17]

The author has described the repopulation of Jerusalem by drawing on the portrayals of the so-called "heavenly book(s)" in very late, and for the most part apocalyptic, or apocalyptically influenced, texts. Gunneweg already observed these parallels with regard to the repopulation of Judah in Ezra 2 (cf. v. 62/Neh 7:64) and proposed that the register functions to underscore the "realized eschatology" of Ezra-Neh.[18] Recently, Schaack has developed Gunneweg's insight.[19] Yet while both restrict their purview to the list itself, it is important to consider the narrative in Neh 7:4ff., for here Nehemiah, after rebuilding Jerusalem, selects the residents of this "expansive and great city" on the basis of the ספר היחש העולים בראשונה he "discovered" (ואמצא) and the names he "found written therein" (כתוב בו, v. 5). The authors of both the list and Nehemiah's account presuppose the late developments in Judaism with which the conceptions of divine bookkeeping elsewhere (primarily in Egypt) were appropriated and adapted. According to many of the biblical – but more often, the non-canonical – witnesses to this development, the names of the "holy" are "written" or "found in a book" for the purpose of admittance to "life" in the purged Jerusalem (cf., e.g., Isa 4:3).[20] Similar to way the apocalyptic movement

---

17 As Kaufmann insightfully pointed out (1977: 377), Neh 7:5-72 is to be understood as Nehemiah's move to support Ezra's handling of the issue of mixed marriages.

18 "Ist das göttliche Heil präsent, so müssen auch die Namen derer, die es erlangen, namhaft gemacht werden können, wohingegen das apokalyptische Buch des Lebens erst 'an jenem Tag' geöffnet werden wird" (1981: 156). On the issue of realized eschatology in Ezra-Neh, see McConville (1986).

19 "Die Ungreifbarkeit der Entstehungsbedingungen der Liste scheint in einem direkten Verhältnis zur Unangreifbarkeit seines Inhaltes zu stehen. Gerade die Episode Esr 2:59-63 zeigt, welche Autorität und unhinterfragt Gemeinde-begrenzende Macht dem Dokument beigemessen wird. Ebenso ungreifbar ist durch die unpersönliche Formulierung in Esr 2,62/Neh 7,64 diejenige Instanz, die das Prüfungs- und Ausschlußverfahren aus der Gemeinde durchführt. [...] Die Analogie zur Funktion des himmlischen Buches im endzeitlichen Gericht ist nur zu deutlich"(1998: 134).

20 That Isa 4:3 constitutes a late text is clear from the relative dating of its context; see most recently the analysis by Becker (1997, esp. p. 293). For references to heavenly booking (some of which are linked specifically to Jerusalem), cf. Ex 32:32f. (belongs to the addition in vv. 30-35); Ezek 13:9; Mal 3:16; Ps 56:9; 69:29; 87:6; 139:16; 149:9; Dan 7:10; 12:1; Neh 3:37; 13:14b; 4 Ezra 6:20; 1 Enoch 81:2; 91:1-3; 103:2f.; 104:1; 106:19f; 108:7; 108:3; 2 Enoch

sought heroic figures for their representatives (Daniel, Enoch, Ezra, etc.), the author of 7:4-72, who may be responding to some sort of (proto-)apocalyptic speculation about a *future* Jerusalem, has presented the historic builder of the *present* Jerusalem choosing the residents of "the Holy City" (11:1) by the selective process of research in the genealogical record.[21]

13.3.2 The Priority of Ezra 2

The most cogent argument one may bring to bear in support of the supplementary nature of 7:4-72 is the likelihood that Nehemiah "found" the list of names that he quotes in vv. 6ff. not in the temple-archives, as is often assumed, but rather in Ezra-Neh itself. Whether Ezra 2 has indeed been cited in Neh 7 is an issue that has long occupied scholars. It is closely intertwined with the theories of the priority of 1 Esdras and the identity of the author of Ezra-Neh with "the Chronicler." All of the various issues cannot be dealt with here and deserve a separate treatment. It suffices to draw attention to a new and more compelling argument for the view that Ezra 2 represents the older text.

Kratz is probably correct in maintaining that this chapter has been interpolated between Ezra 1 and 3 and that the narrative in chap. 1 originally continued directly in 3:8.[22] 1:1-5 appears to have been expanded with v. 6 and then vv. 7-11 based on the supplement in 5:14-15. The beginning of the story in vv. 1-5(6) forms a direct point of contact with 3:8. After reporting that "those who remained" rose up to build the house of God and thus fulfill the decree Cyrus issued in the *first year* of his reign (1:5), the author then describes what happened "*in the second year* of their coming unto the house of God at Jerusalem" (3:8). The redactors responsible for 3:1-7, however, begin the story earlier. Instead of commencing with the laying of the temple-foundation, the builders first erect the altar.

The builders choose an appropriate time to begin this construction: "And when the seventh month came, the children of Israel were in the cities." While six months would probably not have been enough time for all the activities reported in Ezra 1-2, the redactors were not concerned with historical plausibility. The settlement must progress quickly, so that Jeshua and

---

40:13; *Jub.* 5:13; 19:9; 23:32; 30:20ff.; *T. Levi* 5; CD 20:19; 1QH 1:23f.; 16:10; 1QM 1:10; 12:3; 1 QpHab 7:12-14; Luke 10:20; Phil 4:3; Heb 12:22f.; Rev 3:5ff.; 13:8; 17:8. The best work on the theme of "heavenly books" is still that of Koep (1952). Nötscher (1958/9: 409ff.) has postulated a relationship between "heavenly books" and the membership lists and order of precedence in CD and 1QS.

21   For further evidence, see the final paragraph of this section in which we discuss the precise calculations made in 7:4-72.

22   2000: 63f.

Zerubbabel are prepared to build the altar once the seventh month begins. Since precisely this month occupies the pivotal position in the cultic calendar, the reference to the "seventh month" in 3:1 is just as integral to its context as it is to Neh 7:72b (*pace* Williamson).[23] Instead of supposing that the writer of Ezra 3 has "been happy to take it over from his source [Neh 7:72b] as the month most suitable for such an occasion,"[24] it seems that the author of Neh 7:4-72 read Ezra 3:1a as part of the list in 2:1-70. The probability that the list in chap. 2 was inserted *after* the first layer in 3:1-7 (*pace* Kratz) supports this assertion. Upon closer examination of this narrative, one notices that 3:1a has probably been appended to the list in chap. 2. If so, we can account for the change of subject (from "the children of Israel" in v. a to "the people" in v. b) and the rough syntax: V. 1aα is a temporal clause ("And as the seventh month came around…") that introduces v. 1aβ ("…the children of Israel were in cities"). The change of subject in v. 1b ("And the people gathered…") precludes the possibility of subordinating this clause to the temporal clause in v. 1aα.[25]

Significantly, the only parts of 3:1-7 which presuppose that the altar was built in the seventh month appear to constitute late additions to the narrative. For example, v. 4a clearly interrupts the connection between v. 3b and v. 4b; "the daily burnt offering" in v. 4b requires the verb "and they offered" in v. 3b. Similarly, v. 6a brings the account into conformity with the Priestly sacrificial ordinances and adds precision to the general date in v. 1a.[26] Thus, it is quite probable that the earliest layer of vv. 1-7 began with v. 1b ("and the people gathered") similar to the introductions in Neh 8:13 and 9:1.[27] Accordingly, this paragraph was added to 3:8ff. in order to recount the construction of the altar at some indeterminate time in the first year *before* the laying of the temple foundation in "the second year." After the insertion of the list in chap. 2, later hands expanded 3:1-7 with vv. 1a, 4a, and 6a, dating this construction to the sacred seventh month (cf. 2 Chr 7:7ff.).

The proposal is substantiated by a glance at the conclusion of chap. 2, which names the various groups that "were in their cities" (2:70a).[28] The next line repeats "in their cities," yet emphasizes that these groups constituted "all Israel." Why then was it necessary to say a third time that "the children of Israel were in

---

23   1983: 2f.

24   Williamson (1985: 46).

25   This syntactical rule causes immense problems for the priority of Neh 7. Williamson (1985: 41) argues that v. 1aβ is a circumstantial clause and translates v. 1 as a single sentence.

26   The editing of the passage is not confined to these verses. I suggest that the earliest layers are to be isolated in vv. 1b, 3aα, bβ, 6b. Cf. the proposals of Galling (1954: 192f.), Gunneweg (1985: 73), and most recently Steins (1995: 334).

27   The separation of Ezra 3:1a from 1b is supported by the textual tradition of beginning the narrative in Neh 8 with the same clause as in Ezra 3:1b.

28   First in v. a (וישבו הכהנים והלוים ומן־העם והמשררים והשוערים והנתינים בעריהם) and then again in v. b (וכל־ישראל בעריהם).

(their) cities" (3:1a)? The list in chap. 2 could have concluded in v. 70 in the same way as it begins in v. 1 ("every one to his own city"). A closer inspection reveals that the author of 3:1a has not simply repeated 2:70, but has added the date "in the seventh month" (וינע החדש השביעי ובני ישראל בערים). This specification prepares the reader for the commencement of the cultic calendar made possible by the construction of the altar (vv. 2-7*).

Turning finally to Neh 7:72, one notices that the text does not contain the repetitiveness of Ezra 2:70 and 3:1a. While v. b corresponds exactly to 3:1a ("and as the seventh month came around, the children of Israel were in [their] cities"), v. a reads that "the priests, Levites, gatekeepers, singers, some of the people, Nethinim, *and all Israel dwelt in their cities*." In place of the one sentence here, Ezra 2:70 contains two: First, the various groups are said to have "dwelt in their cities" (v. a), and then the author affirms that they represent "all Israel," who "dwelt in their cities" (v. b). The latter appears to be a supplement. That the author of Neh 7:72 has combined the first sentence with the second is indicated furthermore by the addition of the suffix "their" to "cities"29 and the mistakes made with respect to the order of the groups in reformulating Ezra 2:70.30

All these observations substantiate the claim that Ezra 2:70 and 3:1a, which have developed *gradually*, represent the older texts and have been read as a *unity* by the author of Neh 7:4-72.31 Therefore, Nehemiah discovers the "the book of the genealogies of those who came up first" (7:5b), which he employs to enroll the residents of the newly built Jerusalem (7:6ff.), nowhere else than in Ezra 1-6, as Spinoza proposed long ago.32

---

29 Neh 7:72b reads בעריהם, while בערים stands in Ezra 3:1a.

30 In ascribing Ezra 2 and Neh 7 to the same hand and then dismissing them from the interpretation of the "Gesamtkomposition," Karrer (2000: 293f.) does not explain why Ezra 3:1 repeats 2:70 or why Neh 7:72a appears to fuse Ezra 2:70a and b into one sentence.

31 There are additional arguments. For example, Ezra 2 fits much better in its context than Neh 7:4-72. Indeed, the narrative form of Ezra 2:1f., 62-70 and the reference to Nebuchadnezzar (cf. 1:7) suggests that the whole list has been composed for its present context. For further evidence, cf. the eleven names in Ezra 2:2 and the twelve names in Neh 7:7 (as well as the name "Nehemiah"), the better order of the groups in Ezra 2:70a, and "the 245 singing men and women" in Neh 7:67 and "245 mules" in Ezra 2:66 (an *aberratio oculi* of the author of Neh 7:4ff.). For a brief overview of the most important arguments, see Blenkinsopp (1988: 43f.).

32 "Quid inquam clarius ex v. 5 cap. 7 Nahemiæ, quam quod ipse hanc eandem Epistolam simpliciter descripserit? Ii igitur, qui hæc aliter explicant, nihil aliud faciunt quam verum Scripturæ sensum et consequenter Scripturam ipsam negare; quod autem putant pium esse una loca Scripturæ aliis accommodare, ridicula sane pietas, quod loca clara obscuris et recta mendosis accomodent et sana putridis corrumpant. Absit tamen, ut eos blasphemos appellem, qui nullum animum maledicendi habent; nam errare humanum quidem est" (1979 [1670]: 133f.).

13.3.3 The Connections Between 7:1-3* and 11:1-2

According to our proposal, the earlier editions of the building report – before the composition of 7:4-12:26 – presented a sequence of 7:1-3* + 12:27, 43.[33] The analysis in the preceding chapter demonstrated the possibility of isolating the substratum of 7:1-3 to the third-person material vv. 1aαb and 3. Before the insertion of 7:4ff., the narrative would have continued in 12:27ff.* without an interruption by a first-person account. After the addition of 7:1b, the passage refers to the Levites, singers and gatekeepers as individual guilds, thus agreeing with the expansions in 12:45-47 (cf. also משמרת in 7:3b and 12:45).[34]

That 12:27ff. once stood in closer proximity to 7:1-3 is suggested further-more by the connections between 7:1-3 and 11:1-2. With regard to the latter, most recent research on Ezra-Neh assumes that it, or the putative underlying source, represents the resumption of 7:4-5a (or v. 72a) between which a com-piler inserted Neh 8-10. The only problem with this proposal is that it cannot explain why the first-person account does not have a conclusion. One must then resort to the speculative theory that the original continuation was cut short after 7:5 (or v. 72) and replaced by this third-person notice. However, it is much easier to conceive that all of 7:4-72, which contradicts v. 3 in presenting the houses as not yet built (cf. v. 4b), has been inserted between the third-person notices in 7:1-3* and 11:1-2.

In defense of this proposal, we may compare the contents and wording of 7:1-3 and 11:1-2. The first paragraph concludes with the establishment of guards from "the inhabitants of Jerusalem" (ישבי ירושלם, 7:3), and the second begins by reporting that "the princes of the people *inhabited Jerusalem*" (וישבו שרי-העם בירושלם, 11:1).[35] As Blenkinsopp pointed out "the verb *hitnaddēb* [11:2] 'to volunteer' also has military connotations, preparing us for the description of the settlers, lay and clerical, as capable of bearing arms (vs. 6, 14)."[36] 11:1-2 thus

---

33   This represents a common solution to the original context of 12:27ff. The only difference is that we do not suggest that the text has been transposed. Rather, everything between 7:3 and 12:27ff. must have belonged to later editions of the building report.

34   For our analysis of Neh 12:44-13:3, see §14.2.1.

35   7:2 refers to the שר הבירה, which resembles the שרי-העם in 11:1. Although a later hand may have inserted 7:2, the evidence of the redactional activity suggests the proximity of these passages in an earlier edition of the building report.

36   "Once the wall had been built, the provision of a military or paramilitary reserve, supplementing the governor's militia, would have furthered the process of turning the city into a fortress..." (1988: 323). It should also be emphasized that the verb נדב is used for freewill offerings and, when combined with the one-tenth of the population that move to Jerusalem, the sanctity of the temple in Ezra 1-10 extends to the city as a whole (cf. "Holy City" in v. 1). This may be compared to P's presentation of the tribes around the tabernacle (not to mention the analogies with the Temple Scroll), and insofar as the children of Israel in P are mobilized into army regiments, one should not distinguish between the religious

corresponds to the measures described for the security of the city in 7:1-3.[37] The addition of 11:4ff. (with its references to the גבורי חיל) sustained this military tone before the insertion of 7:4ff. conferred a completely new dimension to the description of the repopulation of the city. That 11:1-2 has severed the connection of 7:1-3* to 12:27ff.* is supported furthermore by similarities between 11:1f. and the dedication account (cf. להביאם לירושלם [12:27] with להביא אחד מן־העשרה לשבת בירושלם [11:1]). The designation of Jerusalem as "the Holy City" in 11:1 (cf. also v. 18) may be explained as a development of the *ḥanukkah* of the wall in 12:27 and the purification of the people, the gates and the wall in 12:30 (cf. also 3:1; 13:22a).

Insofar as 11:1f. (and later vv. 4ff.), which concerns the population of the city, stood directly before the account of the dedication in 12:27ff., one may compare the narrative sequence to several ancient Near Eastern portrayals of municipal construction projects. For instance, the so-called "Bull Inscription" Sargon II, in which he recounts the building of Dūr-Šarrukēn, describes the population measures (§§92-97) *after* the building of the walls and gates (§§79-92) and *before* the dedication festivities (§§97-100).[38] The same is witnessed in Assurbanipal's report of the building and dedication of his new capital city, Kalḥu.[39] If these and other parallels, which have been compiled by Hurowitz,[40] indicate that the authors of 11:1-2 (3ff.), as well as of the new-and-improved account in 7:4-72, intended to present the sequence of fortification-» population-» dedication in Nehemiah's building report, one has all the more reason to reject the common assumption that "the editor" transposed the account of the concluding festivities from its original position after 6:15, 16, 19 or 7:3 to its present context after the list of the priests in 12:1-26. It is more tenable to maintain that 12:27ff.* formerly stood directly behind 7:1-3 and was gradually moved by the composition of 11:1-2 (and vv. [3]4ff.); 7:4-73 (and 8:1-10:40); and 12:1-26.

Most importantly, however, the thesis that 7:1-3* continued in 11:1-2 (3ff.) can account for the presence of 7:4ff., the conclusion of which causes scholars so many troubles. Were the author simply supplementing an existing narrative,

---

and military overtones in Neh 7:1-3 and 11:1ff. This applies all the more given the fact that החנרב occurs together with גבורי חיל not only in Neh 11 but also in 2 Chr 17:16.

37 The lot-casting in 11:1 has probably *not* been inspired by 10:35 (*pace* Williamson [1985: 345], Eskenazi [1988: 111ff.], Böhler [1997: 332ff.], and Lipschits [2002: 424-n. 3]), especially since 10:35 appears to presuppose a lengthy redactional history. See the excursus at the end of chap. 9 and the analyses in the following chapter. The commonalities between 10:33ff. and 11:1 (cf. Böhler [1997: 332ff.]) are much easier to explain on the assumption of the priority of 11:1ff.

38 See Luckenbill, *ARAB* II, §122 and Hurowitz (1992: 123), who notes further parallels between the bronze plaque and the reverse side of the stone tablet.

39 See Grayson, *ARI* II 591, 671, 677.

40 1992: 283ff.

then we would not have to presume that "the editor" of Ezra-Neh deleted Nehemiah's original ending. Instead of asserting what cannot be verified, one should first consider the possibility that the author of 7:4ff. has been inspired by the reference to "the Holy City" in 11:1 and composed a new text that presents a more orthodox method of repopulating Jerusalem: According to his view, only the princes of the people originally lived in the city. To expand the population, "the rest of the people cast lots" and "bless those who willingly offered themselves to dwell in Jerusalem." In contrast to the implicit reluctance of settling within the city in 11:1-2[41] and the military nuances of this passage (cf. התנדב and vv. 6, 14), the author of 7:4ff. does not present the city as a fortress and assumes that the Judeans competed for a place of residence within its walls. Hence, he attributes a new manner of repopulating Jerusalem to the one who built the city. However, the divinely-inspired plans ("and my God placed it in my heart," 7:5a) this time do not involve the repair of the fortification (cf. the identical phrase in 2:12), but rather the correct procedures for deciding who should be allowed to live in the new(-ly built) Jerusalem. The lot-casting has been replaced by a more selective approach that permits only those whose names were found in the book that registered the עולים to take up residence in "the Holy City" (cf. 11:1).

Finally, one must explain why it was necessary to include the entirety of Ezra 2. It should be pointed out first that 7:4-72 concludes with an expression similar to the one that introduces 11:1-2 ("and they dwelt"), which suggests that one reason for repeating the list of Ezra 2 *in toto* was to prepare the reader for the transition from "their cities" to "Jerusalem, the Holy City." More importantly, however, the author of 7:4-72 has made significant changes to the list in Ezra 2. According to 11:1, the people cast lots "to bring one of ten to dwell in Jerusalem." In a study of chap. 11, Lipschits has drawn attention to the fact that the numbers in 11:4-19 (3,044) correspond to exactly one-tenth of the sum of the subtotals in Neh 7:6-71 (without slaves and the priests who could not prove their lineage. "The difference of seven persons between the total number (30,447) and the tenth part that came to settle in Jerusalem (3,044) may be explained arithmetically (the exact tenth part is 3,044.7!)."[42] While Lipschits explains these calculations solely on the basis of chap. 11 and 1 Chr 9, it seems more likely that the author of 7:4-72, who adapted Ezra 2 to a new purpose, was responsible for this correlation.[43] This assumption would explain why the

---

41 Cf. the reluctance behind the choice to cast lots in 10:35. Williamson writes: "…this did not mean, however, that the choice was a welcome one. It is therefore probable that those who volunteered were included in the ten percent rather than being added to it, since they reduced the number of those who had to move despite their preference to remain where they were" (1985: 351).

42 2002: 432.

43 This is all the more likely if 1 Chr 9 is a later adaptation of Neh 11. Lipschits does not explain why the direction of dependency must be from 11:1ff. to 7:6ff.. Much easier is the

subtotals of Ezra 2 do not at all correspond to one-tenth of the number of Jerusalem's residents in Neh 11. Considering these numerical differences, it seems that the author of Neh 7:4-72, who severed 7:1-3* from 11:1-2 (and 3ff.), no longer understood the human freewill offerings of 11:2 (המתנדבים האנשים) in its military sense of "enlistment" (as in 2 Chr 17:16) and took the description of the human tithes in 11:1 *literally*. In keeping with the possible apocalyptic influences already noted in 7:4ff., and the concern for numbers and calculations in this tradition, he has presented Nehemiah doing the necessary arithmetic, adding to the subtotals of Ezra 2 and subtracting the number of priests who "sought their register in the genealogy, but were not found" (v. 64). As a result, precisely one-tenth of the inhabitants of Judah moves from "their cities" (7:72) and come "to dwell in Jerusalem, the Holy City" (11:1).[44]

13.3.4 The Late Character of 7:1-3* + 11:1-2

In conclusion to our discussion, it should be pointed out that the fortification of the city in 7:1-3* + 11:1-2 (and 3ff.), although dated to the Persian period in Ezra-Neh, reflects a much later period. The designation עיר הקדש appears only in very young texts (e.g., Isa 48:2; 52:1; 66:20; Joel 4:17; Dan 9:24; 1 Macc 2:7; 2 Macc 1:12; 3:1; 9:14; Sir 36:12; 49:6; Tob 13:9; CD XX 22). Moreover, the closest parallel to Neh 11 (aside from 1 Chr 9) is the description of Jehosaphat's armies in 2 Chr 17:12-19 (cf. esp. vv. 12b and 16), and it is difficult to believe that this text existed before the Hellenistic period.[45] So too, the appendix to chap. 11 in vv. 25-35 appears to presuppose the Maccabean period. Since Hebron was first recaptured from "the descendants of Esau" by Judas (1 Macc

---

supposition that the author of 7:4ff. was cognizant of 11:1ff. and "fixed the books" so that the numbers in 7:6ff. would agree with those in 11:1-19. Yet if Ezra 2 is later than Neh 7, as Lipschits seems to assume, then we would have to suppose that the author of Ezra 2 changed the subtotals of Neh 7. Yet without an apparent reason for making these changes, this assumption is tenuous. The issue of the dependency between Neh 7:4-72 and 11:3ff., however, does not have any bearing on the assertion that 11:1-2 existed before the addition of vv. 3ff. and originally followed 7:1-3*. It is not problematic for our thesis if the one responsible for the changes was the author of 11:4-19. Since, however, one cannot explain why Nehemiah's account concludes after v. 72, it seems more likely that the reason for repeating the entire list of Ezra 2 was to correlate the subtotals with chap. 11.

44 With regard to the (false) sum of the subtotals mentioned in the lists (42,360), Gunneweg pointed out: "Die zuverlässigsten unter den differierenden Daten über die Exulanten enthält die Liste Jer 52,28-30, wo als Gesamtzahl dreier Deportationen 4 600 angegeben wird.... Die Endsumme der Liste ist fast das Zehnfache der Zahl der Weggeführten..." (1985: 66).

45 See Steins' discussion of the problems of dating 1-2 Chr and his arguments supporting the consensus on the continent that it must have been composed sometime during the Hellenistic period (1995: 491ff.).

5:65), Hölscher, Mowinckel, Rudolph, Gunneweg, and Böhler[46] are most probably correct in taking a different approach than that of von Rad, Vogt, and Williamson.[47] The latter treat the list as an idealistic depiction based on Josh 15. While the similarities with Josh 15, which is probably also quite late, are undeniable, the addition in vv. 25-35 may describe the actual borders of Judah after the Maccabean victories. This would agree with the relative chronology of 7:4-10:40. The text 7:4-72 reflects apocalyptic developments, which most likely do not predate the Hellenistic period. The parallels with Ezra 2 created by the repetition of the list seem to have sparked the composition of Neh 8:1-10:30. When read against the backdrop of Ezra 2-3, this literary block witnesses to a growing division between temple and Torah in the Hellenistic period. The prayer in chap. 9, moreover, employs a key expression "at their pleasure" (9:37; cf. v. 24) that occurs elsewhere only in very late texts (Dan 8:4; 11:16, 36; Esth 1:8 and 9:5).[48] The addition of the stipulations in 10:31-40 supports these assertions insofar as a collective observance of the Sabbath year (v. 32b) and a regular payment of the temple tax (v. 33) is not witnessed until the second cent. BCE.[49] The mention of Jojarib in 12:6, 19 – in either the primary strata or the supplements of the passage – is dated by most scholars to the Hasmonean or Maccabean periods.[50] Finally, the external evidence from Ben Sirach, 2 Maccabees, 1 Esdras and *1 Enoch* indicates that Nehemiah's account was widely (and "actively") read in the second century.[51] In light of both this external evidence and the relative chronology of 7:4-10:40, one may, with all due caution, assert that also 7:1-3* + 11:1f.(4ff.), which presents the fortification and population of Jerusalem, does not mirror an Achaemenid administrative policy in Syria-

---

46 Hölscher (1923: 551), Rudolph (1949: 189), Mowinckel (1964[I]: 151), Gunneweg (1987: 148f.) and Böhler (1997: 390f.).

47 See von Rad (1930: 21ff.), Vogt (1966: 68), Williamson (1985: 347ff.), and most recently the literature cited by Lipschits (2002: 430-n. 35).

48 Argued by, *inter alia*, Gunneweg (1987: 126ff.), Mathys (1994), Blenkinsopp (1988: 302f.). Boda (1998) and Bautch (2003: 121ff.) have dated the prayer much earlier.

49 See Kellermann (1967: 40), Williamson (1985: 335), and Gunneweg (1987: 137).

50 Cf., e.g., Hölscher (1923: 553), Rudolph (1949: 192), Mowinckel (1964[I]: 154f.), Kellermann (1967: 108), Gunneweg (1988: 153), and Blenkinsopp (1988: 334).

51 As Blenkinsopp writes with regard to the mention of Nehemiah and Sirach's disregard of Ezra: "We can readily understand the inclusion of Nehemiah, the intransigent opponent of Tobiah the Ammonite, in light of Jesus ben Sirach's attachment to the Oniad priestly house and its contemporary representative Simon II, and in the context of the bitter Oniad-Tobiad rivalry under Ptolemaic and Seleucid rule. We may also suppose that Ezra's singleminded theocratic ideal was uncongenial to the author, who took political realities, and the possibility and desirability of political autonomy, seriously. [...] In this respect he may be seen to anticipate the Hasmonean ideology which looked to Nehemiah as the real founder of the commonwealth and the ideal of political-religious leadership. – The Hasmoneans, who traced their ancestry through the priest Jojarib of the first return (1 Chron. 9:10; Neh 11:10; 12:6, 19; cf. 1 Chron. 24:7), seem to have cherished the memory of Nehemiah" (1988: 55f.).

Palestine (*pace* Hoglund).[52] Rather, it reflects the internal move in Judah toward political autonomy during the Hellenistic period.

The Literary Link between 7:1-3* and 11:1-2 (+ 12:27ff.)

7:1-3* (See the table in §12.3.)
> 4 The city was wide and large, but the people within it were few and no houses had been built. 5 Then my God put it into my mind to assemble the nobles and the officials and the people to be enrolled by genealogy. And I found the book of the genealogy of those who were the first to go up, and I found the following written in it: 6 These are the people of the province who came up out of the captivity of those exiles whom King Nebuchadnezzar of Babylon had carried into exile; they returned to Jerusalem and Judah, each to his town.
> VV. 7-72.

11:1 And the princes of the people resided in Jerusalem; and the rest of the people cast lots *to bring one out of ten to reside in Jerusalem*, the Holy City, while nine-tenths remained in the other towns.

2 And the people blessed all those who willingly offered to reside in Jerusalem.
> 3 These are the leaders of the province who lived in Jerusalem; but in the towns of Judah all lived on their property in their towns: Israel, the priests, the Levites, the temple servants, and the descendants of Solomon's servants. And in Jerusalem dwelt certain of the descendants of Judah and certain of the descendants of Benjamin....
> vv. 4ff.

12:27ff. Now at the dedication of the wall of Jerusalem they sought out the Levites in all their places, *to bring them to Jerusalem* to celebrate the dedication with rejoicing, with thanksgivings and with singing, with cymbals, harps, and lyres....

13.4 The Analogy of the Temple Dedication in Ezra 6:16-22

In this section, we adduce final support for the assertion that the notice 12:27ff.* was the first text to be inserted between 6:17-19 and 13:4ff. before the addition of 7:1-3* + 11:1-2. The most compelling evidence for both the isolation of the dedication account to vv. 27 and 43 as well as the original position of the short notice after 6:17ff. is the analogy of the conclusion to the temple-building account in Ezra 1-6. Both Ezra 6:16-22 and Neh 12:27ff. not only designate the ceremonies חנכות, but they also report in a strikingly similar manner of (1) purification rites, cf. 12:30 with Ezra 6:20; (2) the presence of the priests and the Levites, (3) sacrificial activities, cf. 12:43 with Ezra 6:17; (4) the ordination of the priests and Levites, cf. 12:44 with Ezra 6:18; (5) the "great joy" that accompanies the festivities, cf. 12:43, 44b with Ezra 6:16, 22; and (6) the

---

52 1992: 225f.

centrality of the House of God, cf. 12:40. Given these numerous parallels, it seems rather unlikely that the two passages were composed in isolation from one another.

The analysis in the preceding chapter has shown that the earliest layer of the account, which may be found in the third-person notice in vv. 27 and 43, does not constitute an integral part of the wall-building report. These verses presuppose Ezra 6:16-22 – and thus Ezra 1-6 in its penultimate form. The author probably intended to amplify the parallels between the Neh 1-6 and Ezra 1-6.[53] Within the final form(s) of Ezra-Neh, the building of wall and the centralization of Judah represent the final stage in the building of Jerusalem, which began with the construction of the temple. Now, if the author of Neh 12:27, 43 intended to present the dedication of the wall as the culmination of Ezra 1-6, it would seem that the dedication account has been conceived for the notice of completion in Neh 6:15, just as the account of the temple dedication follows directly upon the notice of completion in Ezra 6:15. There is a problem, however: We have seen that Neh 13:4-31 must have originally been connected to 6:17-19. While Rudolph was most likely correct in postulating 6:17-19 as a supplement to the building report,[54] this paragraph must have been originally conjoined to 13:4ff.[55] Since the assumption is quite tenuous that the account of the dedication has been *transposed* (an approach that renders an attempt to reconstruct the account futile), we conclude that it was *composed* for a context between 6:17-19 and 13:4ff.

With regard to the context of 12:27 and 43, our analyses of chap. 7 have demonstrated the probability that 7:4-72 has been inserted between the third-person notices in 7:1-3* and 11:1-2. As argued in the next chapter, the repetition of the list from Ezra 2 in Neh 7 has inspired the composition of Neh 8-10, which de-emphasizes the centrality of the temple in favor of the Torah. Hence, prior to the composition of 7:4-72 and 8:1-10:40 (as well as 12:1-26), the account of the dedication would have followed directly upon the account of the

---

53   In support of the *opinio communis* that Neh 12:43 builds upon Ezra 3 and 6, Steins writes: "Zwei Parallelen unterstreichen die aufgewiesene Korrespondenz zwischen der Tempel- und der Mauerweihe: Neh 12,43 zeichnet mit dem Motiv des "aus der Ferne" hörbaren Freudenjubels (שמח nif) ein unzweideutig positives Kontrastbild zum "bis in die Ferne' hörbaren 'Lärm der Freude und Weinens' in Esra 3,13. Wie in Esr 6,22 wird dabei festgehalten, daß Gott Urheber dieser Freude ist (שמח pi). Aber der Mauerweihebericht Neh 12,27-43 greift nicht nur mit den Motiven von 'Einweihung und Freude' (vgl. 12,27) Elemente aus dem Bericht über die Grundsteinlegung und Weihe des Tempels auf und faßt sie zusammen, sondern stellt sich betont als Überbietung dieses Geschehens dar: allein fünf Mal wird in 12,43 die Basis שמחה verwendet (vgl. dazu noch 12,27), darunter je einmal in der Adjektivverbindung שמחה גדולה 'große Freude' und in der Konstruktusverbindung שמחת ירושלם 'die Freude Jerusalems'" (1995: 192).

54   Rudolph maintained, however, that Nehemiah himself was responsible for the supplementation of his work (1949: 139).

55   See the arguments in §9.2.2.

security and population measures in 7:1-3* + 11:1-2 (and v. 3ff.). However, it is also likely that a later author added 11:1-2, which agrees with both the description of the defense measures in 7:1-3* as well as the analogies of ancient Near Eastern building inscriptions that present the population of the city before its dedication. Accordingly, this leaves us with only two texts before the notice of completion: 6:17-19 and 7:1-3.

That the account of the dedication originally followed 7:1-3 is a view shared by many scholars. However, one must explain the rough transitions from the notice of completion in 6:15f. and 7:1-3 to the dedication account. Nehemiah begins by reporting that the wall was finished (6:15-16) and then notes briefly that the Judean nobles were in contact with Tobiah during the days of construction (vv. 17-19). Thereafter, he recounts his defense measures for Jerusalem (7:1-3) and finally describes the dedication ceremonies (12:27ff.). Thus, between the notice of completion and the account of the dedication, the paragraphs 6:17-19 and 7:1-3 make for a very disjointed narrative. The recent studies of Karrer and Reinmuth follow Williamson and Throntveit in concluding that the texts 5:1-19 and 13:4-31 have been composed at a later date, yet they fail to address the incongruities inherent in the sequence of paragraphs 6:15-16, 17-19; 7:1-3(4-5a) and 12:27ff.*.[56] Reinmuth, for example, points out the differences between in chaps. 1-4 and 6, on the one hand, and chaps. 5 and 13, on the other.[57] Yet he surprisingly does not point out that 6:17-19, which *cannot* be separated from the account of the building, censures the aristocracy just as much as chaps. 5 and 13 does. If one attributes these chapters to Nehemiah's subsequent literary activities, then the negative tone in 6:17-19 creates even greater dissonance. It leaves the reader hanging inasmuch as s/he does not know how Nehemiah treated the problem posed by the aristocracy.

An alternative to Williamson's and Throntveit's proposal – that Nehemiah added 13:4ff. at a later date – is offered by Kratz's work.[58] While agreeing that the final chapter must constitute an addition to the building report, Kratz does not resort to transposition hypotheses and thus draws the necessary conclusion that 6:17-19; 7:1-3, 4ff., etc. must also be secondary. Observing the analogies

---

56 Williamson (1985: xxvii), Throntveit (1992: 120ff.), Karrer (2001: 145f.), and Reinmuth (2002: 328ff.).

57 "Der Wiederaufbau unter der Führung des Statthalters erscheint dabei zugleich als gemeinsames Projekt der Vornehmen und Vorsteher, der Priester und des Volkes. *Die davon zu unterscheidenden Reformen im Innern der Provinz sind jedoch mit erheblichen Auseinandersetzungen zwischen Nehemia und den führenden Kreisen verbunden:* Schuldenerlaß, Tempelreinigung, Abgabenreform, Handelsverbot am Sabbat und eine Mischehenscheidung in den Reihen des Kultpersonals bringen Nehemia, die kleinbäuerliche Bevölkerung Judas und die niederen priesterlichen und levitischen Gruppen in Opposition zu den Vornehmen und Vorstehern sowie den einflußreichen Kreisen der Priesterschaft" (2002: 335f. – my italics).

58 2000: 69.

with Ezra 6:15, he contends that the dedication account followed originally on Neh 6:15, and everything in between must have been added by later hands.

Though one cannot deny that the account must have once stood in closer proximity to 6:15, it is more tenable, in view of the literary link between 6:17-19 and 13:4ff., to suppose that it did not exist before the composition of 6:17-19. The similarities between 12:27ff. and Ezra 6 indicate that the latter has directly influenced the former. It seems, therefore, that the author intended to present the dedication festivities immediately after the notice of completion, yet did not wish to separate the paragraph 6:17-19 from those in 6:2-4, 5-9 and 10-14, which share a common theme.

Although these paragraphs appear at first sight to be unified, our analysis in §7.4 has demonstrated that they are actually only loosely related. First, vv. 2-4 and 5-9 report that Sanballat and Geshem were *sending* messages and letters to Nehemiah. So too, vv. 10-14 makes plain that God had not *sent* Shemaiah (v. 12) and that Tobiah was the instigator of the attempted calumny. Yet while the latter plays a role in vv. 16-19, the nobles of Judah do not "send" (שלח, six times in vv. 2-14) letters to him; rather the letters "were going (הלך) from" many of them to him.[59] Moreover, the primary antagonist is no longer Tobiah, but rather the Judean aristocrats.[60] This narrative continues in 13:4-9, which recounts "the evil" that Eliashib committed for Tobiah. Apparently, the author of 12:27ff. interpreted 6:17-19, in which Tobiah sends letters (אגרת, cf. v. 5), as inseparably tied to the account in 6:2-14. Making a compromise with Ezra 6:15ff., he found the transition between 6:19 and 13:4 to be the most appropriate place to insert the account of the dedication. Although composed in the third-person, the notice in 12:27, 43* was short enough not to be too intrusive and may even be understood as Nehemiah's *own* words (cf. the third-person accounts in 3:1-32, 5:1-5; 6:15; 13:4-5). Subsequently, the same or a second author added 7:1-3. Considering the third-person substratum (vv. 1aα,b 3) and the introduction ("And when the wall had been built...."), this paragraph appears to presuppose the insertion of 12:27 and 43.

The most compelling evidence for this thesis is provided by 6:19b. After the introduction "in those days" (v. 17a), one would expect only participial expressions. We find these in vv. 17a-19a (as well as in 13:15ff. and 23f., which begin likewise with the phrase "in those days"). In 6:19b, however, the formulation switches to a *qatal* (אגרות שלח טוביה ליראני). Both the sudden change of subject (from the nobles in vv. 17-19a to Tobiah) and the fact that every word in it recurs several times in vv. 1-14 suggest strongly that this clause, which lacks an

---

59   מרבים חרי יהודה אגרתיהם הולכות על־טוביה, v. 17a; cf. also "coming" (באות) in v. b.
60   For the exception in v. 19b, see below.

introductory *waw*, is indeed editorial.[61] As argued in §§7.5.3 and 9.2.2, a redactor added v. 19b in order to integrate the paragraph to the accounts of the enemy's attempts to intimidate Nehemiah in vv. 1-14. With this addition, he has attempted to remedy the open-ended narrative in vv. 17-19a after he separated it from 13:4ff. by inserting new material. And this new material probably consisted of only 12:27ff.*. In the maturation process of Ezra-Neh, the narrative was successively expanded with new introductions in 7:1-12:26.

Thus, in order to explain the interweaving of first-person with third-person accounts in 7:1-13:3, one must begin with the connection between 6:17-19a and 13:4ff. and the gap created by the insertion of the brief notice regarding the dedication ceremonies. This gap gradually widened with the addition of the material in 7:1-12:26.

13.5 Conclusions

In an attempt to reconstruct the growth of chaps. 8-12, we began (§13.2) by demonstrating the priority 12:27 vis-à-vis 11:3ff. and 13:10-13, 14b. According to the conclusion of §12.2.1, the notice in 12:27 belongs together with 12:43 to the earliest layer of the account of the dedication ceremonies. The information in 12:27 that the Levites did not yet reside in Jerusalem contradicts 11:3ff. and 13:10-13, 14b. The best solution to this contradiction is the assumption that 12:27 predates these texts. That the third-person notice in 12:27 is older than the first-person account in 13:14ff. supports our suggestion in §12.1-3 that redactors have inserted Nehemiah's words in 12:31-43 and 7:1-3 into their narrative frameworks.

Turning to 7:1-3, we observed (§13.3) that this paragraph, with its emphasis on the security of the city, forms a literary and conceptual connection to 11:1ff. The disruption of this link by the insertion of 7:4-72, which contradicts 7:3 in presenting the houses as not yet built (cf. v. 4b), has been inserted in order to present a more selective process for populating Jerusalem (§§13.3.1-2). Nehemiah now takes a census to ensure that the future residents of the newly built Jerusalem can identify themselves as the Golah. To prove their genealogy, he employs the roster of the returnees in Ezra 2.

From these findings, it follows that the description of the dedication in 12:27 and 43 was the first text to sever 6:17-19a from 13:4ff. (§13.4). That it does not appear directly after the notice of completion in 6:15f. (as the account of the temple dedication in Ezra 6:16ff.) must be explained as the author's attempt to

---

61 Cf. "Tobiah" three times in vv. 1, 13, 14; "letter" in v. 5; "send" in vv. 2, 3, 4, 5, 8, 12; and "fear" in vv. 9, 13, and 14. Most importantly, the theme of each paragraph is the intimidation of Nehemiah; the addition of v. 19b introduces this theme to vv. 17-19.

position the account as close as possible to 6:15f. without distancing 6:17-19a from the paragraphs in vv. 1-14, all of which share the theme of written correspondence. After severing 6:17-19a from 13:4ff., the redactor noticed that the former paragraph was left dangling. To remedy this situation, he added 6:19b, and by drawing upon the terminology of 6:1-14, he prompts us to read 6:17-19a as part and parcel of the foregoing account.

In the next and concluding chapter, we turn our attention to the final additions of the account of the dedication in 8:1-10:40. Our aim will be both to show that this material was created specifically for its present setting and to examine what it contributes to the final form of the book.

The Gradual Separation of 6:17-19 from 13:4ff.		
Mid 5th Century BCE		*2nd Century BCE(?)*
6:17-19*		
	7:1-3*	
	7:4-72	
	8:1-18	
	9:1-3*	
	9:(4)5-31 + 10:1a, 30aβb	
	10:31-32, 40b	
	10:33ff.	
	11:1-2	
	11:3ff.	
	11:25-36	
		12:1-26
12:27-43*		
	12:44-47*	
	13:1-3	
13:4-9, 14a*		
	13:10-13, 14b*	
13:15-22*		
13:23-31*		

14. The Final Form of the Book in Neh 12:44-13:3 and Neh 8-10

14.1 Introduction

In this concluding chapter, we turn our attention to the final additions to Ezra-Neh in 12:44-13:3 and 8:1-10:40 and examine what these texts contribute to the canonical form of the book. According to the following proposals, which synthesize the findings of our study, the authors of Neh 8-10 portray the preparations for the dedication of the wall in a manner that shifts the focus from the temple and priesthood in Ezra 1-6, 7-8 to the Torah and laypeople. Proceeding from Ezra's new identity as a *sōfēr* in the additions to Ezra 7 and the recognition of the (im)purity of both priests and laypeople in Ezra 9-10, these authors direct the reader's attention away from the temple *in* Jerusalem and to Jerusalem *itself* and the inhabitants of the province. All the activities recounted in the literary complex of Neh 8-10 take place in the seventh month, yet where one would expect a reference to the altar, high priest and sacrifices, there is only Ezra, "all the people," and the reading of the Torah. Whereas Neh 8 provides a contrast to Ezra 3 by portraying a worship service and the celebration of Sukkoth without the temple and sacrifices, the accounts in Neh 9-10 depict "the children of Israel" confessing their sins and initiating a new era in the Restoration with their pledge to the Mitzvoth. We begin by showing that an editor has not given 8:1-10:40 a new literary setting (§14.2). Then in (§14.3) we review the findings of our study and retrace the developments in Ezra-Neh which lead up to the new climax given to the book by the final authors.

14.2 The Youngest Additions to Ezra-Neh

14.2.1 The Paragraphs in 12:44-13:3

Our conclusion that the dedication account has been gradually moved to its present position by the composition of Neh 7-10 is corroborated by the paragraphs in 12:44-13:3, which according to the *opinio communis* constitute redactional supplements.[1] Though not always conceded by past research, these paragraphs are not unified, and we may follow Noth, Rudolph, Kellermann, Gunneweg, and Clines in isolating the earliest layer in vv. 44-45* and attributing the mention of the singers and porters in v. 45, and all of 46-47, to later hands.[2] The redaction of 12:44-47 parallels the additions in 12:28ff., 35f., 41f., which assign the singers a central function at the dedication ceremonies.[3]

Most recently, Reinmuth has posited 12:44 and 13:1-3 as the oldest layer of these paragraphs, which is characterized by "der explizite Verweis auf die Tora (12,44: 13,3) und der Bezug auf die Reformmaßnahmen Nehemias."[4] This proposal is not compelling. Although both v. 45 and 13:1-3 refer to the Torah, the first passage confines its contents, with Ezra 3:1-8 and 6:18, to priestly ordinances. In Neh 13:1-3, "the book of Moses" contains a passage from Deut (23:3ff.), which is read before and followed by "the people." Moreover, התורה in 12:44a, which severs מנאות from לכהנים וללוים, appears to be a gloss. So too, the syntax of 13:1 differs from that of 12:43 and 44. Were 13:1-3 drafted by the hand responsible for 12:44, we would expect a *wayyiqtol* pl. to be followed by ביום ההוא and a direct object.[5] 13:1, however, begins with ביום ההוא and is formulated in the passive voice (נקרא בספר משה באזני העם). Finally, v. 46f. forms a retrospective conclusion (see also שמח in v. 44b with v. 43) after which 13:1-3 comes unexpectedly. Thus, we may embrace Noth's conclusion, which follows the lead of Hölscher and treats *all* of 12:27-47 as older than 13:1-3.[6] The latter paragraph may "als sehr später Zuwachs zu beurteilen sein, der sehr lose mit dem blassen 'an jenem Tag' an das Vorangehende angehängt ist. [...] Es handelt sich wohl um eine späte Lesefrucht aus Dtn. 23, 4-6."[7] This prolepsis serves as a hinge between 12:47 and 13:4ff.

The weighty evidence indicating that 13:1-3 must be younger than the formation of 12:27-47 belies the commonly espoused view that "the editor" of Ezra-

---

1   This consensus takes its point of departure from Meyer's remark: "Der Chronist hat hier einmal empfunden, daß cap. 13 einer Vorbereitung bedurfte, und deshalb 12, 44-47 den Bericht über die Vorrathskammern und die Abgaben für die Priester und Leviten eingelegt" (1896: 97-n. 2).

2   Noth (1943: 131 – "Der Zusatzcharakter von V.46.47 zeigt sich auch daran, daß mit Rücksicht darauf in V.45 'die Sänger und Türhüter' sekundär als offensichtliche Glosse eingefügt worden sind."), Rudolph (1949: 201), Kellermann (1967: 47), Clines (1984: 235 – does not include v. 47 to the redaction), and Gunneweg (1987: 162). See also Hölscher (1923: 558).

3   The identification of the singers with a Levitical *clerus minor* in vv. 1-26 may presuppose the redaction of 12:27-47, in which the singers are juxtaposed with the Levites. In v. 27, the service of the Levites is required, to which the author of v. 28f. responds by depicting the singers assembling. The same can be seen in v. 45: "And they performed the service of their God and the service of purification – i.e., the singers and gatekeepers."

4   2002: 261.

5   12:43a: ויפקדו בים ההוא אנשים על־הנשכות and v. 44a: ויזבחו ביום־ההוא זבחים גדולים

6   Hölscher (1923: 557).

7   Noth (1943: 131).

Neh transposed the account of the dedication to its present context after Neh 8-10. Nehemiah's report in 13:4ff. seems to have inspired the composition of 12:44f.*, and the expansions in 12:46f. agree with the lists in 11:3ff. and 7:5ff. insofar as the singers and gatekeepers are distinguished from that the priests and Levites. This contrasts with 12:1-26 as well as vv. 32-36, 41f., in which the singers have already attained the status of priests. Before the composition of Neh 8-10, and perhaps Ezra 7-10, the expansions in 12:44-47 strengthen the parallels between the dedication of the wall and the conclusion to Ezra 1-6. The expression "in the days of Zerubbabel and in the days of Nehemiah" (12:47) and the late addition of the reference to Ezra (12:36) suggest that Nehemiah and Ezra had not yet established a diarchy corresponding to Jeshua and Zerubbabel.

On the other hand, the author of 13:1-3 clearly presupposes the present shape and placement of Neh 8. "On that day the book of Moses was read in the ears of the people..." (13:1). The only other place in Ezra-Neh that reports a מקרא־התורה is Neh 8:1-10:30. Without 13:1-3, the account of the ceremonies on "that day" in 12:27-45* + 13:4-31 could have stood directly after the lists in 11:1ff. (and then 7:4-72), which portray the population of the city before its dedication, as in several extant ancient Near Eastern building accounts. Both 7:1-3 (after the editing of 7:1b) and 11:1-20 refer to the Levites and gatekeepers as individual guilds, which agrees with 12:27-45 (see also משמרת in 7:3b and 12:45).[8] In 8:1-9:37, the gatekeepers (and singers) do not appear, yet in this section, the reading of the Torah comes to the fore. As contended below, the repetition of Ezra 2 in 7:4ff. has occasioned the composition of chaps. 8-10, which severs 7:1-3* from (11:1ff.) 12:27-47 + 13:4ff. Accordingly, the account of Ezra reading the ספר תורת משה in "the ears of all the people" (8:1ff., cf. v. 3) prepared the way for the expansion of the building account with 13:1-3, which describes the ספר משה being read again "in the ears of the people."

14.2.2 The Literary Setting(s) of 8:13-18 and 9:1-10:40

Taking our point of departure from the evidence furnished by the addition of 13:1-3, we may now examine the composition of the account of the Torah-reading on the first day of the seventh month (8:1-12) and the following texts (9:1-10:40) that expand this narrative. With respect to the provenance of Neh 8-10, few would disagree that the description of the Sukkoth festival in 8:13-18 presupposes the account in vv. 1-12. I submit that a later hand has appended vv. 13-18 in order to illustrate how the community not only read the Torah, but also

---

8   In 11:1ff. the theme of repopulation-measures resumes, which suggests that it was interpolated between 7:4ff. and 12:27ff.*.

discovered a commandment that they followed with innovation and without hesitation.[9]

The evidence for the secondary character of vv. 13-18 is substantial. First, this section concludes in a manner that does not leave the reader waiting for a continuation. The assembly dissolves in order to make merry after the monumental occasion of reading the Torah. After v. 12 the narrative in vv. 13-18 is not only anticlimactic, but also the commands to "go your way" and to "send portions to those without" suggest that the people actually returned to "their cities" whence they came (cf. 7:72). It is therefore difficult to explain their presence in Jerusalem on the immediately following day?[10]

Second, the clues left by the redactions of these texts attest to the supplementary character of vv. 13-18. While the narrative in vv. 1-12 is well rounded, the insertion of v. 2,[11] which dates the events precisely to "the first day," prepares the reader for a continuation reporting further activities throughout the month. Conversely, v. 18a interrupts vv. 17b and 18b by noting that "he read in the book of the Torah of God from the first to the last day...." Since the mere reading of the Torah is not the subject of vv. 13-18, the addition of v. 18a indicates that a redactor attempted to unify the chapter.[12]

Third, the wording of vv. 13-18 differs starkly from that of the foregoing paragraph. While in vv. 1-12, "all the people" (כל־העם – used nine times) initiate the action (cf. v. 1), in vv. 13-18 the leaders of "all the people" gather around Ezra to continue their studies (v. 13). Neither this group nor the priests are mentioned in vv. 1-12, and the simple designation העם, which appears only in the additions of vv. 1-12, is integral to vv. 13-18. These terminological differences may be compared to the different descriptions of the Torah.

If vv. 13-18 have been appended to chap. 8, the account in chaps. 9-10 must be even younger. With respect to the latter, several scholars argue that it may have originally stood closer to Ezra 10.[13] The transition from the glee during the feast of Sukkoth to the mourning on the twenty-fourth of the month is extremely rough. Nevertheless, this approach is difficult to follow. Not only is it implausible that the Ezra narrative recounted the events of one year, but also the statement in 9:2a that "the seed of Israel was separated from all foreigners"

---

9   See Galling (1954: 234) and more recently Kratz (2000: 89).
10 In contrast to the depiction of the former day in which the festivities began before the break of dawn (v. 3), the reader is not told how early this meeting took place.
11 See the excursus at the end of this section for a literary-critical analysis of vv. 1-12.
12 This addition may be compared to the supplement in 6:19b, which assimilates the final paragraph to vv. 1-14. See §13.4.
13 Torrey (1896: 31ff.), Rudolph (1949: 155), Williamson (1985: 308ff.), Kosters (1895: 64ff.), Hölscher (1923: 544). Noth (1943: 148f.) and Kellermann (1967: 32ff.) have argued for the unity of chaps. 8-10.

has most likely been inserted into the passage.[14] Without this statement, however, Neh 9 and Ezra 10 have nothing in common. To be consistent, one would have to argue that notices of separation in Ezra 6:21 and Neh 13:1-3 also originally belonged to Ezra's account.[15] Furthermore, the literary complex in chaps. 8-10 appear to intend to portray a development: Ezra reads the Torah on the first day. On the second day, he assists the leaders of the community in reading the Torah. And finally, "the children of Israel" read the Torah on the twenty-fourth day – without Ezra or the community leaders.[16]

Excursus II: Evidence of Editorial Activity in 8:1-12

The greatest difficulty posed by Neh 8:1-12 is the relationship of v. 3 to the remaining verses. "And he read therein before the street in front of the Water Gate from first light until midday in the presence of all the men and the women and those who could understand. And the ears of all the people were attentive unto the Book of the Torah." This information, according to which Ezra has already completed the reading, is provided prematurely in the narrative. In the very next verses, Ezra has not yet ascended the wooden tower (v. 4), let alone unrolled the scroll (v. 5).

According to a proposal of Bertholet, which has heavily influenced the subsequent explanation of the narrative structure, "die folgenden Verse [vv. 4ff.]

---

14 "And they stood…" (v. 2b) requires the antecedent subject in v. 1. The verb in the *niphal* and the change of subject is intrusive.

15 Ezra 6:21 ("and all that had separated themselves") and Neh 13:1-3 ("and they separated from Israel all the mixed multitude"). The notices of separation throughout Ezra-Neh may be understood as the attempt on the part of their authors to portray each highpoint in the history of the Restoration accompanied by a commitment toward ethnic purity.

16 See Excursus I at the end of chap. 9, where it is argued that 10:1ff. was drafted as a continuation to the prayer (either 9:31 or 9:37). – The date in 9:1, despite insistence of many scholars to the contrary, disagrees with the provision for celebrating Sukkoth for seven (or eight) days beginning with the fifteenth day of the seventh month (cf. Lev 23:39, 41). According to 9:1, the "children of Israel" gathered on the twenty-fourth of the month, yet 8:18b reports that the celebration of Sukkoth lasted seven days and concluded on the eighth with "a solemn holiday" (cf. Num 29:35-38). Had the author of 9:1ff. intended to align 8:13-18 with the instructions for an eight-day celebration in P, we would expect the third assembly to take place on the twenty-second or twenty-third day, yet not on the twenty-*fourth*. In order to understand why they meet at this time, one could compare the reference to the twenty-fourth day with Hag 1:15, 2:10, 18, 20, Zech 1:7 and Dan 10:1-4, all of which portray visions and prophecies being received on this day of the month. Most analogous is Dan 10:1-4, where Daniel mourns (אבל *hit.*) for "three full weeks" in the first month and sees a vision on the twenty-fourth day. In Neh 8:9, the people are discouraged from mourning (אבל *hit.*) on the first day of the month and return to their homes. It seems that this note in 8:1-12 inspired the author of 9:1ff. to resume the theme of mourning, depicting a delay of the time of confession until the twenty-fourth day. Perhaps we should even understand that "the children of Israel" in 9:1 mourned for three weeks, as Daniel, after they celebrated.

bringen die detaillierte Ausführung der allgemeinen Notiz v. 3."[17] Accordingly, the action of v. 3, as well as of vv. 1-2, is not to be understood as happening prior to and separate from the events described in the remainder of the account. Rather, these first three verses represent the author's narrative technique of providing a proleptic summary before the more elaborate and detailed account vv. 4-8. Although the transmitted text may be read as Bertholet proposed, the passage exhibits too many imbalances which suggest that the v. 3 has developed into a prolepsis as the chapter underwent extensive redactions. Thus, one searches vv. 4ff. in vain for a statement reporting that Ezra read the Torah, as in v. 3. While he begins ceremoniously by first opening the book and then blessing YHWH, this responsibility of reading is assumed by the Levites or the people, depending upon how one understands the relationship of v. 7b to v. 8a.[18] Conversely, the former section never mentions the Levites, and the people are depicted as playing a purely passive role: "And the ears of all the people were (fixed) on the Book of the Torah" (v. 3b).

In view of the shortcomings of the suggestion for the proleptic nature of v. 3, it seems appropriate to examine the text diachronically. Surprisingly, this route has been taken by but very few scholars. Some consider Neh 8 as a creation of "the Chronicler." Since sloppy style and contradictions are supposedly his trademark, the otherwise important indications that a text has undergone editing are not considered valid in the case of this chapter. Others admit that there are clues in Neh 8 pointing to the composite nature of the account, but they are sceptical as to the possibility of unravelling the various textual strands. Representing this hesitancy, Williamson writes: "All in all, therefore, it seems best to conclude that this chapter certainly has passed through the hands of the editor of the Ezra-Nehemiah material [...], but that he has covered his tracks sufficiently well to preclude our being able to isolate particular elements which might be his own contribution."[19] The only alternative to Bertholet's suggestion has been made by Hölscher and Mowinckel.[20] They both argued that the doublets in v. 3 – above all, the repetition of the location from v. 1 – indicate that this verse represents a later insertion. Yet, if it was not part of the original version, where then is it said that Ezra actually read from the book? Recognizing this problem, Hölscher alters the first verb in v. 8 from the plural to a singular masculine form: "and he (Ezra) read aloud from the Torah." The decision is, however, completely without support in the versional witnesses, and therefore these scholars have rectified one problem only to create another.

---

17   1902: 69. See also Rudolph (1949: 146), Kellermann, (1967: 27), Williamson (1985: 288).
18   See Veltri (1993).
19   1985: 280.
20   Hölscher (1923: 543ff.) and Mowinckel (1965: 46ff.).

When one examines the relationship of v. 3 to its surroundings more closely, it appears to be actually older than the immediately preceding statement in v. 2. The latter is quite easy to identify as a later insertion, since it repeats details from its context while adjusting their formulation. First, the consistently employed designation for the people in the passage, כל־העם (nine times), is exchanged in this verse for another common term, הקהל. Second, Ezra is not called "the *sōfēr*," as in the foregoing verse as well as vv. 4, 9, and 13, but rather "the priest." Third, the date at the end of the verse, "on the first day of the seventh month," forms a doublet with 7:72. Fourth, the description of the audience, "from man to woman, and all those who could understand what they heard," overlaps with the description of the people in v. 3 ('the men and the women and those who could understand'). Fifth, the masculine suffix of the prepositional phrase from ויקרא־בו in v. 3 does not agree with the feminine antecedent התורה of v. 2. The most likely candidate to which בו refers is the ספר תורת משה in v. 1. All this confirms the suspicion that v. 1 originally continued in v. 3. Without v. 2, however, the transition from v. 1 to v. 3 becomes rough. The call for the book to be brought is followed immediately by the statement that the book is read. That the book is brought is only implied. Although v. 2, with its peculiar wording, is probably not original, the information it provides is exactly what the reader desires. This dissonance was probably one of the factors that motivated a later redactor to fill in the gap in the narration.

Now if v. 2 has been added, it is quite probable that the remaining incoherencies in the passage are the product of editorial work. In the original formulation of the account, it seems that "Ezra, the *sōfēr*" is simply called upon to bring the Torah (v. 1); he then reads it and blesses his audience (vv. 3 and 6). Nehemiah (sic!) finally proclaims the day holy (v. 9* - without "Ezra, the priest, the *sōfēr*") and sends the people home (vv. 9-10) "to make merry" (vv. 10 and 12a).[21]

14.2.3 The Provenance of 8:1-12

Having concluded with Galling that 8:13-18 and all of 9:1-10:40 are later expansions composed for their present context, we are left only with the short account in 8:1-12* and the difficulties created by its historical and literary setting. The problems already begin in Ezra 7, from which the reader knows that Ezra arrived in Jerusalem in the seventh year of Artaxerxes' reign. This passage also describes him as "a *sōfēr* skilled in the Torah of Moses" (v. 6, cf. also vv. 10, 11, 12, 14, 25, 26). In Nehemiah's first-person account, however, this figure

---

21 See Noth (1943: 130) and Kratz (2000: 89).

does not play a role. Why then does he, after some thirteen years, suddenly make an appearance in Neh 8 and perform the task assigned to him by the king ("and teach them that know not [the laws of your God]," 7:25b)? Rather than assuming that Ezra was negligent in fulfilling his duties, the majority of scholars contend that the editor of Ezra-Neh has rearranged his account, splicing a portion of it into Nehemiah's building report. The original literary setting of Neh 8 (or at least vv. 1-12) is said to be either between Ezra 8 and 9 or after Ezra 10. Accordingly, Ezra read the Torah in the year he came to Jerusalem. With this solution, scholars believe that they may rest at ease after having solved a major source-critical problem.

Upon closer examination, however, one must admit that the problem, rather than being solved, has only grown more critical. Whereas before the "naïve" reader could suppose that the primary author of Neh 8:1-12 composed the account for its transmitted context and created what we perceive as an incongruity, the critical reconstructions require that one distinguish between an author, who was motivated primarily by a concern for historical accuracy and who told the story "correctly," and an editor, who was motivated primarily by an ideology or theology and who caused the confusion. In assigning the responsibility for these disturbances solely to the editor(s) of Ezra-Neh, this method seeks to isolate the problem to a tendentious compilation of fundamentally credible accounts.[22]

Instead of treating one problem only to create many more, we must consider the possibility that the authors of Ezra-Neh, rather than rewording, rearranging and deleting their sources, have primarily added their interpretations to them. The consideration of this possibility is rendered necessary not only by the disconcerting nature of any attempt to rearrange a piece of *literature* to the proposed *historical* sequence, but also by the serious weaknesses of the only two proposals for the original setting of Neh 8:1-12, which we examine here briefly.

14.2.3.1 The Evidence of 1 Esdras

According to the first proposal, this text formerly stood directly after Ezra 10, and 1 Esdr has preserved the original arrangement. In a study of the latter work, Böhler shows that the textual differences between it and Ezra-Neh works are not due to the vicissitudes of the transmission process, but should be treated as evidence of the existence of two consciously composed *Rezensionen* of the Ezra material. While the rebuilding of the city is not a central theme of 1 Esdras (its

---

22 This restoration of texts is not confined to the attempts to reorder them: Also those who view these attempts critically often presume that there is an historical substratum to the unbelievable accounts and that one must simply read between the lines to find it.

completion is only implicit in the narrative), the city remains in ruins in MT Ezra 1-10, and Nehemiah is the one who changes this condition. Every reference to the gates, gatekeepers, marketplaces, temple court, etc. are conspicuously lacking in MT Ezra 1-10, yet are present in 1 Esdras.[23] It cannot be mere coincidence, as Böhler argues, that exactly those passages which concern the construction of the *city* are either fully missing (the Nehemiah account) or appear at a different place (the Artaxerxes-correspondence).

Nonetheless, our genetic analyses of Ezra 1-10 make it difficult to assume that this material – or the putative *Vorlage* for 1 Esdras – ever existed independently from Nehemiah's account. In §3.3.3, we have seen how the Artaxerxes-correspondence in Ezra 4 postpones the building of the city until after the temple is built and beautified by Zerubbabel, Jeshua and Ezra. 1 Esdras presupposes the addition of these "letters" to the temple-building account and simultaneously attempts to reinterpret them in keeping with the removal of Nehemiah's report. Moreover, we have observed in §11.2.2 that Ezra 9, before the addition of the third-person narrative in Ezra 10, functioned as a new framework for interpreting the first and final passages (and thus the entirety) of the wall-building account.

Additional evidence for the dependency of Ezra 1-6 upon Nehemiah's account are the several unmistakable analogies between Ezra 4:1-5 and Neh 1-6. The former adapts the שמע-schema from Nehemiah's account (וישמעו צרי יהודה כי־בני הגולה בונים היכל ליהוה אלהי ישראל, Ezra 4:1); the closest parallels are 2:19 and 3:33 (כי־אנחנו בונים את־החומה). Whereas Sanballat, Tobiah and Geshem scoff at the building of the wall, "the adversaries of Judah and Benjamin" desire to participate in the building of the temple (Ezra 4:2). Zerubbabel, Jeshua and the rest of chiefs of the fathers of Israel must spurn their suppliants (v. 3). The analogies between their "elitist" response and the answer Nehemiah gives Sanballat, Tobiah and Geshem (Neh 2:20) are undeniable. Ezra 4:3 inverts Neh 2:20, and the statements resemble each other both stylistically and conceptually.[24]

These arguments are bolstered by several other points: Once the "people of the land" are rebuffed, they began "weakening the hands of the people of Judah" (מרפים ידי עם־יהודה, v. 4; cf. 6:22). This expression is encountered elsewhere in the book only in Neh 6:9 (ירפו ידיהם מן־המלאכה, see also v. 3). The "people of the land" were also "bribing counselors to frustrate their purposes" (וסכרים עליהם יועצים להפר עצתם, Ezra 4:5). A different spelling of the term "bribe" or "suborn" appears in Neh 6:12f. (שכר and שכור instead of סכר).

---

23 1997: 78-108.

24 Cf. Ezra 4:3a (לא־לכם ולנו לבנות בית לאלהינו) with Neh 2:20b (ולכם אין־חלק וצדקה וזכרון)
(ואנחנו עבדיו נקום ובנינו), and Ezra 4:3b (כי אנחנו יחד נבנה) with Neh 2:20a (בירושלם).

Finally, the expression "to frustrate (להפר) their plans (עצתם)" occurs only in Neh 4:9, where the antecedent of "their" is "our adversaries" (צרינו, 4:5; cf. צרים in Ezra 4:1). According to Neh 2:19-20, the division with Sanballat was precipitated by the building of the wall, as Nehemiah denied him "a portion, right and memorial in Jerusalem."[25] The author of Ezra 4:1-3 has interpreted this incident as the beginnings of the (Samaritan?) schism, yet has dated it much earlier, namely to the reign of Cyrus and the beginning of the construction of the temple in Jerusalem.[26]

Now if the authors of the Ezra material intend to balance, augment, reinterpret and correct Neh 1-6 and 13:4-31, then it is impossible that 1 Esdras antedates Ezra-Neh. Böhler's observations with regard to the variant readings indicate that 1 Esdras constitutes a document in the reception-history of Ezra-Neh. The process of reinterpreting and depreciating Nehemiah's account that began with the composition of Ezra 1-8 continues with the revisions made by 1 Esdras in which everything that has to do with Nehemiah and his work has been removed or presented as already complete.

This process concluded as Nehemiah's role came to be identified with that of Zerubbabel. In 2 Macc 1:10-2:18, for instance, Nehemiah does not build the city of Jerusalem; rather, he flourishes directly after the construction of the temple and altar (cf. 1:18), and organizes the dedication of the latter.[27] While his *name* seems to have still held influence for those who created and transmitted the legend, his *work*, as presented in his eponymous account, was fully discarded. In an attempt to win his support for a different view of the Restoration, Nehemiah was given the role traditionally assigned to Zerubbabel. The independent evidence of the Nehemiah legend in 2 Macc 1:10-2:18 witnesses to a dispute in the Hellenistic period with regard to the formative period of the Return and Restoration that centered on the person and work of Nehemiah. It took its point of departure from the composition of Ezra-Neh. The authors of 1 Esdr, instead of continuing to counterbalance Nehemiah's account in the manner of the authors of Ezra 1-6 and 7-8, excised it completely and made the changes to Ezra 1-10 and Neh 8 that left no room for the Restoration project associated with the name of Nehemiah.[28]

---

25   All the examples cited are found also in 1 Esdras (cf. 5:66ff.).

26   Significantly, *Yal.* 2 §234 brings Neh 2:20, 6:2ff. and Ezra 4:1ff. together.

27   See Torrey's essay on 2 Macc 1:1-2:18 (1900), the literature cited in Bergren's article on the Nehemiah legend in 2 Macc (1997), *1 Enoch* 89:72f., *Josippon* I 3.11d-12a, *Sanh.* 38a ("Zerubbabel...his real name is Nehemiah ben Hachaliah"), and S. *'Olam Zut.* (Gelbhaus [1902: 46]).

28   Thus, in keeping with the emphases of the 1 Esdras, the account in 9:37ff. refers to Ezra consistently and frequently as "the chief priest." Cf., e.g., Neh 8:1 with 1 Esdr 9:39. This

14.2.3.2 The Transposition-Hypothesis

An alternative to the approach based on 1 Esdras is the view which Torrey proposed, Rudolph revived, and Williamson popularized,[29] namely that Neh 8 has been transposed from its place between Ezra 8 and 9. This approach has already been touched upon in our discussion of Neh 13:23ff. and Ezra 9, where we noted several major disparities between Neh 8 and Ezra 9. While the princes play a key role in Ezra 9, they are completely absent in Neh 8. So too, the priests are mentioned before the Levites in Ezra 9:1, yet are not found in Neh 8. In the latter text, the author refers to the people nine times as כל־העם – a designation that is missing in Ezra 9. "All the people" in Neh 8 call upon Ezra to bring the Torah (v. 1). They also show their utmost respect, standing when it is opened and mourning after it is read. According to Torrey's solution, the people in Ezra 9 recognize their sins after Ezra's completes his reading (Neh 8). This is false. The princes come to Ezra and report that "the people of Israel" had sinned. Thus, the contradiction created by Neh 8 before Ezra 9 is blatant. Neh 8 presents the people positively inasmuch as they mourn after hearing the Torah read. In Ezra 9, however, they do not even recognize their own sins. It seems, therefore, that the portrayal of the people acting uprightly in Neh 8 always followed the account of them "doing according to the abominations" of the peoples of the lands in Ezra 9 and swearing to change their ways in Ezra 10.

In order to adduce additional evidence for this claim, we need only to observe that Neh 8 does not describe Ezra "teaching" the Torah (cf. Ezra 7:10, 25), but rather "reading" it.[30] Böhler correctly asserts that "[d]ie Gesetzesfeier Esras in Neh 8 ist ja nicht die Bekanntmachung eines Gesetzes…, sondern die Feier einer als ideal dargestellten Gemeinde, die durch Verlangen nach der Tora und Verständnis derselben auszeichnet."[31] Likewise, one must take issue with Williamson that Ezra "offered a new interpretation of it [the Torah] in such a way that the people came suddenly to appreciate its relevance to their own situation in a fresh way."[32] Nothing in Neh 8 indicates that Ezra *interpreted* the Torah or *taught* the people, let alone that the latter "discovered" (מצא) the prohibitions of intermarriage, as in 13:1-3 (see also the "discovery" of the prescription for Sukkoth in 8:13ff.). Now if Ezra does not "teach" in Neh 8, where do we hear that he fulfilled his commission? And for that matter, where do we hear that he appointed magistrates and judges, as Artaxerxes explicitly commanded (7:25)?

---

contrasts with Neh 8 in which he is primarily "the scribe" and only in supplementary passages "the priest" (vv. 2 and 9), yet never "the chief priest."

29 Torrey (1895: 29ff.), Rudolph (1949: 14ff.), Williamson (1977, 1985).
30 In Neh 8, the root למד does not appear, while קרא occurs four times.
31 1997: 201.

Insofar as we lack evidence of later authors who endeavored to assimilate the account to Artaxerxes' instructions to teach and appoint judges (Ezra 7:11ff.), the inconsistencies between the firman and the Ezran narrative do not appear to have disturbed the earliest readers. In contrast to this, many modern readers cannot rest easy with the inconsistencies and attempt to rearrange the text so that Ezra fulfills his tasks. Yet Neh 8 contains nothing whatsoever that matches Artaxerxes' instructions. Williamson seems to be aware of the predicament: "The account of a teaching ministry would…fit very well before Ezra 9, and for this, Neh 8 is the only candidate."[33] Yet had Neh 8 never been written, no one would have ever proposed that the Torah must have been read before Ezra 9 (or after Ezra 10), just as it is rarely, if ever, contended that a notice reporting the appointment of judges is missing at some other place in the narrative. Why then should one not leave Neh 8 where it is presently located and consider the possibility that the Ezra material has only been expanded?

Torrey's solution requires the supposition that the text not only has been transposed from its original context, but also that it has been *reformulated* from the first- to third-person. Although many are not reluctant to embrace such a supposition, the safest approach to the problems posed by Neh 8 is to focus our attention on the transmitted wording of a text. In doing so, it appears that Neh 8 was never reformulated or repositioned.

The account begins by stating that, "as the seventh month came around, the children of Israel were in their cities. Then all the people assembled with a single purpose unto the place that is before the Water Gate" (7:72b, 8:1a). The foregoing statement in 7:72a reads, "and the priests, Levites, gatekeepers, singers, from the people, the Nethinim and all Israel were in their cities." Developing the thesis of Torrey and Rudolph, Williamson contends that an editor, who combined Ezra's and Nehemiah's memoirs, found Neh 7:72b and 8:1ff. after Ezra 8. This editor noticed that the proposed conclusion to the list in Neh 7:72a concluded with a similar statement. "When, therefore, the editor wished, for theological reasons, to include Ezra's reading of the Law in his account of the climax of the work of both Ezra and Nehemiah, his attention was drawn to this particular point by close similarity."[34] While Torrey argued the transposition originated as the error of a copyist and is "due to the close resemblance" of the passages in Nehemiah's and Ezra's account,[35] Rudolph, Williamson *et al.* explain it as the "theological" intention of an editor.[36] Regardless of the reason, the

---

32 1985: 285.
33 Ibid.
34 1985: 286.
35 1895: 34.
36 At first appearances, Torrey's reasoning seems the most implausible. Actually, however, it is much less troublesome than Rudolph's and Williamson's, for Torrey realized that when

belief that Neh 7:72b has been moved to its present context is extremely problematic.

First, it is gratuitous to assume that Ezra must have reported, "as the seventh
month came around, the children of Israel were in the cities" (Neh 7:72b).
According to Ezra 7:9, the date of arrival was in the fifth month. One must thus
explain why it lasted two months before they settled in their cities. Moreover,
one must also account for the fact that Ezra does not use the expression
"children of Israel" in chaps. 7-10; it appears only in Ezra 7:7, and most would
ascribe this verse to an editor. Likewise, Ezra has one aim in mind, namely to go
up to Jerusalem with the Golah in order to deliver the royal donations (7:28).
The entire account in chaps. 7-8 focuses on the trip to *Jerusalem*. Even the third-
person notice in v. 35 refers to sacrifices at the *temple*. Likewise, Artaxerxes made
a decree that allows "the people of Israel" in his kingdom "to go up to *Jerusalem*"
(7:13), not to settle "in their cities." These findings render it difficult to maintain
that Neh 7:72b, which refers to the children of Israel *in their cities*, could have
ever appeared in Ezra 8.

Second, the term in Neh 8:1 for "assembled" (אסף) recurs twice more in the
immediately following passages, introducing the accounts of the gatherings on
the second and twenty-fourth days of the month (8:13 and 9:1). This word
appears only two times elsewhere in Ezra-Neh (Ezra 3:1 and 9:4). The synonym
of "assemble" (קבץ), however, is never employed in Neh 8-10 (nor in Ezra 1-6),
yet it is found five times in Ezra 7-10 (7:28, 8:15, 10:1, 7, 9). And the only text in
these chapters where it is not used appears to represent a late addition.[37] Now if
קבץ is employed consistently in Ezra 7-8 (twice) and 9-10 (thrice), it seems very
unlikely that Neh 8, which employs only אסף, was originally positioned between
Ezra 7-8 and 9-10 and that Neh 9:1ff., which also begins with אסף, followed
Ezra 10.[38]

The transposition-hypothesis requires the assumption that the "the editor"
consistently replaced such an insignificant term as "assemble" with its synonym.
Were insignificant terms simply substituted, then we would have to doubt
whether "the editor" has faithfully transmitted even one word of Ezra's account
in Neh 8-10. And if we cannot be confident that he has not totally revised the

---

scholarship allows an "editor" to *intentionally* rearrange and reformulate texts, it must give up
hope of reconstructing "The Ezra Story in its Original Sequence" (1910: 254).

37 In Ezra 9:4, "every one who trembled at the words of the God of Israel" assemble (אסף)
around Ezra. Were this verse integral, one could not explain that the author of 10:1ff. writes
as if he is reporting for the first time that a group had gathered around Ezra ("Now when
he had prayed...there assembled a great congregation...," v. 1). And there the term קבץ is
used. Moreover, in v. 3b, Ezra "*sat* confounded" and in v. 5, he arises at the evening *minhah*.
As a later reader added an etiology of the *haredim* in v. 4a (cf. 10:3), it became necessary for
Ezra to repeat that he "*was sitting* confounded..." in v. 4b. On independent grounds, Kratz
(2000: 86) has also ascribed this verse to a redactor.

38 Similar questions face those who propose that Neh 8 originally followed Ezra 10.

literary precursors to Neh 8-10, then there is surprisingly no "Ezran sub-stratum" to be discovered. On the other hand, there is still the *transmitted* text of Neh 8-10. Instead of giving up our interpretive task, we need only abandon belief that this editor ever existed. This means that one must begin to take the text at face value and to treat Neh 8-10, with the greatest part of biblical litera-ture, as the work of anonymous *authors* and *redactors* – in contrast to sources and an editor.

The theses that Neh 8 has been relocated from Ezra 8 or 10 are all the more frustrating when one recognizes the simple reason for the use of אסף instead of קבץ in Neh 8-10: The authors of this literary complex wrote with Ezra 3 in view. As noted above, the only other place in Ezra-Neh where אסף occurs is Ezra 3:1, and there we encounter almost a very similar statement found in Neh 8:1 ("As the seventh month came around, the children of Israel were in cities [sic]. Then the people assembled with a single purpose [ויאספו העם כאיש אחד] unto Jerusalem").[39]

As already pointed in §13.3, the original conclusion to Nehemiah's account in 7:4-72 has probably not been deleted. The author of Neh 7:4ff. appears to have simply inserted the text into the narrative of 7:1-3* + 11:1-2 (3ff.) in order to portray the builder of Jerusalem opting for a more selective approach to popu-lating the city: Only those whose names are "found written" in "the book of the genealogy of those who went up in at the beginning" qualify as residents of the newly built Jerusalem. More importantly, it seems that Nehemiah "found" the list nowhere else than in the book of Ezra-Neh inasmuch as Ezra 2:70 and 3:1a manifests three compositional levels: Originally, the list concluded with the statement, "The priests, Levites…dwelt in their cities" (2:70a). Later, a redactor affirmed that these groups represented "all Israel," who were "in their cities" (2:70b). And finally, an even younger hand re-dated the construction of the altar to the most important point in the sacrificial calendar by asserting, "And as *the seventh month* came around, the children of Israel were in (their) cities" (3:1a). The author of Neh 7:4-72 has simplified Ezra 2:70 by combining the two sentences – in a very rough-and-ready manner – into one: "And the priests, Levites, porters, singers, and of the people, and the Nethinim, i.e., all Israel dwelt in their cities." Since it is most improbable that the author of Ezra 2:70 split the one sentence of Neh 7:72a into two, we must concede that Neh 7:4-72 is later than, and directly dependent upon, Ezra 2.

---

39 According to Williamson's two-phase model for the formation of the book, an editor combined Ezra's and Nehemiah's "memoirs," moving Neh 7:72b + 8:1ff. from Ezra 8 to Neh 7:6-72a and reformulating it in the third-person. A second editor then found this combined work in Ezra 7-Neh 13* and patterned Ezra 2-3 according to the structure and wording of Neh 7-8.

The change of subject in Ezra 3:1b (= Neh 8:1a) indicates the beginning of a new unit,[40] and insofar as Neh 7:72b should be read together with the list in vv. 6-72a, the author (as well as the MT) has interpreted Ezra 2:70 and 3:1a correctly. With the insertion of 7:4-72, an earlier author severed the join between 7:1-3* and 11:1-2 (3ff.) and conferred a fully new character to the population measures for Jerusalem. The inclusion of this text created an unmistakable parallel to Ezra 2, although one also observes differences.[41] Noting both the similarities and differences, the author of Neh 8* continued the editorial activity, which began with the inclusion in 7:4ff., by composing the counterpart to Ezra 3. He also introduced the account of the Torah-reading where both lists conclude: "Now as the seventh month came around, the children of Israel were in [their] cities." In Ezra 3, this statement has been inserted to date the construction of the altar to the month when it was most needed, and it replaced the introduction in 3:1b: "And the people gathered themselves together (אסף) with a single purpose in Jerusalem...." It is precisely this older introduction that has been slightly adapted to serve as the beginning of the narrative in Neh 8:1-12 ("And all the people gathered themselves together [אסף] with a single purpose unto the place before the Water Gate...," v. 1a).

In sum, the evidence of the redactional activity in Ezra 2:70 and 3:1 indicates (i) that Ezra 2-3 has directly influenced the use of אסף instead of קבץ in Neh 8-10; (ii) that Neh 7:72b and 8:1-12 have been composed for their *present* literary settings, rather than the context of Ezra 8 or 10; (iii) that this text was always in third-person; and (iv) that a single editor is not responsible for both Ezra 3:1 and Neh 7:72b (*pace* Gunneweg and Blenkinsopp). Accordingly, Neh 7:4-72 first interrupted the account of the security and population measures in 7:1-3 and 11:1-20. The repetition of Ezra 2:1-70 and 3:1a occasioned the composition of a brief response to Ezra 3 in Neh 8:1-12, the earliest layers of which can be isolated in vv. 1, 3, 6, 9* ("and Nehemiah said..."), 10*, and 12a. Because the narrative consisted of only a few verses, the disruption to the account of the repopulation of Jerusalem in 7:4-72 and 11:1ff. was initially negligible. Moreover, the reader would have already appreciated the intended parallels between Ezra 2-4 and the list and narrative in Neh 7-8. Later authors then successively added the material in Neh 8:13-18 and 9:1-10:40 in order to bring out what is only implicit in 8:1-12*. They, not a single editor, are responsible for the forma-

---

40 Most commentators read Neh 7:72b as the beginning of the narrative, creating an almost impossible syntax. The temporal clause in v. 72bα ("And as the seventh month came around") is connected only to v. bβ ("the children of Israel were in their cities"). According to the most common approach, the main clause is 8:1a upon which 7:72b depends.

41 Cf., e.g., the "work" (Neh 7:69) instead of "the House of YHWH" (Ezra 2:68). Not only vv. 68-72 are different , but also the subtotals of each group. The latter is most likely explained as an attempt to match the figures with the statement in 11:1 that one-tenth of the population of the province settled in Jerusalem. See §13.3.3.

tion of Neh 8-10, which constitute the *youngest*, not the oldest, texts in Ezra-Neh.[42] In the following section, we review the results of our study in order to consider, in conclusion, what Neh 8-10 contributes to the reading of the book.

14.3 Concluding Survey

Taking its point of departure from the pre-critical view that everything between Neh 1:1 and 13:31 represent "the words of Nehemiah ben Hachaliah" (1:1a), the present study has developed a new model for understanding the composition of Ezra-Neh according to which the book constitutes a process (a *creatio continua*), rather than a static entity consisting of sources that have been shaped and molded according to the providential plan of one (or two) editor(s). The literary process in Ezra-Neh was initiated by the composition of Nehemiah's report and continued by generations of active readers. Thus, the interweaving of the first- and third-person material in Neh 7-13, which provoked pre-critical scholars to identify Nehemiah as the author of all of chaps. 1-13, is easy to explain if 13:4ff. originally followed 6:17-19 and was first separated by a brief account of the dedication of the wall that was formulated in the third-person (12:27 and 43).[43] While the expansions in 12:44-13:3 bridge the paragraphs in 13:4ff. to the account of the dedication, the units in 7:1-12:26 prepare the narrative for the festivities: A notice reporting what "he said" to the gatekeepers (7:1-

---

42 The question may now be posed, At what point in the composition-history of Ezra-Neh could an author have added 13:1-3 to the account of the dedication? We have seen that the earliest part of Neh 8-10 is to be isolated in vv. 1-12, which has been successively expanded with vv. 13-18*, 9:1-3, vv. 4-37, 10:1-30*, and finally 31-40*. The following observations render it quite possible that 13:1-3 was appended to (11:1ff.) 12:27-47 (13:4ff.) before the existence of 9:1-3 (and thus 9:4-10:40 and 12:1-26): In 8:1-12, Ezra reads the Torah (cf. קרא in vv. 3 and 8), to which "the ears of all the people" are attentive. In vv. 13-18, "the chief of the fathers" gather around him on the second day and discover (וימצאו כתוב ב; cf. 13:1b) the command to celebrate Sukkoth (cf. קרא in v. 18). In 9:1-3, the "children of Israel" assemble once again, this time to confess their sin and read in the Torah (cf. קרא v. 3). In these three scenes, we notice a progression from Ezra who reads (with the Levites; vv. 1-12), to the leaders who read with Ezra (vv. 13-14), and finally to the whole community which has become literate (9:1-3). In 13:1-3, "the book of Moses was read in the ears of the people (נקרא בספר משה באזני העם) and it was discovered (ונמצא כתוב בו)...." The passive voice suggests that the narrative had not yet attained the stage at which the people read without the assistance of their leaders, which contrasts with 9:3 ("and they [= the children of Israel, v. 1] read in the book of the Torah of YHWH their God..."). Furthermore, the expressions "the ears of (all) the people" and "they (it was) discovered," while absent from 9:1ff., appear in both chap. 8 and 13:1-3. If, finally, 9:1-3 were older than 13:1-3, we could not explain that 9:2a (ויבדלו זרע ישראל מכל בני נכר) appears to draw on the formulation of 13:3 (ויבדילו כל־ערב מישראל). It seems, therefore, that 13:1-3 has been added to 12:27-47 as this text followed 8:1-18 (+ 11:1ff.) and before the composition of 9:1ff.

43 See §13.4.

3*) was added to 12:27, which created a new chapter (cf. 7:1 with 4:1 and 6:1).[44] Together with 11:1-2, the report of security and repopulation measures before the dedication ceremonies parallels several ancient Near Eastern inscriptions that describe the foundation of cities.[45] When the lists in 11:3-12:26 were inserted is difficult to determine, yet it is clear that the composition of 7:4-72 presupposes the transformation of 7:1-3 and 12:27ff. into a first-person account.[46] Finally, the repetition of Ezra 2 in Neh 7 inspired the authors of 8:1ff. and 12:44-13:3 to portray how the festivities accompanying the dedication of the wall differed significantly from those celebrated at the dedication of the altar (Ezra 3) and temple (Ezra 6).[47]

The passages in Neh 7:1-13:3 conclude the process of maturation in Ezra-Neh that began with the first additions to the building-account. After the heading in 1:1a, Nehemiah announces that he was a royal cupbearer (1:11b) and recounts a scene in the first month of Artaxerxes' twentieth year when the king approved of his suggestion to be sent to Judah (2:1-6).[48] Upon arriving in Jerusalem (2:11) and inspecting the wall at night (2:15abα), he presented his plans to the rulers (2:16a, 17), who responded enthusiastically (2:18b).[49] To conclude the report, he affirms, "So we built the wall [...] and the people had a heart to work" (3:38aαb), "and the wall was finished on the twenty-fifth of Elul in fifty-two days" (6:15).[50] This short account (perhaps a building inscription) was first expanded in 3:1-32, which fills the gap between 2:18b and 3:38* and commemorates the most prominent contributors to the project.[51] In assigning names to each segment of the wall, the passage illustrates the unity brought to Judah by the restoration of Jerusalem's ramparts. Inasmuch as the high priest and his colleagues initiate the work (3:1), one senses here a tension growing that will propel the composition of Ezra-Neh from its origins to its culmination.

The primary strata of Nehemiah's account continue the emphasis upon the consolidation of Judah that is already found in Nehemiah's speech (2:17) and the names of the donors (3:1-32). As the restoration of the ramparts elicits antagonism, the solidarity of the builders increases. The antagonism begins with Sanballat's reaction to the news of Judeans' activities in 3:33f., which expresses negatively what motivated the Judeans to build according to 2:17. The passages reporting Tobiah's response in 3:35 and the imprecation in 3:36-37 appear to

---

44 §12.3.
45 §13.3.3.
46 §13.4.
47 §§14.2.1-2.
48 §§4.2 and 5.2.
49 §§6.2. and 6.3.1.
50 §§6.3.2.3 and 7.5.2.
51 §§6.3.2.1-3.

have been written for the conclusion in 3:38* + 6:15.[52] Similarly, 4:1-3* depicts a plot by Sanballat and Tobiah, as well as the Arabs, Ammonites and Ashdodites, to come and fight against Jerusalem as they hear that the wall "*had been restored.*" The author of 4:5-9* and 15* has made changes to 3:38 and 4:1, so that the Judeans mobilize *before* the construction is complete.[53] The remedy to the situation of "disgrace" and "reproach" in 2:17 is implicit in the notice of completion in 6:15. However, the animosity evoked by the work on the wall – which was not envisioned in the first editions of the account – necessitated the addition of 6:16 for the denouement of the story (cf. 4:9aβ).[54]

After the insertion of 6:2-4 and 5-9 between 4:15* and 6:15,[55] the redaction of the building report took a radical turn in 5:1-13, 6:10-14, 17-19; 13:4-31.[56] These passages censure the nobles, rulers, priests and prophets during "those days." They confer a new meaning to the two central terms – "evil/affliction" (הרעה) and "reproach" (חרפה) – employed in Nehemiah's speech in 2:17. Before the addition of 13:6 and 13:19-22a, Nehemiah takes these groups to task prior to and during the work on the wall. [57] Thus, by the twenty-fifth of Elul, Nehemiah has not only repaired the ramparts of Jerusalem, but has also introduced aggressive reforms that lay the groundwork for the religious, ethnic and sociopolitical reconsolidation of Judah.

As the building report had attained these proportions, an author recognized the need for a new introduction and thus composed 1:1b-4.[58] This passage not only follows 5:1-19, 6:10-14, 6:17-19 + 13:4-31 in detaching the situation of "affliction" and "reproach" from the condition of the wall, it also identifies the inhabitants of "the province" as "the survivors remaining from the captivity." The new opening scene interprets the transformation of Judah, which is portrayed in the expanded version of the building report, as the Restoration of Judah and "the remnant" after the catastrophe of 587/6 BCE.

While Neh 1:1a and 11b are parts of the first edition of the building account and 1:1b-4 introduces the amplified versions of the work, the prayer in 1:5-11a reflects a view of the Restoration that was originally foreign to the building account.[59] By confessing the sins of Israel, Nehemiah re-identifies "the ones remaining from the captivity there in the province" (1:3) as those whom YHWH had promised to "gather from the uttermost parts of heaven." The story of this return is first told in Ezra 1-6, which probably contains an older narrative (5:6-

---

52 §6.3.2.2.
53 §6.3.2.3.
54 §7.5.2.
55 §7.4.
56 §§7.5.1-3, 8.4, 9.2.2, 10.3.1-2, 11.2.
57 §§9.2.1 and 10.3.
58 §§4.2-3.
59 §§2.2-3.

6:15*) that does not know that the "elders of the Jews" were repatriates. This narrative provided the impulse for the composition of Ezra 1-4 and 7-8 by affirming that already Cyrus commanded the temple to built and that Darius confirmed this imperial decision with an additional decree. After the composition of 1:1-5, 3:8ff.* and 4:4-5,[60] the delay in the completion of the temple is due to the "the people of the land," who frustrate the builders until the reign of Darius (4:4-5 + 5:6ff.). The addition of 4:1-3 dates the schism between Samaria and Judah to the time when the foundations of the temple were laid.[61]

At this early stage in the formation of Ezra-Neh, the friction with Nehemiah's account is minimal. The construction of the temple only precedes the building of the city as whole, which may be compared to the sequence completion of temple/completion of city-wall in LXX 1 Kgs 2:35. So too, the builders in Nehemiah's account are now presented as the descendants of the returnees from the first-year of Cyrus's reign.

The insertion of Ezra 4:7-23, however, shifts the direction radically.[62] Picking up on the priority given to the temple and the imperial favor for this institution, the authors of the Artaxerxes-correspondence present the same king, who later only *accedes* to his cupbearer's wish to build Jerusalem, issuing a decree that prohibits the repatriated Jews from building the city-wall. Later, Darius issues a decree prohibiting any interruption of the work on the temple and providing royal funds to support of the same. And before Artaxerxes takes advantage of his proviso in 4:21 and reverses his decision, he commands Ezra to make Aliyah with "the people of Israel" and to transport funds for the temple (7:11ff.). This tension between the temple and the wall, which takes its point of departure from Nehemiah's censure of Eliashib and the priests, prepares the way for the composition of Neh 8-10.

First, however, the concentration of the earliest editions of Ezra-Neh on the restoration of Jerusalem is adjusted in Ezra 7-8,[63] which closes the gap between the third-person account of the temple-construction in Ezra 1-6 and the first-person account of the wall-construction in Neh 1-13*. While Ezra does not build, he follows the imperial orders to "glorify the house of YHWH which is in Jerusalem" (7:27). For priestly circles, these two chapters provide the proper frame of reference for viewing Nehemiah's achievements and relationship to Artaxerxes.

At this compositional stage, the book quotes a number of "sources:" the list of the returnees in Ezra 2, the Artaxerxes-correspondence in Ezra 4, the Darius-correspondence in Ezra 5-6, the Artaxerxes-decree in Ezra 7, the register in

---

60 §13.3.2.
61 §14.2.3.1
62 §3.3.
63 §5.3.2.

Ezra 8:1-14, as well as Ezra's account itself in 7:27-8:32(?). Against the backdrop of these texts – especially the final example, Nehemiah's account is to be understood as a source integrated with the others into the history of the Restoration. Whereas Neh 1:1a probably represents the original title of – or introduction to – the independent building-report, the reader of Ezra-Neh ascribes this line to the same narrator responsible for the other third-person passages in the book. In following Greek historiography and differentiating between sources and a narrator, the authors of Ezra-Neh have established the model for other Jewish histories from the Hellenistic age, such as the work of "the Chronicler,"[64] 1 and 2 Maccabees, the *Epistle of Aristeas*, the *Jewish Antiquities* of Josephus, and the *Alexander Romance*.[65] The analogies to these works provided the necessary framework for the authors of 1 Esdras to excise Nehemiah's account from the book – for reasons already discussed. Directly influenced by Greek historiography and the witness of 1 Esdras, critical scholars from Spinoza on have read Nehemiah's account as one source among others in Ezra-Neh, instead of recognizing that it constitutes the point of departure for the composition of this history.

With the addition of Ezra 9, the book treats Nehemiah's work much more positively. In contrast to the diarchy of Zerubbabel and Jeshua, Eliashib never enjoyed a harmonious relationship with Nehemiah. The same, however, cannot be said for Ezra, for after the situation in the province takes a turn for the worse (Ezra 9), the erection of the wall, rather than being depreciated, is recognized as the only solution. The notice in 8:35f. concludes chaps. 7-8 with the same-third person style with which it began, yet suddenly Ezra resumes his account and portrays a deficiency in a manner that strikingly resembles the first and final passages in Nehemiah's work (1:1b-4 and 13:23ff.).[66] Herewith, the authors of Ezra-Neh have made plain that the Restoration was not complete once the imperial court had issued a number of decrees promoting the temple. As long as "the people of Israel, the priests and Levites had not separated themselves from the people of the land" (Ezra 9:1), there was still much to be done. Without the late addition in Ezra 10, the next scene in the book transports the reader back to the court of Artaxerxes, where Nehemiah hears about the affliction and

---

64 See Mathys (1997).
65 Grätz (2004: 194ff.) has provided a superb comparison of Ezra-Neh and these works. "Die Darstellung von Geschichte als 'authentischer' Geschichte unter Aufnahme von im Wortlaut zitierten Dokumente zeigt eine Nähe zu griechisch-hellenistischer Geschichtsdarstellung. Die Dokumente haben dabei einen legitimatorischen Charakter; sie können dem Ausweis der besonderen Informiertheit des Autors – und damit der Glaubwürdigkeit der ganzen Geschichte – ebenso dienen wie auch der Legitimation einer bestimmten Geschichtssicht." One must, however, recognize that there is a major difference between Ezra-Neh and Greek historians, such as Herodotus and Thucydides: The latter identify themselves, while the authors of the former remain anonymous.
66 See §11.2.2.

reproach of his compatriots. He petitions for a leave of absence, comes to the province, and repairs the ramparts of Jerusalem. Yet, at every step of the way, he faces the interruptive tactics of Sanballat and Tobiah with whom the priests and aristocracy were connubially allied. Before the wall is complete on the twenty-fifth of Elul, he has removed Tobiah from his foothold in the province (13:4ff.), commanded the city-gates to be closed on the Sabbath to prohibit foreign merchants from continuing their trade with the nobles (13:15ff.), made the inhabitants of the province to swear to abolish their contacts with foreigners (13:23ff.), has "chased away" the descendant of the high priest who was the son-in-law to Sanballat (13:28f.), and has "fenched us about with impregnable palisades and with walls of iron, to the end that we should mingle in no way with any other nations..." (*Ep. Arist.* §139).

Against the backdrop of the tensions between the temple and the wall that have produced Ezra-Neh, one can appreciate what Neh 8-10 contribute to the final form of the book. The composition of this literary complex not only follows the principle that "they who love the Law build a wall around themselves" (LXX Prov 28:4b),[67] but also sets forth the study of the Torah and the confession of "the sins of the fathers" within the newly built walls of Jerusalem as an alternative to the temple and sacrifices performed by a high priest that was in league with the enemies of the Restoration.[68]

We began our study by noting that "Nehemiah's First Prayer" both resembles and omits important aspects of Solomon's prayer at the dedication of the temple in 1 Kgs 8/2 Chr 6.[69] Most importantly, Nehemiah emphasizes faithfulness to the Mitzvoth and does not adopt the identification of "the place where my name will dwell" with the temple. After comparing the prayer with the rest of the book, one may explain its placement in the seams between Ezra 1-10 and Neh 1-13 as the attempt to prepare the reader for the developments in the Restoration that began with the construction of the wall and concluded with the pledge to the Torah.

Just as Nehemiah's prayer avoids a reference to the temple, so does Neh 7-10 appear to deliberately substitute key features in Ezra 2-3. The first paragraph in Neh 8:1-12 begins by declaring that, "all of the people gathered together with one purpose in the place before the Water Gate." This introduction is strikingly similar to Ezra 3:1b, yet there are also significant differences. Whereas כל־העם is

---

67 ...δὲ ἀγαπῶντες τὸν νόμον περιβάλλουσιν ἑαυτοῖς τεῖχος.

68 The final form of Ezra-Neh presents three spheres of sacrality for the province, corresponding to Jerusalem's three building-phases: the altar, the temple, and the wall – which encircles both Jerusalem and Judah. According to our compositional model, this ideological map was inspired by the symbolism of the wall and moved toward the epicenter (the temple and than the altar; Ezra 3:1-6 is one of the latest texts in the book). The Temple Scroll evinces a very similar representation of space.

69 See §2.3.

the subject in Neh 8, Ezra 3 refers simply to הָעָם.[70] Since both scenes are set in "the sacred month *par excellence*,"[71] one would expect the activities described in Neh 8 to revolve around the temple, as in Ezra 3. However, the Water Gate was probably nowhere near the latter.[72] Moreover, the people do not wait upon the high priest to perform the required sacrifices on the altar that Jeshua had built in the seventh month years before (Ezra 3). Instead, they themselves take the initiative, and what they do has little, if anything, to do with the temple: "And they told Ezra, the *sōfēr*, to bring the book of the Law of Moses that YHWH had commanded Israel" (v. 1b).[73] As Ezra complies with their request, he surprisingly does not teach the people, but rather treats "the book" as a cultic object. As he reads "in it," the people listen intently. When he is finished, he praises YHWH, and all the people respond with "Amen" and do obeisance (v. 6). The holy character of the day is stated explicitly in vv. 9-12 (הַיּוֹם קָדֹשׁ־הוּא לַיהוה אֱלֹהֵיכֶם), where the people are encouraged to depart and celebrate.[74] Hence, while Ezra 3 emphasizes the altar and sacrifices, as anticipated in an account of activities on the seventh month, the authors of Neh 8:1-12 have succeeded in mentioning neither. Indeed, the high priest and the sacrifices have been completely replaced by a *sōfēr* (cf. 8:1, 5) and the reading of the Torah.

---

70 If the author of the latter were writing after the composition of Neh 8, as commonly supposed, he would have certainly employed the designation כָּל־הָעָם. That he did not, indicates that Neh 8 represents a development of Ezra 3.

71 Williamson (1985: 46).

72 Cf., e.g., Rudolph (1949:145). Böhler has interestingly observed (1997: 149) that if "das Wassertor wirklich ein profanes Tor war, gar ein Palasttor, wie Rudolph meint, bekäme die Versammlung in Neh 8 einen politischeren Charakter als alle anderen Versammlungen in Esdr α und Esr-Neh, die auf dem Tempelplatz stattfinden." The readers responsible for 1 Esdras seem to have noticed this problem, for they present the people gathering in "the place of the gate *east of the temple*" (9:38). In contrast, the MT in (cf. also v. 3) makes no effort whatsoever to confirm that the meeting was held before the temple. See Böhler's exhaustive discussion (1997: 52, 95-102) of the problems with 8:1, 3 and refutation of Pohlmann's position (1970: 151ff.) that the gate should be associated with the temple. – Willi interprets the passage as reporting the "Konstituierung der Provinz Jehud vollzogen am Neujahrstag des Jahres 444 v. Chr. in Jerusalem" (1995: 116). In support of this approach, he claims that Neh 8 cannot depict a cultic service, because it does not report any sacrifices and presents the congregation assembling before a *city*-gate, instead of a *temple*-gate. According to our approach, the contrasts with Ezra 3 indicate that Neh 8 intends to portray a cultic service in which the temple and high priest are dispensable and have been replaced with the Torah and a *sōfēr*. Nevertheless, these two approaches are not mutually exclusive.

73 Where is the high priest? To this question, 1 Esdras has provided the expected answer: καὶ εἶπον Εσδρα τῷ ἀρχιερεῖ καὶ ἀναγνώστῃ κομίσαι τὸν νόμον Μωυσέως τὸν παραδοθέντα ὑπὸ τοῦ κυρίου θεοῦ Ισραηλ (9:39).

74 The additions to the passage continue in this direction. For example, v. 2 describes Ezra as "the priest" (cf. also "Ezra, the priest, the *sōfēr*" in v. 9a) who brings the Torah before the congregation on the first day of the sacred month. In v. 5, as Ezra opens the book "in the eyes of all the people," the people stand up.

After the day is proclaimed holy to YHWH, the people return whence they came and do not seem intent on returning to witness the traditional cultic activities.[75] Nonetheless, the next paragraph in vv. 13-18 recounts that "on the second day were gathered together the chief of the fathers of all the people, the priests and the Levites unto Ezra, the *sōfēr*, even to understand the words of the Torah." Whereas in vv. 1-12, the priests are never mentioned, they have now joined the leaders and the Levites. And their behavior is just as peculiar as the people's activities on the preceding day: Instead of dictating what was to be done in this most important month of the cultic calendar, they submit themselves to learn from "Ezra, the *sōfēr*." Most noteworthy is the description of the place of assembly. Just as the people did not meet at the temple on the first day, the leaders gather around Ezra on the second.[76] Inasmuch as the latter plays only a passive role and soon disappears from the scene,[77] his function is merely symbolic – representing *concretum pro abstractum* the scribal institution. Moreover, instead of the priests and Levites organizing the activities, the lay leaders head the council and discover that Sukkoth was to be celebrated in the seventh month.[78] Significantly, Sukkoth is also celebrated in Ezra 3:4, yet there the obligatory sacrifices and offering are made on the newly built altar (cf. Lev 23:25ff. and Num 29).[79] In Neh 8, the council not only disregards the precise sacrificial requirements; it also does not recognize the preeminence of the temple. In an innovative reading that combines the prescriptions in the Pentateuch with Haggai's prophecy concerning the construction of the *temple*, the leaders order the people to "go forth unto the mount, bring olive branches…to make booths as it is written."[80] Significant are the places where the people construct the booths: first on the roofs of their houses and in their courtyards, and then in the temple-courts and elsewhere. Thus, not solely the temple, but rather the entire city of Jerusalem is given a place in the activity of Torah observance

---

75 If Ezra, the priest, who had brought monies for the temple (Ezra 8), were the author of this text, one would find difficult to explain the silence with regard to the temple.

76 In Ezra 9:4 and 10:1, Ezra also represents a place of meeting (cf., however, 10:7 and 9). It seems that the author of Neh 8:13 has been influenced by this depiction.

77 V. 18a is probably secondary. See §14.2.2.

78 Galling noted the artificiality of vv. 13-14: "Außerordentlich geschickt wird das Laubhüttenfest dadurch vorbereitet, daß man bei einer Nachversammlung im Hause Esras auf das Laubhüttengesetz stößt."

79 That Lev 23 was unknown to the authors of Neh 8 is unlikely. Indeed, the אך-section of vv. 39-43, which does not contain directions for sacrifices and is closer to Neh 8, could be later than the paragraph vv. 34-36. Cf. also the association of all the feasts with days of offerings in the subsuming remark of v. 37, after which we would not expect the continuation in vv. 39-43. This late editorial activity, which must predate Neh 8, witnesses to a development of new ways of celebrating Sukkoth (i.e., without the priests and sacrifices) in the late Persian and early Hellenistic period. See Rubenstein (1994).

80 Cf. Neh 8:15 (לעשׂת סכת...עלי־זית והביאו ההר צאו) with Hag 1:8 (עלו ההר והבאתם עץ ובנו הבית).

during the seventh month. And the author can proudly invoke the tradition for this innovation. In Deut 31:10-13, which appears to have directly informed the wording of Neh 8, Moses instructs Joshua to read the Torah every seven years at the feast of Sukkoth. After 8:1-12, this command had finally been heeded once again, "for since the days of Jeshua ben Nun (Josh 8:34f.?) to that day, the children of Israel had not done so."[81]

When the people gather again on the twenty-fourth day of the month (9:1ff.) to confess "their sins and iniquities of their fathers" (9:2), they neglect the temple altogether. The thirty-seven verses of the Levites' confession recount Israel's history since the beginning and in considerable detail, yet not once is the temple mentioned.[82] The land (הארץ), Moses, and the Torah have taken its place.[83] After acknowledging that it has lost its national sovereignty because "our fathers" had failed to keep the Mitzvoth, the community then ratifies a pact, promising to adhere to the Torah (chap. 10). And until the final (secondarily appended) stipulations are enumerated (10:33ff.), we wonder whether the temple had fallen into complete oblivion.[84]

The original form of Nehemiah's building report would not have provoked the composition of the greater part of Ezra-Neh, as well as that of 1 Esdras and the Nehemiah-Legend in 2 Maccabees, had it not been transformed into an account of Judah's Restoration and expanded with passages that portray the temple as a place of corruption. The remedy to Judah's reproach is the construction of the wall, various reforms are undertaken for the social and religious consolidation of the province, and the Jerusalemite priesthood is found only to be supporting Judah's enemies. All these factors served as the impulse for the drafting of Ezra 1-6. This section of the book was originally conceived as a

---

81 Galling wrote to Neh 8:13ff.: "So bleibt die Zeit zwischen dem 3. VII und 14. VII für die Vorbereitungen zum Laubhüttenfest frei. Das ist deswegen bemerklich, weil in dieser Periode der große Versöhnungstag am 10. VII fällt (3. Mose 16, 29-34). Warum dieser Tag hier nicht erwähnt wird – sei es nun, daß man an die Zeit Esras oder and die des Chron** denkt – ist nicht sicher zu beantworten." Galling alluded to the answer: "[a]m Versöhnungstag war *die Tätigkeit des Höhenpriesters* nicht zu entbehren" (1954: 235 – my italics).

82 The failure to specify the location contrasts sharply with the prayers made in the vicinity of the temple in 2 Kgs 19:14ff./Isa 37:14ff. and 2 Chr 20:5ff.

83 See Gilbert (1981).

84 In Excursus I at the end of chap. 9, I attempt to show that these stipulations have been added to 10:30 in order to present the community in chaps. 5 and 13 acting in violation of their pledge to the Torah. The stipulations regarding the temple in 10:33ff. represent, as suggested by several scholars, the latest additions to the pact and perhaps the final touches to Ezra-Neh. Their emphasis on the temple indicates the recognition on the part of their authors that this institution had not received attention in Neh 8:1-10:30 (and Neh 1-6). In correcting this situation, these authors take part in (and finish) the dialectical process (between laity/wall and priests/temple) that produced the book of Ezra-Neh. – For the dating of 10:33ff. and the greater part of 11:1-13:3 (the final redactions) to the time of the Maccabees, see the cogent arguments of Böhler (1997: 332ff.), as well as §13.3.4 *supra*.

prologue to the wall-building report, yet the composition of the Artaxerxes-correspondence in 4:7-22 presents the imperial court now searching the record-books, discovering that Jerusalem is a rebellious city (as Nehemiah's nemeses later affirmed), and then prohibiting the construction of the wall. When the court is called upon once again to search the records (5:17), it discovers a decree allowing the temple to be built (cf. 1:1ff.), to which a new decree is added (6:6ff.). After the construction of the temple is complete, Artaxerxes reverses his decision and allows Nehemiah to build the city. Yet before doing so, he commands Ezra to transport funds to Jerusalem in order to "glorify" the temple (chaps. 7-8). Thus, the authors of Ezra 1-6 and 7-8 concede that Nehemiah may have been correct in pointing out the corruption in the priesthood of his time. However, they emphasize that the first repatriates followed the decrees of the Persian kings to initiate the reconsolidation of Judah not with the wall, or even with reforms for the people, but rather with the construction and glorification of the temple.

Upon arriving in Jerusalem, Ezra notices that the support for the temple was not enough, for "the people of Israel" had compromised its distinctive identity by "mingling" with the surrounding nations (Ezra 9:1ff.). In order to remedy this situation, Nehemiah comes from Susa and erects a wall – both by repairing the physical ramparts around Jerusalem and rebuilding the ethnic boundaries around Judah. At the dedication festivities, the priests and Levites purify not just themselves, as in Ezra 6:20, but also the people, the gates, and the wall (12:30). Thereby, they extend their own sanctified status to the city as a whole and its inhabitants. Before the Levites sacrifice (12:43), Nehemiah has discovered a book (7:4-72) with which he selects the future residents of "the Holy City" (11:1). Once their exilic pedigree is confirmed, "all the people" petition Ezra to join Nehemiah and read the book of the Torah (Neh 8:1ff.). As the Torah gradually eclipses the temple in the literary maturation of Ezra-Neh, the community learns how to read for themselves (cf. 8:3 and 18 with 8:8, 13-14, 9:3 and 13:1). And in their respective writings, both the Persian kings and the inhabitants of Judah "search" (בקר/בקש) and "discover" (מצא/שכח) the proper way of reestablishing Judean society (cf. Ezra 2:62, 4:15, 19; 5:17, 6:1-2, Neh 7:5, 64; 8:14, 13:1). This practice of rebuilding identity through active reading is not only portrayed in Ezra-Neh, but it has also produced the book and attracts new generations to search and discover in it.

The Primary Compositional Layers of Neh 1-13

First Stratum:

> 1:1a, 11b; 2:1-6 (without "I prayed to the God of Heaven" in v. 4b; "the consort was sitting beside him" and "I gave him a time" in v. 6), 11, 15 (without "I came through the Valley Gate and returned"), 16a, 17, 18b; 3:38 (without "it was completed until the half of it"); 6:15.
> — *The earliest portions of Nehemiah's building account.*

Second Stratum:

> 2:9b, 12-14, 16b, 18a; 3:1-32.
> — *The register of the builders and isolated additions.*

Third Stratum:

> 2:10, 19-20; 3:33-34, 35, 36-37; 4:1-3, 4-9, 10-17; 5:16-18; 6:5-9, 16.
> — *Supplements which illustrate the positive implications of the building project by way of the negative reactions of the enemy; characterized by the use of the שמע-formula.*

Fourth Stratum:

> 2:7, 9a; 5:14-15; 6:2-4.
> — *First notices which depict Nehemiah as governor.*

Fifth Stratum:

> 1:1b-4; 5:1-13, 19; 6:10-14, 17-19; 13:4-14, 15-22, 22-30a, 31b.
> — *Paragraphs in which Nehemiah (presumably as governor) diverts his attention from the wall and institutes "extramural" reforms before the twenty-fifth of Elul; characterized by the use of זכרה-prayers. At this stage, the building report has become an account of Judah's Restoration.*

Sixth Stratum:

> 7:1-3; 11:1-2, 3ff.; 12:27-47.
> — *Additions related primarily to the population and dedication of the city. They presuppose the composition of Ezra 1-6, which together with Nehemiah's account constitute an expanded history of the Restoration. With its "sources," this history resembles other Jewish histories from the Hellenistic age.*

Seventh Stratum:

> 1:5-11a; 2:8; 7:4-72; 8:1-12; 13-18; 9:1-3, 4-37; 10:1-30, 31-40; 12:1-26; 13:1-3, 30b, 31a.
> — *Final supplements which mirror the friction between temple and Torah and which presuppose the addition of Ezra 7-8, 9 and 10 to Ezra 1-6.*

Bibliography

1. Primary Sources

Baars, W., and J.C.H. Lebram. "1 (3) Esdras." In *Cantica sive Odae—Oratio Manasse—Psalmi Apocryphi—Psalmi Salomonis—Tobit—I (III) Ezrae*. Part 4, fascicle 6 of Vetus Testamentum Syriace iuxta simplicem Syrorum versionem. Leiden: Brill, 1972.

Biblia Sacra iuxta latinam versionem: Libri Ezrae Tobiae Iudith. Rome: Typis Polyglottis Vaticanis,1950.

Biblia Sacra iuxta versionem simplicem quae dicitur Pschitta. Beirut: Typis Typographiae Catholica, 1951.

Budge, E.A.W. and L.W. King. *Annals of the Kings of Assyria*. Vol. 1. London: Longmans, 1902.

Cowley, A. E. *Aramaic Papyri of the Fifth Century B.C.* Oxford: Clarendon, 1923.

Donner, H. and W. Röllig, *Kanaanäische und aramäische Inschriften*. Wiesbaden: Otto Harrassowitz, 1962.

Elliger, K., and W. Rudolph, eds. *Biblia Hebraica Stuttgartensia*. Stuttgart: Deutsche Bibelgesellschaft, 1977.

Gibson, J.C.L., ed. *Textbook of Syrian Semitic Inscriptions I-III*. Oxford, 1971, 1975, 1982.

Grayson, A.K. *Assyrian Royal Inscriptions. I. From the Beginning to Ashur-resha-ishi I. II. From Tiglath-pileser I to Ashur-nasir-apli II*. Wiesbaden: Otto Harrassowitz, 1972-76.

Hanhart, R. *Esdrae liber I*. Vol. 8.1 of Septuaginta, Vetus Testamentum Graecum auctoritate Academiae Scientiarum Gottingensis editum. Göttingen: Vandenhoeck & Ruprecht, 1974.

———. *Esdrae liber II*. Vol. 8.2 of Septuaginta, Vetus Testamentum Graecum auctoritate Academiae Scientiarum Gottingensis editum. Göttingen: Vandenhoeck & Ruprecht, 1993.

Josephus. With an English Translation by R. Marcus in Nine Volumes. VI. Jewish Antiquities, Books IX-XI. LCL. Cambridge, Mass.: Harvard University Press, 1937.

Kittel, R., ed. *Biblia Hebraica*. Stuttgart: Württembergische Bibelanstalt, 1937.

Kraeling, E.G. *The Brooklyn Museum Aramaic Papyri: New Documents of the Fifth Century from the Jewish Colony at Elephantine*. New Haven, Conn.: Yale University Press, 1953.

Lapp, P.W., and N.L., eds. *Discoveries in the Wâdi ed-Dâliyeh*. Cambridge, Mass.: American Schools of Oriental Research, 1974.

Lichtheim, M. *Ancient Egyptian Autobiographies Chiefly of the Middle Kingdom: A Study and Anthology*. OBO 84. Freiburg, Switzerland: Universitätsverlag, 1988.

Luckenbill, D.D. *Ancient Record of Assyria and Babylonia*. I-II. Chicago: University of Chicago Press, 1926-27.

Meiggs, R. and D. Lewis, eds. *A Selection of Greek Historical Inscriptions to the End of the Fifth Century B.C.* Oxford: Clarendon, 1969.

Otto, E. *Die biographischen Inschriften der ägyptischen Spätzeit*. Probleme der Ägyptologie 2. Leiden: E.J. Brill, 1954.

Porten, B. and A. Yardeni, eds. *Textbook of Aramaic Documents from Ancient Egypt*. 4 Vols. Jerusalem: Carta, 1986-99.

Rudolph, W. עזרא נחמיה. Pages 1411–58 in *Biblia Hebraica Stuttgartensia*. Edited by K. Elliger and W. Rudolph. 3d ed. Stuttgart: Deutsche Bibelgesellschaft, 1987.

Tscherikower, V. and A. Fuks, eds. *Corpus Papyrorum Judaicarum*. Vol. 1, Cambridge, MA, 1957.

2. Secondary Literature

Abadie, P. "Le livre d'Esdras: un midrash de l'Exode ?" *Trans* 14 (1998): 19-31.

Ackroyd, P. R. "The Historical Literature." Pages 297–323 in *The Hebrew Bible and Its Modern Interpreters*. Edited by D.A. Knight and G.M. Tucker. Philadelphia: Fortress, 1985

Aharoni, Y. *The Land of the Bible: A Historical Geography. Revised and Enlarged edition*. Translated and edited by A. F. Rainey. Philadelphia: Westminister Press, 1979.

Ap-Thomas, D.R. "The Phoenicians," Pages 259-86 in *Peoples of Old Testament Times*. Edited by D.J. Wiseman. Oxford: Clarendon Press, 1973.

Auld, A.G. "Gideon: Hacking at the Heart of the Old Testament." *VT* 39 (1989): 257-267.

Avigad, N. "Seals and Sealings." *IEJ* 14 (1964): 190–94.

———. "Seals of the Exiles." *IEJ* 15 (1965): 222–32.

———. Bullae and Seals from a Post-exilic Judean Archive. *Qedem* 4. Jerusalem: The Institute of Archaeology, Hebrew University, 1976.

———. "The Contribution of Hebrew Seals to an Understanding of Israelite Religion and Society." Pages 195–208 in *Ancient Israelite Religion: Essays in Honor of Frank Moore Cross*. Edited by P.D. Hanson, P.D. Miller Jr., and S.D. McBride. Philadelphia: Fortress, 1987.

———. "Hebrew Seals and Sealings and Their Significance for Biblical Research." Pages 7–16 in *Congress Volume: Jerusalem, 1986*. Edited by J.A. Emerton. VTSup 40. Leiden: Brill, 1988.

Baltzer, K. *Das Bundesformular*. WMANT 4. Neukirchen-Vluyn: Neukirchener Verlag, 1960.

———. "Moses Servant of God and the Servants: Text and Tradition in the Prayer of Nehemiah (1:5-11)." Pages 121-130 in *The Future of Early Christianity*. Edited by B.A. Pearson. Minneapolis, 1991.

Barag, D.P. "A Silver Coin of Yohanan the High Priest and the Coinage of Judea in the Fourth Century B.C." *Israel Numismatic Journal* 9 (1986-87): 4-21.

Barthélmy, D. *Critique Textuelle de L'Ancien Testament*. Vol. 1 Freiburg, Switzerland: Univ. of Freiburg, 1982.

Batten, L.W. *The Books of Ezra and Nehemiah*. ICC. Edinburgh: T&T Clark, 1913.

Bautch, R.J. *Developments in Genre between Post-Exilic Penitential Prayers and the Psalms of Communal Lament*. SBL.AB 7. Atlanta: Society of Biblical Literature, 2003.

Becker, J. *Der Ich-Bericht des Nehemiabuches als chronistische Gestaltung*, fzb 87. Würzburg, 1998.

Becker, U. *Jesaja - von der Botschaft zum Buch*. FRLANT 178. Göttingen: Vandenhoeck & Ruprecht, 1997.

Bedford, R.R. "Diaspora: Homeland Relations in Ezra-Nehemiah." *VT* 52 (2002): 147-165.

Begg, C.T. "Ben Sirach's Non-mention of Ezra." *BN* 42 (1988): 14–18.

Begrich, J. *Die Chronologien der Könige von Israel und Juda und die Quellen des Rahmens der Königsbücher*. Tübingen: Mohr, 1929.

Bergen, T.A. "Nehemiah in 2 Maccabees 1:10-2:18." *JSJ* 28 (1997): 249-270.

Berquist, J.L. *Judaism in Persia's Shadow: A Social and Historical Approach*. Minneapolis: Fortress, 1995.

Bertheau, E. *Esra, Nechemia und Ester*. Leipzig: Hirzel, 1862.

Bertholet, A. *Die Bücher Esra und Nehemia*. KHC 19, Tübingen-Leipzig: J.C.B. Mohr, 1902.

Bi(c)kerman(n), E.J. "The Edict of Cyrus in Ezra 1." (1946) Pages 72-108 in *Studies in Jewish and Christian History*, Vol. 1, (AGAJU 9/1), Leiden 1976.

————. "En marge de l'Ecriture. I. – Le comput des années de règne des Achéménides (Néh., i, 2; ii, 1 et Thuc., viii, 58." *RB* 88 (1981): 19-23.

Bieberstein, K. and H. Bloedhorn, *Jerusalem: Grundzüge der Baugeschichte von Chalkolithikum bis zur Frühzeit der osmanischen Herrschaft*. Band 1. BTAVO Reihe B 100/1. Wiesbaden: Dr. Ludwig Reichert Verlag, 1994.

Bigwood, J.M. "Ctesias as Historian of the Persian Wars." *Phoenix* 32 (1978): 19-41.

Blenkinsopp, J. "Interpretation and the Tendency to Sectarianism: An Aspect of Second Temple History." Pages 1–26 in vol. 2 of *Jewish and Christian Self-Definition*. Edited by E.P. Sanders. 2 vols. Philadelphia: Fortress, 1981.

————. "The Mission of Udjahorresnet and Those of Ezra and Nehemiah." *JBL* 106 (1987): 409–21.

————. *Ezra-Nehemiah*. OTL. Philadelphia: Westminster, 1988.

————. "Temple and Society in Achaemenid Judah." Pages 22–53 in *Second Temple Studies 1: Persian Period*. Edited by P.R. Davies. JSOTSup 117. Sheffield: JSOT Press, 1991.

————. "The Nehemiah Autobiographical Memoir." Pages 199-212 in *Language, Theology, and the Bible* (FS for J. Barr). Edited by S.E. Balentine and J. Barton. Oxford, 1994.

Bliese, L.F. "Chiastic Structures, Peaks and Cohesion in Nehemiah 9:6–37." *BT* 39 (1988): 208–15.

Blum, E. "Das sog. ‚Privilegrecht' in Exodus 34, 11-26. Ein Fixpunkt der Komposition des Exodusbuches?" Pages 347-366 in *Studies in the Book of Exodus. Redaction – Reception – Interpretation*. Edited by M. Vervenne. Leuven: University Press, 1996.

Boda, M.J. "The Use of *Tôdôt* in Nehemiah XII." *VT* 44 (1994): 387–93.

————. *Praying the Tradition. The Origin and Use of Tradition in Nehemiah 9*. BZAW 277. Berlin and New York: De Gruyter, 1999.

Boecker, H. J. *Redeformen des Rechtslebens im Alten Testament*. WMANT 14. Neukirchen-Vluyn: Neukirchener Verlag, 1964.

Boer, P.A.H. de "Vive le Roi!" *VT* 5 (1955): 225-231

Böhler, D. *Die heilige Stadt in Esdras α und Esra-Nehemia: Zwei Konzeptionen der Wiederherstellung Israels*. OBO 158. Göttingen: Vandenhoeck und Ruprecht, 1997.

Bordreuil, P. "Sceaux Inscrits des Pays du Levant." *DBSup* 66: cols. 86–212.

Boström, G. *Proverbiastudien*. LUA, NF Avd. 1, 30:3, Lund, 1935.

Bovati, P. *Ristailire la Giustizia. Procedure, vocabulario, orientamenti*. Rome, 1986.

Bowman, R.A. "Ezra and Nehemiah." Pages 551-819 in *The Interpreter's Bible*. Edited by G.A. Buttrick. Vol. 3. Nashville: Abingdon, 1954.

Braun, R. "Chronicles, Ezra, and Nehemiah: Theology and Literary History." Pages 52–64 in *Studies in the Historical Books of the Old Testament*. Edited by J.A. Emerton. VTSup 30. Leiden: Brill, 1979.

Briant, P. *Histoire de l'empire perse de Cyrus à Alexandre. 2 Volumes* in Achaemenid History X. Edited by P. Briant, A. Kuhrt, M. C. Root, H. Sancisi-Weerdenburg, J. Wiesehöfer. Paris: Libraire Arthème Fayard, 1996.

Briend, J. "Le Sabbat en Jr 17:19-27," *AOAT* 215 (1985): 23-35.

Brongers, H.A. "Bemerkungen zum Gebrauch des Adverbialen *weattah* im Alten Testament." *VT* 15 (1965): 289–99.

Burrows, M. "The Topography of Nehemiah 12:31-43." *JBL* 54 (1935): 29-39.

Cameron, G.C. "Darius, Egypt and the 'Lands beyond the Sea." *JNES* 2 (1943): 307–13.

Carroll, R.P. "Coopting the Prophets: Nehemiah and Noadiah." Pages 87–99 in *Priests, Prophets and Scribes: Essays on the Formation and Heritage of Second Temple Judaism in Honour of Joseph Blenkinsopp.* Edited by E. Ulrich, J.W. Wright, R.P. Carroll, and P.R. Davies. JSOTSup 149. Sheffield: JSOT Press, 1992.

Carter, C.E. "The Province of Yehud in the Post-exilic Period: Soundings in Site Distribution and Demography." Pages 106–45 in *Second Temple Studies 2: Temple Community in the Persian Period.* Edited by T.C. Eskenazi and K.H. Richards. JSOTSup 175. Sheffield: JSOT Press, 1994.

———. *The Emergence of Yehud in the Persian Period. A Social and Demographic Study.* JSOTSup 294. Sheffield: JSOT Press, 1999.

Cazelles, H. "La Mission d'Esdras." *VT* 4 (1954): 113–40.

Chirichigno, G. C. *Debt-Slavery in Israel and the Ancient Near East.* JSOTSup 141. Sheffield: JSOT Press, 1993.

Clines, D.J.A. "Nehemiah 10 As an Example of Early Jewish Biblical Exegesis." *JSOT* 21 (1981): 111–17.

———. *Ezra, Nehemiah, Esther.* NCB. Grand Rapids. Mich.: Eerdmans, 1992.

———. "The Nehemiah Memoir: The Perils of Autobiography." Pages 124–64 in *What Does Eve Do to Help? and Other Readerly Questions to the Old Testament.* JSOTSup 94. Sheffield: JSOT Press, 1990.

Coggins, R.J. *The Books of Ezra and Nehemiah.* CBC. Cambridge: Cambridge University Press, 1976.

Collins, J.J. *The Apocalyptic Vision of the Book of Daniel.* HSM 16. Missoula: Scholars Press, 1977.

———. *A Commentary on the Book of Daniel.* Minneapolis: Fortress, 1993.

Cross, F.M. "Geshem the Arabian, Enemy of Nehemiah." *BA* 18 (1955): 46-47.

———. "The Discovery of the Samaria Papyri." *BA* 26 (1963): 110–21.

———. "Aspects of Samaritan and Jewish History in Late Persian and Hellenistic Times." *HTR* 59 (1966): 201–11.

———. "Papyri of the Fourth Century B.C. from Dâliyeh." Pages 41–62 and figs. 34–39 in *New Directions in Biblical Archaeology.* Edited by D. N. Freedman and J. C. Greenfield. Garden City, N.Y.: Doubleday, 1969.

———. "The Papyri and Their Historical Implications." Pages 17–29 in *Discoveries in the Wâdi Ed-Dâliyeh.* Edited by P. W. and N. L. Lapp. AASOR 41. Cambridge, Mass.: American Schools of Oriental Research, 1974.

———. "A Reconstruction of the Judean Restoration." *JBL* 94 (1975): 4–18.

———. "A Report on the Samaria Papyri." Pages 17–26 in *Congress Volume: Jerusalem, 1986.* Edited by J.A. Emerton. VTSup 40. Leiden: Brill, 1988.

Dahood, M. "Ugaritic-Hebrew Parallel Pairs." Pages 197ff. in *Ras Shamra Parallels I.* Edited by L. R. Fisher. AnOr 49. Rome: Pontifical Biblical Institute, 1972.

Daniels, D.R. "The Composition of the Ezra-Nehemiah Narrative." Pages 311–28 in *Ernten, was man sät: Festschrift für Klaus Koch zu seinem 65. Geburtstag.* Edited by D. R. Daniels, U. Gleßmer, and M. Rösel. Neukirchen-Vluyn: Neukirchener Verlag, 1992.

Deliceto, G. da "Epoca della Partenza di Hanani per Gerusalemme e Anno della Petizione di Neemia ad Artaserse. Neem. 1,1 e Neem. 2,1." *Laur* 4 (1963): 431–68.

Demsky, A. "Who Came First, Ezra or Nehemiah? The Synchronistic Approach," *HUCA* 65 (1994): 1–19.

———. "Who Returned First—Ezra or Nehemiah?" *BRev* 12 (April 1996): 28–33, 46, 48.

Depuydt, L. "Evidence for Accession Dating under the Achaemenids," *JAOS* 115 (1995): 193-204.

De Fraine, J. *Esdras en Nehemias*, BOT V/2, Roermond, 1961

De Roche, M. "Yahweh's Rîb Against Israel: A Reassessment of the So-Called 'Prophetic Lawsuit' in the Preexilic Prophets." *JBL* (1983): 563-74.

Driver, S.R. *An Introduction to the Literature of the Old Testament.* Edinburgh: T&T Clark, 1898.

Duggan, M.W. *The Covenant Renewal in Ezra-Nehemiah (Neh 7:72B-10:40): An Exegetical, Literary, and Theological Study.* SBL DS 164. Atlanta: Society of Biblical Literature, 2001.

Dumbrell, W.J. "The Tell el-Maskhuta Bowls and the 'Kingdom' of Qedar in the Persian Period." *BASOR* 203 (1971): 33-44.

Ehrlich, A.B. *Randglossen zur Hebräischen Bibel.* Siebenter Band. Leipzig: Olms, 1914.

Eissfeldt, O. *The Old Testament: An Introduction.* Translated by P. R. Ackroyd. Oxford: Blackwell, 1966.

Emerton, J.A. "Did Ezra Go to Jerusalem in 428 B.C.?" *JTS* 17 (1966): 1–19.

———. Review of U. Kellermann, *Nehemia: Quellen, Überlieferung und Geschichte. JTS* 23 (1972): 171–85.

Erbele-Küster, D. *Lesen als Akt des Betens: eine Rezeptionsästhetik der Psalmen.* WMANT 87. Neukirchen-Vluyn: Neukirchener-Verlag, 2001.

Eskenazi, T.C. *In an Age of Prose: A Literary Approach to Ezra-Nehemiah.* SBLMS 36. Atlanta: Scholars Press, 1988. – 1.

———. "The Structure of Ezra-Nehemiah and the Integrity of the Book." *JBL* 107 (1988): 641-656. – 2.

Ewald, H. *Geschichte des Volkes Israel bis Christus.* III/2. Göttingen, 1852.

Fensham, F.C. *The Books of Ezra and Nehemiah.* NICOT. Grand Rapids, Mich.: Eerdmans, 1982.

Fernández, A. "Epoca de la Actividad de Esdras." *Bib* 2 (1921): 424–47.

Fishbane, M. *Biblical Interpretation in Ancient Israel.* Oxford: Clarendon, 1985.

Fitzmyer, J.A. "Aramaic Epistolography." Pages 183–204 in *A Wandering Aramean: Collected Aramaic Essays.* SBLMS 25. Missoula, Mont.: Scholars Press, 1979.

Frei, P. and K. Koch. *Reichsidee und Reichsorganisation im Perserreich. Zweite, bearbeite und stark erweiterte Auflage.* OBO 55. Freiburg: Universitätsverlag Freiburg, 1996.

Fruin, R. "Is Esra ein historisch persoon?" *NThT* (1929): 121-32.

Fullerton, K. "The Procession of Nehemiah." *JBL* 38 (1919): 171-175.

Galling, K. "Assyrische und persische Präfekten in Geser," *PJB* 31 (1935) 86-7.

———. *Syrien in der Politik der Achaemeniden biz zum Aufstand des Megabyzos 448 v. Chr.* Der Alte Orient, 36. Band, Hefte 3-4. Leipzig: J.C. Hinrichs, 1937.

———. *Die Bücher der Chronik, Esra, Nehemia.* ATD 12. Göttingen: Vandenhoeck & Ruprecht, 1954.

———. "Die Proklamation des Kyros in Esra 1." Pages 61-77 in *Studien zur Geschichte Israels im persischen Zeitalter,* Tübingen, 1964.

Gelbhaus, S. *Nehemias and seine social-politischen Bestrebungen.* Vienna, 1902.

Gelin, A. *Le Livre de Esdras et Néhémie.* JerB. Paris. 2. edition. 1960.

Gilbert, M. " La place de la Loi dans la prière de Néhémie 9." Pages 307–16 in *De la Tôrah au Messie* [Mélanges Henri Cazelles]. Edited by J. Doré, P. Grelot, and M. Carrez. Paris: Desclée, 1981.

Gilatt-Gilad, D.A. "Reflections on the Structure of the 'amānāh (Neh 10,29-40)." *ZAW* 112 (2000): 386-395.

Goldstein, J.A. "The Tales of the Tobiads." Pages 85-123 in *Christianity, Judaism and other Greco-Roman Cults*. Vol III. SJLA 12 - 3. Edited by J. Neusner. Leiden, 1975.

Golka, F.W. "Die figura etymologica im Alten Testament." Pages 415-424 in *Wünschet Jerusalem Frieden. Collected Communications to the XIIth Congress of the International Organization for the Study of the Old Testament*. Jerusalem, 1986.

Grabbe, L.L. "Josephus and the Reconstruction of the Judean Restoration." *JBL* 106 (1987): 231-246.

———. "Reconstructing History from the Book of Ezra." Pages 98–106 in *Second Temple Studies 1*: Persian Period. Edited by P. R. Davies. JSOTSup 117. Sheffield: JSOT Press, 1991.

———. "Who Was the Bagoses of Josephus (Ant. 11.7.1 §§297-301)?" *Trans* 5 (1991): 49-55.

———. *Judaism from Cyrus to Hadrian. Vol. 1 The Persian and Greek Periods*. Mineapolis: Fortress Press, 1992.

———. "What Was Ezra's Mission?" Pages 286–99 in *Second Temple Studies 2: Temple Community in the Persian Period*. Edited by T. C. Eskenazi and K. H. Richards. JSOTSup 175. Sheffield: JSOT Press, 1994.

Granild, S. *Ezrabogens literaere genesis undersoegt med searligt henblick paa et efterkronistik indgreb*. Kopenhagen, 1949.

Grätz, S. *Das Edikt des Artaxerxes: Eine Untersuchung zum religionspolitischen und historischen Umfel von Esra 7,12-26*. BZAW 337. Berlin and New York: Walter de Gruyter, 2004.

Green, A.R.W. "The Date of Nehemiah: A Reexamination." *AUSS* 28 (1990): 195–209.

Grol, H.W.M. van "Ezra 7, 1–10: Een Literair-Stilistische Analyse." *Bijdr* 51 (1990): 21–37.

Gunneweg, A.H.J. *Esra*. KAT. Gütersloh: Gerd Mohn, 1985.

———. *Nehemia*. KAT. Gütersloh: Gerd Mohn, 1987.

Haller, M. *Das Judentum*. SAT II/3. 1914. Second Edition. Gottingen: Vandenhoeck & Ruprecht, 1925.

Hengel, M. *Judentum and Hellenismus. Studien zu ihrer Begegnung unter besonderer Berücksichtigung Palästinas bis zur Mitte des 2. Jh. v.Chr.* WUNT 10. Tübingen: J.C.B. Mohr, 1969.

Hensley, L.V. "The Official Persian Documents in the Book of Ezra." Ph.D. diss. Liverpool, 1977.

Hezel, W.F. *Die Bibel Alten und Neuen Testaments mit vollständig-erklärenden Anmerkungen*. Lemgo, 1782.

Hinz, W. *Darius and die Perser Holle*. Vergangene Kulturen. 2 Vol. Baden-Baden, 1976 and 1979

Hjelm, I. *The Samaritans and Early Judaism: A Literary Analysis*. JSOTSup 303. Sheffield: Sheffield Academic Press, 2000.

Höffken, P. "Warum schwieg Jesus Sirach über Esra?" *ZAW* 87 (1975): 184–202.

Hofstetter, J. "Zu den griechischen Gesandtschaften nach Persien." Pages 94-107 in *Beiträge zur Achämenidengeschichte*. Edited by G. Walser. Wiesbaden: Franz Steiner Verlag, 1972.

Hoglund, K. "The Achaemenid Context." Pages 54–72 in *Second Temple Studies 1: Persian Period*. Edited by P. R. Davies. JSOTSup 117. Sheffield: JSOT Press, 1991.

——. *Achaemenid Imperial Administration of Syria-Palestine and the Missions of Ezra and Nehemiah*. SBLDS 125. Atlanta: Scholars Press, 1992.

Holladay, W.L. *Jeremiah 1*. Hermeneia. Philadelphia: Fortress, 1986.

Holmgren, F.C. *Ezra and Nehemiah: Israel Alive Again*. ITC. Grand Rapids, Mich.: Eerdmans, 1987.

——. "Faithful Abraham and the 'amanâ Covenant." *ZAW* 104 (1992): 249–54.

Hölscher, G. "Komposition und Ursprung des Deuteronomiums," ZAW 40 (1922): 161-255.

——. *Die Bücher Esra und Nehemia*. Pages 491-562 in *HSAT* II. 4. Auflage. Tübingen: J.C.B. Mohr, 1923.

Hoonacker, A. van "La Succession Chronologique. Néhémie-Esdras (Suite)." *RB* 33 (1924): 33–64.

Hout, M. van den "Studies in Early Greek Letter Writing." *Mnemosyne* 4th ser. 2 (1949).

Howorth, H.H. "Some Unconventional Views on the Texts of the Bible." *PSBA* 23 (1901): 147-159.

Hübner, U. *Die Ammoniter. Untersuchungen zur Geschichte, Kultur und Religion eines transjordanischen Volkes im 1. Jahrtausend vor Chr*. ADP 16. Wiesbaden: Otto Harrassowitz, 1992.

——. "Die Münzprägungen Palästinas in alttestamentlicher Zeit." *Trumah* 4 (1994): 119-45.

Hunter, P.H. *After the Exile I*. London: Oliaphant, Anderson, & Ferrier, 1890.

Hurowitz, V.A. *I Have Built You an Exalted House: Temple Building in the Bible in light of Mesopotamian and Northwest Semitic Writings*. Sheffield: Sheffield Academic Press, 1992.

Ibáñez Arana, A. "Sobre la colocación original de Neh. 10." *EstBib* 10 (1951): 379–402

In der Smitten, W. Th. *Esra: Quellen, Überlieferung und Geschichte*. SSN 15. Assen: Van Gorcum, 1973.

Ivry, A.L. "Nehemiah 6,10: Politics and the Temple." *JSJ* 3 (1972): 35–45.

Jacoby, F. "Ktesias." In *Pauly Real-Encyclopädie der Classischen Altertumswissenschaft*, ed. G. Wissowa et al., Band 11, T. 2, 2032-73. Stuttgart: J. B. Metzler, 1922.

Jagersma, H. "The Tithes in the Old Testament." Pages 116–28 in *Remembering All the Way...* Edited by A. S. van der Woude. OTS 21. Leiden: Brill, 1981.

Jahn, G. Die Bücher Esra (A und B) und Nehemiah. Leiden: E. J. Brill, 1909.

Janzen, D. "The 'Mission' of Ezra and the Persian-Period Temple Community." *JBL* 119 (2000): 619-643.

——. *Witch-hunts; Purity and Social Boundaries: The Expulsion of the Foreign Women in Ezra 9-10*. JSOT 350. New York: Sheffield Academic Press, 2002.

Japhet, S. "The Supposed Common Authorship of Chronicles and Ezra-Nehemia Investigated Anew." *VT* 18 (1968): 330–71.

——. "Sheshbazzar and Zerubbabel—Against the Background of the Historical and Religious Tendencies of Ezra-Nehemiah." *ZAW* 94 (1982): 66–98; 95 (1983): 218–29.

——. "Composition and Chronology in the Book of Ezra-Nehemiah." Pages 189–216 in *Second Temple Studies 2: Temple Community in the Persian Period*. Edited by T. C. Eskenazi and K. H. Richards. JSOTSup 175. Sheffield: JSOT Press, 1994.

Jepsen, A. "Nehemia 10." *ZAW* 66 (1954): 87–106.

Jeremias, J. *Der Prophet Hosea*. ATD 24,1. Göttingen: Vandenhoeck & Ruprecht, 1983.

Johannesen, E. *Studier over Ezras og Nehemjas Historie*. Kopenhagen, 1946.

Johnson, J.H. "Demotic Chronicle." *ABD* 2:142–44.

Joüon, P. "Notes philologiques sur le texte hébreu d'Esdras et de Néhémie." *Bib* 12. (1931), 85-89.

———. *Grammaire de L'Hébreu Biblique.* Rome: Biblical Institute, 1965.

Junge, P.J. "Hazapartis," *Klio* 33 (1940): 16-17

Kaiser, O. *Grundriss der Einleitung in die kanonische und deuterokanonische Schriften des Alten Testaments. Band 1. Die erzählenden Werke.* Gütersloh: Gütersloher Verlagshaus, 1992.

Kalluveettil, P. *Declaration and Covenant: A Comprehensive Review of Covenant Formulae from the Old Testament and the Ancient Near East.* AnBib 88. Rome: Biblical Institute, 1982.

Kapelrud, A.S. *The Question of Authorship in the Ezra-Narrative: A Lexical Investigation.* SUNVAO 1. Oslo: Dybwad, 1944.

Karrer, C. *Ringen um die Verfassung Judas. Eine Studie zu den theologisch-politischen Vorstellungen im Esra-Nehemiah-Buch.* BZAW 308. Berlin and New York: De Gruyter, 2001.

Kaufmann, Y. *The Religion of Israel: From its Beginnings to the Babylonian Exile.* Translated and abridged by M. Greenberg. Chicago: University of Chicago Press, 1960.

———. *From the Babylonian Captivity to the End of Prophecy.* Vol. 4 of History of the Religion of Israel. New York: Ktav, 1977.

Kaupel, H. "Der Sinn von עשה המלאכה in Neh 2, 16." *Biblica* 21 (1940): 40-44.

Kellermann, U. *Nehemia: Quellen, Überlieferung und Geschichte.* BZAW 102. Berlin: Töpelmann, 1967.

———. "Erwägungen zum Problem der Esradatierung." *ZAW* 80 (1968): 55–87.

Kidner, D. *Ezra and Nehemiah: An Introduction and Commentary.* TOTC. Leicester: Inter-Varsity, 1979.

Kindler, A. "Silver Coins Bearing the Name of Judea from the Early Hellenistic Period." *IEJ* 24 (1974): 73-76.

Klostermann, A. *Geschichte des Volkes Israel.* Munich: C. H. Beck, 1896.

Knauf, E.A. *Ismael. Untersuchungen zur Geschichte Palästinas und Nordarabiens im 1. Jahrtausend v. Chr. 2., erweiterte Auflage.* ADPV 7. Wiesbaden: Otto Harrassowitz, 1989.

Knoppers, G.N. "Sources, Revision and Editions: The Lists of Jerusalem's Residents in MT and LXX Nehemiah 11 and 1 Chronicles 9." *Textus* 20 (2000): 141-68.

Koehler, L. *Lexicon in Veteris Testamenti Libros.* 2 vols. Grand Rapids, Mich.: Eerdmans, 1953.

Koep, L. *Das himmlische Buch in Antike und Christentum*, Theophaneia 8. Bonn: Hanstein, 1952.

Kosters, W.H. *Die Wiederherstellung Israels in der persischen Periode. (Het herstel van Israel in het Persische tijdwak*, 1894). Translated by A. Basedow. Heidelberg, 1895

Kraemer, D. "On the Relationship of the Books of Ezra and Nehemiah." *JSOT* 59 (1993): 73–92.

Kratz, R.G. *Kyros im Deuterojesaja-Buch. Redaktionsgeschichtliche Untersuchungen zu Entstehung und Theologie von Jes 40-55.* FAT 1. Tübingen: Mohr & Siebeck, 1991.

———. *Translatio Imperii. Untersuchungen zu den aramäischen Danielerzählungen und ihrem theologischem Umfeld.* WMANT 63. Neukirchen-Vluyn: Neukirchener Verlag, 1991.

———. "Der Dekalog im Exodusbuch." *VT* 44 (1994): 51-65.

———. *Die Komposition der erzählenden Bücher des Alten Testaments: Grundwissen der Bibelkritik.* UTB 2157. Göttingen: Vandenhoeck & Ruprecht, 2000.

Kugler, F.X. *Von Moses bis Paulus: Forschungen zur Geschichte Israels.* Münster: 1922.

Kutsch, E. "Die Wurzel עצר im Hebräischen." *VT* 2 (1952): 57–69.

————. "Sukkot." Cols. 495–98 in vol. 15 of *Encyclopaedia Judaica*. Edited by C. Roth and G. Wigoder. Jerusalem: Keter, 1971.

————. "'Trauerbräuche' und 'Selbstminderungsriten' im Alten Testatment." Pages 78-95 in *Kleine Schriften zum Alten Testament. Zum 65. Geburtstag*. Edited by L. Schmidt and K. Eberlein, BZAW 168, 1986.

Lande, I. *Formelhafte Wendungen der Umgangssprache im Alten Testament*. Leiden: E. J. Brill, 1949.

Lapp, P. "An Account of the Discovery." Pages 1–6 in *Discoveries in the Wâdi ed-Dâliyeh*. Edited by P. W. and N. L. Lapp. AASOR 41. Cambridge, Mass.: American Schools of Oriental Research, 1974.

Lebram, J.C.H. "Die Traditionsgeschichte der Esragestalt und die Frage nach dem historischen Esra." Pages 103-138 in *Achaemenid History I*. Edited by H. Sancisi-Weerdenburg, 1987.

Lefèvre, A. "Néhémie et Esdras." Cols. 393-424 in vol. 6 of *Dictionaire de la Bible Supplément*. Edited by L. Pirot et al. Paris: Libraire Letouzey et Ané, 1960.

Levin, C. *Der Jahwist*. FRLANT 157. Göttingen: Vandenhoeck & Ruprecht, 1993.

————. "Das Amosbuch der Anawim," *ZThK* 94 (1997): 407-436.

————. "The Poor in the Old Testament: Some Observations," *RT* 8 (2001): 253-273.

Lipschits, O. "Literary and Ideological Aspects of Nehemiah 11." *JBL* 121 (2002): 423-440.

Luria, B.Z. "Men of Tyre also, who lived in the city, brought fish and all kinds of wares (Nehemiah 13:16)" (Heb.). *BMik* 15 (1970): 363-67.

Marquart, J. *Fudamente israelitischer und jüdischer Geschichte*. Göttingen, 1896.

Martin, W.J. "'Dischronologized' Narrative in the Old Testament," *VTSup* 17 (1969): 179-86.

Mason, R. "Some Chronistic Themes in the 'Speeches' in Ezra and Nehemiah." *ExpTim* 101 (1989): 72–76.

Mathys, H.-P. *Dichter und Beter: Theologen aus spätalttestamentlicher Zeit*. OBO 132. Göttingen: Vandenhoeck & Ruprecht, 1994.

Matzal, S.C. "The Structure of Ezra iv-vi." *VT* 50 (2000): 566-569.

McCarter, P.K. Jr. *II Samuel*. AB 9. Garden City, New York. 1984.

McConville, J.G. "Ezra-Nehemiah and the Fulfillment of Prophecy." *VT* 36 (1986): 205–24.

McEvenue, S. "The Political Structure in Judah from Cyrus to Nehemiah." *CBQ* 44 (1981): 353–64.

McEwan, G.J.P. *Priest and Temple in Hellenistic Babylonia*. FAS 4. Wiesbaden: Franz Steiner, 1981.

McKane, W.A. *Critical and Exegetical Commentary in Jeremiah. Volume I. Introduction and Commentary on Jeremiah I-XXV*. ICC. Edinburgh: T&T Clark, 1986.

Meinhold, A. "Die Gattung der Josephsgeschichte und des Estherbuches: Diasporanovelle, I, II." *ZAW* 87 (1975): 306-24; 88 (1976): 79-93.

Meshorer, Y. *Ancient Jewish Coinage, Vol. 1 Persian Period through Hasmoneans*. New York, 1982.

Meyer, E. *Die Entstehung des Judentums*. 1896. 2nd Edition. Hildesheim: Olms, 1965.

Meyers, E.M. The Shelomith Seal and the Judean Restoration: Some Additional Considerations." *EI* 18. (1985): 33-38.

Michaeli, F. *Les Livres des Chroniques, d'Esdras et de Néhémie*. Neuchâtel: Delchaux et Niestlé, 1967.

Michaelis, J.D. *Deutsche Übersetzung des Alten Testaments mit Anmerkungen für Ungelehrte*. Part 13. Göttingen, 1783.

Mildenberg, L. "Über das Kleingeld in der persischen Provinz Judäa. Die Yehud Münzen." Pages 719-728 in *Palästina in vorhellenistischer Zeit*. Weippert, H. Vorderasien II, Vol. 1. München: C.H. Beck, 1988.

Milik, J. "Les modèles araméens du livre d'Esther dans la grotte 4 de Qumran" *Revue de Qumran* 15. (1992): 321-406

Milik, J. and M. Black, *The Books of Enoch. Aramaic Fragments of Qurmran Cave 4*. Oxford, 1976.

Moore, C.A. *Esther.* AB 7B. Garden City, N.Y.: Doubleday, 1971.

Moscati, S. "I Sigilli nell'Antico Testamento: Studio Esegetico-Filogico." *Bib* 30 (1949): 314–38.

———. *The World of the Phoenicians* (tr. A. Hamilton). London: Weidenfeld and Nicholson, 1968.

Movers, F.C. *Kritische Untersuchungen über die biblische Chronik*. Bonn: 1834.

Mowinckel, S. *Stattholderen Nehemia*. Kristiania, 1916.

———. *Studien zu dem Buche Ezra-Nehemia I: Die nachchronistiche Redaktion des Buches. Die Listen*. SUNVAO 3. Oslo: Universitetsforlaget, 1964.

———. *Studien zu dem Buche Ezra-Nehemia II: Die Nehemia-Denkschrift*. SUNVAO 5. Oslo: Universitetsforlaget, 1964.

———. *Studien zu dem Buche Ezra-Nehemia III: Die Ezrageschichte und das Gesetz Moses*. SUNVAO 7. Oslo: Universitetsforlaget, 1965.

Muilenburg, J. "The Form and Structure of the Covenantal Formulations." *VT* 9 (1959): 347–65.

Myers, J.M. *Ezra, Nehemiah*. AB 14. Garden City, N.Y.: Doubleday, 1965.

Naveh, J. *The Development of the Aramaic Script*. PIASH V 1. Jerusalem, 1970.

Neufeld., E."The Prohibitions against Loans at Interest in Ancient Hebrew Laws." *HUCA* 26 (1955): 355–412.

Neuffer, J. "The Accession of Artaxerxes I," *AUSS* 6 (1968): 60-87.

Newman, J. *Praying by the Book: The Scripturalization of Prayer in Second Temple Judaism*. SBLEJL 14. Atlanta: Scholars Press, 1999.

Nötscher, F. "Himmlische Bücher und Schicksalsglaube in Qumran." *Revue de Qumran* 1 (1958/59): 405-411.

Noth, M. *Überlieferungsgeschichtliche Studien. Die sammelnden und bearbeitenden Geschichtswerke im Alten Testament*. 1943. Darmstadt: Wissenschaftliche Buchgesellschaft, 1967.

Oelsner, J. *Materialen zur babylonischen Gesellschaft und Kultur in hellenistischer Zeit*. Budapest: Eötrös University, 1986.

Olmstead, A.T. *History of the Persian Empire*. Chicago, 1948.

Pardee, D. *Handbook of Ancient Hebrew Letters*. SBL.SBS 15; Chico, CA; Scholars Press, 1982.

Parker, R.A. and W.H. Dubberstein, *Babylonian Chronology, 626 B.C.–A.D. 75*. Providence: Brown University Press, 1956.

Pavlovský, V."Die Chronologie der Tätigkeit Esdras. Versuch einer neuen Lösung." *Bib* 38 (1957): 278–305, 428–56.

Perlitt, L. "'Ein einzig Volk von Brüdern.' Zur deuteronomischen Herkunft der biblischen Bezeichnung 'Bruder.'" Pages 27-52 in *Kirche* (FS G. Bornkamm zum 75. Geburtstag). Edited by D. Lührmann and G. Strecker. Tübingen, 1980.

Pichon, C. "La Prohibition des Mariages mixtes par Néhémie (XIII 23-31)." *VT* 47 (1997): 168-199.

Plöger, O. "Reden und Gebete im deuteronomistischen and chronistischen Geschichtswerk." Pages 35-49 in *Festschrift für Günther Dehn zum 75 Geburtstag*. Edited by W. Schneemelcher. Neukirchen-Vluyn: Neukirchener Verlag, 1957.

Pohlmann, K.-F. *Studien zum dritten Esra*. FRLANT 104. Göttingen: Vandenhoeck & Ruprecht, 1970.

Porten, B. *Archives from Elephantine: The Life of an Ancient Jewish Military Colony*. Berkeley and Los Angeles: University of California Press, 1968.

———. *Nechemiah: The Book of Nehemiah, Translation, Commentary and Overview*. New York: Mesorah, 1990.

Pritchard, J.B., *Winery, Defenses and Soundings at Gibeon*. Philadelphia: The University Museum, 1964.

Rabinowitz, I. "Aramaic Inscriptions of the Fifth Century B.C.E. from a North-Arab Shrine in Egypt." *JNES* 15 (1956): 1-9.

Rad, G. von. "Die Nehemia-Denkschrift." *ZAW* 76 (1964): 176–87.

———. *Der heilige Krieg im alten Israel*. 5th edition. Göttingen, 1969.

Rawlinson, G. *Ezra and Nehemiah*. New York: A. D. F. Randolph & Co., 1891

Reich, N.J. "The Codification of the Egyptian Laws by Darius and the Origin of the 'Demotic Chronicle.'" *Mizraim* 1 (1933): 178–85.

Reinmuth, T. *Der Bericht Nehemias: Zur literarischen Eigenart, traditionsgeschichtlichen Prägung und innerbiblischen Rezeption des Ich-Berichts Nehemias*. OBO 183. Göttingen: Vandenhoeck & Ruprecht, 2002.

Rendtorff, R. "Esra und das 'Gesetz.'" *ZAW* 96 (1984): 165-184.

Robinson, G. *The Origin and Development of the Old Testament Sabbath. A Comprehensive Exegetical Approach*. BET 21. Frankfurt a. M., 1988.

Rowley, H.H. "The Chronological Order of Ezra and Nehemiah." Pages 137–68 in *The Servant of the Lord and Other Essays on the Old Testament*. 2d ed. Oxford: Blackwell, 1952.

———. "Nehemiah's Mission and Its Background." *BJRL* 37 (1954–1955): 528–61.

Rubenstein, J.L. "The History of Sukkot during the Second Temple and Rabbinic Periods: Studies in the Continuity and Change of a Festival." Ph.D. diss. Columbia, 1992.

Rudolph, W. *Esra und Nehemia*. HAT 20. Tübingen: Mohr (Siebeck), 1949.

———. *Jeremia*. HAT 12. Tübingen: Mohr (Siebeck) 3. verbesserte Auflage, 1968.

Ruffing, A. *Jahwekrieg als Weltmetapher. Studien zu Jahwekriegstexten des chronistischen Sondergutes*. SBB 24. Stuttgart, 1992.

Saley, R.J. "The Date of Nehemiah Reconsidered." Pages 151–65 in *Biblical and Near Eastern Studies: Essays in Honor of William Sanford LaSor*. Edited by G.A. Tuttle. Grand Rapids, Mich.: Eerdmans, 1978.

Schaak, T. *Die Ungeduld des Papiers. Studien zum alttestamentlichen Verständnis des Schreibens anhand des Verbums* katab *im Kontext administrativer Vorgänge*. BZAW 262. Berlin and New York: De Gruyter, 1998.

Schaeder, H.H. *Esra der Schreiber*. BHT 5. Tübingen: Mohr (Siebeck), 1930.

———. *Iranische Beiträge I*. Halle: Max Niemeyer, 1930.

Schaper, J. *Priester und Leviten im achämenidischen Juda. Studien zur Kult- und Sozialgeschichte Israels in persischer Zeit*. FAT 31. Tübingen: Mohr (Siebeck), 2000.

Schmid, K. *Buchgestalten des Jeremiabuches. Untersuchungen zur Redaktions- und Rezeptionsgeschichte von Jer 30-33 im Kontext des Buches*. WMANT 72. Neukirchen-Vluyn: Neukirchener Verlag, 1996.

Schneider, H. *Die Bücher Esra und Nehemia*. HSAT IV/2. Bonn: Hanstein, 1959.

Schottroff, W. *'Gedenken' im Alten Orient und im Alten Testament. Die Wurzel zakar im semitischen Sprachkreis*. 2d ed. WMANT 15. Neukirchen-Vluyn: Neukirchener Verlag, 1967.

Schunck, K.-D. *Nehemia*. BK AT XXIII/2.2. Neukirchen-Vluyn: Neukirchener Verlag, 2001.

Schwiderski, D. *Handbuch des nordwestsemitischen Briefformulars. Ein Beitrag zur Echtheitsfrage der aramäischen Briefe des Esrabuches.* BZAW 295. Berlin and New York: De Gruyter, 2000.

Siegfried, C. *Esra, Nehemia und Esther.* HK I/6, 2. Göttingen: Vandenhoeck & Ruprecht, 1901.

Smend, R. (Sr.) *Die Listen der Bücher Esra und Nehemia zusammengestellt und untersucht.* Basel: Schultze, 1881.

Smith, M. *Palestinian Parties and Politics That Shaped the Old Testament.* 2d ed. London: SCM, 1987.

Smith-Christopher, D.L. "The Mixed Marriage Crisis in Ezra 9–10 and Nehemiah 13: A Study of the Sociology of the Post-exilic Judaean Community." Pages 243–65 in *Second Temple Studies 2: Temple Community in the Persian Period.* Edited by T. C. Eskenazi and K. H. Richards. JSOTSup 175. Sheffield: JSOT Press, 1994.

Snaith, N.H. "Nehemiah xii.36." *VT* 17 (1967): 243.

Snell, D.C. "Why Is There Aramaic in the Bible?" *JSOT* 18 (1980): 32–51.

Spieckermann, H. "Mit der Liebe im Wort." Pages 157-172 in *Gottes Liebe zu Israel.* FAT 33. Tübingen: Mohr & Siebeck, 2001.

Spiegelberg, W. *Die sogennante demotische Chronik des Pap. 215 der Bibliothèque Nationale zu Paris nebst den auf der Rückseite des Papyrus stehenden Texten.* Demotische Studien 7. Leipzig: Hinrichs'sche Buchhandlung, 1914.

Spinoza, B. de *Tractatus theologico-politicus.* Opera 1. 1670. Edited by G. Gawlick and F. Niewöhner. Darmstadt: Wissenschaftliche Buchgesellschaft. 1979.

Starke, C. *Synopsis Bibliothecae Exegeticae in Vetus Testamentum.* 3. Teil. Berlin and Halle, 1744.

Steck, O.H. *Israel und das gewaltsame Geschick der Propheten. Untersuchungen zur Überlieferung des deuteronomistischen Geschichtsbildes im Alten Testament, Spätjudentum und Urchristentum.* WMANT 23. Neukirchen-Vluyn: Neukirchener Verlag, 1967.

———. *Exegese des Alten Testaments. Leitfaden der Methodik. Ein Arbeitsbuch für Proseminare, Seminare und Vorlesungen.* Twelfth Edition. Neukirchen-Vluyn: Neukirchener Verlag, 1989.

———. *Der Abschluß der Prophetie im Alten Testament. Ein Versuch zur Frage der Vorgeschichte des Kanons.* BTS 17. Neukirchen-Vluyn: Neukirchener Verlag, 1991.

Steiner, R.C. "The *MBQR* at Qumran, the Episkopos in the Athenian Empire, and the Meaning of *LBQR'* in Ezra 7:14: On the Relationship of Ezra's Mission to the Persian Legal Project." *JBL* 120 (2001): 623-646.

Steins, G. *Die Chronik als kanonisches Abschlußphänomen: Studien zu Entstehung und Theologie von 1/2 Chronik.* BBB 93. Weinheim: Beltz Athenäum, 1995.

Stern, E. *Material Culture of the Land of the Bible in the Persian Period 538-332 BC.* Warminster and Jerusalem, 1982.

Stolz, F. *Jahwes and Israels Kriege. Kriegstheorien und Kriegserfahrungen im Glauben des alten Israels.* ATANT 60. Zürich, 1972.

Stuart, D. *Hosea-Jonah.* WBC 31. Waco, Texas: Word. 1987.

Stuckenbruck, L.T., *The Book of Giants from Qumran. Texts, Translation, and Commentary.* TSAT 63. Tübingen: Mohr & Siebeck, 1997.

Talmon, S. "Ezra and Nehemiah." Pages 357–64 in *The Literary Guide to the Bible.* Edited by R. Alter and F. Kermode. Cambridge Mass.: Harvard University Press, 1987.

Thiel, W. *Die deuteronomistische Redaktion von Jeremia 1-25.* WMANT 41. Neukirchen-Vluyn: Neukirchener Verlag, 1973.

Throntveit, M.A. "Linguistic Analysis and the Question of Authorship in Chronicles, Ezra and Nehemiah." *VT* 32 (1982): 201–16.

————. *Ezra-Nehemiah.* IBC. Louisville: John Knox, 1992.

Tigay, J.H. "לִפְנֵי הַשַּׁבָּת and אַחַר הַשַּׁבָּת = 'on the day before the Sabbath' and 'on the day after the Sabbath' (Nehemiah xiii 19)." *VT* 28 (1987): 362-65.

Torrey, C.C. *The Composition and Historical Value of Ezra-Nehemiah.* BZAW 2. Gießen: Rickers'sche Buchhandlung, 1896.

————. "Die Briefe 2 Makk 1,1-2,18." *ZAW* 20 (1900): 225-242.

————. *Ezra Studies. Library of Biblical Studies.* 1910. Repr., New York: Ktav, 1970.

————. "Sanballat 'The Horonite,'" *JBL* 47 (1928): 380-389.

Tscherikower, V. "Palestine under the Ptolemies (A Contribution to the Study of the Zenon Papyri)." *Mizraim* 4-6 (1937): 9-90.

Tucker, G.M. "Covenant Forms and Contract Forms." *VT* 15 (1965): 487–503.

Tuland, C.G. "Ezra-Nehemiah or Nehemiah-Ezra?" *AUSS* 12 (1974): 47–62.

Uehlinger, C. *Weltreich und "eine Rede". Eine neue Deutung der sogenannten Turmbauerzählung (Gen 11,1-9).* OBO 101. Fribourg: Universitätsverlag. 1990.

VanderKam, J.C. "Ezra-Nehemiah or Ezra and Nehemiah?" Pages 55–75 in *Priests, Prophets and Scribes: Essays on the Formation and Heritage of Second Temple Judaism in Honour of Joseph Blenkinsopp.* Edited by E. Ulrich, J. W. Wright, R. P. Carroll, and P. R. Davies. JSOTSup 149. Sheffield: JSOT Press, 1992.

Veijola, T. *Die ewige Dynastie.* Annales Academiae scientiarum fennicae Ser. B. Tom. 193. Helsinki, 1975.

————. "Die Propheten und das Alter des Sabbatgebots." Pages 246-264 in *Prophet und Prophetenbuch,* FS O. Kaiser zum 65. Geburtstag. Edited by V. Fritz et al. BZAW 185. Berlin/New York: de Gruyter 1989.

Veltri, G. "Der Aramäische Targumvortrag zur Zeit Esras: Eine sprachgeschichtliche und historische Frage." *Laur* 34 (1993): 187–207.

Vogelstein, H. *Der Kampf zwischen Priestern und Leviten seit den Tagen Ezechiels. Eine historisch-kritische Untersuchung.* Stettin, 1889.

Vogt, H.C.M. *Studie zur nachexilischen Gemeinde in Esra-Nehemia.* Werl: Dietrich Coelde, 1966.

Volz, P. *Der Prophet Jeremia.* KAT X. Leipzig, 2d ed., 1928.

Walser, G. *Beiträge zur Achämenidengeschichte.* Historia Einzelschriften 18. Wiesbaden, 1972.

————. "Heiraten zwischen Griechen und Achämeniden-Prinzessinen." Pages 87-90 in *Kunst, Kultur und Geschichte der Achämenidenzeit und Ihr Fortleben.* Berlin: Dietrich Reimer, 1983.

Watts, J.W. *Psalm and Story, Inset Hymns in Hebrew Narrative.* JSOTSup 139. Sheffield: JSOT Press, 1992.

Weinberg, J. *The Citizen-Temple Community.* Translated by D. L. Smith-Christopher. JSOTSup 151. Sheffield: JSOT press, 1992.

Weinfeld, M. *Deuteronomy and the Deuteronomic School.* Winona Lake, Ind.: Eisenbrauns, 1992.

Weippert, H. *Palästina in vorhellenistischer Zeit.* Handbuch der Archäologie, Vorderasien II, Band I. Munich: C. H. Beck'sche Verlagsbuchhandlung, 1988.

Wellhausen, J. *Israelitische und Jüdische Geschichte.* 1894. Ninth Edition. Berlin-Leipzig: 1958.

————. "Die Rückkehr der Juden aus dem babylonischen Exil." *GGN* (1895): 166-168.

————. *Prolegomena zur Geschichte Israels.* 1899. Sixth Edition. Berlin-Leipzig: 1927.

Welten, P. *Geschichte und Geschichtsdarstellung in den Chronikbüchern.* WMANT 42. Neukirchen-Vluyn, 1973.

de Wette, W.M.L. *Lehrbuch der historisch-kritischen Einleitung in die Bibel Alten und Neuen Testaments. Erster Teil.* Berlin: Reimer, 1845.

Widengren, G. "The Persian Period." Pages 489–538 in *Israelite and Judaean History.* Edited by J. H. Hayes and J. M. Miller. Philadelphia: Westminster, 1977.

Wiesehöfer, J. "Zur Frage der Echtheit des Dareios-Briefes an Gadatos." *Rheinisches Museum für Philologie* 130 (1987): 396-398.

Willi, T. *Juda-Jehud-Israel: Studien zum Selbstverständnis des Judentums in persischer Zeit.* FAT 12. Tübingen: Mohr & Siebeck, 1995.

Williams, N.A. "Geshem." *ABD* 2:995.

Williamson, H.G.M. *Israel in the Books of Chronicles.* Cambridge: Cambridge University Press, 1977.

————. "The Historical Value of Josephus' Jewish Antiquities XI. 297–301." *JTS* 28 (1977): 49–66.

————. "The Origins of the Twenty-Four Priestly Courses: A Study of 1 Chronicles xxiii–xxvii." Pages 251–68 in *Studies in the Historical Books of the Old Testament.* Edited by J.A. Emerton. VTSup 30. Leiden: Brill, 1979.

————. "Nehemiah's Walls Revisited." *PEQ* 116 (1984): 81-88.

————. *Ezra, Nehemiah.* WBC 16. Waco, Texas: Word, 1985.

————. "The Governors of Judah under the Persians." *TynB* 39 (1988): 59-83.

————. "Judah and the Jews." Pages 145-63 in M. Brosius and A. Kuhrt (eds.), *Studies in Persian History: Essays in Memory of David M. Lewis.*Achaemenid History 11. Leiden, 1998.

————. "Ezra and Nehemiah in the Light of the Texts from Persepolis." *Bulletin for Biblical Research* 1 (1991): 41-61.

Wills, L.M. *The Jew in the Court of the Foreign King: Ancient Jewish Court Legends.* Harvard Dissertations in Religion 20. Minneapolis: Augsburg. 1990.

Winckler, H. "Die doppelte darstellung in Ezra-Nehemia." Pages 458-489 in *Altorientalische Forschungen* II/III, 2, 1902.

Wolff, H.W. *Dodekapropheton 2. Joel und Amos.* BK XIV/2. Neukirchen-Vluyn: Neukirchener Verlag, 1969.

Wright, J.W. "The Origin and Function of 1 Chronicles 23-27." Diss., Univ. of Notre Dame, 1989.

————. "The Legacy of David in Chronicles. The Narrative Formation of 1 Chron 23-27," *JBL* 110 (1991): 229-242.

————. "From Center to Periphery: 1 Chronicles 23–27 and the Interpretation of Chronicles in the Nineteenth Century." Pages 20–42 in *Priests, Prophets and Scribes: Essays on the Formation and Heritage of Second Temple Judaism in Honour of Joseph Blenkinsopp.* Edited by E. Ulrich, J.W. Wright, R.P. Carroll, and P.R. Davies. JSOTSup 149. Sheffield: JSOT Press, 1992.

Yamauchi, E.M.. "The Archaeological Background of Ezra." *BSac* 37 (1980): 195–211.

————. "Was Nehemiah the Cupbearer a Eunuch?" *ZAW* 92 (1980): 132–42.

Zimmerli, W. *Ezekiel 1-2.* Translated by R. E. CLements. Hermeneia. Philadelphia: Fortress, 1983.

————. "Das Phänomen der 'Fortschreibung' im Buche Ezechiel." Pages 174-191 in *Prophecy. Essays Presented to G. Fohrer.* Edited by J. A. Emerton. BZAW 150. Berlin: de Gruyter, 1980.

Zunz, L. "Dibre hajamim oder die Bücher der Chronik." Pages 13–36 in *Die gottesdienstlichen Vorträge der Juden, historisch entwickelt. Ein Beitrag zur Alterthumskunde und biblischen Kritik, zur Literatur- und Religionsgeschichte.* 1832. Repr., Frankfurt: Kauffmann, 1892.

Index of Biblical and Ancient Literature

A. Hebrew Bible

B. Apocrypha and Pseudepigrapha

C. New Testament

D. Elephantine

E. Qumran and Rabbinica

F. Greek Literature

Index of Modern Authors

Index of Subjects